CORE

A Study in the
Civil Rights Movement
1942–1968

CORE

A Study in the Civil Rights Movement 1942-1968

August Meier and Elliott Rudwick

Generously Donated to

The Frederick Douglass Institute

By Professor Jesse Moore

Fall 2000

UNIVERSITY OF ILLINOIS PRESS

Urbana Chicago London

For Clifton W. Henry

A. M.

For two from Southern Illinois University (Edwardsville)
Ernest Schusky and Arthur Stahnke

E. R.

Preface to the Paperback Edition

In preparing for this paperback edition of CORE, it seemed appropriate to survey briefly what has happened to the organization since 1968.[1] During the past seven years black activism has changed dramatically. SNCC disappeared, SCLC declined sharply in size and importance, and the NAACP, with a membership that was growing older and had stabilized in numbers, once more emphasized tactics of fighting discrimination through the courts. Not only have the protest demonstrations disappeared from the streets, but the wave of civil disorders of the late 1960s ceased as suddenly as it had arisen, and the confrontation rhetoric of the advocates of Black Power subsided. Black pressures continued and gains were made in the job market, in southern school desegregation, in the increased numbers of blacks at predominantly white colleges and universities, and in politics. These pressures, however, came increasingly from local and more specialized groups — the Chicago-based PUSH, organized by Jesse Jackson, who had earlier established a national reputation as a SCLC leader; Negro union officials; black student organizations; black caucuses in professional organizations; and most notably, black politicians and their constituencies. In fact, Bayard Rustin's perceptive prediction in 1965 that black protest would have to shift from confrontation to politics has been abundantly borne out.[2] Paradoxically, Black Power has had its greatest success not where it has been used to promote separatism, but where, as in the congressional Black Caucus and the black caucuses within the labor movement and learned societies, it has been used to push for more tangible benefits and greater recognition for blacks within the major institutions of American society.

In this context CORE continued to decline. Its condition was such that the *New York Times,* analyzing the black protest movement on the tenth anniversary of the 1963 March on Washington, described CORE as a "black nationalist organization pushing a philosophy without a program, gaining attention only because of its charismatic leader, Roy Innis." A year and a half later *Time* magazine flatly declared, "CORE has disintegrated."[3] Under Innis's leadership CORE had committed itself to a consistently nationalist position. Yet even at the cresting of black nationalist sentiment in America at the end of the 1960s, the overwhelming majority of Afro-Americans did not perceive separatism to be their goal. And as nationalist rhetoric waned in the course of the 1970s, CORE found itself in an increasingly marginal position.

In the early years of his administration Roy Innis, capitalizing on a confrontation style of activism, appeared in the news on a number of occasions. He deliberately emphasized the gulf between CORE and the NAACP, openly denouncing Roy Wilkins for consistently opposing "the legitimate aspirations of black people." As Innis put it a couple of years later, "In America today there are two kinds of black people — the field-hand blacks and the 'house niggers.' We of CORE — the nationalists — are the field-hand blacks. The integrationists [of the NAACP] are house niggers."[4] Innis made headlines in 1969 by threatening to create disorder with "a locally mobilized army" at the American Bankers Association convention to back up his demands for 6 billion dollars "in reparations" from the banking industry. In 1972, during a gathering of civil rights leaders at the Lyndon Baines Johnson Library for the ceremonies opening the Johnson administration's civil rights papers, Innis successfully threatened to break up the meeting unless allowed to make a speech.[5] More sustained publicity came through CORE's advocacy of separate schools. CORE was one of the organizations pushing New York City in the direction of school decentralization and community control, and to a considerable extent these demands were implemented by the New York City Board of Education.[6] Innis traveled south in 1970, conferring with state governors and other white officials about his plan for separate school districts to be completely controlled by blacks. He thought the plan could be sold to southern officials as an alternative to court-imposed desegregation, and he believed that its constitutionality would be sustained by the Supreme Court. In Mobile, Alabama, which was under a desegregation court order, Innis was accorded a particularly cordial hearing, but in the end the city did not adopt his plan.[7] Not surprisingly, in 1972

CORE and Innis filed a legal brief opposing the efforts of other civil rights organizations to further desegregation of Richmond's public schools by requiring busing between the city and the predominantly white suburban school districts.[8] When the congressional Black Caucus refused to consider endorsing CORE's approach, CORE denounced these members of the House of Representatives as "incestuous, outdated, arrogant, and contemptuous."[9]

Behind CORE's stance of militant black separatism, there was little successful program development. The most substantial project was a federally funded youth job-training program in Baltimore.[10] Although the national office does not make public the number of active chapters, clearly there were very few. Those chapters which were active were largely engaged in working with local communities on such matters as drug abuse and developing black awareness through cultural programs. In 1974 Suffolk County (New York) CORE, for example, sent thirteen youths on a trip to Africa; Lexington (Kentucky) CORE conducted sessions in reading and writing skills for high school dropouts and staged a Miss Black Kentucky pageant; Harlem CORE co-sponsored a bicycle championship contest with the local police precinct community council and joined with the Pan-African Martial Arts Association in co-sponsoring a Karate meet; Los Angeles CORE's major event was an all-day picnic, at which the special attraction was a football game between eleven young women called the CORE-ETTES and disc jockeys from a local radio station.[11]

With a weak domestic program, Innis sought to develop his Pan-African thrust and create ties with the African nations. Upon returning from a four-week trip to Africa in 1971 he announced the establishment of a CORE Department of African Affairs. He wanted to encourage black American financial investment in Africa, to organize black Americans to pressure the American government in support of African interests, and to provide black professionals and technicians for the African states. Innis proposed that black Americans be permitted dual citizenship in the United States and the African countries. The only part of this program that seemed to bear fruit was the idea of sending skilled Afro-Americans to Africa. In 1973 Innis announced that as part of an effort to replace the Asians expelled from Uganda by President Idi Amin, CORE had recruited fifty black technicians due to depart on August 1, but within forty-eight hours General Amin decided not to go through with the project.[12]

As CORE's decline continued in the 1970s a major interest became the publication of *CORE,* an expensively produced glossy magazine which contained little about the organization's activities and programs but which assumed a major place in the organization's budget. The publication was supported by advertisements purchased by major industrial corporations. The organization's financial report for 1973 indicated that out of total receipts of slightly over a million dollars, $433,000 came from the federal government for the Baltimore job-training project, and $421,000, or over two-thirds of the balance, was income derived from the magazine. Direct expenses for the magazine in 1973 amounted to about $270,000, or nearly half of CORE's disbursements for the year, exclusive of the Baltimore project.[13] With little being spent on other activities, the CORE magazine had seemingly become the organization's major project.

Symptomatic of what was happening to CORE was the drastic change in its fund raising. The old direct-mail list of financial supporters so carefully developed over the years grew increasingly less productive. CORE turned to various devices for raising money. For example, by threatening a boycott of the closed-circuit showings of the Muhammad Ali–Joe Frazier heavyweight championship bout in 1971, CORE became a partner for the showings at several sites — netting $20,000.[14] The most important source of funds, however, undoubtedly became major industrial corporations. The CORE annual report for 1973/74 proudly listed as contributors eighty-two nationally known companies, including Standard Oil, Union Carbide, Warner-Lambert Pharmaceuticals, International Business Machines, Xerox, Reynolds Metals, Inland Steel, Bethlehem Steel, and the Crown Zellerbach Paper Company.[15]

Although CORE itself was in a state of decline, the spirit of the organization from its heyday of the 1960s remained alive elsewhere. Across the country former CORE activists were engaged in various types of political work and community organization, epitomized by the careers of men like Missouri congressman William Clay and the architect of the National Welfare Rights Organization, George Wiley.

The most direct offshoot of CORE was, of course, the Scholarship, Education, and Defense Fund for Racial Equality (SEDFRE), which, it will be recalled, had been established in 1962 as a tax-exempt arm of CORE but which had cut its ties with CORE in 1966. Headed first by Marvin Rich and later by Ronnie Moore, SEDFRE functioned as a "non-profit national training and technical assistance organization specializing in community development."[16] It has provided a wide range of programs for a variety of private companies, public agencies, and community-action projects. For example, it held a race relations training workshop for Aetna Insurance

Company executives, and another one for corrections officers in Richmond, Virginia. It has a continuing program imparting management skills for Headstart personnel in the Northeast. It has provided similar assistance to the boards and staffs of a number of community-action agencies ranging from the Beaufort-Jasper Comprehensive Health Center in South Carolina to the Camden County (New Jersey) Community Coordinated Child Care Program. In a year-long project with the United Community Corporation of Newark, New Jersey, SEDFRE helped the board and staff of this formerly federally funded anti-poverty program "to make a successful transition from total government support to economic self-reliance."[17]

Especially striking has been SEDFRE's assistance to newly elected black government officials in the South. Starting with a South-wide conference in 1966, SEDFRE has specialized in helping several key localities where blacks have recently gained political control. Thus in Tallulah, Louisiana, SEDFRE has been of considerable assistance. When CORE's old friend Zelma Wyche became Tallulah's police chief in 1969, SEDFRE provided a four-day seminar in police-community relations. In the following years, under Wyche's leadership, blacks achieved political control of the whole parish, and in 1974 Tallulah elected a black mayor and board of aldermen. The new city officials, who lacked practical experience in running a town government, inherited a substantial municipal debt, and faced serious needs for jobs, housing, sewerage improvement, recreational facilities, and health services. At Mayor Adell Williams's request SEDFRE sent in specialists and held workshops to provide basic skills in town administration. A fiscal management specialist audited the financial records and gave instruction in bookkeeping techniques. A workshop with the mayor and aldermen assisted them in setting priorities and developing budgets, and the black officials emerged with a basic understanding of their legal roles and powers, and assurance that their immediate fiscal problems were under control. Furthermore, they now had a "clear, comprehensive consensus for step-by-step action" in the specific goals and priorities which had been hammered out. Another workshop was arranged to give Tallulah's community leaders advice on how to apply for federal and state monies for which they were eligible.[18]

SEDFRE also concentrated substantial resources in Greene County, Alabama, which as a result of elections in 1968 and 1970 became the first county in the country to be entirely governed by black officials. In this, the county in Alabama with the lowest per capita income, SEDFRE lent its efforts to assist in solving the pressing economic problems and aid the county commissioners in generating new jobs. In the fall of 1970 SEDFRE helped to create the Greene County Economic Development Commission, headed by former CORE field secretary and SEDFRE staff member Spiver Gordon. SEDFRE helped the commission conduct an economic analysis of the county, train staff members, formulate a comprehensive industrial development plan, and obtain funds from the government and private foundations. As a result of this intensive effort, a few corporations decided to locate plants in the county, most notably the Levi-Strauss clothing manufacturers. With SEDFRE's assistance the county also obtained a variety of grants for a public housing project, education, medical services, and job training for high school youths.[19]

An approach very different from SEDFRE's was undertaken by George Wiley, who shortly after resigning from CORE in 1966 took the lead in establishing the National Welfare Rights Organization (NWRO). Predominantly black but including whites as well, this federation of welfare mothers' groups across the country struggled for increased welfare benefits. Wiley, who in CORE had been a leading advocate of attacking the problems of the poor and organizing them in the struggle for their own advancement, demonstrated through his work with NWRO that the poor could indeed be mobilized. Welfare mothers' groups sprang up in slums across the country, as Wiley's tactics both dramatized the issue and substantially increased the financial benefits paid to families in poverty. Exploiting existing legislation through direct action tactics and litigation, NWRO was largely responsible for raising the number of people on welfare in six years from less than 3 million to over 10 million, and in quadrupling appropriations made to Aid to Dependent Children families. NWRO also helped to establish a welfare recipient's right to privacy, overturned residency requirements, and made possible administrative hearings for recipients whose grants were threatened. Friends and enemies alike credited NWRO with a major role in this explosion of welfare aid. By 1972, state officials, alarmed at the growing welfare rolls and burgeoning expenditures, began to cut back and tighten up requirements. Wiley, concluding that the poor lacked the power to fight back singlehandedly, resigned as NWRO's director in late 1972 and formed a more broadly based coalition to struggle for a more equitable distribution of the nation's wealth. But before he could get his Movement for Economic Justice under way, Wiley died in 1973.[20]

Both Wiley's activities in welfare rights and the work of Ronnie Moore and his colleagues in SEDFRE were developments that stemmed directly from the thrust toward community organization and political activism that formed the heart of CORE's "New Directions" in the last part of James Farmer's administration. Other former CORE activists also worked along similar lines. Most of the CORE people who have remained actively involved in the struggle for racial equality have personally eschewed holding political office. But as in the case of Ronnie Moore, they have usually been very sympathetic to the political thrust and have frequently been of direct assistance to blacks involved in partisan politics. Given the growing influence of the Negro vote, they recognized the potential in what Moore has described as a "politics of delivery," as contrasted with CORE's older style of a "politics of confrontation," but they have largely remained ambivalent about personally making the compromises inherent in direct participation in the political process.

A number of CORE leaders of the 1960s, such as Richard Haley, Alan Gartner, Wilfred Ussery, Arthur Zebbs, and Marshall England, held top executive posts in local anti-poverty agencies across the country. Others, like Rudy Lombard, who directed a drug-control program in Washington for several years, and Marvin Robinson, who became executive director of the Interracial Council for Business Opportunity in Dallas, were active in other forms of community work. After SEDFRE gave up its legal program, Carl Rachlin became counsel for Hunter College, where he also teaches a course in law and social action. David J. Dennis, after obtaining a law degree at the University of Michigan, returned to New Orleans and joined Lolis Elie in establishing an integrated legal firm mainly devoted to handling cases for the black poor. Floyd McKissick, assisted by Gordon Carey, with 19.5 million dollars in federal grants and loan guarantees began building Soul City, a new industrial community in a depressed area of rural North Carolina. With Soul City revealing what a Republican administration might do for blacks, McKissick endorsed President Nixon and organized black support for him during the 1972 election campaign.[21]

The work of others had a broader regional or national focus. Weldon Rougeau for a period was director of the Citizenship Education Department of the National Urban League. Kenny Johnson, who had become active in CORE as a local youth participating in the Plaquemine, Louisiana, demonstrations, obtained a master's degree in urban planning at Yale University and is now directing SEDFRE's southern operations. Shirley Lacey, after leaving SEDFRE in 1971, joined the staff of the NAACP Legal and Educational Defense Fund, where she has administered a variety of special projects. Meanwhile, she has been active in Bergen County, New Jersey, politics, serving as the Democratic party district leader for Englewood and surrounding communities; in 1974 she ran for the county board of freeholders. Marvin Rich, after leaving SEDFRE, established a professional fund-raising organization that has as its clients social action organizations like SEDFRE and George Houser's American Committee on Africa. Norman Hill served on the staff of the Industrial Union Department of the AFL-CIO, and then joined Bayard Rustin at the A. Philip Randolph Institute, an organization largely funded by the unions and dedicated to forging an alliance between blacks and organized labor. Early in 1975 Hill succeeded Rustin as the institute's executive director. Ruth Turner Perot became a consultant in program and policy development and human services delivery planning for a variety of agencies like the Office of Human Development, the Office of Economic Opportunity, the National Urban Coalition, and the National Council of Negro Women. Alan Gartner is now associate director of the Queens College Human Services Institute and an editor of the magazine *Social Policy*. The type of work which the institute performs and the kind of involvement which many CORE people have with political affairs are both illustrated by the way in which Gartner drafted — and then proceeded to organize the lobbying for — the full-employment bill which was introduced by Congressman Augustus Hawkins. James Farmer, having served a frustrating two years as an assistant secretary in the Department of Health, Education, and Welfare during Nixon's first term, resigned in disappointment at his lack of influence. After leaving the government, he joined the longtime builder of private interracial residential developments, Morris Milgram, in establishing Partners in Housing. Then in 1973, in cooperation with Howard University and with a $150,000 grant from the U.S. Office of Education, Farmer became director of the Public Policy Training Institute, designed to bring teachers from black colleges together with public officials "to determine how minorities might influence public decisions that affect them."[22]

Some CORE people became directly involved in the new political activism. Robert Curvin, who is now a professor of political science at Brooklyn College, was organizer of the black and Puerto Rican convention which nominated Kenneth Gibson to run for mayor of Newark, and then served as director of Mayor Gibson's transition staff during the early days of the new administration. James McCain, although now retired, remained exceedingly active in community work in Sumter, South Carolina. He has served on the local anti-poverty board and Council for the Aged, and is chairman of the Sumter County Black Political Caucus. The caucus has sponsored candidates for city and county political offices, its most significant victory being the election in 1974 of the first black to sit on the county board of commissioners.

At least three former CORE leaders were elected to their state legislatures — Curtis Graves of the Houston chapter; Ernest Finney, who had been CORE's lawyer in South Carolina; and Hannah Atkins, formerly head of Oklahoma City CORE. Easily the most outstanding example of political activism to be found among CORE leaders is William Clay. Clay's political interests were of long standing, and as noted elsewhere in this book, he had been a St. Louis alderman at the time of his most intense participation in CORE. Elected to Congress in 1968, Clay has been a prominent figure in the congressional Black Caucus and was active in the McGovern campaign of 1972.

Thus although CORE itself has declined, its long-range influence continues. Not only had CORE in the 1960s contributed substantially to the surge toward community organization and political activism, but a number of CORE leaders themselves continued to be active in the cause of racial equality and the advancement of blacks in American society.

NOTES

1. The following discussion is based upon both confidential interviews and the sources cited below.

2. Bayard Rustin, "From Protest to Politics: The Future of the Civil Rights Movement," *Commentary,* XXXIX (Feb. 1965), 25-31.

3. *New York Times,* Aug. 29, 1973; *Time,* XV (Jan. 27, 1975), 12.

4. *New York Times,* Jan. 22, 1969, Oct. 8, 1971.

5. *Ibid.,* Sept. 29, 30, 1969, Dec. 13, 1972.

6. On CORE's role see *ibid.,* Mar. 4, Apr. 30, 1969.

7. Washington *Post,* Feb. 5, Mar. 6, 1970; *New York Times,* Mar. 15, Sept. 7, 9, 1970.

8. Washington *Post,* Jan. 17, 27, 1972, Apr. 3, 1973; *New York Times,* Apr. 29, 1973.

9. *New York Times,* Feb. 11, 1972.

10. *CORE Annual Report 1973/1974* (New York: [1974]), unpaged.

11. Larry Hopper, "CORE Declares War," *CORE,* Holiday Issue, 1974, 35-40.

12. *New York Times,* Aug. 22, 1971, Apr. 5, 21, June 27, 29, 1973.

13. *CORE Annual Report 1973/1974.*

14. *New York Times,* Jan. 17, 19, 28, 1971; Washington *Post,* Mar. 30, 1971.

15. See list of contributors in *CORE Annual Report 1973/1974.*

16. Leaflet, "SEDFRE Seminar Series, 1974-1975." This and the other SEDFRE documents cited below were obtained from the national office of SEDFRE.

17. See "SEDFRE Program Prospectus for Fiscal Year 1974-1975," [1974], and SEDFRE, "To Better Serve the Health Needs of the Poor: Three Training Workshops for Board/Council Members of the Beaufort-Jasper Comprehensive Health Program," 1971.

18. Edward L. Cole, "Police-Community Relations Workshop for Police Officers and Citizens of Tallulah, Louisiana," a SEDFRE report, 1969; Kenny Johnson, Memorandum to Ronnie Moore, Aug. 21, 1974; and Johnson, Memorandum to Mayor Adell Williams, Nov. 26, 1974.

19. "A Proposal for Funding the Comprehensive Economic Development of Greene County, Alabama during the 3-Year Period October 1972 to September 1975," submitted by the Greene County Economic Development Commission with the assistance of SEDFRE Department of Economic Development, Oct. 2, 1972; SEDFRE, "Annual Report to the Greene County Economic Development Commission," Jan. 1973.

20. *New York Times,* Dec. 17, 1972, Aug. 10, 1973; Washington *Post,* Dec. 17, 1972; George Wiley to Welfare Rights Leaders, Members, Friends and Supporters, Dec. 15, 1972, Personal File; and Wiley to Dear Friends, Feb. 6, 1973, Personal File.

21. *Wall Street Journal,* July 31, 1974; Washington *Post,* Jan. 15, 1975; *New York Times,* Oct. 15, 1972, Mar. 9, 1975.

22. *New York Times,* July 7, 1973.

Introduction

This is a study of the rise and decline of one of the leading civil rights organizations of the twentieth century. Utilizing archival materials, manuscript collections in the possession of individuals, black and white newspapers, and over two hundred personal interviews, we have attempted to describe CORE's development, its successes and failures, and the changes it underwent. We have given special attention to tactics, strategies, ideologies, and organizational structure, as well as discussed CORE's major campaigns. We have also tried to place CORE in the context of the larger civil rights movement and to analyze its interrelationships with other black protest organizations.

Because CORE was a federation of essentially autonomous chapters that carried on most of the organization's activity, we have given considerable emphasis to the affiliates and their work. Chapters and local CORE-related movements selected for intensive study were chosen on the basis of two main criteria: their importance in the organization and the availability of materials. In a few cases personal contacts led us to study a smaller chapter. We do not claim that the chapters selected for intensive analysis are a statistically representative sample, but we have included communities in all sections of the country, and we believe that they represent the range and variety of activities and problems experienced by CORE affiliates.

This book could not have been written without the cooperation of James Farmer, George Wiley, Floyd McKissick, Wilfred Ussery, and Roy Innis, who on different occasions generously provided access to the CORE archives. Each of them will undoubtedly disagree with certain portions of the volume, and we are particularly indebted to them because they gave us permission to use these materials without placing any restrictions on our work.

We owe a great deal to the many people who agreed to confidential interviews and took the time to share with us their experiences in CORE and the movement. In addition, a number of them, acknowledged individually in the Note on Sources, also kindly let us consult their own personal papers. These interviews were essential to our study. They provided a vital dimension by supplying information on a variety of topics either completely omitted or only sketchily covered in the written record. Our discussions with CORE chapter and national leaders were especially important for a knowledge of the shifting composition of the chapters and the internal dynamics behind changes in both the affiliates and the national organization.

We are deeply indebted to John H. Bracey, Jr., Robert Curvin, Louis R. Harlan, Gary T. Marx, and Marvin Rich for reading the manuscript in its final draft and offering many helpful criticisms. None of them will agree fully with the contents of this book, but their stimulating comments were exceedingly valuable.

We wish to acknowledge the cooperation of the staffs of several libraries, notably the State Historical Society of Wisconsin and its former director Leslie H. Fishel, Jr.; the Martin Luther King Center in Atlanta, directed by Julius Scott; the John F. Kennedy Library; the Manuscripts Division of the Library of Congress; the University of Washington Library; and the Bancroft Library at the University of California at Berkeley. We also want to express our appreciation for the assistance of Jane Benson, Linda Burroughs, and Helen Peoples of the Kent State University Library, and Howard Smead of the Washington *Post* Library. And we are indebted to Paul Gaston for arranging access to the Southern Regional Council Archives and to John Lewis for granting us permission to use the Voter Education Project Archives.

Albert Gollin kindly let us study the transcript of an interview he had with James Farmer. Three students of ours, Jana Coll, Carol Milligan, and Martha Thompson wrote seminar papers on the protest movement in Cleveland which proved helpful. Alan Uhr's painstaking assistance greatly facilitated the preparation of the index. Barbara Hostetler typed and retyped the manuscript of this volume several times as it underwent revisions; and to her we owe a debt which words cannot adequately express.

Portions of the first chapter of this book originally appeared as articles in scholarly journals: "How CORE Began," *Social Science Quarterly,* XLIX (March 1969) and "The First Freedom Ride," *Phylon,* XXX (Fall 1969). Thanks are due to the editors of both journals for permission to reprint these two articles, almost in their entirety, in this book.

We gratefully acknowledge several sources of support: Southern Illinois University (Edwardsville) and Roosevelt University for sabbatical leaves in 1966–67; the Kent State University Faculty Research Committee for Academic Year Fellowships; the Kent State University Center for Urban Regionalism and its former and present directors, James G. Coke and Eugene P. Wenninger, for facilitating in many ways the research and writing of this book; and the John Simon Guggenheim Memorial Foundation for fellowships aiding the final revision of this manuscript.

August Meier
Elliott Rudwick

Kent, Ohio
August 1972

Contents

MAPS

I

The Pioneers
1942 - 1959

1
How CORE Began
1942-1947

Four organizations provided the backbone for the "Black Revolt" of the 1960's: The National Association for the Advancement of Colored People, the Southern Christian Leadership Conference, the Student Nonviolent Coordinating Committee, and the Congress of Racial Equality. SCLC, which grew out of the Montgomery bus boycott of 1955–56, SNCC, which was the product of the southern college student sit-ins of 1960, and CORE were all identified with the strategy of nonviolent direct action that dominated the black protest movement during the first half of the decade. But it was CORE, considerably older than SNCC and SCLC, which had pioneered in this technique.* It articulated the philosophy and applied the tactics of nonviolent direct action for nearly two decades before the "civil rights revolution" burst upon the national scene in 1960.

CORE played a leading role in bringing about the achievements of the

---

* Certain direct-action tactics, most notably boycotts, had been employed as weapons of black protest from time to time as far back as the antebellum period. However, these acts were undertaken spontaneously, without a self-conscious strategy or ideology of nonviolent direct action, which was a creation of the twentieth century. In fact, the modern protesters were unaware of the nineteenth and early twentieth century use of what would now be described as nonviolent direct action, and indeed, they independently reinvented tactics such as bus boycotts and school boycotts.

next several years. First lending valuable support to the black student lunch-counter sit-ins, it became a major force in the movement with the Freedom Ride of 1961. Subsequently, the organization played a key role in the southern voter registration drive of 1962–64 and in the wave of demonstrations that swept the South during the spring and summer of 1963. Meanwhile CORE, more than any other organization, was responsible for the massive outpouring of direct action against housing, employment, and educational discrimination in the North. Finally, in the person of its national director, James Farmer, CORE provided the black protest movement with one of its major charismatic leaders.

Rooted in the American pacifist movement, CORE began in Chicago during the spring of 1942. Its foundations were laid at a time when growing segments of the white public, stimulated by the ideological concerns of the New Deal for America's dispossessed citizens and by the irony of fighting the racist Nazis while tolerating domestic racism, were gradually becoming more sensitive to the black man's plight. Simultaneously, in the black community, as a result of the legal victories achieved by the NAACP during the 1930's, the encouragement of leading New Dealers like Eleanor Roosevelt, and the obvious contradictions between America's democratic war propaganda and its violation of democracy at home, a more militant mood was becoming widely evident.

In the radical vanguard of this slow shift in sentiment among blacks and whites were the founders of CORE. Products of the Christian student movement of the 1930's, with its deep social concerns, they were a small band of dedicated young pacifists, and members of the Christian-pacifist Fellowship of Reconciliation (FOR). Within the FOR, they belonged to a group which was intensely committed to applying Gandhian techniques of *Satyagraha,* or nonviolent direct action, to the resolution of racial and industrial conflict in America. The FOR, established during the First World War, had long been interested in race relations and numbered several Negroes among its officials. When, in 1940, the radical reformer A. J. Muste became FOR's chief executive, the Fellowship moved beyond philosophical opposition to war to experimenting with nonviolent direct action for social justice in the United States.[1] Among the "peace teams" or "cells" into which the FOR organized its members, there was one established at the University of Chicago in October 1941, which was deeply interested in applying Gandhian principles to racial problems. From the activities of this race relations cell of about a dozen members emerged the first CORE group, the Chicago Committee of Racial Equality.[2]

The race relations cell included four of the six individuals who were mainly responsible for founding CORE, while both of the others were FOR staff members who cooperated closely with the cell.[3] James Farmer and George Houser, who started work at the Chicago FOR office in October, had been prominent in Methodist student circles in the 1930's. Farmer, son of a professor at Wiley College in Texas, had received a Bachelor of Divinity degree from Howard University. There, as a student of Howard Thurman, the noted Negro Methodist pacifist and FOR vice-chairman, he had become "deeply versed in Christian pacifist thinking" and had served part time as an FOR field worker. In the summer of 1941 the twenty-one-year-old Farmer accepted a full-time apppoinment with the Fellowship. Houser, the son of a Methodist minister, was in his third year at Union Theological Seminary when he was sentenced to prison for refusing to register for the draft. After spending a year in Danbury penitentiary he went to the University of Chicago to complete his seminary studies and to work part time as an FOR field secretary. The prominence of Methodists among early CORE leaders, epitomized by the contribution of these two men, one black and one white, was no accident, for the Church was influenced to an unusual extent by the pacifism of the 1930's. As A. J. Muste observed, "The Youth Movement of the Methodist Church . . . is the most progressive of our Protestant Youth Movements."

Two other CORE founders, Bernice Fisher and Homer Jack, both white, were also divinity students at the University of Chicago. Both had been social activists in Rochester when they were in their teens. Jack was studying for the Unitarian ministry; Fisher, an active member of the Baptist Young People's Union, had long been interested in labor and race questions. The remaining two founders were liberal arts students at the University of Chicago. Joe Guinn, a Chicago Negro, who would later be incarcerated as a conscientious objector, was head of the local NAACP Youth Council. James R. Robinson, a graduate student in English, was the only non-Protestant in the group. A white Catholic from upstate New York, his interest in pacifism had been stimulated by reading the *Catholic Worker,* and he had been active in peace circles while an undergraduate at Columbia University. Later, as a conscientious objector, he would serve time in a Civilian Public Service (CPS) camp as an alternative to military service.[4]

The six persons most responsible for founding CORE were all pacifists; three served terms in jail or CPS camp as conscientious objectors. Four were white, two were black. All had been deeply involved in the

Christian-pacifist student movement of the 1930's, whose members also shared an ideological commitment to interracialism and industrial union- ism. Years later a CORE founder recalled, "the 1930's was the pacifist era and the trend in pacifist-Christian circles was on nonviolence as an al- ternative to violence. It was natural that this was combined with Gan- dhism." Unlike the majority of their Christian-pacifist fellow students who changed after American entry into World War II, the CORE leaders remained consistent with their earlier ideology. As heirs of the Christian radicalism of the 1930's not only were they conscientious objectors to war, but they exhibited their social idealism in other ways as well. Half were Socialists, and all of them admired the CIO industrial unions and the di- rect-action techniques of the sit-down strikers. Farmer wrote in 1942, "similar instrumentalities for racial brotherhood in America must be developed." [5] Indeed, the first CORE sit-ins were called sit-downs.

The race relations cell met as a Saturday afternoon discussion group. Its dominant personalities were James Robinson and Bernice Fisher. "All of us," Fisher recalled later, "were afire with the ideas of Gandhian non- violence." The cell's members studied and debated, chapter by chapter, Shridharani's *War Without Violence,* a description of Gandhi's philoso- phy and methods, and they discussed ways of adapting Gandhism to the struggle against American racism. Skeptical of NAACP and Urban League programs and believing that, in Houser's words, discrimination "must be challenged directly, without violence or hatred, yet without compromise," the cell members regarded the Saturday study group as preparation for real action.[6] And an opportunity for action, stemming di- rectly from their experience at the University, was close at hand. Black students found it nearly impossible to obtain housing in the neighbor- hood. It was the black physician and civic leader, Dr. Arthur Falls, later a valued adviser to Chicago CORE, who first described to the young pacifists the operation of the restrictive covenant system, under which property owners signed agreements not to sell or rent to blacks. Inspired by the example of the Gandhian cooperative communities known as "ash- rams," the race relations cell established Fellowship House, an interracial men's cooperative, to challenge the restrictive covenants in the University area. Whites in the cell secured an apartment, and in January 1942, a dozen men, including three or four blacks, moved in. They regarded this act, which the owners did not contest, evidently because the lease ran only six months, as a successful example of nonviolent direct action against residential segregation.[7]

Farmer, although not a cell member, had been active in arranging the strategy for securing Fellowship House. Meanwhile, during the course of his speaking tours of midwestern colleges and southern black campuses, he wrestled with the problem of developing a nonviolent direct-action movement. Early in 1942 he addressed two memoranda to Muste and the FOR National Council, outlining a proposal for a "Brotherhood Mobilization." Farmer called for the inauguration of a nationwide organization based upon Gandhian principles of love and nonviolence. While using FOR cells as nuclei, Brotherhood Mobilization would be an autonomous group that included nonpacifists and hopefully would become a mass movement within a decade. Realizing that all persons would not be equally dedicated, Farmer recommended an elitist arrangement, with three classes of membership ranging from a broad base of those who would lend general support to the few who would participate at the appropriate time in the most radical forms of civil disobedience. Finally, the memoranda, reflecting the ideological milieu in which Farmer moved, articulated a distrust of the capitalist system, urged the formation of consumers and producers cooperatives to finance the mobilization, and even exhibited a Gandhian predilection for handicraft industries.[8] Even though the memoranda and the cell's activities were parallel and converging rather than causally related developments, his proposal gave further stimulation to the FOR's growing interest in race relations, and was in fact discussed at length by the group at the University of Chicago.[9] The first suggestion for a national direct-action movement, the proposal actually bore certain striking similarities to CORE as it later evolved. FOR people often provided the nucleus for early CORE groups, which consisted mainly of nonpacifists, and CORE practice made an elitist distinction between active members and the less dedicated associate members in the organization.

In March 1942, the cell appointed an informal preliminary organizing committee. Because they did not want to be just "another talking club," the committee decided to develop a "concrete action project" first and then, having attracted enthusiastic participants, to create a hard-hitting organization. The project chosen involved an attack on the White City Roller Rink, which exluded Negroes, in violation of the state civil rights law, on the fictitious grounds that it was a private club. One evening in April, a group of twenty-four cell members and friends, including Farmer, sought admission to the rink and thereby disproved the private club claim. The whites were admitted while the Negro and mixed contingents were not. On the basis of this experience, a committee was appointed to negotiate with the rink manager.[10] By today's standards this action seems inconsequential, yet at that time it produced considerable excitement among the participants and their friends. Stimulated by this enthusiasm, fifty people met in late April to form "a permanent interracial group committed to the use of nonviolent direct action opposing discrimination." [11]

Of these charter members, consisting of twenty-two women and twenty-eight men, we have been able to secure data on thirty-nine. They were mostly unmarried people in their early twenties. Of the thirty-nine, twelve were blacks, twenty-six were whites, and one was of mixed Japanese and white ancestry. Most of the whites were university students, mainly at the Federated Theological Seminary at the University of Chicago. Most of the blacks were college graduates engaged in white-collar jobs. The overwhelming majority were Christians; three or four were Jews. About half were pacifists—three of the Negroes and fifteen or sixteen of the whites. The role of the pacifist nucleus was critical. In addition to founding the group, pacifists held most of the offices during Chicago CORE's early years and decisively influenced its philosophy and style.[12]

Thus began this small, interracial, nonviolent direct-action group. Not until June 1942, was the name Committee of Racial Equality chosen. Debating the alternatives in a bull session at Fellowship House, the members rejected the idea of calling themselves the Commiteee *for* Racial Equality; since "racial equality exists, working *for* it would be erroneous. We were a committee of racially equal people. . . ." This name was especially attractive because its acronym, CORE, "meant that we were working at the core of the problem," in contrast to the NAACP and the Urban League whom, the CORE founders contended, were merely attacking the issue at its fringes.[13]

In one sense, early CORE was an elitist organization, and in another it was extraordinarily democratic. From the start, members were required to be well versed in the principles of nonviolent philosophy, to be active in some phase of CORE's work, and to accept the "Action Discipline" which set forth the modified Gandhian methods by which CORE operated. Commitment and dedication were deemed more important than size, and prospective members were carefully investigated and interviewed before being admitted. All this was in direct contrast to the NAACP, where an annual dollar contribution made one a full-fledged member, and active participation was not required. Internally, CORE functioned as a small, tightly knit body that absorbed most of the time and energies of its members. The "Statement of Purpose" and the "CORE Action Discipline" which were adopted after intensive discussions, directed members to "commit themselves to work as an integrated, disciplined group" and provided that "all decisions on general policy shall be arrived at only through democratic group discussion." As Bernice Fisher later recalled, "Democracy became almost an obsession. Hours of debate consumed every meeting." Democratic functioning was facilitated both by frequent meetings and by the holding of elections every two or three months. Gradually, over a period of a half-year, an organizational structure evolved. Each active member was expected to serve on at least one committee or in one of three action units. These units were the real heart of the organization; the members investigated and planned projects against discrimination in schools and hospitals, housing, and places of public accommodation. Ordinarily a member would attend a meeting every week—either of the group as a whole, or of his committee or his action unit. There was constant discussion of philosophy and program, and, except in an emergency, all decisions were approved during membership meetings of the group as a whole.[14] Thus there developed a decentralized, cohesive group of about twenty-five active members. For such people, as was often said of the more dynamic CORE chapters in later years, CORE had become a way of life.

This small band of dedicated activists operated on a shoestring budget, financed by voluntary contributions from the members. There was no central office, and meetings were held at places like the Meadville Theological Seminary or the Good Shepherd Community Center. In addition to regular business meetings, the group was addressed by visiting speakers like Farmer, Howard Thurman, and the black FOR Youth Secretary Bayard Rustin, who had earlier provided helpful counsel to the CORE founders. In warm weather, the Sunday evening gatherings would be preceded by a picnic and folk dancing at the 55th Street promontory.[15]

Gandhian nonviolence and interracial action were the twin ideological beliefs underpinning CORE's organizational structure. As the Action Discipline declared, the nonviolent method "confronts injustice without fear, without compromise, and without hate." CORE literature expressed the belief that direct action should always be accompanied by a spirit of good will toward the discriminator, a frame of mind calculated to change not only his action, but his attitudes as well. As Bernice Fisher put it, "reading 'War Without Violence' was a prerequisite in the early days. We adhered seriously to the steps of Satyagraha." Farmer later recalled that like Gandhi, "We . . . believed that truth alone, the transparent justice of our demands, would convert the segregationists, once they agreed to listen. That was why *satyagraha* as 'the firmness engendered by love' was so essential to our discipline." [16]

The leaders' faith in nonviolence was based on both religious and practical considerations. Fisher once wrote, "As a young Christian I had been caught up with the idea that we should live life now as if the Kingdom of God were at hand. . . . To many of us [nonviolence] was a philosophy of life." Farmer asserted that "at the very foundation of the pacifist philosophy is the Jewish-Christian faith in the universal community," a faith which "urges that putting an end to racial discrimination become one of our major emphases." More pragmatically, nonviolent direct action, as the CORE Discipline put it, "assumes that it is suicidal for a minority group to use violence, since to use it would simply result in complete control and subjugation by the majority group." Farmer and other early CORE leaders like Bayard Rustin expressed grave concern at the increasing talk and incidents of black retaliatory violence; and they sought in nonviolent direct action a program that would provide an alternative to what they deemed the ineffectual NAACP and Urban League.[17]

If nonviolence was one cornerstone of the early CORE ideology, interracialism was the other. As the Statement of Purpose succinctly put it, "CORE has one method—interracial, non-violent direct action." The founders of the organization maintained that it was false to speak of a "Negro problem"—rather it was a human problem which could be eliminated only through the joint efforts of all believers in the brotherhood of man. Bayard Rustin called for whites to imitate Gandhi's attitudes toward the untouchables and to identify with oppressed blacks by becoming an integral part of the Negro community. Among the whites, no one expressed the ideology of interracialism more pungently than Bernice Fisher. As she later recollected: "One of our motivations had been the determination that there should be a thoroughly interracial organization . . . not another Negro group with a token membership of whites." Fisher took her interracialism so seriously that it became a central part of her life. For example, she joined Rev. Archibald Carey's Woodlawn AME Church. She recalled that "Negro bloc voting to us was anathema . . . the building up of the myth of differences." Once, when a noted black cleric spoke of his pride in the historic heroes of the Negro race, she "indignantly claimed the equal right to be proud of them as a part of the human race. Negro History Week seemed mere chauvinism. . . . My avowed intention was to fight for the time that race would be a term of importance only to anthropologists." [18]

Not surprisingly, CORE members displayed ambivalences about what was, at the time, a more celebrated nonviolent direct-action organization —A. Philip Randolph's all-black March on Washington Movement. They admired Randolph's use of Gandhian techniques and his appeal to the masses but had strong reservations about his policy of excluding whites. Rustin in 1942 criticized the MOWM on this ground, but a few months later became "very enthusiastic" about Randolph's plans for a MOWM-sponsored civil disobedience campaign. Subsequently, Rustin explained to skeptics that Randolph's position was justified for two reasons: southern Negroes would not follow northern interracial leadership, and admitting whites into the MOWM meant risking a repetition of Randolph's experience as president of the National Negro Congress, where Communists had seized control.[19] Fisher was vastly inspired by Randolph, whom she revered as one of the few people who "deeply influenced my life," and despite her vigorous interracialism prevailed upon the Chicago Committee to cooperate with the March's program.[20] Farmer also lent his services to the March organization, although in public statements he made thinly veiled criticisms of the movement. He opposed anything that "smacks of racial chauvinism" and declared that "no great and oppressive evil can ever be truly wiped out until those oppressed by that evil, in collaboration with men of conscience everywhere, refuse cooperation with its oppression." As he wrote on another occasion, "The stronger black nationalism becomes in Negro life in America, the farther we are from a real solution to the problem of color. The basic problem . . . is to *break down barriers* of segregation. Trying to break down social and economic barriers of segregation while nurturing mental barriers of segregation is fantastic. But that is precisely what the nationalists are doing. We cannot destroy segregation with a weapon of segregation." [21]

The strategy developed by Chicago CORE was an adaptation of Gandhian techniques to the American scene. Gandhi's method was to start with an attempt to convert the opponent through negotiations and then successively move on to more militant actions. Thus, if negotiations failed, agitation was employed to arouse public opinion against the evildoer. If this did not succeed, there would be parades and other colorful demonstrations, and eventually an ultimatum threatening more radical actions. Before undertaking these steps, the *Satyagrahis* would perform rites of prayer and fasting to purify themselves of their own guilt arising from their previous failure to resist evil practices. Then came picketing, strikes, boycotts, and sit-downs. Finally, if all else failed, outright civil disobedience was employed. Throughout, the *Satyagrahis* would seek to love their opponents and refrain from committing violence, no matter what the provocation, even if this meant accepting death. In borrowing this procedure, the Chicago Committee of Racial Equality omitted certain actions in the series. Because of the organization's small membership, parades survived only as occasional "poster walks." Rites of self-purification were discarded as inapplicable in the United States. Civil disobedience was a subject of discussion, but it was mentioned nowhere in the CORE literature. To have done so might have frightened potential recruits; and in any case its use seemed irrelevant at the time, since CORE in its early years generally operated in areas covered by state civil rights laws and was therefore battling private business rather than government authority. On other points, CORE followed Gandhi rather faithfully, and the Action Discipline stressed the importance of behaving without malice and in a "spirit of good will and creative reconciliation," submitting to assault without retaliating in kind.[22]

The Chicago Committee of Racial Equality in its first year attacked discrimination on several fronts. "Good will" failed the members in the White City Roller Rink case. After considerable discussion they took the matter to court, only to find their skepticism about legal action justified by the judge's unfavorable decision.[23] "Good will" proved more successful when the men living in the second Fellowship House, established late in 1942, were haled into court. Because of the friendly attitude which the co-op's members displayed toward their neighbors, the real estate agent was unable to obtain witnesses to testify that Negroes lived in the apartment, and the case was dropped.[24] Attacking racism at the University of Chicago, CORE took preliminary steps in a long-range campaign against discrimination at the hospital and medical school [25] and eliminated race exclusion at the University barbership. In November 1942, after barbers refused to cut Bayard Rustin's hair, a committee from CORE and the divinity school faculty spoke with the University's business manager; students indignantly threatened a boycott, and an agreement was reached that Negroes would be served.[26]

The greatest effort, however, was put into fighting restaurant discrimination. The majority of Chicago eating establishments observed the state civil rights law, but CORE found some that did not, most notably the Jack Spratt, near the Fellowship House, and Stoner's, downtown. In both cases CORE first strove to negotiate in a spirit of Gandhian good will, but the two proprietors proved adamant. Interracial groups testing the restaurants received a hostile reception. Sometimes they were served at Jack Spratt's, but in an uncivil manner, and in one instance the dishes Negroes had used were smashed by the manager. Stoner's would seat the test groups after a long wait, and then would serve them, as George Houser reported, "meat with egg shells scattered on it, or a plate of food salted so heavily that it could not be eaten, or a sandwich composed of lettuce and tomato cores picked out of the garbage can. . . ." Negotiations having failed, CORE, following Shridharani's outline, undertook to mobilize public opinion against Stoner's through agitation. For one entire week in December 1942, CORE members passed out leaflets to patrons, asking them to protest discrimination as they paid their checks. Accused of picking on Stoner's, CORE investigated the policies of other downtown restaurants and circulated its findings in a leaflet entitled "50 Loop Restaurants Which Do Not Discriminate." In January 1943, four months after the start of the Stoner's campaign, CORE justified the lengthy procedure and suggested that it was about to proceed to the next stage of the Gandhian strategy. Its newsletter announced that "we are an action group, and within the month the investigation will grow into the demanding of justice from any restaurant with such undemocratic policies yet unremedied. Remember technique! . . . Gather facts. Negotiate. Rouse public opinion, and then, if absolutely necessary, and only as a last resort, Take Direct Action. . . ."

Finally, two months later, CORE considered a sit-down at Stoner's, but it quickly became evident that because the group was small, it would not be able to adapt this tactic of the industrial unions successfully to a restaurant seating over two hundred persons. Thus it was decided to delay the attack until June, when the conference which established a national federation of nonviolent direct-action groups brought enough participants into the city. Accordingly, the first sit-in took place in May at the smaller restaurant, Jack Spratt's. Twenty-one CORE members entered at the dinner hour; together with the regular patrons they filled the premises. When white CORE members "politely but firmly" refused to eat until the blacks were served, the manager called the police, who announced they could do nothing. Finally, two hours after the sit-in began, the manager took the orders from the mixed groups, and the first CORE sit-in ended successfully.[27]

The demonstration at Stoner's in early June, in which the delegates to CORE's first National Convention participated, followed a similar pattern. The contrast between CORE's method in these early sit-ins and the character of the direct action of the 1960's is obvious and profound. As James Farmer pointed out,

> When I look back at that first sit-in, I am amazed at our patience and good faith. No action group today would prolong the attempts at negotiation for more than a month before finally deciding to demonstrate. No militant Negro today would dream of trying to persuade a manager to serve him on the grounds that Negro patronage would not be bad for business. We have grown too proud for that. But in those days we were childishly literal-minded. . . . We regarded the sit-in as the successful culmination of a long campaign to reach the heart of the restaurant owner with the truth. What we took to be his conversion was as important as the fact that the restaurant had indeed been desegregated.[28]

CORE's use of nonviolent direct-action tactics in the struggle for racial justice was not unique. Just three weeks before the sit-in at Jack Spratt's, the Howard University NAACP held a similarly successful demonstration at a cafeteria near the University. A year later the Howard group sat-in for three days at a Thompson's Restaurant in downtown Washington, until stopped by the school administration.[29] Moreover, CORE members were aware of others who also had employed Gandhian tactics independently.[30] For example, Farmer was intimately acquainted with a group of white pacifist college students who, inspired by Gandhi, lived on a cooperative farm near Cleveland and, working with an NAACP youth council, during the summer of 1941 successfully integrated a public swimming pool, in the face of a hostile white crowd.[31] A more direct influence on the CORE founders was J. Holmes Smith, a former Methodist missionary in India, where he had been closely associated with Gandhi. A leading mover in the Non-Violent Action Committee which the FOR created early in 1941, he was the founder of the Harlem "Ashram," a small interracial cooperative which the New York CORE chapter used for a meeting place during its early years. The Ashram's major direct-action project was a two-week "Interracial pilgrimage" from New York to Washington in 1942, involving fourteen persons who walked the 240 miles to dramatize the antilynching and antipoll tax bills then before Congress.[32] Finally, and most important, there was the very different March on Washington Movement. Founded in 1941 when Randolph proposed a march to the nation's capital to petition for desegregation of the armed forces and equal employment opportunity in defense industries, the MOWM was national in scope and was based upon the premise that the power of the black masses must be the engine for social change. Although Randolph's strategy was strongly influenced by his experience as a Marxist and a labor leader, it was also consciously modeled on the mass nonviolent Gandhian movement in India. Despite its all-black composition, the MOWM was a key inspiration for CORE people. It not only demonstrated the power inherent in nonviolent direct action by forcing President Roosevelt to create a Fair Employment Practices Commission, but it also encouraged CORE's founders in their hopes that their own organization had the potential of becoming a mass movement.

Seeking to tap this growing interest in the application of nonviolent direct action, the FOR in the autumn of 1942 created a Department of Race Relations under the direction of Farmer and Rustin. While organizing FOR race relations conferences in a number of cities, the two men were able to stimulate the formation of several nonviolent direct-action groups. For example, in Denver, a local Committee of Racial Equality developed after a visit by Rustin. Similarly, in Syracuse, CORE "crystallized" out of an interracial meeting sponsored by the local FOR, at which Farmer spoke. These, and other groups organized in Colorado Springs, Detroit, and New York, attacked discrimination mainly in places of public accommodation. For example, both Denver and Syracuse CORE began their activity by testing restaurants, many of which served Negroes for the first time. Denver CORE then turned to theaters and, pointedly ignoring the ushers who violated state law by directing blacks to the balcony, took seats in the orchestra. The particularly enterprising Syracuse group tested the city's largest hotel, which barred Negroes, investigated discrimination in the Red Cross Blood Bank, and attempted to move a black family into a restricted neighborhood. New York, tackling an employment project, undertook negotiations for sales jobs with the Woolworth Company.[33]

As Farmer and Rustin went about their work, the idea of an FOR-sponsored Brotherhood Mobilization faded into the background, while the more practical idea of developing an independent federation of nonviolent direct-action groups, patterned on the Chicago Committe of Racial Equality, soon became their goal. This necessitated carefully defining

CORE's relationship to the FOR both because Rustin and Farmer were organizing local CORE committees while carrying out their duties for the Fellowship, and because certain FOR leaders wished to retain control of the new organization. CORE founders, particularly Robinson and Fisher, were firm in their conviction that CORE could not have a wide appeal if closely linked to pacifism or to FOR. Farmer, because of his delicate position, urged Fisher to "lay down the *party line* from the Chicago CORE point of view," when supplying information to people planning to form local CORE groups in other cities. "I am counting on you to fill the great gap which, as an FOR secretary, I must for the time being leave. You know—such as not confusing the two issues [CORE and pacifism], etc., etc. I'll be depending upon you to act where my hands are tied." Although FOR national leaders had voted to "endorse" rather than "sponsor" the Brotherhood Mobilization or the local committees which Rustin and Farmer were establishing, John Swomley, FOR's associate director, wanted the Fellowship to take over Chicago CORE and the other groups "with one fell swoop." Only upon Farmer's earnest representations was Muste persuaded to accept "the separation between the FOR and CORE." [34]

While Farmer and Rustin were establishing these groups, Bernice Fisher and the Chicago Committee shouldered the responsibility of organizing the "planning conference" called to create a national organization. Representatives from nine cities assembled at Carey's Woodlawn AME Church the first weekend in June 1943. [35] The bulk of the three-day meeting consisted of a heated debate over the nature of the national organization—whether it should be "a loose federation of organizations . . . permitted to select their own name . . . [and] with few restrictions" upon them, or whether it should have a more centralized structure with all affiliates adopting the name CORE, and their members individually subscribing to the CORE Statement of Purpose. Bernice Fisher led those who argued that, while the heart of CORE activity must be in vigorous local units, a closely knit organization with a paid secretariat was imperative. Her opponents came principally from leaders of the Columbus, Ohio, Vanguard League and the FOR-inspired Baltimore Interracial Fellowship, who insisted on preserving their local autonomy. Both Houser and Farmer urged the compromise which prevailed—create "a loose federation" under which the groups were required to adopt the CORE Statement of Purpose and the Action Discipline "in principle," but did not have to take the name, Committee of Racial Equality. At the end of the conference Fisher expressed her disappointment; she protested that "by making the strings loose enough to meet the needs of the Vanguard League and the Baltimore group, it was so loose that any group could come in." Frank Shearer, head of the Vanguard League, emotionally responded, charging his opponents with "conceit" for acting as though people would "be breaking their necks" to join CORE. Farmer, as conference chairman, brought the delegates together, reminding everyone "that the most important thing is the spirit in which the thing will be executed and that there be spiritual harmony." [36]

Actually there were good reasons for the reluctance exhibited by the League, which would be one of CORE's most important affiliates during the 1940's. In character and in origins it was very different from the other CORE groups. Founded in 1940 as an all-black organization, it was rooted not in Gandhism or pacifism, or interracialism, but in a combination of traditions stemming partly from NAACP legalism and partly from the "Don't Buy Where You Can't Work" campaigns of the 1930's when blacks in several cities mounted successful job boycotts against white-owned ghetto businesses. Its founders were all young "refugees from the NAACP" who condemned the Association for pursuing the "3 T's: Tea, Touch, and Talk." The earliest whites joined toward the end of 1941, and throughout the group's history whites constituted only a tiny minority. Whites came to form perhaps half of the Vanguard League's inner circle, but never held the top positions of leadership. Although there were only a small number of really active participants, the League, which claimed 1500 dues-paying members in 1943, proudly called itself a mass movement. The organization was notable for harassing discriminatory theater and restaurant owners with numerous lawsuits, generally settling out of court in exchange for agreements to obey the Ohio Civil Rights Law. Its leaders disdainfully differentiated their strategy from the less militant tactics of the NAACP because, instead of filing single lawsuits intermittently, they filed them in "job lots"—for example, eight simultaneously, against two downtown theaters in February 1941. Moreover, during 1941–42 the League engaged in extensive negotiations for nonmenial employment in ghetto stores, public utilities, and manufacturing companies. They enjoyed some limited successes. Bell Telephone employed Negroes to distribute phone directories in black neighborhoods, a bakery company outlet replaced its white staff with blacks, Kroger hired five clerks for a ghetto store, and Standard Oil admitted a few Negro trainees in a service station attendant program.[37] In its campaigns the Vanguard

League sometimes resorted to picketing, but it had no awareness of nonviolent direct action as a philosophy; only at an FOR interracial conference in December 1942, did "the League 'discover' that it had been using nonviolent techniques." [38] Thus to the CORE leaders at the Planning Conference, the affiliation of the League was desirable not because of its commitment to Gandhian methods, but because of its record of action and its roots in the black community.

The delegates adopted the name Committees of Racial Equality (the title *Congress* of Racial Equality was substituted the following year), named Farmer as Chairman and Fisher as secretary-treasurer, and selected a committee to carry on the organization's affairs until the next annual meeting. Although this first conclave was able to create only a skeletal national structure, CORE's basic character had been set. The constitution declared simply, "The purpose of the organization shall be to federate local interracial groups working to abolish the color line through direct non-violent [sic] action." Heightening the decentralized nature of the federation was the fact that, owing to the founding convention's deliberate decision, the loyalty of individual members was oriented more toward their local group than toward the national organization. In a calculated departure from the practice of the NAACP, whose national office issued membership cards and retained half of the dues collected by the branches, National CORE lacked a direct relationship with individual members and never even secured membership lists from the affiliates. Also in contrast to the NAACP branches, the CORE "locals" retained nearly all funds which they raised, being constitutionally required to pay the national office only a five-dollar annual membership fee and, beginning in 1945, a contribution amounting to 1 per cent of their annual income. The fact that the affiliates often neglected to send in even those token sums symbolized both their autonomy and their distrust of a strong national apparatus. Indeed, the CORE constitution said nothing about the power of the national body over the local groups, except for giving it the authority to affiliate new chapters and suspend inactive ones. As Houser told the 1945 CORE Convention, "We do not aim for a strong national organization, but for a federation of strong local groups." [39]

Details of the national organizational structure developed as a result of considerable experimentation. Bernice Fisher recalled, "Those first three years, there was no money, no salary, no office of our own, and actually no desire on our part to get institutionalized." The constitution adopted at the 1944 Convention provided for an executive committee elected by the Convention and added three vice-chairmen—one for handling affilia-tions, one for editing the organization's newsletter, the *CORE-lator,* and one for preparing educational literature. Farmer and Fisher were re-elected chairman and secretary-treasurer, respectively. These arrangements proved unsuccessful; the national organization was "practically inactive" for most of the following year because the officers failed to carry out their responsibilities. They were located in several cities and were seldom able to meet, and, in addition, Bernice Fisher became preoccupied with other interests. Accordingly, at the 1945 Convention the whole system was re-vamped, with the institution of a more conventional arrangement of offi-cers (a chairman, a single vice-chairman, a recording secretary, and a treasurer), the creation of the office of executive secretary, and the addi-tion of a Council consisting of the executive committee and two representa-tives from each chapter. This Council, meeting semiannually, was em-powered to make decisions on all important matters between Conventions and had the authority to affiliate new groups. The executive committee, which met more frequently, could no longer make policy but was em-powered to act in emergencies. With the appointment of an executive secretary the structure became more centralized; on the other hand, in creating the Council, CORE leaders were attempting to make the na-tional organization more responsive to its affiliates. The new structure re-mained unaltered until 1949.[40]

George Houser, then stationed at the FOR office in Cleveland, was chosen to fill the new unsalaried, part-time position of executive secre-tary. He assumed the CORE post at a time when the organization's lead-ership was undergoing major changes and when the work of FOR's race relations department was at a standstill. Fisher had withdrawn from ac-tive participation, Rustin was in jail as a conscientious objector, and Farmer had resigned his job with the FOR and stepped down as CORE's national chairman, being succeeded in the latter position by Frank Shearer of the Vanguard League.[41] A year later, however, when Rustin was released from prison, Houser moved to New York, and the two men became co-secretaries of FOR's new Racial and Industrial Department.[42] Concerned about the possible confusion that would arise regarding the relationship between FOR and CORE, Houser was careful to secure a statement reiterating the Fellowship's position that it "in no sense seeks to control C.O.R.E. groups."[43] Although the FOR permitted CORE to operate without interference, Houser's and Rustin's connections with the Fellowship were nevertheless of critical importance. In the first place, by permitting Rustin, Houser, and Houser's secretary to spend considerable time on CORE affairs, the FOR in effect subsidized a part-time secretariat for CORE. Second, CORE's national projects were jointly sponsored by the FOR, with the Fellowship providing a major part of the financing.

As executive secretary, Houser had three major duties. He edited the *CORE-lator;* he gave speeches, especially at colleges, to encourage development of CORE groups; and he tried to strengthen the work of existing affiliates as much as his time allowed. Most of CORE's business was handled through correspondence since Houser's travel was necessarily limited by a very small budget. In fact, it was only on an extended FOR trip in 1946 that Houser was able to visit CORE chapters in the West.[44] In his work for CORE, Houser sought to recommend and persuade; he possessed neither the authority nor the personality to pressure the locals forcefully. He did, however, push strongly for ambitious projects sponsored by the national organization—notably, his "Plan for a Mass Movement" and, later, the Journey of Reconciliation.

Houser, both because he prepared most of the early CORE literature and by virtue of his status as executive secretary, set the tone for the organization's activities over the next decade. He maintained what might be described as a classic Gandhian conception of nonviolent direct action. Believing that the activist, by taking unmerited suffering upon himself, mobilized public opinion and exerted a "redemptive influence upon the wrongdoer," Houser stressed that "a non-violent campaign cannot be considered a total success unless attitudes are changed in the process of changing policies." In thus emphasizing the *reconciling* spirit which was characteristic of FOR, he advocated prolonged negotiations, and using direct action "only as a last resort." As he said, "We frequently tend to think we are not taking action at all unless we are picketing or passing out leaflets. Often action of this sort is an admission of defeat," implying that "all other ways of solving the problem have been exhausted." [45] Finally, Houser was unswervingly dedicated to the ideal of interracialism, which he regarded as essential on both principled and pragmatic grounds. He disapproved of white and black nationalism; he thought interracial action would make it "impossible for race-baiters to say that they were being persecuted [sic] simply by Negroes"; and he believed that blacks and whites "working together in the same organization would undermine the racist theory that the two races cannot mix." Thus, for example, when A. Philip Randolph refused to cooperate with CORE on a

project in the nation's capital because "Negroes of Washington themselves should take the leadership in the fight," Houser uncompromisingly
insisted that the campaign must be thoroughly interracial.[46]

Although CORE was a tiny organization, Houser, inspired by Gandhi,
retained his hopes for a mass movement modeled on the Indian example.
Paradoxically, CORE's founders saw themselves as a well-disciplined, elite
group with rigid membership requirements, while also dreaming of becoming a large-scale, broad-based movement such as the MOWM. Randolph's attempt to revive a floundering MOWM through a call for a
mass civil disobedience campaign in the summer of 1943 had prompted
an earnest discussion among CORE's founders about what the nature of
their own organization should be. Farmer advised that if Randolph's new
campaign turned out to be successful, CORE would have to function as a
small cadre sophisticated in Gandhian strategy. However, if as Farmer
anticipated, the project would fail and the whole MOWM would "practically fold up in a year," then the way would be cleared for CORE to develop its own mass movement. Meanwhile, at his urging, the leaders of
Chicago CORE were proceeding with plans for the first CORE convention on the assumption that their organization would have to function as
a small, elite vanguard. As Houser put it at the time, there was a "unique
place for CORE . . . a place in organizing a small disciplined activity on
the race relations front." [47]

The MOWM rapidly declined as Farmer had predicted, and Houser
soon revived the idea of CORE developing a mass movement. In a memorandum circulated shortly after the 1944 CORE Convention, he urged
that, as a first step in this direction, the organization should sponsor a
year-long experimental project involving two hundred volunteers who
would live in "ashrams or housing co-ops." Before embarking on direct-
action projects, they would receive "intensive . . . spiritual training" for
group discipline and unity. Such a program would bring CORE "to the
attention of the masses of people" and provide a model for the "mass
non-violent approach . . . on a more permanent basis" in cities across the
country. The response of Houser's associates in CORE and the FOR was
only guardedly enthusiastic. Muste favored a less ambitious project engaging about fifty people over a two- or three-month period. Fisher,
wanting to avoid the "pacifist tag," was skeptical of anything involving
co-sponsorship with the FOR. Houser thereupon suggested that several
nonpacifist organizations be invited to join the list of sponsors, and he
recommended holding a summer campaign in Washington.[48]

Unfortunately, the hopes for a Washington project foundered on Houser's inability to obtain the endorsement of a broad spectrum of local racial advancement groups. Accordingly, the CORE Executive Committee chose Chicago as the location for a two-month summer workshop in 1945, and eighteen persons, six of them black, signed up as participants. Plans were laid for a wide-ranging attack on restrictive covenants, job discrimination in department stores, and segregation in the YMCA, to be carried out in cooperation with the Chicago Urban League and other local organizations. When negotiations with obdurate managers of ten department stores revealed that they feared a loss of business if blacks were employed as clerks, workshop members stood outside Loop stores polling customers. Upon finding that two-thirds of those queried said they would not object to black saleswomen, the group persuaded the Mayor's race relations committee to meet with the managers. The summer volunteers tested the YMCA swimming pool, held discouraging conferences with top YMCA officials, and then obtained signatures on a petition urging the "Y" to adopt a policy of nondiscrimination. Finally, the group picketed a Negro apartment complex owned by an outspoken advocate of restrictive covenants.[49]

Out of all this, very little was accomplished, and almost no direct action was attempted. The tactics employed, while based on Gandhian procedures, also clearly reflected the powerlessness and weak position of the workshop, which was small in size and unable to mobilize substantial community support. Yet Houser was convinced that many whites were "waiting for an opportunity" to work with blacks on direct-action projects and, more important, that the "increasingly restless" Negroes would provide the "mass base" for a movement "committed to the interracial principle." In the fall of 1945 he circulated a new memorandum, again urging the establishment of a year-long leadership training project in preparation for a "Mass Non-Violent Interracial Movement." This time, however, conceding that CORE "has neither experienced local leadership nor the financial backing to make it into a mass organization," Houser sought a broad base by proposing to enlist the support of "key people across the country." He even prevailed upon Randolph to agree to call a small, exploratory conference of important leaders, and despite his skepticism of the NAACP actually broached the subject with the Association's Assistant Secretary, Roy Wilkins. Yet, at the meeting in December, members of the CORE Council were pessimistic. They believed that neither CORE, consisting of small groups often with "immature leadership," nor the NAACP, which among whites had the image of being a black organization, would be suitable agencies for mounting a mass interracial movement. Although deciding to participate in the Randolph meeting, the Council abandoned the year-round project as unfeasible, and settled instead for another summer workshop. In the following months Houser's hopes foundered completely. Randolph decided against calling the conference, pleading that the NAACP might fear he was trying to establish a rival organization. And although Houser actively promoted the summer workshop, he was forced to cancel it because only three volunteers signed up.[50]

Houser's vision of creating a mass interracial nonviolent movement died, although the summer institute was revived in 1947 and became a major vehicle of national CORE activity for the remainder of Houser's administration. History proved Houser correct in his view that only by a mass movement could southern segregation be challenged effectively,[51] but CORE in the 1940's was simply too feeble to have created such a movement, even if Houser had accurately gauged the mood of the black masses at the time. In fact, it was just because CORE was so weak that it had toyed with the idea of involving the NAACP and Randolph in the first place. Not until the 1960's did a mass movement such as that envisaged by CORE founders actually develop—and then, CORE played an important, though scarcely dominant role.

Although CORE leaders dreamed of creating a national mass movement, in practice the heart of the organization's activities rested with scattered affiliates or "locals" (a term reflecting the pro-labor orientation of the founders). During the first year of the federation's history seven groups joined: Chicago, Denver, Detroit, Oberlin, New York, Syracuse, and the Vanguard League of Columbus. Thereafter the number rose slowly, reaching thirteen in 1947. Meanwhile, six groups had died.[52] The locals had a strong midwestern tinge. Of the total of nineteen affiliates during this period, nine were from states in the Mississippi River basin: Chicago, Evanston, and Peoria, Illinois; Minneapolis, Minnesota; Kansas City, Missouri; Kansas City and Lawrence, Kansas; Lincoln, Nebraska; and Bartlesville, Oklahoma. One was in Detroit, and four were in Ohio: Columbus, Cincinnati, Cleveland, and Oberlin. Only three were in the East—Syracuse, New York City, and Philadelphia; and two were in the West—Denver and Los Angeles. None was in New England or the South. In size, these groups, with the notable exception of the Vanguard League, were typically small, fluctuating between fifteen and thirty members. This fact reflected both the amount of interest they were able to generate in their local communities and, more important, their selectivity in admitting new members. Chicago CORE set the model. From the beginning it was a closely knit group of highly committed individuals; in September 1943, it formally established two types of membership: "active" and "associate." The latter, being unwilling to participate regularly in action projects, were not given the right to vote.[53] Many other chapters soon instituted this distinction, and in time it became the general practice.

In composition, there was variation in membership of the different CORE chapters. White and black members alike were usually well-educated people drawn from middle-class occupations, although the Vanguard League boasted of its black working-class base. Bartlesville, Oklahoma, Kansas City, Kansas, and Kansas City, Missouri, affiliates were composed of middle-aged persons, but the majority of CORE members were young—in their late teens and early twenties. College students were an important element. An early member recalled that the campuses were the places where "recruiting was done in those days." Between a third and a half of the affiliates were essentially college-student groups, some of the most active people in the Vanguard League were graduate students at Ohio State University and many of the other chapters had substantial student contingents. Although CORE chapters were, almost by definition, interracial, they ranged from the overwhelmingly black Vanguard League to groups in Philadelphia, Minneapolis, and Cincinnati, which complained of the difficulty of securing blacks. In the Kansas City, Kansas, chapter there were almost no whites, while in the Kansas City, Missouri, group there were almost no blacks. The college groups were mainly white, although when Lincoln, Nebraska, CORE was first organized in 1945 it was divided equally between the races.

While CORE members were predominantly white, blacks were prominent in chapter leadership. The chairman of Denver CORE was Dr. Clarence Holmes, a black dentist and long-time civic leader who had founded the Denver NAACP in 1915. Rev. Robert Kelley was the first chairman of Minneapolis CORE; both Harriett Lane, another chairman of Minneapolis (and in 1949–50 chairman of National CORE), and Gerald Bullock, a chairman of Chicago CORE, were schoolteachers; A. C. Thompson, chairman of Evanston CORE, attended Roosevelt University and later became a businessman. Lynn Coleman, co-chairman with Houser in early Cleveland CORE, was a policeman; Juanita Morrow, later chairman in Cleveland, was a journalist. The top leaders of the Vanguard League were all upwardly mobile college graduates on their way to professional careers. Frank Shearer worked in the state auditor's office and obtained a degree from the YMCA Franklin College of Law. Barbee William Durham was a pharmaceutical chemist at Ohio State University's Reagent Laboratory. Eugene Stanley, a state civil service employee and a graduate student at Ohio State University, became a professor at North Carolina A. & T. College in 1947.[54]

Although the exact role played by the pacifists is difficult to assess, such individuals, mainly white, continued to function as a creative minority. Pacifists, many of whom were FOR members and field secretaries, provided the most dynamic leaders for several chapters, notably, Denver, Cleveland, Detroit, and Kansas City, Missouri. One of the black founders of the Vanguard League, Barbee Durham, was sufficiently inclined to pacifism to have joined the FOR in the late 1930's, and the first whites admitted to the League were drawn from the Fellowship and the American Friends Service Committee.[55] On the other hand, from the beginning tension developed over the fact that many pacifists—as well as some nonpacifists—were more concerned with the philosophical emphasis upon loving and converting the enemy, upon reconciling whites and blacks, than with the employment of nonviolent and direct action such as picketing and sitting-in. Bernice Fisher warned about the danger of being primarily interested "in converting the exploiter [rather] than in ending the exploitation," and at the 1944 Convention she became disturbed about some of the people joining CORE: "One of our most perplexing problems is the caliber of the individuals we are attracting. They are more interested in being nonviolent than in hitting the race question; many misinterpret the technique in terms of 'education.' " At the opposite extreme were other members who viewed "direct nonviolent action only as a useful method of a minority group who have too often found violence self-defeating." Fisher, while acknowledging that "breaks in discipline" were more likely to occur among the latter, also recognized that they brought to CORE "a refreshing challenge and perspective." As she put it, "CORE, integrated, hardhitting and vital, can grow only through a creative balance of the elements within it."[56]

The locals displayed wide variations in the amount of activity they undertook. A few appear to have done nothing beyond holding meetings. Those furthest south were naturally timid. The affiliates in Bartlesville, Oklahoma, and Kansas City, Missouri, adopted the name Committee on the Practice of Democracy because, as a black leader of the latter group said, Kansas City was "not yet ready for the name CORE." Neither chapter engaged in actual direct action. In Bartlesville, where the group had been founded by the town's librarian, the principal project was to help bring in a Negro physician "who is accepted in the white hospital." But as one member said, "In a southern town like Bartlesville, something is accomplished when whites and Negroes meet together as friends." [57] Elsewhere the more vigorous affiliates typically met biweekly and even weekly, involving much of the members' time. Yet even the busiest chapters like Chicago, Columbus, Cleveland, Detroit, and New York, operating with volunteers and facing an indifferent if not hostile public, were limited in what they could achieve.

Those groups which reported a significant amount of activity invariably worked on public accommodations campaigns, and such projects consumed nearly all the energies of many chapters. Their appeal may be explained by the blatant visibility of the discrimination and by the fact that in most places where CORE operated, the establishments involved were especially vulnerable to direct action because they were clearly in violation of state civil rights laws. Several of the CORE affiliates had projects to integrate the YMCA. New York CORE, for example, negotiated and petitioned for half a year and then, beginning in January 1945, the group picketed the monthly meetings of the "Y" Board of Directors. By June, however, no progress had been made and the effort died in discouragement. Restaurants were a particularly popular object of attack. In Detroit the chapter enlisted support from black unionists and tried to integrate eating places near the automobile factories. The 1944 CORE Convention, meeting in Detroit after the race riot that took thirty-four lives, conducted a sit-in with some trepidation at Trainor's restaurant. The apprehension surrounding this demonstration was recorded by Bernice Fisher:

> The action project was particularly important because Walt [Jackson] made such an issue of the danger involved, and the fact that we were in Detroit! Against the prospect of milder restaurant testing, the group chose the Trainor sit-down! And it was a thrilling experience in spite of not being served—3 white outsiders joined in. . . . The feeling of solidarity was good.

Elsewhere chapters reported victories. During 1943–44, Chicago CORE ended discrimination at several establishments. Los Angeles CORE was so successful that by 1947 it observed, "We have reached a point where small restaurants are more or less routine." [58]

Except for one instance in Detroit, arrests were not part of the experience of restaurant demonstrators, but they did occur with frequency at places of public amusement. In August 1943, police arrested seven members of the Denver chapter at a downtown theater. The CORE action had, however, effectively exposed the illegality and immorality of the theater owners' policy, and the commissioner of public safety convinced the owners' to relax their jim crow practices for persistent Negroes. [59] In Chicago, police arrested twelve persons who staged a "stand-up," blocking the ticket counter at the White City Roller Rink. Several weeks after this first recorded instance of a CORE group using such obstructive tactics, the rink finally opened, thus bringing to a successful conclusion in early 1946 CORE's very first public accommodation project begun four years earlier. [60] Less fortunate was the outcome of a sustained campaign against Cleveland's Euclid Beach Amusement Park, where in August 1946, the project collapsed after three CORE people were manhandled, clubbed, and kicked by park police. [61]

Although discrimination in employment was much harder to fight than discrimination in places of public accommodations, because it was more difficult to prove and, except in a few places, not forbidden by law, half of the affiliates engaged in job projects. Two chapters attacked the transit industry. In 1944, Syracuse CORE, a university-based affiliate, polled people waiting for buses and found 97 per cent of them favorable toward hiring black drivers. Negotiations with the company followed, but when the students left Syracuse at the end of the spring semester, the project was dropped. [62] In Columbus the Vanguard League worked unsuccessfully between 1943 and 1945 to persuade the streetcar company to hire Negroes. Reluctant to picket, the League appealed fruitlessly to the United States Employment Service and the War Manpower Commission. [63] More frequently CORE locals focused on the department and variety stores. Customers were polled and inconclusive interviews were held with stalling store managers in cities like Chicago, Cleveland, and Detroit, all without success. [64] There was only one victory against job discrimination—a modest success flowing from a joint effort in which Chicago and Evanston CORE collaborated with other groups during 1946–47 in a campaign against Wonder Bread Bakeries, which had a large market in the Negro community but employed blacks only in menial ca-

pacities. The picket lines soon petered out, but the boycott lasted nearly
a year, ending when Wonder Bread hired five black truck drivers.[65]

Half of the locals also attempted to do something about segregated
housing, and two of them sought to attack jim crow schools, but none
found techniques adequate even to begin to grapple with these serious
problems. Syracuse CORE interviewed officials at the local housing authority, urging them to explore ways in which a few other cities had tried
to promote integration. The Detroit affiliate and the Vanguard League
helped secure legal assistance for black families attempting to move into
lily-white neighborhoods. Chicago CORE sent a delegation to testify before a state legislative committee considering a restrictive covenant bill.
New York used direct action: during the winter and spring of 1946–47 its
main project was to picket financial institutions which discriminated
against blacks in financial mortgages.[66] The chapters in Columbus and
Chicago both made elaborate investigations of their local school systems
and publicized their findings widely. The Vanguard League, protesting a
situation where residential segregation and deliberate gerrymandering
consigned one-third of the black children to jim crow schools, appeared
at school board meetings and even campaigned against a bond issue. Chicago CORE in 1944 charged that the Negro schools were overcrowded—
often on double session—while white ones had empty classrooms. Rebuffed by the educators and refused an interview with the mayor,
twenty-five CORE supporters staged a poster walk at City Hall.[67]

Chicago CORE also continued its earlier campaigns against discrimination at the University of Chicago and the Red Cross blood bank. CORE
discovered that the University, through its membership in several "neighborhood improvement associations," actually contributed money to evict
Negroes who had moved into apartments covered by restrictive covenants. Moreover, black patients were seldom admitted to the University
hospitals, and the medical school's Negro students could not intern there.
For over a year CORE repeatedly attempted negotiations. Ignored by
President Robert Hutchins, the members on one occasion sought to embarrass him; stationing themselves outside a meeting where he was giving an address, they passed out copies of their report òn University discrimination. Meanwhile, protesting against the Red Cross practice of
segregating the plasma of black and white donors in its blood bank,
CORE members distributed leaflets urging, "When you give your blood,
register your protest against this Jim Crow policy." The local also circulated a pamphlet asking other CORE groups to undertake a similar cam-

paign; Syracuse and Oberlin were the only ones to respond. But, like Chicago, they failed to move the Red Cross which, ironically, owed its blood bank program to the scientific research of a black man, Dr. Charles Drew.[68]

Clearly, concrete achievements were modest. Success occurred almost entirely in places of public accommodation and recreation. Accomplishments in jobs were negligible; efforts on schools and housing were failures. And New York CORE's unique attempt to influence national legislation—a pilgrimage to Washington in 1944, modeled on J. Holmes Smith's earlier march—to protest the filibustering against the antipoll tax bill, made scarcely a ripple.[69] In fact only half the affiliates can be said to have registered any victories at all.

Several factors account for CORE's record of accomplishment. The climate of white public opinion was such that, except for restaurants, few discriminators felt themselves under strong pressure to modify their policies. Nor did substantial numbers of people in the black community as yet perceive the potential for change offered by CORE's approach. Given this context it is not surprising that the small CORE chapters seldom attracted much attention in the black or white press or in other media of mass communication. Moreover, as Fisher had discerned, the tendency for chapters to focus on the reconciliatory aspects of their strategy could also have negative consequences. They took seriously Houser's advice that nonviolence should "incarnate the spirit of understanding, of good will, of humility," [70] and in fact during these first four years only half the chapters attempted to move beyond negotiation. Sometimes discussions with discriminators did indeed eliminate racist practices, but on numerous occasions, when testing and negotiation produced no results, CORE locals failed to follow through with more militant tactics and allowed projects to peter out. Many members it seemed had an affinity for intellectually oriented activities such as investigation and discussion at the expense of action in the streets. Such tendencies were of course reinforced by the sense of powerlessness stemming from CORE's small size and public apathy. Yet it should be emphasized that CORE leaders, while often disappointed, did not become disillusioned. Unlike the activists of the middle 1960's who in their discouragement with the rate of change turned their backs on CORE's ideology of interracial nonviolent direct action, the organization's early members had only a modest set of expectations. It must not be forgotten that in the 1940's all the racial advancement groups put together were achieving only very limited gains. Given the milieu of the period, both friends and foes regarded CORE's successes as significant.

Like National CORE, the local groups maintained strong ambivalences about the "conservative" NAACP and Urban League, yet nevertheless worked with them on occasion. The degree of actual cooperation between CORE affiliates and other racial advancement organizations varied with circumstances. In Chicago, CORE collaborated with the Urban League and other groups in developing its department store employment campaign and the Wonder Bread boycott. Philadelphia also pushed its proposal to attack job discrimination in department stores through a coalition of local organizations, although unfortunately this broke down amid mutual recriminations before a campaign could be launched.[71] The founders of the Minneapolis group had originally seriously considered joining the NAACP, but had decided to choose the relatively unknown CORE "rather than wasting our time fighting the reactionary elements" in the local NAACP branch which had "done little but talk." Yet Minneapolis CORE worked with the NAACP to eliminate discrimination in a bowling alley, and was one of several CORE affiliates that collaborated with the Association's branches in local coalitions seeking state and city FEPC legislation.[72]

CORE locals in this period—and throughout the organization's history —were marked by instability. Even the busiest and most successful chapters typically exhibited a pattern of intensive activity followed by decline, ending either in a revival or dissolution. Not surprisingly, college affiliates had particular difficulties, both because the transient quality of student life discouraged continuity and because college groups often had an image of youthfulness and immaturity. Lincoln, Nebraska, CORE conducted a successful year-long campaign to open a downtown cafeteria, but then merged with the Social Action Council of Lincoln in the summer of 1946 "to avoid the stigma of adolescent irresponsibility which we feared had become attached to CORE." [73] Undoubtedly, the most important factor accounting for the vigor of individual chapters was the quality of their leadership, the presence of creative leaders often being critical for the development of action programs. Thus, following the departure of Houser and a few other key persons from Chicago in the spring of 1944, the original Committee of Racial Equality faced difficult days, and when Bernice Fisher moved to Detroit some months later, the affiliate practically collapsed. The dynamic Syracuse CORE chapter enjoyed periods of vigor when the pacifist student Robert Vogel served as its leader in 1942–43 and again for a few months after his brief return from CPS camp at the beginning of 1944. During the following school year, the group met regularly, but no leader emerged to match Vogel's capabilities, and the affiliate accomplished very little, disbanding in November 1945.[74] When Cleveland CORE's founder, George Houser left the chairmanship in 1946, its high level of activity was maintained by Juanita Morrow, a black journalist and experienced direct actionist who had been prominent in the sit-ins of 1943–44 at Howard University. Cleveland CORE's decline dates from her departure in mid-1947. Yet dedicated leaders in themselves did not necessarily produce viable affiliates. New York CORE included a half-dozen highly committed individuals, but it mainly held lengthy meetings and had a generally meager action program.[75] Cincinnati was plagued by leadership wrangles and infighting, centering upon the aggressive and blunt personality of Nathan Wright, the Negro chapter chairman and Episcopal Church social worker.[76] In Los Angeles the factionalistic personality of the dynamic black chairman Manuel Talley split the group, and the original affiliate ceased functioning after Talley seceded with his supporters to form a rival chapter.[77]

In three instances, problems with left-wing organizations either destroyed chapters, as in Detroit, or seriously weakened them, as in Columbus and Chicago. From the very beginning CORE leaders had an anticommunist policy, both because they feared the kind of infiltration that hurt many reform organizations in the 1930's, and also because they considered it poor strategy "to mix our issues." [78] Wishing their movement identified exclusively with the cause of racial equality, they contended that linking CORE with other matters such as pacifism or communism alienated many who otherwise would be supporters. Yet the communist problem cropped up occasionally. In an affiliate like Cleveland, with Juanita Morrow's strong, skillful leadership, communist attempts at infiltration were repulsed without much difficulty.[79] In contrast, CORE chairmen in Columbus and Chicago, faced with their chapters' loss of momentum, welcomed help from the Marxists. Thus as the Vanguard League declined after World War II, several white CIO unionists—some of whom were later alleged to be Communists—became active in the group. Under their influence the noted black Communist Benjamin J. Davis, Jr., was invited to address the opening rally of the League's 1947 membership drive. A furor led by Barbee Durham followed, and the invitation was withdrawn. But the controversy only accelerated the demise of the League.[80]

Chicago CORE, after a year of inactivity, was revived in the autumn of 1945 under the chairmanship of the black schoolteacher and NAACP leader, Gerald Bullock. Finding few members interested in action, he dropped the chapter's rigid selection procedures and made a broad appeal for new members to which the Trotskyist Socialist Workers Party (SWP) responded. Difficulties with them became apparent during the second (and successful) campaign against the White City Skating Rink. The Trotskyists dominated the demonstrations, and the CORE chapter voted in January 1946 to refrain from requesting pickets to obey "even a watered down discipline." When Houser learned of participation by SWP people, he warned Bullock that the SWP was not committed to nonviolence. To allay Houser's criticism about distributing circulars which referred to the campaign as a joint CORE-SWP project, subsequent publicity listed as sponsors a broad-based coalition of civil rights, labor, and radical organizations. Houser was still disturbed, because he knew that elsewhere Trotskyists had subverted other organizations for their own purposes. By late summer 1946, the *Chicago CORE-News,* edited by a Trotskyist, espoused retaliatory violence and carried notices like "No Regular CORE meeting this Friday. Everybody out to the SWP Rally." Meanwhile, "the violent vs. the non-violent approach [was] being . . . argued" at meetings, with many people in the affiliate, now swollen to nearly five hundred dues-paying "members," ridiculing nonviolence. In early 1947 University of Chicago students, discouraged by the Trotskyists' tactics, withdrew to form their own campus chapter. As activity declined, the Trotskyists drifted away. But by then the chapter was moribund, and ultimately it was disaffiliated.[81]

Houser's handling of the Trotskyist situation in Chicago CORE—his inability to intervene beyond writing hortatory letters—clearly revealed the limited authority of the national office and the virtual independence of the chapters. Houser was also dismayed at the lack of coordination between national and the chapters, and among the affiliates themselves. As he wrote in the fall of 1946,

> There is practically no contact between the groups except as an occasional bulletin is sent [to chapter officers] from the volunteer national secretary. . . . Practically no financial support comes to the national office from the local groups. Last year this amounted to

$113.00. . . . There is no contact between national office and the rank and file members of the affiliated groups. . . . Members of CORE in various cities know practically nothing about what is happening nationally. It is impossible to support an organization on the basis of this national scheme.[82]

Houser, although committed to a democratic federation of autonomous groups, doubted that CORE could ever become an effective mass movement, as he and other founders had envisaged, without a national program and a full-time salaried staff. Personally he found the CORE job increasingly burdensome and time-consuming, and he frequently regretted that financial stringencies prevented the hiring of a full-time executive secretary to replace him.[83] Yet the chapters were skeptical about strengthening the central office, and in particular they proved unwilling to finance a paid staff or a meaningful national program.

National CORE's budget was indeed miniscule. Office expenses in 1945–46 ran about $100 a month.[84] The organization's small income came mainly from sporadic contributions and direct mail appeals. In December 1945, Houser reluctantly recommended that the locals support the central office by agreeing to enroll their members in the national organization, with the dues split equally between the chapters and National CORE. This idea, which to many members suspiciously resembled the practice of the centralized and bureaucratic NAACP, was received less than enthusiastically, and the 1946 Convention in effect tabled the proposal. Yet a few months later national CORE leaders, determined to develop a viable national program, tried again. The Executive Committee decided to develop a project attacking southern transportation segregation and to raise $7000 to staff an office and hire a full-time executive secretary. Houser believed that some money could be collected by using the mailing lists of sympathetic organizations, with an appeal signed by well-known members of the advisory committee that had been inaugurated in 1945. Hoping to cajole the chapters into permitting national to send similar appeal letters to people on their "contact lists," he offered the affiliates the option of handling such a mailing themselves. But except for Cleveland none of the chapters was willing to cooperate. Thus, although Houser had written the black pacifist Wilson Head inquiring if he would be interested in the position, the national financial drive foundered, and no executive secretary could be employed.[85]

These setbacks notwithstanding, CORE went ahead with the proposed national project, the Journey of Reconciliation, a two-week interracial foray into the South designed to test compliance with a recent Supreme Court decision against segregation in interstate travel. For several years a small but growing number of blacks had been challenging the jim crow transportation laws by attempting to occupy accommodations reserved for whites. The most celebrated of these protests involved the arrest and conviction of Irene Morgan for refusing to vacate a front seat on a bus traveling from Virginia to Maryland, In June 1946, the Court ruled that it was unconstitutional for the Virginia legislature to require segregation on interstate motor carriers. Negroes soon discovered, however, that the bus companies did not intend to alter their seating practices.[86]

To CORE and FOR activists, this situation demonstrated the inherent limitations of legalism, and provided an excellent opportunity to prove the value of nonviolent direct action. The possibilities of a Journey were first explored at the autumn 1946 Executive Committee where Houser and Rustin, who were starting their jobs as co-secretaries of the FOR's Racial-Industrial Department, had a leading role in the extensive discussions. With Muste encouraging them to take on the campaign, it became a joint CORE-FOR venture. In fact the very name, Journey of Reconciliation, grew out of conversations among FOR staffers. For CORE the project promised to be of inestimable value. It would be "a real national campaign," conducted by the organization's central office, in contrast to the purely local projects of the affiliates. This project, it was hoped, would provide CORE with a national image, arouse the energy of the chapters, and bring in money to finance both the development of new groups and the employment of an executive secretary.[87]

On the basis of consultation with southern friends, Houser and Rustin subsequently scrapped the original idea of taking the Journey as far south as New Orleans. Fearing the enormous potential for violence in Alabama, Mississippi, and Louisiana, they decided to confine the trip to the upper South.[88] In January 1947, the two men made a preliminary tour of the area. They were able to persuade three North Carolina white radicals to join them on the Journey, and to arrange for other forms of assistance from local blacks, who agreed to feed and house the travelers, sponsor rallies, and provide legal assistance. For example, out of more than thirty speaking engagements during the Journey, nearly all were before black church, college, and NAACP groups. Former national CORE treasurer Eugene Stanley, then teaching at North Carolina A. & T. College, handled local arrangements in Greensboro. NAACP branches at key stopovers were particularly friendly.[89]

Not surprisingly, given the ambivalent relationships between CORE and the NAACP, the Association's relationship to the Journey was a complex one. Toward the end of November 1946, Thurgood Marshall, the Association's chief counsel, publicly warned southern blacks to be wary of "well-meaning radical groups" who had asked his advice about applying Gandhian tactics in the South. Marshall, apparently unaware that FOR and CORE had decided to confine the Journey to the upper South, sternly declared that "A disobedience movement on the part of Negroes and their white allies, if employed in the [deep] South, would result in wholesale slaughter with no good achieved." Shortly afterward, NAACP executive secretary Walter White declined an invitation to be one of the "prominent individuals" signing FOR's financial appeal to underwrite the Journey.[90] Nevertheless, even though it did not give "active support," the Association supplied a list of contacts in branches located along the Journey's route, thus providing CORE with an entree to NAACP leaders in the South which proved inestimably helpful.

The group of sixteen men who left Washington on April 9, 1947, consisted of eight whites and eight blacks. Among the latter, in addition to Rustin, were William Worthy, an official of the New York Council for a Permanent FEPC; Conrad Lynn, New York attorney active in civil rights causes; and three men from Cincinnati—Nathan Wright, the chapter leader; Andrew Johnson, a law student; and Wallace Nelson, who would later become a key CORE staff member. Eugene Stanley joined the trip for the leg from Durham to Chapel Hill, and lost his job as a result. The whites included two CORE founders—Houser and Homer Jack, executive secretary of the Chicago Council Against Racial and Religious Discrimination; Igal Roodenko, a New York printer; and two functionaries of the socialist-oriented Workers Defense League—Joe Felmet of Ashville, North Carolina, a southern representative of the organization, and James Peck, editor of the League's news bulletin, who would subsequently become an influential figure in national CORE.[91] It is noteworthy that all the whites and half of the blacks were pacifists. Thus, as was true of CORE's founding, the organization's first major national project really depended on the initiative and idealism of a small group of pacifists.

Just before embarking upon the Journey, the participants spent two days in Washington, where they received intensive training in nonviolent philosophy and techniques. For hours on end they engaged in sociodramas, acting out the appropriate responses to be taken in the face of abusive behavior by bus drivers, policemen, and hysterical segregationists. The two-week bus trip which followed took the group to Virginia, North Carolina, and Kentucky. Its members generally split into two parts, one going by Trailways, the other by Greyhound. No efforts were made to integrate facilities in stations, rest rooms, and restaurants, but they incurred twelve arrests in challenging seating arrangements.

Although they experienced no trouble in northern Virginia, when the demonstrators reached Petersburg, Lynn was arrested after refusing to move from the front section of a Trailways bus, and released on a twenty-five-dollar bond. The next arrests came on the third day of the Journey, in Durham, where Johnson and Rustin were apprehended for refusing to give up their front seats. Also arrested in this incident was Peck, who left his seat in the middle of the bus and declared, "If you arrest them you'll have to arrest me too, for I'm going to sit in the rear." The three were taken to the police station where they were later released without being charged.

The incident which provided the most violence potential and resulted in the most important legal case of the Journey occurred at Cargill, a mill town just outside Chapel Hill. Johnson and Felmet were arrested for being seated together in front. Thereupon Rustin and Roodenko, who were in the rear, walked forward, occupied the seat which the other pair had just vacated, and were themselves promptly arrested. Peck, standing outside the bus, was hit by several taxi drivers; one of them declared, "They'll never get a bus out of here tonight." After the men were released on fifty-dollar bonds, Charles Jones, a white Presbyterian minister, hurriedly drove them to his home for safety. They arrived there, followed by two taxicabs filled with angry whites armed with sticks and rocks, and shortly afterwards, an anonymous telephone caller told the minister, "Get those damn niggers out of town or we'll burn your house down. We'll be around to see that they go." Fearing bloodshed, the interracial group almost immediately left by car traveling over the back roads to Greensboro.

The remainder of the arrests occurred in the Trailways bus station in Asheville, North Carolina, and on the final leg of the trip at Culpeper and Amherst, Virginia. At Asheville, Peck, and a black rider from Chicago, Dennis Banks, were arrested and held on one-hundred-dollar bonds until their trial the following day, where they were represented by Curtis Todd, a Negro lawyer of Winston-Salem. Neither the judge nor the state's attorney was acquainted with the Morgan decision, and they actually borrowed Todd's copy to read in the courtroom. Despite that fact, both men were sentenced to thirty-day terms on a road gang.[92]

As significant as the arrests, in the view of the participants, was the fact that most of the time they were able to violate transportation segregation without being apprehended. Generally the bus drivers did not know about the Morgan decision. Their ignorance of it was also shared by the police, who, when summoned, were usually "polite and calm." While some whites threatened violence, none occurred except at Chapel Hill, and Rustin and Houser reported that most of the white passengers, rather than reacting strongly, "were apathetic." Negroes were "cautious" —often fearful—upon seeing the black testers in the front seats, but when it became evident that the latter were not being molested, many black passengers "tended to move from the rear forward, too." To account for what they regarded as the minimal tensions and scarcity of violence on the Journey, Houser and Rustin stressed the interracial composition and the nonviolent, disciplined behavior:

> . . . We can not over-emphasize the necessity for this courteous and intelligent manner while breaking with the caste system. It is our belief that the reason the police behaved politely stems from the fact that there was not the slightest provocation in the attitude of the resisters. On the contrary, we tried at all times to understand their attitude and position first. . . . Another reason for the lack of tension was the interracial character of the group. We did not allow a single situation to develop so that the struggle appeared to be between white and Negro persons, but rather that progressives and democrats, white and black, were working by peaceful means to overcome a system which they felt to be wrong.[93]

Thus their experience confirmed the faith of these early CORE leaders in the reconciliatory philosophy of the CORE Action Discipline.

The authorities in North Carolina dropped the charges in all of the cases except those for the four arrested in Chapel Hill. The case was handled by local black lawyers, and because of CORE's and FOR's slender financial resources, the North Carolina Conference of NAACP branches and a committee of prominent Durham Negroes raised the necessary money. At the trials in June 1947, in Chapel Hill Recorder's Court, the two Negroes involved, Rustin and Johnson, received small fines, while the two whites, Roodenko and Felmet, were given the maximum sentence of thirty days on the road gang. The case was appealed, and in March 1948, after an all-white jury deliberated for twenty minutes and sustained the convictions, the county judge increased the sentences of the blacks to the same thirty-day road gang terms meted out to the whites. Ten months later the State Supreme Court upheld the lower courts.[94] Houser and Rustin hoped that the NAACP would carry the Chapel Hill case to the Supreme Court, but after studying the trial transcript the Association's attorneys concluded that, because of the unsatisfactory way the North Carolina lawyers had examined the defendants in the lower courts, the record was "not full enough" to carry the case further.[95] In March 1949, with Johnson having decided that he was "both mentally and physically unprepared to serve thirty days on the road gang," the other three men returned to North Carolina to serve their sentences. With time off for good behavior, Rustin, Felmet, and Roodenko were imprisoned for twenty-two days of arduous labor.[96]

What was the significance of the Journey? Several years later, James Peck, looking back on the event, described it as "perhaps the most unique and outstanding undertaking CORE has ever made." Its actual impact, however, is difficult to measure. CORE and FOR never claimed that it led to transportation desegregation. Atlantic Greyhound officials maintained that since the state laws were still in force in regard to intrastate travel, as a "practical" matter they had to continue to segregate all black passengers. Thus the faith that nonviolent direct action would succeed where legalism had failed was misplaced. For the immediate future the principal fruit of the Journey and the jail sentences was the "publicity." Houser and Rustin proudly noted that it "received a good deal of publicity, most of it quite fair in both the daily and the Negro press. That there has been a larger amount of interest is indicated by the many meetings which have been held since the project was finished, where there has been an enthusiastic response, as well as by the demand for copies of the complete report." More important, the Journey, by placing a spotlight on nonviolent direct action, functioned as one of the many events that gradually were to make this type of protest respectable, even fashionable. Peck observed in 1954, seven years afterward, that he still found that the Journey interested his audiences more than anything else.[97]

From an organizational point of view the Journey scarcely produced the results hopefully anticipated. CORE was somewhat more widely known, but it still lacked a substantial national image; and there was no evidence that the Journey stimulated the growth of CORE and its chapters. In fact, the organization's finances were so weak that in the end the responsibility for the Chapel Hill cases came to be viewed as FOR's. The

Journey only temporarily invigorated the program and activity of the national office. But it functioned as a dramatic high point, a source of inspiration to CORE for years to come. Finally, fourteen years later it served as the model for the famous Freedom Ride of 1961, which projected CORE into the forefront of the civil rights movement.

2
Growth and Disintegration 1947-1954

Inspired by the Journey of Reconciliation, the fifth national convention met in 1947 at CORE's birthplace, Chicago, in an optimistic mood. For the first time in the organization's history, nearly all the affiliates were represented. Approving ambitious plans for expansion, the delegates amended the constitution to provide for an unpaid field representative who would establish new affiliates and adopted the Executive Committee's proposal of a $6900 budget to permit the employment of a part-time fund raiser and a full-time executive secretary. Despite their support of the budget, however, the chapters were still unwilling to accept the necessity of surrendering enough of their autonomy to provide the minimal financing for National CORE. Reluctant even to pay the 1 per cent tax which they owed the central office, the delegates intensely debated alternative ways of raising money. In the end they referred the problem to the Executive Commiteee, with the pointed proviso "that any ideas . . . adopted by them . . . which change the basic practices of CORE . . . be subject to submission to the groups for approval." [1]

With this limited mandate the Committee went ahead hopefully. At its next meeting William Worthy was appointed to the temporary salaried post of Action Director. Worthy, a black pacifist and a Journey participant was expected both to raise funds and to develop a "creative action program." At the same time, preliminary planning was begun for an ambitious attack on segregation in the armed forces, the YMCA, apartment complexes owned by the Metropolitan Life Insurance Company, and southern transportation. Correctly anticipating that mail appeals would provide only a modest amount, the Executive Committee resurrected the idea of dual local-national memberships as the only feasible way to finance a paid executive secretary. Houser seriously urged the chapters to consider this plan, carefully reassuring them that "the national organization would not usurp the freedom of action of local groups," which would still be "the basic unit [s] of CORE." [2] Yet their response was still negative. Nor was Worthy able to raise much money.[3] Moreover, none of his action projects proved fruitful, and in fact, most of the ambitious program projected by the Executive Committee was never seriously attempted.

Accordingly, CORE continued to wrestle with the closely interrelated problems of finance, national staffing, and chapter development. Time and again, the affiliates would agree on the desirability of hiring a paid staff but would refuse to provide the needed money. For example, the 1949 Convention passed a motion to employ a full-time worker "as soon as possible" but defeated another motion that would have required each local to give national 20 per cent of its gross income. Although in the preceding year all the affiliates combined had paid only $353, the delegates so zealously guarded the principle of chapter autonomy that they rejected Houser's desperate plea to permit him to send financial appeal letters to their members twice a year in order to enlarge the CORE mailing list of only four hundred names.[4]

As a consequence the national office continued to depend primarily upon outside donors. Thus in 1949–50 chapter payments were $437, while individual donations amounted to $1528. In 1950 the constitution was amended to increase the affiliates' contribution to national from 1 per cent to 10 per cent of their annual income, but the chapters resisted, and while individual giving held steady during the following year, income from the chapters actually dropped. The sizes of the donations were small: a list of "contributions of sizeable amounts" from 1949 through 1952 showed that only forty-five individuals had given a total of $20 or more during these four years.[5] Contributors received the *CORE-lator,* which beginning in 1949 was printed rather than mimeographed in order to create a more favorable impression upon potential donors. In its original format, the *CORE-lator* had served largely as a house organ for the benefit of the affiliates, carrying financial statements, reports of executive committee meetings, and detailed summaries of projects that would be instructive to other locals. The new printed version, edited by James Peck, and pitched to financial contributors, was deliberately less informative; it simply publicized CORE's more dramatic actions and achievements.

Meanwhile, CORE leaders had not given up the idea of hiring a fund raiser, and in 1951 the Convention authorized the employment of James R. Robinson on a part-time basis.[6] Robinson put CORE's financial soliciting on a fully professional basis: he expanded Houser's earlier policies of exchanging contributor lists with other organizations like the FOR, the American Civil Liberties Union, and the War Resisters League, and he increased the number of appeal letters signed by well-known advisory committee members.[7] Through Robinson's work, the importance of individual gifts as a source of income became more marked than ever. During the fiscal year 1953–54 chapter payments were a mere $152, while individual donations totaled nearly $5000. Although at first the results of his work had been modest, cumulatively they paid off. CORE's income for the year ending June 1, 1954, rose to a high of $7000; and the CORE list, which had stood at 1000 when Robinson took office in October 1951, had nearly doubled to over 1900 three years later.[8]

While CORE was grappling with its fiscal difficulties, it was simultaneously attempting to solve the vexing problems stemming from the looseness of the organization's structure and the inadequate coordination between the national office and the chapters. As already noted, the 1947 Convention created the office of field representative, charged with "travel[ing] on behalf of CORE, helping to interpret CORE to interested people, and to organize new groups."[9] Rustin, whom the 1947 Convention selected for the new position, was a logical choice, but his duties with the FOR made it impossible for him to travel very far from New York. Adding a second field representative in 1948 the Convention chose the black chairman of Los Angeles CORE, Manuel Talley, to service the Far West. Unfortunately, this appointment only exacerbated the organizational problems since the dynamic Talley, who had gone to prison during World War II rather than serve in a jim crow army,[10] created serious difficulties. For a second time he led a faction that broke away from Los Angeles CORE to form a new chapter. As field representative he refused to recognize the authority of the executive secretary or the Council, and he set up an unauthorized "Western CORE Federation" which posed a schismatic threat to the national organization. Finally, in 1950, having lost all support among the national officers and hemmed in by new regulations specifying the responsibility of field representatives to the executive secretary and the Council, Talley severed his relations with CORE.[11]

Thus far the field representative system had not accomplished its purposes, and in an effort to provide more effective coordination between the national office and the affiliates, the 1949 Convention not only increased the authority of the executive secretary over the field representatives but also made a number of other significant structural changes. At Houser's recommendation it expanded the number of field representatives to six. At the same time the delegates tried to involve the chapters more directly in the formulation of national policy. The 1949 amended constitution, in fact, specifically declared that "Policy decisions shall be made at the Convention," and provided that affiliation and disaffiliation required approval of two-thirds of the chapters, rather than leaving the decision in such matters up to the Council. In addition the Council, which directly represented the affiliates, was also strengthened by the abolition of the Executive Committee. Some chapters, most notably New York CORE, believed that this Committee, selected by the national chairman, was unrepresentative and had become too deferential to Houser's views. Finally, in order to encourage chapter attendance at the Council meetings and make it a more viable institution, the number of delegates from each affiliate was reduced from two to one, thereby encouraging attendance through reduced transporatation costs.[12] These innovations, however, did not strengthen CORE as had been anticipated. In fact, over the next two years, the organization began to decline. The field representative system continued to function poorly; by the spring of 1951 it was clear that except for Wallace Nelson, who spent two or three days a week visiting colleges, the representatives were doing almost nothing. Moreover, the important chapters in Boston, Berkeley, Cleveland, and Columbus had become "pretty much inactive," while the Brooklyn College and Denver chapters had gone out of existence.[13] Clearly, something had to be done.

Accordingly, in March 1951, New York CORE circulated several new proposals among the affiliates. The chapter was convinced that the "loose" structure created when CORE began was "organizationally destructive," and that this and the lack of a full-time paid executive produced a "slipshod relation between local and national" and minimized national's assistance to the affiliates. New York's memorandum recommended hiring a full-time fund raiser immediately. It was hoped that his work would soon enable CORE to employ salaried organizers and make it possible to free the organization from its dependence on FOR. While New York CORE leaders insisted that nothing in these proposals would threaten chapter autonomy or democratic control of the organization, if, as they strongly urged, affiliates would regularly send delegates to conventions and council meetings, others were not so certain. Thus, the Minneapolis chapter, operating on the assumption that a democratic CORE required a "loose federation of autonomous groups" as provided at the founding convention, and fearing that a professional staff would ultimately mean bureaucracy and centralization, was not dismayed at the prospect of maintaining the old arrangements. Moreover, believing that for the foreseeable future the organization's financial condition made it "unrealistic" to hire a salaried worker, they did not view the connection with FOR as a "pressing problem." What eventuated was a compromise. Acting upon the Council's recommendation, the 1951 Convention authorized both a full-time "subsistence" field worker, and as already noted, a part-time fund raiser. This was CORE's final attempt under the Houser administration to grapple with the problems of creating a viable program and providing a coordination between the national office and the local groups.[14]

Robinson accepted the financial job, and the new position of field worker went to a local chapter leader and participant on the Journey of Reconciliation, Wallace F. Nelson. The son of a Methodist minister, Nelson had attended Ohio Wesleyan, where he was active in the student Christian movement. A conscientious objector during World War II, he served two years in prison, being released after going on a three-and-a-half-month hunger strike protesting the injustices of the penal system. He then moved to Cincinnati, where he was a founder of the local Committee on Human Relations, which became a CORE affiliate, and joined the Peacemakers, an anarcho-pacifist group that encouraged civil disobedience to draft laws and refusal to pay income taxes. With his background of pacifism and anarchism Nelson was hardly the ideal choice for New York CORE, a chapter that wished to see CORE disassociated from pacifism and, far from supporting anarchistic principles, favored a more centralized, tightly knit organization. The New York CORE leaders, who had nominated Nelson for the job, were fully aware of the potential problems involved in his appointment. But Nelson was the only field representative who had taken his duties seriously, and no one else wished the position with its low subsistence salary.[15]

Meanwhile, over the years, CORE leaders had maintained their commitment to developing a strong national program. Their most important efforts were the summer interracial workshops, held annually from 1947 until 1954 in cooperation with the FOR. All were located in Washington except for the 1948 institute in Los Angeles. The workshops' principal purpose was to train individuals who had the potential for leadership in their local communities. Though teaching the theory of nonviolence, the workshops were action-oriented. CORE was the first, and for many years —until the emergence of SCLC—the only organization to hold such institutes. The workshops were only partially successful. The number of participants, never large, declined over the years from a maximum of thirty in 1947 to an average of about ten in the early 1950's. Many were white college students who never became active in CORE. Although several early participants became leaders in CORE's District of Columbia affiliate, for the most part the workshops neither produced new groups nor built leadership in old ones.[16] These summer institutes undoubtedly made CORE better known; they helped to desegregate Washington, demonstrating that nonviolent direct-action methods could be applied in a community lacking civil rights laws; and their main significance was that they produced CORE's first action-oriented border-state affiliate— the year-round Washington Interracial Workshop.

Other efforts to develop a national action program proved frustrating. The chapters, sensitive about their autonomy and preferring to confine themselves to local projects, were reluctant to give support. National leaders proposed coordinated action against segregation in the armed forces, jim crow in southern transportation, and job discrimination, but in each case they were ineffective because of indifference in the affiliates.

Thus, for example, after the 1947 Convention went on record in opposition to the jim crow peacetime draft, Action Director William Worthy urged CORE to support the protest being mounted by A. Philip Randolph's Committee Against Jim Crow in Military Service and Training. Taking into account the objections of many CORE members who were reluctant to endorse an all-black demonstration in Washington, Worthy told them not to make a "fetish of 'interracialism,'" but to spearhead their own local interracial poster walks and picket lines. But CORE chapters were not interested, and the project was dropped. Then, in March 1948 Randolph electrified nonviolent activists when he told the Senate Armed Services Committee that he would lead a civil disobedience campaign if military segregation were not abolished. Pacifists Houser, Worthy, Igal Roodenko, Rustin, and Peck thereupon dramati-

cally announced that if the draft were extended without prohibiting segregation, they would not only refuse to fight, but they would decline to
pay their income taxes as well. CORE support, however, foundered on
the reluctance of the chapters to engage in civil disobedience. The 1948
Convention voted overwhelmingly to endorse the Randolph proposal
but, significantly, it was only by a narrow margin that the delegates
agreed to urge the affiliates to actually participate. The entire protest
collapsed in August when President Truman issued his Executive Order
to begin integration of the armed forces and Randolph called off the
campaign. Rustin and others distrusted Truman's assurances and vowed
to continue the battle, but except for the Minneapolis chapter, the
CORE affiliates were only too glad to follow Randolph's cue.[17]

Worthy, Rustin, Houser, and Peck, all of whom had been on the Journey of Reconciliation, continued to press the issue of interstate transportation segregation. In November 1947 Worthy urged CORE groups to
focus public attention on the matter by seeking arrest through demonstrations in northern railroad stations which sold jim crow reserved seats
on trains bound for the South. After Worthy had left the organization,
the Executive Committee voted to proceed with the protest, but, except
for one occasion when Houser and a few others handed out leaflets outside
New York's Pennsylvania Station, CORE people ignored the project completely.[18] Not until 1949 did New York state authorities, pressured by
NAACP and other groups, require termination of the odious practice.
Similarly, a few stalwarts still continued to carry on the fight against bus
segregation. Peck and Rustin, each one an owner of a share of Greyhound stock, attacked the issue through the company's annual stockhold-
er's meetings. In 1948 they startled the gathering by raising the question
from the floor. In 1950 and 1951 they picketed the meetings; and in 1952
they again spotlighted the issue from the floor, this time forcing the
firm's executives at least to discuss it. The Greyhound campaign brought
CORE considerable publicity, but nothing more. Over the years other
proposals made at CORE conventions for combating interstate transportation segregation were all shelved. In 1955, eight years after beginning
their campaign, Rustin (who by then had left the FOR and CORE to
work with the War Resisters League) and Peck were again vainly picketing the Greyhound annual meeting.[19]

Lack of support among the chapters also undermined suggestions for a
national employment project against one of the large corporations. Executive Committee meetings and conventions between 1948 and 1951 dis-

cussed the feasibility of attacking a consumer-oriented company like A&P or Carnation Milk, which would be vulnerable to a boycott. But the idea always foundered on the difficulty of coordinating the activities of widely separated CORE affiliates.[20] Epitomizing National CORE's predicament —and its powerlessness—was the final attempt at a national project, the innocuous Pledge Brotherhood campaign. This campaign, conducted annually, from 1950 through 1954, during February, "Brotherhood Month," was directed primarily at white church people. Thousands of leaflets were circulated which the recipients were to sign and return to the CORE-FOR office, thus committing them to perform some act during the month that would demonstrate opposition to jim crow. Originally, Houser had hoped that their pledges would be a springboard for direct action, and in fact the idea had occurred to him in Durham, North Carolina, where he met black students boycotting jim crow theaters. But in practice, the pledge functioned not as a stimulus to direct action, but only as "a means of education for the individual." Nor did the annual project help CORE financially as anticipated. Although the pledge forms were supposed to build up CORE's mailing list, only a few hundred individuals bothered to sign and return them each year. Thus, Pledge Brotherhood, despite the considerable effort expended upon it, was merely a symbolic exercise which was discontinued after 1954.[21]

Clearly, the principal locus of CORE activity remained with the chapters, and there it flourished for a few years following the Journey, only to decline precipitously during the early 1950's. The number of affiliates rose from thirteen in 1947–48 to twenty in 1950, then dropped to seventeen the next year, and hovered around eleven thereafter. CORE chapters were still youthful and small. The typical adult participant was in his midtwenties, and about one-third of all the chapters during this period were composed predominantly of college students. Overwhelmingly white, these college chapters were particularly numerous in 1947–49 when Houser often visited campuses, but they continued to be relatively unstable, typically fading away after a brief flurry of activity.[22] In size, most groups ranged from fifteen to thirty active members. Requirements for joining, which had become fairly well standardized, generally called for a term of probation of up to two months during which time the initiate participated in chapter activity and studied CORE philosophy, the approval of the membership committee, and, finally, a vote by the entire affiliate. St. Louis CORE, stricter than most, required a ten-week probationary period and approval by two-thirds of the membership. Anyone who thereafter became inactive was relegated to the status of "Friend of CORE." [23]

Of the twenty-nine different groups affiliated in this period, about half were in the Midwest; the rest were almost equally divided among the northeastern, western, and border states. Although CORE was thus basically a northern organization, it exhibited a new interest in forming chapters in the southern and border areas. The 1949 Convention, acting upon Rustin's recommendation, passed a resolution that "immediate action be taken toward the setting up of CORE groups in key locations in the South," and Nelson, during his three years as paid field worker, twice attempted to organize groups in North Carolina and Virginia.[24] Such efforts proved abortive, and CORE was unable to establish a southern beachhead. On the other hand, with public accommodations largely settled as an issue in the North, the emphasis of CORE activity shifted to the border states. In fact the organization's most impressive developments occurred in Washington and St. Louis.

The Washington Interracial Workshop and St. Louis CORE were organized about the same time—the former in 1947 at the end of the summer workshop, and the latter in January 1948. At the maximum each had twenty-five members, the majority of whom were in their twenties. In other respects the two groups were rather different. The one in Washington was founded by a member of the first summer institute—Lynn Seitter, whose father had been influential in moving the National Council of Methodist Youth to a pacifist position during the 1930's—and the Workshop through much of its history was dominated by pacifist leadership. The guiding spirits in its first few years were two white pacifist couples— Robert and Lynn Seitter Kirk, and Don and Grace Ito Coan. During the early 1950's they shared influence with two whites employed at the Census Bureau, Albert Mindlin and Lillian Palenius, and a black schoolteacher, Constance Perry. At first the group, largely composed of government workers, was mainly white. By the 1950's the majority of the membership was black, yet the leadership continued to be predominantly white; both Negro and white members of the Workshop have indicated that efforts to involve blacks more substantially in the group's leadership structure were inhibited by differences in education and previous participation in organizational work. During the chapter's most active period in the early 1950's it was loosely divided into two white-led but interracial factions, one headed by the Kirks, the other by Mindlin, while a smaller group of blacks, centering around the Perrys, operated as an independent force outside the white-dominated groupings. In a period when CORE's interracial values generally shaped the behavior of most of its members, the Washington affiliate was probably unique in experiencing overt evidences of interracial tensions. Several of the Negroes complained that many of the white members failed to take an uncompromising stand against segregation. These critics were resentful at such incidents as white members discussing films they had seen at downtown theaters which excluded blacks, suspicious that whites might be slipping out during sit-ins to have a meal at a nearby—and segregated—restaurant, and worried about indications that whites might be meeting informally to outline chapter strategy. In fact, Constance Perry's brother, Leon Whitt, a medical student at Howard University, resigned, charging the whites with hypocrisy. However atypical the Washington Interracial Workshop may have been in this respect, like most CORE chapters it had an erratic career, marked by irregular outbursts of activity.[25]

In contrast, St. Louis CORE, founded by Bernice Fisher, was an unusually energetic and stable group with a labor union orientation instead of a pacifist one. The chapter which was about half black in membership, was solidly middle class. Although, as in Washington, the whites were somewhat better educated and generally held better jobs than the blacks, the leadership structure was thoroughly integrated. The principal figures included Charles Oldham, a young white labor lawyer; two Negro school teachers, Marian O'Fallon—who later married Oldham—and Wanda Penny; Walter Hayes, a black postman; Henry Hodge, a black college student; two white students, Marvin Rich and Joe Ames—who in 1951 became a union official—and the latter's wife, Billie Coil Ames. This highly cohesive St. Louis chapter would prove unusually influential in CORE's history, with about half of these individuals subsequently becoming prominent in National CORE.

Despite the differences, the campaigns of both affiliates epitomized the tedious, time-consuming, and protracted character of CORE projects in this period. They reveal the tenacity of the CORE activists who, given their powerlessness and their commitment to the Action Discipline's reconciliatory spirit, were willing to proceed gradually as they sought both to end discrimination and convert the discriminator. While St. Louis tended to justify its procedures on the basis of practicality, and the Washington affiliate was more prone to stress the philosophical aspects of nonviolence, the experience of both groups illuminates the spirit and style of CORE's operations in its early years and merits careful examination.

Washington, the almost completely segregated national capital, was a symbolically important location for conducting nonviolent direct-action projects. As early as 1944 the FOR had held a race relations institute there, and a weak, unaffiliated CORE group was established, but it became defunct by 1946.[26] CORE returned to the city with the interracial workshop led by Houser and Rustin in July 1947. For this first summer, CORE chose to concentrate on restaurants maintained by religious institutions because of their vulnerability to a moral attack. Testing and negotiations integrated the Methodist Building Cafeteria on Capitol Hill, but three days of sit-ins at the YMCA coffee shop produced only an avowal that the Y board of trustees would consider serving blacks. A local CORE group, which also called itself the Washington Interracial Workshop was established at the end of the summer and held a sit-in at the Greyhound bus terminal restaurant as its first project. It then followed up on the YMCA project, conducting a rising crescendo of demonstrations which culminated in a February 1948 sit-down involving thirty-seven people. On the basis of an encouraging conference with Y officials the next month, a moratorium was declared. But when the Y remained adamant, enthusiasm could not be revived. With this failure the Workshop's momentum had been lost, activity languished, and the group died.[27]

The local Workshop was revived early in 1949 by Don Coan, a west coast journalist who returned to Washington to pursue graduate work in sociology at Howard University. The chapter resumed negotiations with the YMCA, which quietly integrated its coffee shop a year later.[28] Working with the local NAACP branch, members sat-in and desegregated the Greyhound restaurant in July 1949. The 1949 summer workshoppers, led by Houser, turned their attention to the exclusionary practices of the Trans-Lux, a downtown movie house. In orthodox CORE fashion they began with an open letter to the owner and distribution of leaflets outside the theater. Finally, in August, after the summer participants had departed, the local affiliate placed "a standing interracial line before the ticket window," a technique which drew public attention to the discrimination without preventing people from purchasing tickets. In keeping with the chapter's reconciliatory method, Coan emphasized to the theater manager that "our sole aim in having these waiting lines is the end of racial discrimination at the Trans-Lux theater. We are not trying to make the theater lose business." Coan believed that these "quiet" demonstrations "aroused more sympathy" than picketing, and as he advised

Houser, "Our approach all along has been one which would least antagonize the management." Always ready to negotiate, Coan journeyed to New York in November, where he, Houser, and James Farmer met with the theater's national officers. On the basis of assurances that the movie house would change its policy if even one competitor did, the sparsely attended demonstrations were discontinued, and the group instead tried to confer with the Loew's chain. After this company refused to negotiate, waiting lines were placed outside their F Street theater. Subsequently the campaign dragged on for many wearisome, inconclusive months. During the summer of 1950 the "waiting line" strategy was revived, and in an effort to prove that desegregation would not hurt profits, movie patrons were polled outside the theaters. An overwhelming majority indicated they would not object to a nondiscriminatory policy. Accordingly, a year after the campaign began, Houser hopefully wrote to the Trans-Lux company, pointing out that a change would entail "absolutely no risk." [29] Rebuffed again, in the fall the chapter shifted its attention to an easier target—the Playhouse, one of a chain of three art theaters, whose manager was sympathetic to CORE's goal. In fact, the other two movie houses in the chain were the only ones outside the ghetto open to blacks. Ultimately, after seven months of persistent efforts, the tactics which had failed elsewhere produced a victory.[30]

Meanwhile CORE's Washington affiliate had found a formidable competitor in the Coordinating Committee for the Enforcement of D. C. Anti-discrimination Laws. Created in 1949, this organization sponsored the Thompson Restaurant case, which sought to challenge black exclusion by invoking a recently discovered 1872 ordinance that forbade segregation in places of public accommodation. In addition, the Coordinating Committee employed direct-action techniques in an enormously successful campaign to open eating facilities at downtown Seventh Street stores heavily patronized by blacks. Goaded by this competition, the Washington Workshop again began to test restaurants in the spring of 1950. In cooperation with the summer institute, a special effort was made to integrate the Sholl cafeteria; in July, fifteen demonstrators—including Houser himself—were arrested while waiting for service at the steam table, even though they purposely did not block others behind them. The Sholl project accentuated the rivalry between CORE and the Coordinating Committee, which complained that the arrests jeopardized the Thompson case then before the courts. The fact that many in Washington, including CORE Workshop leaders, regarded the Committee as infiltrated by Communists only increased the mutual resentment. By September, Lynn Kirk was so discouraged by the Workshop's lack of activity and the vigor of its rival that she thought her own group might be dead in six months.[31]

The summer workshops of 1951 and 1952, directed by Wallace Nelson and again closely coordinated with the activities of the local group, sought to integrate the public playgrounds and the lunch counters of the Whelan drug store chain. Despite a sit-in campaign which lasted more than two years, the Whelan project—like the one at the Trans-Lux theater—failed.[32] But a new departure, and one that produced dramatic publicity as well as significant victories, was the attempt to desegregate two public playgrounds which, although located in mixed neighborhoods, excluded blacks.

It was Nelson who set up the strategy for the playground projects, which were notable for their pioneering use of two techniques that CORE would not seriously attempt to employ again until the 1960's: civil disobedience and "community organization." He taught the Workshop members how to involve the grass-roots people—"exploiting neighborhood sentiment and energy by door to door canvassing and forming a citizens committee to lead the fight, and the marshalling of community resources." By the end of July 1951, he had organized a "pilgrimage" of parents and children to the Hoover playground, whose directors angrily closed it down. Yet the campaign was a success, for when the playground reopened a few months later, it was desegregated.[33]

In the autumn, the Washington affiliate turned to the Rosedale playground. First securing neighborhood support, the workshoppers formed the all-black Rosedale Citizens Committee. Frequent pilgrimages followed; but these dwindled to a handful of people after white hoodlums dragged a woman off the grounds and beat a male demonstrator outside the playground gates. Week after week, often accompanied by an interracial team of two CORE women—Lillian Palenius and Constance Perry—the tiny band of parents and children went to the playground, where they sometimes faced violence but were usually simply ignored. In June 1952, after a Negro youth climbed Rosedale's fence one night and drowned in the swimming pool, the black citizens were galvanized into intensive action. The campaign went into high gear with mass meetings, picketing of the recreation department, and for the first time, coverage in the daily newspapers. Into this tense setting stepped the members of the 1952 workshop, led by Wallace Nelson. On July 17, ten workshoppers and two members of the Citizens Committee were arrested while standing before the gates, seeking admittance to the playground. Employing a technique which Nelson had first used in Cincinnati a few months earlier, the CORE people resisted arrest by going limp, and they refused to post bond after they arrived at the jail, where eight of them went on a brief hunger strike. More pilgrimages to and more picketing at the recreation department followed. But the authorities were still adamant. Then, beginning in early September, black children climbed over the playground fence daily. On one occasion a gang of white youths armed with baseball bats met them, and in the ensuing melee severely beat a Negro adult who tried to intervene. Rushing into his house and grabbing a gun, the man began firing into the air. The incident became front-page news, the playground was closed, forty organizations testified at a recreation board hearing, and in October the Rosedale playground was finally desegregated.

But the workshoppers, committed to nonviolence, were frightened and angered by the firing of the gun, and their vocal criticisms estranged them from most of Rosedale's black community, which deeply sympathized with the man who pulled the trigger and which was infuriated by the Workshop's lack of support for him. A number of the Rosedale citizens in fact believed it was the crisis engendered by the shots that finally opened the playground. As CORE chairman Albert Mindlin put it, with most of the chapter members unable to empathize with the Rosedale people, CORE and the community, in a "psychological struggle between non-violence and violence, met in a head-on collision." Although the Workshop at this point had a majority black membership, many Rosedale residents now perceived it as a predominantly white alien group because its leaders were mainly whites. Thus, although black Workshop members fully supported the nonviolent principle, the disagreement was perceived by the grass-roots blacks as an ideological polarization along racial lines. The Rosedale Citizens Committee itself was torn by internal conflict, and its chairman, Ruth Shirley, was forced out because she "became identified in the minds of the others with 'those hypocritical whites,' an ofay-lover." Although Rosedale playground was integrated, CORE had only a handful of friends left in the neighborhood.[34]

The Rosedale campaign with its recriminations exhausted the Washington CORE affiliate. The group thereafter accomplished little, and the leaders were soon fighting among themselves. The Supreme Court in June 1953, handed down its decision in the Thompson case, ruling restaurant segregation illegal in the nation's capital. Other places opened soon afterward—two theater chains doing so in October, following renewed demonstrations during the summer. With the public accommodations issue in the District thus essentially solved, the 1953 and 1954 summer institutes, both again led by Wallace Nelson, attempted to attack employment discrimination. Investigations and negotiations were carried on with department, grocery, and dime stores. But no direct action occurred, partly because of the Workshop's weakness and partly because a few black clerks were hired. By 1954 only seven people volunteered for the summer workshop, and National CORE decided to terminate these annual institutes. In turn, the tired local group, lacking the stimulus of the summer projects, withered away and disbanded in early 1955.[35]

St. Louis CORE, the organization's other major border-state affiliate, was in many respects a model chapter. It adhered closely to the CORE Discipline and to the procedures Bernice Fisher had created in Chicago. Members were required to devote an extraordinary amount of time to the group's projects; the chapter even met weekly, rather than biweekly as was the practice in other cities. Democratic procedure was ensured by holding elections every three months. Billie Ames explained, "Often a person willing to work along with CORE is hesitant about taking on responsibility—particularly such responsibility as being chairman or secretary. In St. Louis we have adopted the plan of electing officers every three months. We find people will take on responsibility for a short period and also find this a good way of getting participation from a number of people." [36]

For its first six years, St. Louis CORE concentrated almost completely on downtown eating facilities. After testing many restaurants and easily opening the YMCA and YWCA cafeterias, they decided in July 1948 to focus on the Stix, Baer, and Fuller department store, whose owners had reputations as humanitarian civic leaders. For several months CORE members distributed leaflets urging customers to complain to the store's management. Then, beginning in May 1949, about twenty-five people sat-in once or twice weekly. As the weeks passed the owners became more adamant, and in December, after sixteen months of negotiations and demonstrations, St. Louis CORE finally gave up. As Billie Ames wrote, "We then swallowed our pride, retreated and went to work on lesser stores." [37]

Having desegregated three major drugstores simply through testing even before withdrawing from the department store campaign, the chapter decided that lunch counters at dime stores were more vulnerable targets. When, after a brief sit-in and picketing in December 1949, Woolworth said it would change its policies if competing chains did the same, CORE held a store managers' conference in the vain hope of obtaining simultaneous desegregation. For the next five months the group conducted sit-ins at the Woolworth store downtown. Then in May the affiliate began picketing branch outlets in the Negro neighborhoods. Thus pressed, and after months of continued negotiation, Woolworth opened its downtown basement cafeteria on a limited basis, allowing blacks to purchase only salads and sandwiches. In March 1951, the chapter held several demonstrations at the steam counter, but the store held firm. During the summer, CORE held intensive demonstrations at other downtown variety stores, and by autumn all four chains had agreed to serve an interracial group on a once-a-week "controlled test" basis. A year later the number of weekly tests, by agreement with the managements, was increased to two (five at Woolworth's), and in early 1953, more than three years after the project first began, two Sears Roebuck outlets, the Greyhound terminal, and all but one of the downtown dimestores completely desegregated their eating facilities.[38] Encouraged by these victories, St. Louis CORE returned the following year to the attack on the department store lunchrooms. Conferences with the managers of two stores led to controlled testing, and by March 1954, Stix finally opened its first floor and Famous-Barr allowed Negroes to eat in the basement dining room.[39] In retrospect Billie Ames observed, "Little did we know when we started that campaign that it would take six years to complete." While certain dining facilities in all the department stores still remained closed to blacks, the group congratulated itself upon the essentially successful completion of its drive against the downtown establishments.[40]

All this was accomplished by a mere handful of people. As Billie Ames once wrote to a discouraged Kansas City CORE member, "If you have ten people really working, you are doing very well. There have been many times when fewer than ten people carried the load of work of our group." These efforts demonstrated what a small, dedicated band could do in a border city like St. Louis, characterized by black apathy and white indifference and hostility. The group was a model of respectability and decorum. Participants were informed, "Men are to wear shirts and ties. Correct posture should be remembered." Rather than risk arrest, they withdrew from demonstrations when business firms called the police. Operating in a border city with a southern tradition, lacking a real power base, and facing a public that was moving only slowly toward recognition of the black man's civil rights, St. Louis CORE evolved a method that brought limited but solid gains. Thus the chapter's gradualist procedures were clearly justified in the minds of its members. "Controlled testing," although hard work, was an approach "that cannot be easily ignored or scoffed at by management yet results in complete though gradual change. But there is also an understanding that it is better to test for several months or even a year and end up with a complete change in policy than it is to have 18 months of demonstrations as we did at Stix [department store] and end up in complete defeat. Though the testing is presented to the manager as a means of education [for the public], we consider it more as a foot in the door," making it "easier to push him a little further. . . . We have discovered a damned good foot in the door tactic." [41] Compared to the direct actionists of the 1960's, their style may seem timid, yet it should be borne in mind that they were people who refused to retreat in the face of harassment such as a physical assault from Gerald L. K. Smith's Christian Nationalists and the burning of a Ku Klux Klan cross on Billie Ames' lawn.[42]

Even this especially viable affiliate experienced the typical CORE pattern of decline. The chapter wished to move wholeheartedly into a fight on job discrimination,[43] but their one project, directed at the A & P; involved no direct action and resulted in the hiring of one black cashier in 1954 only after months of negotiations.[44] As Billie Ames reported, "We don't have enough action to keep fringe members active and have had a terrific slump in the number of people attending meetings." She had learned the lesson that "demonstrations will attract more people to your group." By early 1954 she was doing almost all the work, and recognized the unhealthy condition of an affiliate that would fall apart "if I were not there to push them." [45]

Elsewhere in the border states, active CORE chapters developed in Baltimore and three university towns in Kansas and Missouri. During 1947–48, a student group at Lawrence, Kansas, experienced a "stormy history" in trying to desegregate places of public accommodation. Although barred from the University of Kansas campus, the chapter gained enormous publicity through its theater and restaurant sit-ins, and was able to open local movie houses. Both this group and one at Wichita, composed mainly of students at Friends University, were defunct by the autumn of 1950.[46] Nevertheless, a couple of years later, with St. Louis and Washington having shown the viability of CORE-type action in a border setting,

Wallace Nelson was sent into Maryland, Kansas, and Missouri on an organizing tour. One group which he initiated in Kansas City, Missouri, proved weak and never even affiliated, and an embryonic student chapter begun at Lincoln University, a black institution in Jefferson City, Missouri, foundered because of the opposition of the school administration.[47] Two other chapters which he helped to establish—Columbia, Missouri,[48] and Baltimore, Maryland—conducted victorious lunch-counter campaigns. Baltimore, in fact, turned out to be one of CORE's most active affiliates. Organized in January 1953, largely on the initiative of a white pacifist Herbert Kelman, a psychologist at the Phipps Psychiatric Clinic, its success lay in its ability to recruit from a broad spectrum of people. The membership of about twenty-five or thirty was unique, for in addition to the usual types of middle-class whites and Negroes, its members included a black minister and his wife, and a significant contingent of upwardly mobile black trade unionists who were active in the International Ladies Garment Workers Union. Going directly to work at the dime stores both downtown and—with Negro Morgan State College students—at the Northwood Shopping Center, the chapter had within months opened all the chains except Grant's. And Grant's finally desegregated in May 1954, as the result of the combined pressures of a New York CORE picket line at the company's Harlem outlet, negotiations by Rustin and Peck at Grant's national headquarters, and a demonstration at its annual stockholders meeting. As a result, the Baltimore CORE chapter, hitherto existing very much on the fringes of the city's racial advancement organizations, temporarily achieved respect and recognition in the local black community.[49]

In the North, the locals varied widely in the amount and scope of activity which they undertook, and overall their accomplishments were relatively modest. The most important student chapter was the University of Chicago affiliate, which flourished in 1947–48. In late 1947 it revived the campaign against the University hospitals, engineering a two-hour walk out by a thousand placard-carrying students. Among the nonstudent chapters, New York was clearly the most energetic. This group tested two large apartment developments, sought to secure nonstereotyped roles for blacks on TV, carried out a long campaign of negotiations and picketing that desegregated a YMCA in Brooklyn, and launched dramatic demonstrations to desegregate the swimming pool in a New Jersey amusement park.[50]

With the general elimination of restaurant, hotel, and theater segrega-

tion in the North, the chapters gave more attention to pools and amusement parks. On these projects, where CORE was directly challenging the
prejudices of young working-class whites, the organization experienced
more physical harassment than in any other campaigns prior to the
1960's. For example, members of Los Angeles CORE, who made the desegregation of the Bimini Baths their major interest during 1948, sometimes faced violence when they sought to buy tickets, and once the management even used fire hoses on them. Nevertheless, the Baths finally
opened that autumn. In 1952 the Cleveland chapter singled out the
Skateland Roller Rink, where eight years earlier hooligans had given
Houser and other CORE members rough treatment. The new project
ended abruptly when the black pacifist chairman, Eroseanna Robinson,
was tripped by white youths and broke her arm.[51] During the summers
of 1947 and 1948, New York CORE members suffered over sixty arrests
while conducting "stand-ins" at New Jersey's Palisades Amusement Park
swimming pool, with the police often using blackjacks on the demonstrators. Although litigation accompanying the direct action produced a
court decision in 1949 that upheld a black man's right to buy a ticket to
the pool, it was not until New Jersey passed a new civil rights law specifically including swimming pools that the chapter was able to force the
Park authorities to cease their discrimination.[52]

More radical were the tactics employed by the Cincinnati CORE affiliate, the Committee on Human Relations. Drawing members from two older
CORE groups—the all-black West End Civic League, which had specialized in employment campaigns against ghetto stores, and a weak, predominantly white college chapter—it also included several individuals
from the anarcho-pacifist Peacemakers, particularly Wallace and Juanita
Morrow Nelson. The CCHR's major project, a dramatic effort to integrate the Coney Island Amusement Park, was particularly significant because it used militant techniques which were later popular in the 1960's.
In May 1952 about fifteen persons attempted to gain admittance, blocking both the ticket window and the entrance. Police dragged the Nelsons
away, releasing them a few hours later. The following month another
group, including the Nelsons and Mrs. Ernest Bromley, wife of a white
pacifist minister who had participated in the Journey of Reconciliation,
again tried to enter. On this occasion the Nelsons practiced total non-
cooperation when arrested. They went limp, were dragged into a police
car, and then carried into jail, where they and Mrs. Bromley went on a
nine-day hunger strike. Bound over to a grand jury they proudly "stood

mute," refusing to answer any questions. Later that summer CORE held another demonstration at the park, but by then the group had entered a decline that would lead to its disaffiliation. The initiative passed instead to the NAACP, which won a lawsuit that finally desegregated the park in 1955.[53]

The Palisades Park and Coney Island campaigns illustrated the important role which CORE's direct action often played in furthering the cause of civil rights even where the organization's own project did not produce a victory. In both instances it was CORE which had effectively publicized the moral issue through its dramatic confrontation with park authorities and local police. Others then pressed the cases in the courts and legislatures. In New Jersey the inclusion of pools and amusement parks in the public accommodations law was largely due to the activism of New York CORE. Similarly in Cincinnati the NAACP's successful intervention came only after CORE had brought public attention to the problem.

CORE groups in Chicago, Omaha, Wichita, Los Angeles, San Francisco, and Berkeley placed considerable emphasis on employment projects. In 1947–48 the Chicago chapter spearheaded a drive against Goldblatt's department store. Picketing was initiated in February 1948, but since Goldblatt's, which was heavily patronized by Negroes, had a better employment policy than other State Street stores, CORE soon found itself charged with antisemitism. Actually it was Goldblatt's record which had led CORE to believe that it was a place where more jobs could be won easily. Enthusiasm on the part of the cooperating organizations soon fell off, however, and by March CORE noted that "We have had our hands full just trying to keep one picket at one door at all times." [54] In California there was a flurry of CORE activity between 1947 and 1950 due to the aggressive organizing of Manuel Talley, who prodded the affiliates into undertaking employment projects.[55] A San Francisco chapter established in 1948 picketed a Lucky chain grocery store in a ghetto area for four months and gained two jobs there. Then after three months of negotiations and picketing it secured one job at another market.[56] The Los Angeles chapter participated in a coalition headed by the NAACP which for months picketed a Santa Monica Sears Roebuck store that refused to employ blacks, and subsequently the Berkeley group was similarly unsuccessful when it organized a picket line and boycott against the Sears outlet in Oakland.[57] More fruitful were the efforts Talley stimulated in Wichita, Kansas, where he led a workshop in 1949. Following through on his suggestions, the affiliate, which had previously fought segregation in theaters and the YMCA, secured two jobs at a Safeway store after five weeks of picketing.[58] Meanwhile, Talley had turned to his most ambitious project—a California boycott against the Carnation Milk Company. But he had few followers, and James Peck, who visited the West Coast during this period, reported that despite Talley's "delusions of grandeur" the Carnation campaign "seems impossible to accomplish with an organization the size of CORE." Talley's drive in fact progressed slowly; and even when, more than a year later, he announced that the company had hired six blacks in nonmenial jobs in Berkeley and Los Angeles, his claims of "snowballing boycott action on a statewide scale" had little basis in reality.[59]

The chapter which made the most sustained efforts against employment discrimination was the De Porres Club of Omaha, Nebraska, and ironically its best work was done prior to its affiliation in 1952. The Club, founded five years before, was a college-based group at Creighton University and CORE's only chapter at a Catholic institution. The organization's first projects had included integration of a Catholic parish school and assistance to a black family moving into a hostile white area whose residents soon accepted them as neighbors. Embarking upon its first job campaign in 1951, the Club picketed and organized a successful six-week boycott of the local Coca-Cola plant, obtaining two positions and a pledge of future fair employment. Successes followed at three laundromats and a dairy, though a year's agitation failed to secure any jobs with the transit company. The group's most intensive project after affiliating with CORE was another year-long effort, including boycotting and picketing, against an ice cream parlor chain, which was concluded when the company hired its first black saleswoman in 1954. Throughout its history the chapter, guided by a remarkable Jesuit priest, Father John P. Markoe, maintained a warm relationship with local Negro leaders, obtaining on appropriate occasions the cooperation of a number of ministers, the NAACP, and the Omaha Urban League, then headed by Whitney Young.[60]

In retrospect it is clear that beginning around 1950 CORE chapter activity entered a slump. Manuel Talley's departure signaled the end of significant work in California. Not only did Los Angeles fall apart after the rebuff he met at the National Convention, but Berkeley, the only other active affiliate in the state, folded a few months later in the wake of its unsuccessful Sears campaign. With the San Francisco group having died by 1949 after being denied affiliation because of Trotskyist infiltration, all that remained in California were two weak college units—one in Pasadena, so conservative that members wishing to engage in direct action had to join an NAACP picket line, and a new Los Angeles CORE initiated in 1952.[61] Elsewhere old-line CORE groups were dying. The Vanguard League, already wracked by the Communist issue, was virtually defunct and was finally disaffiliated in 1951. In Chicago, where the chapter had been similarly weakened by wrangling over the Trotskysists, activity dropped sharply after the Goldblatt job campaign backfired, and by 1950 the group was practically moribund. Denver and Minneapolis chapters proved unable to conduct viable campaigns and were disaffiliated in 1951 and 1954, respectively. Cleveland CORE limped along, but after the abortive attempt to revive it with the roller rink project in 1952, the frightened group fell apart and died.[62] The Washington Interracial Workshop, beset by internal leadership squabbles, became a small coterie that did little beyond holding meetings. Even the strongest groups— Omaha, St. Louis, and New York—were in trouble. The De Porres Club had suffered a serious cleavage in 1952, after a visit from Wallace Nelson when he openly declared his belief that Communists should not be excluded from CORE. The sharply divided group did decide to affiliate with CORE, even though many members were unhappy with Nelson's statements. Yet the Club had been greatly weakened by the controversy which in the long run killed the chapter.[63] The New York and St. Louis affiliates seemed exhausted. And while the new Baltimore chapter displayed considerable vitality, most of Nelson's other efforts to establish viable new groups in the border states failed.

Decline in the vigor of existing affiliates was itself scarcely unusual in CORE history, but the inability to establish new chapters was a new phenomenon. At the 1952 Convention, where most delegates reported a decline in chapter membership, Houser admitted, "CORE is stronger as a principle than as an organization." Over the next two years the deterioration continued, and in 1954 Houser declared that CORE was in "a weaker position" than ever before. Until the 1950's there had always been new groups to replace moribund ones that were disaffiliated. But in the year between the 1953 and 1954 Conventions not a single new group had joined. At the same time CORE's slight base in the black community was eroded seriously, a situation reflected in the failure to recruit blacks to the most important posts in the national organization. Most of the field representatives were Negroes, undoubtedly indicating CORE's concern with the need for more black members. But after 1950 the top officials were overwhelmingly white. Farmer served as national chairman in 1950–51, but he was unable to give the position the time required. While the field representatives continued to be mostly blacks, Farmer's successors were all whites, as were nearly all the other elected national officers.[64]

The fact that even affiliates with strong leaders encountered serious difficulties suggests that CORE's problem in the early 1950's stemmed mainly from its complex interrelationships with the changing social milieu. Two paradoxes were operating there. On the one hand, the demise of a chapter might result from either a defeat in the face of an intransigent discriminator or from a victory that left the group unsure about what to do next. On the other hand, CORE was functioning in a context where there was both a growing—and encouraging—recognition of the black man's civil rights and also a discouraging threat to reform organizations posed by the McCarthyite anticommunist hysteria.

As throughout CORE's history a sense of failure often precipitated or hastened a chapter's decline. The experiences of Berkeley, Cleveland, and Chicago in this period are cases in point. Very different were the kinds of organizational problems stemming from CORE's victorious public accommodations campaigns and the shifting public sentiment which made these possible. The Truman administration was inaugurating several important innovations; the Supreme Court was promulgating a series of favorable decisions on cases involving restrictive covenants, interstate transportation, and public education, while simultaneously the northern and border states were becoming more susceptible to pressures from civil rights organizations. Northern CORE groups like Minneapolis and Denver, and even New York, having witnessed the virtual disappearance of the public accommodations problem, were not prepared to attack other issues such as employment. Those that did not die altogether carried on a weak action program. The situation in Washington, though more complex, was essentially similar. The Interracial Workshop, faced first with the competition from the energetic Coordinating Committee and then with the disheartening denouement of the successful Rosedale Playground campaign, found its original goal of ending jim crow in the nation's capital basically accomplished with the Thompson restaurant decision and floundered in its search for other projects. When the Workshop finally disbanded in 1955 one long-time member commented, "In many minds was the feeling that the Workshop had outlived its usefulness to the community; we had had a role to fill and had filled it; the need for nonviolent direct action was over." [65]

Especially illuminating was the experience of St. Louis CORE. One reason for its crisis in 1953–54 was the successful conclusion of its lengthy campaign to desegregate dining facilities in downtown stores. It was not that the attainment of this particular objective left St. Louis CORE members with the feeling that they had accomplished their larger goal. It was not that this tiny, dedicated band felt exhausted after nearly a half-dozen years of intensive effort, although this fact played a role. Nor can it be said that the chapter was at a loss because it did not know which issue to choose next—for the members clearly perceived employment to be that issue. Rather they felt that the affiliate was not in a position to attack this problem. For one thing, employment was traditionally the province of the Urban League and St. Louis CORE hesitated to alienate a racial advancement organization which had strong roots in the black community, and with whom they had enjoyed good relations. But more important, they regarded their techniques as inadequate and inappropriate for this type of campaign. Actually what they lacked was power. Gandhian —and labor union—tactics like picketing and boycotting could be effective in obtaining jobs only where a large number of people lent their support. But in the early 1950's equal employment opportunity did not enjoy the same legitimacy that the white public was increasingly according the idea of equal treatment in places of public accommodation. Moreover, although leaders in both CORE and other organizations were familiar with the "Don't-Buy-Where-You-Can't-Work" campaigns which blacks had mounted with some success against ghetto stores during the 1930's, at midcentury the prospect of mobilizing the black community to undertake massive boycotts was seldom perceived as a practical possibility. In any event, as Manuel Talley's experience with the Carnation Milk project suggested, an organization as small as CORE, without deep roots in the black community, was unlikely to be the agent of such a campaign. Unable to appeal to the conscience of white America, or to tap the potential economic power of the masses of black consumers, CORE lacked the leverage needed to redirect its resources into significant employment projects.

CORE's difficulties, meanwhile, were compounded by the anticommunist scare that swept the country during the early 1950's. It has already been noted that CORE, from the very beginning, had feared infiltration by Communists and Trotskyists largely because its leaders had always believed that the surest way to alienate potential supporters was to be identified with other unpopular causes. In Houser's words, CORE's strategy had consistently been to "work on the principle that no stand would be taken on any issue that did not have to do directly with the race issue." Moreover, CORE had always distrusted the revolutionary Marxists because they used reform organizations as fronts to be destroyed when they could no longer be controlled—a phenomenon with which liberals and pacifists had become very familiar during the New Deal and war years. But now strong external pressures were also pushing CORE to articulate a vigorous anticommunist position. As Houser explained, CORE members were often unfairly labeled Communists "because we are, in carrying on a resistance campaign to jim crowism, bucking the main currents of our culture." [66]

As early as 1948 the post office loyalty board had mistakenly pinned a subversive label on Los Angeles CORE for participating in a coalition containing alleged Communists. Worried, Houser and the Executive Committee drafted a "Statement on Communism" for discussion at the 1948 Convention. The delegates voted unanimously not to affiliate "Communist-controlled" groups, enacted procedures for disaffiliating chapters which had fallen under Communist domination, and "approved in principle" the statement which Houser had circulated. Deploring the Red Scare, this document declared that CORE should make clear its own solid organizational reasons for excluding revolutionary Marxists. Since the Communists' primary commitment was to advancing Soviet interests through the use of "any kind of tactics, including violence, treachery and political maneuvering without principle," rather than to waging an uncompromising fight for racial equality, "any degree of Communist influence" in CORE groups would be "destructive" to the organization's "central principles." While there was no "fool-proof way" to exclude Communists, CORE groups were advised to avoid working with Communist-front organizations and to require that CORE members and officers be fully committed to the CORE Discipline.[67]

This action on the part of the 1948 Convention, however, by no means solved the problem. It neither prevented conservatives and racists from continuing to attack CORE as Communist controlled, nor did it completely eliminate the possibility of infiltration. Bartlesville, the CORE affiliate in Oklahoma whose approach was so mild that it actually eschewed direct action, collapsed when, following a speech by Bayard Rustin there in 1950, local conservatives charged its chairwoman with

Communist sympathies and secured her dismissal after over thirty years as town librarian. Two years later CORE leaders, particularly those in St. Louis and New York, became suspicious that the newly formed Pittsburgh affiliate was infiltrated with Communists. When Houser visited Pittsburgh at the convention's request, he found the members agreed on the antithesis existing between communism and non-violence, but nevertheless divided over whether to bar Communists. Some felt that exclusion would be aping Senator Joseph McCarthy, while others denied that it was "red-baiting" to insist on knowing the basic philosophy of individuals who would be functioning in the group. After months of discussion, early in 1953, the Pittsburgh chapter tightened its membership admission procedures but, wracked by the divisive issue, it dwindled in size and activity, and in October voted to disband.[68]

The Pittsburgh situation and the anxieties associated with the cresting of McCarthy's career resulted in further action at the 1952 Convention. While basically reaffirming the 1948 "Statement of Communism" the delegates deleted the denunciation of the Red Scare, on the grounds that CORE was a civil rights rather than a civil liberties organization. Still hoping that appropriate procedures would effectively bar Communists without reducing CORE to witch-hunting, the convention added to the constitution the requirement that a national officer must visit prospective groups before they could be considered for affiliation.[69] For the remainder of the decade CORE was not troubled with attempts at infiltration by revolutionary Marxist organizations. On the other hand, despite its vigorous anticommunist position, CORE suffered considerably from the McCarthyite hysteria of the period. The Red Scare, by labeling radical reform groups subversive, seriously impeded CORE's growth. Ironically, at the very time that the Truman administration and the federal courts were according increasing recognition to the black man's rights, CORE, largely because of its tactics and radical image, enjoyed less public acceptance and attracted fewer members than ever before.

The decline in the number of chapters and in their activity and size was so demoralizing that there was an almost inevitable tendency for CORE leaders to criticize each other. Internal differences over tactics, the communist issue, and CORE's future crystallized in a conflict over Wallace Nelson which polarized the organization and by 1954 had brought it to a serious schismatic crisis. One side was led by the St. Louis and New York City chapters, united against Nelson; arrayed in his defense were principally Nelson's own Cincinnati affiliate and the Washington Interracial Workshop. Nelson was indeed vulnerable. The effectiveness of his work in organizing and helping chapters was hotly debated, and in fact his reports indicated that his accomplishments were modest.[70] Clearly the climate of public opinion worked against CORE's organizational efforts, but Nelson's opponents maintained that in addition he actually frightened potential CORE groups by publicly expounding his own unpopular views on anarchism, pacifism and the communist issue. They insisted that, despite his attempt to distinguish between his and CORE's positions, audiences nevertheless interpreted Nelson's remarks as official CORE doctrine.

Nelson in fact deeply believed that CORE should be an organization that was radical beyond the racial issue, and he stated his position vigorously both within CORE and to potential recruits. In the first place, he not only propagandized on behalf of his anarcho-pacifist views but, as we have seen, employed a kind of civil disobedience by practicing non-cooperation with lawmen when arrested. He refused to accept arrest willingly and advocated going limp against the police since they were "part of the enforcing power of discrimination." In 1953 his supporters sought to make the CORE Action Discipline conform to his antistatist views by deleting the sentence which read, "If a CORE member faces arrest, he will submit willingly to such arrest by a legally constituted official." Second, although as an anarchist and pacifist he had profound ideological differences with the Communists, Nelson's notion of freedom placed him in direct conflict with CORE's efforts to exclude them. As he declared, "A belief in the democratic way of life . . . implies a willingness to take the risk, a calculated risk, of free expression for everyone, including those who preach a totalitarian creed." Nelson charged that in seeking to prevent infiltration CORE was "in danger of surrendering to the current hysteria," and he even argued that CORE with its youthfulness and flexibility and its lack of "respectability" was one of the few organizations which was in a position to aggressively fight the Red Scare and "do something toward checking this hysterical wave of McCarthyism."[71]

Robinson, the Oldhams, and their associates believed that the policies which Nelson articulated would simply retard the cause of racial equality. Alarmed at CORE's decline, they insisted that the organization must actually cultivate greater respectability and thereby gain greater acceptance. Robinson, although one of the pacifist founders, held that if CORE were to appeal to a larger segment of American society, it must deliberately outgrow its "cult image" and lose its identification as an organization radical about anything but the race issue; its mission for the 1950's should be to "pitch itself through liberals to liberals rather than as once, through pacifists to pacifists and a few liberals." Not only was Nelson naïve in thinking that Communists could sincerely subscribe to the CORE Discipline, but the organization could not afford to ignore the anticommunist hysteria or to frighten off potential supporters with a public attack on McCarthyism. "How," Robinson wanted to know, "can a tax-resister, a person who is rather generally anti-police, etc., appeal to the non-radical liberal?" St. Louis chapter leaders were particularly upset at Nelson's position on police action, since their practice was to avoid arrest at all costs, even to the point of terminating demonstrations when arrests seemed imminent. And the entire anti-Nelson faction held that "going limp," while perhaps suitable for a pacifist demonstration, was an "extreme" and "illegal method" which violated the Discipline and forfeited public support. In fact New York CORE, anxious to erase CORE's pacifist image and to show that the commitment to nonviolence was not a "total philosophy," proposed deleting from the Discipline the statement that "the nonviolent method assumes the possibility of creating a world in which nonviolence will be used to a maximum degree." Instead, the chapter urged simply substituting a sentence indicating that nonviolent direct action "is a technique for developing a racially-integrated society in America." [72]

Nelson and his supporters had no use for the attempt to make CORE respectable. They denounced their opponents for an "overconcern with 'respectability,'" holding that "no direct action can be respectable in these times. 'Respectability' under these circumstances can easily come to mean less principled action on our part." Albert Mindlin of the Washington Interracial Workshop was not himself a pacifist, yet he questioned the theory that trade union-oriented liberals would rush to embrace CORE if it dropped the pacifist image.[73] Even Houser, who as the organization's chief executive, had become extremely discouraged by the struggle to attract new members and form new groups, was unmoved by the respectability argument. He sympathized with Nelson's basic civil libertarian philosophy and had also once been a tax resister himself, paying only a small portion of his income tax in 1951 as a protest against the Korean War.[74] Houser had composed the Statement on Communism, and he thought that Nelson was unwise to raise the McCarthyist issue;

yet he had great admiration for the field worker's idealism and integrity. Although Houser attempted to play a mediating role in the controversy, throughout Nelson retained the executive secretary's support.

During the spring of 1953, Nelson's opponents decided to mount a full-scale attack at the forthcoming annual convention. The lengthy debates at the conclave resulted in a distinct compromise. In regard to the Discipline's philosophical statement about nonviolence, New York CORE largely won its point when the conference deleted the pacifist-sounding clause and substituted an innocuous one proposed by Houser. On the question of cooperating with the police in submitting to arrest, the delegates adopted another compromise offered by Houser, providing that an individual could refuse such cooperation if the group had previously agreed to take this position. But when Lula Farmer, James Farmer's wife and a leading member of New York CORE, threatened that her chapter would disaffiliate because this would be changing CORE's "basic nature" by "sanctioning opposition to law as such," the conclave postponed a decision until the following year. Finally, intending to impose restraints on Nelson, the convention required all national officers to "clearly present CORE's position" to the public, and empowered the National Council to appoint additional, though unpaid, field representatives. Although the delegates also decided that hereafter all field representatives must be approved by a two-thirds vote of the annual conference, Nelson enjoyed such personal respect that despite the reservations held by many he was reelected to his post.[75]

This 1953 Convention settled nothing—either about Nelson or CORE's future. In the following months the controversy worsened, erupting into personal attacks between Nelson's partisans and opponents. As Catharine Raymond, Houser's secretary and CORE's national treasurer, later described the tension-laden atmosphere of 1953–54, there was "in our midst a bitterness and suspicion of each other's motives that is bad and . . . fairly new. . . . If we saw two or three people talking between sessions, we . . . immediately jump [ed] to the conclusion that they were hatching up something." Houser, trying to reconcile the two "camps" and thus "avoid a knock-down drag-out at the convention," hoped that as a compromise Nelson could be retained as a paid field worker responsible for a limited territory. Warning Nelson's opponents that the field representative had substantial support in the Baltimore, Washington, and Columbia, Missouri, chapters, he urged acceptance of this proposal before "real damage" was done to the organization. Robinson, however, reiterated his "complete opposition" to Nelson holding any office and declared that he, like a number of others, would resign from CORE if necessary.[76] In what Houser later described as "fast maneuvering . . . to clip Wally's wings," St. Louis and New York prevailed upon the autumn Council meeting to appoint three additional unpaid field representatives, all of them anti-Nelson. The Council further isolated him by restricting all of the field personnel, including James Farmer who had been appointed at the Convention, to work in specific geographic areas. Nelson's critics, however, were still not entirely satisfied. Oldham wrote, "Our group is solid in replacing Wally if someone else can be found." Yet the anti-Nelson faction faced a tactical problem, since they had not a suitable candidate to replace him as full-time paid subsistence worker. They considered Bernice Fisher ideal, but she preferred to work for the CIO in Chicago.[77]

Early in 1954, Houser's resignation from the FOR, by requiring a reorganization of the National CORE structure, provided Nelson's opponents with the opportunity they were seeking. Houser's position in the FOR had been growing increasingly precarious. As early as 1951, the Fellowship began to move away from activism in the racial and industrial fields, and two years later, about the time Muste retired, the FOR Program Committee recommended that "staff time on CORE should be eliminated as rapidly as possible." The Fellowship, by permitting both Houser and Catharine Raymond to spend much of their time on CORE, had contributed significantly to the organization's survival. Clearly, with this support now being withdrawn, and with CORE's old critic John Swomley now head of FOR, Houser would be unable to remain as CORE's executive secretary. Meanwhile he was becoming increasingly interested in assisting the South African resistance movement, and early in 1954 he announced his intention to resign from his positions in both FOR and CORE in order to organize the American Committee on Africa.[78]

A few days later Houser met with representatives from the New York chapter and approved their proposals for reorganizing the national structure. The duties of executive director were now to be divided. The popular Billie Ames would be asked to become group coordinator—handling correspondence and acting as a liaison between the chapters. Peck, in addition to editing the *CORE-lator,* would prepare and mail all CORE literature, while Robinson would continue to take care of finances. In addition to providing for CORE's administrative needs, Robinson was hopeful that through this arrangement "the Wally problem might work itself out without so much of a fuss." Since the group coordinator's part-time salary would about equal Nelson's subsistence pay, it was clear that CORE could not afford to pay for both. Soon afterwards the CORE Council recommended that the convention adopt these proposals for structural reorganization. On Houser's reluctant motion the Council also urged the Convention for financial reasons to eliminate the paid field worker position but to re-elect Nelson as an unpaid part-time representative. Houser thereupon began preparations for an extended trip to Africa, and in April Ames assumed many of his responsibilities.[79]

Houser's conciliatory stance did not spare CORE the "knock-down drag-out" he had hoped to avoid. Shortly before the convention, New York CORE mapped out its "strategy on ridding CORE of Wally Nelson." One member was assigned to lead the floor fight, while others talked to key delegates informally, stressing Nelson's weaknesses. New York delegates were directed to vote against Nelson for anything: "Stick to one slate as far as anti-Nelson forces are concerned," they were told, "but try to nominate more than one person of the opposition in order to split votes. . . . LOVE EVERYONE AND VOTE AS INSTRUCTED!!" Although both sides engaged in "a good deal of politicking," the Nelson forces condemned New York CORE's attempts to "line up votes in advance" as more evidence of "lack of good will" and a "struggle for power." Such accusations did not disturb James Robinson: "Of course, 'struggle for power' is always involved in any organization and on almost every major issue. But it is bad only when issues are used for personal power advancement, and I think none of us on the anti-Wally side are guilty of that." [80]

Basically the 1954 Convention settled things to the satisfaction of New York and St. Louis CORE. To the dismay of the Nelson forces the delegates sidestepped the issue of noncooperation with the police by eliminating from the Discipline all references to the subject. They approved the new structural arrangements and the appointment of Billie Ames as paid group coordinator. At the same time they abolished the post of paid field worker. Four unsalaried field representatives were elected—two from the anti-Nelson faction and two who were friendly to him. But Nelson himself could not muster the necessary two-thirds majority vote. In a moving and dramatic climax, his wife, Juanita Morrow Nelson, who had herself been a prominent CORE leader for nearly a decade, resigned the post of secretary to which she had just been elected.

The organization which Billie Ames inherited was a shambles— important leaders were on the verge of resigning and the chapters were weak and inactive. Ironically, in the very year—1954—that the NAACP won its landmark school desegregation decision from the Supreme Court, CORE was at its lowest ebb. Viewed as more radical than the NAACP, CORE suffered more from the McCarthyite hysteria. And the crest of McCarthyism came at the very time that the public accommodations issue had been pretty well solved in the North and West, leaving CORE floundering tactically—unable to adapt its techniques to housing and employment problems of the North, or to establish a foothold in the South. The convergence of these two developments produced a weak organization, wracked by internal conflict.

On the other hand, the NAACP's victories in the school cases and other desegregation litigation reflected a long-range improvement in the climate of public opinion. This shift had been dramatized by President Truman's position on civil rights during the 1948 election, and his subsequent actions—desegregation of the armed forces, appointment of the first black federal circuit court judge, and creation of a fair employment contracts committee. While the McCarthy ascendancy during the early years of the Eisenhower administration marked a setback for civil liberties, the drift of public sentiment toward greater support of civil rights continued. Nothing made this fact more evident than the enormous popular favor enjoyed by Martin Luther King and the Montgomery Bus Boycott which began in December 1955. True, the changes in public sentiment had ironically been part of the complex of factors which accounted for CORE's temporary decline in the early 1950's. Nevertheless by the end of the decade, growing public acceptance of both racial equality and nonviolent direct action enabled CORE to enjoy a substantial revival that laid the groundwork for its flowering in the 1960's.

3

Nadir and Revival
1954-1959

.

It was with a sense of dismay that Billie Ames, fearing that the "hard feelings" between the two factions would destroy what was left of CORE, assumed her new job as group coordinator. Enjoying cordial relations with people on both sides, Billie Ames was the one person who might have been able to unite the disputants behind the CORE banner. But even she was stymied. Nelson and his wife submitted their resignations, and Catharine Raymond, who had backed him, warned, ". . . if the present trend toward a power struggle in CORE is not halted, I for one am not going to stay in longer than this year." [1] Seeking to boost morale and prevent groups from disaffiliating, Ames actively pursued the convention's mandate to mount a second Journey of Reconciliation into the South. Tentatively renaming the proposed trip "Ride for Freedom," she suggested an itinerary that extended as far south as Birmingham. But the project fell through after the NAACP refused to extend the support it had provided in 1947; it advised CORE to give up the trip altogether because the Association's attorneys anticipated a favorable Interstate Commerce Commission ruling on a case against the jim crow railroads. Although Ames countered that the South would simply flout the decision, making the "Ride for Freedom" imperative to "dramatize and publicize" the ruling, CORE leaders were reluctant to offend the NAACP and so tabled the project.[2] Meanwhile the Nelson faction was losing interest in CORE. Raymond resigned as national treasurer in 1955. Ames had persuaded the Nelsons to withdraw their resignations, but they both retreated to the sidelines and officially severed relations with CORE in 1956. Moreover, the chapters in Cincinnati, Chicago, Washington, and Baltimore were deeply disaffected. The Washington Interracial Workshop, which was already in the doldrums, voted to disband in March 1955, and a year later Nelson's own Cincinnati local was finally disaffiliated because of its inactivity.[3]

The number of affiliates remained small, fluctuating between seven and nine over the period from 1954 to 1957, and most of them were nearly extinct. Only four—New York, St. Louis, Chicago, and Evanston —sent delegates to the 1955 CORE Convention, and even they reported scarcely any activity. Chicago, with virtually a paper membership, had for years been "primarily a social group," and during 1956 it suffered from an intense factional fight over an anarcho-syndicalist clique headed by Joffre Stewart, a young black who upset other CORE members on their few demonstrations by wearing unconventional clothing and distributing political tracts. More significantly, the previously active New York chapter was, according to Robinson, similar to Chicago CORE in that it was "very busy now doing practically nothing but meetings, parties, etc." It did manage to stir itself for one or two days to join ten other organizations in a picket line against the discriminatory employment policy of the local office of the Automobile Association of America. Clearly aware of the weaknesses of CORE and the other groups, the AAA agreed merely to hire four blacks as temporary clerks. By the end of 1956 both the half-dozen active members of Chicago CORE and the "dormant" New York chapter were reduced to occasional restaurant testing.[4]

St. Louis CORE also went downhill. An attempt to integrate a few sandwich shops dragged on for months, while efforts to end jim crow in movie houses proved dilatory and ineffective.[5] The chapter did have one successful employment project in 1955—three black cashiers were hired at two supermarkets whose customers were heavily Negro.[6] Because progress was so slow and piecemeal—and because the group lacked the strength to carry on direct-action projects—it spent many months in unsuccessful lobbying for passage of a municipal public accommodations bill.[7] Matters deteriorated still further after Billie Ames left CORE in 1955. The Oldhams tried to keep the group going but lacked the great amount of time she had been able to give. By the spring of 1957 St. Louis

CORE, once the most viable chapter in the entire CORE movement, was "temporarily defunct." [8]

Even the most active chapter, Baltimore CORE, encountered serious problems. This affiliate, at the time composed of about a dozen members who were chiefly young professional people, continued to press forward on the public accommodations issue. In January 1955 it ended a successful eight-month lunch-counter campaign against the Reed drug store chain, and in mid-1956, after many weeks of negotiations and picketing, desegrated a restaurant located at the edge of the principal black business district.[9] It also began two protracted, frustrating campaigns that would engage the chapter for years—picketing the annual All-Nations Day celebration at the exclusionary Gwynn Oak Amusement Park, and, as its major effort, initiating an intensive direct-action struggle against the White Coffee Pot chain.[10] Meanwhile the chapter became embroiled in a factional conflict over whether an avowed Trotskyist should be allowed to distribute political leaflets at CORE demonstrations and to remain in the group. By 1957, with this clash still unresolved, Baltimore CORE had become so weakened that its members could not even agree to hold an election for chairman.[11]

Nor did an attempt to reinvigorate CORE work on the West Coast prove very fruitful. The leading chapter there was Los Angeles CORE, which was revived in the summer of 1955 through the conscientious efforts of Herbert Kelman, then at the Center for Advanced Study in the Behavioral Sciences, and at the time the only one of the elected field representatives who devoted much time to the organization. He formed a new group of ten members, chiefly white pacifists and chaired by Henry Hodge, a black social worker who had formerly belonged to St. Louis CORE and who would later become national vice-chairman. Although Kelman urged them to undertake the complex task of attacking housing and employment discrimination, the chapter preferred to start with a successful attempt to secure service for blacks at the Union Passenger Terminal barber shop. When the group did turn to the job issue, they were unable to go beyond generally fruitless negotiations with several companies. By the time they obtained sales positions for two blacks at a downtown department store in the spring of 1957, the chapter had nearly folded.[12]

CORE leaders, acutely concerned about the parlous state of existing affiliates and the failure to develop viable new ones, attributed the organization's weakness in large part to the decline of discrimination in public accommodations in the North and West, and felt that "as the jim crow line recedes southward, CORE groups should follow." Clearly, short of creating successful techniques for challenging northern job and housing discrimination, the logical place for CORE to continue its work was in the South, and for this a paid field organizer was essential.[13] In fact, ever since Wallace Nelson's defeat, the employment of a salaried field staffer had been regarded as a matter of the highest priority.[14] The system of unpaid, elective field representatives was a failure, since individuals occupying that position only occasionally carried out their responsibilities. In James Peck's words, "unless we can find a field representative who will help start new groups, the future is dim." If CORE were not to fold, "something has got to be done—and quick." [15] As a temporary stopgap, Billie Ames and Marian Oldham attempted to revive activities in the border states. They briefly reinvigorated the remnants of the Kansas City and Columbia, Missouri, chapters, and early in 1955 were contemplating a trip to Louisville in hopes of demonstrating that CORE could function in an upper South city.[16]

At this juncture things worsened when in March 1955, Billie Ames, for urgent personal reasons, was compelled to resign from CORE. In May Houser called a meeting of a few CORE stalwarts in New York to assess the organization's prospects. "The atmosphere was extremely pessimistic," Robinson reported afterward, and small comfort was derived from the fact that things were "no worse than a year ago." Houser, in his despair, urged that the usual spring financial appeal be skipped. Robinson and Lula Farmer, however, disagreed. Ironically, even though CORE activity was at its nadir, there was more money than ever—$2200—in the national treasury, and Robinson anticipated that another appeal would bring in enough funds to warrant hiring a national field organizer.[17] A few weeks later the annual convention voted to create this position, which was filled in December with the appointment of LeRoy Carter, a black former NAACP field secretary.

The thrust of Carter's work was clearly intended to be in the South. The hopes of Robinson and other CORE leaders had recently been raised by the appearance of a chapter in Nashville, organized by FOR members and composed largely of black college students.[18] At the same time Martin Luther King's Montgomery bus boycott, which began in December 1955, and soon hit the national headlines, added a new dimension to CORE thinking. The South was now clearly where the publicity was, and Montgomery also suggested the great potential for nonviolent direct action in that region. The FOR sent a representative to assist Dr. King, and the War Resisters League dispatched Bayard Rustin.[19] CORE likewise attempted to associate itself with the new movement, assigning LeRoy Carter to Montgomery as an observer. The *CORE-lator* reported his meeting with King and published a photograph captioned, "LEADERS OF THE CORE-TYPE PROTEST IN MONTGOMERY." Readers who failed to get the point about CORE's supposed contribution to King's boycott movement learned, "The CORE technique of nonviolence has been spotlighted to the entire world through the effective action which the Montgomery Improvement Association has been conducting." The delegates to the 1956 CORE Convention told themselves that with Montgomery, "the CORE technique has come of age," and that vigorous efforts to create affiliates in the upper South would enable CORE to play an important role. Anxious to establish a base in the South, and realizing the unlikelihood of attracting white participation there, the 1956 Convention made a significant departure from past CORE policy by deleting the interracial requirement from the CORE constitution.[20]

Carter, on his first assignment, early in 1956, visited not only Montgomery but also two other cities in the midst of nonviolent direct-action campaigns, Tallahassee and Orangeburg. His principal task, however, was to organize groups in the less repressive tier of states in the upper South. There his efforts proved disappointing to CORE. For example, of his brief stay in Memphis he wrote, "It is my opinion that integration in Memphis is a long way off and that something sensational will be required to motivate the masses of people to action." He found the Nashville chapter frightened by the possible consequences of direct action; and in fact the weak affiliate could get no further than conducting a test at a jim crow drive-in theater.[21] "Convinced that the amount of courage required for the formation of a CORE group in the South is rare," Carter reported to the 1956 Convention that "my time was spent in lectures to small groups and conferences with individuals on the power of nonviolence." [22] Subsequently Carter sparked a temporary revival of Kansas City CORE, but field trips to Detroit, Chicago, and the West Coast were unproductive. Meanwhile CORE's experience with Ralph Blackwood, a white pacifist hired in January 1957 as a "half-time field organizer" to service the Midwest, proved no more fruitful. The preceding year Blackwood had developed in Hutchinson, Kansas, an active chapter of thirty-six members—the largest in the whole organization, and as field organizer he visited other Kansas towns, forming a few small incipient units consisting mainly of blacks. But in every case the attempt to end restaurant exclusion ended in failure and in the demise of the local group. Soon afterward, in April 1957, both men resigned from CORE.[23]

Thus in the spring of 1957 CORE was where it had been in 1954— without any field staff, and still grappling with the problem of creating new and viable chapters. It was an organization dominated at the top level by a handful of dedicated whites—national chairman Charles Oldham, group coordinator and national treasurer Lula Farmer, finance secretary James Robinson, and *CORE-lator* editor James Peck. But Robinson, now the most influential figure in CORE, remained confident that the organization had great potential for developing in the South if a competent Negro organizer could be found. Clearly the introduction of an explicit racial criterion for the post of field secretary was a departure from CORE's traditional ideology of selecting officers without regard to race. Yet as Robinson observed, "A dynamic Negro organizer is essential to the build-up of CORE." Indeed, Blackwood had been hired only after a Negro, the FOR official and future state superintendent of education in California, Wilson C. Riles, had rejected the position.[24] In Robinson's view CORE had been "missing the boat" by not moving aggressively into the South, for participation in the southern civil rights movement would give CORE "a much larger operation" and a national image, making the organization "synonymous with direct non-violent action throughout the United States." And for CORE "to establish rapid contact with southern protest actions . . . a fieldworker who is Negro has a strong advantage over one who is white," since southern blacks "have learned not to expect support from white people and . . . realize that white 'Yankee' help provides a handle for the Citizens Council to use." [25] Several more blacks were asked to consider the field secretary position, but discouraged by the organization's bleak prospects, they all declined. It was not until the autumn of 1957, when CORE secured James T. McCain that its push into the South really began.

Paradoxically, in the years after 1954, when CORE was perilously close to demise, its income continued to rise, owing chiefly to Robinson's aggressive efforts. Anxious to see the organization acquire an office and expand its staff, he urged a "speedup" in money-raising—printing more literature, sending out more financial appeals, selling December holiday cards, and publishing the *CORE-lator* more often. The *CORE-lator* maintained an energetic public image for CORE's financial supporters, and it sometimes even stretched the truth to give an impression of vitality among the affiliates. Thus in January 1957 Oldham confided to Peck that "the plain and simple truth . . . is that [St. Louis CORE] has not been doing anything"; yet the following month the *CORE-lator* portrayed St. Louis as busy working to integrate department store restaurants and to obtain a local FEPC ordinance. Meanwhile Robinson, as finance secretary, composed and sent out letters to thousands of prospective contributors, which typically exploited the headline-making developments in the southern black protest movement. Thus during the fiscal year 1956–57, 40,000 copies of a Martin Luther King pamphlet on the Montgomery struggle were mailed with CORE appeal letters. One of them, over the signature of A. Philip Randolph, —whose name proved singularly effective with potential contributors—proclaimed, "Success of the Montgomery boycott suggests that CORE, with its techniques, might be a significant help in the Deep South. . . . To enable CORE to explore the possibilities of spreading the spirit and technique of nonviolence I ask your help. . . ." [26]

Robinson's work was so successful that, although payments from the chapters remained miniscule, the number of individual contributors nearly doubled between 1954 and 1957—rising from about 1900 to about 3400. At the same time the total receipts showed a gratifying rise. During the fiscal year ending May 31, 1955, CORE's income was $8200, while expenses were $6700. A year later income was $12,000, expenditures $7500. Robinson, heretofore an advocate of giving priority to building a financial reserve as a prerequisite for developing a program, now shifted gears. He was a strong force in persuading the 1956 Convention to spend some of the surplus and adopt a budget for the next year that included a planned deficit of $2100, in order to subsidize an expansion of field work. Accordingly, because of the employment of field organizers, expenditures more than doubled during the fiscal year ending May 31, 1957, to over $16,100. Yet Robinson's appeals were so productive that income rose to $16,000 and the deficit was only slightly more than $100.[27]

Meanwhile, in the vacuum created by the small number of affiliates, their lack of power, and the absence of satisfactory field organizers, a more centralized structure was appearing at the national headquarters in New York. This innovation was recommended by Robinson, who urged the formation of a "central committee of an active sort to plan and carry through the many steps needed to [expand CORE] . . . and to present CORE as a national integrated movement rather than a loosely connected agglomeration of local groups." He and other leaders agreed that an executive committee whose members were all located in one city could more effectively discharge key functions and serve as a base on which to build a revitalized and dynamic CORE than could the widely scattered members of the Council who met together only occasionally. Accordingly, in March 1956 the Council appointed a committee of New Yorkers— Houser, Lula and James Farmer, Peck, Robinson, and Carter—"to act on immediate situations as they arise." At the same time the group coordinator's office, which since Billie Ames' departure had temporarily been serviced by a member of St. Louis CORE, was transferred to New York, and Lula Farmer was named to the position. By November, Robinson asserted that this small executive committee—later known as the National Action Committee—"in effect is running CORE . . . as it is not possible to have National Council meetings, etc., frequently enough." [28]

The moribund state of the affiliates which had encouraged the creation of this extra-legal body was demonstrated even more dramatically by the 1957 CORE National Convention. Aside from four national officers, only three other persons appeared—evidence extraordinary that there were no longer any truly functioning local groups. But there was an operating national body, the National Action Committee (NAC), which met regularly in New York. Robinson, Lula Farmer, James Peck, and Charles Oldham were determined to prevent CORE from dying, having faith that it could make a great contribution to the cause of racial equality. The way out of the dilemma was to overhaul the constitution, giving legal recognition to the powers which had developed in the NAC and enabling the national office to continue soliciting funds for projects that would hopefully stimulate new chapters. Consequently, the Convention directed Robinson to draft a new constitution spelling out the Committee's functions. The NAC, required to meet at least ten times a year and consisting of a small group of officers, staff members, and persons appointed by the national chairman, all of whom were located near the New York office, was authorized to "handle day to day decisions between Councils and Conventions, including matters of personnel and policy . . . to initiate and develop action programs and projects in the name of the national organization." [29]

The Convention also asked Robinson to take the post of executive secretary, which he accepted in September. He started off with better finances and a tighter organizational structure than had Houser. These factors combined with his own drive and vision and the changing landscape of race relations, especially in the South, accounted for the growth and achievements during his period in office. Robinson, in fact, took charge at a dramatic juncture in the southern integration struggle. Violence greeted the beginning of school desegregation in Nashville and Little Rock—the dynamiting of a newly integrated school in the Tennessee city, the calling of soldiers to enforce integration in the Arkansas capital. The rush of events in the South confirmed his judgment that CORE should bend its efforts toward developing affiliates there; the parallel growth in national concern for the black man's rights was reflected in the success of CORE's fund-raising appeals, which permitted the organization to increase its staff, expand its work in the South, and stimulate the revival of CORE activity in the North. Thus between 1957 and the end of 1959 was laid the basis for CORE's prominent role in the civil rights movement of the sixties.

Robinson, who assumed the duties previously assigned to both the group coordinator and the finance secretary, devoted half his time to fund-raising and promotion; the other half was given to corresponding with groups, setting up Council meetings and conventions, and coordinating the activities of CORE's new field secretaries. Peck continued to handle the *CORE-lator,* while Lula Farmer, who had been treasurer since 1955, spent much time at the office doing the bookkeeping. Robinson also worked very closely with the NAC and with national chairman Oldham. Although Oldham was in St. Louis, he kept abreast of developments through an extensive correspondence and had a share in all important decisions.[30]

At the heart of CORE's revival was the growth of the national staff. First came the hiring of new field workers. In October 1957, very soon after he took office, Robinson was joined by James T. McCain, a former high school principal in Clarendon County, South Carolina, who had served for many years as president of the Sumter, South Carolina, NAACP branch. After his dismissal from the school position in 1955 because of his NAACP activities, McCain had worked for a moderate interracial reform group, the South Carolina Council on Human Relations, before coming to CORE. In 1958 the convention authorized the employment of a second field secretary, and Gordon Carey, a white man, was hired in August. Carey's background bore a striking resemblance to CORE leaders of an earlier period. The son of a Methodist minister, he had been a leader in the Methodist Youth Fellowship and the Youth FOR, and he had served a year in CPS camp for refusing to report for induction. Since 1951 he had been active in Pasadena and Los Angeles CORE, and was national vice-chairman in 1956–57. Meanwhile as program and activity expanded, CORE leaders felt the need for a more professional public relations program, since as Robinson frankly observed, press releases were never systematically distributed, and except for the *CORE-lator* the organization had "virtually no publicity set-up." [31] Finally, in October 1959, Marvin Rich was appointed to the post of community relations director to handle public relations and special fund-raising. Rich, who was married to a Negro, had been one of the founders and a former chairman of the St. Louis chapter. At the time he joined the CORE staff he was working in New York, securing political and financial support for Histadrut, the Israeli Labor Federation, and since late 1956 he had been on the NAC. As community relations director Rich aimed "to establish the image of CORE as a major race relations organization" ranking in stature with the NAACP and SCLC.[32] After his appointment, regular publicity releases were sent out, and CORE began to receive steady attention in the black press.

With the expansion of the national staff, costs rose abruptly, and the campaign for money was augmented accordingly. At the end of 1957 CORE's monthly expenses jumped from about $350 to about $2850. At first Robinson seemed overwhelmed by the fund-raising aspect of his job, being "slightly worried" about the "somewhat risky expansion" CORE had undertaken, and finding that "promotional fund-raising . . . often pushes other work into the background for days at a time." Between June 1957 and March 1958 some 39,000 letters went to members of other liberal organizations, and 1131 new donors were added to the CORE list. By then CORE had come to appreciate the need for more elaborate promotional materials. In an expensive "two color printing," tens of thousands of copies of *This is CORE* and *CORE Rules for Action*—a retitling of the "CORE Action Discipline" for wider appeal—were circulated.[33] In the most ambitious and successful publicity effort CORE had ever undertaken, Robinson, through Bayard Rustin's intercession, persuaded King to sign an appeal letter; accompanied by a pamphlet, *A First Step Toward School Integration,* describing Nashville CORE's assistance to the first black pupils who attended white schools there, nearly a hundred thousand were mailed to prospective donors late in 1958.[34] Overall the results were gratifying. Between mid-1958 and mid-1959, CORE doubled its list of contributors from about 4500 to more than 9000.

Now, more than ever, there was an effort to enlist the Advisory Committee in CORE's fund-raising campaigns. Because the Committee was regarded as such an important means of creating an image for CORE among possible contributors, there was serious concern over the fact that it was difficult to persuade prominent blacks to serve on it. King agreed to join the Committee in 1957, but despite attempts to attract more distinguished Negroes, the group remained about two-thirds white.[35] Nor was the endeavor to use the Advisory Committee as a device through which CORE could attract support from the labor movement especially successful. Unions were chary of giving to a "small unknown" organization; for example, Walter Reuther of the United Automobile Workers, had declined to serve in the mid-1950's, and in 1959 an approach through A. Philip Randolph to James Carey, Secretary-Treasurer of the Industrial Union Department, AFL-CIO, similarly failed. However, at the end of the year Jerry Wurf of the American Federation of State, County, and Municipal Employees did accept membership, thus joining Randolph, Harold Gibbons of the Teamsters, and Charles S. Zimmerman of the International Ladies Garment Workers Union.[36] Yet efforts to exploit these union contacts for fund-raising proved disappointing. During 1959 labor organizations gave $1347 (up from $695 in 1958), of which the ILGWU and the AFSCME contributed the major part.[37]

In order to build up CORE as rapidly as possible, the organization embarked upon a policy of spending to the limit of its income, withdrawing from the reserve account to meet current expenses, and then sending emergency appeal letters.[38] During the fiscal year ending May 31, 1958, income had increased by 50 per cent, but expenses had risen even faster; CORE had collected $24,700 but had spent $25,200. By July, there were so many unpaid bills that the NAC even considered deferring payment of salaries. Yet a few weeks later Gordon Carey was added to the staff.[39] As income continued to grow, so did the organization's obligations. In the spring of 1959 Carey observed, "We have the largest budget ever and more money than ever before, but with constantly expanding program and staff, it isn't near enough. . . . We are acting on faith and may even take on a new employee." During the fiscal year ending May 31, 1959, the total income of $62,000 only slightly exceeded expenses. Nevertheless, CORE optimistically set its 1959–60 budget at $103,500 and began spending commensurately. Although money was now coming in at a higher rate than ever, it became clear that the organization had overestimated what it would raise, and in January 1960, Robinson announced that the staff would take a "voluntary" pay reduction.[40] Yet clearly, in increasing CORE's annual income more than sixfold while directing vigorous efforts to expand CORE's activity, Robinson had accomplished a considerable feat.

The heart of Robinson's program was the aggressive development of local chapters—the responsibility of the two field secretaries, McCain and Carey. Since McCain preferred to be in the field rather than in the office, Carey handled the planning of field trips for both men. Their work was arduous and often discouraging. Because of CORE's modest financial resources, they ordinarily traveled by bus and roomed either with local CORE members, or more frequently, at the YMCA. For communities where no CORE group existed, McCain and Carey used the list built up by Robinson's financial appeals, and before a field tour they wrote letters to contacts along the route, soliciting help in forming a local affiliate. Upon arrival in a city, the field secretary would telephone the handful who had replied affirmatively, inviting them to a small gathering. Such a collection of individuals, even if finally drawn to a meeting, often did not produce a suitable nucleus for a functioning local group. All too frequently those who expressed interest did not genuinely desire to engage in direct action, and on the basis of some hard experience in northern Virginia, Robinson advised his field secretaries to proceed promptly to action. "We should not wait for those who want to study first; if they are sincere in their interest, they will come in once action starts. . . . CORE's action program itself, once it is in motion, is more persuasive to prospective members than any amount of study and talk." [41]

In deploying McCain and Carey, CORE faced an important question of strategy. Should it put all its resources into developing groups in the South or should it assign the field secretaries to the North and West as well? During Robinson's first year the efforts of the two men were concentrated exclusively in the South, and consequently, as Robinson frankly informed the 1958 Convention, CORE had failed to organize new affiliates in the northern, western, or border states. With the convention's disaffiliation of long-inactive groups in Chicago, Omaha, and Hutchinson, only five chapters were left in addition to the ones McCain had been organizing in South Carolina: St. Louis, New York, Los Angeles, Baltimore, and Nashville. In a spirited debate at the NAC meeting in October, Peck and Rich urged that organizational resources be expended almost exclusively in the South, while James Robinson, vigorously supported by the black attorney and New York CORE leader, Tom Roberts, argued for a dual thrust, pointing out that integrated housing and open employment were becoming salient issues in the North. In the end the

NAC backed Robinson, deciding to keep McCain in the South but to have Carey revive field work in the North and West.[42]

Another problem of strategy which CORE faced as it created new chapters was maintaining the organization's interracial character. In the South and to some extent in the border cities it was difficult to attract whites; in other areas there was the old problem of securing black members. The March 1958 Council meeting expressed concern over the "mono-racial" character of the new South Carolina groups which McCain was forming, but agreed that such units were unavoidable until sincere whites could be found to join. A year later, after all-black chapters had been affiliated in Charleston, West Virginia and in East St. Louis, Illinois, the question was again discussed by the Council. Both Robinson and Anna Holden of Nashville, who was one of CORE's few white members in the South, emphasized the need to maintain CORE's traditions as an interracial organization. But South Carolina delegates, not surprisingly, insisted that they could not secure white participation, and in a compromise statement the Council decided that whites should be involved as soon as possible except in the smaller towns of the deep South. The CORE staff remained worried. Robinson wrote to the Oldhams: "The characteristic 'mood' of CORE and some of its techniques as well require an interracial membership, and I am concerned that the recent Council seems to underscore a trend toward becoming a largely Negro group." At the very least, he believed, efforts should be made to induce "a few token whites" to join. Carey declared that the decision of the 1956 Convention to facilitate the southern work by removing the interracial requirement had actually created "a danger . . . that we may tend to look for Negroes when organizing a group rather than looking for good persons regardless of color. This tendency is a dangerous one and could radically alter the nature of CORE unless carefully guarded against." The matter was again discussed at the 1959 Convention, and afterward McCain fruitlessly sought to locate white members for the groups in Columbia and Rock Hill, South Carolina. Basically it was unrealistic to think that whites would participate in most of the southern chapters; the fact that two finally joined the Sumter, South Carolina, affiliate was an exception that left the fundamental possibilities unchanged.[43]

In contrast, the West Coast groups in Portland, Oregon, and the San Francisco Bay area which Carey organized in 1959 all complained of a paucity of black members. For example, the college-based Berkeley CORE for all its annoyance with the "do nothing" local NAACP branch,

admitted that the latter organization had "the necessary lines of communication" with the black community which CORE so obviously lacked.
To an unhappy leader of Richmond, California, CORE, Carey wrote,
"In the North a good many of our groups suffer from lack of adequate
Negro participation. In the South they suffer from lack of whites—it
about compensates itself. I do not mean that Negro participation is not
important because [being] interracial is the heart of CORE. However,
some of our most effective groups have been quite heavily white. Usually
when a group gets involved in *significant* action projects it will build up
its membership from both groups." [44]

In creating a base in the South, CORE leaders found that, for the most
part, it was not feasible to employ the traditional kind of direct-action
confrontation epitomized by the sit-in. In the upper South they sought to
facilitate the enforcement of the 1954 Supreme Court decision on public
school desegregation. In the repressive state of South Carolina, CORE,
stimulated by the provisions of the 1957 Civil Rights Act, intended to secure the franchise for southern blacks and concentrated on helping people register to vote. Only in Florida did the chapters undertake the kind
of direct-action projects against places of public accommodation that had
been most characteristically associated with CORE. Overall the results
were mixed; but by 1960 CORE had clearly established a foothold in the
South.

Nashville was the only CORE affiliate in the South established before
Robinson became executive secretary. The "prime mover" [45] of this interracial chapter was Anna Holden, a white Floridian employed in social research at Fisk University. With a membership hovering around ten, the
chapter encouraged black parents to send their children to schools recently desegregated by federal court order. In a climate of intimidation
and even violence, interracial CORE teams reassured frightened black
adults and escorted the children during the first three days of school in
the autumn of 1957. Only thirteen Negro youngsters attended school
with whites, but their presence was a beginning of school integration
which Nashville CORE had helped to make possible. At the opening of
the following school year, CORE again visited homes and offered escorts;
this time thirty-four of three hundred eligible black children braved harassment to attend the previously all-white schools. Thereafter, however,
Nashville CORE declined, and finally disintegrated with the departure of
Anna Holden for graduate study in Michigan in the middle of 1959. [46]

At first Nashville CORE's efforts to achieve peaceful school integration inspired the NAC to encourage the same methods and hopefully establish a CORE affiliate in another southern community under court order to desegregate. Virginia appeared to be a place where success seemed within easy reach, but would, in fact, prove elusive. In December 1957 McCain had been dispatched to Alexandria, but the whites on CORE's mailing list who had replied affirmatively to Robinson's inquiries "hesitate [d] at anything approaching direct action." [47] Yet in view of the well-publicized massive resistance campaign against school integration, leaders like Robinson and Rich were "insistent that CORE be represented during the anticipated ruckus," [48] and several months later CORE tried again. Responding to a letter from Harry A. Reid, a forty-year-old Negro realtor and insurance agent, Robinson sent Carey and McCain to Norfolk. Although the two men went together as an "interracial team" in order to avoid the recurrence of the all-black groups which had appeared in South Carolina, this objective was only partly fulfilled. In September 1958 they created interracial chapters at Norfolk and Portsmouth—both chaired by Negroes and consisting chiefly of middle-aged professional and business people; but when the two organizers returned to Virginia a couple of months later, their work at Suffolk and Petersburg resulted in all-black groups.[49]

In Petersburg, Carey and McCain met the Baptist minister, Wyatt Tee Walker, head of the local NAACP branch and a close associate of Martin Luther King. Walker urged CORE to organize a march on Richmond to protest the governor's action in closing the public schools to avoid integration. Robinson and other CORE leaders had already considered such a demonstration, believing that it had immense possibilities both as a method of fighting the massive resistance of the Virginia segregationists and as a tool for building CORE. Carey, in fact, anticipated that "this March for Integration might be just the ticket to really put CORE before the entire state if not the entire South." [50] At CORE's request Walker agreed to coordinate the "Pilgrimage," which was cosponsored by the Virginia State Conference of NAACP branches and endorsed by Martin Luther King. On Emancipation Day, January 1, 1959, nearly two thousand persons, almost entirely black, but including a couple dozen whites, marched in the rain across Richmond to the Capitol. The governor, however, refused even to meet the delegation. Not only was there a frigid reception at the Capitol, but there were also misunderstandings with the NAACP, which, in CORE's view, failed to pay its share of the expenses but received most of the publicity.[51] Disappointed in the fruits of the project, Robinson wondered if it had done anything to help build CORE in Virginia. His doubts were, indeed, well founded, for by the spring of 1959 all of the fledgling groups in Virginia except the one in Norfolk were dead.[52] Thus, despite all its efforts, National CORE had little to show in Virginia.

Meanwhile McCain had been working assiduously to build CORE in South Carolina. Although CORE leaders hoped that his broad contacts there would provide the organization with an entré into the deep South, from the beginning Robinson worried that the situation in South Carolina "may mean a different type of group," engaging in "a distinctly different kind of project." [53] His analysis proved correct. The nine groups McCain was to form in the state between 1957 and 1959, except for the group in Sumter, were composed exclusively of blacks, worked only on voter registration, generally lacked a distinct CORE identity, and essentially remained outside the CORE tradition of direct action. Not that South Carolina had entirely escaped direct action by the black community. In 1955 blacks in the Negro college town of Orangeburg had inaugurated a vigorous, though unsuccessful boycott against white businessmen because they had withdrawn credit from Negro merchants who had signed a petition to integrate public schools. Two years later, the Negroes in the small industrial city of Rock Hill mounted a bus boycott which, like the famous campaign in Montgomery, forced the local transportation company out of business.[54] Boycotts, which avoided direct confrontation with the oppressive whites, seemed far more feasible in the deep South than CORE-style sit-ins. In fact, the environment of the region during the late 1950's was so repressive—with the rise of the White Citizens' Councils and the persecution of the NAACP—that many black protest leaders regarded voter registration work as a type of direct action. Martin Luther King's Crusade for Freedom was concentrating on just this type of activity at the time. Moreover, even to use the name "Congress of Racial Equality" was dangerous in the deep South, and at Robinson's suggestion, most of the groups formed in South Carolina made the CORE acronym stand for Committee on Registration Education.[55]

In December 1957 McCain began holding voter registration "institutes" in Columbia and Sumter, instructing Negroes how to fill out an application form and accompanying them to the county courthouse. In the course of the next ten months he shuttled back and forth across the state—from Charleston in the East to Greenville in the West and from Ridgeland, seat of Jasper County in the South, to Cheraw, the seat of Chesterfield County in the North. Creating a close liaison with the long-established Palmetto State Voters Association, but depending primarily upon the contacts which he had made earlier during his tenure as president of the black state teachers organization, McCain conferred with local preachers and businessmen, addressed mass meetings of potential voters, instructed registration workers, and by October 1958 had created seven CORE groups.[56] The potentialities of this kind of activity were seen in mid-1958 in Marion, where eight of the county's fourteen precincts had been organized under the direction of CORE members, and where the mayor, "elected to office by the Negro vote," told a committee of CORE protesters that he would take immediate steps to employ blacks at City Hall in other than menial positions. It was in Sumter where McCain reported the most dramatic progress when, as early as February 1958, blacks captured all the offices of a Democratic Party precinct. By May, the Strategy Committee composed of CORE and other cooperating organizations announced that black registration stood at nearly 1200, and in June CORE found its endorsement solicited by two whites running for city council and state assembly.[57] In most respects, however, Sumter CORE was much like the other groups. It was small, about ten members, was composed entirely of blacks, had a minister as chairman, and engaged only in voter registration. It lacked CORE's distinctive program and its chairman also headed the Sumter County Grass Roots Registration Drive, an organization whose activities duplicated those of the chapter. Similarly, elsewhere CORE officials were leaders in NAACP registration campaigns. The chairman of Spartanburg CORE was Rev. I. DeQuincey Newman, president of the South Carolina State Conference of NAACP Branches.[58]

Robinson was disturbed both because the new groups, formed by McCain on the basis of his old NAACP contacts, lacked commitment to CORE and because they shunned CORE-style direct action.[59] Some NAC members even questioned whether McCain should continue to limit his activities to the state, but most agreed that the voter registration project in the deep South was valuable for promoting CORE's public image elsewhere in the country. In May 1958 potential contributors found letters in their mailboxes saying, "In the South today, registration has become the key issue in the civil rights struggle. . . ." [60] However, the 1958 CORE Convention, held on St. Helena Island, South Carolina, a site selected for its proximity to the fledgling chapters, confirmed Robinson's apprehension. Several did not even bother to send delegates. For all of McCain's endeavors, only two units—Sumter and Clarendon County—had been affiliated by the time of the convention. The others were patently unready for affiliation, although the conclave, anxious for some evidence of organizational progress, voted to refer the applications of Columbia and Greenville to the chapters for approval.[61] Disturbed, both Robinson and the NAC directed McCain to create affiliates that would be clearly distinct from the NAACP, and to develop direct-action projects. Nevertheless, despite McCain's efforts identification with CORE remained weak, and for the most part he was unable to convince the groups to move beyond voter registration. He understood their fears and declared that this kind of activity was actually radical for South Carolina.[62] Yet, dubious as was their standing as CORE chapters, the five unaffiliated units were accepted by the Council, which needed to demonstrate to itself and to the public that it had an action program in the South.[63]

Occasionally, McCain did succeed in pushing a few of these affiliates beyond voter registration. In Columbia, during the fall of 1958 he and several CORE people lunched without interference at the airport restaurant, used the main public library, and sat in the front section of local buses. In January 1959, McCain was with members of the Greenville group when they conferred with city officials to protest against the long-established custom of assigning blacks to the city auditorium's jim crow balcony. The Negroes were able to convince the authorities to create a separate area downstairs as well. Robinson was unhappy and notified McCain that such acceptance of segregation, even though it might represent improvement over previous conditions, was "in direct contradiction to what CORE stands for," and symbolic of the fact that "we are not building a consciousness of CORE as a national movement in South Carolina." [64]

A fortuitous event offered CORE an opportunity to initiate a genuine direct-action demonstration and to exploit the confused relationships and overlapping leadership of CORE and NAACP in the state. In October 1959, Jackie Robinson, the baseball star, a guest of the South Carolina NAACP, was threatened with arrest along with his welcoming party for using the "white" waiting room at the Greenville airport. In the group was Rev. J. S. Hall, Jr., an NAACP officer as well as chairman of the local CORE affiliate. The incident aroused the city's blacks, and Marvin Rich saw an opportunity for encouraging CORE-type action and receiving valuable publicity for it. Robinson and Rich offered Hall the services of McCain for staging a pilgrimage and protest march on the airport. McCain, who persuaded the preacher to rename his group Greenville

CORE, organized the march, which was co-sponsored by the Greenville Interdenominational Ministerial Alliance, the NAACP State Conference of Branches, and an impressive list of civic and protest leaders from around the state, including Rev. I. DeQuincey Newman and Rev. C. A. Ivory, the leader of the Rock Hill bus boycott and a man prominent in both NAACP and CORE. After a rally in Hall's church, hundreds participated in the pilgrimage to the terminal on a chilly New Year's Day in 1960. Officials had refused requests for protection and had urged that the demonstration be called off. The apprehensive marchers, who feared violence, were surprised to find that the mayor provided a motorcycle escort, and that state police were on guard at the airport. Even more unexpected, and particularly heartwarming, upon their arrival at the airport, the demonstrators were greeted by over 300 sympathetic whites, mobilized by the South Carolina Council on Human Relations, who joined them in a brief service of song and prayer. A few days later the terminal was quietly desegregated.[65]

Throughout, Robinson continued to have misgivings about the South Carolina work. At the end of 1959 he was again admonishing McCain that some of the groups still conducted registration drives that were not even known as CORE campaigns. He threatened to "cut down on time allotted to you in South Carolina . . . further unless we get more sense of tie-in with the national organization." The victory at the airport demonstration notwithstanding, Robinson worried that the NAACP seemed to get more publicity from it than CORE. Still, CORE could boast of three active groups in the state, Rock Hill, Greenville, and Sumter. All had done important voter registration work, and two of them had moved on to direct action in the field of employment. Sumter CORE had sent teenagers to test lunch-counter service at local drug stores, and the Sumter and Greenville groups had both negotiated for jobs at retail stores and were contemplating boycotts. On the other hand Robinson's fears eventually proved justified in the case of Greenville, for the following year the chapter there dissolved because, as a careful student of the black protest movement in that city observed, "its leadership was simply the leadership of the local NAACP wearing new hats."[66]

The southern state where CORE went furthest in attacking the public accommodations issue was Florida. There, affiliates were established at Miami and Tallahassee, and the summer interracial workshop was revived in 1959. In Miami, racially the most progressive city in the state, the formation of a CORE group was precipitated by a federal court decision admitting four black children to a previously all-white school. Inspired by Anna Holden's pamphlet on Nashville, Mrs. Philip Stern, wife of a Miami Beach physician, asked that a field representative be sent to Florida. Robinson jumped at this opportunity to enter such a "strategic city," which he hoped would produce not only an interracial CORE affiliate, but would also provide the "nucleus" for a summer institute.[67] Early in 1959 McCain and Carey organized the Greater Miami Committee of Racial Equality. In its first few months this thoroughly interracial chapter consisted of nineteen people, about 40 per cent of them black. Most of the members had been recruited by McCain or were Jewish friends of Mrs. Stern—the most important of whom was Shirley Zoloth, wife of a successful businessman. The chairman was Dr. John Brown, a thirty-six-year-old Negro doctor who was also a vice-president of the NAACP.[68]

Instead of attacking the school issue, the chapter began its activities in April with brief sit-ins at downtown variety store lunch counters. But fear of a legislative committee's forthcoming investigations of the NAACP and the threat of repressive laws caused a loss of momentum. By summer Miami CORE was suffering from low morale and did little aside from becoming involved in the interracial workshop held in September.[69] This first Miami Action Institute, led by McCain and Carey, suffered from poor coordination with the local CORE affiliate. Nevertheless, Robinson was pleased with the work of the workshop's twelve participants. They first engaged in voter registration under McCain's direction, canvassing door to door in the black community, and then they turned to their major project—sitting-in at the lunch counter of one of Miami's department stores. For five days the sit-ins continued, and a short time before the Institute ended the management agreed to serve blacks on a trial basis. When the store reneged on this promise, the local chapter followed through with another week of sit-ins which reached a climax when Carey and two others were arrested. Robinson eagerly urged stepping up the pressure, but by then, Miami CORE, shaken by the unsatisfactory relations it had sustained with the summer workshop, was in disarray. With the affiliate unable to resume sit-ins, the atmosphere at meetings became one of pronounced hostility and recriminations. Although the group was reorganized in October, sit-ins were not revived and in January 1960 the new chairman, A. D. Moore, a black insurance executive who would later serve as treasurer of National CORE, complained, "It seems that all the officers and board members . . . are too busy to conscientiously and effectively do a job in CORE." [70]

In the long run the most important fruit of the Miami Action Institute was the founding of an affiliate in Tallahassee. At the request of one of the workshop's Negro participants, Patricia Stephens, who was a student at Florida A. & M. University, CORE sent McCain to Tallahassee in the fall of 1959. There he met "in a semi-secret atmosphere" with fifteen blacks and three whites, most of whom were students at local universities. Tallahassee had already witnessed a major direct-action campaign during 1956–57, a bus boycott inspired by the events in Montgomery. Led by Rev. C. K. Steele, the effort had eventually petered out in the face of intransigeance on the part of the local authorities. Subsequently, however, many cities in the Atlantic coastal states had quietly desegregated their buses following the United States Supreme Court decision that brought victory to Montgomery's blacks, and accordingly the fledgling Tallahassee CORE decided to first address itself to the transportation problem. Test teams met little resistance when they integrated the city's local buses and the ticket lines at the Greyhound terminal. But the Trailways personnel refused to serve Negro CORE members at ticket windows in the white waiting room. CORE also tested a dimestore lunch counter, but after being rebuffed, the group reluctantly decided that the city "was not ready for such a bold transgression of tradition." [71] Although Tallahassee CORE seemed unprepared to launch a major campaign, its activities were evidence of the rising dissatisfaction among black students in the South. A couple of months later this dissatisfaction suddenly emerged as a major protest movement. And in this movement the Tallahassee affiliate played an important and creative role.

In the border region CORE formed three new groups—two all-black ones in Charleston, West Virginia, and in East St. Louis, Illinois, in 1958, and an interracial, university-based affiliate, composed largely of teachers and clergymen, in Lexington, Kentucky, in 1959. All of them worked on public accommodations. McCain also journeyed to Louisville in the hope of creating a chapter there, but he found that the NAACP had already preempted the direct-action strategy with some lunch counter testing. The Charleston and Lexington chapters held sit-ins and successfully desegregated several variety store lunch counters. [72] East St. Louis CORE, led by Homer Randolph, a black high school teacher who had become dissatisfied with the inactivity of the local NAACP, tested numerous restaurants with varying results, conducted one victorious sit-in, and brought successful litigation against the local Howard Johnson outlet. [73] Similarly, the declining Baltimore chapter still devoted itself to public accommodations, continuing campaigns it had begun earlier,[74] while the new Washington chapter, an interracial group of a dozen members, organized in the autumn of 1958, ignored a plea from the national office to inaugurate an employment project and instead spent all its time pressing the central YMCA, which finally accepted blacks as members.[75]

The most important chapter in the border states—and indeed in the country as a whole—was still St. Louis CORE, which in a marked revival of activity not only continued its work on public accommodations but together with the NAACP began an imaginative attack on job discrimination. Much of St. Louis CORE's vigor was due to the participation of William Clay, who had been responsible for organizing the St. Louis NAACP Youth Council in 1955 and for building it into an effective direct-action organization.[76] Elected to the St. Louis Board of Aldermen in 1959, he would become Missouri's first black congressman a decade later. In 1958, after twelve months of negotiations and demonstrations had finally opened all the remaining dining facilities at the department stores, the CORE chapter broadened its efforts to include other major restaurants. Clay was among those arrested for disturbing the peace at the one Howard Johnson in the area that still barred blacks; afterward CORE conducted daily picket lines with as many as fifty participants until the manager obtained an injunction limiting picketing.[77]

Meanwhile during 1957–58, the small CORE affiliate found it advantageous to pursue its job campaigns under the auspices of an umbrella group known as the St. Louis NAACP Job Opportunities Council, in which both Oldham and Clay were active.[78] As a matter of fact the relationship between the NAACP and CORE was quite close in this period, with Clay joining CORE, and Oldham serving on various NAACP committees. The Job Opportunities Council began its work with an attack on the supermarket chains. Ten days of picketing in January 1958 resulted in an assurance that the A & P would hire blacks in all capacities; conferences with the Kroger chain led to a similar promise several months later. Toward the end of the summer a joint CORE-NAACP motorcade and the threat of mass picketing produced a promise from the Famous-Barr department store to process job applications without regard to race.[79] More coercive tactics were applied in the year-long campaign against the Taystee Bread Company, which employed blacks in menial capacities only. In this case, it was only after the NAACP and CORE had mobilized grocers in ghetto areas that the company promised to consider qualified blacks for better positions. Following several conferences the protesters became convinced that Taystee was stalling and thereupon asked grocers to display signs in their windows saying, "We Don't Sell Taystee Bread Due to Discriminatory Employment Policy." Thus pressed, Taystee hired three Negro production workers and two route salesmen in May 1959. Five other bakeries took similar action after being contacted. By January 1960, CORE claimed that about twenty Negroes held production and clerical jobs in the bakeries.[80] The gains thus secured were in absolute terms, small, yet in the context of the times these agreements were considered a major step forward. It was not until the 1960's that it became clear how limited and tokenistic they had been.

Outside of the South and border states CORE's activity was concentrated in a few cities of the Northeast and in an attempt to revive the work on the West Coast. Chapters were still small, weak, and essentially unsure of the appropriate way to fight racism. The trouble as Carey once described it was that "we are challenged in the North to adapt our techniques to the subtler, more difficult problems of prejudice and discrimination in employment and housing. The time-tested techniques of the sit-in and the other patterns of direct action do not meet the needs of these new situations. We must find new ways of fighting the old enemy who is clothed in a very different apparel." The situation facing many CORE chapter leaders was poignantly illustrated by the Berkeley affiliate, where the white collegians whose sympathy for Gandhian principles drew them to CORE were unable to understand how his methods could be applied and soon became disillusioned. One Berkeley leader writing at the end of 1959 summed up the group's dilemma: in employment the chain stores hid behind tokenism and denied discrimination; in housing, discrimination was pervasive, but since the city was already 25 per cent black, CORE members believed that a campaign against residential segregation patterns would only drive whites out and make the community black, thus working against the goal of integration.[81]

The NAC urgently desired to utilize CORE techniques in the fight against job and housing discrimination in the North. Robinson succinctly expressed its point of view when he warned, "The challenge lies in making CORE work in large northern cities—and unless we can do this, CORE is outmoded except in the border and southern states." [82] In fact, his first project upon assuming the post of executive secretary was to initiate and coordinate a demonstration at New York City Hall on behalf of the Sharkey-Brown-Isaacs Bill, which, enacted in December 1957, became the first municipal fair-housing law in the country. Side-stepping the broad coalition of organizations who were lobbying for the bill but were unwilling to engage in more radical tactics, Robinson and New York CORE, with support from the NAACP and American Jewish Congress, mounted a picket line of three hundred persons. As they marched around City Hall, a delegation headed by Jackie Robinson conferred with Mayor Wagner. The demonstration received substantial publicity, and CORE proudly claimed considerable credit for the law's enactment.[83]

Nevertheless, despite much vigorous encouragement from the national office and the field secretaries, most chapters found it difficult to translate the obvious need for projects on jobs and housing into concrete action. Thus, for example, as late as January 1960 Robinson observed that "employment is an emphasis which is essential and has . . . been largely lacking in CORE, with the exception of St. Louis." [84] The organization's oldest affiliate, the mainly white New York City chapter, was able to do little. Its three housing committees accomplished nothing; the chapter concentrated its efforts on a vain attempt to secure higher paying jobs for blacks on the airlines. Eastern, United, and American refused even to discuss the matter, and New York CORE's action consisted of picketing a recalcitrant airline office and conducting a poster walk to congratulate TWA for hiring its first black stewardess.[85] Across the country in Los Angeles the story was only somewhat better. The chapter still suffered from "the old problem of lacking the one person who will devote most of his free time to CORE." Picketing of Anheuser Busch and Budweiser in a joint CORE-NAACP campaign for truck drivers' jobs in the spring of 1958 failed to break up the Teamsters' exclusionary practices. Feeling too small and impotent to use more direct action, the chapter confined itself mainly to testing motels and negotiating with their owners. Twelve motels agreed to accept black guests, and CORE filed lawsuits against a few others who remained recalcitrant. Lacking the power needed to launch a direct-action campaign against housing discrimination, the affiliate's one project in this area was to provide all-night protection for a black family which was threatened with violence after moving into a white neighborhood. Los Angeles CORE was fully aware of the importance of attacking housing discrimination and "token employment," but its members continued to feel that adequate tactics to fight these problems remained to be developed.[86]

CORE put forth considerable energy in developing new affiliates, but the results were disappointing. Work was revived in Cleveland and Boston, but the two small groups, though interested in housing discrimination, spent months groping and doing nothing.[87] On the West Coast CORE first sent Vice-Chairman Henry Hodge on two futile trips to form a viable chapter in Seattle. Subsequently, in the spring of 1959, Carey made a western field trip that was no more successful than Hodge's had been in Seattle, but he did succeed in establishing weak, predominantly white groups in Portland, San Francisco, and Berkeley.[88] All three groups attempted to attack racism in jobs and housing but, because of inadequate leadership and techniques, all remained impotent and frustrated. For their first project the Berkeley chapter decided to work for white-collar jobs in grocery chains, but after four meetings they were still in the "investigatory stages" and requested information from National CORE on the methods utilized by other groups; two months later they had not progressed much further. Not surprisingly the Bay-area groups did not last long. By the summer of 1959, San Francisco group was inactive, and six months later the Berkeley affiliate had reportedly "disintegrated like wet toilet paper." [89]

Even though nearly all the new affiliates in this period were established by national CORE field staff, the old pattern of chapter autonomy persisted. Few affiliates contributed financially to the national office. Despite an urgent appeal signed by Oldham, by the end of 1959 only five had given anything toward their constitutional assessments since the fiscal year began.[90] This problem was the subject of perennial discussion at councils and conventions, but nothing was done about it. Moreover, despite repeated urgings most affiliates failed to send delegates to national meetings. At the 1959 Convention only about one-third of the chapters were represented. Robinson was worried, fearing that the increasing difficulty of communication would produce a wide divergence in types of CORE locals and militate against the democratic functioning of the national organization.[91]

At the same time a threat to the organization's internal democratic structure was developing as a result of a preponderance of staff influence on the National Action Committee. In November 1959 the NAC members themselves decided that the Committee was impairing "democratic functioning" because it contained "too large a proportion of staff members." Six of the ten people on the NAC—Robinson, Rich, McCain, Peck, Carey, and Lula Farmer—were employees of the organization. All of them, except for McCain who was usually far from New York, were present at most of the Committee's meetings. In contrast, the other four members—Houser, Roberts, Carter, and James Farmer—attended relatively infrequently. Since under the constitution the NAC, which shared policy-making authority with the National Council and Convention, met at least ten times a year, while the other two bodies each convened only once, it is no exaggeration to say that the staff-dominated NAC held the major levers of power in the national organization. At this point the problem posed by the composition of the NAC was only beginning to emerge in the consciousness of CORE leaders. Subsequently, as the number of chapters continued to grow, it would become a serious and divisive issue with which the organization would have to grapple.

CORE in January 1960, on the eve of the outbreak of the southern black student movement, was still a small organization. Nor did the organization's leaders foresee rapid growth in its size or influence in the near future. As Marvin Rich put it, "CORE is not and will never be a mass organization." As a matter of fact, CORE was still having trouble keeping its affiliates alive. The January 1960 CORE Council discussed the "rise and fall of local groups," and both Carey and McCain emphasized that the heavy demands upon their time prevented adequate supervision, thus contributing to the demoralization of many new chapters.[92] On the other hand CORE had grown significantly. Thus, as of July 1958, there were eight chapters. In the following year and a half, while CORE disaffiliated several inactive locals, the number of affiliated chapters more than doubled to nineteen. Meanwhile, between the 1958 Convention and the January 1960 Council meeting the CORE list of contributors almost tripled from about 4500 to 12,000.[93]

By then CORE was planning to expand its work in the Mid-west and particularly in the upper South. For years there had been talk of organizing in North Carolina; thus, for example, the sentiment among the NAC members in April 1959 was that "North Carolina should get some attention. . . . there is much work to be done there." [94] In December, Carey was laying plans to make a field trip to Durham during the first week in February. He observed that

> CORE has been expanding rapidly during the past couple of years.
> This growth . . . is an indication of the spread of revolution across
> the South—and an acceptance of nonviolence as a worthy method
> by many persons who had never heard of it a few years ago. It was
> only natural that CORE should profit from this increased interest in

direct action. . . . As the 'border' moves South CORE must move with it. It is in areas such as North Carolina where we can legitimately expect the greatest rate of progress and where traditional CORE techniques are most applicable.[95]

Two months after Carey described this ferment the southern college student sit-ins would begin in Greensboro, North Carolina. Both Carey and McCain were on the scene—McCain working with CORE's predominantly student chapter in Tallahassee and Carey arriving in North Carolina a few days after the demonstrations erupted there. Suddenly nonviolent direct action became the dominant strategy of the black protest movement. CORE was in a position both to lend the students valuable assistance and, simultaneously capitalizing upon the new popularity of the technique in which it had pioneered, to move itself closer to being a major civil rights organization.

II

CORE
and the Sit-ins
Come of Age
1960

4

CORE
and the Black Student
Movement

On February 1, 1960, four students from North Carolina A. & T. College sat-in at a Woolworth lunch counter in downtown Greensboro, igniting a major southwide protest movement. Within a week sit-in demonstrations broke out in Durham and Winston-Salem. By February 14 they had spread to eleven more cities in four other states, including half a dozen places where CORE had been active previously: Rock Hill and Sumter, South Carolina; Norfolk and Portsmouth, Virginia; Tallahassee, Florida; and Nashville, Tennessee. By April, there had been sit-ins in seventy-eight southern communities, and two thousand youth had been arrested.[1]

The effects of these student demonstrations on the civil rights movement—and on the Congress of Racial Equality—were momentous. They speeded up incalculably the rate of social change in the sphere of race relations; broke decisively the NAACP's hegemony in the civil rights arena and inaugurated a period of unprecedented rivalry among the racial advancement groups; made nonviolent direct action the dominant strategy in the struggle for racial equality during the next half-decade, and set in motion a train of events that propelled CORE into the front rank among Negro protest organizations.

CORE—like the NAACP and SCLC—immediately grasped the importance of the student demonstrations and rushed to give assistance and guidance to the new activists. As a consequence, it expanded its foothold in the South, meanwhile pioneering in another innovative tactic—the "jail-in." At the same time, the courageous example of the black youth and CORE's sponsorship of sympathy demonstrations in the North helped the revival of CORE work there. Moreover, the excitement generated by the sit-ins boosted CORE's income, enabling the organization to enlarge its field staff greatly, and thus to take further advantage of the broadening opportunities. Yet CORE's rapid growth produced serious internal tensions that culminated in a major change in the organization's leadership at the end of the year.

CORE was not without some indirect influence on the action of the four youths who sat-in at the Greensboro Woolworth store on February 1. Actually they had been encouraged to take this step by a local white businessman, who served on the executive board of the city's NAACP branch and who knew of CORE's methods through reading Houser's pamphlet, *Erasing the Color Line*. As the sit-ins grew in size during the following days, the young college students appealed for help to the president of the Greensboro NAACP, Dr. George Simkins. Simkins lacked experience in nonviolent direct action, but admired CORE's work, and on February 4 he telephoned the CORE national office for aid.[2] With Robinson out of town at the time, Rich and Carey decided upon a two-fold course—to send both Carey and McCain into the Carolinas, and to assist in the North by negotiating with dime store managements and organizing sympathy demonstrations on behalf of the Greensboro movement. Carey immediately left for Greensboro; McCain, who had been working with the Tallahassee chapter, was dispatched to Rock Hill, while Rich and Peck held conferences with Woolworth and Kress executives in New York, unsuccessfully urging them to desegregate their lunch counters.[3] On February 12, Rich asked all CORE chapters around the country to picket their local dime stores, and the next day the first sympathy demonstration was held in Harlem by New York CORE. As Robinson proudly told the CORE chapters, "We were the first organization to give assistance in North Carolina when the sit-ins began. We were the first to picket in the North. We were the first to call for a nationwide boycott. We were the first to enter into negotiations with the managements of the chains."[4]

Robinson hoped that Carey and McCain would stimulate further sit-ins, interest adult groups in supporting the students, create new CORE chapters, and keep the lunch-counter demonstrations nonviolent. Outbreaks of black retaliatory violence against hostile white bystanders in Chattanooga, High Point, and Portsmouth worried Robinson and other CORE leaders, who feared that this would discredit the movement. In the Portsmouth case Robinson arranged immediately for a workshop to teach black high school students who had fought with white harassers "direct action along the lines developed by Gandhi." To the chairman of the newly formed Raleigh Citizens Association, Robinson wrote, "One of our concerns is that the student protests are developing so rapidly that action occurs without much preparation and without much background in the use of nonviolence. Nonviolence has proved to be the essential ingredient in winning advances wherever feeling runs high and the opposition open and disposed to the use of rough tactics." CORE leaders were concerned with inculcating among the students their own commitment to the Gandhian spirit and tactics. As Oldham put it, "We must widen and deepen the understanding of nonviolent direct action so that soul force, the Satyagraha of Gandhi, develops and transforms our society." [5]

Meanwhile Carey had arrived in North Carolina, where he acquainted young activists with CORE's philosophy and tactics. Simkins introduced him to Attorney Floyd McKissick of Durham, who, thirteen years before, had briefly participated in the Journey of Reconciliation. Carey helped McKissick and the students organize the demonstrations that broke out on February 8th in Durham, and in the course of the next few weeks the two men travelled over the state setting up non-violent workshops.[6] Carey worked with college students in Greensboro and Raleigh, and advised high school youth in Chapel Hill and High Point. He achieved considerable publicity for CORE following his arrest in Durham on February 9 while sitting-in at a dime store with North Carolina College students. The press pounced upon the presence of this "outside agitator" and publicized his travels about the state. Carey himself described his exhilaration during the first weeks of the North Carolina sit-in,

> ". . . CORE has been on the front page of every newspaper in North Carolina for two days. CORE has been on radio and TV every hour. . . . I can't move without the press covering my movement. Jim McCain phoned tonight that Rock Hill is joining the protest on Saturday. Raleigh is joining on Monday. . . . I will probably be speaking at a mass meeting on Thursday with Rev. Fred

Shuttlesworth * in Greensboro. Last night I spoke at a mass meeting in Durham. . . . In fact, invitations to speak have been so numerous that I cannot possibly accept them all. We are attempting now to co-ordinate all the various movements. . . . Everyone here is looking to us for leadership. When CORE did act on the national negotiations and the NAACP failed to do so we pulled a real coup.[7]

McCain, during February, similarly shuttled back and forth among the Carolina cities, though without the fanfare that accompanied Carey's visit. He first went to Rock Hill, South Carolina, to advise Friendship Junior College students. His work bore fruit on Lincoln's birthday, in the first demonstrations in South Carolina, when over one hundred Rock Hill students held sit-ins and picketed downtown variety and drug stores. Next day, Tallahassee CORE, which McCain had been encouraging a couple of weeks earlier, held its first sit-in. As these two demonstrations were taking place, McCain was busy assisting the North Carolina students. Several days later he was back in the Palmetto state, this time at Orangeburg, offering the students suggestions on how to promote sit-ins there. On February 25, when McCain was again in North Carolina consulting with leaders of the Raleigh movement, the Orangeburg students, inspired by the example of Rock Hill, held their first sit-in. This act was the prelude to massive demonstrations culminating in a march the following month in which police used fire hoses and tear gas and arrested nearly four hundred—the largest number jailed in any city up to that time. Thomas Gaither, one of the top leaders of this campaign, so impressed CORE officials that he was soon afterwards added to the field staff.[8]

McCain's role was thus to encourage the students and advise them in the techniques of nonviolent direct action. As a middle-aged black man with deep roots in the area, he was also useful in rallying adults to the cause and running interference with the NAACP, which like CORE and SCLC was anxious to guide the student movement. The Association sent its youth secretary, Herbert Wright, to stimulate direct action on the part of NAACP college chapters and youth councils. All three organizations jockeyed for influence at a conference of student leaders in Durham on February 16, and afterwards Robinson privately criticized Wright for trying to control it for the NAACP's benefit. There were also reports that Robert Saunders, field secretary of the Florida NAACP, had urged the

---

* Fred Shuttlesworth, leader of a bus boycott in Birmingham in the late 1950's, and a prominent associate of Martin Luther King.

Tallahassee branch not to cooperate with CORE. McCain, who as usual tried to smooth over conflicts with the NAACP, attended an NAACP regional conference in Memphis a few days later and resolved this particular misunderstanding. Gloster Current, the Association's director of branches, even invited McCain to attend a staff meeting where CORE was warmly praised.[9]

Publicly, CORE spokesmen preached interorganizational harmony, taking the view that, contrary to reports in the press, CORE's advocacy of direct action was in no way a denigration of the NAACP's valuable contribution to the civil rights movement. Privately, however, they recognized that after the southern student movement began in February, "Everywhere under the surface there were conflicts between the NAACP and other race relations organizations." CORE leaders were especially annoyed at the NAACP's claim—based upon variety store demonstrations sponsored by the Oklahoma City NAACP Youth Council in 1958—to have started the southern student sit-ins.[10] In the end, none of the adult groups succeeded in dominating the new movement. NAACP college chapters and youth councils often undertook vigorous variety store campaigns. Nevertheless, many of the militant youth were skeptical of the Association, viewing it as a legalistic organization dominated by a timid black bourgeoisie. SCLC was at first more influential with the students, and called the conference held in Raleigh over the Easter weekend at which SNCC was organized. But from the beginning the youth wanted to be independent of SCLC, and as the months passed they grew increasingly critical of King, coming to regard him as not being sufficiently militant.

CORE likewise was limited in the role it played. Despite all of the effort expended in aiding the student activists, with scarcely half-a-dozen new southern chapters CORE at the end of the year had little to show in the way of organizational expansion. Everywhere the students displayed a desire to control their own affairs. For example, a member of the Baltimore CORE chapter, which found itself upstaged by the Morgan State College-based Civic Interest Group, reported, "I suppose the Morgan students are typical of the active students all over the country—they prefer to be independent, and although we offered our services, we were not called on." Clearly, the southern youth, appropriating the technique in which CORE had pioneered, took the initiative, seized the headlines, and bypassed the older organizations. Both CORE and SCLC, despite their past contributions in the use of nonviolent direct action, like the

NAACP, found themselves in the position of attempting to get on the student bandwagon. CORE's relationship to the southern youth was summed up in a letter Robinson sent to student leaders when he wrote: "CORE is proud of you. . . . If there is *anything* we can do to help, please feel free to call on us." [11]

CORE's most impressive—albeit unsuccessful—activities during the spring of 1960 were in three southern communities where it had already established roots: Rock Hill, Sumter, and Tallahassee. McCain succeeded in forming CORE chapters both at Friendship Junior College in Rock Hill, whose students continued to sit-in and picket until the end of the school year, and at Morris College in Sumter, where demonstrations began on March 4. Members of the adult CORE groups in these two towns raised funds to cover bonding and legal expenses, and in Sumter they helped coach the youth prior to their first sit-in. In a mass meeting in Rock Hill, where the militant NAACP president Rev. C. A. Ivory worked closely with CORE, nearly 850 Negroes voted a boycott of eight discriminatory establishments. And in the following weeks McCain succeeded in forming CORE chapters at both colleges.[12]

The demonstrations sponsored by Tallahassee CORE were notable because of their interracial character and because they introduced a militant new tactic—the jail-in. The chapter sponsored its first sit-in on February 14 when black students from both Florida A. & M. University and the local high school sought service at Woolworth's. During their second sit-in the following week, eleven were arrested. For the demonstrations which followed, the group secured the participation of several white Florida State University students. The campaign climaxed on March 12. Several were arrested at Woolworth's, and Pat Stephens rushed to the Florida A. & M. campus urging students to "march on Woolworth's and McCrory's" and "fill the jails if necessary." A hundred followed her downtown, where nearly a score were arrested at McCrory's. A second contingent marched toward Woolworth's but found their way blocked by club-wielding whites. The demonstrators returned to the University, regrouped, and, joined by nearly a thousand young men and women, marched again. But this time they were dispersed by police with a tear gas barrage.

The police repression and the impending court trials led CORE to suspend further demonstrations. A few days later the first sit-inners who had been arrested were found guilty of disturbing the peace and unlawful assembly. Rather than pay their fines, Pat Stephens and four others chose to remain in the county jail for sixty days, thus becoming the first activists to undertake a jail-in. Reflecting the religious and Gandhian arguments articulated by Martin Luther King which provided the philosophical underpinning for the southern student movement in this period, the jailed youth believed that their example of unmerited suffering would help to convert the oppressors and bring about social change. As Pat Stephens expressed it in a statement she issued from her cell: "We could be out on appeal, but we strongly believe that Martin Luther King was right when he said, 'We've got to fill the jails in order to win our equal rights.' "

With the students incarcerated, the black community boycotted the downtown area. But by then the CORE chapter, intimidated by the convictions and fearing administrative discipline by Florida A. & M. authorities, had lost much of its drive. On the other hand, because of its militant and interracial character, the Tallahassee affiliate was exceedingly important for National CORE. It provided the one CORE campaign during that tumultuous spring which received significant attention in the black press. The organization's literature played up the chapter's activities to the hilt. As early as March, the national office had widely disseminated a pamphlet about the Tallahassee sit-ins, and Robinson privately commented, "This should be helpful in showing our CORE people across the nation how excellent the Negro-white cooperation was in Tallahassee—a point the papers tend to overlook." When the five who had chosen jail were released, National CORE sent them on a speaking tour, where they appeared at meetings sponsored by universities, Jewish groups, labor unions, and other organizations across the country from Baltimore to Los Angeles.[13]

Another important student protest with which CORE was associated occurred at Baton Rouge. McCain spent a few weeks there during April, in response to a plea for help from the Southern University activist leader, Major Johns. Johns summed up the new mood of militance among black youth and their belief in the moral power of nonviolence when he told his fellow students, "No longer can we endure the back door of public places, the denial of equal job opportunities, the right to vote or any privilege granted to a full citizen. . . . We will strike the moral conscience of the white man and not his physical body. Let the echoes of the Christian principles he taught . . . and the shocking realization that, in the words of Jefferson, all men are created equal . . . ring in his own ears." [14] By the time McCain reached Baton Rouge, a dra-

matic series of events had occurred. On March 28, seven students, including senior class president Marvin Robinson, were arrested for sitting-in at
a Kress dime store; nine more were arrested the next day, and on March
30 Major Johns led a gigantic protest march of 3500 students to the state
capitol. Although even the local press reported that the marchers were
"very orderly," the University expelled Johns and all who had been arrested. The student body thereupon voted to boycott classes until all
were reinstated. McCain found the local community leadership "split
down the middle" over whether to back the students in the struggle with
the university administration, and, as in the Carolinas, he sought to unite
skeptical adults in support of the youth: "I tried to convince the leaders
that the biggest blow against segregation in the South would be to rally
behind the student leaders in asking all students to leave Southern University." This time, however, McCain's efforts proved unavailing. Many
Negroes ignored the call for a dime store boycott, influential alumni
closed ranks behind the school's president, and the student walk-out collapsed.[15] Although these Southern University demonstrations thus ended
so inauspiciously, they had important consequences for CORE. Major
Johns and Marvin Robinson joined CORE's field staff,[16] and, even more
significant, CORE established contacts that would later prove crucial in
the organization's extensive work in the Louisiana parishes.

As in the deep south, so in less repressive areas on the region's periphery, CORE usually was able to mount viable programs only where it had
already established firm roots. Thus in Norfolk and Nashville the militant banner passed to the black college student groups, while in Atlanta
a new and unaffiliated interracial CORE chapter was unable to make
headway in the face of the well-organized student movement.[17] Because
Kentucky seemed a promising place for CORE expansion, the New York
headquarters assigned two new field secretaries to work there. But their
accomplishments were limited—even in Louisville, where they concentrated their greatest efforts, only a weak group was established. On the
other hand, national publicity surrounding the sit-in movement produced an energetic new affiliate in Columbia, Missouri, and stimulated
vigorous action in existing chapters in Lexington, Kentucky, Charleston,
West Virginia, and Miami, Florida, all of which won lunch-counter
struggles they had been pursuing sporadically for months prior to the
sit-ins at Greensboro. In April, Miami CORE inaugurated interracial
demonstrations that continued until August when twenty-eight variety
stores agreed to serve everyone without discrimination. The Charleston

affiliate was involved in a twenty-month campaign which ended when the Diamond department store opened its lunch counter to all in May. Between February and August, the integrated Lexington chapter, led by its new chairman, Julia Lewis, a black nurse, sponsored a boycott and sit-ins which finally produced the desegregation of the four variety stores, Walgreen's drug store, and several restaurants.[18]

At least as valuable to the southern students as the aid given by the field secretaries were CORE's supportive actions in the North. New York, where the first demonstration was held in Harlem on February 13, and St. Louis, where the chapter picketed two Woolworth stores a week later, were probably the first northern CORE affiliates that went into action on the national office's call for a boycott and sympathy protests.[19] Soon the campaign had been extended to include all the variety store chains, and a wide spectrum of race advancement, union, student, and Jewish organizations were participating in demonstrations across the country.

For the national office the variety store demonstrations served a dual function: they simultaneously aided the southern student movement and stimulated CORE activity in the North. For example, Carey informed Henry Hodge of Los Angeles, "This action in North Carolina provides the best opportunity CORE has ever had for developing additional groups," and Robinson advised the affiliates, "Here is your opportunity to build your own group on a live issue of national importance. DON'T MISS IT." [20] In Philadelphia where, at the end of February college students had assumed the responsibility for picketing Woolworth's, Robinson suggested that this was "an ideal time" to form a new group, and a preliminary organizing meeting was held a few weeks later. Almost simultaneously the energetic Ann Arbor Direct Action Committee, led by Anna Holden, was founded as an outgrowth of dime store demonstrations, while in Berkeley CORE was reactivated by two University of California students who drew sixty people to a meeting at which they decided to set up a picket line at Woolworth's. Nor did National CORE leave matters entirely up to spontaneous actions; it sent McCain to the West Coast in March, where he assisted chapters in Portland, Berkeley, and Los Angeles. He was interviewed by the mass media, and during his stay in Los Angeles spoke before numerous church and civic groups. "If CORE were not known on the West Coast before my trip, I am sure that it is now," he observed.[21]

Elsewhere the variety store demonstrations became a staple activity. In Chicago, where McCain and Carey had initiated a new chapter of about a dozen members in January 1960, the group sponsored weekly protests at various locations on the west and south sides. Los Angeles CORE, whose picketing was coordinated with a coalition which included the NAACP, the ILGWU, the UAW, the American Jewish Congress, and other organizations, reported that "picketing the Woolworth and Kress stores had consumed the major portion of activity recently." [22] Most elaborate was the campaign in New York, where the national office provided direction for the impressive outpouring of support from many sources. Robinson assigned first Carey and later Darwin W. Bolden, a black graduate of Yale University Law School, to coordinate the protests. They regularly disseminated lists of picket line locations in the New York metropolitan area, and held weekly "picket line coordinating meetings" which attracted representatives of cooperating New York organizations and which usually presented southern students as guest speakers. There were dozens of demonstrations each Saturday at variety store outlets throughout the city—thirty-five were scheduled for the first Saturday in April, and sixty-nine stores were picketed three weeks later. Ministers and unions lent their support. Twenty-five prominent black and white clergy marched outside a Woolworth store on Fifth Avenue on Maundy Thursday. Labor leaders on the Advisory Committee solicited the participation of union members, the ILGWU furnishing as many as eight hundred pickets for a single afternoon. The campaign was still going strong in the middle of May, with CORE able to mount fifty-nine picket lines, several of them under the sponsorship of NAACP branches and college chapters.[23]

The participation of other organizations in the dime store picketing was not without its problems. In mid-March the NAACP's national office urged all its members to give full support to the student movement, and in some cities the Association's branches provided CORE with lively competition. Berkeley reported that while at first the local NAACP had refused to cooperate, subsequently for a number of weeks its demonstrations outclassed those of the CORE affiliate. In Philadelphia it was the strong NAACP branch rather than the puny CORE chapter which ceaselessly picketed Woolworth's month after month through the autumn. The chapter in San Jose, California "solved the problem" of NAACP competition when the NAACP agreed to sponsor the picketing on alternate weekends.[24]

Sometimes difficulties arose because many CORE people disliked the manner in which other groups, not versed in the Rules for Action carried out their picketing. In Boston, university students initiated the demonstrations, and created a broad-based coalition of labor, liberal and civil rights organizations known as EPIC (Emergency Public Integration Committee) to coordinate the sympathy protests. Adults from the CORE chapter were critical of the aggressive and noisy style of the college youth, who constituted the majority of the participants. The students in turn labeled the CORE people "too cautious, too conciliatory, and too committed to a 'pacifist' orientation." New York experienced comparable problems, with demonstrators often dressing informally, singing and chanting on the lines, exchanging insults with hecklers, and even blocking store entrances. Some of these matters were discussed at a New York CORE meeting in February. Robinson emphasized that "well-dressed pickets were received more favorably by the public than those who carried casual dress to an extreme." There was also a debate over the propriety of chanting; while Marvin Rich's wife, Evelyn, maintained that a quiet line was more effective, some disagreed, and one woman asserted that silent lines were better suited to white neighborhoods than to Harlem. Two days later the national headquarters issued "Suggestions For CORE Pickets": "To win public support it is important that the picketers be neat and well dressed and that the line be orderly. . . . Sometimes you may wish to chant slogans. At other times this may not be appropriate. But in no case should the slogans be abusive. . . . The entrances should never be blocked (we try to keep customers out by moral force—not by physical force). . . . No matter what the provocation we remain calm and courteous to all. We do not respond to hoots or to jeers. Our strength lies in our moral force." This did not, however, resolve the issue of people from other organizations violating traditional CORE decorum. In March, CORE demonstrators complained about an "extremely noisy" picket line on 125th Street and its "lack of discipline." When a leader of the Lower Harlem Tenants Council defended the shouting of slogans which had at certain points turned into jeering and wisecracking, Robinson reluctantly compromised and recommended singing as a substitute.[25]

Although it would be impossible to determine how much influence the northern supportive activities had in affecting the decisions of the variety store managements, CORE could legitimately take much of the credit for the desegregation that occurred in the South. The organization's leaders believed that the sharp drop in sales which Woolworth reported in March 1960—down 8.9 per cent from March 1959—was attributable to the boycott it had called. On March 16 the lunch counters in San Antonio were the first to open to blacks; in the following weeks St. Louis CORE which had entered into negotiations with the regional managers of two dime store companies, secured agreements desegregating McCrory's outlets in the border states and Woolworth stores in a wide territory in the Southwest. By the end of July, when the Greensboro stores began to serve Negroes, integration of at least some facilities had occurred in 27 southern cities. Three weeks later, when Oldham arrived in New York to negotiate with dime store executives, changes had been reported in 90 towns in 11 southern states, and by the following spring the number of cities reporting changes had risen to about 140. Nearly all of this progress had taken place in states on the periphery of the region—in North Carolina, Virginia, Tennessee, Kentucky, Texas, and southern Florida. In Tallahassee, Rock Hill, and Sumter, as in other communities across the deep South from South Carolina to Louisiana, conditions remained unchanged.[26]

Events in the South dominated the discussions at the 1960 Convention, the best attended Convention thus far. The mood was optimistic: as Carey informed the delegates, the organization was "rapidly gaining the image now of being a major race relations group." Wyatt Tee Walker delivered the keynote address, praising the southern direct actionists as "the untouchables who are America's destiny." [27] To more effectively connect CORE with the southern movement, the organization brought a number of student activists to the conclave. Darwin Bolden, Major Johns, and Pat Stephens served as a Committee on Strategy for the Student Movement, and the delegates approved their recommendation that CORE make more aggressive efforts to guide and coordinate the protest activities of the southern students.[28] Although it soon became evident that SNCC would dominate the scene and that CORE with its limited resources would have to confine its work with southern college students to a few areas, principally in South Carolina and Louisiana, relating to the student movement remained for several months a major preoccupation of CORE leaders. In pursuit of this goal they assigned most of their growing field staff to the South, and sponsored the second Miami Action Institute in August.

The Institute was viewed as so important that Carey, McCain, and even Robinson himself were on hand to lead it. Over half of the thirty-five participants were southern college students, including several who later played prominent roles in CORE; the bulk of the remainder were student activists from the North. Reflecting CORE's continuing concern with the philosophical aspects of nonviolence, the Institute's lesson plan provided for the study of the following topics: "Gandhi and his 'insistence on truth' . . . varying views on non-violence—way of life or technique? coercion vs. non-coercion. . . ." The most notable feature of the Institute was CORE's further experimentation with the jail-in or "jail-no-bail" tactic. Seven members of the group, including Robinson, were arrested at a lunch-counter sit-in, and refusing to accept bail remained behind bars for the ten days preceding their trial. When they finally appeared in court, the protesters were given suspended sentences. Although the incident lacked the drama of the first jail-in in Tallahassee, CORE promotional literature employed it to project an image of an organization in the tactical vanguard of the civil rights revolution.[29]

In regard to staff, CORE had taken steps to augment and restructure its field personnel within weeks after the first Greensboro sit-in. By April, Carey had been promoted to "field director," and the number of field secretary positions was increased from two to five. To the 1960 Convention delegates Carey exulted that for the first time CORE had "a real field staff." There was considerable turnover largely because the first new field secretaries had been hastily recruited. Of the ten field staff who were hired during the rest of the year all except one were black males; the majority were college students. By autumn, CORE had established a relatively permanent staff of five field secretaries. In addition to McCain it included two black youths who had participated in the Miami Institute jail-no-bail sit-in—Thomas Gaither, and Joseph Perkins, a graduate student at the University of Michigan, active in the CORE affiliate there; Richard Haley, forty-five-year-old treasurer of Tallahassee CORE who had been dismissed as a music professor at Florida A. & M. because of his participation in the movement; and Genevieve Hughes, the first woman on the CORE field staff, a white person in her twenties who had been working for Dun and Bradstreet and had led the dime store boycott committee of New York CORE. Better than any of the others, Gaither expressed the outlook of the southern student movement of this period, rooted in Christian and American democratic principles and dedicated to the practice of nonviolence. He once wrote: "Our nation can have only one law and that we all say is the United States Constitution. . . . How can we forget the America envisioned by Washington, Lincoln and Jefferson?" Beyond the Constitution there was a law "that is greater than any law the mind of man can envision and that is the law of Universal Love and Brotherhood. As a Negro, I feel sorry for my irrational white brothers who are sinning against God and destroying the very principles upon which this nation was conceived." Gaither was "proud" of the way blacks had acted on demonstrations: "It is my sincere hope that the Negroes will continually realize that violence will not solve this problem. . . . The task of the Negro now becomes that of loving our oppressor with a love so strong that we may save his soul from destruction." [30]

During the latter part of the year a large share of field staff resources was devoted to New Orleans, where a new and vigorous chapter was initiated, and to South Carolina, where the work culminated in a major jail-in at Rock Hill early in 1961. The strategy considerations guiding the deployment of CORE forces in the South were articulated by Carey, who pointed out that "if we are to really crack the Deep South, then we must have concerted and continued action in South Carolina since that is where most of our strength lies at present," and that "If . . . we are successful in New Orleans, this will be one of the first times that interracial direct action has penetrated so far into the Deep South on a consistent planned basis. What happens in New Orleans can be meaningful to the entire South." [31]

Early in the summer Marvin Robinson went to New Orleans where he helped to form an interracial group composed primarily of black and white college students. The chapter was headed by Rudy Lombard, a black Xavier University senior who would later become CORE's national vice-chairman. Six members of the new group attended the Miami Action Institute, and by the time they returned to New Orleans they found the chapter already planning its own lunch-counter campaign. The first action came in September, when five blacks and two whites were arrested several hours after they began a sit-in at Woolworth's. These arrests galvanized the local black community. The NAACP Youth Council picketed Woolworth's the next day; the Consumers' League, an Urban League-inspired adult group which had been demonstrating since the spring for jobs at downtown stores, endorsed CORE's action; and the following Sunday, collections at Negro churches netted $700 to help finance the CORE project.

Sensing the momentum which CORE had achieved, New Orleans' Mayor deLesseps Morrison banned further picketing and sit-ins. What followed was a series of efforts by national CORE leaders to persuade the chapter members that, if they did not let Morrison frighten them, theirs could become the number one civil rights organization in the city. Both McCain, on the scene, and Robinson, from New York, urged the affiliate to resume direct action quickly, but to refrain from entering a coalition with other groups, in order, as McCain put it, "to maintain itself in the prime position." Thus Robinson advised Lombard that "It is always a strong action to repeat a sit-in after an arrest. . . . The group itself will gain most from action it carries out on its own and under its own name." A few days later Lombard and three other CORE members were arrested while sitting-in at a McCrory lunch-counter in defiance of the mayor's order. Lombard, influenced by his experience at the Miami Institute, refused to accept bail for six days, "Hoping to make the community more conscious of racial discrimination." Scarcely had Lombard been released from jail when McCain and four leaders of the Consumers' League were arrested for further violating the mayor's order by picketing for jobs at a Dryades Street shopping center.

National CORE placed high hopes in the possibilities of this renewed campaign. It advanced the chapter $3500 toward bail costs, and Rich flew down from New York to confer with black community leaders in an attempt to stimulate a major New Orleans dime store protest. While there he spoke with three young black lawyers—Robert Collins, Nils Douglas, and Lolis Elie—whom Lombard had secured to represent the arrested chapter members. Rich was especially impressed with these men, who would in the future handle most of CORE's legal work in Louisiana. And the very first case they took, Lombard's arrest for sitting-in at McCrory's, produced a major decision when the United States Supreme Court in 1963 reversed his conviction. Yet for the short run the results in New Orleans were disappointing to National CORE leaders. After school reopened in late September 1960 the sit-ins tapered off, the energies of the chapter were largely taken up with the litigation stemming from the first sit-ins, and two CORE secretaries sent to the city to develop a program around the tense school desegregation situation, then much in the news, were unable to rekindle enthusiasm.

In long-range terms, however, the New Orleans lunch-counter demonstrations proved exceedingly valuable for CORE. Not only did the organization establish a fruitful relationship with Collins, Douglas, and Elie, but by the spring of 1961 the chapter would revive and once again make an important contribution to major CORE campaigns. Finally, and most important, the New Orleans affiliate proved to be an unusual source of leadership in future years. Lombard, possessed of unusual warmth and personal magnetism, became CORE's highly popular national vice-chairman, while other members of the chapter—David J. Dennis, Jerome

Smith, George Raymond, Jr., Oretha Castle, Mat Suarez, and Ronnie M. Moore—held the key positions on CORE's field staff in Louisiana and Mississippi. The chapter's role in CORE in fact, was comparable to that played in the larger southern nonviolent movement by the Nashville students who supplied outstanding activist leaders like Diane Nash, John Lewis, and James Bevel as well as imparting an extraordinary dynamic to southern activism between 1960 and 1963. The creative contribution which both groups made was rooted in their sophisticated knowledge of pacifist thought and their unparalleled dedication to Gandhian methods of nonresistance—derived in the case of Nashville from the leadership of the black Methodist pacifist student at Vanderbilt Divinity School, James M. Lawson, and in the case of New Orleans mainly from the teachings of the exlongshoreman and former Southern University student, the 21-year-old pacifist Jerome Smith. As one member of the New Orleans chapter, who later played a prominent role in CORE, recalled it, "The chapter had a deep Gandhian philosophy. . . . All the members were prepared to die if necessary. In fact we spent hours talking about Gandhian philosophy and willingness to give our lives. We would not eat and talk for days as a means of acquiring discipline." The spirit of this small band of about twenty active members was exemplified by chairman Lombard who informed a citywide mass meeting at the end of September 1960 that arrests and jail-ins, far from frightening the activists,

> have only strengthened our determination to persevere, in our fight
> [for] liberty and equality. We believe that all men are created
> equal and endowed by their Creator with certain unalienable rights.
> . . . As chairman of New Orleans CORE, I spent six and a half days
> in jail to let the nation and world know, that we the citizens of New
> Orleans are demanding our freedom and are willing to pay the
> price. No man can imprison the desire to be free. I speak with confi-
> dence when I say, not even the threat of jail shall silence the cry of
> the Negro for liberation from the imprisonment of segregation.[32]

Meanwhile McCain and Gaither had been devoting most of their time to South Carolina. During the early part of the summer Gaither was helping demonstrating students in Columbia and Orangeburg, and in Rock Hill CORE leaders were arrested while sitting-in at McCrory's. Since by autumn things were at a standstill, Gaither, to "get the movement started again," returned to South Carolina in October, established a new CORE group in Orangeburg, and reorganized the Sumter students for a new series of sit-ins which began later in the month.[33] In both towns trouble developed with the NAACP, despite the fact that in May the NAACP state field secretary, Rev. I. DeQuincey Newman, had promised that the Association would cooperate with CORE in South Carolina "to see that the student movement does not lag." Now, however, Newman warned the youths, many of whom were active in both organizations, to resign from CORE on the grounds that dual membership was forbidden. Newman was inaccurate—he himself had been active in both CORE and the NAACP in the late 1950's. Nevertheless, in Orangeburg his ploy succeeded, despite Gaither's efforts to counteract it, and by December the CORE chapter there was "totally inactive." On the other hand, in Sumter, where the chairman of Morris College CORE was also president of the NAACP college chapter, the students refused to disaffiliate themselves from CORE and heatedly announced that they would neither participate in any NAACP project nor allow the NAACP to take credit for recent sit-ins in which the youths were arrested. Newman warned that if the students persisted, their support in the Sumter black community would dry up completely. When McCain heard about this threat he was infuriated and told local black leaders, "if there was to be a fight between NAACP and CORE . . . Sumter would be split straight down the middle." McCain's firmness actually prevented a showdown and he reported triumphantly, ". . . we have blown holes in whatever plans Newman might have had in taking our students away from us." The NAACP, he continued, had been deprived of the opportunity to "cash in" on the youths' action projects. With unity restored, both the NAACP and CORE backed the students in the dime store boycott and their demands for jobs as well as lunch counter integration.[34]

Meanwhile Gaither, although dissatisfied with the "poor leadership" and "apathetic attitude" of black collegians throughout South Carolina, was laying plans for a major jail-in project. CORE leaders favored this tactic partly because by circumventing the need for bail it conserved the organization's very limited financial resources. More important, they believed that the act of staying in jail, through dramatizing the courage of the activists, would both galvanize the local black community into militant protest and awaken the conscience of many northern whites to a degree that mere arrests by themselves could not accomplish.[35] Accordingly National CORE sponsored a statewide student workshop in December, where Gaither, who had participated in the Miami jail-in, gave special emphasis to the value of the jail-no-bail technique. The Orangeburg workshop's most immediate effect was seen in the escalation of demonstrations which followed in Rock Hill, culminating in CORE's widely publicized jail-in of February 1961.[36]

Having previously reactivated the Friendship Junior College chapter, Gaither now instituted daily sit-ins and picketing at the Rock Hill dime stores, while simultaneously undertaking the difficult task of recruiting students for the jail-in. He recalled that for those who finally agreed to participate, "Making a decision to go to jail for the first time was not easy. In some cases, it meant leaving a girlfriend; in others, antagonizing parents who had little understanding of nonviolent action and much fear for their children's safety," and who might also be fired from their jobs for their children's action. Finally on the morning of January 31, almost exactly one year after the Greensboro sit-in, Gaither and nine students headed downtown toward two dime stores. Later he recollected their feelings vividly: " . . . As we walked uptown, some of us wondered whether any of our group would change his decision on the way and withdraw. None did." Scarcely had they taken seats at McCrory's lunch counter when the police appeared and roughly hauled them off to jail. Locked in cells, "We started singing freedom songs and spirituals. . . . We slept on bare steel bunks, which bruised our bones but not our morale. . . ." The next day they were convicted of trespassing and sentenced to thirty days hard labor on the road gang or one-hundred dollar fines. Only one of the ten elected to pay the fine. "Surprise and shock filled the courtroom when it became known that we had chosen to be jailed-in. The only thing they had to beat us over the head with was a threat of sending us to jail. So we disarmed them by using the only weapon we had left . . . jail without bail. . . . It upset them considerably."

In prison the youths irritated the guards with their singing. On one occasion when the prisoners sang a spiritual with the lines, "Before I'll be a slave, I'll be buried in my grave," the guards placed all of them into a single cell, ordinarily used for solitary confinement, where they were left for several hours, and fed only bread and water. They were then assigned to a work gang loading topsoil on dump trucks. When it became evident several days later that they were being forced to do more work than other prisoners, the youths resisted with a slow-down. Agitated jail officials returned them to the punishment cell, where they promptly went on a hunger strike. This, added to the loss of sleep resulting from lying on the bare floor of the cramped cell, made the prisoners "feel miserable." On the third day the authorities, worried by possible adverse publicity, reassigned them to the road gang for the remainder of their sentence, after indicating to the protesters that the abuse of which they complained would not be repeated.[37]

The Rock Hill jail-in made national headlines, ironically, in large part because SNCC became involved in it. SNCC, which from its inception had backed the jail-in technique, had never actually carried it out. At a SNCC conference in October 1960, James Lawson, had reminded the delegates of their earlier pledge: "We lost the finest hours of our movement when we left the jail for bail. . . . Perhaps we can never again recover. . . ." As soon as it learned about CORE's jail-in, the SNCC steering committee, anxious for its own organization to be regarded as the most militant in the movement, issued a call for students to assemble at Rock Hill. Four prominent SNCC leaders rushed there, were arrested, refused to pay fines, and began serving thirty-day jail terms. A few days later, SNCC sent forty others to conduct dime store picketing. They also held a kneel-in at five churches, and along with several hundred others, participated in a motorcade to the York County prison farm where the CORE and SNCC men were serving their terms.[38]

The Rock Hill jail-in did not desegregate the lunch counters, but in the history of the southern movement and CORE, it was an event of considerable significance. As soon as the arrestees had chosen jail, Carey notified all CORE leaders; and at the Council meeting later that month Farmer described Rock Hill as "the 1961 Greensboro." Once Gaither and the others were released CORE exploited their celebrity status. For example, in New York, labor leaders were invited to meet the young people at a fund-raising luncheon.[39] Coming during a lull in student activism, the Rock Hill campaign also provided a sense of momentum to a movement that was slowing down. It furnished the inspiration for student jail-ins in Lynchburg and Atlanta that February.[40] Most important, Rock Hill was the model for the jail-in strategy of the Freedom Rides of 1961, and several subsequent major campaigns which CORE conducted in the South.

In other parts of the South CORE staff had mixed results in their attempts to encourage activity. It proved generally difficult to revive CORE work in Florida. The Miami group became moribund, while in Tallahassee, Haley reported that demonstrations were not renewed: "Enthusiasm is at the low ebb . . . the natural reaction of the non-criminal types to the imminence of jail." In Jacksonville, he discovered that white students were the nucleus of a weak group, but the NAACP Youth Council had already pre-empted the sit-in strategy in that city. Only in St. Petersburg, where Pat Stephens had helped to form a CORE chapter, did

Haley find action. He reported a demonstration during November at McCrory's; in January the group succeeded in desegregating lunch counters of a dozen stores in this, the most liberal Florida city north of Miami.[41]

CORE's efforts achieved more in West Virginia and Kentucky. In the autumn, field secretary Joe Perkins organized new groups in Huntington, West Virginia, and in Richmond and Covington, Kentucky; all three carried out demonstrations in public accommodations during the ensuing months with some limited success. Most outstanding was the work of the Lexington chapter which was picketing the theaters almost daily at the time he arrived in October. Perkins found that all the downtown drug stores, dime store lunch counters, and restaurants had been desegregated, and that Lexington CORE had obtained four cashier jobs at supermarkets.[42]

In Louisville, on the other hand, complications prevented the development of a viable CORE chapter, although the small affiliate eventually provided a vital stimulus for the city's black protest movement. Despite the fact that field staff had invested considerable time in Louisville the preceding spring, the small interracial group labored under great difficulties because of its association with Carl and Anne Braden and AME Bishop C. Ewbank Tucker. The Bradens, who were officers in the Southern Conference Educational Fund, were widely charged with being Communists not only by racists but by many in the civil rights movement as well; while Bishop Tucker, who supported them vigorously, had quarreled with nearly all of the other local black leaders. The Bradens had arranged for Tucker to invite Len Holt, the Norfolk attorney who briefly served as a CORE field secretary, to the city, where he formed a largely high school student chapter in April. Not surprisingly the Louisville NAACP attacked the group, and CORE's national leadership dealt with the Bradens most circumspectly, advising field personnel not to accept food or lodging from them. Ultimately the Bradens agreed not to have any "formal association with the chapter." [43] Meanwhile, during the late spring and early summer the group had concentrated its efforts on holding small demonstrations protesting the policy of the Kaufman-Strauss department store tearoom, where one of the chapter's young black leaders was arrested in August. Nevertheless Louisville CORE, consisting of a small band of black adults, white liberals and pacifists, and high school students of both races, proved unable to make any impact or gain any support from the black community, and when Perkins visited the city in the autumn he found that it had lapsed into inactivity. As a result of his prodding, however, the group, by the end of the year, had renewed picketing and stand-ins at the department store restaurants in an action that would provide the catalyst for a major campaign by Louisville blacks in 1961.[44]

Simultaneous with this expansion of CORE work in the South, the number of northern chapters also increased—spontaneously during the spring in the wake of the dime store sit-ins, and at the initiative of field secretaries in the latter part of the year. Their work, however, proved varied and uneven. Well-established groups like Ann Arbor, Boston, East St. Louis, St. Louis, and New York were active continuously. On the other hand, Los Angeles and Berkeley, busy in the spring were in a state of decline by fall, doing little but maintaining a few picket lines; Washington CORE was inactive; and Baltimore was so dormant that in December Carey sent out inquiries to local contacts in order "to help build Baltimore CORE." [45] Despite the enthusiasm generated by the southern sit-ins, the attempt to revive chapters in three major northern cities—Philadelphia, Cleveland, and Chicago—was only modestly successful. Chicago, although active, remained small and split by internal conflict; Cleveland was a failure; and in Philadelphia, the group formed in March as a result of the Woolworth picketing suspended its projects after a few months, but revived late in the year. Similarly, field secretaries reported that new groups in Detroit, Columbus, and Cincinnati were quite weak —in the two Ohio cities in fact the chapters would have had difficulty in mounting any program without the participation of militants in the local NAACP branches.[46]

One problem facing northern chapters generally—and an important reason for the inactivity which characterized some of them—was the declining interest in the dime store boycotts and demonstrations. As early as the summer they were clearly not going too well, and National Chairman Charles Oldham, who had taken charge of the negotiations with the chain managements, was in fact under some pressure to "suspend" the national boycott, even though so much lunch counter discrimination still remained. Chapter members in Boston, St. Louis, and Berkeley had urged ending the boycotts, and in city after city the sympathy demonstrations had dropped off sharply. Partly this was a reflection of the fact that, as the sit-ins waned, northern sympathizers were no longer prodded by the drama of the southern movement. Moreover, as Robinson acknowledged, "After all, it is difficult to expect the same people to picket week in and week out for a very long period of time." A Chicago CORE member put her finger on another part of the problem when she wrote, "We found most people concluded that the battle was over—they had read the papers which said that a large number [of southern lunch counters] had desegregated." [47] Yet both the CORE National Action Committee and the NAACP, with whom Oldham consulted, were reluctant to break faith with the southern activists by publicly calling off the campaign.[48] Instead they allowed the campaign to peter out gradually. Even the unusually dedicated Ann Arbor group, which for months insisted on maintaining its picket lines, though they were functioning only on a symbolic and ineffective level, reported in November that the demonstrators had been withdrawn. On the West Coast the lines also "tend[ed] to numerical anemia." In New York by January 1961, when the boycott coordinating committee met for the first time in several months, the number of weekly picket lines in the entire city had dwindled to six, "and most of them not large." [49]

As the dime store campaign waned, CORE chapters, like many other organizations in the North, became deeply involved in assisting another southern cause—the embattled black sharecroppers of Fayette and Haywood counties in southwestern Tennessee. Since late 1958 these farmers, organized into the Fayette County and the Haywood County Civic and Welfare Leagues, had carried on a voter registration drive so successful that the white community retaliated with severe economic repression. Many were deprived of credit at the local white-owned grocery stores, and over three hundred were evicted from the plantations. With Fayette-Haywood achieving national publicity, CORE swung into action in the summer of 1960. The national office sent an observer, and at his recommendation Robinson asked all affiliates to cooperate with an NAACP boycott against the Gulf and Texaco companies whose distributors had refused to supply blacks in the two counties. More important was the material aid which CORE chapters sent to the beleaguered sharecroppers. Thus the Ann Arbor, Michigan, affiliate donated $377 to purchase flooring for the "Tent City" which a dozen of the evicted families had established. Chapters in Los Angeles, St. Louis, New York, and Chicago formed relief committees which rushed food, medicine, clothing, and money to the Fayette and Haywood County Leagues. The most active was undoubtedly the CORE-sponsored Chicago Emergency Relief Committee for Fayette County, which over a period of about five months sent about sixty tons of food and clothing. In January 1961 National CORE increased its efforts, assigning field secretary Richard Haley to the area. For several months he sought to settle an unfortunate factional dispute that disrupted the Fayette League, but without success. With the movement in that county a shambles, and national concern fading, Haley departed, and CORE turned down further requests for assistance. On the other hand, CORE aided the pacifist Eric Weinberger who, working with the dispossessed farmers on the viable Haywood County League, organized a cooperative which produced leather tote bags for sale among northern sympathizers of the civil rights movement. Weinberger himself suffered extraordinary physical harassment from local police and was eventually forced to leave the county. But the tote bag cooperative, despite the farmers' lack of business experience, brought to the families involved more than ten thousand dollars by the end of 1962. More important, it served as an inspiring model that would influence the thinking and program of CORE activists and other civil rights workers in the South during the course of the following years.[50]

Valuable as were the supportive actions on behalf of the southern protest movement, from the beginning the national office stressed that these projects should be regarded by northern CORE groups not as ends in themselves but as a base upon which to build a program aimed at battling discrimination in their own communities. And while the South continued to command the bulk of their attention well into 1961, the affiliates of the North and West did put greater effort into attacking local concerns and problems.

In the more conservative border cities discrimination in places of public accommodations and recreation was still a major issue. However, it was evident that CORE's demands for desegregation had achieved an unprecedented degree of legitimacy, since public authorities were often intervening on behalf of the protesters. The Cincinnati chapter ended discrimination at two swimming pools and several eating places. East St. Louis continued its assaults on exclusionary restaurants. It sought to convince the county prosecuting attorney to take action under the state law, on one occasion even picketing the courthouse. At the same time the chapter sponsored sit-ins at the restaurants themselves, and the demonstrations climaxed in November 1960 with the arrest of twenty-two persons—an action which finally brought the mayor's intervention and the desegregation of the remnant of proprietors still violating Illinois' civil rights law. In Columbia, Missouri, the largely university-based chapter picketed discriminating establishments, and after a sit-in which involved the arrest of five CORE members several restaurants opened voluntarily. Meanwhile the St. Louis affiliate, whose vitality had been enormously strengthened by the southern sit-ins, brought its twelve-year-old public accommodations campaign to a successful conclusion. In October, after months of negotiations, the St. Louis Restaurant Association passed a resolution urging its members to adopt a nondiscriminatory policy, and shortly afterwards the arrest of black high school students at a downtown cafeteria produced the mayor's intervention and the opening of all the restaurants. More rarely in this period northern chapters addressed themselves to surviving discrimination at recreational facilities. During the summer Columbus CORE demonstrated at exclusionary swimming pools, while the Ann Arbor group conducted stand-ins at an all-white beach, filed complaints with the county prosecutor, and had the satisfaction of seeing the beach opened to blacks several months later.[51]

CORE's national headquarters hoped that the northern chapters would move aggressively against employment discrimination. As city after city in the upper South began to desegregate its lunch counters, the organization's leaders became more sure than ever that "a national employment movement patterned after" the student sit-ins could succeed.[52] And a few chapters, most notably St. Louis which sustained its earlier interest in this issue, did undertake job projects. St. Louis in fact was the first CORE group to channel the enthusiasm generated by the dime store sympathy boycotts into an employment campaign. Its agreements with Woolworth's and McCrory's in the spring of 1960 provided not only for the opening of lunch counters in several border states but also for a change in employment practices in the St. Louis outlets. McCrory's promoted a Negro dishwasher to counter supervisor, upgraded two bus girls to waitresses, and reserved the next two sales openings for blacks, and Woolworth's hired Negro sales-clerks in several stores. Meanwhile, since January, St. Louis CORE leaders had been holding extensive discussions with banks, department stores, and other retail establishments. Deciding that it lacked the strength to embark upon direct action to back up its demands, the chapter carried on a protracted series of negotiations which, in the climate of mass demonstrations elsewhere obtained some significant concessions. By the end of the year it had obtained over twenty white-collar jobs in downtown businesses—including two at the Bank of St. Louis, the only financial institution in the city to drop its color bar, and three at a furniture store, where the victory had required fifteen negotiating sessions extending over a period of more than a year. Other chapters which attempted employment projects failed to duplicate St. Louis's accomplishments. In the latter part of 1960 the East St. Louis affiliate undertook its first job campaign, fruitlessly picketing a drug store in the ghetto which refused to hire a black clerk. Nor was New York CORE any more successful in negotiating with the Chase Manhattan Bank.[53]

A few northeastern groups engaged in projects to combat housing exclusion. Of these the most active was Boston CORE, which not only attempted to secure enforcement of the state's recently enacted fair housing law but blended new militant methods with the reconciliatory spirit reminiscent of CORE in its earliest years. When the manager of a suburban tract told a black engineer that all the apartments were already rented, Boston CORE sent in "testers," who proved that there were indeed available accommodations. Confronting the owners with the evidence, CORE was told that the discriminatory practice reflected the wishes of the tenants. Thereupon the chapter industriously polled more than two hundred tenants, 80 per cent of whom indicated that, in fact, they did not mind having a Negro neighbor. Only as a last resort, after failing in further negotiations, did CORE appeal to the Massachusetts Commission against Discrimination. A short time before the Commission's hearing in June, the black engineer was told he could have the apartment. In another case the following month, after a developer refused to consider a black businessman's application, the affiliate conducted the first housing sit-in. According to the chapter chairman, Boston CORE sought "not merely to bring about grudging compliance with the law, but also through negotiation to help convince the Campanelli Brothers that their fear of Negroes is irrational and immoral." Whether or not the owners experienced any moral transformation, they were ordered by the Massachusetts Commission against Discrimination to sell a house to the black man.[54]

Boston CORE's example prompted the national office to hold a housing workshop in New York that summer. New York CORE and the newly organized Brooklyn chapter trained members as "housing testers" and held a sit-in at a Brooklyn real estate office in August. Although further direct-action against housing discrimination in the New York area would not take place for another year, Long Island CORE, stimulated by the workshop, inaugurated a "Freedom Dwellers" campaign. Seeking to open the suburban housing market, the chapter, which met in the almost totally white community of Levittown, compiled and circulated a listing of white homeowners willing to sell to blacks.[55]

Clearly 1960 had witnessed substantial expansion of CORE. At the time of the annual convention in July there were twenty-four chapters; by November eleven additional groups had applied for affiliation, eight others were "active but not yet affiliated," and six more were in the process of being formed.[56] The location of the affiliated chapters indicates that CORE in 1960 was markedly southern. Eight groups were in South Carolina, two in Florida, nine in the upper South and border states, and only five were in the North and West. Five of the eleven that had applied for affiliation were in South Carolina and Louisiana; the other six were from California and the North. On the other hand, of the groups in various stages of formation but which had not yet requested affiliation, nearly two-thirds were in the North and on the West Coast—a fact that prefigured future trends in CORE's chapter growth. Affiliates, maintaining CORE's traditionally rigorous membership procedures, were still small, ranging in size from a dozen to a high of about forty for the Ann Arbor Direct Action Committee. As earlier, the chapters in the North were mostly predominantly white, and, although the important Tallahassee and New Orleans affiliates were interracial, most of the southern groups were still entirely black.

The expansion in CORE activity was accompanied by a sustained and rapid growth in income, although the organization continued to spend to the maximum of its resources and Robinson feared that, with the novelty of the sit-ins wearing off, financial support might drop. For the year ending May 31, 1960, CORE raised more than $144,000. In the following months contributions came in at a faster rate than ever—$110,000 between June 1 and December 1.[57] As in the past, CORE obtained considerably less than 1 per cent of its funds from the affiliates ($715 in fiscal 1959–60). Financial contributions of labor organizations, although still small, increased from $815 in 1958–59 to over $6100 in 1959–60, of which the Industrial Union Department, AFL-CIO, and the Dressmakers Joint Council of the ILGWU gave $1000 each. Symbolic of CORE's new status among the unions was the fact that James B. Carey, head of the Industrial Union Department, Eugene Frazier, president of the United Transport Service Employees (Red Caps), and Arthur Goldberg, special counsel to the AFL-CIO, agreed to join the Advisory Committee. Special fund-raising also helped swell the total. In June, Eleanor Roosevelt sponsored a luncheon for CORE, at which $5000 was raised. Direct-mail appeals still provided the bulk of CORE's income. In the spring 200,000 appeal letters were sent out over the signature of the popular black singer, Harry Belafonte, urging the public to finance the services CORE was rendering to the southern students. *Cracking the Color Line*—sprightly, shorter than the older *Erasing the Color Line,* and reflecting CORE's new militance in its title—was widely distributed for promotional purposes. The results were gratifying, for the CORE list of associate members reached a total of 20,000 at the end of 1960—a rise of 8000 since February.[58]

CORE's rapid growth brought enormous internal strains within the organization. Even the efficiency which Robinson gave to CORE's affairs suffered. The rapid build up in office staff produced a situation that led Robinson to observe, "The office does not function smoothly, and we must experiment with new employees in different ways until we can achieve a solution." In the rush to aid the southern student activists in the spring of 1960, the additional field secretaries were not only recruited hastily, but they were sent into the field without extensive formal indoctrination in CORE philosophy and traditions. Serious difficulties arose with two of them, and they both resigned after complaints were received from local CORE leaders. Replying to criticism at the 1960 Convention, Robinson assured the delegates that improved screening procedures would be used in the future. When National CORE sent the Tallahassee jail-inners on tour, the arrangements were slipshod. In Cleveland and Chicago, Bill Larkins was forced to use his limited time to develop his own speaking engagements; while in Berkeley, CORE members were "annoyed at the very short notice we received of Bill Larkins' trip to the Bay area. Because of the short notice . . . we did a poor job of lining up speaking engagements for Bill." [59]

CORE's growth also produced increasing dissatisfaction with the organization's structure. Complaints came from some chapters that the staff and the staff-dominated NAC constituted an oligarchy which made unilateral decisions without consulting the affiliates. Robinson and other NAC members themselves recognized the growing seriousness of the situation; as he put it, "so many decisions had to be made by the National Action Committee that the Committee became more important than in the past . . . and . . . should be reconstituted." The greatest pressure for change came from the Los Angeles chapter, whose leaders called for "more service and a closer connection" with National CORE,[60] which they regarded as guilty of neglect and bumbling. For example, they were infuriated about the New York headquarters' arrangements for Major Johns' speaking tour in their city. His engagements were sponsored by the Los Angeles Civil Liberties Union, which refused to coordinate his visit with the CORE affiliate.[61] Henry Hodge charged that, despite his position as national vice-chairman, CORE policies and actions were determined without consulting him: "I haven't the slightest idea of what goes on and why." As a partial solution to the problem, the chapter proposed the creation of a regional office in California, a suggestion which Robinson opposed on the grounds that CORE's limited resources should be concentrated in the South.[62] At the 1960 Convention the openly critical Los Angeles representatives generated "lots of floor fights" and later complained that Carey, Robinson, and Lula Farmer tried "to squelch" their ideas and proposals. The delegates, however, did authorize the NAC to establish branch offices "as the need arises," with "first consideration going to the West Coast." Moreover, after considerable discussion about the composition of the National Action Committee, they adopted a compromise formula limiting the number of staff votes at NAC meetings to three. Nevertheless, staff dominance of the NAC had not been really eliminated. Not only did staff attend NAC meetings more regularly than the others, but the new CORE constitution actually gave the three top executives what amounted to a veto power over the nominees proposed by the national chairman for positions on the Committee.[63]

The tensions and frustrations of the rapidly expanding organization faced with unprecedented demands upon its resources, taxed the strength and patience of the staff and estranged Robinson from Carey and Rich. The dispute involved disagreements over how best to run the organization in order to assure continued growth. And, most important, it reflected a feeling that Robinson could no longer adequately represent CORE in its relationships with other civil rights organizations or the larger society.

There was resentment over Robinson's concern for "bureaucratic details" and his manner of handling field and office staff. Rich and Carey disliked Robinson's "intrusion" into their "areas of responsibility." Both they and the other administrative and field staff thought him "absolutely petty" for requiring them to sign in and out and to report "minute details of how one spent his time when on CORE business." Rich and Carey also deplored what they regarded as Robinson's failure to appreciate that CORE was no longer a small, obscure organization. In particular they considered him "too thrifty" and insensitive to the fact that, if CORE were to take advantage of its new opportunities, it must depart from its parsimonious style and be willing to spend money more freely. For example, Rich was particularly irritated by Robinson's insistence that CORE send speakers on trips only where other organizations agreed to pay the transportation costs. This not only angered local affiliates, who often were not asked to help sponsor such tours, but, Rich contended, actually resulted in reduced income. As one example of the kind of expense Robinson "finds very difficult to approve," Rich cited a recent fifteen-dollar expenditure to help put William Clay, St. Louis alderman and CORE member, on a television program, which reaped dividends when it was shown in Louisville, New York, and Atlanta. Rich declared that Robinson simply could not understand that it was "essential sometimes to make an investment. . . ." Robinson, on the other hand, was annoyed by the "looseness" which had crept into office operations and the undisciplined work habits of some new clerical employees, and he even considered hiring an office manager to restore efficient operations. More aware than anyone else of the difficulties involved in raising CORE's operating expenses, the executive secretary was appalled at the mounting expenditures on such items as telephone and travel. Contending that his opponents were overly concerned with rivalling the NAACP as a "big" civil rights organization, he declared that CORE's department heads were spending money too freely and were, in fact, encouraging financial crises as a way of pressuring the public into giving CORE more money. Robinson himself had sponsored deficit spending when the organization's fiscal situation permitted it; but fearing that CORE could spend itself back into obscurity, he maintained that solid growth required a substantial financial reserve.

While Rich and Carey readily conceded Robinson's superior abilities as a fund raiser, they contended that in other ways his personality impeded CORE in its external relationships. Rich asserted, "He is not an adequate image of the forceful, aggressive yet responsible organization. He is unable to meet with the leaders of other organizations and represent us. He is inadequate as a public figure in the press or on television and radio." His critics took the position that, if CORE were to be a front-rank civil rights organization, it required someone who was not a bureaucratic-administrator type like Robinson but rather "a leader of men," an "impressive public speaker . . . capable of addressing large audiences," someone who could supply image and charisma.[64]

Anxious to obtain a respite from office tensions, Robinson left for a European vacation in October. Writing from aboard ship, he urged Rich to consider taking another job. Carey and Rich decided that the time had come to oust Robinson and, after consulting Peck and Lula Farmer, called upon national chairman Oldham for assistance. Oldham wanted Robinson to remain as executive secretary "unless there is so much conflict in the office that it means a replacement of the entire staff if he stays." But since Robinson was not "particularly popular" with the chapters, and since Rich intended to resign immediately and warned that Carey and even perhaps McCain would soon leave, Oldham, like Peck and Lula Farmer, agreed to back their position.[65]

Even though Robinson possessed some support among the nonstaff members of the NAC, the decision to remove him as executive secretary had essentially been made. In December Oldham, vice-chairman Henry Hodge, and secretary Anna Holden came to New York to participate in discussions with the staff and NAC on the matter. First they decided to eliminate the position of executive secretary and to appoint Robinson membership director, restricting his work to direct fund-raising. Then they created the new post of national director. In considering a successor to Robinson, there was unanimity that the man must be black, if he were to successfully project CORE in the movement and relate the organization to the black community. In Carey's view this was imperative because, with the three top posts all held by whites, CORE itself had not been projecting an integrated image. Yet the NAC felt that in specifying race as a qualification for the post they were departing from their old ideology of color-blind interracialism, and they did not want to admit this publicly. Consequently, the final version of the NAC minutes deliberately omitted any mention of the explicit color specification that the Committee had established for the job.[66]

As the NAC well knew the reorganization which it had engineered was quite unconstitutional. Only the Council or the Convention, not the NAC, could choose the administrative head of CORE; only the convention had the power to abolish a post or create a new one. What had occurred was a staff-engineered coup d'etat. It was curious that this should have happened in an organization that was so proud of its internal democracy and the autonomy and power of its chapters. But the very looseness of the tie between the chapters and the national office helped make the coup possible. In these circumstances, the oligarchic machinery—the staff-dominated NAC—which Robinson had himself created to enable

CORE to survive, and which he had used so effectively to promote the organization's growth during his period in office, now became the instrumentality through which he was removed.

Among the names considered by the search committee over the following weeks, the two with the strongest support by the NAC were Martin Luther King and James Farmer. A number of people thought that King would make the ideal choice. He was the person most prominently identified with nonviolent direct action; he would have supplied the much needed charismatic leadership; and his strength among blacks would have complemented CORE's image of being a largely white organization. King was offered the position, but the NAC was not surprised when he decided to remain with SCLC. As Rich had anticipated, Farmer would be the man to whom the NAC would turn. Farmer was indeed a natural choice: his previous role in CORE, his commitment to nonviolent direct action, his supreme ability as a speaker, all made him extremely qualified. He became CORE's national director as of February 1, 1961.[67]

The resignation of Robinson and the appointment of Farmer marked the changeover from the bureaucratic leader to the charismatic leader. CORE thus acted in a way very different from many social movement organizations, where charismatic leadership initiates the movement and paves the way for a period of stabilization characterized by bureaucratic leadership. In CORE, the process worked the other way. Robinson took a weak organization and developed it to the point where it needed more than a hard-working bureaucrat if it was going to continue to grow. His achievements were essential to CORE's future. His success had been partly due to the change in the climate of race relations, and to the growing popularity of nonviolent direct action among southern Negroes, but his accomplishments cannot be overestimated. He had created an effective national organizational structure, a superb fund-raising machinery, and a solid financial base. But the external environment that had promoted Robinson's work now undermined his position. Robinson had brought CORE to the point where to make further rapid progress and to achieve greater prominence and effectiveness, another kind of leadership was needed. Robinson played an essential role in laying the groundwork for CORE's greatness under Farmer; Farmer himself supplied that other necessary ingredient—a charismatic leader who could make CORE a major influence among the Negro protest organizations.

III

Ride Toward
Freedom
1961-1963

5

The Freedom Ride and Its Consequences

Securing James Farmer as national director was part of a broad effort to make CORE better known and give it a more important role in the civil rights movement. Simultaneously, CORE was searching for a major campaign that would propel both the organization and its new director into the headlines. The project chosen was the Freedom Ride of 1961—the most momentous single event in CORE's entire history. Its architects could scarcely have anticipated its success; it rejuvenated the southern protest movement, pushed CORE suddenly into the ranks of the leading civil rights organizations, and made Farmer a black leader of national stature. The Freedom Ride also revived older chapters and generated many new ones. It accelerated tendencies begun with the Woolworth boycott and furthered CORE's attempts to establish roots in the northern cities. The importance of the Freedom Ride for both CORE and the civil rights movement was incalculable.

Like the Journey of Reconciliation, on which it was consciously modeled, the Freedom Ride was precipitated by a Supreme Court decision. In this instance it was *Boynton v. Virginia,* which, handed down in December 1960, extended the prohibition against segregation in interstate travel to cover terminal accommodations as well as the trains and buses. A short time thereafter, CORE's staff began considering the possibilities of a second Journey, and Farmer, upon taking office on February 1, 1961, announced that CORE would soon spread nonviolent direct action from lunch counters to buses and stations. The CORE Council, convening soon after, amidst the excitement of the Rock Hill jail-in, endorsed the staff's proposals. These plans, which called for a dozen persons to challenge segregation as they traveled by day and address mass meetings along the way at night, bore an obvious likeness to the 1947 Journey. There were, however, major differences: the Freedom Ride would penetrate the deep South, it would focus on terminal facilities, and the riders would pledge, if arrested, to remain in jail rather than accept bail or pay fines. Thus tactically the Ride was the culmination of the use of the Gandhian jail-no-bail principle first employed in 1960 and most recently applied with such stunning effect at Rock Hill. In April 1961, Tom Gaither, following the procedure used by Houser and Rustin in 1947, made a preparatory trip along the proposed route. He arranged rallies and overnight housing and exerted special efforts to secure assistance from local NAACP leaders, whose responses ranged from outright refusal in Richmond to an unusually sympathetic welcome from the Greensboro branch headed by Dr. Simkins. After a twenty-minute stopover at Anniston, Alabama, Gaither prophetically described the place as "a very explosive trouble spot without a doubt." [1]

Thirteen individuals—seven blacks and six whites—assembled in Washington for training; they departed via Trailways on May 4 in two interracial groups. Of these only Peck had been on the Journey of Reconciliation fourteen years before. Three others—Farmer and field secretaries Joe Perkins and Genevieve Hughes—were also CORE staff members. As was often the case on CORE projects, the whites and blacks presented rather different profiles. Aside from Farmer, who was forty-one, none of the Negroes was over thirty; in fact, most were products of the southern student sit-in movement, as were nearly all of the half-dozen blacks who joined the Ride along the route. John Lewis, twenty-one-year-old member of the Nashville Christian Leadership Conference, who had already been arrested five times and would later become SNCC's national chairman, summed up the spirit of these youths when he wrote on his application blank that he would willingly sacrifice his June graduation from theological seminary because "at this time, human dignity is the most important thing in my life. This is [the] most important decision in my life, to decide to give up all if necessary for the Freedom Ride, that Justice and Freedom might come to the Deep South." The whites were older than the blacks, ranging in age from twenty-eight to sixty-one. The oldest were Mr. and Mrs. Walter Bergman, retired Detroit school administrators, long-time Socialists and active in the ACLU and the Committee for a Sane Nuclear Policy. Indeed, most of the whites were associated with peace organizations—another contrast with the Negroes, among whom only Farmer had been identified with this cause.[2]

While traveling through Virginia and North Carolina the riders insisted upon their rights to use terminal waiting rooms and lunch counters, and successfully challenged, usually without serious incident, the segregation that still prevailed despite the Boynton decision. An arrest, however, occurred in Charlotte when Perkins was apprehended at a shoeshine chair; he was acquitted two days later. Violence erupted first in South Carolina, at the Rock Hill Greyhound station on May 9, when a mob at the entrance of the white waiting room beat John Lewis and Albert Bigelow, a fifty-eight-year-old white architect and pacifist who had commanded the ship *Golden Rule* in a protest against atomic testing in the Pacific. The next day Henry Thomas and Peck were arrested after attempting to eat at a white luncheonette in Winnsboro, South Carolina; they were released from jail seven hours later. Arriving in Atlanta on May 13 the riders found the restaurant at the Greyhound station closed but were able to dine at the Trailways terminal.[3]

Next day the riders left for Birmingham despite warnings from Fred Shuttlesworth, the noted SCLC leader, that a mob planned to meet them there. Actually violence broke out even before the Riders reached Birmingham. As the Greyhound bus pulled into the station at Anniston, an angry mob with chains, sticks, and iron rods began breaking windows and slashing the front tires. The bus finally departed, but several miles out of town the mob intercepted it; the rampage of window-breaking which followed came to a climax when someone tossed an incendiary bomb into the bus. As it burst into flames, the passengers escaped amid almost unbearable smoke and heat. The police made a belated appearance, and later refused to guarantee protection from another mob waiting outside the hospital where the riders were treated for smoke inhalation. Shuttlesworth had to dispatch a convoy of cars from Birmingham to rescue them. Meanwhile, the group traveling on the Trailways bus fared no better. As their vehicle was about to depart from Anniston, eight white men boarded and tried to shove Ike Reynolds and Charles Persons, a Morehouse College student, out of the front section. Peck and Bergman tried to intervene but were knocked to the floor and beaten, Bergman suffering permanent brain damage as a result. When the bus arrived in

Birmingham, another mob struck Peck and Persons with metal pipes; both were badly injured, and Peck, knocked unconscious, required over fifty stitches. In view of these experiences the riders seriously debated whether to go on with the Journey. They concluded that their only choice was to continue, and amid a hostile crowd, sought to board a bus for Montgomery, but no drivers would transport them. Even after they canceled their plans to complete the trip by bus, bomb threats and an angry crowd forced the suspension of all plane traffic from the airport, where they were delayed for six hours until Justice Department attorney John Siegenthaler could arrange for their departure on a special flight to New Orleans.[4]

Disappointed that CORE was prematurely terminating the Ride, black student leaders in Nashville quickly decided that the project should continue, proving to the world that violence could not halt the Negro revolution. Events thus paralleled the sequence at Rock Hill, where SNCC enthusiasts had also seized upon what was originally a CORE project. In fact, on May 17, the day after the first group of Freedom Riders disbanded in New Orleans, John Lewis, Henry Thomas, and eight other SNNC youths left Nashville for Alabama. They were detained overnight by police when they reached the outskirts of Birmingham. The Nashville students were then shipped back to Tennessee but, with their number augmented, they promptly returned to Birmingham and sought to board a Montgomery bus. The drivers again refused to make the trip and not until the morning of May 20 was there one who, assured by state and federal authorities that his vehicle would not be attacked, agreed to make the trip to the state capital. When the Riders emerged from the Montgomery bus terminal, however, they were savagely assaulted by a large crowd. The situation was now so serious that the Kennedy Administration, which had thus far sought to avoid open intervention, was forced to order in six hundred marshals. Next day, Martin Luther King rushed to the city, where he addressed a mass meeting of 1200 persons at Ralph Abernathy's First Baptist Church. Besieged by a howling, rock-throwing mob, the frightened audience was forced to spend the whole night in the church, until the national guard finally dispersed the rioters.[5]

Feeling upstaged by King and the students, the NAC moved quickly to rejoin the project which CORE had initiated. On May 23 Farmer, who had left the Ride at Atlanta to attend his father's funeral, arrived in Montgomery where he found that black youths, including several members of New Orleans CORE, were already gathering to continue the trip into Mississippi. Since CORE obviously could not, at this point, dominate the proceedings, it joined with SNCC and SCLC in forming the Freedom Ride Coordinating Committee. The objective of this coalition was to "fill the jails of Montgomery and Jackson in order to keep a sharp image of the issue before the public," and thus force Attorney-General Kennedy to protect the rights of interstate travelers. In a dramatic joint press conference, King, Farmer, and the Nashville student leaders announced that despite threats of violence the Ride would be resumed. The following day Farmer and twenty-six other riders ate in the white dining room at the Montgomery Trailways station, and then departed in two heavily guarded buses for Jackson, Mississippi, where they were arrested for attempting to use the white facilities. When they were found guilty of breach of peace, they refused to pay their fines and began serving sixty-seven-day terms in jail.[6]

Meanwhile, the Attorney-General had urged a temporary cessation of the Rides to provide a "cooling-off period." The civil rights organizations, however, were determined to keep the heat on. Farmer subsequently told a journalist, "We had been cooling off for 100 years. If we got any cooler we'd be in a deep freeze." In fact, before leaving Montgomery, he had urged CORE supporters throughout the country to join the Ride. On the day Farmer and the other riders were convicted in Jackson, King, who had not gone on the Ride, speaking for the Coordinating Committee rejected Kennedy's request. A new phase of the Rides was about to begin. As Farmer later expressed it, what had started as a plan to use a small interracial band to raise the moral issue would spontaneously become "a different and far grander thing than we had intended. . . . Instead of seeking token arrests to spur legal and administrative action, we began to fill the jails of Mississippi." [7]

To National CORE, Farmer in a Mississippi jail had tremendous symbolic value. He had been absent during the mob violence in Alabama, but the Mississippi jail-in restored the primacy of his leadership—and of CORE's—in the Freedom Rides. In fact, the joint sponsorship arrangment notwithstanding, the major responsibility for recruiting, financing, and coordinating the Riders fell upon CORE, and Farmer's incarceration greatly facilitated the organization's efforts. In early June, Rich enthusiastically informed Farmer that "More and more freedom riders should be moving toward Jackson in the next two weeks—and we have the money to get them there!" CORE field secretaries were already deployed at key southern cities to assist riders: Tom Gaither in Montgomery, Jim

McCain in New Orleans, B. Elton Cox in Atlanta, and Richard Haley in Jackson. In Chicago, Los Angeles, and several other cities, local CORE chapters helped to organize contingents of volunteers. Under the circumstances training was limited; one man who came with a San Francisco area group in June, recalled: "Our 'training' in New Orleans consisted of an afternoon of lectures. . . . With the best will in the world he [McCain] could not prepare us for the unknown. . . . As the crush of Riders streamed through the New Orleans check-point, the most that could be accomplished was to reduce confusion. . . . It was a heroic effort at organization improvised under the most difficult conditions." [8]

Although the protesters did not succeed in filling the Mississippi prisons, the call for more Freedom Riders resulted in the arrest of 328 persons in Jackson by the end of the summer. With another 35 jailed in Houston, in Shreveport, and on two well-publicized trips of clergymen and labor leaders to Florida, the total number of people arrested surpassed 360.[9] The list included prominent SCLC and SNCC leaders like James Lawson, C. T. Vivian, Wyatt T. Walker, John Lewis, Stokley Carmichael, Diane Nash, and James Bevel, and several who were later to play prominent roles in CORE. Two-thirds of the Riders were college students; three-fourths were males; slightly more than one-half were black, mostly from the South. A substantial number were ministers and rabbis, and many others, especially among the southern blacks, had strong religious motivations. Among the whites, Jews and Quakers were disproportionately represented, while only a few were Catholics. The commitment of many Riders is illustrated by a letter which Farmer received at the end of the summer, thanking him for the chance to go to jail. The young white man noted that it was not easy to be behind bars, "but it is nothing compared to the lifetime of suffering and embarrassment that 20 million Americans must face because their skin is black. In a speech at Dayton, Ohio, last Sunday, you spoke of the white freedom riders and said 'they are doing something they don't have to do.' I would like to correct you. *We do have to be Freedom Riders.* We must do this for God, for Humanity, and for our country." [10]

Such sentiments were severely tested during the weeks of incarceration. After sentencing the first Riders to arrive in Jackson were sent to the county jail, where facilities were filthy, the food execrable, and the guards hostile. Charles Oldham, who visited the prisoners there in June, found incredibly crowded conditions; for example, fourteen women were occupying a thirteen-by-fifteen-foot cell and sleeping on a damp concrete floor. Mary Hamilton, a young black woman from the West Coast who would later become a CORE field secretary, reported "Our blankets all smelled of urine. The sheets were soiled . . . and the mattresses were very dirty." The men antagonized the guards by singing freedom songs. Several were thrown into the "sweat box," but the singing continued and the group was later transferred to the county prison farm where they were assigned to work long hours in the fields in one hundred degree weather. Individually interrogated upon arrival, those who did not answer to the guards' satisfaction were beaten. One rider recalled, "Outside we could hear the questions, and the thumps and whacks, and sometimes a quick groan or a cry." Reverend C. T. Vivian of Chattanooga refused to say "Yes, sir," and left the room with blood flowing from his head.[11]

The stream of Freedom Riders into Jackson quickly overtaxed the city and county jails, so that beginning June 15 male riders were sent to the state penitentiary at Parchman, where under orders from Governor Ross Barnett they were confined to the maximum security wing. Later a hunger strike by the female riders, who demanded to be treated like the men, produced their transfer to the state penitentiary also.[12] At Parchman blacks and whites were segregated but housed in the same blocks, with two or three prisoners placed in each six-by-nine-foot cell. Farmer reported that there was little physical violence, except for a few individuals "who refused cooperation with the prison system. Wrist breakers and cattle prods were used on them and they were dragged across the floor in great pain." On the other hand, there was, as he put it, considerable "psychological violence." Food was greasy and inedible. Confined to their cells for the whole time except for semiweekly trips to the showers, they were allowed no exercise periods, games, cigarettes, or reading matter. They had, as one rider recalled, "nothing but time, endlessly advancing in minutes, hours, days." To make the days pass more quickly the men "desperately tried to stick to a rough schedule." After breakfast "came devotions—a period of prayer and song usually led by one of the ministers. This was followed by a special time period set aside for debate and argument. . . . After lunch came the 'quiet hour,' to sleep away the interminable afternoon. After dinner there were devotions, including singing, once more and then blessed sleep—if it came." As Farmer later told the press, the singing especially exasperated the guards who for punishment would take away the Riders' mattresses, forcing them to sleep for nights at a time in their underwear on the steel bed frames, "with fans going full blast to freeze them at night"; when the mattresses were returned the fans were turned off and the windows closed, "causing the heat to be unbearable, making it difficult to breathe." When the women prisoners heard of this treatment, they too sang and were similarly punished. Farmer was impressed by the Riders' indomitable spirit and recalled a young black's reply after guards threatened to remove his bedding: "Come and get my mattress. I will keep my soul." Nevertheless, there were serious morale problems among the men, reflected in the "bitter wrangling about tactics" which threatened to undermine their "precarious solidarity." To overcome this, elaborate procedures were created under Farmer's leadership to facilitate democratic decision-making on the cell block, with discussion and voting conducted in orderly fashion from cell to cell. But in the end, individuals followed their own strategies—some defiantly going into a solitary cell, others embarking on hunger strikes, and others trying to obey orders and serve out the weeks as comfortably as possible.[13]

The Freedom Rides saddled CORE with enormous financial and legal problems. Rather than serve the full jail sentence, the overwhelming majority of the Riders elected to leave prison after thirty-nine days—the maximum time one could stay in jail and yet appeal—thus requiring CORE to provide bail money. By the end of July CORE had spent $138,500 on the Rides, chiefly in bail and legal fees, but this was only the beginning. On August 4, initiating what appeared to be a deliberate effort to drive CORE into bankruptcy, the Mississippi authorities directed the organization to have all 196 persons thus far released from jail back at Jackson for arraignment in ten days. CORE went on "emergency footing" and 190 returned, only to be informed at the arraignment that they would be tried two a day, thus requiring CORE to pay more money to bring them all back again. Moreover, after the trials were held, the jail terms were generally doubled to four months and fines tripled to $1500. When this pattern of more stringent sentences became clear, Farmer announced that he would withdraw his own appeal, serve the remainder of his sentence, and advise others to do the same. But the courts foiled this tactic by ruling that appeals for new trials could not be withdrawn. Then CORE found that all bonding firms doing business in Mississippi, fearing reprisals, refused to supply surety bonds.[14] CORE, faced with the prospect of having to raise $372,000 for bail, was forced to borrow heavily.[15] The NAC also asked the Riders to plead *nolo contendere,* which would result in a suspended sentence and a $200 fine. This arrangement was accepted by 118, and although CORE paid the fines, a substantial saving did result. A handful decided to serve their entire jail sentences, but most of the others insisted on appealing to the higher courts. Fortunately in November 1961 the NAACP Legal Defense Fund agreed to advance much of the bail money and assumed the actual trial costs. The trials themselves extended from August 1961 to May 1962. Ultimately, attorneys for CORE and the NAACP Legal Defense Fund appealed the action of the Mississippi courts to the Supreme Court of the United States, which in April 1965 reversed the convictions.[16]

While the legal cases stemming from the arrests took years to settle in the courts, the Freedom Ride itself had largely solved the interstate transportation issue within a matter of months. Essentially what happened was that the strategy originally projected—arousing enough public pressure to make the federal government act—proved successful. The executive branch was certainly not anxious to intercede, given the delicate balance of forces upon which Kennedy's election rested, but as early as May 29 the Attorney-General asked the Interstate Commerce Commission for an order abolishing segregation in interstate transportation. CORE Counsel Carl Rachlin testified at an ICC hearing several weeks later, but since the proceedings dragged on, CORE staffers and Nashville student leaders began making tentative plans for a spectacular civil disobedience demonstration in Washington. Then on September 22 the ICC issued its order prohibiting jim crow facilities in interstate travel.[17]

The order, which became effective on November 1, was at first often evaded in the deep South. Field secretaries Cox, Haley, Gaither, and McCain tested terminals across a broad territory. They were refused service in places like Shreveport, Louisiana; Jackson, Mississippi, and Albany in southwest Georgia, but they experienced no difficulties in South Carolina, Florida, or north Georgia, and were even served at station lunch counters in Montgomery, Birmingham, and Anniston, Alabama. Certain recalcitrant communities became objects of concerted attacks by SNCC and CORE activists; SNCC challenged bus station segregation in Albany, precipitating a major campaign there during 1961 and 1962, while New Orleans CORE members tested towns in southern Mississippi. At the end of November, five members of the chapter arrived in McComb, a town already tense as a result of SNCC voter registration activity. At the station they were met by a mob which barred them from the white waiting room; Freedom Rider George Raymond and others were kicked; Jerome Smith, who had served eighty days at Parchman after refusing bail, was beaten with brass knuckles; field secretary Gaither was knocked down several times. Finally, on December 1, 1961, three Baton Rouge CORE members successfully integrated McComb's bus terminal, and by the end of 1962, CORE was satisfied that the battle of interstate travel basically had been won.[18]

The Freedom Ride not only had a momentous impact on the patterns of southern segregation; it also exerted an influence impossible to exaggerate upon the civil rights movement itself. For the first time the mass media recognized CORE as a major race relations organization. In Farmer's words, the Freedom Rides "catapulted CORE into fame." CORE's new prominence provided fresh challenges to the NAACP. CORE's achievements also caused further realignments and rivalries among the Negro protest organizations. Roy Wilkins, impressed with CORE's new stature, visited Farmer in the Jackson jail, and invited him to address the NAACP's convention. In his speech CORE's national director paid tribute to the NAACP for its half-century of "blazing trails through the jungles of bigotry," but indicated that in his view the initiative had now passed to the nonviolent direct actionists. And a few months later, Alan Gartner exulted over *Life* magazine's recent "description of us as a tough equality organization. I think for the first time it was CORE and not the NAACP whose comments were sought on a court case—a sign of the times." [19] In the South, the Rides both sparked a revival of the becalmed nonviolent movement, and also heated up the antagonisms among the direct-action organizations themselves, exacerbating the growing rupture between SNCC and SCLC. In fact it was SNCC's very floundering which led its leaders to eagerly latch onto CORE's Rock Hill jail-in and Freedom Ride. Having salvaged the latter, they became angered at King's seeming lack of militance and his failure to help CORE bear the expenses. At one meeting of the short-lived Freedom Ride Coordinating Committee, King even appeared open to the idea of halting the Rides, thus infuriating the young activists. Ella Baker, SNCC's adult advisor, recalled, "They came back from the Freedom Rides with the terrible feeling that the angel had feet of clay." [20] More important, CORE's leaders took pardonable pride in having stimulated the surge of direct action that followed in Mississippi, Alabama, Georgia, and Louisiana.[21] In fact, in CORE and SNCC, veterans of the Freedom Ride provided much of the leadership for both the action programs in the deep South during 1961–62 and for the later Voter Registration Projects which proved so significant to the civil rights movement.

The Freedom Ride greatly influenced the development of CORE over the next two years. It dominated the proceedings of the 1961 Convention, provided an unprecedented entré into the deep South, and inspired intensified activity in the North. It sparked substantial growth in the chapters and caused a remarkable rise in CORE income, which thereby facilitated a rapid expansion of CORE staff. Organizational growth exacerbated the existing internal problems and produced new ones, and thus paved the way for some important structural changes within the organization. These developments were accompanied by subtle changes in direction and ethos. In the North CORE moved more energetically into housing and employment projects; in the South the organization worked increasingly in voter registration. And all of these campaigns enlisted for the first time substantial numbers of working-class Negroes. The rapid influx of newcomers—an increasing proportion of them black—was largely responsible for the first stirrings toward black separatism and the earliest expressed skepticism of nonviolence. More general was a quickening sense of immediatism that found expression in the escalation of demands—most notably for compensatory, preferential employment; in a mood of impatience with negotiations; and in a rising use of more militant tactics like blocking entrances and driveways, conducting all-night "dwell-ins," and dumping garbage on city hall steps. All of these developments would come to full flower only later; but they were rooted in CORE's changing activities and constituency during the aftermath of the Freedom Ride.

Although the chapters supplied much of the thrust for CORE's militance and for the shifts that were occurring, part of the explanation for change also lies in the character of James Farmer's leadership. In seeking a director who would "be an adequate image of a forceful, aggressive yet responsible organization," and "an impressive public speaker" who could effectively represent CORE to the civil rights movement and the nation, CORE leaders chose well when they selected Farmer. Farmer himself conceived of his role as making CORE "a national force" that would function as the "cutting edge" of the civil rights movement. Except for Martin Luther King, he was the most charismatic of all the civil rights leaders. He embodied a rare combination of extraordinary oratorical ability and equally extraordinary physical courage. Whether in the banquet hall or at a street corner rally, Farmer could move a crowd. With his magnetic and authoritative manner and his deep resonant voice, he captivated audiences, alternately making them laugh at his wry and ironic anecdotes, indignant at his recount of injustices, and eager to contribute money or march on city hall. On TV and at press conferences, he came across equally well. Unlike King, he did not tend to retreat into grand generalizations and evasive moralizing. With his eyes flashing and his voice edged with righteous indignation, he knew how to parry hostile questions and even turn them to CORE's advantage. Just as important were the courage and leadership he demonstrated in direct-action campaigns—as on the Freedom Ride and at Plaquemine, Louisiana, in the summer of 1963 when he only narrowly escaped death. Both as spokesman and as activist, Farmer symbolized CORE to the public as a militant, creative force in the black protest movement.

These same attributes were crucial to his success as a leader within CORE also. He saw himself as a "personification of action" for the chapters, filling innumerable speaking engagements to raise money, getting new affiliates off to a good start, and assisting in local action projects. For example, in a typical instance, Farmer visited Grand Rapids, Michigan, to aid a fledgling chapter that was about to initiate a campaign against housing discrimination. As anticipated, he attracted a large audience at a public meeting and received maximum publicity in the mass media. Speaking on TV he "gave the appearance . . . of a man who was confident of his own ability and of the ability of the local CORE chapter to act, not just to talk." Thus his very presence always helped local affiliates by bringing attention to their work. Moreover he added to his stature by joining local demonstrations; such participation made him a popular and respected figure among the members. Compared to M. L. King and to Roy Wilkins, Farmer was approachable—called "Jim" even by acquaintances—and he identified himself with the hardships and sacrifices of his followers. Thus as at Parchman and Plaquemine and the New York World's Fair, he not only went to jail with CORE members, but, unlike King, who tended to be bailed out quickly, he stayed in jail. He served the thirty-nine days in Mississippi and announced his willingness to return and complete his prison term; two years later he remained in a Plaquemine jail instead of participating in the March on Washington; and he was the last one bailed out in the World's Fair demonstration of April 1964.

Yet Farmer displayed limitations as an administrator. Throughout his career the sharp contrast between his administrative and speaking abilities had been evident. One journalist summed it up, "Even Farmer admits that his calling is oratory, not bureaucracy." When the NAC's search committee, interviewing him for the post of national director, asked him to name his most serious limitation, he frankly referred to his weakness as an administrator. Once Farmer accepted the job, this became painfully evident. On the one hand, he stubbornly supported people loyal to him, even when other CORE leaders believed that this sacrificed organizational interests. For example, he vigorously defended Gordon Carey from charges of inefficiency until the forces for his removal grew irresistible. On the other hand, Farmer was often indecisive, postponing many important decisions for months. Such delays occurred partly because he was frequently away on lengthy speaking tours; often he would wearily return to face a mountain of accumulated business. But by personal inclination, he usually acted only under pressure. Thus, for example, Oldham, anxious to integrate the Southern field staff, not only discussed the matter with Farmer himself but also urged McCain and Peck to do the same. "I know that Jim only moves under pressure and the more individuals that approach him with suggestions along this line the more receptive he will become to making a move himself." Simultaneously, Oldham wrote Farmer's warm friend Alan Gartner that while he did not want to appear to be "maneuvering behind Farmer's back," he thought that the national director "must be persuaded to move in certain directions and it is up to those who feel changes are important to discuss them with him." One close associate of Farmer has explained, "Jim was not a mover or originator of things. In this respect he was a bit like King. Jim needs a structure and organization around him to force him to take positions of leadership." Farmer, in fact, saw himself less as an initiator of policy than as one who carefully gauged trends within the movement and, when the time seemed appropriate, helped to push CORE into new directions he thought desirable. Wishing to relate democratically to the chapters and their leaders, extremely sensitive to shifting nuances and changing orientations in CORE and in the black protest movement generally, Farmer attempted less to direct CORE policy—though at times he did that— than to place the organization in the vanguard of the movement.

Farmer brought great gifts to CORE. He was an integrative force; throughout nearly all of his administration he was a figure around whom most of the leaders and the rank and file could rally, diverse though their opinions sometimes were. To the outside world he projected CORE as a militant—but not radical—action-oriented organization. Singularly combined in Farmer was the capacity to inspire loyalty and commitment among CORE's members and thus mobilize them for action, and the ability to attract vital support from the growing white public sympa-

thetic to the cause of civil rights. Without him—or someone like him—
CORE would have been a minor appendage in the civil rights crusade of
the 1960's.

Farmer's limitations as an administrator created a leadership vacuum
which to a considerable extent was filled by Marvin Rich. The latter's
community relations department—which combined both publicity and
fund-raising—grew even more influential after Robinson resigned in October 1961, and direct-mail solicitation was added to Rich's responsibilities. Rich and Carey had been the key figures in bringing Farmer in as
national director, and he often turned to them for advice. More important was Rich's own particular combination of talents: administrative
abilities which made his department the most smoothly functioning in
the organization; a willingness to formulate policy proposals and take the
initiative in urging others to adopt them; and a tact which made him almost as good a salesman of his own ideas within CORE as he was of
CORE to the outside world. Possessed with a long record of commitment
to the cause extending back to the days when he helped found St. Louis
CORE, knowledgeable and articulate, dedicated to the organization without desire for personal publicity, working long hours at the office while
Farmer was of necessity out of town much of the time, responsible for
financing CORE's program, Rich wielded an informal influence with the
national staff and the NAC Steering Committee far beyond that of the
usual publicity or fund-raising director. Department heads often consulted Rich before initiating new projects requiring substantial expenditures of money. With Rich possessing an initimate knowledge of all aspects of CORE's operations, Farmer also found his counsel especially
useful. Rich's power, however, should not be exaggerated. Farmer lis-
tened carefully to a number of people, and was sensitive to pressures
from a wide range of sources. During this period, moreover, there was a
basic consensus on most matters among CORE leaders in the national office and on the NAC. Yet in CORE's heyday, Rich and Farmer were the
two most influential persons in the organization.[22]

Rich's unusual position was based in considerable degree upon his
competence as a fund raiser, and his task was greatly facilitated both by
the quickening of public interest in civil rights and CORE's own dramatic contribution to the protest movement. Financial receipts, which
had lagged in early 1961, picked up tremendously with the Ride. Both
Robinson's direct-mail operations and Rich's special fund-raising produced an income of over $228,000 from June through August 1961—

nearly as much as the amount raised during the entire previous fiscal year. Speaking tours for the Freedom Riders, theater benefits, cocktail parties, jazz concerts, and rallies were all held during the summer; the first CORE art auction in May had brought in $11,000; a four-hour "telethon" netted nearly $30,000.[23] Eleanor Roosevelt lent her name to a mail appeal during the summer which proved highly successful, and subsequently served as chairman of a luncheon conference in October. In the following months, celebrities like Dick Gregory, Dizzy Gillespie, and Joan Baez appeared on CORE fund-raising programs. Members of the Advisory Committee also played a far more important role than previously. Lillian Smith, a major speaker at the 1961 Convention, often sent in money which she had raised from speeches and wealthy admirers. James Baldwin, another Committee member, made three speaking tours between October 1961 and May 1962, raising thousands of dollars for CORE.[24] Donations from unions rose from $13,500 in the year ending May 1961 to about $40,000 annually over the next three years, a significant increase though nowhere near what CORE leaders had hoped. Chapter financial contributions continued to be minimal, with few paying even their constitutional assessment. But associate memberships zoomed from nearly 26,000 in May 1961 to 40,000 by February 1962, reaching a total of over 52,000 at year's end, and 61,000 by by June 1963. CORE's income more than doubled, from $240,000 during the fiscal year 1960–61 to $607,000 in the fiscal year 1961–62.[25] As usual, increased income went hand in hand with overextended financial commitments and continued fiscal crisis. In February 1962 Farmer sent an appeal letter announcing, "Our financial cupboard is bare; today there is only $2081 in the bank. Unpaid bills total $25,540." Rich was "constantly juggling to bring in a few extra dollars to meet bills as they come due." CORE faced problems even in meeting its payroll, and in the summer of 1962 the staff went on half-pay. The situation remained critical during the autumn and winter, and by February 1963 had deteriorated to the point where the reserve fund and checking account were nearly depleted and bills totaled $62,000. By then the excitement of the Freedom Rides had worn off and CORE fund-raising lagged, as it had after enthusiasm waned for the sit-in movement. Although the level of the donations remained far higher than it had been in the months prior to the Freedom Ride, income dropped to $520,000 during the fiscal year 1962–63. With spending at an all-time high the organization's debts had almost doubled by May 1963 to an unprecedented $120,000.[26]

Even more than CORE's increased income, the rapid growth in number of its chapters in the North testified to CORE's rising prominence and popularity. The Freedom Ride revitalized the older affiliates and influenced the creation of new ones. During the summer, as Carey noted, "almost every local chapter . . . reported that it has benefited from the Freedom Rides." In June a St. Louis CORE member proudly observed,

> Our schedule for the week runs something like this: Tuesday night . . . committee meeting; Wednesday night meeting with Alton group (in Alton); Thursday night, meeting with St. Louis County group (in Webster); Friday evening, picket line in conjunction with county group at Toll House; Saturday noon, picket line at Toll House; Saturday night, picket line at White Castle; Sunday noon, picket line at Toll House; Sunday night, St. Louis CORE meeting. Like Charlie Oldham always says, "you have to be a little crazy to be in this group."

From Boston, Alan Gartner reported, "Freedom Ride parties are going over big around Boston—hold a party, invite your friends, charge admission—anywhere from $2.50 to $5.00 a head. . . . There are quite a few scheduled for this coming week." To create public pressure for change, chapters from coast to coast—often with the help of unions and other sympathetic groups—picketed local Greyhound and Trailways terminals. Detroit CORE demonstrated in front of the city's Federal Building, and New York CORE sponsored a public fast at the Statue of Liberty.[27] Meanwhile new groups sprang up spontaneously. In the New York metropolitan area alone during the summer and fall of 1961 the number of chapters increased from three to nine. At the National Convention held in September fifteen were affiliated, bringing the total to fifty-three. Of this number, twenty-eight had been added since the beginning of the year. The pace of new affiliations remained high into the first part of 1962, and eight more were approved at the February 1962 Council. Thereafter the number stabilized, rising slightly to sixty-eight on the eve of the 1963 Convention—the loss of momentum, like the simultaneous decline in income, reflecting a temporary lull in the protest movement. The majority of these new groups were located in the North and West, with the largest concentrations in California and metropolitan New York. By 1963 only about one-third of the chapters were southern.[28]

Meanwhile the chapters also grew in size, though they continued to remain esentially small, intimate groups. In the summer of 1961 the largest ones on the West Coast—Los Angeles, San Francisco, and Seattle—had about thirty active members each; Denver and Columbus had about fifteen each; New York, the largest one at this time, claimed somewhat under fifty. When Chicago CORE, which had twenty-three members at the time of the Freedom Ride, reached what was for CORE the phenomenal total of more than one hundred members at the end of 1961, the chapter decided to preserve the old cohesive and intimate style by dividing the affiliate into five units coordinated by an executive committee. A year after the Freedom Rides started, the three largest West Coast chapters each reported forty to fifty members, with an average attendance at meetings of between twenty-five and thirty; Denver and Columbus membership had risen to twenty-five; Detroit, St. Louis, Boston, New Haven, and suburban Long Island each claimed between thirty and forty members. And while the very active Brooklyn CORE still consisted of about twenty-five members, the New York chapter had almost 60. As late as April 1963, Brooklyn had a total of thirty-five members.[29] The fact that CORE groups remained quite small was due at least partly to deliberate policy. Field staff were instructed to zealously maintain CORE's tradition of "closed membership," and prior to affiliation chapters were required to include in their constitutions provisions limiting active membership to those who served a probationary period, participated in action projects, received approval from two-thirds of the chapter, and committed themselves to following the CORE Rules for Action.[30]

The growing scope of CORE's activities demanded—and the rise in CORE's income made possible—expansion in the legal and field work, with a concomitant growth in staff. During the summer of 1961, Rich hired as assistant community relations director William Larkins, former chairman of Tallahassee CORE; a year later he was replaced by another young black, Robert Gore, who had been an administrative assistant at the FOR. Litigation became so burdensome that in the spring of 1962 the NAC placed on retainer both Carl Rachlin, who had previously been contributing his services without recompense, and the New Orleans black law firm of Collins, Douglas, and Elie.[31] Most substantial was the increase in the field staff. In June 1961, three original Freedom Riders were added to the payroll: Edward Blankenheim, a white carpenter and member of Tucson, Arizona, CORE; Henry Thomas, nineteen-year-old Howard University student and former chairman of the Washington Nonviolent Action Group; and B. Elton Cox, a black Congregationalist minister and protest leader from High Point, North Carolina, with whom Carey had worked during the lunch-counter sit-ins in February

1960. Joe Perkins had departed from the staff, but with the addition of McCain, Haley, and Hughes, the number of field secretaries was brought to seven. In the autumn, Fredricka Teer, a Negro social worker who had been active in the Woolworth boycotts; Norman Hill, a young black who had been working with the Chicago Socialist Party and A. Philip Randolph's Negro American Labor Council; and David Dennis, a black Freedom Rider from Louisiana, were hired.[32] There was considerable instability among the field staff—both because of CORE's financial situation and the demanding nature of the work. The majority of field secretaries did not stay more than twelve or fourteen months, and their number fluctuated,[33] ranging between five and ten in the two years which followed the Freedom Ride. Always suffering from a serious shortage of field staff, and pressed both by fiscal exigencies and the desire of youthful activists to serve even on an unpaid basis, CORE leaders in the fall of 1962 created the "Task Force." The Task Force which consisted of individuals who could work for periods from four months to a year on a weekly subsistence salary of twenty-five dollars, supplemented the regular field staff, principally in the South.[34] By June 1963 there were fifteen Task Force workers, with about equal numbers of black and white, consisting mainly of college-age youth from both the North and the South. The new field secretaries, on the other hand, were recruited principally from among southern black activists. This was because CORE had long before decided that Negro organizers could best build the organization in the South and, more importantly, because the student protest leaders provided a natural source of dedicated, well-qualified personnel. Ronnie Moore, Jerome Smith, and David Dennis were among the most outstanding of the southern Negroes recruited in the two years after the Ride; another black Freedom Rider, Mary Hamilton, would also play an especially important role in developing the southern program. Some of the long-time CORE leaders like Charles Oldham were still deeply concerned that "the interracial aspects of our organization" would be jeopardized because virtually all new field staff were black. Yet to executives at the national office, who were in direct contact with the needs of the chapters and the southern program, the use of Negro field secretaries seemed appropriate to the realities CORE faced. As one of them has recalled, "We assumed black field staff was something that had to be." [35]

The organization's growth compelled CORE leaders to grapple with two important dilemmas: the old question of an oligarchic staff-dominated NAC, and new bureaucratic problems stemming from the enormous burden of work now placed upon the field department. As Farmer told the National Convention in September 1961, the Freedom Ride brought CORE not only new opportunities but serious internal difficulties as well.[36] Both matters led to major structural reorganization.

The most immediately pressing issue was the one involving the National Action Committee. The attack on the power of the national staff was led by New York CORE chairman and Northeast Regional Representative, Gladys Harrington, a black social worker who had formerly been a leader in the Tallahassee bus boycott. In addition to the genuine dissatisfaction with the organization's structure, the estrangement from the national office was fed by the resentment which James Robinson and his New York CORE friends had for the Farmer administration. Robinson, in fact, was now bitterly denouncing the very centralized system he had created. Harrington and other New York delegates to the 1961 Convention charged that a small clique on the NAC headed by the Farmers and the Riches held tight control of the organization. In support of this contention they complained that for over a year the national headquarters had deliberately kept the affiliates uninformed of organizational transactions by failing to circulate NAC and Council minutes. More important, they maintained that the February 1961 Council had unconstitutionally reversed the decision of the 1960 Convention by raising the number of staff votes on the NAC from three to five. In order to re-establish control of the national organization by the local chapters, New York CORE specifically proposed that NAC appointees should be restricted to those active in the affiliates, and that "no one in the immediate family of national officers and staff should be eligible for an elective or appointive position." The last proposal was directed at the wives of Farmer and Rich, who both sat on the NAC. On the convention floor, Harrington unsuccessfully sponsored a constitutional amendment which would have placed the regional representatives on the NAC and thus given the chapters more power. In the flush of Farmer's new charisma following his imprisonment, New York CORE posed no real threat. Yet Harrington raised important issues, and the delegates unanimously instructed the national officers to recommend changes in the NAC to the 1962 Convention.[37]

The NAC itself was stung by the criticism. Minutes were thereafter mailed regularly. To give "some distribution in terms of representation" Oldham added to the Committee Alan Gartner of Boston CORE, who had effectively backed the Farmer administration at the Convention, and

Laverne McCummings, chairman of Philadelphia CORE. Although Harrington felt vindicated by these appointments, she expressed concern that day-to-day decision-making was still in the hands of a small staff clique. Indeed, staff members, who had far better attendance records than non-staff members, still predominated at these NAC meetings.[38] Moreover there were persistent objections to the fact that NAC members, rather than being elected, were appointed by the national chairman. Accordingly, after much internal discussion, an amended constitution was passed by the 1962 Convention providing for a drastic overhaul of the organization's structure. Replacing both the National Action Committee and the National Council was a *National Action Council,* which convened semiannually and from which would be drawn a Steering Committee to meet monthly in New York. The NAC would consist of twenty-two people: the national director, the five elected officers, the *CORE-lator* editor, two members from each of five geographical regions, and five "co-opted members" selected by these seventeen individuals. The composition of this new body thus clearly eliminated all staff from voting except the national director and reflected a growing sentiment for regionalization by guaranteeing representation to all sections of the country. Yet, although all NAC members were free to attend Steering Committee meetings, those who came regularly were from the Northeast—the national director, the two representatives from that region, and the five "co-opted" members who invariably lived within 250 miles of New York. Despite the democratic aims of the 1962 constitutional amendments, a small group of northeastern leaders still basically controlled policy—a situation epitomized by the fact that Oldham, in distant St. Louis, had less power than previously, while Gartner, who was personally close to Farmer and lived not far away in Boston, became more influential at the national level than any other chapter leader.[39] Other important chapter leaders from the Northeast who became very influential in National CORE by virtue of their membership on the Steering Committee were three blacks, Robert Curvin of Newark, Shirley Lacey of Englewood, and George Wiley of Syracuse. Moreover, the staff, controlling the day-to-day operations of CORE and providing the chief source of information for the Steering Committee still possessed the biggest voice in the decision-making process. Yet the new structure, which lasted through the Farmer administration as CORE's basic governing framework, provided the potential for a redistribution of power from the staff to the NAC that would ultimately have important consequences.

Less success attended the organization's efforts to cope with staff problems created by an increase in the number of employees and the volume of work, and by the fact that the new staff members, generally preferring action in the streets to pencil-pushing in an office, were openly skeptical of conforming to bureaucratic routine. Indeed for the field staff particularly, but also for national office personnel, participation in direct-action projects and willingness to face violence and jail were as important a qualification as technical competence. The Field Department, overwhelmed by the growth in the number of staff and chapters under its jurisdiction, felt the strains most severely. Accordingly, upon the recommendation of a management consulting firm, Farmer, with the NAC's approval in January 1962 ordered a sweeping revamping of the national office. Haley filled a newly created post, assistant to the national director, designed to free Farmer for better coordination of CORE's affairs. More important, the Field Department was divided into an Organization Department to service the affiliates and supervise the field staff and a Program Department to manage staff training and execute special projects. Carey became program director and McCain became director of organization; Norman Hill and Fredricka Teer were named as their respective assistants.

These arrangements not only set the basic structure of CORE's national office during the remainder of Farmer's administration, but also provided for greater black representation in CORE's administrative hierarchy. Farmer, Rich, and Carey all had recognized the desirability of securing a higher proportion of blacks in executive positions. Moreover, there was pressure stemming from an undertow of dissatisfaction at the 1961 Convention where Farmer's critics expressed objections to the continuing predominance of white leadership at the national level. McCain and Haley were promoted to their new posts on the basis of their maturity and experience, but these appointments, like those of Hill and Teer, and the new field secretaries mentioned previously, clearly served to strengthen CORE's image as a black protest organization, and to assure Negroes a greater role in the policy-making process.[40]

Not everyone was completely satisfied with these new developments, or with the reassignment of valued field secretaries to administrative duties at the national office. Although concerned about imposing a "bureaucracy" on CORE which might result in inhibitions to spontaneity, Farmer, Rich, and others had concluded that the price of growth and maximizing limited resources was a more elaborate organizational arrangement. As Rich observed at the time, "We may be a little over-bureaucratic at this point, but, if we continue to grow, we shall require this structure." But a few leaders were very critical. Peck and Vice-Chairman Rudy Lombard, who had been asked by Oldham to propose financial economies, argued for sharp curtailment of the "topheavy" bureaucracy, eliminating the Program Department and the post of assistant to the national director, and the reassignment of McCain and Haley to the field. Moreover, the new structure did not accomplish the intended improvement in clerical efficiency, and the concern that both the Organization and Program Departments had with staff-training and chapter programs provided overlapping and even conflicting jurisdictions. McCain, who personally would have been delighted to "go back to the field," thought that combining the two departments under one director with two assistants would "cut down duplication and . . . lead to better coordination." To Rich this duplication was symptomatic of a larger problem of general inefficiency accompanying CORE's growth: "We do not coordinate between the departments at all well. Mailings go out from one department which affect another but are never seen by the other. Each department seems bent on doing the best possible job in its own field and the hell with everyone else." [41]

Along with the increasing complexity of structure came a new effort toward standardization of procedures. This was most evident in the steps taken to systematize the work of the field staff. Until late 1961 staff assignments were made on a spontaneous, ad hoc basis, with field secretaries constantly being shifted from one part of the country to another before they could develop a solid CORE program in any one place. In October Carey, after considerable consultation with other leaders, made individual field secretaries responsible for specific geographical areas. A few months later, McCain, as the new Director of Organization, reorganized the system further, dividing the country into seven regions, each one of which would be served by at least one field secretary. By April McCain had opened an area office in San Francisco and placed field secretaries in six of the regions. Actually these arrangements never became fully operable. It did not prove feasible to service all areas at once, both for financial reasons and because there was a strong feeling that field staff should be concentrated in the South.[42]

A thrust toward efficiency and standardization was also evident in the Organization Department's procedures, although it was stymied both by the rapidity of CORE's expansion and by the antibureaucratic bias of many chapters and new staff members. The young activists recruited to the field staff were often resistant about submitting reports. McCain requested a "daily log" and at least one detailed weekly report to help him keep in touch with the field. He also attempted to have field staff funnel all their communications to national administrators through his department. The staff balked, and by October 1962 McCain was requiring only a monthly report, although insisting that it was "absolutely necessary" to submit weekly expense receipts and to "keep the national office notified of your whereabouts at all times." The field secretaries again resisted, and months later McCain was still requesting weekly expense reports, and still warning that the auditors would disallow reimbursements without receipts.[43] Similarly, in trying to create a "tightly knit" organization, McCain sought regular reports from the affiliates, but their cooperation was erratic, leaving National often ignorant of their affairs. "We have a list of 65 CORE groups but really know so little about most of them," wrote McCain's assistant in January 1963.[44] On the other hand, the Organization Department had its own efficiency problems and failed to either adequately service the field secretaries or maintain effective communication with chapter leaders. From Boston, Gartner complained that even routine notices were not being sent him. And on the West Coast Fredricka Teer, who became West Coast regional field secretary in November 1962, reported that the affiliates had "very little awareness of the fact that CORE is a national organization," while she herself received almost no copies of national office correspondence with chapters in her jurisdiction. She lamented that she was "completely on my own without much relationship to the National Office. . . . the last to know what's going on." [45]

Inefficiency and resistance "to anything that even smacked of bureaucracy" were prevalent in other sectors of the national office. In the spring of 1962, Carey informed Farmer of "a laxity" in dealing with personnel, which caused low productivity and morale. Many of the clerical staff were arriving a half-hour late and departing a half-hour early, the switchboard was operated carelessly, and "our entire stockroom, supply, mailing, and shipping system is in a terrible mess. . . ." The clerks were behind in filing correspondence, and letters went unanswered for months. With discomfort Farmer wrote a Brooklyn church in December 1962, "We are deeply embarrassed to find that our receipt for your $100 contribution last June has not been mailed." CORE's accountants complained about numerous mistakes in the financial records: "The record keeping is much poorer than in the past. . . . There appears to be inadequate su-

pervision of overloaded bookkeepers." Clora Coleman, the office manager, repeatedly admonished the clerical staff about excessive absences,
overly long lunches and coffee breaks, and radio-playing in the office, but
the clerks continued to resist her efforts at reform.[46] Thus CORE's attempt to retain the efficiency established under Robinson and simultaneously move toward a greater degree of bureaucratization to cope with the
organization's increasing size and complexity was a difficult fight. At the
very time that CORE leaders tried to rationalize procedures, the orientation of many new personnel, combined with Farmer's style of administration and the strong antibureaucratic tendencies in the chapters, actually
eroded the orderliness which had existed earlier.

These problems notwithstanding, the Freedom Ride transformed
CORE into a major organization operating at the very center of the
black protest movement. With its expanding membership and growing
resources, CORE moved aggressively against racism in both the North
and the South.

6
CORE in the South

In the two years following the Freedom Ride CORE broadened the scope of its activities. Moving increasingly away from the public accommodations issue its program emphasized housing and job problems in the North and included an important voter registration program in the South. In the southern and border states much still remained to be done about public accommodations, and CORE sponsored major campaigns against hotels and restaurants which excluded blacks. However, encouraged by the Kennedy Administration and private philanthropy CORE also joined other civil rights organizations in inaugurating a large-scale voter registration drive among the disfranchised black masses.

Public accommodations had ceased to be a problem in the North, except for mopping-up operations in a few midwestern cities, and there it was mainly amusement places which still discriminated. During 1961 CORE chapters from Rochester and Detroit to Cincinnati and East St. Louis sponsored demonstrations—often jointly with NAACP Youth Councils—against roller rinks and swimming pools. The members of the energetic East St. Louis chapter suffered thirteen arrests while picketing bowling alleys in January, ended exclusion from the city's public pool after a swim-in with the NAACP, and victoriously completed a three-year restaurant desegregation campaign. The new Cincinnati CORE chapter returned to the battle against the Coney Island Amusement Park whose pool still excluded blacks; after twenty-six were arrested while seeking admission to the pool in May 1961, the management agreed to change its policy, thus bringing to a final conclusion the drive which Wallace Nel-

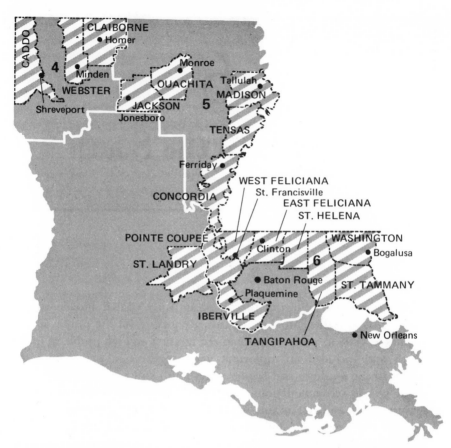

Louisiana: Map of the Fourth, Fifth, and Sixth Congressional Districts, selected parishes and cities. From *Congressional District Data Book* (Districts of the 88th Congress): A Statistical Abstract Supplement, Washington, D.C.: U.S. Government Printing Office, 1963.

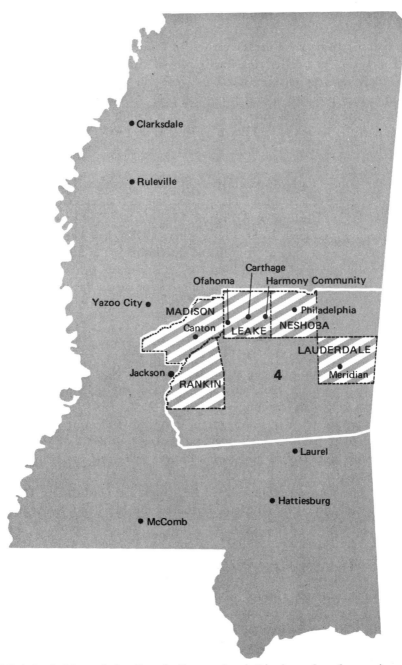

Mississippi: Map of the Fourth Congressional District, selected counties and cities. From *Congressional District Data Book* (Districts of the 88th Congress): A Statistical Abstract Supplement, Washington, D.C.: U.S. Government Printing Office, 1963.

son had begun nearly a decade earlier. In Columbus, a year of stand-ins and picketing at a roller rink finally proved victorious in October; but the following year chapter members were still being pelted and spat upon as they picketed a local swimming pool. As late as 1963 Cleveland CORE achieved success after picketing for a month in an effort to integrate facilities for white and black patients at St. Luke's hospital.[1] Yet by the end of 1962 reports of such demonstrations in the North had practically disappeared.

In the border states discrimination in public accommodations continued to be more of a problem. The participants in National CORE's 1961 summer Action Institute at Arlington, Virginia, attacked segregation in local restaurants. Even in St. Louis, where CORE had been unusually effective, it took a chapter sit-in to end discrimination at a local bowling alley in the spring of 1962. Kansas City, considerably behind St. Louis, had more numerous demonstrations, culminating on the day the 1964 civil rights law took effect in a barbershop sit-in at the hotel where the CORE Convention was being held.[2]

The most important border-state campaign was a National CORE project to desegregate Maryland restaurants in Baltimore and along U. S. Route 40, the main highway at the time between New York and Washington. In September 1961, after reading about the indignities suffered by African diplomats traveling on this road, Wallace and Juanita Nelson led a restaurant sit-in in northeastern Maryland. Following their arrest they refused to pay the small fine, and during fourteen days in jail attracted wide publicity by going on a hunger strike and practicing total noncooperation. Aroused, CORE initiated the Route 40 Freedom Ride project. The national office enlisted help from the northeastern CORE chapters and other organizations, including the Maryland NAACP, although Baltimore CORE bore the brunt of the local effort. A Ride scheduled for November 11, 1962, was postponed when the Governor's office informed CORE that a majority of the restaurants had agreed to desegrate within two weeks. Pressed by the student activists of the Baltimore Civic Interest Group, who felt that CORE had sold out by accepting even this compromise, CORE hastily redirected the manpower which had been mobilized for the Freedom Ride to "Project Baltimore." For three successive Saturdays in November and December, hundreds of demonstrators, mainly northeastern college students, tested and picketed Baltimore restaurants—all to no avail. Meanwhile no further progress had been made on Route 40, and accordingly the Freedom Ride was finally held on December 16, with eight hundred demonstrators participating. Most of the proprietors refused to serve them.[3] Undaunted, Baltimore CORE members continued to press the issue, and with the Civic Interest Group employed direct action across Maryland in a lengthy campaign for city and state public accommodations laws. Their efforts, together with NAACP lobbying, paid off in June 1962 with a Baltimore city ordinance, and the following year with a state law that covered half the counties.[4]

Further south, of course, public accommodations remained salient. CORE sought both to attack this problem and use it as an issue around which to expand its base in the region. Victories against discriminatory proprietors were secured mainly in southern Florida and in the upper South states of Kentucky and North Carolina. Organizational expansion, encouraged by foundation grants for voter registration as much as by CORE's own attempts to create direct-action projects, came principally in places where CORE had already been active—South Carolina, Louisiana, northern Florida, and North Carolina— and in Mississippi, where the Rides gave CORE an entré. Elsewhere as in Alabama, Tennessee, and Arkansas, CORE's work was singularly unproductive, leading neither to the desegregation of public accommodations nor to the creation of a solid organizational program. Moreover, even where CORE staff mounted major campaigns in the South, chapter development was often disappointing.

CORE officials were deeply concerned over the organization's inability to establish a large number of strong southern affiliates and to expand into states where it had previously not been active. The National Action Committee seriously considered allocating additional staff to the South,[5] even though two-thirds of the field secretaries were already assigned there. As CORE leaders saw it, their limited resources were a serious drawback to the organization's development in a region where extreme racist repressiveness provided serious impediments to the formation of direct-action groups. CORE's failure to establish itself in more places in the South following the Freedom Ride's phenomenal success was also in part because of the competition from other civil rights organizations. Both SNCC's youthful dynamism and more particularly, King's unequaled charisma and well-financed operations created major problems.

Actually organizational competition was a two-edged sword. On the one hand, it stimulated CORE to greater effort, for example, in the Freedom Ride when the young Nashville enthusiasts prompted CORE to continue the project. On the other hand, rivalry seriously limited both CORE's ability to establish itself in many communities and the amount of publicity it was able to obtain. In late 1961 when SNCC and Martin Luther King brought national attention to the nonviolent direct-action campaign in Albany, Georgia, CORE sent Haley to the scene to establish a beachhead there. He was unsuccessful, but CORE leaders, in part because they were so impressed with the publicity produced by the mass marches and arrests which accompanied King's presence, embarked upon similar demonstrations in Baton Rouge. Unfortunately for CORE, without King the important Baton Rouge project received relatively little attention in the press. McCain, returning from a southern trip in the spring of 1962, concluded that "King & Co., are stealing the show without producing—even in South Carolina, where CORE has done all the work. . . ." What CORE needed were "mature representatives who can sell CORE as well as King, etc., sell SCLC." [6] But to the general public Farmer's charisma never matched King's. Similarly, CORE's appeal could never equal the organizational charisma of SNCC. Consequently, CORE's dedicated field staff neither received the recognition they merited, nor, except in unusual circumstances, did they succeed in building CORE programs in areas where SNCC or SCLC was strong.

CORE's public accommodations projects in Kentucky actually began well before the Freedom Ride and were in fact a continuation of the wave of activity which had started in 1960. In Louisville, department store restaurant stand-ins by the tiny local CORE group had ignited a major campaign in February 1961. Taken up first by the NAACP Youth Council, the project soon came under the sponsorship of a community-wide coalition, which boycotted the entire downtown area in a massive drive to desegregate all the places of public accommodation. A dramatic series of demonstrations followed which produced seven hundred arrests, and which by June had integrated nearly every establishment in the center city.[7] Compared to the NAACP Louisville CORE received little credit for the campaign it had precipitated, and the chapter failed to grow. Simultaneously, Lexington CORE was engaged in seven months of stand-ins at downtown movie theaters, which ended successfully in May. CORE's national office took an especially active interest in this project. Farmer and Rich personally pressed the Schine Theater management; furthermore, in Rochester, Genevieve Hughes organized mass demonstrations against the chain which, faced by picket lines in other up-state New York cities as well, finally capitulated.[8] Lexington CORE turned at once to restaurant discrimination, but meeting organized resistance suffered a discouraging decline. By the end of 1961 a field secretary sadly reported that the Kentucky chapters "are all extremely weak," suffering from "lack of leadership, lack of direction, lack of an action program." Meanwhile, Richard Haley on a Florida trip found the situation there also depressing. Only Miami, which would successfully conclude a year-long campaign of theater stand-ins the following spring appeared to be viable in late 1961.[9]

Yet at this very time, capitalizing on the enthusiasm engendered by the Freedom Rides, CORE attempted a major assault upon segregation in the deep South. Carey sent Gaither first to Rock Hill and then to Jackson to reactivate direct action in South Carolina and Mississippi; he dispatched Henry Thomas to Alabama to establish a CORE base there; and the national office deployed substantial forces in Baton Rouge. In South Carolina, Alabama, and Mississippi the results were disappointing, and only in Baton Rouge was CORE able to launch a full-scale campaign. Yet the importance of these efforts organizationally should not be overlooked, signifying as they did CORE's assigning top priority to eliminating segregation and building chapters in the South.

Disunity in the black community foiled CORE's attempt to revitalize the movement in Rock Hill; but in Alabama and Mississippi failure to create viable affiliates was caused more by white repression than by opposition from other protest organizations. Soon after the jail-in in February 1961, the Rock Hill group had for a brief period courageously resumed demonstrations at downtown lunch counters, amidst violence by white hoodlums. At the end of the year, hoping to revive a flagging movement and create racial unity behind a downtown boycott, Gaither arranged a second jail-in, but his plans disintegrated when black community leaders dissuaded the arrested students from staying in jail.[10] Meanwhile Henry Thomas was attempting to organize CORE groups in Alabama, where, except for the college student sit-ins in 1960, SCLC affiliates had dominated the protest movement ever since Alabama had enjoined the NAACP from operating. Faced with SCLC hegemony in Birmingham and Montgomery, Thomas could establish a chapter only at Huntsville, where in January 1962 students from Alabama A. & M. College commenced sit-ins at the dime store lunch counters. National headquarters rushed Haley to the scene, and the month-long campaign that followed was characterized by extreme harassment and repression. There were forty-nine arrests, with sentences up to ninety days; Thomas suffered severe burns after hoodlums poured mustard oil on the seat of his car; and a local white CORE participant was sprayed with the same substance after being forced from his home at gunpoint. The black business and professional men became frightened and withdrew support. Then the state secured an injunction prohibiting CORE from conducting business in Alabama, thus successfully quashing the organization's efforts to establish a base there.[11] In Jackson, Mississippi, events were less dramatic, but equally fruitless. Gaither arrived in January 1962 and revived the floundering group of black high school students known as the Jackson Nonviolent Movement which SNCC workers had originally created to recruit local people for the Freedom Ride. Yet it proved impossible to find a project that would exert leverage on the local authorities without promptly landing the demonstrators in jail, and that summer, after four members were arrested while picketing at the post office in a forlorn effort to secure federal intervention against segregation at the city courthouse and on the local bus line, the group collapsed.[12]

The Baton Rouge campaign emerged from the inspiration of twenty-one year old David J. Dennis, a sharecropper's son who was attending Dillard University on scholarship when, swept up in the lunch-counter sit-ins, he had joined New Orleans CORE in November 1960. A veteran of the Freedom Ride, he organized a CORE chapter in his home town of Shreveport following his release from Parchman Penitentiary in the summer of 1961. He and others were soon arrested for attempting to integrate the Shreveport bus terminal, and the chapter, hampered by severe repression ranging from mistreatment of the jailed activists to the firebombing of the church where CORE meetings were held, lapsed into inactivity.[13] Dennis himself was not discouraged. He believed that students at the southern Negro colleges were ready to act, and envisaged a major campus-based CORE program.

Joining the CORE staff as a field secretary in November 1961, Dennis went at once to Baton Rouge, organized a chapter, and in collaboration with the national office made plans for a full-scale attack on the downtown dime stores. New Orleans CORE leaders, headed by their chairman Jerome Smith, arrived to help with workshops on nonviolent action, and national sent both Cox and Rich to assist. Fearing a reoccurence of the events of 1960 when staunch adult support was lacking, care was taken to secure preliminary approval from local ministers and other leaders. As anticipated the white merchants refused to negotiate, and a boycott and sit-ins began on December 10. Encouraged by the announcement the next day that the U. S. Supreme Court had overturned the conviction of Southern University students arrested in the 1960 demonstrations, CORE proceeded as planned.

On December 14, Dennis and twenty-two students, including chapter secretary Weldon Rougeau, were arrested for picketing which was in violation of a new state antidemonstration law. With bond set at $1500 each, the students, refusing bail, embarked on a jail-in. That evening Cox and chapter chairman Ronnie M. Moore, a Southern University student, addressed a rally of more than 3000 on the campus, announcing a march downtown next day to protest the arrests. Although just before the march Moore himself was apprehended by police for operating a sound truck without a permit, Cox led two thousand students, walking eight abreast, the seven miles to the East Baton Rouge Parish jail. Upon arriving at the courthouse they pledged allegiance to the flag, prayed briefly, and sang "We Shall Overcome." Cox then urged them to seek service at downtown lunch counters. At this point the students in the jail began singing, "O Students, don't you weep, don't you mourn," and the demonstrators responded with clapping and yelling. The police dispersed them using dogs and tear gas, and later Cox and fifty others were arrested. A few days afterward, nearly three hundred more persons, mostly students, were arrested while on a mass sympathy march in New Orleans, organized by the CORE chapter there. Arriving in Baton Rouge, McCain was impressed with the support that welled up in the community, in contrast to 1960. The adults were "up in arms over the use of tear gas and dogs" and collected more than $3000 to help the youths.[14] National CORE contributed an additional $3500 bond money, and soon after the new year all of the arrested youth had been bailed out. Moore and Dennis, as leaders, chose to be the last ones released, even though they had both been severely manhandled by the guards. Two weeks later the University authorities expelled seven members of Baton Rouge CORE, temporarily shut down the school, and had Moore and Rougeau arrested on charges of being on campus illegally. When the University reopened forty-five activists were barred from returning, but the student body was now so demoralized that an attempt by Marvin Robinson to lead a school boycott fizzled.[15]

The ambitious Baton Rouge campaign had ended in failure, but CORE was far from through with the courts. At the end of January, Cox was sentenced to twenty-one months in jail and fined $5700 for obstructing public passage and picketing a courthouse. Soon afterward Rougeau and Moore, already awaiting trial for trespass and disturbing the peace, found themselves slapped with additional charges of criminal anarchy, which carried a maximum penalty of ten years. Carey, Jerome Smith, and two students from Baton Rouge obtained an appointment with assistant attorney-general Burke Marshall, who was disturbed by the "grossly excessive bail." Yet the Justice Department concluded that there were no grounds for intervention under federal law. By the time CORE was able to raise the $20,000 bail to release them in mid-March, Moore and Rougeau each had been imprisoned for a total of seventy-eight days, most of the time in solitary confinement. Although all charges against Rougeau were dropped, and the conspiracy charges against Moore were never brought to trial, the latter ultimately served a thirty-day sentence for violating the sound truck ordinance.[16] The Cox case, on the other hand, reached the U. S. Supreme Court, which in January 1965 finally overturned his conviction in a landmark decision declaring unconstitutional the vague breach of peace and disorderly conduct statutes, and, in Rachlin's words, "greatly expanding the scope of permissible speech in basic demonstration situations." [17]

Despite the drama of the campaign, the severity of the charges against Cox and Moore, and the enormity of the bail, CORE faced the unpleasant fact that contrary to its hopes the media of mass communications paid little attention to the Baton Rouge story. The scenario was practically identical to the one King had used in Albany, and which he would apply brilliantly in Birmingham and Selma—select as a target a community dominated by racist officials likely to employ severe repression; mount a well-organized campaign galvanizing thousands of blacks into action; and supply detailed information to cooperative mass media. Baton Rouge had most of the right ingredients; nevertheless, the demonstrations, lacking the presence of Martin Luther King and the mystique of SNCC, were largely ignored by the press. To generate national pressure against judicial harassment in Baton Rouge and elsewhere in the South, CORE invited prominent Americans like Eleanor Roosevelt, A. Philip Randolph, Kenneth Clark, Walter Reuther, and Norman Thomas to serve as a "Commission of Inquiry into the Administration of Justice in the Freedom Struggle." With Mrs. Roosevelt as chairman, these hearings were held in Washington in May 1962. They produced some striking testimony from southern activists about southern white intimidation, abetted by police and judges, and complaints of an indifferent Justice Department and FBI. But to CORE's dismay, the news media did not give this event much coverage either.[18]

The pattern of intense activity followed by precipitous decline, which, as in earlier years, continued to be common among CORE chapters, became the fate of the once-lively Louisiana affiliates at Baton Rouge and New Orleans. Enjoined from engaging in street demonstrations, the small group of people remaining in Baton Rouge CORE after the expulsions from Southern University resorted to a series of "hit and run" sit-ins which led to the desegregation of the dime store lunch counters in August 1962.[19] But the affiliate, already weak and now facing opposition from the NAACP and other civic groups, soon became dormant. The New Orleans Chapter, on the other hand, while not experiencing the repression which had occurred in Baton Rouge, suffered from the departure of several of its ablest leaders: Rudy Lombard, who left to attend graduate school at Syracuse University in the fall of 1961; David Dennis; and Jerome Smith, who became a CORE field secretary the following spring. New Orleans CORE's program was further hurt by a controversy that arose in early 1962 when the black chairman, Oretha Castle, stung by criticism of interracial dating among CORE people voiced in a letter to the local black newspaper, suspended several members. Haley revoked the suspensions but advised against further dating across the color line on the grounds that it was a divisive issue in both the chapter and the black community. But the damage had been done, and the chapter never regained its earlier vigor. Direct action tapered off sharply, and the group was forced to work through a broad-based coalition of black advancement organizations that finally secured the desegregation of the lunch counters by the autumn of 1962.[20]

In part because of defeat and sheer exhaustion, and in part because foundation grants for voter registration absorbed the energies of CORE field staff in South Carolina, Louisiana, and Mississippi, direct action thereafter ground to a halt in the deep South, and CORE, in continuing the struggle against segregation, focused its attention on North Carolina and Tennessee. CORE's interest in the latter state was revived at the invitation of a group of courageous adults in Lebanon, a town near Nashville in location, but far behind the state capital in its racial climate. Arriving in July 1962, Mary Hamilton organized a chapter consisting chiefly of middle-aged people. Operating amidst a fearful black community and harassment from white hoodlums, the group, with the assistance of several

staff members, picketed a downtown theater for months and staged a
boycott which obtained a few supermarket jobs. Despite CORE's considerable investment in the community, by the spring of 1963 this dedicated
little chapter, wearying of expending so much effort for so little, began to
decline. By then, also, CORE's efforts to establish affiliates in Memphis
and Chattanooga had foundered on the vigor of direct-action-oriented
NAACP branches.[21]

If CORE, faced with NAACP opposition, was unable to expand into
the major cities of Tennessee, just the opposite occurred in North Carolina. It not only committed substantial resources to the state, but it also
received valuable assistance from old friends like Dr. Simkins of Greensboro and Attorney McKissick of Durham, and even from Roy Wilkins.
Thus fortified, CORE sponsored the last of its national public accommodations projects, the Freedom Highways campaign of 1962; created flourishing chapters at Greensboro and Durham; and established the base for
massive North Carolina demonstrations in the spring of 1963.

For the "Freedom Highways"—a natural southward extension of the
Route 40 Freedom Ride—CORE chose to focus on the Howard Johnson's chain—a highly visible target, vulnerable to a boycott from sympathetic northern tourists. Originally the organization announced an ambitious campaign along the major highways from Washington to Miami.
Thus threatened, and pressed also by Miami CORE and NAACP, Howard Johnson's had desegregated sixty-seven restaurants in Florida and a
dozen more in the upper South by the end of May. At this point CORE
decided to confine the project to North Carolina, where success seemed
most likely. Because the organization had practically no chapters in the
state, field secretary Cox organized groups in Raleigh, Greensboro, and
Burlington-Graham, which tested Howard Johnson restaurants and
staged "flush-ins" that desegregated washrooms in public buildings. In
addition, CORE recruited thirty experienced activists from all over the
country to lead the Freedom Highway demonstrations. To get more
black North Carolinians involved, Farmer sought the help of local
NAACP branches, and Roy Wilkins pledged wholehearted cooperation.[22]

Demonstrations began in August at Durham, where four persons were
charged with trespassing at a Howard Johnson's restaurant; they served
thirty days in jail rather than pay a twenty-five-dollar fine. Following up
on this action, Farmer and Wilkins led a thousand blacks and some
whites in picketing the restaurant where the arrests had taken place.
Meanwhile, three hundred protested at a Howard Johnson's in Raleigh,

where they were drenched with hoses, and a large demonstration in Statesville—a backward town untouched by the 1960–61 campaigns— resulted in twenty-one arrests. The next evening Farmer and a Statesville minister led a mass march of six-hundred to the jail where they held a prayer meeting, despite a thick fog of insecticide laid by the police. All told, arrests during the month-long campaign totaled ninety-three; all but two refused to pay their fines and went to jail instead. James Peck, who participated in the Durham demonstrations, was impressed with the contrasts between Freedom Highways and the Journey of Reconciliation fifteen years earlier. Not only was there a new black militance, but, despite the arrests, the white public was now far more tolerant. He reflected "how this type of protest in a place like Durham would have been inconceivable 15 years ago." While a few passers by made abusive comments, "neither they nor the police molested us. In 1947 we would have faced violence on that street. . . ." At a cafeteria stand-in the authorities refused to interfere, and a number of customers even told the manager they supported the demonstrators. "Most unthinkable of all in 1947," he concluded, would have been the mass demonstration in which a thousand people risked arrest for trespassing on Howard Johnson's property.[23] Given the context of diminishing white resistance, and faced with nonviolent direct action of massive proportions, Governor Terry Sanford conferred with Farmer, McKissick, and other local CORE and NAACP officials and appointed a committee of prominent North Carolina citizens in an effort to promote desegregation. Although the conference actually brought no direct results, the campaign had opened half of the Howard Johnson's restaurants in the state by late August.[24] Further pressures, however, including demonstrations by CORE chapters at Howard Johnson's outlets at thirty northern cities in October, proved unavailing, and the stalemate ended only with the massive southern campaigns of the spring of 1963, which desegregated virtually all of the chain's restaurants.[25]

Organizationally the North Carolina campaign had important consequences, even though CORE's attempt over the following months to create an extensive network of chapters foundered on personality conflicts among the field staff and on what Carey called the "naive" assumption that the organization had the resources to work the entire state.[26] During the Freedom Highways project most of the local NAACP branches had given excellent cooperation to CORE, and particularly because of Wilkins' participation, the public impression was that the two organizations were co-sponsoring the project. Yet all along, the state NAACP president Kelly Alexander, sensing that CORE intended to use the campaign to expand its base in North Carolina, had been unfriendly, and at the Association's state convention in October he openly charged that CORE was trying to take the young people away.[27] The attack had some substance, for many members of the Greensboro NAACP Youth Council had transferred to the local CORE chapter, while in Durham the Youth Council, whose advisor was Floyd McKissick, took the name "Durham NAACP-CORE." [28] The struggle with Alexander embittered McKissick, who handled legal cases for both organizations, and several months later he withdrew from the NAACP, thus paving the way for his election to the CORE national chairmanship at the 1963 Convention.

Meanwhile two extraordinarily vigorous affiliates appeared in Durham and Greensboro—the two cities where CORE had captured the loyalty of the young NAACP activists. The Durham chapter devoted its energies to fighting job discrimination, while Greensboro carried out the most sustained public accommodations program of any southern CORE group. In a major campaign to desegregate the city's restaurants, the Greensboro affiliate adopted the strategy employed with success previously at Louisville—inaugurating large picket lines at two leading cafeterias and calling a boycott of the entire downtown area. In November the demonstrations reached a climax, with arrests for sitting-in totaling 117. After the first two cases drew thirty-day jail sentences, McKissick arranged a compromise, and direct action was suspended while the mayor appointed a committee to persuade the restaurants to desegregate. But by March 1963, when negotiations still showed no results, CORE turned to picketing City Hall, and subsequently resumed the protests downtown in what would become one of the year's most dramatic campaigns.[29]

Along with its demonstrations in the South, CORE also embarked upon a major effort in voter registration. The Freedom Ride not only revived nonviolent direct action, but also played an important part in crystallizing the creation of the Voter Registration Project (VEP), through which the leading racial protest organizations, encouraged by the federal government and foundation grants, participated in a large-scale drive to register the disfranchised black masses of the South. From the time the Kennedys took office, they strongly favored a massive voter registration campaign, believing that until blacks formed a major part of the constituency of southern congressmen, no significant civil rights legislation could be passed. Moreover, Kennedy administration officials had been impressed by the results of voter registration drives that they had encouraged in several northern black communities prior to the 1960 election; they perceived possibilities for creating an enlarged bloc of black voters in the South who would support Kennedy in 1964. Simultaneously, leaders of the biracial Southern Regional Council (SRC) were also urging that a voter-registration program be accorded the highest priority. Then in May 1961, the Administration found itself in an embarrassing position resulting from the enormous publicity stemming from the Rides. It was in this milieu of heightened interest in voter registration, combined with the sense of crisis produced by the Freedom Ride that the idea of a foundation-financed voter-registration campaign developed. The proposal actually emerged out of informal discussions between Burke Marshall, Assistant Attorney-General for Civil Rights, and Harold Fleming, head of the newly established Potomac Institute and former director of the SRC. The Potomac Institute's funding source, the Taconic Foundation, created by Stephen Currier, had been concerned for some time about encouraging Negro voting in the South, and now indicated a warm interest in assisting civil rights organizations to mount a broad-based attack on the problem.[30]

The NAACP which had already sponsored voter-registration programs in a number of southern cities, was approached first. On May 15, the day after the bus burning at Anniston, Roy Wilkins, conferring in Washington with Robert Kennedy and Burke Marshall, vigorously urged federal protection for the Riders, and at the same time discussed the NAACP's and the Administration's mutual interest in voter registration. On June 9, at a conference in Capahosic, Virginia, attended by both southern activists and Justice Department officials, the subject of voter registration, along with other matters, was discussed informally. A week later, on June 16, at the invitation of the Kennedy Administration, representatives of SNCC, SCLC, the National Student Association, and CORE met with the Attorney-General in Washington. With Farmer imprisoned in Mississippi, CORE sent Carey and Rachlin. Kennedy asserted that in his opinion voter registration projects would be a far more constructive activity than freedom rides or other demonstrations. He assured the conferees that necessary funds would be available through private foundations, and that Justice Department personnel, including FBI teams, would provide all possible aid and cooperation. While many activists in CORE, SNCC, and SCLC were suspicious of Kennedy's proposal, seeing it as a calculated attempt to divert them from direct action, others had already concluded that direct action was no panacea, and that voter registration would provide a necessary basis for further progress.[31]

Thus the groundwork was laid for discrete approaches from the Taconic Foundation which, like the Kennedys, was anxious to avoid all publicity on the matter. Farmer himself was quietly contacted a short time after he left Parchman penitentiary. On July 28 he and top leaders of the Urban League, NAACP, SCLC, and SNCC met with SRC and Taconic officials, Burke Marshall, and Harris Wofford of the White House staff who "spoke of the concern of the President." Plans were unveiled to channel foundation monies for voter registration through the SRC, and the conferees were assured that the Justice Department would act to protect civil rights workers and those who attempted to register.* Farmer

* The nature of the Justice Department officials' assurances subsequently became a matter of considerable controversy. The civil rights organizations maintained that the Administration's representatives promised protection for activists and local citizens attempting to register. They charged treachery and deceit when the Justice Department failed to fulfill this promise. Government officials, however, have asserted that they had simply committed themselves to give all the aid and support they could. The Department, faced with FBI investigators who often exhibited hostility toward the civil rights workers, and with what it regarded as the limited federal intervention permitted by law, proved helpless in most cases of intimidation and violence. Undoubtedly, also, the political power of the southern bloc in Congress, which dictated the appointment of racist federal judges, increased the reluctance of the Justice Department to intervene. Documents in the Burke Marshall Papers indicate that the Civil Rights Division was aware from the beginning that reprisals from southern whites were likely, and that when these occurred, quick court action and the use of federal marshalls would be necessary. (See especially Burke Marshall to Deputy Attorney-General Byron White, July 14, 1961, Marshall Prs.) But time and again, the Division secured investigations, only to decide that the nature of the evidence and the provisions of federal law precluded any action. (See Burke Marshall to Leslie Dunbar, director of SRC, August 16, 1961, Marshall Prs, for typical instance. On problems with FBI investigations, see, e.g., Marshall to Robert Kennedy, June 5, 1964, Marshall Prs.) CORE's staff in Mississippi found that they could easily reach John Doar, Marshall's First Assistant in the Civil Rights Division, to discuss their problems; but while he was always sympathetic and tried to be helpful, there was little he could do (interview). The authors of the most comprehensive account of the VEP noted that only twice prior to the Voting Rights Act of 1965 did the Justice Department take legal action to protect civil rights workers. The Justice Department, on the other hand, pointed to the increased number of lawsuits it filed against county registrars and against sheriffs and other county officials who intimidated blacks attempting to register. Yet writing in 1964 to the mother of a northern youth participating in a Mississippi summer project, Burke Marshall admitted the existence of "a law enforcement problem to which there is no completely satisfactory answer." (Pat Watters and Reese Cleghorn, *Climbing Jacob's Ladder: The Arrival of Negroes in Southern*

committed himself to securing CORE's participation; emphasizing that direct action and voter registration were "not mutually exclusive," he pointed to CORE's past experience in South Carolina. At the September 1961 CORE Convention only a handful of the delegates were aware of these delicate negotiations and of the fact that Farmer had formally requested of SRC substantial grants for work in South Carolina and Florida. Nevertheless, at Farmer's recommendation the Convention approved initiation of a nonpartisan voter registration campaign in the South.[32] In effect, the delegates thus ratified what proved to be an exceedingly important policy decision by the national office. As the program's scope became evident, not all CORE people were eager to participate. Skepticism was especially prevalent among the field personnel, many of whom at first questioned devoting organizational resources to voter registration, and wanted the project to be only "an experiment for CORE." Like many SNCC workers they were exclusively committed to boycotts and demonstrations, and not until later were they able to comprehend McCain's insistence that in the oppressive southern states, voter registration, by confronting a hostile white majority, was indeed direct action. The matter was also debated at the CORE Council, where Anna Holden, in particular, maintained that voter registration was not "relevant to the problem of breaking down discrimination in the rural areas of the South." She reminded her colleagues that CORE was "a direct action group and not . . . a political organization."[33]

With Kennedy officials actively encouraging every step, the Voter Education Project finally got under way in April 1962. Designed to last two and a half years, it cost $870,000, nearly all of which came from the Taconic and Field Foundations and the Stern Family Fund. With less than 25 per cent of the southern blacks registered at VEP's start, the drive was expected to achieve substantial change in time for the 1964 presidential election.[34] The man chosen to administer this program was Wiley Branton, a skillful attorney from Pine Bluff, Arkansas, who had been counsel in the Little Rock school cases and one of CORE's lawyers for the Freedom Ride trials. Faced with the usual competition among civil rights groups, he abandoned most of his early efforts to encourage joint projects. Instead, he usually arranged to have an organization funded to operate registration drives in localities where it was already well established.

Politics [New York, 1967], 61–62; Marshall to Gilbert Harrison, Oct. 30, 1963, Marshall Prs; Marshall to Simeon Booker, March 12, 1964, Marshall Prs; Marshall to Mrs. Alice Lake, July 14, 1964, Marshall Prs.)

Thus CORE was awarded money for work in parts of Louisiana, Florida, Mississippi, and South Carolina.[35]

In Miami, Florida, where there was no white opposition, CORE in a whirlwind campaign led by Weldon Rougeau registered 3400 in the autumn of 1962. Elsewhere the going was tougher, especially in Louisiana, where CORE was assigned the Sixth Congressional District. There, blacks who attempted to vote faced intimidation as harsh as any place in the South, and only 600 were registered during the VEP's first year. In these resistant areas CORE's procedure was similar to the one used in South Carolina during the late 1950's. The first step was house-to-house "canvassing," explaining the importance of registering; next came instruction in filling out registration blanks. These training "clinics" were held at cooperative churches and whenever else possible at special offices opened by CORE. The third step involved accompanying applicants to the courthouse.[36]

In South Carolina the CORE chapter which McCain had organized at Sumter, initiated the new wave of voter registration activity in February 1962 under the leadership of McCain's old friend, Frank Robinson. In April Robinson started to service the surrounding counties, where he was able to secure assistance from friendly ministers. Sumter officials tried to discourage the blacks by changing registration dates and procedures. In Bishopsville the home of a registration worker was bombed. But Robinson, who had himself been forced out of his real estate and home-building business when sources of credit were shut off because of his registration activities, persisted. By the end of the summer CORE had registered nearly 1400 in Sumter and Lee counties. As the campaign expanded during the following months, harassment and delaying tactics were stepped up, especially at Kingstree, in Williamsburg County, where only 4 per cent of the eligible blacks were registered. The registrar there opened his office only one day a month and admitted one person at a time, subjecting him to such intimidating questions as, "Who sent you here?" and "Who do you work for?" CORE countered with "mass stand-ins" in March and April 1963. On April 1, 250 men and women lined the streets from 9 until 4:30, but only 11 were allowed to fill out applications. Protests lodged with the Justice Department were ignored. Nevertheless, at the end of the first year of the South Carolina project, CORE was able to announce that it had added 3700 voters to the rolls.[37]

The task in South Carolina was simple compared with the challenge faced in Louisiana and Mississippi. In Louisiana, four parishes had completely excluded blacks from voting since the turn of the century, while many rural parishes which had, beginning in the 1940's, allowed them to vote, purged thousands in 1956–57 after the Brown Decision. When CORE started its Sixth Congressional District project in 1962, registrars were putting up all the roadblocks they could. Like the Delta counties in Mississippi, the rural Felicianas represented extreme cases of the oppression of a black majority by a white minority.[38] Although between one-third and one-half of the eligible Negroes had been able to register in most of the district, total disfranchisement existed in West Feliciana, while in East Feliciana only 1 per cent of the Negroes were on the rolls.

With CORE having produced only modest results on its first Louisiana voter education project in Baton Rouge during the spring and summer of 1962, Branton diverted the organization from the city to the district's rural parishes. Consequently, responding to a request for help from W. W. Harleaux, an elementary school principal and president of the Iberville Parish Industrial Voters' League, CORE moved its state headquarters to the town of Plaquemine in October.[39] Ronnie Moore, who headed CORE's work in Louisiana, found himself located in a parish where only about a third of the eligible blacks were registered. Even worse was the fact that Negroes were completely powerless in the municipal elections because the ghetto in the "Back of Town" area had been gerrymandered outside of Plaquemine's boundaries. CORE workers found most blacks living in shacks lacking running water and indoor toilets, on unpaved and unlit streets, with sewage ditches running through the front yards. Poor though they were, Plaquemine's blacks raised $500 toward the purchase of an automobile for the CORE staff and spent $250 more for subsistence salaries. Working with adults like Harleaux and several young local Negroes (most notably twenty-three-year-old Spiver Gordon, who later became a valued CORE field secretary), in about a month Moore accompanied his first group of registrants to the courthouse.[40]

Moore soon branched out to the neighboring parishes of Pointe Coupee and St. Helena, and by March 1963 he had registered a total of 307 people. On the other hand, in the Felicianas, he was unable to counter the "apathy and fear" and convince any blacks to go to the courthouse.[41] Indeed as the work continued, even more subterfuges were used by the authorities. In Iberville Parish blacks who had high school diplomas were not permitted to register, and when Spiver Gordon, with three years of college education, appeared, the registrar closed the office early, slamming the door in Gordon's face. In April when CORE tried to register

138 in Pointe Coupee Parish, 92 were turned down, including three schoolteachers. At Tangipahoa Parish, a black high school graduate asked the registrar if he had passed the test, and was told, "You didn't flunk, you just got to come back some other time." Complaints sent to the Justice Department were ignored. Even a trip by McCain to confer with Burke Marshall in Washington proved unproductive. Finally Moore wrote McCain: "The Justice Department ain't doing a d--- thing. . . . If we don't stop the denials, voter registration in Louisiana will come to a standstill." [42] These difficulties notwithstanding, Moore refused to become discouraged, and when applying for renewal of the VEP grant, CORE ambitiously planned expansion into additional parishes.[43]

Difficult as voter registration was in Louisiana, it was conducted under even greater obstacles in Mississippi, where CORE closely coordinated its activity with SNCC staffers led by the legendary Robert Moses. As early as the summer of 1961 Moses, a former New York schoolteacher in his late twenties, had inaugurated a SNCC voter registration project at McComb that received considerable publicity when whites employed violence in an attempt to intimidate the activists. CORE had toyed with the idea of sending in field personnel to help, but drew back rather than risk incurring SNCC's resentment, and the organization's first involvement in Mississippi voter registration did not come until the spring of 1962, when it shared a three-month VEP grant in Jackson with SNCC and NAACP. Although hampered by a moribund CORE affiliate, lack of a car, and rivalries with the NAACP, David Dennis, who was CORE's representative on this project, doggedly persisted.[44]

VEP did not renew its subsidy for a CORE field secretary in Mississippi, but Dennis convinced CORE leaders to keep him in the state, where he became one of the principal architects of the coalition known as COFO—the Council of Federated Organizations, which handled VEP grants in Mississippi. Aaron Henry, a Clarksdale pharmacist and head of the state NAACP, was COFO's president; Robert Moses became director, while Dennis served on both the Steering and Financial committees.[45] Dennis worked in widely scattered parts of the state, attempting each week to participate in COFO projects at Hattiesburg and Laurel in the South, and at Cleveland and other communities in the North. He traveled five hundred to a thousand miles weekly, using buses and hitching rides. One field report in October 1962 noted, "During a day I interview around 20 families [canvassing for voter registration], visit leaders in a community, teach voter registration, or speak in assemblies." In Hattiesburg, despite intimidating calls and harassing arrests, the COFO clinics and door-to-door canvassing continued, and by October forty people had attempted to register. Dennis played a leading role in expanding the work to Laurel, where 250 were registered in six weeks, making it the most successful project in the state.[46]

In the heavily black Delta counties of northwest Mississippi, Dennis reported, "we were constantly harassed. . . . Some families who attempted to register were evicted from their homes in Sunflower County by landowners. Several homes were shot into in Ruleville, Mississippi, by hoodlums which resulted in the injury of several people. Threatening phone calls plagued the workers. . . . Some people were threatened by police officers if they attempted to register. Traffic violations against [civil rights] workers climbed steadily." Dennis was particularly concerned about the economic reprisals. Besides being thrown off plantations, many were removed from welfare rolls and denied federal surplus commodities. Organizing a Christmas relief campaign, he sent an appeal to CORE contacts which brought in five tons of food and clothing.[47] While such an emergency program was helpful, he recognized the long-range need for economic self-sufficiency. Impressed by the Gandhi methods and Eric Weinberger's example at Haywood County, Tennessee, Dennis in March 1963 organized eighteen women into the Ruleville Cooperative which made blankets, throw rugs, and aprons for sale in the North. This cooperative, located near Senator James Eastland's plantation, excited special interest in circles sympathetic to CORE and COFO.[48]

From June 1962 to April 1963 Dennis worked single-handedly for CORE in five Mississippi counties. On numerous occasions he was arrested for alleged traffic violations and other flimsy charges. Once, after leaving a night meeting at Clarksdale he was stopped by a highway patrolman. Refusing to say "sir," he was repeatedly cursed and threatened. "During the conversation . . . [the officer] made several gestures toward hitting me with his night stick. I always addressed him with a 'yes' or 'no,' and I told him that I was going to continue until he stopped calling me nigger." Fortunately Wiley Branton was in town and got Dennis out of jail the next morning. Yet imbued with the Gandhian philosophy, he saw positive possibilities in his arrests: "The last three times that I have been arrested I have also been able to accomplish something greater than anything that I can think of. For instance, when the officers arrest me they are always nasty and threatening, but I have been able to leave each time with all involved laughing and joking with each other. When I see

them on the street they wave and smile. We have been able to communicate in an understanding manner and to agree on things that would surprise the average person. If each time I am arrested I can accomplish
this, then I welcome an arrest every hour of the day." In a letter to
McCain, he revealed the courage and almost millenarian faith which sustained him, "They [the southern whites] are making their last stand,
Jim, and if we survive it we'll be seeing a new day soon. . . . New leadership is arising and it is not from the white collar man but from our
'down to earth' people. They are people in the rural areas and areas
where there is great pressure from the whites. The people are tired, Jim,
and they are beginning to stand up for what they want. It's what I have
been dreaming of." [49]

CORE's work in the South—like that of other civil rights
organizations—was stymied by the ambivalence of President Kennedy's
policy, which encouraged the voter education drive but, faced with southern power and the negative attitudes of FBI investigators, failed to protect civil rights activists and blacks attempting to register. In August
1962 Haley and representatives of other civil rights organizations tried
without success to convince the Attorney-General to intervene on behalf
of peaceful demonstrators. The civil rights workers' problems were further exacerbated by President Kennedy's appointment of racist federal
district court judges—like Harold Cox in Mississippi, a close friend of
Senator Eastland, the influential chairman of the Senate Judiciary Committee. At Rachlin's request, Eleanor Roosevelt personally took up
CORE's complaints with the Attorney-General and the President; the
former insisted that while there had been some disappointments, "we
make every effort to make sure that the new judges we have appointed
recognize their responsibility and are willing to do their duty," while the
President explained that "he recognized the situation," but "did not know
what could be done" in view of Eastland's power in the Senate. Marvin
Rich observed to Lillian Smith that Kennedy "has done ever so much
more than Eisenhower. . . . Yet, when measured against our expectations and against the awesome rush of events he has done little." From
the point of view of southern activists, this was an understatement. In
fact, their disillusionment with the executive branch, which they believed
had promised them protection in their voter registration work, was an
important cause of their later radicalization. In the summer of 1962 some
CORE leaders considered the possibility of staging "aggressive nonviolent
action" against the Kennedys, but the organization pulled back, fearing

that a militant demonstration in Washington might produce damaging repercussions from the White House. Thus CORE, like other civil rights organizations saw no way to force the President to stop appeasing southern congressmen and to start providing safeguards for civil rights activists and voter registrants.[50]

Accordingly the VEP brought only limited achievements in the deep South at the cost of enormous suffering. Nevertheless, a determined CORE decided that the program must continue and, in fact, be expanded.[51]

7

New Directions in the North

While the southern staff was becoming deeply involved in voter registration, the northern chapters were beginning a serious attack on the problems facing the black ghettos. The national office was largely responsible for the direction in which CORE moved, but, in contrast to the South, where staff provided most of the motivation, in the North much of the dynamism and initiative came from the chapters themselves. To move from supportive demonstrations for the southern campaigns into northern employment and housing projects was a natural progression. When Farmer informed the 1961 Convention that northern CORE groups could not survive merely "on sympathy with the South," he not only articulated the staff's views but with his usual sensitivity reflected the swell of sentiment in the chapters as well.

Yet ironically, as activities on behalf of the southern campaigns tapered off, the northern affiliates were at first often bewildered about how to apply direct action to employment and housing, and, despite the experimentation of the previous year, floundered as they contemplated the complications involved in developing projects for their own communities. Farmer himself conceded that CORE "has not yet devised enough techniques or used enough imagination" in fighting northern discrimination. The experience of Berkeley CORE in the spring of 1961 was not unusual. Feeling incompetent to combat employment discrimination, the chapter chairman asked the national office for "methods, procedures and examples of attack." "If our group is typical," he wrote, such material would be "invaluable to northern CORE groups." At the end of the year Genevieve Hughes found that the six-months-old San Francisco chapter "completely lacked an action orientation," and its meetings reminded her of NAACP branches. It had no employment project and the housing committee, far from being involved in direct action, was "working to get a housing ordinance passed." Even as late as 1962 some generally effective chapters sometimes lacked self-confidence as they surveyed the vast sea of northern discrimination. A Boston leader commented: "At the moment we have no employment project. We are in the process of making a decision to concern ourselves—the exact nature of our commitment is not yet clear. . . ." [1]

To provide chapter leaders with the experience and assurance necessary for handling local problems, National CORE sponsored training conferences and convention workshops. Genevieve Hughes led weekend institutes in California in December 1961, and the national office sponsored two ambitious summer programs—a housing workshop in Boston in 1961 and a housing-employment institute in Columbus in 1962. Because it reached more people, the weekend institute proved to be preferable, and accordingly a series of two-day regional conferences was held in the winter of 1962–63. [2] Mainly, however, the chapters developed techniques to fight northern racism through trial and error, displaying considerable originality in inventing appropriate tactics, and borrowing freely from each other. During 1961 and 1962 most of them expended more effort on housing campaigns than on any other activity. Job discrimination also had a high priority, and by 1963 it became the most popular target for CORE demonstrations. De facto segregated schools and police brutality were also objects of concern, but did not achieve salience until 1963 and 1964.

Prior to the latter half of 1963, CORE housing projects were practically all devoted to securing homes and apartments for middle-class blacks in white neighborhoods. CORE people in this period were thinking more in terms of breaking up the ghettos than in making them more livable. New York CORE placed its emphasis on interracial housing in order to "secure to the residents of New York City the benefit of shared living by families of varied background." As Farmer put it when launching a CORE campaign in Grand Rapids, "Our objective is not merely to provide more housing, but to provide integrated housing, an open city and an open society." Of course, CORE members knew that beyond constitutional rights lay racism's bitter legacy of inadequate schools, poverty, and rat-infested, overcrowded tenements, but they sought to attack racism's most overt symbol—segregation. Although in actual practice, few blacks had the money, inclination, and stamina to move into white neighborhoods, many projects did, nevertheless, aid individual middle-class Negroes in finding homes outside the ghettos.[3]

CORE chapters used a variety of tactics in their housing campaigns, not all of them direct action. Long Island CORE's earlier program of circulating lists of white homeowners willing to sell without regard to race was also adopted by Seattle, and both chapters placed a number of black families in previously all-white neighborhoods. More popular was "Operation Windowshop," which involved guiding groups of Negroes on tours of suburban developments to look at model homes. First tried by Philadelphia and Los Angeles CORE in the late spring of 1962, "Operation Windowshop" was widely borrowed across the country. Generally, chapters undertaking such projects found Negroes reluctant to move from the ghetto, a situation "lamentable but quite understandable," as a Syracuse CORE member expressed it. Philadelphia CORE's experience was typical: "Our CORE complainants were very few, just a handful and mostly people looking for a halfway decent row house on the fringes of the ghettto. We always suggest that they go and look at the new developments in the Northeast (which is 100% white), but only one or two have gone up there. We tried to conduct an 'Operation Windowshop' through the churches, NAACP, etc., but were totally unsuccessful. In about four Sundays, we got about five carloads of onlookers." [4]

Direct action in the form of picketing and sit-ins was not widely employed on housing projects prior to 1962. Brooklyn CORE, however, proved to be a major exception. Over the July 4, 1961, weekend members of the New York and Brooklyn chapters conducted a sit-in at a Brooklyn rental office, which ended when an apartment was obtained for Clarence Funnyé, who later became chairman of New York CORE. In the autumn Brooklyn CORE held victorious sit-ins at the Lefrak Realty Company and the Ira Management Corporation. At the former, a succession of demonstrations starting in October came to a climax several weeks later with an eighteen-hour sit-in. CORE had vowed to stay until the two black applicants received apartments. In the other instance a twenty-five-hour sit-in secured a Brooklyn apartment for a medical secretary. The following year Brooklyn CORE's most dramatic housing project involved a seventeen-day "dwell-in," with members bringing card tables, sleeping mats, and other furniture into an apartment at a development which refused to rent to a black IBM supervisor.[5]

With Brooklyn having set such an example, other affiliates followed. In January 1962, the University of Chicago CORE took up an issue that had continued to defy solution ever since CORE's founders had established their Fellowship House twenty years before. Charging the University with maintaining a discriminatory off-campus housing list and barring Negroes from apartment buildings it owned, the student activists conducted a two-week campaign, demonstrating daily at the University's real estate office—where over thirty arrests occurred—and sitting-in round-the-clock outside the president's chambers. The campaign ended when the University administration threatened to suspend the students while simultaneously appointing a faculty committee to study the issue. Although it was some time before the committee made its report and the University halted the discrimination, the chapter quite properly took pride in the change that ultimately resulted.[6] The following summer Philadelphia CORE staged a sit-in at a new housing development and, as a result of subsequent negotiations, obtained an antidiscrimination agreement with the home builders association. In the course of the next seven months Newark CORE picketed a suburban complex which had turned down a Negro applicant; the Washington affiliate picketed both the offices of Morris Cafritz, a leading developer in the nation's capital, and the homes of two District of Columbia commissioners demanding they issue an order barring housing discrimination; the Bergen County, New Jersey, chapter held a dwell-in with a black family who had been similarly rejected, and Syracuse CORE engaged in a sit-in that secured an apartment for two African students.[7]

Meanwhile the Ann Arbor, Michigan, affiliate was conducting a sustained campaign against a tract known as Pittsfield Village, whose manager refused to rent to an interracial couple. Other groups in town were pressing for a municipal fair-housing ordinance, but CORE, convinced that such legislation would come only after long delays, believed that direct action was required. Under the leadership of Anna Holden, the predominantly white chapter created the Ann Arbor Fair Housing Association (AAFHA) in order to secure substantial support from the black community. Commencing in January, AAFHA sponsored eight months of demonstrations—daily picketing, Sunday marches through Pittsfield Village, and mass protests at the company's Detroit headquarters. With

sympathetic politicians adding to the pressure, the first black family finally moved into Pittsfield Village in August 1962. CORE, which officially
merged with the AAFHA that autumn, continued in its efforts. By the
spring of 1963 three Negro families were living in Pittsfield Village, and
another had moved into the Orchard Hills subdivision.[8]

The western chapters were slower than the eastern ones in utilizing direct action on housing projects. Only occasionally, notably in Denver,
had instances of picketing occurred during 1961, and Genevieve Hughes,
after conducting a housing institute for California groups at the end of
the year, concluded that most of them were "rather timid about sit-ins.
. . . The West Coast is two years behind the East Coast in the use of direct action in housing." A few months later the hitherto lethargic Los
Angeles affiliate became the first CORE chapter in the West to engage in
a housing sit-in, with a demonstration at a development in Monterey
Park, where a black physicist was denied a $24,000 home. This campaign,
which ended successfully after nearly five weeks, was the forerunner of
other massive suburban housing sit-ins sponsored by Los Angeles CORE
that summer and autumn, and for more than a year after. At a development in Wilmington, where forty were arrested in the fall of 1962,
CORE members conducted a dwell-in lasting several days, and after
being removed by police, returned to hold a "dwell-out." Sitting with arms
and legs interlocked in passive resistance, they refused to cooperate with
law officers, who were forced to "unscramble" them and drag them limp
to the paddy wagon. The chapter's most ambitious project was directed
against the prominent suburban developer, Don Wilson. This campaign
in which 250 arrests were made lasted for over eighteen months until it finally petered out in late 1963.[9]

Only in rare instances did chapters involve themselves with the housing needs of the black poor. During the winter of 1961–62, New Haven
CORE, in a particularly dramatic campaign to help lower-class blacks
uprooted by urban renewal, introduced a new technique, the "sit-out."
This tactic, which originally called for slumdwellers to obstruct traffic by
sitting-in the street, was first proposed at a meeting of the New Haven
NAACP. When several branch officials objected, Blyden Jackson, a
twenty-seven-year-old black factory worker and former Marine drill in-
structor, withdrew with his supporters and founded New Haven CORE.
This new chapter, though confining its demonstrations to sitting on the
curbs without blocking traffic, held two sit-outs involving hundreds of
blacks in October and November 1961, to back up their demand for a

fair-housing ordinance which they expected would make decent dwellings available to slumdwellers. After the bill was defeated the following February, CORE members staged a sit-in at City Hall and blocked the corridor until police removed them. In another new departure, New York University CORE in the spring of 1963 turned to helping slumdwellers secure correction of housing code violations. Cooperating with the East Side Tenants Council, CORE filed complaints with the city and began picketing slumlords to force them to repair their buildings. Neither the activities of New York University CORE nor the techniques employed by the flamboyant, charismatic Jackson brought the changes sought. But the demonstrations were significant because they prefigured both an escalation of tactics and CORE's involvement with the rent strike movement in 1963–64.[10]

As CORE's thrust grew more militant in the two years following the Freedom Ride, employment projects changed in several respects. At first the principal targets were retail stores, but by the spring of 1963 CORE chapters were beginning to attack banks, the construction trades, and major consumer-goods manufacturers. While picketing and the boycott were the forms of direct-action universally employed, as early as the summer of 1962 the use of more extreme tactics, bordering on civil disobedience, appeared. Finally, a marked evolution in CORE's demands occurred. There was an escalation in the number of jobs demanded, and a shift from seeking nondiscriminatory practices to requiring agreements which guaranteed "compensatory" or preferential employment policies.

At first CORE groups, put off by employers who professed an inability to locate qualified blacks, frequently assumed the burden of seeking applicants. In 1961 Berkeley CORE advertised in the press for Negroes willing to fight discrimination. New Haven CORE, having negotiated with Sealtest, Wonder Bread, and other companies, made the rounds of school placement directors.[11] In one of the most successful CORE employment campaigns conducted prior to 1963, the Philadelphia affiliate actually did recruit people for the jobs. This chapter, which had been revived when the national office dispatched two field secretaries to the city at the end of 1960, undertook as its first project an attack upon the Horn & Hardart restaurant chain. Vigorous CORE picketing produced a fair hiring agreement in April 1961. By November, however, the chain had obtained only three black waitresses and one cashier, and CORE resumed picketing. The following January a sit-in at the company's executive office finally brought its officials to the negotiating table. When the management, who agreed to train six Negroes as waitresses and hire three more black cashiers, claimed that it could not find qualified individuals, CORE conducted a search, and by November 1962 the company had hired thirty-two black waitresses and five cashiers.[12] Philadelphia was clearly exceptional, however, and as CORE grew more militant, furnishing black applicants became increasingly unacceptable. The question was debated at the 1962 Convention, and soon the practice virtually ceased.

Prior to 1963, CORE chapters, possessed of limited power, generally made what in retrospect seem like minimal demands; and the results were highly mixed, with many failures and token victories as well as some significant successes. Not one of New York CORE's employment projects brought worthwhile gains. For example, the negotiations with the *Daily News* resulted in only vague promises. In East St. Louis, the small CORE chapter felt powerless to use direct action; instead, with several Baptist ministers it spent many disappointing months in negotiations with ten major employers that brought a total of five jobs. In Los Angeles, CORE also worked through coalitions. The picketing and boycotting of a beer company over several months in 1961 and 1962 brought the hiring of three black driver salesmen; and nearly a year of picketing the Greyhound Bus Terminal finally led to the employment of two Negro bus drivers in August 1962. Berkeley CORE negotiated for months with Hinks Department Store, whose manager adamantly refused to employ even one black salesperson. Finally in December 1961 the chapter resorted to picketing and boycotting, and in a few days Hinks hired two Negroes. The Washington chapter, by threatening boycotts, obtained promises of nondiscriminatory hiring in 1962 from several downtown clothing stores, a major drug store chain, and the District of Columbia Transit Company. Its claim to a significant victory in the transit case, however, was challenged by other black organizations because the agreement provided no specific guarantees. Vague promises which CORE and other groups obtained from the Potomac Electric Power Company toward the end of the year were also unsatisfactory, and CORE chapter chairman Julius Hobson announced that the blacks refused to accept it. But with few people willing to man the picket lines, the project was allowed to lapse.

The Boston affiliate, having negotiated with Sears and Trailways in 1961, decided that its limited resources permitted direct action only against the bus company. For four months the chapter picketed the terminal before obvious defeat in early 1962 forced suspension of the campaign. Ironically, several weeks later Trailways hired its first black agent, though not the drivers which had been demanded. The experience was so discouraging that Boston CORE ventured gingerly into further job projects early the following year, obtaining one position at Sears and the promise of policy change at Filene's Department Store. Other affiliates, while proudly reporting their successes, were, like Boston, apologetic because "We have been satisfied too long with token employment." Detroit CORE, which helped a few blacks secure jobs and promotions at the Detroit *Free Press* in late 1962, declared, "While we realize this is a small number . . . it is significant because it indicates an active implementation of their fair employment policy." And when, in early 1963, several months of negotiations brought a handful of retail positions at three establishments, the chapter welcomed this "step in the right direction" because it compared favorably with the previous year's even more miniscule job victories.[13]

Retail stores, particularly chain supermarkets which had numerous ghetto outlets but hired few blacks, became natural targets because, in Seattle CORE's words, of their "vulnerability . . . to economic pressure," [14] and some of CORE's most active chapters concentrated on such firms. The Seattle chapter achieved substantial success with this type of employer, but elsewhere CORE's experience showed only too well how limited was its power to make more than a dent in racist employment policies, particularly when—as in Denver, St. Louis, and Columbus—their efforts were undercut by rivalries with other civil rights organizations.

The Seattle and Denver affiliates conducted campaigns against both the Safeway grocery chain and downtown retail stores. But where Seattle CORE maximized its small resources by uniting with the NAACP and the Baptist Ministerial Alliance, Denver CORE lacked such support and even incurred the hostility of the local black newspaper. In October 1961, the Seattle coalition, pushed by CORE, launched a boycott and picketing campaign that won five positions at Safeway—the first job victory of a West Coast chapter. Given the limited employment achievements of the chapters around the country, Seattle CORE considered the project a highly successful one, and Genevieve Hughes enthusiastically described the campaign as "a real model of CORE action." In contrast, Denver CORE was at first fearful of attacking a national corporation like Safeway. Then, enouraged by winning three jobs from a local food chain in the spring of 1962 and prodded by Genevieve Hughes, they informed Safeway that since 5 per cent of its business came from blacks, a similar percentage of its employees should be black. But fearing that it had little support, Denver CORE delayed picketing, and by June, when it finally decided to demonstrate, the demands had been scaled down to five jobs "as a token of good faith." Rich now warned against accepting tokenism, for in the onrush of events what had looked like an exciting victory in Seattle in November 1961, appeared inconsequential eight months later. But without help from the black press and the NAACP, Denver CORE reluctantly settled for the five openings.[15] In the campaigns which followed, the contrast between the two chapters became accentuated. Denver picketed a downtown department store and won three sales positions. Seattle CORE, continuing to enjoy excellent rapport with local black leaders, exhibited greater confidence and ambition. Over the course of eleven months of negotiations, the chapter obtained twenty jobs at J. C. Penney, and by the end of 1962 had opened another forty positions in chain supermarkets.[16]

In St. Louis and Columbus, where both CORE chapters focused their efforts on Kroger Supermarkets, conflict with the local NAACP produced a situation even worse than Denver's. St. Louis CORE, after passage of the city's public accommodations law in 1961, made employment its primary concern, and in June 1962 began picketing the Kroger offices. Three weeks later four black butchers were hired, and more skilled jobs were promised. But after the company reneged, St. Louis CORE demanded a long-range preferential hiring policy so that at least 15 per cent of the employees in all departments would eventually be black. In September a picket line was resumed with support from the St. Louis NAACP Youth Council and from Alderman William Clay's 26th Ward Democratic organization. At one point the picketing was briefly interrupted when Clay and Lucian Richards, St. Louis CORE chairman, were arrested while distributing leaflets. The project collapsed in December when Kroger made a private agreement with the adult NAACP branch and other local black leaders. Meanwhile in Columbus, where CORE had begun picketing Kroger's in September, the NAACP had also reached a separate, unilateral understanding with the company. Rich was infuriated. "If . . . the NAACP will sell out then there is little you can do unless you want to really blast them," he fumed impotently. Since neither chapter wished to engage in an open fight with other black protest leaders, both reluctantly dropped the Kroger project. In St. Louis, the defeat adversely affected CORE's morale: newer members, searching for scapegoats, criticized "old fogey conservatives" like Marian and Charles

Oldham, and because of the dissension expressed at chapter meetings some older members ceased attending.[17]

As the public accommodations issue began to recede in the South, CORE groups in New Orleans, Kentucky, and North Carolina started turning their attention to employment problems. Here also results varied. In 1962, CORE chapters in Covington, Kentucky, and Charleston, West Virginia, secured a few jobs at downtown stores, while the Lexington, Kentucky, affiliate persuaded the local transit company to hire a black bus driver.[18] Louisville CORE, helped by the presence of two field secretaries, mounted a highly effective boycott against Sealtest and Coca Cola. However, as a result of being undermined by Bishop Tucker's enemies in the Urban League and NAACP, and on the local black newspaper, in June 1962, ten weeks after the drive had started, the boycott was at a standstill and the CORE chapter was "racked with conflicts" from which it never recovered. In New Orleans the chapter participated in a coalition that conducted a boycott a short time before Easter 1963 that brought an agreement to hire forty-five blacks in thirty-eight downtown stores. About the same time there was an equally impressive boycott in the smaller city of Durham against sixteen stores which refused to place Negroes in sales positions. Within three weeks, fifteen had been hired.[19]

Meanwhile National CORE, paralleling tendencies in the chapters, debated the issue of preferential hiring. When the February 1962 Council meeting discussed the advisability of insisting that employers hire a specific percentage of blacks, several members attacked the idea as discrimination in reverse which amounted to a quota system. By the end of the year, however, CORE leaders had overwhelmingly endorsed the principle, and a set of preferential employment guidelines was drawn up for the staff and chapters. Observing that "traditionally, many CORE groups have taken a 'soft' approach to management," this document urged the chapters to make "very specific demands which far exceed tokenism," and to insist that "it is management's responsibility to locate, select, train—if necessary—and hire nonwhite employees." Amplifying upon the subject in a letter to a Denver CORE leader, Carey explained, "CORE has begun recently to change its 'line' on the national level. Heretofore, we used to talk simply of merit employment, i.e., hiring the best qualified person for the job regardless of race. Now, National CORE is talking in terms of 'compensatory' hiring. We are approaching employers with the proposition that they have effectively excluded Negroes from their work force for a long time and that they now have a responsibility and obligation to make up for their past sins." For the national office the turning point came in December 1962 when it sponsored a New York area boycott of the Sealtest Dairy Company and won a preferential hiring agreement. Although blacks comprised only about 1 per cent of Sealtest's 1400 employees, the company refused to consider CORE's compensatory demands. As Lincoln Lynch, Long Island CORE's black chairman and a member of the negotiating committee, asserted, "We are trying to drive home to all businesses that the negative policies of yesterday and even the positive policies of yesterday are not going to survive." National CORE's two-month boycott, conducted with the help of local college students and the New York metropolitan area chapters, ended when Sealtest promised to hire ten blacks immediately and give "initial exclusive priority to all job openings, except those of contractual obligations during 1963 to Negroes and Spanish-Americans." [20]

While national's stance toward employers was thus becoming more militant, a few chapters were prefiguring important future changes in the style of job campaigns. The range of targets began to broaden. St. Louis and especially Long Island CORE attacked major banking institutions. In the early part of 1962, after surveying St. Louis's leading financial institutions and finding only six blacks in nonmenial jobs, the local CORE affiliate by threatening direct action obtained the first teller position for a Negro. A year later, following the national office's initiative in the Sealtest campaign, Long Island CORE negotiated preferential hiring commitments at two banks. According to the agreement with Meadowbrook National Bank, thirty blacks and Puerto Ricans would be hired within four months, and 50 per cent of future openings would be reserved for them. Another CORE precedent was established in April 1963 when the Philadelphia affiliate took up the fight against discrimination in the powerful building trades unions. In the opening of the campaign, the chapter protested job exclusion in the construction of a municipal office building by picketing Mayor James Tate's home and twice sitting-in at his City Hall reception room. As a result, in early May Tate temporarily halted work on the building.[21] Tactically, the most significant departure in employment campaigns was made by Brooklyn CORE, which in its Ebinger Bakery project adopted techniques that seemed radical at the time. The several-month-old drive came to a climax when seven Brooklyn CORE members were arrested in August 1962 for blocking trucks at the company's garage. Some of them went limp and had to be carried by the police, apparently marking the first time a CORE affiliate had used this technique since Wally Nelson had demonstrated at Coney Island Amusement Park in Cincinnati a decade before. Brooklyn CORE proudly regarded the thirteen jobs it obtained at Ebinger's as an important breakthrough.[22]

De facto segregation of black children in inferior, overcrowded schools was not a major focus of attack during the two years following the Freedom Rides, even though the National CORE conventions in this period discussed the subject and Farmer strongly urged the 1962 conclave to apply direct-action tactics to this problem.[23] While some chapters, as in Philadelphia and Los Angeles, confined their protests to giving testimony at school board hearings,[24] several CORE affiliates did dramatize the issue through direct action. Beginning in 1960 Chicago CORE picketed the school board periodically, urging free bus transportation from overcrowded ghetto schools to underutilized white ones instead of building new jim crow schools. When in the autumn of 1962 the Chicago school board purchased mobile classrooms in ghetto areas, southside CORE picketed the site where they were being erected. Across the country in the Bay area, the Oakland and Berkeley CORE chapters also picketed their boards of education when school opened in September 1962.[25]

To deal with school board recalcitrance, a few chapters improvised other techniques. In February 1962 Bergen County, New Jersey, CORE held an all-night sit-in at the Englewood City Hall which resulted in the arrests of eleven, including three National CORE staff members: Norman Hill, his wife Velma, and Gordon Carey. The following August chairman Lincoln Lynch and two other Long Island CORE members dramatized an NAACP de facto school segregation case by staging an all-night vigil in the superintendent's office. And the next month members of the San Francisco affiliate sat-in at the Board of Education overnight.[26] Moreover, a few chapters experimented with boycotts. In September 1962 Brooklyn CORE, in collaboration with Reverend Milton Galamison's Parents Workshop for Equality in New York City Schools, led a small group who withdrew their children from black schools and held a twenty-six-hour sit-in at the Board of Education, thus successfully pressing officials to find vacancies for the youngsters in predominantly white schools. A short time afterward, Mr. and Mrs. Jerome Bibuld, an interracial couple who were members of Brooklyn CORE, kept their children out of a nearly all-black school for several months. In February 1963, after the Bibulds were convicted of violating the compulsory attendance law, they and a half dozen other chapter members staged a week-long round-the-clock sit-in at the Board of Education, which resulted in the transfer of their children. The Bergen County, New Jersey, and Syracuse, New York, affiliates went even further. Securing the support of other local civil rights organizations, both chapters led boycotts against jim crow elementary schools in September 1962. In Syracuse, the one-day boycott brought a school board commitment to study the problem, and more than a year later the two predominantly black schools were closed. In Englewood, where the three-day boycott of the Lincoln school produced no action from the Board, CORE called a second boycott in February 1963, and a few months later Lincoln ended its career as an all-black institution. Thus, although school segregation had been a central issue for only a handful of chapters, CORE had pioneered in tactics that would involve hundreds of thousands of children in the great school boycotts of 1963 and 1964.[27]

Only a few chapters took up the question of police brutality. The problem was spotlighted for a brief time by widely publicized attacks upon blacks by Jackson, Mississippi, police dogs during the summer of 1961. The Rochester CORE and local NAACP Youth Council jointly sponsored a demonstration to protest intimidation by the canine patrol in their city; and in September, delegates at the 1961 CORE Convention, held in Washington picketed a police station over the same issue. A year later, East St. Louis CORE demonstrated at police headquarters protesting brutality and jail segregation. By then some CORE leaders had begun to view police brutality as a grievance that could be used to rally lower-class blacks to CORE. Thus in November 1962, Eugene Tournour, a white midwestern field secretary, upon hearing of a case in which patrolmen had beaten a fifteen-year-old youth, urged the Kansas City chapter to organize a protest which would publicize police mistreatment and mobilize the black community behind CORE. The following month, second National Vice-Chairman Earl Walter similarly told the NAC that an important lesson could be learned by recalling how Los Angeles blacks had rallied to the Black Muslims after several of their members had been shot by the police earlier in the year. Walter declared that because police brutality aroused such deep resentment, it "can be used to bring CORE closer to the Negro community." But neither the CORE chapters nor the national office made the issue salient at this time.[28]

As CORE thus developed techniques and programs to attack the problems of blacks in the North, it was simultaneously being propelled toward a greater concern with working-class Negroes and the black poor.

The employment campaigns benefited many individuals who had no more than a high school education; a few of the housing projects were directed toward helping working-class blacks; and the attack on defacto segregated schools was an attempt to alleviate the inferior education available to the slumdwellers. CORE also hoped that these efforts would attract increasing numbers of working-class people to the organization. There was, in fact, considerable anxiety over what was regarded as CORE's inadequacy in relating to the black community, both because of the organization's disproportionately white membership and the predominantly middle-class status of people, whether white or black, who were attracted to CORE.

In racial composition there was a sharp contrast between the chapters in the South, where CORE staff no longer seriously attempted to recruit white members, and those in the North and West, which were typically predominantly white, and as in Berkeley CORE, "not solid in the Negro community." In 1961 the preponderance of whites in the North was still so marked that Carey reassured a concerned member, "You should not be disturbed about the apathy of the Negro community in participation in CORE. This is a problem that every group faces throughout the North. It is unfortunate; it is difficult to deal with . . . but it is always possible to develop an interracial group in spite of this." A black undergraduate who belonged to Columbus CORE wrote the Ohio State University campus newspaper that he was "bitter" because so few of his fellow Negro students would turn out for a CORE rally, and because the CORE picket line at the Rollerland Skating Rink "consists largely, if not completely, of caucasians."

The difficulty persisted. Early in 1962 a young white professor, recently fired from the University of Missouri because of his CORE work, was "very discouraged" because so few Negroes had joined the local chapter. Chicago Southside CORE's black chairman lamented, "We have not had the support we hoped for from the community. . . . We are continually looking for some new approach to this problem but at this point we really have not met with too much success." As late as the spring of 1963 all except two demonstrators on a Chicago CORE picket line were whites. At that time, even the highly effective Boston chapter was still overwhelmingly white.[29]

There were also widespread misgivings about the bourgeois character of most of the chapters. For example, in early 1962 a field secretary described the black members of Kansas City, Missouri, CORE, who actually formed a slight majority of the affiliate, as "out of touch" with the Negro ghetto. In January, the newly formed New York Metropolitan Area Coordinating Council of CORE chapters overwhelmingly passed a motion offered by Lincoln Lynch that the organization must make itself "more attractive to 'rank and file' Negroes." A 1962 Convention workshop resolved that "CORE is primarily middle-class, and to broaden our base we must begin to concentrate on the needs of the working class." At the time CORE was indeed "middle class," although on the whole the Negroes were not as economically secure or had as much formal education as the whites. A careful student of CORE in this period, Inge Powell Bell, found that the Negroes she queried were "highly mobile." Typically "children of semi-skilled or unskilled working-class fathers," they "had risen to professional or clerical jobs." She noted that whites, on the other hand, generally came from upper-middle-class backgrounds. They were mostly from the "liberal intelligentsia," and disproportionately Jewish— one-third of her white respondents were of Jewish ancestry. Our own interviews with national and chapter leaders provide substantial support for her conclusions. Of course the make up of the membership varied widely. The Negro office holders in Brooklyn CORE in the fall of 1962, all of them in their thirties and early forties, occupationally ranged from a mailman and a bus driver to a university professor. Some affiliates, such as Boston and Seattle, numbered few Jews among their white activists. Southern black members were generally poorer and had less formal education than those in the North. The socio-economic background of CORE people was not too different from that of active NAACP members, although CORE ranks included practically no black clergymen and few who were active in black churches and lodges. In fact, as one prominent northeastern CORE leader put it, "Unlike the NAACP, you won't find CORE people in the churches." But what chiefly distinguished CORE members from those involved in other racial advancement organizations was their desire to engage in direct action. Many of them had been active previously in the NAACP, but found their local branches slow-moving. For example, Rochester CORE's first chairman, Flora Harris, was a white social worker who had been vice-president of the local NAACP branch, and in Newark, CORE's chairman Robert Curvin was a black social worker who had been president of the Rutgers University NAACP chapter.[30]

Several factors accounted for CORE's difficulties in securing support within the black community, particularly from "grass-roots people." Although CORE's militance elicited considerable admiration, few were willing to risk arrest on demonstrations. CORE's highly educated and largely white membership projected an image that discouraged many blacks from joining. Some in CORE even worried that interracial dating alienated potential black members. The fact that so many of the chapters met outside the ghetto only reinforced the impression that CORE lacked ties to the black community. For example, Bergen County CORE met at the Ethical Culture Building in Teaneck; Rochester CORE met at the First Universalist Church; and the Ann Arbor and Kansas City, Missouri, affiliates met at Friends Meeting Houses. Furthermore, in some cities CORE had a radical reputation that offended many blacks. Occasionally, as in Lexington, Kentucky, where the black chairman desired the resignations of white pacifists who "frightened" the community by propagandizing for nonpayment of income taxes, activities of white radicals were at the root of the problem. More frequently the alienation stemmed from the very militance of CORE's style. In Kansas City some Negroes charged the affiliate with irresponsibility for calling demonstrations at the drop of a hat and acting as if militant tactics were more important than securing effective change. In many towns, the more conservative black leaders regarded CORE people as "rabble-rousers." [31] Probably the most important reason for CORE's difficulties in sinking roots in the Negro community was the entrenched position of established—and from CORE's point of view, often conservative—organizations and leaders, particularly the NAACP and the black politicians. The NAACP not only had a distinguished reputation among most blacks for militant advocacy of Negro rights, but it enjoyed close ties with religious and fraternal organizations and, in some cases, black politicians as well. Lacking these advantages, CORE often found it difficult to make much headway among blacks.

Various CORE policies existed to secure greater participation from the Negro community in general and from "grass-roots people" in particular. As CORE stepped up its employment campaigns in the North, it attracted increasing numbers of working-class blacks. The fact that most of the chapter chairmen were black was largely due to the desire to create an image that would encourage Negro participation. As one Los Angeles CORE member recalled, "There was the feeling that when we presented our face to the public it should always be a black face." [32] In the Northeast, by 1962, except for Boston and Columbus, every important chapter had a black chairman—for example, Blyden Jackson in New Haven, Shirley Lacey in Englewood, New Jersey; Oliver Leeds in Brooklyn; Gladys

Harrington in New York; Lincoln Lynch on Long Island; Robert Curvin
in Newark; Louis Smith in Philadelphia; Arthur Evans in Cleveland;
Walter Carter in Baltimore; Julius Hobson in Washington; and George
Wiley in Syracuse. There and on the West Coast many chapters which
were overwhelmingly white had black chairmen: Harold Brown in San
Diego, which was nearly two-thirds white; Earl Walter in Los Angeles,
which was three-fourths white; and Wilfred Ussery in San Francisco
CORE, which was four-fifths white. Seattle CORE, with the exception of
only one year, had black chairmen throughout its history. Nearly all of
these leaders were middle-class professionals. Curvin, Carter, Walter, and
Harrington were social workers, Ussery was an architectural designer,
Lynch a flight operations officer at British Overseas Airways, Brown a
school teacher, Hobson a federal civil service employee, and Wiley a
chemistry professor. A few were employed in nonprofessional occupations: Louis Smith was a vacuum cleaner salesman, Leeds a proofreader,
Jackson a skilled factory worker and Woody Faddis, the chairman of
Oakland, California, CORE, was a janitor. Finally some chapters inaugurated active programs of recruiting in the black ghettos. Many members
sought speaking engagements in black churches and clubs. A number
moved their meeting places to Negro neighborhoods, or opened storefront offices in slum areas; some did both. Seattle CORE met from the
beginning at the black YMCA; by 1961 Boston and New York were meeting in the ghettos. In New York CORE, some were opposed to opening a
Harlem office in September 1961 because "if we are trying to break down
the walls of the ghetto, we should not establish ourselves in its heart."
But the majority felt differently; as the newly hired executive-secretary of
the chapter put it, "We are desperately trying to get more Negroes involved. That's why we moved to Harlem. Much of the program has been
aimed toward the bourgeois, the educated. We're not going to get off the
ground that way." [33] In 1962 Philadelphia, San Francisco, and other
chapters moved to the "heart of the Negro community." In March New
Haven opened a storefront office, and later in the year the Ann Arbor affiliate moved from the Friends Center to the Laborers' local meeting hall
to "strengthen ties with the Negro community." In early 1963 the Cleveland chapter began meeting at a church in the Hough area, and the St.
Louis and Syracuse chapters secured ghetto headquarters. While others
did not move their meeting places until 1964, and a few not until 1965,
by the spring of 1963 the trend was well under way.[34]

Over the months the northern and western chapters recruited more black members. Although most of them possessed a white majority, as early as 1962 there were, in addition to the previously all-black East St. Louis CORE, two overwhelmingly Negro groups outside the South: the Oakland, California, affiliate and the one recently organized in Cleveland. From its beginning in 1960, the Brooklyn chapter had been about half black. A few others, like Philadelphia, were shifting from a white to a black majority. In less than three years the Philadelphia chapter underwent an evolution in membership characteristics that took as long as a decade in other chapters. Revived at the end of 1960 under the leadership of a black pacifist school teacher, Ruth McIntosh, this predominantly white chapter quickly underwent a cleavage between its "pacifist" wing and an "actionist" wing critical of "too much philosophizing" at the expense of moving at once into concrete projects. The pacifists were pushed to the sidelines and the actionists, who were largely ADA- and trade-union-oriented whites, vigorously sought Negro working-class members. With the election of Louis Smith as chairman in 1962, the affiliate became working class both in membership and in orientation. St. Louis had also succeeded in building a membership that was majority black by 1962. Elsewhere, most of the chapters were still unhappy over their inability to attract grass-roots blacks. A Syracuse CORE leader noted, "In our few recruiting attempts which involved canvassing the 'ward' and speaking in several churches, we have been notoriously unsuccessful. Perhaps our orientation was wrong. . . . We are attempting to revolutionize a staunchly Republican city . . . where the Negro leadership itself has not demonstrated much dynamism." [35] While the proportion of working-class people gradually rose in the period after the Freedom Ride, only a few chapters recruited them in significant numbers—Philadelphia, Oakland, New Haven, and Brooklyn.

Among the chapters Brooklyn CORE was in the vanguard of those developing projects to help the black poor, while at the national office assistant program director Norman Hill was the individual most responsible for pushing the organization to address itself to their plight. Deeply concerned with the problems of the Bedford-Stuyvesant area, Brooklyn CORE fought not only for employment and school integration but also for adequate garbage collection, enforcement of health and sanitary codes, and court action against slumlords. Fifteen chapter members were arrested picketing Beth-El Hospital in support of striking black and Puerto Rican workers during June 1962. The following September the affiliate held "Operation Cleansweep," in which forty persons dumped garbage on the steps of Brooklyn Borough Hall to dramatize the dirty streets and infrequent trash pickups. Hill meanwhile convinced the NAC Steering Committee to create task force projects in the ghettos of Bedford-Stuyvesant and Newark during the summer of 1963. Conducted with the cooperation of the Brooklyn and Newark chapters, they were "an attempt to develop a grass-roots approach toward the elimination of the everyday reality of discrimination in the ghetto, an effort to involve people where they are in militant, direct nonviolent action on their concrete problems." Hill believed that the crucial question to ask about any proposed CORE program was, does it encourage "an approach which leads to more roots in the Negro community, which begins to make civil rights a reality for the great bulk of Negroes who are working-class." [36] There were, it should be emphasized, important differences between Hill and the officers of Brooklyn CORE, differences that would eventually make them bitter enemies. Hill was a Socialist, thoroughly wedded to CORE's traditions of interracialism and nonviolence. Brooklyn CORE by this time was a highly activist mix of black exrevolutionary Marxists from the 1930's and 1940's, black slum youth, and young white militants. They were less firmly committed than Hill to nonviolence or the Rules for Action, and they would soon be inclining toward black separatism. Yet in key respects—their support for militant, innovative tactics, and their deep commitment to involving CORE with the problems of the slumdwellers—Hill's vision and Brooklyn CORE's actions bore striking resemblances to each other.

In their differences as well as their similarities, the views of Hill and the Brooklyn CORE leaders were symptomatic of a whole series of fundamental changes taking place in CORE ideology and strategy—changes that involved not only a stress on the grievances of the black poor, but also an escalation of tactics, the beginnings of an erosion in the commitment to nonviolence, and a tendency toward black separatism. These trends were themselves the fruit of several developments—both internal and external to the organization. The rapidly rising expectations that followed the sit-ins and freedom rides produced an impatience with the rate of social change. At the same time, outside of CORE there were the well-publicized activities of the Black Muslims, combining an ideology of nationalism with a rhetoric of violence. Finally, CORE's rapid expansion brought an influx of new members, many of them black, unfamiliar with CORE's traditions but attracted by its militance.

It should be pointed out that these developments in CORE were confined almost entirely to the North. Southern blacks had experienced demonstrable progress. Less secularized than the inhabitants of the Northern ghettos they were still deeply influenced by the Christian world view epitomized by Martin Luther King. Only in New Orleans did the CORE chapter experience the ideological changes that were beginning to appear in the North.

Demonstrations in this period generally retained their previous style. Only rarely were picket lines or sit-ins disorderly, and these were quickly disavowed by National CORE. After Farmer heard about the boisterous foot-stamping accompanying the Englewood school board sit-in of February 1962, he declared, "In my opinion it violated CORE discipline and the principle of nonviolent direct action. . . . Under no conditions would we approve of such a tactic. We would approve of a sit-in—quiet, peaceful, and orderly, but not a noisy disruption of the proceedings." Yet all over the country there was an increasing tendency to shortcut some Rules for Action—to reduce the period of negotiations to a minimum and turn to demonstrations quickly. A long-time member of Baltimore CORE wrote to Farmer early in 1962 deploring the chapter's "strong leanings" toward imitating a local student group's style of "practically all action and very little negotiation." [37] CORE people were becoming impatient with extended conferences; they were now committed to eliminating discrimination quickly, not to reconciling the discriminator.[38] A tone of disrespect often crept into negotiations with businessmen and public officials. For example, Louis Smith, preparing to mount the demonstrations over building trades discrimination, wrote Philadelphia's Mayor Tate that CORE could only believe he was "putting politics before the welfare of the Negro citizens of this city," and warned that the chapter would "allow" him just twelve days to suspend contracts for the new municipal building which was being erected.[39]

More unusual but clear-cut evidence of tactical radicalization foreshadowing what later became standard practice, were such demonstrations as the all-night school sit-ins in Englewood, San Francisco, and Malverne; the University of Chicago CORE's camping outside the president's office; Los Angeles CORE members locking arms and legs, compelling police to force them apart and drag them to the paddy wagon; New Haven CORE's City Hall sit-in where members blocked doorways until pushed away by police. It was Brooklyn CORE, however, that was most consistent in its application of new tactics—the blocking of trucks at Ebinger's Bakery, the going limp in the hands of the police, the seventeen-day dwell-in at the housing development, and the dumping of garbage at Brooklyn Borough Hall. Such tendencies toward civil disobedience at this point were still minor in CORE, but as early as the fall of 1961 its possibilities were discussed by the members of CORE's field staff. They felt that since civil disobedience lacked "popular acceptance," a chapter should employ it only "with the overwhelming approval . . . of the group." Yet the staff predicted that "Perhaps the more controversial techniques will have to be adopted as the problems become more subtle, i.e., housing and employment, especially in the North. . . . People might have to resort to more shocking methods of protesting." [40]

CORE was increasingly becoming known for militance and action rather than for nonviolence. Alan Gartner was ambivalent about Boston CORE's reputation as "those wild young kids." "This image is not a bad one, at least to the extent that it means we are activists in a community long on talking and meeting. [But on the other hand] we continue to be somewhat derelict in a deep understanding of CORE philosophy." In Philadelphia, Louis Smith commented that his chapter, concerned only with practical matters, put "very little emphasis on theoretical discussions" of nonviolence.[41] Moreover, largely due to external influences some CORE people were beginning to question the very principle of nonviolence. Not only were Malcolm X's sardonic references to nonviolence achieving wide publicity, but the example of the North Carolina black militant, Robert Williams, also had a profound effect.

Williams first achieved prominence in the late fifties after his dismissal as president of his local NAACP branch for advocating retaliatory violence; subsequently he concluded that blacks could secure their freedom only through the calculated use of revolutionary force. CORE became involved in the situation in Monroe, North Carolina, when seventeen Freedom Riders visited Williams there in August 1961. In the ensuing days the Riders inaugurated nonviolent protest demonstrations which precipitated violence from hostile crowds and culminated in the alleged kidnapping of a white couple. In the aftermath Williams fled first to Cuba and then to China, not returning to the United States until 1969. Meanwhile, in 1964 others including John Lowry, a Freedom Rider from New York, were sentenced to long prison terms on the kidnapping charges.[42] Because of Williams' advocacy of violence, and the revolutionary and nationalist ideologies of two defense groups that sprung up—the all-black Monroe Defense Committee and the more influential Trotskyist-oriented Committee to Aid the Monroe Defenders (CAMD)—CORE tried to steer clear of entanglement. But the national office felt some responsibility for Lowry, and more important the issue attracted much sympathy among chapter members who regarded Williams as a victim of racist repression and admired his highly militant rhetoric. Accordingly, CORE from the beginning handled the Monroe case gingerly. Thus in April 1962 Farmer advised the chapters gently that the NAC opposed endorsement of the CAMD since Williams "never repudiated violence." Nevertheless, at least a few affiliates such as Cleveland and Greensboro lent their assistance to the CAMD.[43]

Although the issue of tactical violence vs. nonviolence did not become widely discussed in civil rights circles until mid-1963, it was a matter that disturbed Farmer and other CORE leaders as early as the spring of 1962. When a contributor complained about hearing a CORE spokesman say that the organization was not bound by nonviolent methods if they failed to work, Farmer replied that CORE's commitment to nonviolence was irrevocable and anyone using other means "will no longer be part of CORE." A few weeks later, while addressing the Princeton FOR, he confessed that CORE found it difficult to control some of its members. Noting that "we are troubled by hate," he described "the angry young men of the present generation" who were now doubting "the non-violent direct action ideals." As a solution, he urged the expansion of CORE's training program. In money-raising appeals for the 1962 summer workshops, Farmer attempted to convince the public that the organization could guide direct actionists on a sure road of nonviolence. Despite the fact that the summer volunteers recruited for Freedom Highways were nearly all experienced nonviolent activists, the national office opened the project with a two-week training session in nonviolent theory and practice, and this subject also received prominent attention at a housing workshop in October.[44] Nevertheless, the problem persisted. In 1962 two field secretaries on the West Coast admitted to a social researcher that in meetings with CORE groups "we don't talk about nonviolence anymore." Wilfred Ussery, head of San Francisco CORE and later national chairman, told the local school board in September 1962, "The crucial point for the Negro is that on the one hand, with respect to violence, he is not starting anything. But on the other hand he may be ready to start something if he doesn't get his demands immediately. . . . I am trying to convey an appropriate sense of urgency . . . this country is on the brink of blowing up over the issue of second class citizenship." Not surprisingly, with the dedication to nonviolence beginning to erode at the local level,

National CORE continued its efforts to offer as much education on the subject as practicable.[45]

An issue that was quite distinct from CORE's commitment to nonviolence but one that in practice was often viewed as closely intertwined with it was CORE's stance on interracialism and black nationalism or separatism. Because of the association of retaliatory violence with nationalism in the speeches of Williams and Malcolm X, the two ideologies were often considered practically coterminous during internal organization discussions and in the statements of CORE leaders. But for CORE people "nationalism" covered a range of ideas, not all of which were always espoused as part of a separatist ideology. At one extreme were the frankly anti-integrationist programs of consistent nationalists like the Black Muslims, with their advocacy of territorial separatism and black institutions as ends in themselves. Although as shall be seen, a number of CORE members were intrigued by the Muslims, this kind of nationalism did not become a significant force in the organization until 1965 or 1966. More appealing to CORE people in the early 60's were two other doctrines, both largely stemming from the successes of the civil rights revolution— an intensified racial pride and a growing belief that blacks, not whites, must be the leaders in the movement to secure the black man's freedom. Neither of these views was inherently anti-integrationist; race pride was not usually coupled with a separatist philosophy, and emphasis upon the importance of black leadership in CORE was by no means necessarily indicative of hostility toward whites. In fact, as we have observed, since the late 1950's CORE had increasingly believed that to effectively recruit from the black community, and especially from among the grass roots, black leaders were essential. Certainly the mainly white group that had engineered the selection of Farmer as national director for precisely this reason, were not nationalists and they were actually deeply dedicated to CORE's interracial traditions. The very paucity of Negroes at top positions in CORE's national hierarchy as late as 1961 was sometimes cited as evidence for a lack of interracialism. In the early 1960's moreover, when it became almost universal for chapters to regard a black chairman as tactically essential, few members felt that this compromised CORE's interracialism, and whites continued to play important roles in other chapter offices. Yet some of the sentiment behind the demand for black leadership was ideological rather than tactical, and was motivated by a distrust of all whites, even those in CORE. The motives behind the thrust for black leaders were often mixed, and it is frequently difficult if not impossible to discern the degree to which they were based on tactical or on nationalist considerations.

In some chapters the role of whites was being discussed as early as 1961–62. In Newark CORE in 1961 there was a brief but intense debate over restricting the chairmanship to blacks, with the advocates of this position arguing that only in that way could the chapter relate effectively to the local black community. The group decided that a black chairman was essential, elected Robert Curvin to the post, and thereafter functioned as one of the most integrated chapters in the organization, even in the mid-1960's when many other affiliates seriously questioned white participation. In New York early in 1962, chairman Gladys Harrington— who had been critical of Farmer's appointment in part because he had a white wife—went beyond the position taken by Curvin and his followers in Newark when she publicly stated that civil rights organizations "should basically be run by Negroes," and several months later Brooklyn CORE had an intensive discussion of the subject. A number of whites agreed with this position. One in the Brooklyn chapter observed, "Many Negroes simply will not allow their civil rights struggle to be led by whites," a view to which he "wholeheartedly subscribe[d]." Yet certain whites functioned very effectively in this chapter; thus in the early fall of 1962, of the nine officers and committee chairmen, three—the vice-chairman, the secretary, and Arnold Goldwag who occupied the important post of action chairman—were white. In some cases the debate was fueled by strong ambivalences if not outright hostility toward the whites in CORE. In May 1962, Fredricka Teer reported that in the Baltimore chapter several influential blacks "have expressed strong anti-white feelings." A few months later Haley was sufficiently troubled to comment that one of the recent "unfortunate developments . . . has been that Negroes more and more tend to be suspicious of white participation." Thus began in a small way a discussion that would ultimately eliminate whites from active membership in CORE.[46]

In a few chapters, such changing attitudes toward whites produced cleavages. As early as 1961 in a very unusual case Detroit CORE actually broke apart on the issue. The controversy began because of concern that the affiliate was overwhelmingly white. Although the chapter divided into two factions, there were actually three points of view on the subject. At one extreme was a small group that took the position that CORE should be an all-black organization. Allied with them was a larger group that believed CORE should be interracial but mainly black-led, with white officers pledged to represent "the Negro point of view." The other faction denounced these doctrines as racist violations of CORE's color-blind traditions and withdrew to form Metropolitan Detroit CORE. Only under considerable pressure were the two factions, both of which were interracial, reunited into one chapter, which thereafter operated as a well-integrated unit for the next four or five years. In New Orleans CORE, the previously mentioned controversy over interracial dating ended in the exodus of most of the white members, who "insisted that interracial socializing was central to CORE's goals, while most Negro members felt that this was peripheral and expendable if it hurt the group's standing in the Negro community." In decline, the affiliate's members asserted a pride in their blackness and African origins, complained that "We've let whites set our values," and denounced the light-skinned Negroes prominent in rival civil rights groups as bourgeois conservatives who were ashamed of Africa.[47]

Meanwhile influences from avowedly nationalist groups began propelling some CORE members toward a separatist philosophy. Especially important was the public renown gained by the Black Muslims through the meteoric rise of Malcolm X. Even black integrationists resonated to the biting rhetoric of the celebrated minister who led the Nation of Islam's New York Temple. Malcolm's charismatic appeal was evident in the reaction of CORE's assistant community relations director Robert Gore when he witnessed a debate between Malcolm and Bayard Rustin in 1962:

> I came away . . . with mixed feelings. . . . Being a pacifist, a Negro, and one who has been involved in the racial struggle lately I expected to be "with" Bayard all the way and "against" Mr. X completely. My mixed feelings were the result of the discovery that I was applauding more for Malcolm X than I was for Bayard Rustin. . . . There is no question in my mind but that Bayard presented the saner attitude, but the amazing thing was how eloquently Malcolm X stated the problems which Negroes have confronted for so many years. . . . I must confess that it did my heart a world of good to sit back and listen to Mr. X list the sins of the white man toward the black man in America.[48]

CORE's official position on the Muslims was unequivocal. Farmer wrote to a concerned inquirer, "The Muslims are all black and CORE is interracial. The Muslims are separationists and CORE is integrationist. The Muslims do not reject violence as a solution; CORE does." Speaking in Grand Rapids he stated, "Theirs is a movement of despair. They represent the view that America will not and cannot implement its democratic ideals. CORE is a movement of hope that America can live up to its credo." [49] However, many CORE people had a real respect for the Muslims, and there was much communication and debate between the two organizations. Chairman Olly Leeds and a number of others belonging to CORE's vanguard chapter in Brooklyn greatly admired Malcolm X. Even Farmer himself declared that, while "they would not make good members of CORE," the Muslims were not "subversive in any sense." [50] He accepted Malcolm X's invitation to speak at a Harlem rally on unemployment, and both he and Floyd McKissick appeared in formal public debates with the celebrated Harlem minister.[51] A number of chapters also maintained considerable contact with members of the sect. Malcolm X addressed meetings sponsored by CORE groups in New York and Hartford, while local Muslim ministers met with chapter leaders in places like New Orleans, Baltimore, and Philadelphia. In New Orleans, CORE and the Muslims frequently interacted because the Muslims had their greatest influence upon the two population segments in which the chapter was involved—the lower-class people and the students. New Orleans CORE members were about equally divided between those sympathetic and those unsympathetic toward the Muslims. One observer reported, "In the struggle to radicalize the [New Orleans] Negro community, Muslims were seen more as allies than as competitors," dramatically exposing white racism and criticising the middle-class black leadership.[52]

San Francisco CORE was influenced even more deeply by the Nation of Islam. Compared to the Muslims' ringing denunciations of white racism, CORE's "love thy neighbor thing" seemed tepid to many Bay-area blacks. Western field secretary Genevieve Hughes reported that local CORE people were put "on the defensive" by articulate black nationalists who "cut a wide swath" in the San Francisco Negro community, and within the chapter there appeared a black nationalist contingent whose leader personally wavered between the Muslims and CORE.[53] CORE officials attempted to counter the Muslims by stressing more fiery rhetoric and sponsoring discussion groups on Negro "identity," which in effect became forums for the exploration of black nationalism.[54] Because of the nationalists' challenge there was considerable sentiment within the chapter for giving more leadership positions to blacks, and Hughes urged the National CORE office to dispatch a black field secretary to the region. Farmer, hearing of "the rather serious strife there," called a meeting of all the Bay-area chapters when he visited California in October 1962. As this session made abundantly clear, to the Bay-area CORE people the Muslims were a challenge because of their two-fold appeal to the black man's sense of identity and to the alienated black poor. The complex ambivalence of many black CORE members was revealed in the vehement remark made to Farmer at this gathering: "*All* Negroes have a foot in the door of nationalism and CORE must accept that—it's tied into the need of the black man to change his imagery. . . . Besides, discrimination is a secondary problem compared to the need for a psychological solution to the problem: to dig being black—do you dig that? As Negroes become whole, lines of communication with whites have to be kept open—that's why I dig CORE." Others kept referring to the ability of the Muslims to attract the masses. "CORE has failed because we are afraid to get down on the street with those masses of people who are really seeking something. The people most vulnerable are the people seeking for identification, and we don't reach them," while the Muslims did. Farmer in replying, maintained that there was no "contradiction between the search for identity and CORE. . . . We can have this identity and still be for integration." [55]

While nationalism was as yet a minor theme in the CORE movement, unquestionably the Nation of Islam's appeal to the black poor and the dramatic way in which it called attention to their plight reinforced the tendency of CORE people to stress the problems of the slumdwellers and to engage in fervent criticism at the organization's inability to attract large numbers of them. One sociologist who studied the organization in this period stated that "The Muslims' greatest challenge to direct actionists was their insistence on speaking for the lower classes . . . and their outstanding success in recruiting these elements in the Northern cities." At CORE's national office, Norman Hill viewed his proposals for dealing with the needs of the black poor as a way to combat the Muslims' threat to integrationist civil rights organizations. As he put it, only projects like the Sealtest campaign, which attacked the "pattern of discrimination in all job categories," would "provide a direct alternative to the Muslims in terms of aims, programs, and results." [56] Yet ironically Hill's own plan of community organization would in the long run actually strengthen the separatist forces in CORE and finally pave the way for their domination.

All these shifting trends were closely related to changes in CORE's membership. There were still some of the old-line liberals, Socialists, and even a few pacifists—white and black. There was also a handful of revolutionary Marxist types of both races. A growing number of young white student activists, ranging from liberal to radical, were being attracted to CORE by its idealism and militance. And there were increasing numbers of both middle-class and working-class blacks, whose commitment was to no particular political ideology, but who wanted to get things done—and quickly.

The result was to increase tensions within the organization. As Farmer told the 1962 Convention, "We no longer are a tight fellowship of a few dedicated advocates of a brilliant new method of social change; we are now a large family spawned by the union of the method-oriented pioneers and the righteously indignant ends-oriented militants. . . . Our problem is the constant internal tension between means and ends." Farmer was fond of this formulation of the contrast between the "means-oriented idealists," grounded in the philosophy of nonviolence, and the "ends-oriented militants," the "New Jacobins," disillusioned with America's equalitarian rhetoric who viewed nonviolence as an expendable tactic. Optimistically, he consistently maintained that this tension was organizationally valuable, and indeed necessary. "Without the Young Turks the movement could never have grown to mass proportions, and without the idealists it could not have developed revolutionary dimensions. The anger of one without the disciplined idealism of the other could have produced only nihilism." [57] Yet Farmer oversimplified considerably. Rather than two, there were many points of view in CORE. All were dedicated to racial equality, and by 1963 all were agreed that CORE's top priority in the North should be the problems of the slum-dwellers. But there were wide differences over ideology and tactics—involving especially the whole tradition of nonviolence and interracialism, as well as the legitimacy of techniques like obstructing traffic and going limp in the hands of police. Occasionally, Farmer feared that the new strains within CORE were becoming explosive. For the present, however, there were no well-defined ideological factions, only tendencies of which the participants themselves were not always fully aware, as they groped for ways to move beyond constitutional rights and attack the deep-seated problems of the black poor.

By the spring of 1963 converging forces had brought CORE to the point where it would embark upon a major series of campaigns to aid the northern ghetto dwellers. In addition CORE, with increased support from philanthropic foundations, was poised for expanded voter registration efforts in the South, at the very time that direct action was also experiencing a revival there. The fruit of all these influences would be the explosion of black protest activity throughout the country which followed Martin Luther King's Birmingham campaign during the spring of 1963 and propelled CORE to the zenith of its career.

IV

CORE
at its Zenith
1963-1964

8

Direct Action: High Tide and Decline

In 1961, CORE's Freedom Ride had been the great symbolic event that set the tone of the entire black protest movement for months. In contrast, during the period of CORE's greatest activity the important symbolic events—the Birmingham demonstrations of May 1963, the March on Washington a few months later, and the Mississippi Freedom Democratic Party's Challenge to the seating of the state's "regular" delegation at the Democratic National Convention in August 1964—were all occasions in which CORE played only a supporting role. The sixteen-month period between the Birmingham demonstrations and the Convention Challenge delimitated a distinct phase in CORE's history during which time the entire direct-action movement crested and started to recede.

Martin Luther King's Birmingham campaign coincided with the inauguration of an extraordinarily vigorous era of direct action. In the following months CORE involved more people than ever before, heightened its demands, conducted massive and tactically more radical demonstrations in both the North and South, and mounted major voter registration campaigns against overwhelming odds in Mississippi and Louisiana. Compared to previous years, the Freedom Movement made enormous strides; yet its very successes only revealed how much more needed to be done. Consequently, there was an increasing feeling of pessimism that eroded the faith in direct action and the commitment to nonviolence and interracialism. The rejection of the demands of the Mississippi Freedom Democratic Party at the Democratic National Convention crystallized this disillusionment with CORE's traditional strategy. Although it was not fully recognized then, the events of the summer of 1964—the large-scale rioting in Rochester and New York City, and the failure of the Convention Challenge—symbolized the end of an era both for CORE and for the civil rights movement.

In the spring of 1963, as in 1960, the Negro protest movement became suffused with a new militance. "Freedom Now!" became the slogan. Like the Greensboro sit-ins the Birmingham demonstrations both epitomized the change in mood and became a major stimulus for direct-action campaigns across the country. As Farmer told the 1963 Convention at Dayton, "Twenty years ago there were just a few of us. Today . . . hundreds of thousands of people are now marching and [thousands are] sitting-in." [1] Again, like the spirit behind the 1960 sit-ins the new sense of urgency reflected a revolution in expectations. For blacks the achievements of the intervening three years now seemed like mere tokenism. Wilfred Ussery of San Francisco CORE observed, "Birmingham brought a drastic revision in our thinking. You can nibble away at the surface for a thousand years and not get anywhere." [2] A complex amalgam, the new mood in part involved what Farmer called "a spiritual emancipation"—a pride in being black, an optimism over what black bodies could accomplish through creative dislocation. Yet there was also a spirit of angry defiance, and a spreading tolerance for violence. In June 1963 Farmer insisted that CORE intended to channel the energy of discontent nonviolently, but he warned that the cities were "explosive," and predicted that "It will be a long, hot summer." As the black journalist Lerone Bennett observed, "the burning militance of the Birmingham leaders . . . pinpointed a revolutionary shift in the attitudes of the Americans called Negroes." [3]

CORE was an active participant in the demonstrations that swept the South during the spring and summer of 1963. There the heightened militance was evident in the numerous mass jail-ins, the involvement of all strata in the Negro community, the jeering at white policemen, and a disposition to meet violence with violence. Moreover, as Bayard Rustin observed, "The package deal is the new demand." Instead of fighting for one reform at a time, the pattern was simultaneously to make a number of demands that typically included integration of buses, public accommodations, schools, public buildings, and recreational facilities; an end to police brutality; and an equal employment policy in city halls and down-town stores.[4] Even before Birmingham, CORE chapters in North Caro-lina were experiencing an upsurge in direct action. Subsequently CORE led major projects in Gadsden, Alabama; Plaquemine, Louisiana; Talla-hassee, Florida; and the North Carolina Piedmont, as well as playing an important role in campaigns sponsored by SCLC in Birmingham, by SCLC and SNCC in Danville, Virginia, and by the NAACP in Jackson and Clarksdale, Mississippi.[5]

Yet, as so often happened, these other organizations—especially SCLC—received the limelight, a situation epitomized in May 1963 by CORE's William Moore Memorial Freedom Walk. Moore, a white mailman, was murdered in Alabama on April 24 while on a one-man walk from Chatta-nooga to Jackson protesting southern segregation. CORE leaders had ad-vised Moore, a member of the Binghamton, New York, chapter, against this demonstration, but in the atmosphere of crisis that followed his death the Steering Committee immediately planned a Freedom Walk along the route he had planned to take. SNCC also rushed to the scene, and a small interracial band led by Richard Haley left Chattanooga on May 1. As they proceeded along the highway, hostile whites threw stones and bottles, and upon reaching the Alabama state line the marchers were arrested. When Eric Weinberger went limp, state troopers repeatedly shocked him with electric cattle prods. Refusing to accept bail the walk-ers spent a month in Kilby State Prison. For a brief moment CORE lead-ers hoped that this project would become another mass movement like the Freedom Ride, bringing federal intervention and spotlighting the or-ganization's contribution. But even though a second group was arrested, Birmingham seized the national headlines aborting the impact of the ar-rests and jail-in sponsored by CORE.[6]

Because the Freedom Walkers had been first detained in the county jail at Gadsden, CORE had established useful contacts there which en-abled the organization to mount a major campaign in the city. Mary Hamilton, who had coordinated the Walk and then was jailed in the Bir-mingham demonstrations,[7] returned to Gadsden, where she was soon joined by three other CORE workers. Organizing local protest groups and the SNCC and SCLC staffers assigned to the city into a coalition known as the Gadsden Freedom Movement, they announced a broad-ranging package of demands including complete desegregation of buses, hotels, restaurants, schools, and parks, and merit employment in downtown stores. There followed a series of demonstrations notable for the use of radically new tactics and civil disobedience, followed by savage police repression.

Direct action involving sit-ins, picketing, and daily marches began on June 10. With as many as 700 participating, demonstrators blocked entrances of business establishments, conducted "snake dances" through downtown stores, and held a lie-in that completely covered the sidewalk in front of a drug store. A week after the direct action began, CORE field worker Marvin Robinson, addressing hundreds of protesters on the police headquarters lawn, vowed a campaign of massive civil disobedience in defiance of a court injunction against disruptive demonstrations. Next day, over 450 persons, headed by Robinson, marched into the courthouse, where they were all arrested. That night as 300 blacks held a vigil on the courthouse lawn, state troopers dispersed them with clubs and electric cattle prods. In the course of the following week Martin Luther King arrived in town, urging an overflow crowd to sustain the drive, and another 100 people were arrested for violating the injunction. Yet the firmness of the authorities, and the trials of the hundreds who had been jailed, sapped the movement's energy, and on July 1, following desegregation of the local buses and a pledge by the white officials to negotiate the other issues, the blacks suspended direct action. Further negotiations failed, and despite the reluctance of some of the civil rights staffers in Gadsden, who feared more police violence which would only crush the movement, another campaign was organized. To help revive the protest, Farmer flew in for a mass rally. But on August 3, when marches were resumed, state troopers with cattle prods moved in before the demonstrators even reached downtown, beating them and arresting 700.[8]

As in other places this kind of determined repression completely exhausted the protesters. CORE had neither gained the publicity that King had found in Birmingham nor moved the blacks of Gadsden much closer to freedom. The campaign was a failure and tied up the local movement in litigation for two years. The most celebrated case was that of Mary Hamilton, whose contempt citation for refusing to answer the prosecutor when he addressed her as "Mary" was reversed by the U. S. Supreme Court.[9] By the time the charges against the others were overturned, the 1964 Civil Rights Act had desegregated the city's public accommodations.[10]

Meanwhile in Florida and North and South Carolina there was an escalation of campaigns previously begun by local CORE affiliates. Extending over the summer and into the following fall and winter, these demonstrations produced results ranging from marked gains in Durham to utter failure in Tallahassee. In both Carolinas CORE now faced considerable competition from action-oriented NAACP branches, especially in South Carolina, where CORE's old rival I. De Quincey Newman was now a dedicated activist and led a vigorous NAACP that sponsored dramatic projects in the state's leading cities. In McCain's hometown, however, Sumter CORE did provide major initiative, joining with the local ministers and NAACP in demanding not only nonmenial jobs and desegregation of public accommodations but also street paving, lighting, and sewers in the grossly under-serviced Negro areas. For months there were daily picket lines, sit-ins, and mass marches with as many as four hundred participants. The variety stores desegregated their lunch counters, and a handful of black salesclerks were hired. But the Sumter merchants and the city administration rejected the protesters' other demands, and what in 1960 or 1961 would have been hailed as a substantial victory proved, in the heightened expectations of the period, a frustrating experience.[11]

In North Carolina, where the campaigns CORE had previously started in High Point,[12] Greensboro, and Durham reached dramatic heights in May 1963, the spring and summer months proved to be soul-stirring times. The gigantic demonstrations, unaccompanied by the severe repression that occurred in Alabama and Louisiana, or even in nearby Danville, Virginia, greatly enhanced both CORE's public image and the pace of desegregation. Yet CORE's aim of achieving fully "open cities" was not realized, and during the fall and winter the organization's campaigns for complete desegregation in High Point, Greensboro, and Chapel Hill ended, from CORE's point of view, as discouraging failures.

Involved in CORE's North Carolina strategy were both a radicalization of tactics, in the form of deliberately courted mass arrests, and a broadening of goals to include the usual package of demands.[13] First came Greensboro, where action against restaurants had been renewed in March. The number of participants reached more than a thousand a night, and arrests totaled 940 between May 15 and 18. Meanwhile the movement exploded at High Point and at Durham where on May 18 over a thousand marched to the City Hall and 130 were arrested for sitting-in during the first of three nights of massive demonstrations. At this juncture Farmer arrived to help coordinate the three campaigns. As a national figure he played a delicate role in relation both to the local black leadership, which guarded its autonomy, and to the white public, which blamed the protest movement on outside agitators. He was employed to best advantage at mass rallies and in heading the line of march in demonstrations. In Greensboro he described himself to the press only as an adviser to the coalition CORE had created. Addressing a jammed meeting of 1200 people in that city on May 19, Farmer likened the current unrest to a "second Revolutionary War": "This drive for freedom is spreading all over the country. . . . There can be no stopping now." Afterward Farmer led 2000 in a march through downtown Greenboro to the old city rehabilitation center where 600 students were incarcerated. In Durham, that same night, 700 persons were arrested for sitting-in at the Howard Johnson's parking lot. Next day Governor Terry Sanford angrily declared that in encouraging mass arrests CORE was going too far. Farmer retorted, "I'm serving notice to the Governor that we haven't gone far enough," and as he predicted arrests continued to mount. When a truce was called in Durham on May 21, nearly 1500 had been jailed; at Greensboro by this time the total was 1300. A boycott of Greensboro's merchants was inaugurated, and Farmer led daily marches involving thousands until a truce on May 25. The spotlight then shifted to High Point, where he addressed a rally inaugurating nearly a week of mass marches.

Finally, CORE declared a moratorium in all three cities, after biracial commissions had been appointed. The Durham committee secured the desegregation of nearly all places of public accommodations and the dropping of charges against those arrested. Although McKissick was publicly critical of the failure to achieve school integration or an FEPC ordinance, privately the city's blacks felt that a great deal had been accomplished. In High Point also, the biracial committee obtained the desegregation of nearly all the hotels and restaurants. In Greensboro, however, negotiations broke down and demonstrations were resumed at the beginning of June. The mood of frustration and the enormous support that the activists now enjoyed throughout the city's black community was revealed when the chaplain of North Carolina A & T. College told a rally that black moderates were changing, "If something is not done by tomorrow, we are going to jail and just sit back and let you radicals take over." On June 5, 500 singing, shouting, and dancing youths, led by A. & T. student body president Jesse Jackson, marched downtown and sat on the main thoroughfare in front of City Hall. Field secretary

Ike Reynolds * told the cheering protesters, "We'll take over the city tomorrow." And the following night Jackson led 850 in a sit-down at Jefferson Square which led to 278 arrests. This escalation of tactics had the desired effect: the mayor met hurriedly with the city's economic leaders and issued a strong statement urging complete desegregation of all public accommodations. The blacks again suspended demonstrations, and the next week 50 restaurants, motels, and theaters agreed to desegregate. Greensboro Negroes extended the truce until September 1.

Although much had been achieved in these cities and through less publicized NAACP activity in other North Carolina towns as well, CORE was anxious to see the job finished. Accordingly it sponsored renewed campaigns at High Point and Greensboro, and in addition sought to secure a public accommodations ordinance in the largely desegregated town of Chapel Hill. All three efforts ended disastrously. In High Point, where two downtown theaters and a few restaurants proved recalcitrant, demonstrations were renewed at the end of August, and in about two weeks escalated to the point where police were arresting hundreds of Negroes and using tear gas to scatter a threatening mob of 2000 whites. These events brought both blacks and city officials to another truce. In Greensboro, on the other hand, where CORE claimed that over half the restaurants and nearly all the hotels still barred blacks, it was only with the greatest difficulty that demonstrations were renewed in September. The two earlier waves of activity had exhausted the black community, the city government had passed a punitive parade ordinance and had insisted on proceeding with the trials of those previously arrested, while the Negro middle class was no longer willing to support direct action. The picket lines that were finally mustered numbered fewer than twenty people, and the movement soon withered away. Although CORE won the "Blocking the Street Cases" the following spring, in Greensboro, as in

* Isaac Reynolds, a black member of Detroit CORE, had been added to the CORE staff after participating in the Freedom Ride. He had recently played a small, though vital, role in the Birmingham demonstrations, working closely with King's lieutenant, James Bevel, in organizing the youngsters for the marches. In early May, at a critical juncture when King wavered because of pressures from the Kennedys to hold off further demonstrations, Bevel and Reynolds, ignoring King's wishes, slipped the children out of a church and marched them downtown to jail in the most brilliant maneuver of the campaign. (Isaac Reynolds to Farmer, April 26, 1963; interview with Reynolds in *New America,* May 31, 1963; Rich to Robert Tyler, May 27, 1963, CA; interviews).

High Point, the complete desegregation of public accommodations took place only when the 1964 Civil Rights Act went into effect.

In Chapel Hill, an ad hoc interracial coalition led by John Dunne and Pat Cusick, two white students, and Quinton Baker, a black student and president of the state NAACP youth conference, had organized large-scale demonstrations over the summer. But frustrated by the intransigeance of the city council, and factionalized by tactical differences between the liberal adults who favored a moratorium and the activists who did not, the committee had fallen apart by autumn. With McKissick's assistance, Dunne and Cusick founded a CORE chapter in October, and, unable to revive activity on their own, joined with the NAACP and other groups to form the Chapel Hill Freedom Committee. Marches and sit-ins began in mid-December, and by the beginning of the year arrests totaled over 200. On January 13 the aldermen again refused to pass the ordinance, and the following day Farmer arrived to put the campaign into high gear, promising "massive action" if Chapel Hill did not become an "open city" by February 1. Governor Sanford angrily threatened to use "every resource" to meet these "brazen threats" against Chapel Hill. Privately he urged CORE leaders to meet with him, but McKissick rejected this invitation. Demonstrations were renewed on schedule, with the blocking of store entrances, lie-ins, and street sit-downs. The climax came on February 8 in two mass marches, traffic tie-ups on four major highways, and two sit-downs at the busiest downtown intersections. With "no tangible success," and with arrests having reached a total of more than 700, the Chapel Hill Freedom Committee halted demonstrations—ostensibly to give the aldermen another opportunity, but actually because the movement's finances and morale had collapsed. CORE found itself saddled with a huge debt to the bonding company, and although the cases against most of those arrested were ultimately dismissed, the movement's leaders served prison terms that in a few cases were as long as twelve months.[14]

Like the chapters in the North Carolina Piedmont, Tallahassee CORE was a group whose activity was intensified in the wake of the Birmingham demonstrations. Revived late in 1962, the affiliate led a sit-in campaign that finally desegregated the bus stations and the dime store lunch counters by the end of the year. The chapter turned at once to an attack on the movie houses, stepping up the project in May when 50 persons, "undeterred by a threatening gang of whites armed with sticks, belt buckles and hammers," were arrested while standing-in at the State Theater. In response to an injunction obtained by the management, CORE embarked upon civil disobedience, and over the next three days 222 more youths were arrested. The court thereupon undercut the movement by suspending the contempt citations and simultaneously sharply restricting the number of pickets permissible. Not until fall did CORE again violate the injunction against massive demonstrations, and this time 354 persons, mostly Florida A. & M. students, were jailed. Another 100 were arrested in a mass demonstration outside the jail where they ignored the sheriff's order to disperse. By then even the most militant ministers, like Rev. C. K. Steele, who had led the city's bus boycott in the 1950's, were unsympathetic with CORE's tactics. With the chapter leaders in jail and the movement demoralized, conservative preachers and the Florida A. & M. administration took over and persuaded three-fourths of the students to accept suspended sentences. The jail-in collapsed, and National CORE had to pay $11,000 in fines. The chapter itself sank into factionalism and inactivity, and the theaters remained jim crowed until the Civil Rights Act of 1964.[15]

Both the activists' strategy of civil disobedience and mass arrests, and the authorities' methods of crushing the protest movements in Tallahassee, Chapel Hill, and Gadsden, were even more spectacularly evident in Plaquemine, where Farmer himself only narrowly escaped bodily harm. In August, CORE and the Voters League, seeking a major confrontation and jail-in at Plaquemine, inaugurated downtown marches to dramatize demands for the annexation of ghetto areas into the city, equal job opportunities, and desegregation of schools and courthouse facilities. The sheriff at first permitted a brief prayer service at the courthouse, but as the demonstrations grew larger civic officials changed tactics, and turned both to the courts and to repressive violence. On August 19, Farmer led a mass march of 500 which was dispersed by police who used tear gas and arrested Farmer, Ronnie Moore, and the principal local leaders. National vice-chairman Rudy Lombard now took charge, and confrontations continued despite a federal court injunction. Matters came to a climax when mounted troopers rode into a crowd of demonstrators, assaulting them with electric prods. With a total of 232 now arrested, detention facilities were overtaxed as CORE had planned. But the police chief foiled the jail-in strategy by persuading many to leave on their own recognizance.

Farmer and the leaders now accepted bail in order to regroup their forces, and demonstrations began anew. Over 300 youths marching toward the sheriff's home were gassed and trampled by mounted troopers. As in Birmingham, the black community was galvanized into unprecedented unity by this cruelty. The ministers, who except for Rev. Jetson Davis had previously opposed the movement, now joined it. On September 1, after a mass rally at Davis's Plymouth Rock Baptist Church, the protesters, again defying the courts, started downtown. The demonstration turned into a melee when white onlookers began yelling insults at the blacks and urging the police to "string them up now." Fearing violence, Lombard climbed on a car and pleaded with the Negroes to leave, but some ran down the street tossing rocks at houses, while the mass of marchers surged toward the square. Police charged into the crowd with tear gas, firehoses, and electric prods. Farmer, at the church, recalled, "I watched the Negroes coming back, those who could run, bleeding, hysterical, faint, some of the stronger ones carrying the injured. The nurse started to bandage the wounds and the rest of us began to sing 'We Shall Overcome.'" Then as the injured were being moved into ambulances, 40 mounted police rode up, shooting tear gas and forcing everyone back into the church. As firehoses flooded the building the fleeing blacks were arrested. Troopers began a house-to-house search for the leaders, particularly for Farmer, who was in the parsonage. They shattered the building's windows with tear gas cannisters, and as Farmer later wrote, "almost everyone inside was blinded and choking. The screaming was unbearable. . . . We tried to telephone for help, but the operators were not putting through any outgoing calls from the Negro section. . . . We could hear the screaming in the streets as the troopers on horseback resumed their sport with the cattle prods and billy clubs." Scores of people escaped from the parsonage and jammed into a nearby funeral home. When police kicked open the door demanding Farmer, he was saved only by the courage of the owner who ordered the troopers to leave because they had no warrant. Although the surprised lawmen withdrew, the blacks feared that if they returned Farmer would be seized and possibly killed. Accordingly he was hidden in a hearse with Moore and Davis. With an armed escort following in a car behind them, the three men were driven over the back roads to safety at New Orleans.[16]

Like SCLC in Birmingham, CORE was successful in creating a dramatic confrontation at Plaquemine with a repressive white officialdom. CORE had brought in its charismatic national spokesman to draw the media's attention and mobilize the local blacks, and had forged an extraordinary unity that produced massive demonstrations, transcended class lines, and resulted in the arrests of 400, including respected community leaders like the school principal W. W. Harleaux and physician Bertrand O. Tyson. Yet unlike Birmingham—and to CORE's disappointment—this campaign neither received much publicity nor galvanized the White House to intervene.[17]

CORE's victories in the South during 1963 paralleled those of the other activist organizations. In the peripheral areas the revival of direct action to integrate public accommodations proved remarkably successful, and, as Marvin Rich observed, "No other period in our history can show such quick changes." In the deep South, on the other hand, the campaigns ended in cruel repression. Yet these southern drives aroused nothern white sentiment and thus paved the way for the 1964 Civil Rights Act, which finally solved the public accommodations issue in the South. Farmer himself cited 1963 as the year which attracted many "white friends and church and labor groups to the front in the fight for freedom." [18]

The events of the spring and summer of 1963 brought to a climax a concern growing among white churchmen for some time. Especially instrumental in mobilizing white support was the interfaith National Commission on Religion and Race, a group of laymen and clerics organized in January 1963. Their first project—the last of the great direct-action drives against public accommodations in Maryland—was to help Baltimore CORE in its old battle to integrate the Gwynn Oak Amusement Park. On July 4, about 300 demonstrators, recruited by Baltimore CORE and the Commission, and including nationally known clergymen, were arrested at Gwynn Oak. Nearly 100 more were arrested the following Sunday. Although Baltimore County Chief Executive Spiro Agnew almost undermined the mediation efforts of the local human relations commission by charging that it favored the protesters, the park's owners capitulated, and in late August Gwynn Oak admitted its first blacks, eight years after CORE began holding annual demonstrations there.[19] From this project the churchmen moved into playing a prominent role in the 1963 March on Washington and the subsequent lobbying for the Civil Rights Act. The March, supported by predominantly white church groups and leading white clergymen, symbolized the entry into the civil rights movement of an important segment in the American population —the hitherto indifferent white moderates.

The March on Washington also symbolized a growing—though temporary—tendency toward cooperation among the protest organizations themselves. There was a widespread feeling among Negroes that the clashing groups could accomplish much more if their forces were united;

and Stephen Currier, the principal financier of the VEP, added the leverage of philanthropy to encourage a drawing together of the competing organizations. Yet, as the March on Washington also showed, such cooperation came at the cost of considerable compromise and was precarious at best. Because CORE was skeptical of working closely with the NAACP and Urban League, its role in the March tended to be peripheral.

At first it appeared that CORE would have a prominent part in the project. In the spring when A. Philip Randolph, acting on a suggestion of Bayard Rustin, issued a call for the March on Washington, CORE's Steering Committee agreed at once to be a co-sponsor.[20] Then, as the number of participating organizations grew, the focus and style of the March changed. The original emphasis on jobs lost its top priority largely because at SCLC's request the principal goal became passage of the Civil Rights Bill. While CORE and SNCC, enthusiastic about the possibilities for militant direct action and perhaps a sit-in at the capitol, readily supported the March, the NAACP and Urban League hesitated, and King, pressured by Kennedy, considered withdrawing. In the end all of the major advancement groups endorsed the March, but the price of unity was a loss of militance in tactics. What resulted, under Rustin's direction, was a great rally of nearly 250,000 blacks and whites—the most moderate of the techniques in Gandhi's arsenal. Norman Hill received a leave of absence to work with Rustin, and Farmer served as one of the March's co-chairmen. The CORE chapters varied widely in their support. Due to the moderation of tactics some had lost their enthusiasm, and a few were openly critical; yet for others the March provided a major focus of activity. Yet without this modification of tactics, the NAACP and Urban League certainly would not have participated, and it is likely that the March would not have taken place at all.[21]

Meanwhile, early in the summer, encouraged by the prospects of increased grants from Currier and other philanthropists, the major racial advancement organizations had created the Council for United Civil Rights Leadership. For about a year under Council auspices, the top civil rights leaders met periodically for frank discussions of their disagreements. Yet neither this effort nor Rustin's attempt to maintain the March on Washington organization actually proved viable. Differences in style, a desire for complete autonomy, and concerns over publicity made it difficult to sustain such coalitions. Thus CORE's Steering Committee rejected Hill's plea to work closely with Rustin on behalf of the civil rights legislation. The Committee expressed the view that because any project carried on through broad coalitions "will necessarily be at a lower pitch than typical CORE actions . . . we should define . . . the restricted limits of broad cooperation within which we feel it is safe to work." [22]

In the North the Birmingham crisis, coming, as Rich observed, at a time of "new ferment in the entire civil rights movement," precipitated an enormous outpouring of direct action and fiscal support. Many northerners, blacks and whites, flocked to join CORE both as active and associate members. Others, already in CORE, became more deeply involved than before. For example, Ruth Turner, a black Cleveland school teacher who had first become active in CORE while a graduate student at Harvard in 1961, gave up her job to devote full-time to the Cleveland chapter because "Birmingham brought about the rather sudden decision" that she "could no longer continue teaching German in a time like this." Not long afterward, her future husband, Antoine Perot, found himself "hooked" by the March on Washington, and switched from the NAACP in which he had been active, to CORE, which he felt was the organization directly confronting issues in Cleveland.[23]

Since the chapters continued to give National little money—only $11,000 during fiscal 1964—the heart of CORE's fund-raising remained the mailing list of "associate members," which jumped from 61,000 in June 1963 to 70,000 less than three months later.[24] About 95 per cent of these contributors were white, and they were disproportionately Jewish. On a list of the largest contributors—"The Extra Special Specials," and on another list of substantial donors, "Tip-top contributors in New York City area," the majority of names were also Jewish.[25] In addition, special projects swelled the total. Celebrities like Odetta, Nat "King" Cole, Frank Sinatra, Dean Martin, Sammy Davis, Jr., and Dick Gregory gave benefit performances, while the third annual Artists for CORE exhibition cleared over $40,000.[26] Thus the crescendo of activity during the spring and summer of 1963 had an impact similar to the Freedom Ride. Receipts for six months ending November 30, 1963, were $502,000— almost as much as was raised in the preceding twelve, and for the fiscal year 1964 CORE's income reached $886,000.[27] In turn this improvement in CORE's financial picture permitted a dramatic growth in the size of the staff, from forty-nine in June 1963 to somewhat over ninety by the spring of 1964. This figure encompassed about thirty clerical workers, twenty-five administrative and professional staff, including field secretaries, and forty full-time task force workers. The most notable single staff addition in this period was Carl Rachlin, who in January 1964 resigned from his law firm to become full-time CORE counsel.[28]

Simultaneously, there was an explosive increase in the number and size of CORE chapters. Field secretary Chet Duncan wrote exuberantly to McCain in July 1963, "The entire western region has come to LIFE!" Located overwhelmingly outside the South, and as earlier, most numerous in the New York metropolitan area and California, the new CORE groups generally sprang up spontaneously. Between June and October, twenty-six affiliates were added, making a total of ninety-four, or about a 40 per cent increase since Birmingham. By the 1964 Convention the total had reached 114. Equally dramatic was the expansion of individual chapters. A Los Angeles CORE leader noted, "Birmingham has done the recruiting for us," and not long after another elated member exclaimed, "The Action Committee meeting which was held last Monday was so huge, it looked like a membership meeting." Across the country, in Brooklyn, membership soared from thirty-five to one hundred over the summer of 1963.[29]

Such growth was frequently accompanied by more impersonal relationships and an inability to socialize adequately the many new members in CORE's traditions. Thus Toledo CORE, which within a few months grew from a handful of "stodgy adults" to nearly 50 "dynamic young people—all anxious to do the things that the CORE chapters they read about in the national press do," suffered "growing pains, . . . loose organizational methods, new people every meeting asking questions . . . that were asked at the last meeting." The Kansas City, Missouri, chapter, which over the summer tripled from about 20 to 60 active members, felt "the dire need of a trained CORE worker" to meet "the tremendous need for . . . further orientation in CORE's philosophy." Similarly, a Seattle CORE member worried in October that his chapter was "growing faster than we can assimilate the numerous capable new people and ideas and is becoming a big structure." As other Seattle leaders later recalled, it became increasingly difficult to function democratically. Committees began acting autonomously and working on many different projects simultaneously. Soon it was impossible to police the many agreements and to keep tabs on what was happening in the chapter. The process of segmentation that occurred in the larger affiliates was illustrated by Berkeley CORE; with the housing and employment committees each numbering dozens of active and probate members, several subcommittees were created to undertake different projects. As a former leader in Boston CORE expressed it, with relations becoming more impersonal, "the old days of a tightly knit, intimate group had passed." [30]

Although the chapters grew markedly, CORE at its height remained a remarkably small organization, with an estimated 3000 to 5000 members.[31] At their peak large chapters like Detroit, San Diego, Washington, Newark, and New Haven, had between 75 and 100 active members; Cleveland and Harlem membership reached about 150. Claims of much higher memberships, like 400 in Washington, 1100 in Los Angeles, were inflated, reflecting either an effort to give CORE a powerful image in the mass media or abandonment of the traditional distinction between active and associate members.[32] Most of the affiliates, however, even the most active, were relatively small. One observant student concluded that between 1961 and 1964 the average chapter size had grown from about 25 to 50.[33] The striking thing was that CORE's few thousand active members accomplished as much as they did.

In part, of course, this was due to the fact that on action projects the strength of CORE chapters was augmented by sympathizers, who now frequently outnumbered CORE participants. Thus, in a major demonstration at St. Louis's Jefferson Bank during the summer of 1963, of the 150 participants only 30 were CORE members. All over, the number of people on picket lines sky-rocketed, and as in the South, it was not unheard of for thousands to participate in marches. Berkeley CORE was able to obtain a few hundred to picket Montgomery Ward instead of the usual handful before Birmingham. Under the leadership of Seattle CORE and NAACP, about 1000 marched downtown to protest employment discrimination at the Bon Marche Department Store and other retail outlets; a few months later Seattle CORE, over a three-day period, found more than 200 people to picket the Washington Real Estate Board. At a suburban housing development Los Angeles CORE had enough supporters in the summer of 1963 to run three long picket lines on weekends. What was true of the West Coast was typical elsewhere. In July, Farmer and Roy Wilkins led a march and rally of 25,000 Clevelanders in a protest against employment discrimination in the building trades.[34]

Demonstrations were not only on a larger scale than before, but they involved more militant tactics than generally used in the past. There was greater impatience than ever with negotiations. Former field secretary and Freedom Rider Genevieve Hughes, who was still an active member of Berkeley CORE, feared that the Bay-area chapters demonstrated without deliberation: "The trouble is these people disdain listening to anyone in politics, hate facts, never investigate, and just rush in with direct action whenever they don't like what is going on." [35] By the summer of 1963 both large-scale arrests, numbering at times in the hundreds, and highly dramatic techniques had become standard procedures, while chapters now widely used tactics which they proudly referred to as civil disobedience. Fairly typical was the action of the Newark chapter, which in its employment campaigns blockaded a construction site and virtually closed a diner in a sit-in where CORE people loudly sang freedom songs and blocked the doors with a picket line. Frequently activists showed disdain for the authorities by resisting arrest and going limp in the hands of police. At an exclusionary Kansas City amusement park, when twenty CORE people were arrested, they had to be carried to the paddy wagons and then into the jail. Elsewhere other innovative techniques were employed. On July 4, Long Island CORE "had a picket, kneel-in, and sit-down at Jones Beach which tied up motor and pedestrian traffic," to publicize their demand for more park jobs. In the New York construction-trade campaign, CORE members were among the hundreds sitting down in front of trucks and bulldozers, chaining themselves to doorways, and even climbing cranes and girders. Similar tactics were used in Chicago against de facto school segregation and in Syracuse against jim crow urban renewal policies. In another innovation, California CORE members held a marathon sit-in at the state capitol, and at one point blocked the entrance to the legislative chambers.[36] For many participants these tactics not only reflected a very real sense of outrage at social injustice but had an expressive as well as instrumental function. Nothing showed this more clearly than the loud singing and chanting on many picket lines, and the sagging of morale when a victory came through negotiations rather than through direct action. Yet these demonstrations made the issue of racism in the North salient as it had never been made before.

As the radicalization of tactics and the escalation in the size of the demonstrations indicated, CORE affiliates were characterized by a new sense of confidence. In the words of a Syracuse chapter leader, the Birmingham crisis had supplied "added leverage" to their local efforts. Public sentiment in the white community was such that in Grand Rapids, Michigan, where the NAACP and the Urban League had been stymied in trying to obtain a fair-housing ordinance, a virtually defunct CORE chapter succeeded simply by threatening mass demonstrations. Elsewhere the dislocation created by direct action in Birmingham was used as a cautionary tale in dealings with public officials. Denver CORE leaders informed Colorado's governor that "the situation in Denver in its potential may not be better than Birmingham." The Ann Arbor affiliate warned that "the seeds of Birmingham exist in every city." Moreover, CORE chapter officials were beginning to talk less about morality and more about power. Attorney Robert Curtis, chairman of St. Louis CORE, declared that the job struggle with local banks was "a war that's to be fought in terms of power. I believe we have to fight with the same type of weapons as the man with his foot on our neck." A San Francisco CORE publication observed, "This entire country is shaking with awe before the anger of the Negro people." Hughes, catching the sense of invincibility of many CORE members, especially newer ones, observed that "Civil rights is so red-hot just now in the Bay area that the white folks are scared out of their minds. We can do anything we want. Every newscast is 60% civil rights." And she concluded, "I may be outdated in my notions and it may be that the day has finally come when no matter what CORE does or how it does it, it still wins." [37]

CORE's new vigor in the North produced greater interaction with other racial advancement groups, particularly the NAACP. In the South, where SNCC and SCLC were located, organizational rivalry was often muted by two circumstances: the deliberate tendency of individual organizations to operate in territory where others were not active and the policy of extreme repression by white authorities which made disunity an expensive luxury. In the North, without these inhibiting factors, CORE's militant activism often posed a threat to NAACP branches. In certain cities, notably in San Francisco, for a period, CORE worked well with the Association, but generally the relations between CORE chapters and the local NAACP ranged from indifference to hostility.

Problems with the NAACP were of two types: complaints of conservatism in some cases and resentment of militance in others. In Boston the two organizations were friendly competitors, sometimes allies. "We thought of them as old fogies, co-opted by the power structure," recalled one chapter leader. In Cleveland CORE activists had to use considerable pressure to get the NAACP involved in demonstrations against de facto school segregation. In Newark, where several NAACP leaders held high positions in the city government, CORE people found the branch so hopelessly conservative that they simply ignored it as much as possible. In Seattle and St. Louis, previously cordial relationships with NAACP groups were disrupted by heightened CORE militance. Seattle NAACP officials, appalled at CORE's obstructive tactics, angrily discontinued co-operation, while in St. Louis NAACP leaders publicly condemned CORE's use of civil disobedience. In some other cities CORE clashed with the NAACP just because of the latter's militance. In Baltimore the aggressive NAACP branch, anxious to dominate the local civil rights scene and willing to use direct action, proved a vigorous competitor. In New York, not only did Herbert Hill, the NAACP labor secretary, ener-getically encourage branch participation in the 1963 construction demon-strations, but also, to CORE's annoyance, he personally received consider-able attention in the mass media for his militance. Meanwhile in Philadelphia NAACP branch president Cecil Moore nearly upstaged CORE's campaign for employment in the building trades by sponsoring his own demonstrations. When CORE criticized him for accepting a token number of jobs, Moore warned the black community that CORE was a "completely negligible" group of agitators trying to increase their own prestige.[38]

Such conflict was inevitable, given the competition for members and money which the civil rights organizations needed to sustain their respec-tive programs. Moreover, the rivalry frequently proved functional, since in its attempts to outdo one another, each civil rights organization was often stimulated to work with greater vigor than would otherwise have been the case. Yet frequently, where mobilization of the entire black com-munity seemed necessary, chapter leaders participated in coalitions with the NAACP and others. Only rarely, however, did durable alliances re-sult. The Newark affiliate, for example, worked closely on a number of specific campaigns with the Newark Coordinating Council, a group of anti-NAACP leaders headed by the maverick politician George Richard-son, although the chapter always carefully retained complete autonomy and control over its own actions. More unusual was the situation in Bos-ton, where Alan Gartner was informally involved in a unique team that included two militant black leaders—Noel Day, executive director of St. Marks Community Center and Rev. James B. Breeden, vicar on racial af-fairs for the Protestant Episcopal Diocese. This group, the moving force behind the coalition known as the Massachusetts Freedom Movement, dissolved only after its leaders had left Boston. Generally, however, exper-iments with coalitions were short-lived. CORE people usually became un-happy because they were either elbowed aside by those with a more mili-tant image or stymied by the foot-dragging of the more conservative groups.

In Baltimore, where the competing organizations periodically formed united fronts for specific goals such as passage of a municipal civil rights bill, the militance and ambition of CORE and its rivals—the NAACP and the Civic Interest Group—prompted each to pursue a vigorously independent course that undercut any long-range alliance. CORE did work with the student-based CIG on several projects, but except for the Route 40 Freedom Ride this cooperation was on CIG's terms not CORE's. In Chicago, the chapter played a crucial role in the early school demonstrations but was latter upstaged by the angry militance of Lawrence Landry, head of Chicago Friends of SNCC, and then practically buried in the broad-based coalition, the Chicago Committee of Community Organizations. In New York, participation in the Citywide Committee for Integrated Schools foundered on the personality of its chairman Rev. Milton Galamison, whose rhetoric was more militant than CORE's, and in the end the national office joined the NAACP in opposing the feisty clergyman.

The Cleveland United Freedom Movement, on the other hand, exemplified a problem about which CORE leaders often complained—a coalition in which others tried to blunt CORE's aggressive style. Actually the UFM had originated under the aegis of the NAACP, which pre-empted plans developed by CORE and other militants to create such a coalition. Once the UFM had been formed, CORE pressed for a confrontation on the school segregation issue, pushing a reluctant NAACP into direct action. Yet, while the NAACP went along with demonstrations against the board of education, it was CORE which supplied most of the manpower. Brooklyn CORE, unable to secure enough pickets for its job construction demonstrations at the Downstate Medical Center, appealed to a group of black ministers. The clergymen, most of whom belonged to the NAACP, recruited the people and then took over the leadership of the project as well. The Brooklyn chapter not only complained that its position had been usurped but, when the ministers reached an agreement with Governor Rockefeller, accused them and the Brooklyn NAACP of "selling out" for tokenism. The NAACP counctercharged that CORE was too unsophisticated to know when to stop demonstrating and start negotiating; deprived of mass support CORE gave up after a few more days of desultory picketing. In Berkeley the chapter's effort to secure black unity similarly backfired. Seeking support in their negotiations with Shattuck Avenue merchants, it conferred with several Negro groups including the NAACP, but the Chamber of Commerce undermined this strategy by negotiating separately with the other black leaders, who settled for less than CORE demanded.[39]

Interrelated with the growth of northern CORE activity was the deepening CORE commitment to move beyond the issue of racial integration to the problems of the black poor. As Farmer observed, "We are fighting on two fronts. We are trying to break down segregation and we are trying to make facilities in segregated areas as good as possible." Harlem, he said, would not soon disappear, and, while CORE should help those blacks who wished to move into white neighborhoods, the organization should also work to make the ghetto "a decent place to live." CORE, Farmer maintained, needed to "broaden our base" by making special efforts to recruit among the masses, both "to provide CORE with roots in the community" and to "cope with the specific problems in the ghetto." [40] Norman Hill, who became Program Director in September 1963, continued to promote a "ghetto-orientation" among the chapters; during the winter of 1963–64 he held numerous regional conferences to provide the affiliates with the philosophical perspectives and practical tactics for helping the slumdwellers. In addition to this encouragement from the national staff, the affiliates also were motivated strongly by the dynamics of the movement itself. Spurred on both by the successes that had thus far been achieved and by the enormity of the problems still unsolved, the chapters ambitiously plunged forward. They launched dramatic demonstrations against job discrimination, fostered rent strikes against slumlords, worked with other groups in school boycotts, and initiated action against police brutality. And while many affiliates stayed within the traditional style of CORE activism, eschewing disorderly conduct and civil disobedience, others were characterized by an unprecedented and escalating militance.

During the post-Birmingham era, campaigns against job bias were the most common projects among the northern and western chapters—and generally the most successful. Although CORE groups were concentrating principally on retail stores, banks, and the construction trades, they were attacking a broader range of targets than ever. And in these projects the radicalization of both goals and tactics was readily apparent. Compensatory, "preferential" employment had become a universal demand; the employer, Farmer told the 1963 Convention, "is now obligated to find a qualified Negro." Impatience among the chapters was pervasive. For example, Dayton CORE's deadline in negotiating with downtown merchants during the spring of 1963 was "a maximum of 30 days," its leaders declaring, "We don't intend to spend weeks negotiating." Letters from St. Louis CORE to businessmen explictly threatened speedy direct action, and chairman Robert Curtis announced that his group would meet with several bankers to inform them "exactly how many Negroes we want hired immediately." Calling for a Christmas boycott of downtown stores, San Francisco CORE in November declared, "We in the Congress of Racial Equality know that the Negro community is fed up with the scraps and crumbs the power structure has heretofore been willing to dole out with respect to jobs. . . . Stores that are unwilling to meet with CORE and reach agreement by Thanksgiving, "will be subject to a wide range of direct action, designed to obtain immediate concessions for the Christmas season."

Syracuse CORE epitomized the changing stance of the affiliates in mid-1963. In June, a chapter leader requesting information on how to conduct employment projects, confessed to the national office that past complaints of job discrimination had not been pursued because of ignorance about ways to proceed. Yet only weeks later the affiliate had successfully completed the Hotel Syracuse employment project, using tactics that previously would have been summarily rejected: "marching through the hotel singing [and] sitting down in the lobby . . . [for] a general CORE meeting." Such tactics caused "great public resentment. . . . This has come as a mild shock, since we previously have counted on public support. . . . But one wonderful accomplishment: last year, when we picketed the school board on de facto segregation, everyone thought this was terrible. Now, everyone talks in terms of 'why don't you *just picket,* why do you have to SING, SIT-IN, and DO ALL THOSE HORRIBLE THINGS?' " The hotel settlement upstaged the local NAACP branch, and a delighted CORE member crowed, "CORE is THE civil rights group now." [41]

From Long Island and Baltimore to Seattle and San Francisco retail stores were still an especially popular object of attack. Some chapters, caught up in the zeitgeist, thought they had the power to tackle an entire downtown commercial district. Affiliates in Dayton, San Francisco, and Lexington, Kentucky, saw nothing extraordinary about negotiating with representatives of twenty to thirty important stores, while Berkeley CORE demanded speedy agreements from nearly two hundred stores in an eight-block stretch of Shattuck Avenue. CORE members in Dayton, Lexington, and St. Louis, after fruitless picketing on the sidewalks, began parading through major department stores. The Lexington group sat down in the aisles and sang freedom songs, while the St. Louis chapter added a new embellishment by stuffing CORE leaflets into merchandise. In all three cities these new tactics brought arrests. In St. Louis CORE resisted the police by blocking vehicles and lying down under police cars. Although the merchants had summoned the police, they nevertheless took steps to modify hiring policies. In Lexington, twenty stores quickly offered fifty white-collar jobs, which the CORE chapter accepted. In San Francisco, where CORE was picketing only two firms, thirty agreed to recruit aggressively and train black employees. In St. Louis, Berkeley, and Dayton, however, CORE's militant stance was undermined by other black leaders. The Dayton chapter spurned a settlement similar to Lexington's as "tokenism," causing a breach in the coalition there; St. Louis CORE, contending that the stores must show "tangible evidence" of hiring more blacks, rejected an NAACP demand to call off the boycott and negotiate further; the Berkeley affiliate was unhappy over the modest agreement which the Shattuck Avenue merchants, under pressure from CORE's Christmas boycott, had negotiated with a black city councilman instead. Although CORE leaders in these communities accordingly dismissed the results of their campaigns as unacceptable tokenism, they had actually secured gains which a year earlier would have been viewed as major accomplishments. For example, in Berkeley fourteen businesses signed with CORE, including Hinks Department Store, which the chapter would later point to as a model example of an equal opportunity employer.[42]

Indeed job settlements were typically greater than before. Chapters returning to companies with whom they had dealt in earlier years often made striking gains. In the spring of 1963 Berkeley CORE, charging that Montgomery Ward had not progressed beyond tokenism, demanded the hiring of thirty-five Negroes within a month and eighty-five more within the next four months. Ward's lawyers tried to secure an injunction against the mass picketing, but the judge proved sympathetic to CORE. In compliance with a precedent-setting court-supervised agreement which provided for regular reports and special recruitment policies, Ward hired about seventy-five blacks within several weeks, about half in sales positions.[43] Denver CORE's month-long picketing at Safeway brought twenty jobs—four times the number gained in its previous timid encounter with the company. Detroit CORE, which in its 1962 campaign against Kroger supermarkets won only vague promises, found in July 1963 that several Saturdays of picketing brought thirty-one jobs, including management trainees, truck drivers, and office workers. By the following spring Kroger and another local chain had together hired over two hundred blacks. The mid-1963 Seattle CORE-NAACP boycott of the Bon Marche ended with the hiring of fifteen full-time and part-time blacks; within two months the total had risen to forty, while nearly fifty had been hired at several other department stores. With pride Seattle CORE leaders announced that in its two years of existence, the chapter had opened 250 white-collar jobs to Negroes. Equally impressive was Baltimore CORE's campaign against Stewart's Department Store which, after three months of picketing, agreed to increase black sales personnel from five to forty and to upgrade two Negroes to executive positions. And as often happened, other downtown Baltimore firms, wishing to avoid CORE picket lines, had meanwhile rushed to modify their employment practices, which resulted in an estimated two hundred new clerical and sales jobs. Long Island CORE negotiated substantial settlements with three local shopping centers; merchants at the Mid-Island Plaza in Hicksville, for example, promised in March 1964 to increase their nonwhite employment by one hundred within three months. The most outstanding victory against a retail chain occurred in New York—in a case where direct action was not used at all. In late 1963 National CORE and a committee representing local CORE chapters, NAACP branches, and Puerto Rican groups won a preferential agreement from A & P to hire four hundred blacks and Puerto Ricans over the next two years, virtually filling all their turnover needs in the clerk category.[44]

The A & P agreement had its impact on the West Coast, which developed its own innovative tactic—the "shop-in." * The Bay-area chapters became dissatisfied with the settlement they had negotiated over the previous summer with Lucky supermarkets, providing as it did for an affirmative hiring policy rather than a specific number of jobs. Picketing against the chain began in February 1964, and several days later came the first "shop-in." Demonstrators filled shopping carts with merchandise, which they abandoned after the items had been rung up by cashiers. Fol-

---

* Actually a "buy-in" sponsored by an NAACP Youth Council had occurred in an East St. Louis supermarket in late summer of 1963. As undoubtedly happened many times in the course of the nonviolent direct-action movement, specific tactics were independently "invented" in widely separated communities. (See Elliott Rudwick, "Fifty Years of Race Relations in East St. Louis: The Breaking Down of White Supremacy," *Midcontinent American Studies Journal,* VI [Spring 1965], 12; East St. Louis *Journal,* Sept. 13, 15, 1963; East St. Louis *Crusader,* Sept. 13, 19, 1963.)

lowing the mediation of Mayor John Shelley, Lucky's promised to hire about sixty blacks in the next few months, and many chapters become convinced that obstructive tactics were a useful shortcut. The "shop-ins" were employed against two grocery chains in Seattle a short time afterward and again brought quick agreements.[45]

Retail stores were highly vulnerable to boycotts and to the disruptive tactics of nonviolent demonstrations. In contrast, defeat and frustration followed CORE's efforts against the building trades unions, highly cohesive organizations that were insensitive to the ideological appeals of the activists and invulnerable to consumer boycotts. The attack on discrimination in the construction trades had begun at Philadelphia in the spring of 1963 and now spread to a few other northeastern cities.* In Newark and New York as well as Philadelphia, obstructive demonstrations forced the intercession of public officials, who temporarily stopped construction and secured from the unions promises that were never fulfilled. In May 1963, after CORE conducted its second sit-in at the Philadelphia City Hall and the NAACP threatened massive picketing, Mayor Tate ordered a temporary halt on work at the Municipal Services Building, explaining that the actions of the two organizations "made us fear another Birmingham." Then, with CORE insisting that 15 per cent of the skilled jobs should be reserved for blacks, the NAACP made a private agreement with the unions and contractors, and several black craftsmen were hired. CORE returned to City Hall for a fifty-four-hour sit-in, the Tate administration announced that contracts with discriminatory contractors would be scrapped, and the craft unions promised to accept qualified black journeymen and apprentices. Newark CORE provided most of the drive behind an extended direct-action campaign, first against the building of a new high school in the summer of 1963 and several months later at the site of the new Rutgers University Law School. After the intercession of the mayor and the governor, an understanding between the unions and the demonstrators was reached.[46] In New York, where the mammoth

---

* Such demonstrations were not entirely new. In August 1960, the East St. Louis NAACP had picketed a public housing site; in fact, there were rumors that they planned to bring construction to a halt by "sitting down" on the equipment. (East St. Louis *Journal*, Aug. 9–11, 14, 21, and 16, 1960.) Our combing of the black press and the *New York Times* uncovered only one instance of a construction site sit-down outside the East during 1963 and 1964. In July 1964, two St. Louis CORE members were arrested after they climbed ladders surrounding the St. Louis Gateway Arch, which was then being erected. (*Argus*, July 17, 1964.)

demonstrations were sponsored by coalitions of CORE chapters, NAACP branches, and other organizations, picketing began at the site of the new Harlem Hospital June 1963. Under pressure the mayor quickly suspended work. Later in the summer CORE members were among the thousands picketing the construction of the Downstate Medical Center in Brooklyn, the Rochdale apartment development in Queens, and the Rutgers housing project in lower Manhattan. More than eight hundred were arrested while lying down on muddy streets and locking arms in attempts to block cement mixers and supply trucks. Several people mounted girders; at Rochdale, four chained themselves to a crane sixty feet above the ground. Refusing to cooperate with the police, scores went limp and were dragged to the paddy wagons. Meanwhile, sit-ins lasting more than six weeks were conducted in City Hall and in Governor Rockefeller's New York office. Through the governor's intercession, the construction unions agreed to facilitate the entrance of blacks, and hundreds were processed, expecting to become apprentices or journeymen. Yet as in Philadelphia and Newark, only a handful were accepted, all the unions having violated the agreements. Epitomizing the problem was the experience of four Negro and Puerto Rican plumbers, whose appearance at a New York construction site in April 1964 led white plumbers to walk off the job. In anger and desperation, East River and Bronx CORE members sealed off the plumbers union offices for several days.[47]

The attacks on bank discrimination, although not always as successful as CORE chapters hoped, nevertheless obtained significant results. These projects, which all aimed at achieving a substantial black presence in white-collar positions, ranged tactically from the staid picketing in Boston to flamboyant techniques used in St. Louis. Taking their cue from the successful employment of obstructive tactics in an NAACP-sponsored bank project at East St. Louis,[48] St. Louis CORE decided to disrupt business at the Jefferson Bank, long under attack by civil rights groups. In late August 1963 when the financial institution rejected CORE's demand of four jobs within fourteen days, many demonstrators, defying a restraining court order, blocked the main entrance, sat on the floor, and obstructed the tellers' windows. During the following weeks over one hundred were arrested. Fifteen were sentenced to jail terms of sixty days to one year. Alderman William Clay, for example, spent nearly four months behind bars. Yet in the months after CORE's campaign, eighty-four blacks obtained white-collar jobs in fifteen St. Louis financial institutions, including Jefferson Bank.[49] Boston had even greater success, though it used none of these tactics. In February 1964, after several months of negotiations, agreements were reached with the Merchants National and Shawmut National banks which brought 150 white-collar positions. A few days later, over one-hundred pickets appeared at the First National Bank, which had rejected CORE's demands. Picketing ended after nearly two months, when the institution employed forty-three blacks, bringing to nearly two hundred the total hired by fiduciary institutions since September 1963—the time that Boston CORE first began this project.[50]

Even more ambitious was the campaign conducted by the California chapters during the spring and summer of 1964 against the Bank of America, the world's largest privately owned bank. With its statewide system of nearly nine hundred branches and 29,000 employees, few of them black, the Bank of America was an ideal candidate for coordinated action on the part of the California affiliates. The company refused to supply racial employment statistics to the chapters' Bank of America Negotiating Committee headed by William Bradley, chairman of San Francisco CORE, or to accede to CORE's demand that it hire 3600 nonwhites during the next year. Picketing began toward the end of May, but probably because of the demoralization stemming from punitive court action in recent Bay-area demonstrations the project lacked the enthusiasm which had marked earlier job campaigns. Picket lines around the state typically did not exceed thirty to fifty people and petered out after a few weeks, and tactics were usually nondisruptive. However, in San Diego, CORE members, defying a court injunction, were arrested after sitting-down in the bank lobby and blocking the front entrance, and ultimately chapter chairman Harold Brown served nearly sixty days in jail. In late summer Bradley announced a "suspension" of the project, stating that CORE had to accept less than its original demands because of chapter apathy. Yet, although the bank would not concede the validity of CORE's accusations, nearly 240 blacks had been hired in white-collar categories between May and July.[51]

CORE chapters across the country were attacking a wide variety of employers. Long Island CORE, during the summer of 1963, followed up its traffic tie-up at Jones Beach with further demonstrations in the Park Commission's office, which produced promises of a "concentrated effort" to hire more blacks.[52] Boston CORE in 1964 sought and secured white-collar jobs in insurance companies; demonstrated at the Howard Johnson's and Hayes-Bickford restaurant chains, obtaining a preferential hiring agreement from the latter; and, concerned also about opening blue-collar jobs, engaged later in a unique though futile campaign to break the color line practiced by the firms collecting the city's garbage.[53] A number of chapters tackled consumer-goods manufacturers and, more rarely, utility companies. Dairies proved quite vulnerable. St. Louis CORE, for example, acting in coalition with other groups, secured preferential hiring agreements with two milk companies in July 1963, providing that the majority of new employees would be black until 15 per cent of the total work force was Negro.[54] Beer manufacturers and utilities, however, were usually more resistant. In late 1963 both East St. Louis and San Diego CORE used obstructive tactics against local power companies, but the campaigns bogged down in litigation over court injunctions.[55] The New York Metropolitan area chapters boycotted and demonstrated in an effort to obtain blue-collar jobs at the Schaefer Beer Company, but ran into a stone wall of union resistance.[56] Perhaps the most brilliant victory against the consumer-goods industries was New York CORE's "TV Image Campaign," led by Clarence Funnyé. The goal was to secure integrated commercials, thus both obtaining jobs for blacks and changing the racial perceptions of millions. Organizing selective purchasing committees among churches and fraternal orders, Funnyé's group threatened leading companies with a consumer boycott. By October 1963 a dozen corporations were making integrated commercials.[57]

The Newark affiliate, working on several projects simultaneously, was probably unique in its focus on utilities and major industries. In November 1963 the chapter picketed the Western Electric Company and jammed the switchboards with a "phone-in." Western Electric upgraded several black employees and developed a compensatory program of black recruitment. Newark CORE next moved against New Jersey Bell Telephone Company, which had many black female operators but no Negroes among its skilled male employees. After CORE broke off negotiations and threatened direct action in March 1964, the company committed itself to a recruiting program that would guarantee substantial black representation among telephone linemen and installers hired in the future. Similarly, aggressive tactics were adopted with Sears-Roebuck and the Hoffman-LaRoche Pharmaceutical Company; at the former, CORE picket lines marched through the store singing freedom songs, and at the latter demonstrators chained themselves to the gates. Both companies signed preferential hiring agreements. In some cases simply the implied threat of direct action brought results. Thus negotiations were enough to secure agreements with both the Pabst Beer Company, which added black salesmen to its staff, and the Mutual Benefit Life Insurance Company, which substantially increased the employment of Negroes in white-collar positions. Yet organized labor at other breweries proved resistant to all of the chapter's efforts, while negotiations with employers like General Electric and Engelhard Industries were inconclusive. In part, these failures were a reflection of the general decline in job campaigns and direct action throughout the country by mid-1964.

Across the country, the San Francisco Bay-area chapters also moved rapidly from one major campaign to another—from chain supermarkets to the Sheraton-Palace Hotel, to automobile dealers, to the Bank of America. Most of these projects were notable for their use of obstructive tactics by large numbers of demonstrators which brought hundreds of arrests, the repeated intervention of the mayor of San Francisco, and favorable hiring agreements. On the heels of the supermarket shop-ins, came the San Francisco Sheraton-Palace Hotel project, sponsored by the Ad Hoc Committee, consisting of NAACP, CORE, and other groups. These demonstrations, manned primarily by college students, culminated in March 1964 in a massive night-long action—the largest one held in San Francisco up to that time. Fifteen hundred participated, picketing on the outside; marching through the lobby chanting, singing, and shouting; and finally sitting down and blocking the hotel's entrances, leading to 167 arrests. Mayor Shelley's mediation brought a preferential hiring agreement under which the San Francisco Hotel Employers Association set a goal of increasing employment of nonwhites to about 15 per cent of the work force. A week afterward, a massive sit-in took place at the Cadillac showroom on Auto Row, resulting in 107 arrests. Then 226 more were arrested at Lincoln-Mercury and Chrysler, and the Mayor's special committee arranged another preferential hiring agreement, covering major auto showrooms in the city. By then the California CORE chapters had already launched negotiations with the Bank of America, and the Bay-area affiliates quickly entered into their final job project—the anticlimactic campaign already described.[58]

While employment had replaced housing as the most salient activity among CORE affiliates, the actual amount of effort devoted to the latter also rose substantially. Housing projects exhibited clear regional variations: the western chapters continued to emphasize breaking down of discrimination in white neighborhoods, an effort in which they were joined by activists in the Washington, D. C. metropolitan area, while northeastern affiliates began concentrating on upgrading tenements in the black ghetto. The drama of the demonstrations, the creative innovations in tactics, and the tenacity of CORE groups notwithstanding, the results proved to be limited.

No chapter received more publicity from its housing efforts than the Los Angeles affiliate, which continued its major campaign against a builder of upper-middle-class residential tracts. Enthusiasm for this project, which received warm support from the NAACP and other groups, reached a high pitch during the summer of 1963. Two hundred were arrested during a two-week period, and on one Saturday a thousand people participated in a mass march to one of the suburban tracts. Despite this pressure and an injunction which the state attorney-general secured against the builder, the case ended in inconclusive litigation in the courts.[59] In Seattle there was also a protracted campaign against a racist real estate firm. In March 1964, after the chapter had conducted windowshops and unsuccessfully lobbied for a fair-housing ordinance, it began sit-ins at the Picture Floor Plans Company. Tactics escalated with each passing weekend. For the first time in Seattle CORE's history, youthful activists chanted and sang, shouted insults, and pushed and shoved when the locked door was opened to admit a customer. The salesmen grew more hostile and when one struck a demonstrator, the affiliate suspended the project. The day after a court injunction halted all picketing against realtors.[60] Meanwhile, beginning in the summer of 1963, Prince George's County, Maryland, CORE, a new chapter outside the District of Columbia, had been conducting massive picketing and sit-ins at the Levittown development in Belair. This series of demonstrations ended after those who were arrested while sitting-in were convicted and fined on trespassing charges and the management secured a permanent injunction restricting the demonstrators' access to the Levitt properties. Although a few home owners privately sold their properties to blacks, the Levittown management adamantly retained its "white only" policy. Nearby, the Washington CORE chapter was only slightly more successful after it stepped up its direct-action tactics against apartment developers. Several dwell-ins during the summer of 1963 at buildings managed by the Cafritz company proved fruitless. But a year later CORE sit-ins at the Trenton Park apartments produced seven arrests, an agreement to rent to two black families who had previously been rejected by the management, and the promise of a nondiscriminatory policy in the future.[61]

In the summer of 1963, at least four affiliates mounted major direct-action campaigns to support the struggle for fair-housing legislation. Two were successful, although in the case of California the law was subsequently overturned by a referendum. In Ann Arbor many organizations supported the proposed municipal ordinance, but without the pressure of the demonstrations led by CORE, it probably would not have been enacted. Protests from May through September 1963, with picket lines numbering as many as eight hundred participants, culminated in a series of City Hall sit-ins that produced sixty-eight arrests. Dissatisfied with the weak ordinance that resulted from these endeavors CORE would subsequently resort to further direct action until a new law was passed early in 1966 covering nearly all of the city's housing.[62]

Elsewhere in Ohio, California, and Colorado, attention focused on the state house. In Columbus during June and July 1963, CORE and other organizations held sit-ins in the governor's office and the House chamber. Rev. Arthur Zebbs, the black Columbus chapter leader who directed the action, chained himself to a seat in the House gallery for over eight hours. A few days later, demonstrators, including chairman Ruth Turner of Cleveland CORE, staged an all-night vigil at the governor's office, while Bruce Klunder, a young white minister and Cleveland CORE's vice-chairman, conducted a one-man sit-in at the House chamber. After the legislature killed the fair-housing bill, Columbus CORE conducted more sit-ins at the capitol, and held nightly picket lines outside the executive mansion in a futile effort to revive the legislation.[63] In California at the end of May 1963, seeking enactment of the Rumford fair-housing bill, demonstrators from several CORE chapters began a marathon round-the-clock sit-in in the state capitol. Daily at noon the protesters would link hands in a circle around the rotunda and sing "We Shall Overcome." On the sixteenth day, with the bill stalled by a senate committee, demonstrators blocked the main entrance of the legislature's upper house. A week later when the law passed, CORE claimed a substantial victory. But real estate interests sponsored a referendum on the act. Although civil rights groups galvanized for the campaign, with CORE in twenty-six cities holding simultaneous demonstrations in January 1964 and engaging in intensive voter registration activities among black citizens, the Rumford Act was defeated in November. Two years later the California Supreme Court overturned the referendum's prohibition on fair-housing legislation, but CORE and other civil rights groups had suffered a demoralizing defeat.[64] Nor were Denver CORE's efforts any more encouraging. The chapter's direct action at the capitol, sitting-in at the Governor's reception room during the day and sleeping on the marble floor outside at night, reaped a good deal of publicity but failed to elicit his support for a strong housing law.[65]

In the Northeast, CORE chapters were turning from housing campaigns benefiting middle-class blacks to projects serving lower-class people. The New Haven affiliate explained in September 1963: "CORE recognizes the necessity of pressure to obtain homes in decent areas for those Negroes who, in a sense, have 'got it made.' . . . But the true housing problem is the problem of the slum tenant, the poorest paid worker, the family on welfare, the family on ADC." In New Haven, Boston, New York, Philadelphia, and other cities, CORE sent inspection teams into slum buildings to document and publicize complaints of inadequate heating, broken plumbing, vermin, and other health and safety violations. At first, direct action was confined to picketing landlords' offices or homes, but with progress slow or nonexistent, several chapters over the course of the year turned to a variety of other tactics. Philadelphia CORE dramatized conditions by unloading debris near a slumlord's suburban home. New York University CORE members, angered by lenient housing inspectors and judges, were arrested when they dumped on City Hall plaza a truckful of junk found outside rat-infested tenements. The Long Island chapter, battling on behalf of migratory farm workers living in shacks, dumped garbage at the Riverhead City Hall and staged a mass protest march downtown. New Haven CORE members held a sit-in at a grocery owned by a slumlord, and when evicted by the police they blocked traffic for two hours on a heavily traveled thoroughfare. On another occasion five members of the chapter were arrested in an unsuccessful effort to prevent the eviction of a black family. The protesters then brought the household effects to the Green in downtown New Haven, where seven more were arrested in a scuffle with the police.[66]

A few chapters sought to grapple with the problems posed by urban renewal, which removed blacks from deteriorated areas without usually providing suitable alternative dwellings. Charging that Negroes were simply being shifted to other slums, nearly one hundred Syracuse CORE members and supporters protested during the summer of 1963 by blocking bulldozers, sitting on cranes, and halting demolition work at urban renewal sites. Philadelphia CORE, demanding the suspension of townhouse construction in renewal areas until the evicted black tenants received low-cost dwellings, tried to damage the mayor's chances of re-election by sitting-in at the city's relocation bureau. New Haven CORE, asking for prompt repairs of city-owned tenements and the refunding of rents to relocated tenants, held a mass rally to embarrass the mayor shortly before Election Day. Disobeying police orders to confine their protest to the sidewalk, the pickets blocked buses and cars on a busy street.[67]

Under the glaring publicity which CORE thus brought to the problem, public officials did in some cases afford temporary redress of grievances. On Long Island the authorities in Riverhead obtained other housing for the migratory workers. Syracuse CORE reported that its efforts produced pledges from the city administration to relocate in nonsegregated areas the blacks forced out of urban renewal neighborhoods. Pressure from the New Haven and Philadelphia chapters produced sufficient intervention from municipal authorities to force some landlords to make repairs on their properties. In Philadelphia, particularly, Mayor Tate criticized subordinates for not taking vigorous action against slumlords, and he stepped-up inspections and prosecutions.[68] However, the CORE groups generally found that the concessions wrung from landlords and public agencies were only transitory.

A few other affiliates, particularly in New York City, used a more militant tactic—the rent strike. Once widely employed in the 1930's but only sporadically thereafter, use of the rent strike reached a feverish pitch in late 1963 and early 1964. Following the initial enthusiasm, however, it proved to be only a palliative. During the spring and summer of 1963, the New York University, Columbia University, and Brooklyn CORE chapters had helped tenants file complaints with the city's Buildings Department, and in the summer Norman Hill directed "pilot projects" in Newark and Brooklyn which sought to organize tenants for possible strikes. Although the New York Buildings Department had in some instances reduced the rents, and the Sanitation Department had cleaned up outside the Eldridge Street tenements after NYU CORE's trash-dumping episode, for the most part, CORE's efforts were stymied. Even after Farmer personally protested to city officials about the numerous violations of a particular slumlord, the man received only a token fine. With CORE groups still merely talking about the possibilities of rent strikes, the Northern Student Movement, an interracial organization of college and university youth, inaugurated one in Harlem during September. Inspired, the affiliates quickly followed this example. On October 1, 1963, NYU CORE announced that the East Side Tenants Council on Eldridge Street had started a strike, and a month later it proudly claimed that 110 tenants were giving National CORE their rent to hold in escrow. Enthusiastically backing the tactic, Farmer warned of a citywide strike of 10,000 families. Brooklyn CORE began rent strikes early in December, and soon after came the explosion of rent strikes in Harlem, under the leadership of long-time organizer of tenant protests, Jesse Gray.

CORE's cooperation with Gray was slight, but with the "rent strike fever" getting front page attention, "an extraordinary sense of exhilaration and even of historic destiny" gripped young CORE activists, as they moved rapidly to expand their activities. As one student CORE leader said, "everyone caught the fever—Rent Strike. No one knew about the legal consequences, or the amount of work involved. It seemed like the thing to do . . . the only way to beat the landlord." Brooklyn CORE claimed scores of buildings on strike; and soon Columbia University, CCNY, Bronx, and the East River chapters were involved. During the height of the enthusiasm political leaders and public agencies improved some conditions in a number of tenements. Brooklyn CORE in particular remedied many tenant grievances, largely because a sympathetic judiciary ruled that those in uninhabitable buildings need not pay rent. Yet the euphoria was short-lived. The mass media lost interest after newsmen discovered that the tenant movement was not as large and powerful as its leaders had publicly proclaimed. The courts quickly reverted to old legal evasions, which destroyed the morale of the tenants. In the words of a careful student of the subject, one CORE group after another dropped the rent strikes, "exhausted by the endless routine of court appearances, frustrated by the impossibility of actively involving slum tenants in complex legal procedures, [and] unable to sustain the militant atmosphere of the early days." Two professors at the Columbia University School of Social Work, who were close observers of the rent strike movement, later recalled: "When CORE organizers failed to resist the eviction of a family on the Lower East Side, other striking tenants, fearing that they also would be turned out, hysterically demanded the rent money from their escrow accounts. That event broke the strike in the CORE stronghold on Eldridge Street." By the autumn of 1964 the New York rent strike movement had practically disappeared.[69]

A few other northeastern chapters also led rent strikes, although nowhere on the scale of New York. Cleveland CORE began its first one in December 1963; a few months later the chapter claimed major concessions from two apartment house owners, and there were seven other buildings on strike. After careful investigations revealed violations in numerous buildings, Boston CORE conducted a month-long rent strike which ended when a slumlord made repairs on six Roxbury apartment houses.[70] Elsewhere in the country CORE affiliates discussed the possibilities of rent strikes but took little action. Chicago's Metropolitan CORE chapter, which actively sought to organize slum tenants, wearily concluded: "The job of organizing tenants was not an easy one, and while the idea of rent strikes was a good one, to successfully pull them off would require lots of time and energy on the part of everyone." [71] All over, organized action among the poor was difficult to sustain. At best tenant organization and rent strikes were difficult to carry out successfully, even where the laws were relatively favorable to tenants as in New York. In most places, landlords could easily evict the strikers, and remained unmovable. And even where successes were recorded, once the pressure was off, the gains often proved illusory.

At the very time that housing and employment campaigns were reaching their zenith, de facto school segregation also became a paramount issue for many chapters in the North. As Farmer told the 1964 Convention, "Our demand, categorically, must be quality integrated schools." [72] Struggles on this issue were conducted from coast to coast and involved tactics ranging from picketing through sit-ins to mammoth boycotts. Rather than proceeding on their own, the affiliates almost everywhere worked together with other organizations. Such coalitions in school campaigns were probably a necessity, given the fact that indifferent or recalcitrant school boards, subjected to intense counterpressure from northern segregationists, would not even vaguely consider policy changes without a unified front among the civil rights organizations. Moreover, the effectiveness of the most dramatic tactic used—the school boycott—required massive pupil participation, which a small group like CORE could not obtain by itself.

CORE often provided the ":cutting edge" in the use of direct-action against school segregation. At St. Louis it was CORE leaders like Charles Oldham and William Clay who, by blocking the buses, protested against the segregation of black pupils in the receiving schools to which they were being transported. CORE thus pushed the local umbrella group into demonstrations. Within weeks the coalition's attack broadened to include the whole system of de facto school segregation, and the campaign culminated in the early summer of 1963 with a mass march on the school board.[73] In Los Angeles in September, CORE was the spearhead for direct action by the broad-based coalition of seventy-six organizations, when eight chapter members conducted a sit-in and hunger strike for several days at the Board of Education building. Subsequently, vigils and "study-ins" were conducted, with hundreds of youths sitting-in the corridors during board meetings, and in November, CORE held a "sing-in" that broke up the session.[74] Meanwhile the Long Island and Brooklyn chapters escalated tactics in campaigns started earlier. In June and July Brooklyn CORE held a marathon three-week sit-in at the State Commission for Human Rights, which culminated in a blockade of the main entrance of the Board of Education. These actions finally won permission for two more black children to transfer to predominantly white schools outside their neighborhoods. In Malverne, Long Island, at the end of the summer, police arrested half a dozen CORE members for sitting-in at a predominantly white elementary school, and on the first day of classes the chapter led a boycott of a black elementary school.[75]

CORE's most important demonstrations on the school issue during 1963 occurred in Chicago, bringing to a climax a concern that went back to the first Chicago CORE's poster walk for integrated education twenty years before. Now dramatic actions resulted in nearly two hundred arrests. In July the chapter began a week-long sit-in at the office of the school board president, threatening to hold massive demonstrations at all-white schools if the board failed to redraw boundary lines. Several days later, when police attempted to prevent some protesters from reentering the building, a pushing, shoving, and kicking melee resulted, injuring a number of demonstrators and policemen. Veteran CORE people regarded these techniques as unnecessarily extreme, and the chapter chairman, Sam Riley, publicly apologized for the violence and resigned his post, saying, "I believe there should be more discipline among the demonstrators." Nevertheless, even more disorder accompanied CORE's renewed action in August—this time in cooperation with a black neighborhood group at a ghetto construction site where mobile classrooms were being installed. The protesters demanded that the Board of Education transport black children to available classroom space in predominantly white schools rather than add "portables" to segregated schools. On August 2, in a driving thunderstorm dozens were arrested during a muddy "lay-down," blocking trucks, earth-moving equipment, and police cars. Tactics were escalated as demonstrators chained themselves to construction equipment, and reached a climax a few days afterward when one hundred more were arrested. Some protesters threw stones at police; others kicked and cursed while being carried to patrol wagons. The publicity thus generated forced the board to dismantle the mobile classrooms at the disputed site. However, they were simply moved to other locations where CORE mounted short-lived protests that quickly spent themselves. The chapter's pre-eminent role in direct action against the school administration had now ended. Nevertheless, CORE had made the de facto segregation issue salient and paved the way for the famous Chicago school boycotts that followed.[76]

CORE chapters participated in the school boycotts in at least seven cities. Involving nearly the entire Negro school population in their respective communities, these demonstrations were quite different from the single-school boycotts carried out previously in the smaller cities of Syracuse and Englewood. Boston, in June 1963, was the first place to have a citywide boycott. Chicago, in November, gave the tactic nationwide publicity. The movement crested in February 1964, with a second boycott in both Chicago and Boston, and similar demonstrations in New York and Cincinnati. There followed another New York school boycott in March, two more in Kansas City, Kansas, and Cleveland in April, and one in Milwaukee in May.[77] All were sponsored by broad-based coalitions which varied greatly in their stability and in the role that CORE played. .

In Boston, Alan Gartner was a key person on the committee that sponsored the two boycotts; chapter members engaged in neighborhood organizational work, walked the picket lines, and assisted in the "Freedom Schools." [78] In Chicago, CORE played a minor role as one of the large number of groups participating in the Coordinating Council of Community Organizations.[79] In New York, where CORE was an important partner in the Citywide Committee for Integrated Schools, the first boycott, coming at the height of the excitement over the rent strike movement, pulled 464,000 pupils out for the day. Thereafter the direct-action campaign against segregated schools in New York declined. Dissatisfied with Rev. Milton Galamison's leadership, the national offices of CORE and the NAACP withdrew their endorsement from the second boycott held in March. Although several CORE chapters, including the militant Brooklyn, Bronx, and Harlem groups, actively supported it, only about 300,000 students stayed out of school.[80]

In Cleveland, CORE was chiefly responsible for promoting the campaign conducted under the auspices of the United Freedom Movement. There, direct action began relatively late—in January 1964, after the Board of Education had reneged on an agreement to cease segregating pupils being bussed from overcrowded black schools. Round-the-clock sit-ins at the Board reached a climax on February 3 when the protesters stopped elevators and blocked doors and stairways. Most of those arrested were CORE members. Criticized for such tactics, the Cleveland affiliate defended its "civil disobedience": "One of the best CORE traditions is the breaking of certain laws to show that a higher law is being violated. . . . Our determination demonstrated that if the Board of Education did not serve *all* the people, it should not be allowed to function." [81] In March the Board integrated the transported children, but to end the busing, it accelerated the building of three new ghetto schools. At CORE's urging, the United Freedom Movement demanded suspension of the construction, and early in April demonstrations began anew. On the fifth and sixth, forty-six protesters, including CORE executive secretary Ruth Turner, were arrested while attempting to halt the erection of these schools. To keep the cement mixer trucks moving into the area, police resorted to pushing and shoving the activists out of the way, and next day the chapter's vice-chairman Bruce Klunder was killed by a bulldozer which accidentally rolled backward as he lay crouched behind it. Shortly afterward a court injunction barred further interference with construction. In response the United Freedom Movement organized a boycott on April 20 in which 75,000 youngsters—92 per cent of the black student enrollment—were absent. Nevertheless in the autumn the new school opened on the site where Klunder had died.[82]

As in Cleveland, so nearly everywhere else, the school campaigns failed. St. Louis, where the school board did move to increase integration, was an exception, although even there CORE militants were dissatisfied. In Cincinnati, Los Angeles, and New York, the direct-action campaigns ended in inconclusive negotiations with the school boards.[83] In Boston the movement's failure was symbolized in 1965 by the re-election of Louise Day Hicks, the flamboyant leader of the Board's antibusing faction. Several factors contributed to these disappointing results. Not only did the protests generate intense white counterpressure, but there were also key factors at work in the black community and the nature of the protest itself. Grass-roots blacks were more interested in improving ghetto schools than in sending their children to distant integrated ones.[84] The boycotts themselves, limited to symbolic one-day stay-outs, lacked the sustained pressure needed to change basic policy. Finally, the coalitions, which included highly diverse organizations, proved unstable. A boycott required enormous planning and neighborhood work, yet when it was over the effects were miniscule.

If CORE found it difficult to grapple effectively with school segregation, the organization faced even greater recalcitrance when it tackled police brutality. Although the frequent abuse of police power had always been present in black neighborhoods, the issue, which became a major one for some affiliates by 1964, grew in salience for several reasons. The use of police dogs in the Birmingham demonstrations had aroused enormous concern. As CORE became more involved with the problems of the black poor, it recognized the importance of police brutality and its usefulness as a grievance around which to organize the slumdwellers.[85] Finally, the northern chapters' use of civil disobedience and going limp placed them in direct confrontation with law-enforcement agencies. Uncooperative demonstrators were dragged to the patrol wagons and in some cases they even tussled with the arresting officers. This created situations which reinforced the policemen's reputation for brutality already rooted in the facts of ghetto life. Beginning with the large-scale direct-action projects of the summer of 1963, CORE affiliates increasingly charged police with violence against demonstrators. At the Downstate Medical Center in Brooklyn, pickets complained of unnecessary roughness and beatings. In Manhattan, mounted policemen were accused of riding their horses over demonstrators who sat down on the sidewalk. New York CORE chairman Gladys Harrington declared that "horses in New York are no different than police dogs in Birmingham." Pickets at the Jefferson Bank in St. Louis were pushed and dragged into patrol wagons. Demonstrators in Chicago were shoved down the stairs at the Board of Education Building. In the Los Angeles housing protests, arrested activists were handcuffed, taken to an overcrowded jail, and forced to sleep on benches or on the concrete floor.[86]

Affiliates employed various tactics to spotlight the problem. In October 1963 San Francisco CORE members participated with other organizations in a mass march on city hall, consisting of two hundred people, in protest against a recent egregious incident of police brutality. Early in 1964 several members of Syracuse CORE were arrested for sitting-in at the police chief's outer office. About the same time Cleveland CORE picketed police headquarters, and in the summer it demonstrated at City Hall demanding a civilian review board. In March, Brooklyn chapter chairman Isaiah Brunson and Bronx chairman Herbert Callender handcuffed themselves to a grill outside the office of the police commissioner. A few weeks later these men and others were removed by police after they sat down in the corridor outside Mayor Wagner's office, protesting police brutality and other issues. They were removed by the police.[87] National CORE, in assigning a full-time field secretary to the task, played a key role in helping mobilize support for a bill to establish a New York City civilian review board. After the Harlem riot of July 1964, which erupted following a CORE demonstration at a precinct station in protest against the police slaying of a black youth, CORE pressed even harder for such a board.[88]

CORE's use of direct-action tactics was at its zenith for almost a year following Birmingham. Street demonstrations for desegregated public accommodations, compensatory employment, and integrated suburban housing reached their peak during the summer and early autumn of 1963, while the rent strike and school boycott movements came to a climax over the winter of 1963–64. There were, it is true, local exceptions as well as important regional variations. The western chapters, which often lagged behind the eastern affiliates, did not embark upon their most ambitious employment demonstrations until 1964, and failed to sponsor rent strikes or school boycotts. Yet for the relatively brief span of ten to eleven months, CORE groups energetically carried on a veritable cascade of campaigns against a broad range of discriminatory practices. And as they did, the militance of their tactics escalated.

These tactical changes were especially well illustrated by the succession of projects in the San Francisco Bay area. In the pre-Birmingham era, a leader of the University of California chapter recalled, "Image was all-important. Suit and tie was the standard direct action costume. Talking and smoking were forbidden on picket lines." * In the autumn of 1963 "a significant turning point" came with the job campaign at Mel's Drive-In restaurants in Berkeley and San Francisco. Not only were the picket lines manned by CORE and other organizations of unprecedented size, but "The notion of trying to maintain a respectable image was almost entirely demolished. . . . There was singing, shouting, clapping, smoking, talking, walking two abreast, dancing, and all types of dress on the line." Scuffles broke out as police officers forced the demonstrators, who had

---

* Certain chapters were still insisting on proper decorum as late as 1964. Milwaukee CORE directed demonstrators that there would be "no talking whatsoever" on picket lines and that participants should dress "comfortably but neatly." Women were specifically forbidden to wear slacks or shorts. (Milwaukee CORE, "CORE Demonstration Rules" [1964], Milwaukee CORE Prs.)

linked arms and gone limp, into the paddy wagons. Victory came following "two large waves of sit-ins and arrests," described proudly as "civil disobedience." [89] Thereafter Bay-area demonstrators "put increasing pressure on their leaders for escalation of tactics," and in February 1964, CORE introduced the supermarket shop-ins, to the consternation of the black Baptist ministers who were San Francisco CORE's close allies. When this campaign had been won, chapter chairman Bill Bradley announced that in the future such "civil disobedience would be resorted to when other tactics failed." To him the lesson of the supermarket shop-ins was clear: because CORE's new strategy had "forced" shoppers and community leaders alike "to assume a positive role . . . a solution which formerly did not exist . . . was suddenly brought into being." [90] Such tactics, as already seen, came to a climax with massive civil disobedience at the Sheraton-Palace Hotel and Auto Row demonstrations.

Meanwhile CORE chapters from Gadsden and Chapel Hill to Syracuse and Chicago had also resorted to obstructive methods in the name of civil disobedience. Among other techniques there had been increasing experimentation with the blocking of traffic arteries—at Greensboro and Jones Beach during the summer, twice at New Haven in the autumn, and at Chapel Hill in February 1964. More famous was the Triborough Bridge demonstration held by New York's East River CORE chapter in March 1964. To call attention to the unsafe and overcrowded East Harlem schools, chairman Blyden Jackson and several other members sat down on the bridge, halting traffic during the late afternoon rush hour.[91] A month later came the debate over the most controversial tactic ever proposed by a chapter—Brooklyn CORE's threatened stall-in on the opening day of the New York World's Fair.

Brooklyn had long been in CORE's tactical vanguard, and as in the second New York school boycott, which the affiliate supported, it and the national office had recently been at odds on various matters. For example, in January, when the chapter publicly called a Negro trial judge an Uncle Tom and threatened "massive civil disobedience" to bring New York to "a complete standstill" until a demonstrator whom the judge had sentenced was released, Farmer and the Steering Committee condemned this violation of CORE's Rules for Action.[92] Then, on April 7, against the wishes of the national office, Brooklyn CORE announced its plan to tie up traffic on the highways leading to the Fair. Although the NAC, polled by phone next day, voted to suspend the affiliate, Brooklyn CORE refused to give up the project. A short time afterward the Steering Committee, in a lengthy meeting that lasted at Farmer's apartment until 4 a.m., unanimously confirmed the chapter's suspension on the grounds that the proposed stall-in, lacking "clear and direct targets," would bring "social dislocation without direction," would provide "no relevant confrontation with those responsible for discrimination," and "would tend to polarize the nation racially and split the Negro community." [93] The affiliate, however, had considerable support within the other New York area chapters, and only after hectic negotiations and frantic meetings was the national office able to persuade most of them not to endorse the stall-in. Brooklyn CORE, nevertheless, maintained a bold front and threatened that two thousand cars would run out of gas on the highways. But except for a few chapter members who were arrested when they tried to halt a subway train, the stall-in failed to materialize.[94] Nevertheless, faced with the challenge from Brooklyn, Farmer and the Steering Committee had arranged their own "major project," directed at specific targets inside the fairgrounds. Nearly three hundred were arrested, including Farmer, who was apprehended for blocking the entrance to the New York City Pavilion. As a "symbolic act" he refused to cooperate with law enforcement officers, who carried him to a police van.[95]

The escalation in tactics, epitomized by the proposed stall-in, reflected an underlying change in perspective that affected both the larger civil rights movement and CORE itself. The greater the achievements, the clearer it became how much remained to be done and how little, relatively speaking, had been achieved by the quieter, more "respectable" forms of nonviolent direct action. As Farmer said at a staff meeting called to discuss the stall-in, "As the Civil Rights struggle increases, so has the frustration of the Negro people." The failure to obtain "Freedom Now" in the South during the summer of 1963 and the limited victories that followed the hard-fought campaigns in the North, produced a crisis over tactics in the nonviolent direct-action organizations. The spirit of disillusionment that began to spread in the left wing of the protest movement was first evident in SNCC; by April 1964, about the time of the stall-in controversy, outspoken militants, including Milton Galamison, Lawrence Landry, Jesse Gray, and Brooklyn CORE chairman Isaiah Brunson, formed a group called ACT. ACT, promising action where other organizations lagged, lambasted other leaders for siding with the white establishment and decried efforts to dampen demonstrations such as the stall-in. Men like Landry and ex-Freedom Rider Stokely Carmichael, who was now rising in the SNCC hierarchy, argued that "the white power structure" would never voluntarily accord blacks their rights, and that Negroes would have to take by force whatever they were going to get. A concerned Farmer wrote to A. Philip Randolph, "The left, the right and Malcolm X are all seeking to polarize the nation. The demagogic leadership of which you speak becomes a tool, wittingly or unwittingly, of the polarizers. It is an extremely dangerous situation." While ACT rarely moved beyond rhetoric and proved to be not an organization but a loose collection of militant spokesmen, it did reflect a growing stridency and alienation in the black protest movement.[96]

CORE was in flux, torn between attachment to its traditional style and the imperatives of a changing movement. As the somewhat millenarian expectations surrounding Birmingham and the March on Washington started to fade, the stress CORE leaders were under became evident. For example, shocked by the persistence of repressive violence in the South, NAC member Mark Dodson, former chairman of Long Island CORE, wrote in the autumn of 1963, "The whole approach of nonviolence . . . and of civil disobedience, needs to be worked on and evaluated and expanded. . . . We need new and/or modified approaches to put to rout the insipid idea of waiting on and for laws. . . . We . . . thought that the Birmingham demonstrations would certainly do something. . . . Just where are we now? Waiting for 'mass violence' and 'mass death?' " CORE people debated the legitimacy of some of the more·extreme tactics, even as they welcomed strategies that might do for the North what the Freedom Ride had done for the South. Thus some veteran members of the organization had misgivings about methods which they believed would antagonize the public and damage rather than advance the cause. A one-time Freedom Rider, who recalled the "different spirit in 1961" when picket lines "were marked by a sense of dignity and [when] the spirit was one of non-violence" complained to Farmer that many New York demonstrations in which she had participated during the summer of 1963 "are undignified both in dress and demeanor, and the underlying feeling is one of hostility." When the new style of protesting emerged on the Mel's Drive-In restaurant project, " 'Experienced' civil rights demonstrators didn't know what to think. Some stayed away; some tried to instruct the line in [what they regarded as] proper conduct; some joined in." Western field secretary Fredricka Teer urged the California chapters against disruptive tactics on behalf of the Rumford Fair-Housing Bill. She, like the bill's black sponsor himself, thought that sit-ins at the Capitol could only hurt its chances. When the demonstrations took place any-way, Teer observed, CORE "got a lot of publicity . . . and that seems at this stage of the game to determine effectiveness." As B. Elton Cox noted at the time Chicago CORE members were disorderly in the Board of Education campaign, many activists were no longer abiding by the Rules for Action.[97]

National officials, attributing the changes to the influx of new members who were attracted as Farmer often said, "by CORE's militance rather than its non-violent philosophy," [98] were divided in their responses to the changing style of demonstrations. McCain, upon returning from a western tour in the autumn of 1963, was disturbed about the new CORE groups who "have not spent much time going over CORE's philosophy, history, and techniques of nonviolence, therefore their activities have not always been in the 'CORE spirit.'" Rich also deplored certain new departures. Agreeing with the one-time Freedom Rider whose apprehension was cited earlier, he wrote, "There was a very different spirit in Mississippi in 1961. We're trying to rekindle that spirit." To a contributor who protested the Lucky store shop-ins, Rich replied, "I agree with you about the supermarket demonstrations. We do want our chapters to try new methods but with the CORE spirit." [99] Farmer, on the other hand, believed that "the means of maintaining the discipline of nonviolence have got to be tightened," but usually justified the new tactics, as did Carey. On a visit to the West Coast, Farmer endorsed the state capitol demonstration, and in New York he defended the members who had blocked entrances and business activities. "We have had our rights blocked for 100 years. It is time for all Americans to realize how it feels to have your way blocked." Speaking on CBS-TV he insisted that this type of action violated neither the CORE constitution nor the Rules for Action. Similarly, Farmer approved of the Triborough Bridge sit-down, which he called a "classic" example of civil disobedience.[100] Undoubtedly these varying responses of CORE's leaders reflected the different roles they played, and the essentially different publics to which they addressed themselves. Rich spoke primarily to old CORE friends and, more importantly, financial donors. As he wrote privately to a Seattle CORE leader after the shop-ins there, "I don't know how many thousands of dollars the shop-ins have cost us, but they have." [101] Farmer, on the other hand, was basically concerned with legitimizing CORE's tactics to a broad public in order to pave the way for the acceptance of CORE's demands. He was also reflecting the outlook of an important part of his constituency in the chapters. As a symbol of CORE militance he would necessarily have to speak to that militance.

The division of opinion, the uncertainty and anguish about the newer tactics was best revealed in the debates over the proposed Brooklyn stall-in. In discussions with the New York area affiliates, Farmer first spoke against the stall-in, then reluctantly went along with the rising sentiment for it, and later in the NAC Steering Committee he reversed himself again.[102] Even after the Committee's unanimous decision to suspend Brooklyn CORE and denounce the stall-in tactic, National CORE was attacked in New York by Bronx, New York, Columbia University, Yonkers, and the Long Island affiliates. CORE members in north Jersey were greatly divided. The Bridgeport, Connecticut, group, though publicly backing National CORE, was "split right in half" and one leader of the chapter reported, "emotionally almost all of us favor" the stall-in, believing that Brooklyn CORE represented the attitude of the black masses. From Louisiana, Mimi Feingold, a white task force worker, though entertaining reservations about the practicability of Brooklyn's project, observed: "What struck me, regardless of the advisability of the stall-in was that it challenged the thinking of people at every level of the power structure which, in itself, is a very valuable thing. . . . It is imperative, it seems to me, that precisely those people who think this country has made substantial strides toward granting Negroes civil rights (such as Pres. Johnson) be constantly made aware of the impatience of hundreds of thousands of people. . . ." Delegates to a Western CORE Regional Conference overwhelmingly endorsed the stall-in. The conference also devoted a session to civil disobedience—a technique which many participants supported vigorously. One Los Angeles delegate declared, "Civil disobedience is effective. Sometimes lesser means are not. . . . We're moving into areas where there is no more one-to-one relations with our adversary. We are dealing with bigger entities like cities, etc. . . . We're hitting institutions, not individuals. We have to use harder force." [103] In view of the substantial sentiment supporting Brooklyn, Farmer administered only a light wrist-tapping and made special efforts to win the personal loyalty of the disaffected militants. Brooklyn CORE's suspension was lifted on May 1, when the affiliate was placed on probation for ninety days. Herbert Callender, the Bronx CORE chairman who had vociferously backed Brooklyn, was appointed a field secretary in August. A short time afterward Farmer nominated Brooklyn CORE leader Olly Leeds to the NAC.[104]

The opposition of many CORE officials to Brooklyn's plans was rooted in pragmatic more than ideological considerations. Some Steering Committee members were ambivalent; and, indeed, the objection was not based on the tactic itself, but upon the fact that the stall-in was not directed against specific targets. Brooklyn CORE, in defending its position, challenged Farmer to differentiate between the Triborough Bridge demonstration which he approved and the stall-in which he did not. Since both involved traffic stoppages and neither was directed at the specific agents responsible for discrimination, clearly the only essential distinction lay in the scale of the two projects. As Alan Gartner explained, "The considerable autonomy which CORE chapters enjoy would under normal circumstances permit such activity. However, the scope of the [proposed stall-in] protest, and the form in which it was to take place, made it a matter for national CORE's concern." Farmer himself openly said at the time that his opposition was based not on principle but on questions of strategy and timing.[105] In the view of CORE's national leadership, the stall-in, compared to which the Triborough Bridge demonstration was but a pinprick, would have aroused enormous resentment among many sympathetic whites and would have exacerbated CORE's financial problems, without the slightest chance of remedying any specific evils. It would have articulated CORE's militance brilliantly and made clear the growing anger and alienation in the black community, but Farmer concluded that, given the social climate of 1964, it would have produced a serious setback for CORE and the civil rights movement.

Ironically the debates over the stall-in came at the very time that direct action had passed its apogee. In fact, the World's Fair project was the last major demonstration which CORE sponsored in New York City; and in most other areas across the country the use of this technique was in precipitous decline. This was due to a paradoxical combination of achievement and failure. As had happened with the lunch-counter sit-in movement of 1960, so by the autumn of 1963, both the victories in the upper South and the dismaying failures and repression in the lower South, seemed to pretty much exhaust, temporarily at least, the potentialities for nonviolent direct action in that region. It is likely that a wave of demonstrations aimed at completing the battle against jim crow public accommodations would have subsequently arisen had it not been for the passage of the 1964 Civil Rights Act. This law was in itself a legislative milestone made possible by the wave of activism which had swept the South in the spring and summer of 1963. Meanwhile victorious job campaigns in the North also provided a significant record of accomplishment. Yet both the substantial desegregation which had occurred in southern public accommodations, and the new willingness of many northern business firms—which had learned from companies experiencing direct action—to make concessions simply through negotiations with CORE, created a vacuum that left activists searching for new situations in which to apply nonviolent techniques. On the other hand, aside from gains in employment projects, the northern CORE chapters seldom experienced substantial progress. School segregation and police brutality seemed almost immune to attack; rent strikes and urban renewal demonstrations produced at best only temporary relief; drives for suburban fair-housing, where successful, brought merely token victories for the middle class; and even in the case of jobs, the highly publicized construction-trade campaigns led only to broken promises. Moreover, in some cases where public officials were sufficiently determined, repressive actions effectively crushed even the most militant demonstrations, not only in southern communities like Gadsden, Tallahassee, Plaquemine, and Chapel Hill, but also in a number of northern cities. In situations such as Seattle's fair-housing campaign, and the Cleveland school site lie-in, court injunctions were enough to discourage continuation of disruptive tactics. In other instances, of which noted ones were the St. Louis bank project and the San Francisco Sheraton-Palace and Auto Row campaigns, punitive court action against arrested protesters broke the back of CORE's nonviolent direct-action program. Finally, it was becoming evident that even where social change had occurred, CORE's demonstrations had not significantly affected the life chances of the black poor.

For all these reasons direct action, while by no means discarded, had sharply declined by the spring of 1964. Though still emotionally committed to this technique, CORE people were by then seriously engaged in the search for new approaches that might better fulfill their quest for equality.

9

Battle for the Ballot

CORE's most substantial efforts to register blacks in the South were made between the summer of 1963 and the summer of 1964. The organization expanded existing projects in Louisiana, South Carolina, and Mississippi and developed a new program in the rural counties of north Florida. Of these campaigns, the most dramatic was the COFO-sponsored drive in Mississippi, which came to a climax in the celebrated Challenge to the seating of the lily-white "regular" delegation at the Democratic National Convention.

The transition from direct action, which had crested over the summer of 1963, to voter registration, which dominated the southern protest movement during the following year, was facilitated by the foundation-encouraged VEP inaugurated earlier. The flow of disbursements from the VEP's Atlanta headquarters was now accelerated. National CORE, stimulated by these grants and pushed by the southern staff, committed increasing resources to the region.

Most of the field secretaries were still stationed in the South, and practically all of the growing task force, which now formed the backbone of the staff in the area, was also located there. This large contingent of southern workers, faced with frightening repression in most of the places where they were assigned, acted as an influential pressure group within CORE, forcing the national office and the Steering Committee to send in even more aid. For example, during the spring of 1963, David Dennis, frustrated by the NAC's reluctance to supply him with additional field staff, appealed directly to VEP director Wiley Branton for funds. CORE's leaders were distinctly annoyed but under this pressure speedily assigned black Freedom Rider George Raymond, a former member of New Orleans CORE, to assist him. Thereafter, with the Mississippi program almost perpetually in crisis, Dennis' fervent, often tearful, pleas for further support, proved nearly irresistible.[1] Again, southern field workers vigorously urged the opening of a regional office; during a meeting in October 1963, they accused the national headquarters of being in "the position of an absentee landlord of a revolution," unable to feel "the needs and anxieties of the people that we live and work with." In response to persistent prodding, the NAC in March 1964 placed Haley, who had been serving since the preceding autumn as associate national director, in charge of a new regional office in New Orleans.[2]

As previously, the funding policies of the VEP meant that CORE's voter registration work was confined to South Carolina, Florida, Louisiana, and Mississippi. Only in Mississippi, where Branton withdrew VEP assistance late in 1963 when it became evident that it was virtually impossible for more than a trickle of Negroes to register, did CORE entirely finance its own project. In all four states the scope of CORE's activity expanded considerably—to include nineteen counties in South Carolina, the rural northern Florida areas as well as Miami, the entire Fourth Congressional District in Mississippi, and the northern parishes in addition to the Sixth District in Louisiana.

In South Carolina the CORE staff increased black registration substantially, despite the stalling registrars who kept their books closed except for a few days each month. Williamsburg County continued to be the most notorious; in October 1963, for example, of the 319 Negroes who waited outside the courthouse, only 55 were admitted to the registrar's office. Nevertheless, monthly registration in CORE's area rose from 400 in May 1963 to a high of 1900 in January 1964, and CORE proudly recorded a total of 16,000 registered in the year ending June 1, 1964.[3] Not unexpectedly, in urban Florida the results were better. Weldon Rougeau led two campaigns in Miami that placed 9400 persons on the books and, cooperating with the NAACP, helped with another successful drive in Tallahassee.[4] But it was different in the rural north Florida project which Pat Due initiated in the autumn of 1963. Operating for the next two years in five counties where blacks voted either not at all or in miniscule numbers, CORE workers faced foot-dragging registrars, harassing police, and occasional beatings and rifle shots from angry whites.[5] Although their difficulties were compounded by trouble with the NAACP, whose state office pressured several local leaders into withdrawing invitations to CORE registration staffers,[6] the work finally got under way, and during July and August CORE was able to register a total of 2700 persons. For Pat Due, the demonstration of CORE interracialism partly compensated for the relatively limited results: "This has been the first time that people have lived, eaten and worked interracially in these areas. . . . When we first came to Gadsden County, for example, in January, it was an unusual and disturbing sight for local people, white and Negro, to see us interracially. Now . . . officials and most of the populace are accustomed to it. Some public accommodations have opened without direct action because workers insist upon eating together in both white and Negro establishments." [7]

While in terms of numbers placed on the rolls CORE's greatest accomplishments were in South Carolina and Florida, its most ambitious efforts were concentrated in Louisiana and Mississippi. In both these states civil rights workers and local citizens who attempted to register continued to face unprecedented physical harassment and intimidation. The situation was so serious, and federal authorities so ineffective in providing protection that in November 1963 the NAC unanimously decided to investigate the possibility of "a freedom ride against the Justice Department." [8] The well-known Mississippi voter registration program received the lion's share of the publicity, but CORE's important contribution in that state was obscured in the public eye just because it was operating as part of a federation in which SNCC played the pre-eminent role. Accordingly, CORE decided to place its heaviest emphasis on Louisiana, and with Ronnie Moore in charge, hoped to make that state a showcase of CORE's activity.

Voter registration in Louisiana's Sixth District became the organization's chief summer project in 1963. An interracial group of forty summer task force workers, recruited from across the country, assembled at Plaquemine in July. After a two-week training program that saturated Iberville Parish with rallies and church appearances, neighborhood canvassing, training "clinics," and daily trips to the courthouse, the task force fanned out into half a dozen other parishes. In the relatively urbanized Tangipahoa Parish, the main problems were rivalry among the local black organizations and their fear of militant outsiders. But most of the canvassing was done in villages and hamlets and among isolated farmers on dirt roads, where intimidation was so serious that despite Moore's numerous protests to the Justice Department, only 452 were registered by the time most of the task force departed from the district late in August.[9]

At Clinton, the tiny East Feliciana Parish seat, the registrar's unconcealed hostility was unnerving; he admitted only one person at a time, set rigid identification requirements that few Negroes could meet, and usually flunked the few whom he permitted to take the tests. Out on the streets blacks heard veiled threats, " . . . boy, you got to live here. Don't get pushed up to doing things against white folks." Within a week after CORE's arrival, three blacks lost jobs for attempting to register. Police constantly patrolled the homes of citizens who provided CORE people with living quarters. A white task force worker from Newark, Mike Lesser, was jailed simply because he accompanied Negroes into the registrar's office. So great was the intimidation in this parish that the black Masons asked CORE to stop using their hall as a voter instruction center. Despite the fear and the subservient "Uncle Toms," there were a few courageous blacks who housed the CORE staff and whose cooperation made the work possible. Seventy-four-year-old "Mama Jo" Holmes opened her home in Clinton for daily "clinics," and her example was followed by three small Baptist churches.[10]

Concerned at these developments, local officials effectively halted the registration program through a court order obtained at the end of the summer, enjoining CORE—"a rabble-rousing Communist-front"—from further activity in the parish. As a substitute strategy, a radical young white task force member stationed in Clinton proposed to generate pressure on public officials by mounting a boycott against the local white merchants. Although the local blacks were reluctant to violate the injunction, he prevailed upon them to inaugurate the campaign in October with the slogan, "If you can't vote with the ballot, vote with your dollar." On the first day of picketing thirty-nine were arrested for defying the court order, and soon afterward the leaders of the movement were indicted for "conspiracy to commit intimidation." The boycott gradually petered out, and by the end of the year CORE's program in East Feliciana Parish was practically dead.[11] Not until the following May, when the authorities, fearing federal court intervention, finally scrapped the injunction, was CORE able to again operate effectively in the parish.[12]

In neighboring West Feliciana Parish, where CORE workers experienced similar harassment, efforts begun during the summer of 1963 produced an important symbolic victory in the autumn, when the first Negro in over six decades signed his name to the voter registration rolls. In August, Ronnie Moore and Rudy Lombard had prevailed upon a rural minister, fifty-five-year-old Joseph Carter, to challenge the registrar. For daring to question the official who had just turned him down, Carter was arrested on a "disturbing the peace" charge. This incident and Carter's subsequent lawsuit against the registrar and sheriff for violating his civil rights, galvanized the local blacks, who took a new interest in CORE's campaign, and daily attendance at the "clinics" rose from below ten to above one hundred by the end of September. On October 17, with Justice Department observers stationed across the street, Carter and forty-two black farmers presented themselves at the courthouse. Not until they had waited outside for five hours, amid the taunts and threats from white hangers-on, did the registrar finally let him into the office. A short time afterward Carter "came out of the courthouse walking briskly, smiling, with his voter registration certificate waving." [13]

Only four others were admitted to the registrar's office that day, and all were turned down. There followed a recurring pattern of physical harassment and intimidation from whites that was countered by an extraordinary display of courage from the blacks. A few hours after leaving the courthouse two of the men were warned by their landlord that they would be killed if they tried to register again. Nevertheless, thirty blacks appeared at the courthouse next day; only a handful were allowed in, but three obtained certificates. That night whites fired into the house of the bus driver who had brought the applicants to town. Again, on the next registration day the blacks returned. Not long afterward, one man's house was burned at the very moment he was registering. Yet the Negroes persisted. Moore regularly sent complaints to the Justice Department, which at the end of October finally filed suit against the registrar, and in early November, when the books closed, the number of blacks on the rolls had risen to thirteen.[14]

By then, while other forms of harassment continued, physical attacks had generally ceased because the Negroes started carrying guns and threatened to retaliate. Three days after Carter registered Moore warned, "Negroes have vowed to shoot on sight any white face which appears on their property after dark. . . . Unless Negro citizens are protected and their civil rights guaranteed, blood, both black and white, will be shed." Mike Lesser, writing to a friend, described the arming of the blacks in West Feliciana Parish:

> But the really beautiful thing to see and be a part of is the movement—the spirit, the people, the courage, and the shotguns. We hold instruction clinics in a Masonic Hall . . . two evenings a

week, and if any hostile white folks should ever try to approach the
place without warning they would find themselves faced by 15-20
high-powered, long-range shotguns. . . . At first when we started
going to the courthouse some of our people were beaten and threatened. But as soon as Negroes started carrying shotguns . . . the attacks stopped and haven't resumed. . . . Incidentally, so you don't
get the wrong idea, we are preaching nonviolence, but Ronnie
Moore and I and the other workers can only preach nonviolence,
and practice it. We cannot tell someone not to defend his property
and the lives of his family, and let me tell you, those 15-20 shotguns
guarding our meetings are very reassuring.[15]

In Iberville Parish, meanwhile, where about half the eligible voting-
age blacks were now registered, Moore and Harleaux directed their energies to other goals: obtaining the annexation of the "back-of-town"
ghetto into Plaquemine and entering into the arena of partisan politics.
In pursuit of the former, CORE and the Voters League followed up on
the direct-action strategy employed during the summer. Because the injunction against street demonstrations was still in effect, they decided, as
had been done in Clinton, to inaugurate a boycott against retail merchants. Two stores were forced to close, but the campaign failed to move
the intransigent public officials.[16] Another effort at direct action, a student strike precipitated by the dismissal of a lunchroom worker whose
child had participated in the summer demonstrations, was equally unproductive. The students, who practically closed down Plaquemine's black
high school for several days, also demanded the desegregation of parish
schools. Using tear gas and cattle prods, the police routed the youths,
who marched to the school board and picketed the white high school,
and with the expulsion of thirty-five of them, the strike was broken.[17]
Meanwhile, the number of blacks now registered afforded some hope that
Negroes could be elected to office, and a slate of black candidates was
fielded in the autumn elections. Most of the black ministers refused to cooperate, and Moore complained that the "old Negro power structure . . .
bitterly opposed any possibility of a Negro running for public office." Although all of the black candidates lost in the December primary, the venture was not without its gains, notably the defeat of the incumbent
sheriff and congressman, two "leading cattle-prod wielding politicians,"
who had taken prominent roles in the repressive tactics employed against
the demonstrators in the summer of 1963.[18]

By the end of 1963 Moore could look back upon a certain amount of
accomplishment. Yet in Marvin Rich's words, the Louisiana program was

"somewhat disappointing." The number registered during 1963 was only about one-fifth of that in South Carolina.[19] In Clinton the boycott had only embroiled CORE in the courts. In Plaquemine the accelerated voter registration campaign and the demonstrations had neither elected blacks to office nor secured the incorporation of the Negro areas into the town. In an attempt to revive work in Shreveport, CORE had run into NAACP resentment and police repression, while the New Orleans CORE group remained quite lethargic.[20] And even in Iberville and the Felicianas the task force found themselves doing most of the work because they could not develop much indigenous leadership.[21] Moreover the repression was demoralizing. In Plaquemine the authorities' handling of the school strike once again brought fear and discouragement. By December 1963 a black field worker, Bill Brown, sadly reported that throughout the district local participants were "exhausted and fast losing faith in the effectiveness of the movement." Another task force worker, Freedom Rider Mimi Feingold, summed up the pessimism that pervaded much of the staff. She complained that the people had been so beaten down that, "We've got to travel many miles, spend much time just talking, before we convince one Negro to go to the registrar's office. In a typical week I contact 150 people, train 60, send 18 to the registrar's office, and have 9 of them get registered." Sadly she noted that the "social revolution" which the VEP had appeared to promise was a long way off.[22]

This sense of limited attainment did not deter the irrepressible Ronnie Moore, who continued to advance ambitious long-range plans. Advising CORE to avoid places like New Orleans where competition between organizations was debilitating and to concentrate instead on North Louisiana where, since SCLC efforts had flopped, the situation was ripe for CORE, he sent staffers to scout the northern parishes, and by December the first task force workers had established headquarters in Monroe. During the following months CORE not only created a firm base in the Monroe area but also expanded its work in the Sixth District. Yet despite these efforts, during the first five months of 1964, in all of CORE's Louisiana projects only 942 could be registered, only a slight improvement over 1963, when CORE had averaged about 150 a month.[23]

The program in the Sixth District, in fact, continued to labor under serious difficulties. In Plaquemine the conservative black leadership which opposed CORE reasserted itself. Opposition from a number of black ministers destroyed a job boycott at a new shopping center. Even the Iberville Parish Industrial Voters League split, with some leaders now attack-

ing W. W. Harleaux and uniting with CORE's other critics to form a
competing League.[24] In the Felicianas, even though CORE chapters had
been established at the parish seats, developments were also discouraging.
With VEP activity effectively curtailed by the tactics of the registrars,
who kept their offices closed, neither affiliate was very active. A test of
the public library at Clinton promptly landed task force worker Mimi
Feingold and a half-dozen youths in jail.[25] In order to counter the climate of intimidation the staff decided to attack the Princeville Canning
Company, which they believed to be a key element in the West Feliciana
Parish "power structure." In February 1964, the company withheld new
contracts from many sweet potato farmers, arguing that they had failed
to meet production quotas the preceding year. In this repressive environment, CORE workers erroneously concluded that the cannery was trying
to destroy black farmers who exercised the right to vote. Actually, those
who lost contracts included whites as well as blacks, nonregistrants as
well as registrants. The task force workers failed to negotiate with the
company, and convinced CORE headquarters to mount a boycott against
the cannery's products. In the end the whole project misfired. Announcing that Princeville had refused "to make a contract with any Negro
farmer who had attempted to register," James Farmer urged CORE chapters across the country to pressure supermarket chains into joining the
boycott. To prevent further economic damage, the cannery reiterated its
innocence, and began purchasing all the potatoes which the noncontract
growers produced. By then National CORE officials recognized their
error, but since a public admission would be "rather embarrassing," they
announced that a victory had actually been won.[26]

In North Louisiana, where the Ku Klux Klan flourished, the intimidation was even worse than in the Sixth District. As Ronnie Moore wrote,
"North Louisiana is rough, so ask those who believe to pray for us." [27] In
the industrial town of Monroe itself where, as in East Feliciana, the overwhelming majority of black voters had been purged in 1956-57, fear
impeded CORE's voter registration efforts. Police frequently held task
force workers for interrogation and tried to intimidate a Negro restaurant owner who served the interracial team. In January 1964 a cross was
burned outside the house where two staff members lived. Accordingly,
the middle-class NAACP leaders, who had originally invited CORE to
help with registration, grew timid, and only after the organization established contact with several working-class leaders in the Olin-Mathieson
paper plant was CORE able to sink firm roots in the community. CORE

helped the workers file complaints with federal authorities against discrimination at the factory, and in turn, a Negro union official who headed the Independent Voters League cooperated closely with CORE's registration efforts. "Clinics" were established at two churches, and despite the registrar's tactics, CORE, assisted by the black union locals and enthusiastic high school volunteers, painstakingly registered 137 people during January. Yet thereafter, with the registrar's office closed much of the time, police intimidation and adult fear prevented further advances.[28]

From Monroe, CORE workers probed into nearby parishes, like Tensas, the last one in Louisiana where not a single black was registered. Oppression was so extreme in Tensas that local black leaders refused CORE's offer to send field staff. In Tallulah, seat of neighboring Madison Parish, CORE found another kind of problem. There blacks voted in substantial numbers but were pressed to support the police chief's political machine. CORE workers, welcomed by Zelma Wyche, a barber and the town's most influential Negro, were immediately ordered out by the police chief.[29]

Terrorism was also extreme in Jonesboro, a small industrial town not far from Monroe, and the seat of Jackson Parish where, as a result of the purge of the voting rolls in 1956, only 20 per cent of the eligible black population was registered. People there were afraid to go to the courthouse even though the registrar was under court order to cease discrimination. Ultimately, once CORE's program got under way with the cooperation of the local Progressive Voters League, the blacks, as in West Feliciana Parish earlier, responded to white violence with armed self-defense. Early in July, Moore and Lesser, leaving an evening meeting at Jonesboro, were blocked on a rural highway by four carloads of whites. Moore turned suddenly and raced back to Jonesboro at nearly one hundred miles an hour, pursued by the other cars. The two men took refuge in CORE's office, as their would-be assailants circled the block shouting obscenities. Neither local law enforcement officials nor the FBI responded until Marvin Rich in New York City contacted FBI headquarters. Afterward, armed local black leaders insisted on personally escorting Moore and Lesser back to Monroe. About three weeks later KKK members burned crosses throughout the parish. That same evening, fifty hooded men, headed by a sheriff's patrol car, marched through Jonesboro's black section holding burning torches, and about one hundred armed whites converged on the jail where two civil rights workers were being held on trumped-up charges. The mob was dispersed only after

Marvin Rich awakened presidential assistant Lee White, who asked the Justice Department to intervene. These incidents confirmed the belief of many blacks that an armed defense was imperative, and they organized the Deacons for Defense and Justice to protect civil rights workers and the black community.[30]

In this context of persistent intimidation, CORE in 1964 sponsored its second Louisiana summer project. The forty task force workers, assigned to nine parishes, faced the usual run of harassment, ranging from menacing phone calls and bomb threats to actual physical assault. On at least two occasions Moore futilely telegraphed Attorney-General Kennedy demanding protection and an immediate investigation.[31] Not surprisingly the summer produced only modest advances in registration. In a vigorous effort during June at Monroe and Jonesboro, the staff canvassed 3800 blacks and convinced 1100 to attend "clinics"; of these, 198 sought to register, but only 55 were accepted. In the Felicianas, a court order reopened the books, which had been closed for months, and the registrars actually permitted a few to register. Although Mimi Feingold was "still deeply impressed by the beauty of those who do take a stand . . . [and by the] simple determination that will lead a man to give his life, if necessary," in fact, intimidation from local whites continued to discourage potential applicants. All told, over the three summer months, 1070 blacks were registered in CORE's Louisiana projects; over 3000 others had attempted to register but were denied.[32] Similarly, testing places of public accommodation after the Civil Rights Law went into effect in July met with distinctly mixed results. In St. Helena and Pointe Coupee Parishes, despite appeals to the FBI and the U. S. District Court in Baton Rouge, Negroes were consistently refused service at the restaurants. At Jonesboro, fifteen were arrested for trying to use the city swimming pool, and twenty-four others for seeking service at the public library. In Monroe about thirty-five youngsters were also arrested at the library, and one theater closed rather than admit blacks; yet some Monroe restaurants accepted Negro patronage, and a number of local bus drivers permitted blacks to sit in front.[33] In Plaquemine people ate at all lunch counters except one, and even there, after returning with the police chief, they were served.[34]

Thus in the second year of the VEP, CORE's Louisiana staff, working closely with small-town blacks in the most oppressed areas of the state, had struggled against enormous odds to register a trickle of people. Only in Iberville Parish had CORE been in a position to take the next logical step and venture into partisan politics. In contrast, in the neighboring state of Mississippi, where the climate of repression and the accretions in registration were similar to those in Louisiana, CORE, as part of the COFO coalition became involved in a much more varied program. Establishing community centers and Freedom Schools, the Mississippi CORE staff began to concern themselves with the broader needs of the local communities and to experiment with a strategy that would later become popular as "community organization." At the same time CORE co-sponsored a unique attempt at organizing blacks into a cohesive political unit —the Mississippi Freedom Democratic Party.

The Council of Federated Organizations, a state-wide coalition of racial advancement organizations that remained viable and effective for more than two years, was a unique phenomenon in the history of the civil rights movement. The preponderant influence in COFO was wielded by CORE and especially SNCC. SCLC's participation was slight. The NAACP's major contribution came through the role which Aaron Henry played as the Council's president. COFO's two top administrators were program director Bob Moses of SNCC and assistant program director David Dennis of CORE. SNCC dominated the executive committee and staffed four of the state's five Congressional districts. CORE had two of the eight seats on the executive committee and was responsible for one district. Most of COFO's budget came from SNCC, with CORE financing its own district and part of the costs of the state headquarters at Jackson.[35] The stability of the coalition was largely due to Mississippi's repressive racial climate, which made differences among organizations seem inconsequential and unity imperative if the movement was to survive and accomplish anything. As one CORE field worker put it, "We can't mess around with petty organizational disagreements and with separate loyalties when the OUT THERE aspect is so pressing." More important, COFO's success was also due to the personalities of Moses, Dennis, and Henry, all of whom were "movement-oriented" and thus able to submerge minor organizational interests for the welfare of the larger movement. Thus Dennis, in appealing to VEP for money, once informed Wiley Branton that it made no difference whether the funds were funeled through CORE or COFO.[36]

Dennis personally identified himself more with COFO than with CORE, and for him working closely with SNCC therefore posed no difficulties. Yet the interaction with other organizations in COFO inevitably involved delicate problems which were of keen concern to National

CORE. Not only did CORE's contribution in Mississippi tend to go unreported to the public, while SNCC garnered most of the credit, but problems also arose over the fact that CORE's Fourth District staff was partly responsible to COFO. Thus, Haley commented, the arrangements place a "hardship on the Fourth District staff," since "as part of a state operation, it must work with COFO; [while] as part of a national body it must work with CORE." For example, Dennis' responsibilities in the statewide operation took him away from his purely CORE duties, so that, as McCain once wrote Haley, there was the persistent problem of "how far Dave will become involved in supervising COFO or CORE's activities." To CORE's Mississippi staff such considerations seemed trivial and narrow-minded. Bob Moses sometimes made decisions regarding the Fourth District when Dennis was unavailable, just as Dennis made decisions for other projects in the state. SNCC staff were assigned to CORE's area, and CORE staff in turn sometimes worked in other congressional districts. The CORE field workers even proposed that the national office channel its funds for the Fourth District through the state COFO office: "We want a willingness on the part of national CORE to approach staff problems differently. There can be no artificial division between salaried CORE workers . . . and workers with other groups." Because of his COFO connection, Dennis operated with greater autonomy than any other project director. In contrast to Ronnie Moore, who regularly submitted formal plans to the national office for approval, Dennis consulted national only when he wanted assistance in implementing plans he had previously charted with the COFO staff.[37]

Two other sources of tension between the national office and Dennis were inadequate financing and the lack of legal assistance. Actually, the NAC had initially been ambivalent about keeping Dennis in Mississippi because, during his first year there, no CORE chapters had been formed.[38] Moreover, once committed to expanding his work in the state, it became clear that whatever money went to Mississippi was at the expense of projects elsewhere. Southern programs just as meritorious as COFO—and often, as in Louisiana and North Florida, laboring under conditions just as repressive—needed more funds and staff than the national office could provide. More serious was the problem of legal aid, a need not limited to Mississippi. Throughout the South only a pitifully small number of lawyers would accept civil rights cases. Into this vacuum stepped the National Lawyers Guild, which aggressively volunteered its help to various civil rights groups. National CORE leaders eschewed cooperation with the Guild, fearing that its identification as a Communist front might damage the movement and believing that the dramatic tactics of some of its lawyers were more often show than substance. SNCC and COFO eagerly accepted the Guild's assistance, and although the presence of Collins, Douglas, and Elie made the use of Guild attorneys unnecessary in New Orleans, the need was so critical in Mississippi that CORE's southern staff also found its offer tempting.[39] The failure of CORE either to supply lawyers or to permit the Mississippi staff to use the Guild left Dennis "bitter . . . and dissatisfied." [40]

Despite the organization's perennial financial problems and the requirements of other programs, National CORE leaders responded to the Mississippi staff's pleas and usually allocated more resources to the state than was planned. Dennis, by making appeals to the NAC rather than to the national staff officials who were normally responsible for allocating funds to various programs, capitalized on the strong emotional identification that CORE people had with the Mississippi project. Over the months CORE increased its investment in the Fourth District, stepped up financial contributions to the Jackson office, and raised the number of staff in the state to eleven by January 1964 and to eighteen during the following summer. At Rich's suggestion, CORE did insist, however, that the Fourth District project maintain a distinct CORE identity rather than allow itself to be obliterated in COFO.[41] Meanwhile, during the spring Carl Rachlin had taken steps to secure better legal service. With assistance from the American Civil Liberties Union, the NAACP Legal Defense Fund, the American Jewish Committee, the American Jewish Congress, and the National Council of Churches, he organized a volunteer group known as the Lawyers Constitutional Defense Committee (LCDC). That summer, the LCDC opened offices in Jackson and Memphis that rivaled the services which the Guild was providing from bases in the same cities. With additional LCDC offices in four other southern towns, all of them staffed by lawyers from across the country, Rachlin was able to say with pride: "For the first time since major civil rights demonstrations have commenced in the South, we have nearly adequate legal assistance in all significant areas." [42]

Financed by a short-term VEP grant, CORE's first beachhead in Mississippi's Fourth District was established in June 1963 at Canton, the seat of rural Madison County, where nearly three-fourths of the population was black—but where only a handful were allowed to register.[43] In setting up their office the CORE staff of five headed by Dennis and George

Raymond obtained the enthusiastic support of a prosperous black businessman, C. O. Chinn. Chinn courageously rented them a building and continued to help despite harassment from authorities that eventually drove him out of business. Twice he was jailed on false charges of carrying a concealed weapon; on the second occasion Chinn was incarcerated for six months. It was such repression that made most other Canton Negroes fearful. Early interest in CORE quickly waned in the face of constant police surveillance, the dismissal of some supporters from their jobs, and the county registrar's refusal to certify most of the applicants CORE brought to the courthouse. Because, as in other southern towns, ministers were key leaders, field staff expended much effort recruiting them, but only two agreed to lend assistance. The CORE workers themselves lived in constant fear of attack, especially after the police began searching people at meetings and broke into the office late one night, leaving the place in shambles. Nevertheless, the staff persisted. The spirit of dogged determination in the face of white terrorism that characterized the CORE workers were reflected in the report of Mat Suarez, a former leader in New Orleans CORE: "Tension is building downtown and it appears as though something will be done soon to prevent us from working down there. Some threats have been delivered to me by word of mouth. In the past week over 150 homes, barbershops, etc., [were] visited and numerous persons spoken to and taught how to register. Most of them will have to be revisited." [44] Yet, during one week in late June the task force reported that although eighteen blacks were turned away at the courthouse, twelve succeeded in registering.

Although during the summer only a few people had been able to register, Dennis and his staff enthusiastically participated in the COFO-sponsored "Freedom Election," held in November. Designed to educate blacks about the potential power of the ballot, to unite them in a cohesive statewide political organization that might ultimately challenge Mississippi's power structure, and to call national attention to the wholesale disfranchisement of Negroes, this project consisted of a "mock" election in which Aaron Henry ran for governor.[45] Amidst a barrage of police harassment, Dennis and Raymond toured the state on the candidate's behalf. At Yazoo City police arrested task force worker Lenora Thurmond for distributing leaflets, and jailed Raymond for "reckless driving," handcuffing him "so tightly that the circulation was cut off in his hand." [46] During the Freedom Vote itself police frightened many away from the polls, and in Canton so few came that CORE staffers brought the forms out to the streets. Nevertheless, one-third of Madison County's Negro adults participated, while, statewide, 82,000 cast ballots for Henry.[47]

Directly after this impressive demonstration of the black Mississippians' interest in the ballot, COFO committed itself to an expanded program of political action, community centers, and Freedom Schools, all intended to "build a basis of power to effect radical changes in the political and economic set-up on the state." At the heart of COFO thinking was the challenge to the regular Democratic Party of Mississippi which reached its climax at the National Democratic Convention.[48] The community centers were an outgrowth of Dennis' and other COFO workers' deep concern about finding solutions to pressing socio-economic problems. Since the summer of 1963 Dennis had been urging the establishment of centers that would teach techniques of running farm and store cooperatives. In addition these would offer library facilities, vocational and citizenship training, and classes in black history (so blacks could be "aware that they have much to be proud of"). It was hoped that the centers would gain mass support for COFO, and provide "a dynamic focus for the development of community organization."[49] And summer Freedom Schools were to be instituted to provide cultural experiences lacking in the black public schools of Mississippi, and to raise the level of political consciousness among the youth. As SNCC staff member Charlie Cobb, who was responsible for incorporating the Freedom School concept into COFO's planning, said, "What they must see is the link between a rotting shack and a rotting America."[50] The entire project would reach a climax in the summer of 1964, when the COFO staff would be joined by a thousand northern volunteers.

In the following months CORE strove to carry out the COFO program both in Canton and at a new base in Meridian, the state's second largest city. In Canton, CORE stepped up its campaign. Adopting a tactic earlier used in Louisiana, it sought to force the town's retail merchants to put pressure on the registrar, by calling a boycott in January against twenty-one stores. The success of the boycott caused authorities to respond by arresting nearly all the civil rights workers for violating an anti-leafleting ordinance.[51] Meanwhile other forms of intimidation continued unabated. Police officers stood outside voter registration meetings taking photographs, demanding to see driver licenses, and following participants when they departed. Raymond was warned to leave town, Dick Jewett, a white task force worker from New York, was arrested for "reckless driving," and two local youths assisting in canvassing were jailed and beaten. To counter the boycott, city officials urged suppliers to stop delivering goods to black merchants. Thus grocer George Washington, treasurer of the Canton Movement, found that wholesalers removed his gasoline pumps and canceled his meat supply.[52]

Hoping to bring federal pressure on the registrar by attracting national news media to Canton, and at the same time to galvanize local blacks, the Canton staff utilized a tactic employed in other COFO projects at Greenwood and Hattiesburg: "Freedom Day" demonstrations that mobilized hundreds of Negroes at the courthouse in open defiance of white officialdom. The first of Canton's three Freedom Days, the one on February 28, was a major COFO effort, enlisting the assistance of SNCC, and NAACP, and even the local black ministers. National CORE assigned extra field secretaries to the project. The FBI and the Department of Justice, the National Council of Churches, and the mass media all sent observers. About 350 adults, some in their seventies and eighties, led by CORE field secretary B. Elton Cox and the NAACP state field secretary Charles Evers marched to the courthouse. To a *New York Times* correspondent, the long lines of blacks waiting stiffly on the walk, with over a hundred armed lawmen standing guard, epitomized the failure of the Civil Rights Acts of 1957 and 1960. With the spotlight on Canton, the authorities avoided arrests or other repressive tactics but permitted only five to take the registration test. Yet Dennis was pleased because through the mass media's presence the nation had seen how Mississippi officials prevented blacks from voting. Moreover, as he had hoped, within a week the Justice Department filed a suit against the registrar.[53]

The Canton Movement was now in high gear. Twenty-six hundred black teenagers immediately followed up the courthouse demonstrations with a one-day school boycott to protest overcrowded, substandard conditions.[54] Although the authorities promptly responded by arresting twelve civil rights workers, the blacks sustained their pressure. Negroes appeared daily at the registrar's office, and a second, though less dramatic Freedom Day, was held March 13. A short time afterward federal judge Harold Cox directed the registrar to process at least fifty applicants each registration day.[55] Yet it proved difficult to sustain the momentum. The store boycott faded, the local whites continued their harassment, the legislature enacted a law to prevent more Freedom Days, and few people were now willing to risk going to the courthouse. In May shots were fired into CORE headquarters. The task force, discouraged and demoralized, became enmeshed in internal conflicts and blamed George Raymond, the project director, for ineffective leadership.[56] Hoping to revive the Canton project, CORE scheduled a third Freedom Day on May 29, in defiance of the new legislation. To give the occasion heightened importance, Farmer arrived to address a rally, which was surrounded by scores of intimidating police. This time the authorities prohibited marching to the courthouse, the representatives of the mass media were absent, and fifty-five were arrested.[57] Thus at the end of CORE's first year in Canton, there were few accomplishments, and harassment was, if anything, on the rise.

In the face of such intimidation and discouraging results, CORE's Mississippi staff, though increasingly embittered, retained a remarkable faith and commitment in the possibility for social change. As David Dennis told the rally just before the final Freedom Day, "We have got to stand up and shout out loud, that this country is a country for freedom. . . . If we want this country to stand up for freedom, we've got to make it that way [ourselves]. Right now it's a lie. . . . I'm tired of the [white] people in this particular state saying I don't want this and I don't want that. . . . I'm tired of President Johnson . . . playing politics with my freedom." The evil political structure of the state which harmed both blacks and whites, he continued, must be changed. Blacks should no longer beg for their rights. "We're demanding this time. . . . We're demanding in a nonviolent manner, but we are still demanding to be first-class citizens. . . . We know deep down in our hearts what we have to do. . . . We've got to sweat, we've got to bleed, a lot of us are going to have to die for it. But you might as well die at once . . . and get it over with." [58]

The repression in Canton had scuttled Dennis' attempt to establish a community center,[59] but in the less violent atmosphere of Meridian the work actually focused around such a facility. The Meridian office was headed by Mat Suarez, CORE's delegate on the COFO executive committee and COFO coordinator for the Fourth District, and the community center, begun in January, was directed by two white task force workers, Mickey and Rita Schwerner. The Schwerners, deeply affected by the Birmingham demonstrations, had become members of New York's Downtown CORE in June 1963, and a short time afterwards both were arrested at the Manhattan demonstrations against building trades discrimination. In his application to CORE, Schwerner, a young social worker, had declared, "I am now so thoroughly identified with the civil rights struggle that I have an emotional need to offer my services in the South. . . . In essence, I would feel guilty and almost hypocritical if I do not give full time for an extended period. The vocation for the rest of my life is and will be to work for an integrated society." [60]

The Schwerners' first weeks were difficult. Although white harassment was absent at the beginning, some black adults opposed the project, fearing it would stir up tensions. Accordingly, as was true in many other southern towns, the activists reached the community through the youth. First Mickey, with the aid of several young Negroes, built shelves for the thousands of books donated from the North. Especially helpful was twenty-one-year-old James Chaney, a high school dropout from a broken family who would become Schwerner's closest colleague. By the beginning of February, young people were coming to borrow books, and Rita was holding well-attended story hours for the children. By then, also, registration efforts had gotten under way; Schwerner and Chaney were canvassing with the help of a couple of high school students. Attempts to involve adults fizzled until March, when Rita hit upon sewing classes as a recruitment device. Using cloth donated from the North, she quickly developed a program which became so popular that within a few weeks participation was restricted to those who had tried to register. By April, two additional black Mississippians had been added to the staff, and the time appeared ripe for direct action. Sit-ins were held at the bus station lunch counter, and a job boycott was inaugurated against a few retail establishments. Several pickets were arrested outside the stores, including Schwerner and Lenora Thurmond, a young black Mississippi task force worker.[61]

As the civil rights campaign accelerated, harassment became a serious problem. In April, at the very time that Suarez and the Schwerners were meeting in the parsonage, a cross was burned near the church of the only clergyman who supported the movement. CORE workers received threatening phone calls at night, the utilities in their living quarters were periodically shut off, and finally they were evicted. Early in June, Haley wrote to Schwerner, "Obviously the tension is gradually rising as your activities probe more deeply into direct action. I am pushing very hard for the national office to set up a high level Justice Department conference to discuss specific protective measures." [62] Violence rose not only in Meridian but all over Mississippi as the time approached when hundreds of northern volunteers would arrive for the COFO summer project. In Canton, on the night following the May 29 Freedom Day, a Negro storekeeper was beaten by two policemen; not long afterwards bombs exploded outside CORE's headquarters and on the lawn of the Pleasant Green Holiness Church, a rallying center for the Freedom Day demonstrations.[63]

Haley kept pushing National CORE leaders to press for federal protection and suggested that Farmer personally urge top people at the Justice Department to send federal agents to Mississippi. In early June, Farmer vainly sought an appointment with Attorney-General Robert Kennedy. A conference which LCDC officials secured with Assistant Attorney-General Burke Marshall and representatives of the FBI produced only disconcertingly "inconclusive" results. Rachlin sadly predicted that only a major crisis would force the Administration to intervene. And in fact intervention came only after the brutal murder of Schwerner, Chaney, and the summer volunteer, Andrew Goodman.[64]

Since February the Meridian staff had been canvassing the surrounding rural areas. In June, several days after Schwerner and Chaney had convinced fearful Negroes in the Longdale farming community to sponsor a Freedom School, several of them were beaten and their church was burned. On June 21, when Schwerner and Chaney learned what had happened, they went to investigate, accompanied by Andrew Goodman. The three were returning to Meridian when they were arrested. Released several hours later they disappeared. Pressed by the enormous publicity that followed, the White House ordered a massive investigation, and a month and a half later the three bodies were recovered. Only then did Farmer obtain the high-level conference he had sought. Meeting with him and Mrs. Chaney, Lyndon Johnson gave assurances that scores of additional FBI agents were now in Mississippi and would unofficially protect civil rights workers.[65]

For the Mississippi Three it was, of course, too late. For Dave Dennis, who delivered a eulogy at Chaney's funeral, the white terrorism had triggered a rage and bitterness that contrasted sharply with the optimistic spirit that had characterized his first year in Mississippi. "I'm sick and tired of going to the funerals of black men who have been murdered by white men," he said. "I'm not going to stand here and ask anyone not to be angry, not to be bitter tonight. We've defended our country. To do what? To live like slaves." Then with his voice rising he cried out, "Don't just look at me and go back and tell folks you've been to a nice service. Your work is just beginning. And I'm going to tell you deep down in my heart what I feel right now. If you go back home and sit down and take what these white men in Mississippi are doing to us . . . if you take it and don't do something about it . . . then God damn your souls!" Stepping back from the pulpit he broke down, tears streaming from his face.[66]

During the summer CORE, with the assistance of the northern volunteers, expanded its work considerably. Robert Gore and Rudy Lombard were placed in charge of the Meridian and Canton projects, while Freedom Schools, rudimentary community centers, and political programs were initiated in two other rural counties—Neshoba, where the murders had occurred, and Leake.[67] The volunteers, most of whom were white, learned—like the civil rights activists there before them—to live in constant fear. The presence of FBI agents diminished, but far from eliminated the terrorism. Arrests on a variety of charges, threatening phone calls, telephone lines going dead, and police surveillance of COFO buildings were routine. Nine black churches were damaged or destroyed by bombs and arson in CORE's district alone.[68] For CORE, the deaths of the Mississippi Three made the Meridian Community Center of profound symbolic importance. Lenora Thurmond assumed direction of the facility, continuing the activities begun by the Schwerners, working particularly with the younger children. Especially popular were the ten Freedom Schools CORE opened in the four counties. These taught classes in remedial English, the arts, social sciences, and mathematics that went beyond the limited offerings of Mississippi's black high schools, and, most important, courses dealing with the Freedom Movement and Negro history. Asking such questions as, "What does the majority culture have that we want? What do we have that we want to keep?" these schools sought to instill racial pride and to develop in the students "a sense of themselves as a people who could produce heroes." A sequence of sessions with high school youth at the Pleasant Green Freedom School in Madison County included discussion of "what they don't like about their [public] schools," the Black Muslims, "the origins of slavery and of the poor white-Negro relationship as it exists today," and "the power structure." Most of the schools were housed in modest quarters. A summer volunteer in Canton wrote, "I'm sitting in what we've turned into a Freedom School—a one room wooden church. . . . Most of the windows are half paneless. The only seats resemble picnic benches. One lamp, hung from the ceiling. . . . A colored U. S. map, a few Freedom posters, some prints torn from an old calendar have brightened the room a little since we came." [69]

The major thrust of COFO's summer program centered on the campaign to challenge the Mississippi delegation at the 1964 Democratic Party Convention. By the end of the previous year COFO had developed a multifaceted strategy: running black candidates for Congress in the regular Democratic Party primaries; seeking participation in the Democratic precinct and county conventions; and creating the Mississippi Freedom Democratic Party to challenge the white political structure by running independent candidates in the general elections and trying to unseat the all-white state delegation at the Democratic National Convention. This strategy was intended to dramatize the illegal exclusion of blacks from the political process, and thus provide a convincing argument for the recognition of MFDP as the legal Democratic Party in Mississippi.

By March these plans had been put into operation. Dave Dennis, assisted by Dick Jewett, coordinated the Challenge at the Jackson office, and Ella Baker, adviser to SNCC, handled affairs at the Washington end. Late in April a statewide convention got the Mississippi Freedom Democratic Party off the ground, and selected Aaron Henry as chairman. COFO chose four congressional candidates to run in the June Democratic Party primaries. Although their effort was symbolically important, all of them lost as was expected, since few blacks were allowed to vote. The experience of Annie Devine, an active CORE worker in Canton and member of the MFDP State Executive Committee, was typical. After arriving at the poll with her registration certificate, she was denied a ballot and told to leave. A week later, registered blacks attempted to participate in a number of Democratic precinct meetings. Excluded in most cases, the Negroes held their own precinct meetings and selected delegates to the county conventions. Again almost all were barred. In Meridian, though the black delegates were permitted to attend, their credentials were not recognized. In Canton, Devine and four other blacks were at first unable to find the convention, which did not meet at the legally designated place. Upon locating it, they were actually informed that no county convention was being held.[70]

So pivotal in COFO strategy was the campaign to challenge the seating of the Mississippi delegation at the 1964 Democratic Party Convention that efforts to register blacks at the county courthouses virtually ceased by summer. Instead blacks were encouraged to register in the Mississippi Freedom Democratic Party, and considerable effort was devoted to creating an organization modeled upon the state's white political parties, in order to strengthen MFDP's claims of being the legitimate state Democratic Party. Thus, for example, CORE's summer staff in Meridian registered about 4000 in the MFDP and created a precinct organization covering the city and parts of the surrounding county.[71] In August, after precinct and county meetings were held around the state, 240 delegates assembled in Jackson for the state MFDP convention. In sharp contrast to the white state Democratic organization, which planned to support the Republican candidate, Barry Goldwater, they pledged loyalty to the National Democratic Party and its platform. Their most important act was to choose the delegation for the National Convention; headed by Aaron Henry it included Annie Devine as secretary.[72]

As early as May, Farmer had announced that National CORE would press for MFDP's seating. While welcoming this move, COFO officials insisted that MFDP must make all its own decisions. National CORE leaders would have liked some role in formulating the strategy, but after considerable internal debate, agreed to endorse whatever actions MFDP finally took. The Steering Committee decided that, if the Democratic Convention refused to seat the challengers, CORE would conduct direct-action demonstrations "timed and coordinated with SNCC and MFDP." [73] In the meanwhile, SNCC had secured Joseph Rauh, the noted civil liberties attorney, who prepared a brief challenging the seating of the "regular" Mississippi delegation, on grounds of disloyalty to the Democrats in past presidential elections and flagrant denial to blacks of the right to vote and to participate in party affairs. Actually, MFDP relied heavily on a moral appeal. Testifying before the Convention's platform committee, Farmer denounced the intimidation that disfranchised most black Mississippians. And in televised hearings before the credentials committee, FDP delegates described the heartbreaking brutality experienced in Mississippi, producing a ground swell of sympathy across the nation and in the committee. Yet they had underestimated Lyndon Johnson. Prior to the Convention the President had proposed seating the MFDP delegation as honored guests but giving credentials to the state's party regulars if they pledged to back the Democrats' national ticket. On the other hand, MFDP and its supporters on the credentials committee urged seating those delegates from both groups who took the loyalty pledge and splitting the votes between them. But Johnson's political arm-twisting eroded MFDP's support on the committee and secured the adoption of a symbolic compromise providing that two MFDP representatives would be seated as delegates-at-large.

The MFDP delegation rejected the compromise in a tense session, while on the Boardwalk in Atlantic City in front of the Convention Hall CORE led thousands in a round-the-clock vigil to demonstrate support for whatever stand MFDP decided to take. Within the Freedom Party there were those like Henry who, moved by the arguments of Rauh, King, and Rustin, were inclined to accept it as a valuable symbolic victory which legitimated MFDP's basic claims and set the stage for the wide inclusion of blacks at the 1968 Convention. On the other hand, CORE and especially SNCC staffers emphatically pressed for rejection of the offer and closed off a discussion of other alternatives. They reminded MFDP people that they were in Atlantic City to show unequivocally the illegality of the white Mississippi delegation and that the compromise provided no real relief. Farmer's advice reflected his own ambivalence. Refusing to urge either acceptance or rejection of the arrangement explicitly, he reminded the delegates that turning it down meant embarking on the difficult task of operating a third political party in Mississippi. Although Farmer had hedged in his presentation, among MFDP leaders he was widely interpreted as favoring acceptance of the compromise. Farmer's ambiguity reflected divisions within CORE and among CORE's supporters—between those who regarded the compromise as tangible progress, presaging significant future change, and those militant purists, many of whom made SNCC their reference group, who considered any compromise a "sell-out." [74]

For the southern CORE staff, the convention experience was both disillusioning and liberating. Disappointed with the decision and the white liberals who had backed it, they dismissed with finality such "false friends" as Rauh, who had advised approval of the compromise, and Walter Reuther, who had pressed Martin Luther King to urge its acceptance. They proudly believed that COFO had created an independent grass-roots political organization which bypassed Mississippi's "established" black leaders who had accommodated locally to the "white power structure" and nationally to the white liberal leadership of the trade unions and the Democratic Party. The experience at Atlantic City only served to confirm the loss of faith in the Democratic Party's leadership which had earlier resulted from the Administration's failure to fulfill the guarantees of protection given at the start of the Voter Education Project. In the southern CORE staff's view, social change could come only through an independent movement that would "remain a threat to the power structure." [75] Their alienation from the mainstream of American society was clearly evident and reinforced the mounting disillusionment that was becoming prevalent among CORE activists in the North.

10

Winds of Organizational Change

Although CORE's expansion and vigor in 1963 and early 1964 were unprecedented in the organization's history, the old problems and weaknesses remained. Income rose dramatically, but CORE still operated on a deficit; office staff efficiency continued to decline, and there were signs that field staff was becoming alienated from the national office; structural problems arising from chapter autonomy remained unresolved. At the same time, CORE was faced with increased questioning of nonviolence and interracialism that threatened to undermine the very essence of its traditions. Finally, by the spring of 1964 it was beginning to be evident that direct action itself was a limited instrument, that the ultimate bounds of what it could achieve may have been reached. Together, these developments produced a crisis from which CORE has never really recovered.

CORE's fiscal operations were still conducted on the assumption that income would continue to rise. And as earlier, the organization, operating in a crisis atmosphere and still characterized by extraordinary spontaneity, spent to the very limit of its resources and beyond. The sudden rise in receipts following the Birmingham campaign wiped out CORE's debt only temporarily, for the organization continued to expand activities faster than income. In early 1964 CORE was in trouble because by increasing its efforts in Mississippi and Louisiana at the southern staff's urgent request its resources had become overstrained.[1] CORE was in such a financial bind that it was forced to depend largely on volunteer or quasi-volunteer field workers and attorneys. In the South the organization was so lacking in money that it had to rely mainly on task force workers and was unable to promote to the rank of field secretary even directors of important countywide projects. Fortunately Rachlin displayed an extraordinary ability to secure volunteer legal help, creating a statewide panel of lawyers to advise the California CORE chapters, and the Metropolitan Defense Committee to provide counsel to New York area affiliates.[2] And in the South, where the few lawyers willing to help CORE— Murphy Bell and Collins, Douglas & Elie in Louisiana, Tobias Simon in Florida, Floyd McKissick in North Carolina—were unable to take on time-consuming cases without some remuneration, the organization constantly had difficulty paying even the modest fees charged.

By 1964, CORE's financial plight was worse than at any time in its history. In March, with unpaid bills totaling more than $50,000, the Steering Committee meeting had to be canceled. Even after the spring drive, CORE ended the fiscal year with a deficit of $27,000. As Farmer informed CORE field workers, in this "desperate" situation the administrative staff at the national office had "agreed to defer every other paycheck during the summer." Thereafter things grew worse. During July and August, the widespread public sympathy and outrage over the Chaney-Goodman-Schwerner murders, produced a temporary spurt in donations, with receipts actually being somewhat higher than they were the preceding summer. Yet, though CORE raised $281,000 in the four months ending September 30, the expensive summer projects and the unprecedented size of the staff left the organization with a $102,000 deficit for this period.[3]

Although CORE was nearly a million dollars a year operation, the top leaders were never able to develop the bureaucratic controls that they believed desirable and essential for an organization of its size. Robert Penn Warren, who visited the national office in mid-1964, observed, "Nothing here reminds you of the headquarters of the NAACP or the Urban League—not the sodden cigarette butts and old gum wrappers on the floor of the hall, nor the creaky elevator, nor the waiting room with bulging and broken cartons stacked in a corner, nor the grime-stained plaster. . . . There was a jumble of offices, everything seemed disordered, untidy, improvised . . . but with some sense, all the same, of a busy order in the operation." What Warren did not see, were the stacks of unanswered letters that kept piling up with each mail delivery. "We are too darned inefficient," Marvin Rich complained in a memo in July 1964. Clora Coleman was still trying to stop tardiness in the mornings and protracted lunch hours in the afternoons, and still threatening disciplinary action which was rarely taken.[4] The staff in the field also resisted direction, which they defined as bureaucratic intrusion. Organization Department director James McCain and the new national chairman Floyd McKissick were concerned that field secretaries were often impairing CORE's image by dressing in a "sloppy" manner. To their annoyance one even appeared barefooted at a St. Louis bank demonstration. In February 1964 the two men instructed the staff that they "must appear neat at all times. . . . For example, at negotiations, business meetings and conferences with public officials, it is expected that male field secretaries wear a tie and coat." Field reports and statements of expenses had become so "spasmodic and incomplete" that McCain warned in the summer of 1963, "No more expense advances will be sent to the field staff unless your expense blanks are in the office and up to date, with receipts attached. . . . At least once a month we should get a written report on your activities. . . . Our auditors have told us that we cannot go on sending out money unless it is accounted for." Several months later he had to send a similar directive, but regular reports now came only from field staffers on projects financed by VEP which required the reports as a condition of the grants.[5]

Nor was the Organization Department itself functioning adequately. The transfer of the task force to its jurisdiction in the autumn of 1963 only added to the problems of an already overburdened staff at the national office. The department was no longer even keeping such records as up-to-date lists of chapter chairmen. Field workers failed to receive needed materials. Chet Duncan, the new western regional field secretary, for example, protested that the national office had not sent him press releases nor advance information that Farmer had scheduled a visit to his area. Echoing Fredricka Teer's earlier complaint, Duncan noted, "I am always the last to know what's going on." [6] More important, because most of the staff was assigned to the South, the chapters in the North and West received only irregular visits. Even affiliates in crises which requested immediate assistance were put off. For example, in September 1963, Kansas City, Missouri, CORE asked for help in setting up a much needed training program, but nearly three months passed before the national office sent "a very belated reply" indicating that nothing could be done at the time. McCain realized that "lack of servicing" was an important reason that many chapters had internal difficulties or were unable to mount viable programs, but, given the limitations of his staff, there was little he could do.[7]

The inadequacy of field services only reinforced the affiliates' sense of autonomy and the "growing cleavage between the national office and the local chapters." A subject for discussion at a staff meeting in September 1963,[8] this problem appeared in its most acute form during the stall-in crisis. A less dramatic but equally important manifestation of the cleavage was the negative attitude held by many CORE people toward the National Conventions. Leaders of many strong affiliates, busy with local affairs, often did not deem it worthwhile to attend. Consequently, a disproportionate number of less active individuals who could afford the time and money tended to show up at these gatherings, which were, therefore, not genuinely representative of chapter membership. At the 1963 Convention, few affiliates had submitted delegate accreditation forms, and individuals without any credentials—even from inactive chapters—were seated. The same loose style characterized the 1964 Convention, even though a credentials committee attempted to tighten up the procedures.[9]

The chapters, anxious to retain their autonomy, were hesitant about working closely with other affiliates. As a member of Columbia University CORE observed, "CORE's autonomous chapter organization is both an asset and a liability," freeing people from "following the direction of a national office which could become rigid in its control, but also too often producing a situation where chapters, even when the need was urgent, were unwilling to support each other's projects." There were a few significant examples of successful interchapter cooperation in the New York area, most notably in the construction trades demonstrations, the A & P project sponsored by the national office, and the first school boycott. Yet the attempts to create a viable New York Area Metropolitan Coordinating Council foundered, and CORE's experience in both the second New York school boycott and the stall-in crisis illustrated the limitations of chapter cooperation and the extraordinary difficulties which the national office faced when its perception of organizational interests diverged from that of some of the chapters. The West Coast groups showed more skill and initiative in working together. Although the San Francisco Bay Area Coordinating Council which Fredricka Teer had tried to develop did not meet after the spring of 1963, a California Conference of CORE Chapters which was established not long afterward, sponsored coordinated picketing of the California Real Estate Association and joint statewide negotiations and demonstrations against the Bank of America. Then, in the spring of 1964, following up on recommendations made by national vice-chairman Wilfred Ussery, the organization's San Francisco office sponsored the first western regional CORE conference.[10]

While the thrust for regional organization mainly came from western leaders, the national office also strongly believed in coordinated regional efforts. Simultaneously, national leaders were grappling with structural problems stemming from the challenge to their authority which had been posed by Brooklyn CORE and by Julius Hobson, chairman of Washington, D. C. CORE. Hobson, charged by members of his chapter with un-democratic, authoritarian leadership, had refused to obey NAC directives to change his course, but only after interminable discussion had the NAC finally removed him from office.[11] In each case the national office's actions had been hesitant and uncertain, in part because it lacked effective constitutional machinery to deal with recalcitrant affiliates. Accordingly, both the advantages of regional coordination and the need for maintaining a minimal degree of authority over the essentially autonomous chapters indicated that the organization's structure should be tightened. In his report to the 1964 Convention, Farmer, referring to the "splintering from within" which accompanied "all revolutions," called for structural changes to weld the organization into "a unified and coordinated whole." The Convention overwhelmingly approved constitutional changes proposed by the national office, strengthening procedures for disciplining problem affiliates. Five Regional Action Councils were created to initiate regional projects, resolve disputes within and between chapters, and advise national on disciplining affiliates who violated CORE's constitution and by-laws. Presiding over these Councils were regional vice-chairmen, who also enjoyed membership on the NAC.[12] In actual practice the constitutional revisions did not provide the cement that had been anticipated. On the one hand, despite the new controls, the chapters essentially remained as free from national regulation as before. On the other hand, although endowed with considerable authority, the Regional Action Councils did not materially influence the CORE movement. By the latter part of 1964, CORE's momentum was slowing down. In this context these councils and the regional conferences they sponsored were forums for discussion rather than initiators of coordinated action projects or mechanisms to "tighten up our organization." Fundamentally, the old structural problems arising from chapter autonomy, which had existed from CORE's earliest days, remained.

Autonomous though they were, the chapters had an enormous impact on the organization's changing ethos. Increasingly, CORE's national leaders had to grapple with the erosion of the commitment to interracialism and nonviolence, and while this tendency arose to some extent in the South, its chief source lay in certain influential chapters in the North and West. Not only did many of these affiliates operate in a situation where nationalist and radical spokesmen resonated to a large audience, but, more important, the dynamics of the chapters' own experiences propelled them in new directions.

The feeling that blacks must hold the leadership posts in CORE became more widespread. It should be emphasized, however, that, as earlier, this view was held with varying degrees of intensity and was based on varying rationales. Some felt that chapter chairmanships and the top national positions should be held by blacks only, with whites having free access to other offices. On the other hand, some—a small minority whose numbers were increasing substantially by mid-1964—inclined toward the belief that whites should be excluded from all decision-making or policy-making positions, that they should serve as foot soldiers and followers in the Negro revolution. Some argued on purely pragmatic grounds that CORE could never establish rapport with the black poor as long as whites remained prominent, while for others the commitment to Negro leadership was rooted in deep emotional feelings that blacks should run the movement for their own liberation.

The latter view, which would not reach its peak until later, paradoxically was derived both from a rising self-confidence among black activists and from the resentment and embarrassment caused by a recognition that whites contributed so much. This resentment stemmed from several and even contradictory sources: from the feeling that whites, because they could always escape to suburbia after brief encounters with oppression in the deep South and in the northern slums, lacked serious commitment and a real understanding of the black man's needs and perspective; from annoyance at the paternalism of certain white members, who believed that they knew what was best for blacks; from an awareness that in some cases it was ironically the whites who predominated at demonstrations, while it proved difficult to mobilize the black community; from the realization that white members were often better educated and more articulate, and therefore more adept at handling certain administrative routines and negotiating with white businessmen and civic leaders, than were many blacks. To some extent differences in life style led to misunderstandings. As one field secretary recalled, "proper," upward-striving blacks disliked the informality of many upper middle-class whites who, when visiting Negroes' homes, casually did such things as putting their feet on coffee tables. Underlying the black-white tensions in CORE was the fact that blacks often joined not because they were interested in fostering interracial friendship but because they saw CORE as an effective instrument for attacking the white oppressor. For some the sins of the white enemy loomed so large that, as one black chapter chairman recalled, at times just the presence of hostile white onlookers at a demonstration triggered intense resentment at white CORE members who were picketing alongside him. In practice, of course, motivations were often very mixed, involving a new sense of black pride and identity, ambivalent or embittered feelings toward whites in the organization, as well as practical considerations of mobilizing the black community.[13]

In the South during this period, overt manifestations of doubts about using white staff arose only in Mississippi. Dennis consistently preferred black field workers, in part because he believed they could relate more readily to the black community, in part because they were less visible to the local authorities, and especially because he considered it important that field workers be symbols to the people among whom they worked. Mississippi blacks felt so impotent and inferior, that it was essential for them to learn that they did not have to depend upon whites, but could develop their own leadership. On the other hand, he highly valued Mickey Schwerner and Dick Jewett and gave them positions of considerable responsibility. Like Mike Lesser who for a while directed CORE's program in North Louisiana, and Mimi Feingold, who after a year in St. Helena and the Felicianas was appointed to head the work in those parishes, Schwerner and Jewett exhibited a profound empathy with the communities in which they lived, displayed an ability to listen well and work with others in an equalitarian spirit, and earned the profound respect both of their black colleagues and the local Negroes. Jewett established extraordinary rapport with Negroes in Canton, and, even though the opposition of many black COFO staffers to white administrators made Robert Moses reluctant to bring Jewett to the state headquarters as Dennis' assistant, most black activists preferred field work to office routines, and Dennis arranged the appointment when Moses was away.[14] This hostility to white leadership in COFO reflected tendencies in SNCC, where as early as 1961 spokesmen like Stokely Carmichael were insisting that an exclusively black leadership was imperative. Two years later this view had developed into what SNCC's influential adult adviser, Ella Baker, described as "something akin to black nationalism," and by the spring of 1964 a "nationalist caucus," drawn mainly from staffers of northern origins, had emerged in SNCC. Whites became targets of hostility; they were increasingly excluded from social gatherings and their motivation was openly questioned.[15]

At the end of 1963 the COFO staff went through considerable debate over the advisability of bringing hundreds of northern whites to the state for the following summer, and doubts were raised about the value of whites working among Mississippi blacks altogether. Local Negroes generally welcomed the help of the white volunteers. But many COFO people resented the fact that violence against white activists was more likely to bring publicity and federal intervention than was intimidation of blacks, and feared that articulate and well-educated white college students might usurp leadership roles. Dennis observed that one reason for the bitterness which he and the Meridian Negroes expressed at Chaney's funeral was the realization that, if Schwerner and Goodman had also been black, the national outrage would have been far less. Moses, who at the time favored an integrated movement, pointed out that the leadership issue particularly rankled: "Negro students, you know, actually feel this is their own movement. This is the strongest feeling among the Negro students—that this is the one thing that belongs to them in the whole country, and I think this causes the emotional reaction toward white people coming in and participating." [16] With the large influx of northern whites early in the summer, the problem was exacerbated by fancied and genuine incidents of white paternalism and insensitivity, and the Freedom Summer turned out to be a mixture of interracial brotherhood and interracial tension. Illustrative of the tensions and misunderstandings that arose was the experience of one white girl stationed at CORE's Canton project, who reported to friends that she had met resentment on several occasions when she had felt it necessary to "completely re-do press statements or letters" written by black co-workers. "Furthermore, I'm a northerner; I'm white . . . I'm a college graduate; I've not 'proven' myself yet in jail or in physcial danger. Every one of these things is a strike against me as far as they are concerned. . . . I either overlook or purposely and pointedly misinterpret their occasional thrusts of antagonism; I think twice or more before asserting myself or pronouncing my opinion on any affair in which they have more experience." Although she generally avoided unpleasant incidents, one misunderstanding produced an antiwhite tirade lasting a quarter of an hour.[17]

In the North as in the South, many blacks experienced ambivalence on the question of the proper role for whites, and CORE's old interracialism did not die an easy death. Resentment was mixed with respect; the wish for independence with the need for the energies, money, and expertise of whites. Some blacks in Boston CORE resented Alan Gartner because he was so "terribly competent"; yet his commitment and militance were unquestioned; he operated with unusual skill and effectiveness in chapter affairs, in negotiations, and in relationships with the city's black leaders; and no one challenged him for the chairmanship. Gartner, the last white chairman of a major affiliate, was clearly exceptional. As one careful student of CORE has written, "By 1964 it had become almost impossible for a white person to be elected chairman of a chapter, though one might serve as chairman of a committee." [18] Indeed, many black chapter chairmen, though believing that black leadership was desirable, sought support from active whites, appointed them to important committee posts, and maintained relationships of genuine cordiality with them. For example, in Long Island CORE, Lincoln Lynch worked to prepare blacks to take over positions of leadership. Nevertheless, whites remained sufficiently visible among his principal supporters and key committee chairmen, for some blacks to complain that whites played too large a role in the chapter. Ruth Turner, the influential leader of Cleveland CORE who became national secretary in 1964, publicly stated that control of the chapter should be in black hands, and that whites, rather than participate in policy-making, should play "a strong supportive role." Yet she worked well with many whites, a few of whom continued to hold key committee chairmanships and to serve on both the chapter's Executive Committee and its chief policy-making body, the Action Committee.[19] Generally, however, such posts tended to be increasingly reserved for blacks. In Philadelphia as early as the autumn of 1963, Ed Hollander was the only white person in the chapter's hierarchy. In California five of the six members of the prestigious Bank of America Negotiating Committee were black. In New York CORE, there was also a strong feeling that only blacks should lead. Although about half the people attending chapter meetings were white, few held office and the affiliate selected an all-black delegation, including alternates, to the 1964 Convention.[20] On the other hand, it should be emphasized that in many CORE groups discussions about the appropriate role for whites did not arise, and whites were well represented in chapter offices.

An important factor reinforcing the emphasis upon black leadership was CORE's increasing concern with the problems of the ghetto poor. As chapters began working with slumdwellers, they often anticipated—and frequently met—an initial suspicion against white workers; moreover, they sometimes found themselves criticized by black groups—not always nationalist—on whose turf they were now competing. Whites themselves often doubted their ability to establish rapport with the black poor. Accordingly, as CORE affiliates became more involved in rent strikes and community organization projects, the role of whites in the chapters was frequently brought under question. In practice, however, black CORE leaders found some white workers extremely effective in the slums and highly adept at organizing blacks. One northeastern chapter officer recalled how delighted and surprised whites were when they achieved success in such efforts. Illustrative of the ambiguity characterizing many slum-organizing projects was the experience of Cleveland CORE. When, in the autumn of 1963 the chapter launched a program directed at black slumdwellers and opened an office in Hough, it also committed itself to a policy of black leadership in the civil rights struggle. Although this stance, adopted after considerable internal discussion, was based upon the rationale that only blacks could effectively relate to the masses and genuinely articulate their needs, nevertheless under the direction of black housing chairman Antoine Perot tenant-organizing was done by interracial teams, some of which were headed by whites. A number of the whites proved highly effective at this task. This was not, however, regarded as a contradiction of the black leadership principle since blacks made the basic policy decisions. As the sociologist Inge Bell has suggested, in an increasingly race-conscious ghetto the new emphasis on organizing the black community had the effect of lessening the role of whites in CORE.[21]

By late 1963 the drift of sentiment was strong enough for the black leadership issue to be used in several contested chapter elections. Because they involved blacks running against other blacks, the controversies took the form of charging certain candidates for chairman with being dominated by whites. For example, in the Chicago affiliate, when West Side unit chairman Samuel Riley was challenging the incumbent chapter head Milton Davis, some Riley supporters accused Davis of being a pawn of the affiliate's white Socialists. Riley, a blue-collar worker with an over-whelmingly black constituency that included many grass-roots people, projected an image of being closer to the masses than Davis, chairman of the South Side unit, who was employed by the University of Chicago and had a substantial white following from the University area. In Washington CORE several months later, when a group led by black Freedom Rider Roena Rand tried to oust black chairman Julius Hobson, the latter charged that he was being crucified by "white liberals who are psychologically not attuned to take orders from a Negro." More complex was the three-way election in the Harlem chapter at the close of 1963, in which chairman Gladys Harrington was challenged by Blyden Jackson, former New Haven CORE chairman, whose supporters included an interracial Socialist group allied with Norman Hill, and Marshall England, a black social worker, whose candidacy was pushed by Roy Innis. Innis, a vigorous advocate of male leadership and black nationalism, liked neither the prospect of a new term for Mrs. Harrington nor the possibility of Jackson with his white Socialist friends replacing her. The popular England—who by no means shared Innis' ideology—finally won the hotly contested election. Jackson and his backers seceded to form East River CORE; yet ironically, months later after breaking with Hill, Jackson resigned as chairman of the new affiliate, charging that Hill's white Socialist friends in the chapter "are trying to take over the show." [22]

The trend toward black leadership was also evident on the National Action Council, where the proportion of Negroes steadily increased. Blacks formed slightly over half of the NAC elected in 1962, two-thirds of the Council chosen in 1963, and four-fifths of those elected in 1964. Upward mobility of whites into the ranks of the Council had disappeared; only one new white face was on the Council in 1963 and no new ones at all in 1964. By then the NAC contained only five whites, all of whom had given lengthy and valuable service to the organization. Four of them had been prominent in CORE since before the Freedom Ride. In contrast, the black NAC members displayed considerable mobility within the organization's leadership. Six of the fourteen Negro members in 1963–64 and eleven of the twenty black members in 1964–65 were new to the Council. And except for Ruth Turner, all of the new black members elected in 1964 had joined CORE since the Freedom Ride—most of them within the last two years. Their elevation to the NAC was indicative also of a noticeable—and growing—circulation of membership on that body. In 1963, about one-third of the NAC members were new, while in 1964 the proportion had risen to nearly one-half. As a group, the new black members—including Ruth Turner of Cleveland, Harold Brown of San Diego, Shirley Lacey of Englewood, New Jersey, Chris Sprowal of Downton CORE, John Due of Tallahassee, and George Wiley of Syracuse—were notable for their militance. Yet they were highly varied in their viewpoints, and while individuals like Wiley and Lacey would remain committed to CORE's interracial traditions, certain key individuals among them, particularly Brown and Turner, would, along with national vice chairman Wilfred Ussery, play a critical role in turning CORE toward black separatism.

The thrust for more black leadership in CORE and the growing hostility toward whites holding top positions had reached the point as early as the summer of 1963 where Farmer believed an accommodation to it was necessary. A few months before the Convention, Adam Clayton Powell had raised the issue of alleged white domination of the major civil rights organizations. Disagreeing, Farmer told reporters that whites in the movement were "just as dedicated as Negroes and have just as much right and responsibility to share in this field." But at the convention, Farmer, ever sensitive to the ebb and flow of sentiment among his constituents, acted to prevent Alan Gartner, whom he described as "brilliant and dedicated" and "a close friend," from running for the national chairmanship. Originally Gartner, who had often acted as an effective champion of the national office's views on the NAC and at Conventions, had been the choice of both Farmer and the outgoing national chairman, Charles Oldham. But just prior to the Convention, Farmer concluded that it would be wise to have a black man occupy the post. Various names were suggested, including Rudy Lombard and Lolis Elie, but Farmer, at Carey's urging, endorsed Floyd McKissick. In Farmer's words: "I knew that at that stage of our struggle he [Gartner] could not be chairman, and that if he ran, the convention would not only defeat him but might turn from the really able Negroes available to a rabid racist, who would raise the divisive racial issue on the floor. So I gathered our staff together along with Mr. Gartner and told him that if he insisted on running, I would fight him on the floor of the convention." Gartner himself, once Farmer's views became evident, quickly agreed to step aside. Others, both white and black, out of a mixture of their great respect for Gartner and a commitment to CORE's interracial traditions, were slower to accede to Farmer's arguments. As Farmer recalled,

> We argued painfully and tearfully for hours. What of CORE's principles of interracialism and color-blindness? Some accused me of being a black nationalist, though the candidate did not. "Why can't

he run? Is he competent or isn't he?" Well, Mr. Gartner agreed not
to run and a floor fight was averted. . . . I was personally saddened
by the cost of our decision. For, no doubt, we had denied this man
categorically, because of color, and this was not at all like us. Yet I
defend the compromise.[23] *

Despite the changing role of whites in many chapters and the flap over
the national chairmanship, most CORE leaders continued to believe that
whites still had an important part to play in the organization. At that
same convention, Gartner defeated a black man in the election for treasurer, and Ralph Rosenfeld, the white chairman of Detroit CORE, was
elected secretary. Gartner, deeply loyal to CORE and Farmer, accepted
the situation gracefully. At the same time he expressed the hope that
"While it may be naïve of me, I believe that in CORE, at least, we
should seek to pay as little attention as possible to racial distinctions. As
to the general public, I think we ought to present, in every way possible,
an image and a reality of interracialism." Farmer agreed, declaring that
through its interracialism CORE could help prevent the possibility of "a
dangerous racial polarization" in the country. Haley was also concerned.
Once when a white staff member was reluctant to represent the national
office at a demonstration in Maryland, Haley declared, "I, myself, have
become a little upset by what seems to me to be our bending over back-
wards to establish the CORE image as a Negro organization. This is not
a true picture of CORE either in its philosophy or its physical make-up.
Consequently, I have been insisting lately that more official public appearances for CORE be assigned to white staff members." Other steps
were also taken by the national office to counteract what they perceived
as growing black nationalism. A workshop for delegates at the 1963 Convention discussed "Interracialism and the Meaning of Nationalism," and
the subject was on the agenda of both the staff meeting in September and
the Program Department's area conferences during the following
months.[24]

---

* CORE leaders interviewed on this critical event are not in agreement about
the seriousness of a threat from an anti-administration candidate running for
national chairman on a platform of opposition to white leadership. The person
referred to was Julius Hobson, whose candidacy was backed by Gladys Harrington and others. While it is not possible at this date to obtain a precise picture
of how the leaders involved in the discussions lined up, it appears that Rich,
McCain, Oldham, Elie, and Lombard all supported Gartner, while Carey was
McKissick's chief backer, along with Farmer. The debate was so emotional that
both Carey and Lombard are reported to have broken down in tears (interviews).

CORE remained throughout this period the most interracial of all the civil rights organizations. Even though only two of the twelve field secretaries were white and there was a policy of recruiting nearly all the task force from among southern black activists, during the summers the field staff was augmented by a substantial infusion of northern white task force workers, and, more important, several whites still held top posts at the national office: Lula Farmer, the bookkeeper, Peck, Carey, Rachlin, and Rich. Yet as time passed, efforts to maintain CORE's interracialism lost their vigor. In fact by the spring of 1964, although Farmer still insisted that "We don't see how we can fight for an open society through a segregated organization, and this is a policy position we intend to maintain," he had nevertheless concluded that because "there are many, many Negroes who will not work with an interracial organization because of their suspicion of whites . . . white liberals must be willing to work in roles of secondary leadership and as technicians." [25]

White activists in the CORE affiliates were divided on how to respond to the push for a diminution of their role. There were many, especially among those who had been in the organization for several years, who were firmly rooted in CORE's interracial philosophy and had serious objections. One long-time leader in a New York State chapter recalled that, when talk developed that whites should resign from committee chairmanships, "some of us who were in leadership positions were unwilling to step down—we felt it was a racially-oriented thing that had no basis in an organization dedicated to wiping out racial discrimination. We had been heavily involved—we had knowledge and dedication— tested for a number of years, and we did not relish being pushed aside." Some felt that withdrawing from policy-making roles and simply accepting without question the decisions of black leaders amounted to a form of servitude. Others were ambivalent. A white member from Baltimore accepted the idea of black leadership but resented what she considered the calculated snubs of some blacks and their complete disregard of the contributions of many whites: "I sincerely do not believe that white people should have key positions in CORE, but I do think that when they make the kinds of sacrifices that white people have been making, they should at least be respected and appreciated." Others fully supported the demands of those who wanted blacks in all the responsible positions and whites in strictly secondary roles. In Cleveland, Bruce Klunder's widow, Joanne, thoroughly agreed that whites should not "participate in the leadership or help plan the strategy" in the chapters, and she believed that

> The civil rights movement is, basically, a movement by, and for Negroes. Though every right-thinking white person should . . . involve themselves in the struggle . . . no white person should make an effort to "take over" the movement. . . . On the matter of "If the movement seems wrong, what then?" I suppose that this is a question that each white person has to answer for himself. But I think that we always have to be aware that we are not Negroes and that we have not had the years of experience with repression, therefore we cannot really know whether the Negro's strategy for freedom is "right" or "wrong."

There were also those whites described by Farmer as "rabid black nationalists," who not only said that it was the duty of white CORE members to serve only as foot soldiers and followers but, convinced of their own racial guilt, found a masochistic pleasure in hearing all whites, themselves included, denounced as evil racists. One "white black nationalist" popular with the inner circle of Brooklyn CORE urged the black chairman of another chapter to run against a white incumbent for a seat on the National Action Council—in order to get rid of the "goddam white members." [26]

Meanwhile CORE leaders were becoming concerned about the possibilities of black retaliatory violence. By mid-1963 northern chapter chairmen like Louis Smith of Philadelphia and Gladys Harrington of New York viewed their cities as "bombs" and "powder kegs" ready to explode with the advent of summer. At a convention workshop, Harrington predicted that "we're going to have hell in Harlem this summer." In the South there were sporadic outbreaks of violence accompanying the campaigns in Birmingham and elsewhere, and staff reported that in self-protection blacks were coming to mass meetings and demonstrations with revolvers and knives. As one delegate commented, "It is not easy to tell a man who is being beaten not to reach for his gun or knife." Not surprisingly, therefore, a short time before the convention a special workshop on mass violence and nonviolent philosophy was placed on the agenda in order to explore such nonviolent themes as "willingness to suffer" and "Is love really necessary?" and, on a more practical level, to help chapters stem violent outbreaks from onlookers and enraged demonstrators. A convention resolution criticizing federal officials in particular warned America of "impending retaliation and mass violence." Southern Negroes were "increasingly arming themselves for the purpose of self defense," while in the North white oppression had produced "a rising, explosive anger which has already expressed itself in skirmishes in Harlem, and which has the potential of erupting into large scale racial warfare." [27]

Farmer empathized with these sentiments, but time and again he reminded the Convention that CORE's nonviolent policy must be absolutely enforced in racial demonstrations. Elsewhere he expressed concern that, as the movement attracted more poor blacks—in itself a desirable development—violence was likely to occur, posing a threat to the public's acceptance of CORE and endangering the very existence of the civil rights movement. "Widespread violence by the freedom fighters would sever from the struggle all but a few of our allies. It would also provoke and, to many, justify such repressive measures as would stymie the movement." [28] Privately, National CORE leaders tried to orient chapters and staff on the importance of adhering to nonviolence at demonstrations. At an NAC meeting in November 1963, members discussed developing "means for emphasizing the need of return to nonviolent philosophy and practice in local groups." In January the Steering Committee directed that chapter chairmen be told to refrain from issuing public statements that "are not in keeping with CORE philosophy." [29] The area conferences sponsored by the program department included discussions of nonviolent philosophy. National officers were also painfully aware that some of the new young field staff, especially among the task force, lacked such training; a four-day staff conference in February 1964 included a session on "Nonviolent Perspectives and Interracialism" led by Bayard Rustin.[30]

National CORE was faced with a long-range shift in sentiment, rooted in a number of causes. Outside of CORE there was the continuing propaganda of Malcolm X and Robert Williams, joined in the spring of 1964 by the rhetoric of ACT's leaders. Of these, Malcolm X, who in March 1964 broke with the Muslims and formed his own group, the Organization of Afro-American Unity, was easily the most influential.[31] More important were factors directly connected with the activities of the CORE chapters and staff: the acute need for protection of civil rights workers and local citizens involved in the southern campaigns; the fact that direct-action projects often achieved success only after some social disorder and even incidental violence occurred; an influx into the organization of young militants, both white and black, who were not interested in CORE's traditional approach; and a rising impatience with the pace of social change.

The terrorism perpetrated by southern whites and the failure of the Department of Justice to live up to its commitment to protect those attempting to exercise the basic democratic right of voting, produced both serious disillusionment with the Kennedy and Johnson administrations and a growing belief in the necessity of armed self-defense. Both Martin Luther King and Aaron Henry had armed guards around their homes at night for protection. Organized armed defense tactics arose among Negroes with whom CORE worked in Louisiana, as previously indicated. In Mississippi some COFO staffers began to carry guns, and in January 1964 Dennis warned Attorney-General Robert Kennedy, with whom he had many times vainly pleaded for protection, "The Negroes shall not watch their families starve, be jailed, beaten, and killed without responding to protect themselves. You have proven by your refusal to act that we have no other recourse but to defend ourselves with whatever means we have at our disposal." In fact, as early as May 1963, the dedicated nonviolent activist, Jerome Smith, who, as a disciple of Gandhian tactics, had probably spent more months in jail and been beaten more often than any other CORE member, pointedly informed Robert Kennedy in a heated personal encounter that he was not sure he could stay nonviolent much longer. Smith concluded his remarks to the shocked attorney-general by exclaiming, "When I pull the trigger, kiss it good-by."

Dennis, who had formerly encouraged people to take beatings on the theory that this would help them reach the white man's heart, by the spring of 1964 began to have doubts about his pacifist philosophy. People he knew were getting shot, the FBI was doing nothing about it, and the attitude of Mississippi whites remained unchanged. Dennis felt increasingly guilty as individuals whom he had advised not to use guns got hurt or killed. Although Dennis himself never carried a weapon, after the Chaney-Goodman-Schwerner murders he and other CORE field staff in the state no longer told people that they should not defend themselves.[32] It should be stressed that in the minds of both local activists and CORE workers using guns to protect homes and meeting places, or carrying a weapon while going about one's ordinary daily activities, in no way implied a lack of commitment to nonviolence on demonstrations. Yet all the talk of violent retaliation marked a new dimension in CORE's internal discussions, and in time the distinction between defense of one's person or property and violence as a tactic would begin to erode for many CORE people, especially in the North.

Already, indeed, the experiences of many northern CORE members were causing them to drift subtly to a position which questioned the assumptions underlying the nonviolent direct-action tactic. Not only did the rapid circulation of membership bring into the chapters substantial numbers of people who were contemptuous of CORE's earlier style, but the momentum of the civil rights revolution, the climate of opinion epitomized by the slogan "Freedom Now!", radicalized many CORE veterans. By mid-1963, no matter what Martin Luther King might say, it seemed clear to CORE activists that nonviolent direct action really worked, not simply because it dramatized the moral issue, but because it also created enough social disorder to force concessions from recalcitrant businessmen and public officials. CORE pamphlets still stressed the importance of good will and negotiations. But in practice, the affiliates operated with calculated coercion—boycotts, nonviolent social dislocation in the streets, and even spontaneous violence from white racists and black onlookers. For example, demonstrations staged by Long Island CORE against a discriminatory real estate agency brought the intervention of city officials and a victory for CORE only after the actions of white counter-demonstrators created an explosive situation. And in Prince George's County, Maryland, CORE, the chapter's militant wing even welcomed the possibility of violence from youthful white hoodlums. Actually it was because a growing segment of white public opinion, particularly among influential elites, endorsed the essential justice of CORE's demands that businessmen were often persuaded to change their policies, that public authorities failed to employ repression, or, as in the South, often used it at the cost of embarrassing publicity and occasional federal intervention. Yet the moral dynamic behind the success of their tactics became secondary in the minds of CORE activists. Paradoxically, moreover, their inclination to perceive coercion, not a moral appeal, as the source of progress was subsequently reinforced by disappointing failures and the continuing frustration of rising expectations. Embittered at the inability of nonviolent direct action to solve the basic problems of the black poor, some of them angrily began to conclude that black America could never be liberated from white oppression except through force and, if need be, violence.

With disorderly demonstrations and even accidental violence sometimes bringing victory, the distinction between direct action and violence began to disappear both in the mind of the general public and among many CORE activists. Although with few exceptions CORE demonstrations stayed within the letter if not the spirit of the Rules for Action, violence occasionally occurred, precipitated sometimes by nonmembers and at other times by CORE people not fully committed to the organization's philosophy. For example, in Chicago at a Board of Education demonstration during the summer of 1963, two young black participants who did not belong to CORE tried to seize the billy clubs of police officers moving in against the protesters. In February 1964 at a Cleveland school board sit-in, some CORE members were criticized for kicking and pummeling policemen. In New Haven, where a traffic-blocking street demonstration in November 1963 resulted in a "bottle-throwing riot" between blacks and the police, leaders in the black community denounced the white chairman of the affiliate's housing committee for precipitating the incident by standing in the middle of the street and urging on the rebellious youths. Afterward, "shocked" National CORE officers sent in two field secretaries to work intensively with the chapter. The whole trend was well illustrated in extensive discussions about the stall-in at the April 1964 Western Regional Conference, where many engaged in rhetoric suggesting that they no longer distinguished between outright violence and the disorder created by the more extreme varieties of civil disobedience. Some conferees proposed a West Coast stall-in that would tie up traffic on five San Francisco area bridges. When objections were raised about the dangers of blocking ambulances and fire engines, a number of participants retorted, "it is the white man's time to suffer. . . . CORE has changed. . . . We are engaged in a war in which the enemy [must] be crushed." One man, who had long been associated with California CORE chapters, wrote to Farmer that among "a sizeable faction" of the leadership an "atmosphere of lightly-suppressed violence" prevailed. Several expressed the feeling that CORE must "abandon its dedication to non-violence" or lose out to groups preaching violent retaliation. "When questioned as to the advisability of 'semi-violent' tactics, these persons said, 'It works, it gets results.' " Clearly the discussion was limited to rhetoric. Indeed, rather than moving toward violence, the California chapters' own subsequent tactics became more moderate. Yet unquestionably the psychological commitment to nonviolent direct action was dissolving.[33]

The issue of violence vs. nonviolence became highly publicized in the case of Cleveland CORE. Early in April, Malcolm X, who had been urging blacks to form "rifle clubs," spoke at a public meeting sponsored by the affiliate. Predicting that Negroes would liberate themselves by "the ballot or the bullet," he asserted that, with the government unresponsive, armed self-defense was necessary. The following night chapter member Lewis Robinson, charging that police failure to protect activists from physical attacks by hostile whites at previous school demonstrations proved the need for Cleveland's blacks to protect themselves, announced that he would, indeed, form a gun club. Two days later came the tragic death of the Reverend Klunder; afterward angry blacks looted, broke windows, attacked cars, and threw rocks at the police. Ruth Turner and other CORE leaders urged the crowd to disperse and helped to prevent a more serious outbreak. In the soul-searching that went on within the Cleveland chapter during the following weeks, the whole issue of violence and self-defense was hotly debated. In reality, as in California this entire question was a rhetorical and ideological one, for Cleveland CORE's next project, a protest against police brutality, was very restrained. Turner herself repudiated Robinson's proposal for a gun club. To her, nonviolent direct action was a method of "channel[ing] justifiably intense feelings" of oppressed people to bring about creative and constructive change. Yet she also felt that there was a point when resentments could not be deflected into nonviolent directions: "I'm . . . realist enough to know that if wide-scale violence breaks out I would no longer be in a position to curb it." [34]

Similarly, in mid-1964 Los Angeles CORE chairman Art Silvers declared, "Our patience is nearing an end. The forces of hate and love are lining up. No one can forestall violence unless immediate federal intervention is extended, particularly in the South." For their part, National CORE leaders kept trying to grapple with the problem posed by the increasing talk among CORE members of the inevitability if not the acceptability of violence. At the NAC meeting just before the 1964 Convention some members evinced reservations about nonviolence, but Farmer and other top officers clutched more fervently than ever to the organization's traditional position. McKissick, for example, asserted that nonviolence was what "makes CORE significantly different from other civil rights organizations . . . we need a cadre who believe in nonviolence and can communicate this belief to the masses." Rudy Lombard, noting that "traditions of violence and nonviolence exist side by side in the Negro community," felt that it was incumbent upon CORE to make "the meaning of Gandhi" relevant to blacks.[35] This issue, however, continued to be debated. In fact CORE's problems with the rising rhetoric of retaliation among chapter members were epitomized by the events which precipitated the Harlem riot.

Following the shooting of a black teenager by a white New York police lieutenant on July 16, CORE groups in the city went into action with a peaceful protest march of hundreds of the slain youth's schoolmates. Then, on the night of the eighteenth, three affiliates held a rally in Harlem demanding the lieutenant's arrest. Among the speakers was Chris Sprowal, chairman of Downtown CORE, who in a rhetoric now used by a number of CORE chapter chairmen announced, "It is time to let 'the man' know that if he does something to us we are going to do something back. . . . I belong to a nonviolent organization, but I'm not nonviolent. When a cop shoots me, I will shoot him back." Afterward CORE spokesmen joined a march to the precinct station. As the police set up barricades they scuffled with members of the crowd; sixteen demonstrators including two CORE speakers were arrested; people threw bricks and bottles, and the riot had begun. During the disorders Farmer and teams from the Harlem and Brooklyn chapters urged residents to clear the streets. Farmer persisted even after being booed by some nationalists.[36]

In the aftermath, more and more chapter leaders justified the riots as a form of protest. Hal Brown, chairman of San Diego CORE and a new member of the NAC, angrily predicted more black violence as the response to "minimal" progress "at the discretion of the white community." Similarly, Walter Brooks, vice-chairman of New Haven CORE, warned, "as Harlem . . . explodes, so might New Haven. The choice is yours. As the militant, the conservative, the Uncle Tom are saying in seemingly different languages—Mister Charlie, you the power structure—We are tired—GET OFF OUR BACK—OR— — —." Such statements led many whites to feel that CORE's actions fomented disorders. Farmer defended the organization from those who confused direct-action protests, even though they were often less "disciplined" than formerly, with race riots. While he opposed demonstrations "whose only possible consequence is mob violence," he insisted that the "decrease of discipline" accompanying "greater mass participation" should not lead CORE to "abandon all but the most polite demonstrations." In Farmer's view, "if demonstrations are in danger of courting violence," the solution lay not in halting them but in "perfect[ing] our ability to control the more undisciplined participants and to spread our teaching. . . . [W]e cannot turn back, and we will not renounce the masses." [37]

As Farmer's comment suggests, CORE spokesmen attributed the changes in the organization's ethos to a rapid rise in membership, especially among blacks, and to increasing participation of the black poor in CORE activities. Actually, the situation was more complex. For one thing, both the revolution in expectations and the rhetoric of people like

Malcolm X had an impact upon CORE. Moreover, the thrust for changes in CORE's style came from several sectors of its membership. Nevertheless, it was indeed true that the organization's traditional philosophy was being undermined largely by its rapid growth after the Birmingham incident. Rich wrote a worried Seattle CORE leader as early as the summer of 1963, "All of our chapters are having problems with expanded membership. It's easy enough to get new members but far more difficult to train them in nonviolence." [38] This trend was in turn accompanied—and facilitated—by a breakdown in the distinctions between active, probationary, and associate members, and in the practice of orienting prospective members in CORE ideology.

In the rush to mount demonstrations, there was neither the time nor often the inclination to follow past entrance procedures, and many chapters discarded the old rules governing probate members. Moreover, Norman Hill and others vigorously argued that, if the organization was to interest the black poor, orientation in CORE philosophy should be scrapped as a requirement, contending, "grass roots people could hardly be attracted by philosophical and intellectual discussions that they regarded as boring and irrelevant." By the spring of 1964, many affiliates had stopped teaching CORE ideology and requiring sustained participation in action projects as prerequisites for membership. They were measuring membership growth simply on the basis of dues payments. In Chicago, for example, any participant in a project could immediately become a full-fledged member by paying a nominal fee. Queens, New York, CORE proudly announced to the national office, "We now have 110 paid members." Some affiliates continued orientation but only in a prefunctory manner. Hill himself believed in a strong training program for people *after* they joined a chapter. In practice, however, fewer and fewer members received any effective education in CORE principles.[39]

Where formerly the chapters consisted of small groups having some knowledge of CORE traditions and characterized by a basic consensus, they now contained many people whose commitment to the Rules for Action was superficial or even nonexistent. In these circumstances some nationalists and revolutionary Marxists entered without challenge; more important, large numbers of youth, without any particular ideology, but open to the militant rhetoric of both nonnationalist and nationalist varieties, joined the organization. The NAC in November 1963 discussed the "breakdown of CORE discipline" produced by the "vast growth in membership," and asked Farmer to write to the affiliates about the problem.

A few days later Haley informed Downtown New York CORE, which was contemplating formal removal of most of its membership requirements,

> Recently, some of our large chapters have experienced internal conflict at least partly because of lax standards of membership. It is the intent of the National Office to emphasize the CORE Rules for Action as the nucleus of a policy of nonviolence. You will be urged to participate in more workshops on nonviolent philosophy. You will be urged—even while seeking more and more members—to train them more and more thoroughly before granting actual membership. All of this being true, I hope you can see that it is hardly consistent with CORE policy for any local chapter to weaken its membership criteria.

The tone of Haley's letter was revealing: in an organization so dedicated to chapter autonomy, National could only cajole, not command, and the membership requirements, like the commitment to other CORE traditions, continued to erode.[40]

This expansion in membership increasingly depended on recruitment from the black community. CORE spokesmen, wanting their organization to have a black image, and under criticism for their relatively high proportion of whites, tended to overstate the number of black members and estimated that CORE was about half black by the end of 1963 and majority black by the summer of 1964.[41] Our interviews with chapter officials suggest, however, that CORE was still over half white as late as mid-1964. Actually, the affiliates exhibited a wide range in racial composition and displayed considerable variation in the rapidity with which they moved toward a black majority. While the number of all-black affiliates did not grow and was still concentrated almost entirely in the South, nearly all of the northern chapters experienced a rise in the proportion of Negroes among their members. In fact, a number of heretofore mainly white chapters now became majority or predominantly black.

Thus San Francisco CORE, which had been 20 per cent black in 1962, had equal numbers of whites and blacks at the end of 1963, and with chairman Bill Bradley's aggressive recruitment in the Negro community it had become predominantly black by mid-1964. Brooklyn CORE, which remained about half white until the summer of 1963, experienced a heavy Negro influx and became overwhelmingly black at that time as a result of the Downstate Medical Center demonstrations. The Baltimore chapter, preponderantly white as late as 1961, had a membership evenly divided between Negroes and whites in the summer of 1963; by the middle of 1964 it had a black majority. Both the Columbus and Detroit affiliates had also been mainly white in their first years; by the spring of 1964, however, they were each about 60 per cent black. In the Newark chapter, where the ratio of white and black had been about half and half until late 1963, the proportion of blacks among the active members rose to two-thirds in early 1964. In the unique case of Cleveland, the chapter, which began as an all-black group and attracted a number of whites so that by the spring of 1963 it was nearly half white, thereafter recruited mainly Negroes; at its height in the spring of 1964 it was about two-thirds black.

A number of chapters remained half or more white, although the proportion of blacks in them was clearly growing. In upstate New York, where most of the cities had small Negro populations, the chapters as well as participants on demonstrations remained mostly white. Even Syracuse CORE, which made particularly concerted efforts to recruit blacks, still was not more than half black at the end of this period; and of the nearly one hundred people arrested during the summer of 1963 urban renewal demonstrations there, nearly four-fifths were white. Seattle CORE, similarly located in a city with a small black community, at its height in 1964 was somewhat over half white. New Haven CORE, which drew its members from Yale University and from the Dixwell Avenue ghetto, remained about half white. In Boston and on Long Island, the proportion of Negroes in the chapters rose, but they retained slight white majorities. In California the situation was about the same. Berkeley CORE, like Syracuse and New Haven, was heavily influenced by the presence of a university community; although the town had a substantial proportion of Negroes, the chapter was about three-fourths white as late as 1964. At San Diego, in the autumn of 1963, the affiliate was still about three-fourths white; an influx of Negroes followed the chapter's gas company project, and thereafter its membership hovered around 60 per cent white. Los Angeles also remained majority white and envied San Francisco's success at relating itself to the black community. Of the eight Los Angeles CORE members who went on a hunger strike to protest de facto school segregation in September 1963, seven were white. The fact that, despite the growth of Negro membership, these chapters were still composed of white majorities was a matter of considerable concern. At the January 1964 California Conference of CORE chapters there was much talk about the need to get more black members, and delegates raised such questions as:

"What motivates Negroes to come out and participate? Why don't they respond even when adequate publicity is given to a project? What devices should we use?" Actually, despite such self-criticism, the trend toward a predominantly black membership was well established in the CORE chapters by the middle of 1964.[42]

There was considerable self-criticism within CORE chapters for their continued failure to attract "grass roots" people into the organization. While in practice chapters approached the problems of the slumdwellers —and their recruitment into CORE—with varying degrees of intensity, it became increasingly common for them to open offices in the ghettos. As a Cleveland CORE leader stated when the chapter established its Hough center in September 1963, "It is necessary to build a strong base in the black community. A few dedicated people, however militant, will not win. We need a great many people, well organized and informed, who can be militant at the polls, at the stores, in their own organization work, as well as in the streets."

Even for chapters which moved vigorously in this direction, the gap between intention and accomplishment was substantial. Syracuse CORE by the summer of 1963 had opened a ghetto office and elected as chairman Bruce Thomas, a factory worker and "ex-wino," as he often described himself. Thomas led CORE members on walks through black neighborhoods, urging citizens to join CORE's projects and "speak for themselves." Though there was a temporary flurry of interest, a sustained program was not possible, nor did many slumdwellers join CORE. It was a source of concern to the chapter that in the civil disobedience demonstrations connected with the urban renewal project only a handful of ghetto residents participated. During the summer of 1964, Syracuse CORE did experience a brief dramatic success in helping tenants at a public housing project block the Greyhound Bus Company from building a hazardous terminal nearby. But after this victory the affiliate went its own way and the black poor went theirs. Newark CORE, beginning in the summer of 1963, maintained a ghetto storefront office to develop a closer relationship with the residents; yet, despite its concern with the problems of the slums, the chapter's major thrust continued to be against job discrimination, and it failed to establish rapport with "the grass roots." Philadelphia CORE sought out juvenile gang members, who promised to give up their weapons if the chapter could convince city officials to establish adequate recreational facilities; but after the initial explorations the project died. In the case of New Haven, which had a long record of interest in the slumdwellers, a field secretary reported that the affiliate's black leadership had failed to mobilize the community. Marlene Wilson of Columbus CORE criticized her group's inability to get involved with grass-roots people; she attributed the problem to the affiliate's concerning itself with the de facto school segregation issue, in which the black poor were not interested, rather than undertaking projects which the black poor considered relevant; "I look out the window and see the Negroes in the streets and I try to tell our members that a lot of them don't know what de facto school segregation is or that we're even in business to try to do something about it. I try to tell them that there's something wrong and unreal about a group of people who are part of an organization that is dedicated to the attainment of civil rights, human rights and dignity for our people, [who are] standing right outside our door and we don't seem to care if they even know we're there." Even the Cleveland CORE chapter, which spoke of developing in the black poor "self-initiative and self-action, for housing, education, jobs, and against police brutality," paid little attention to the job issue, and recruited few lower-class blacks through its school demonstrations, its rent strikes, and its picketing against police brutality.[43]

Although the community organization programs thus remained largely at the stage of rhetoric, and when undertaken generally failed to attract significant numbers of grass-roots people into CORE, there were cases where chapters were able to recruit from among the black poor. In Chicago, unemployed ghetto youth participated in the school-site demonstrations, and some joined the Metropolitan CORE affiliate which seceded from Chicago CORE in late 1963. Boston proudly cited the example of a welfare mother, recruited through a rent strike project, who became a very active member in the chapter. Blyden Jackson, as head of East River CORE, repeating his earlier success in New Haven, established a militant affiliate composed of committed whites and grass-roots black youth. In Brooklyn a group of unemployed youth formed a clique around Isaiah Brunson, who became chairman in the autumn of 1963.[44] On the other hand, our interview data suggest that most of the new black members were drawn from the ranks of blue-collar workers and more commonly from the lower and middling ranks of white-collar people. They were thus individuals with stable working-class backgrounds.

Accordingly, the sources of CORE's changing ethos were varied. CORE was recruiting blacks from all social strata who were attracted by the organization's militance and not by its earlier identification with nonviolence and interracialism. At the same time, as has been pointed out in other contexts, veteran CORE members reflected the changing mood of the black community and their own impatience with the "more respectable" methods they had previously used. Finally, many of the whites in CORE, especially the young college students who joined after Birmingham, provided an important impetus for the change in the organization's style.

Thus it would be an oversimplification to attribute the escalation of tactics in 1963 and 1964 to black influence alone. In Gadsden, Greensboro, Plaquemine, and other places in the South the growing militance was rooted in the heightened expectations of the black community. Similarly, in the North such black-dominated and largely working-class chapters as Philadelphia and Brooklyn contributed much to the radicalization of tactics; and in St. Louis some of the young adult black members were responsible for the use of civil disobedience at the Jefferson Bank demonstrations, and practically everyone sentenced to jail as a result of the campaign was black. On the other hand, a major source of the dramatic techniques used in Chicago against the mobile classrooms were white University students, who were joined by local ghetto youth. In the San Francisco Bay area, most of the demonstrators in the series of campaigns beginning with Mel's Drive-In Restaurants and culminating in the Sheraton-Palace and Auto-Row projects were whites, although local black militants played a key role. In Syracuse, where it proved difficult to mobilize large numbers in the black community, most of the participants in the hotel and the urban renewal demonstrations were white, although Negro leaders like George Wiley were influential in determining the strategy. In Seattle the advocates of militant tactics on the Picture Floor Plan project and on the shop-in campaigns included young white activists as well as black. New York's Triborough Bridge demonstration was a product of East River CORE, a racially mixed chapter of lower-class young blacks and middle-class white Socialists. And in New Haven a white Trotskyist, who talked incessantly about the need to create confrontations with the police, was a leading figure in the street-blocking tactics that produced the "riot" of November 1963.

As the preceding discussion suggests, whites and blacks were ranged on both sides of the major issues facing CORE. Serious cleavages developed in a number of chapters, but these did not involve racial polarization. Not only did whites often agree that they should play a subordinate role, but in many chapters the issue had not yet been raised, and where it was, the whites who had objections withdrew rather than engage in an open struggle. The schisms, which were especially divisive in places like Harlem, Queens, Chicago, Los Angeles, Seattle, New Haven, and St. Louis, revolved around tactics and program. The battles were essentially joined between people who regarded themselves as militant and their opponents whom they called "middle class" or "respectable." To some degree the factional problems involved differences in style, with the challengers often displaying a stridency that contrasted sharply with earlier CORE practice. Often personality clashes were also involved—and in places like Washington and Dayton were sufficient to divide a chapter severely. But tactics and organizational direction were basic sources of conflicts and were debated intensely, even in cities like Cleveland and Detroit where skillful or charismatic leadership guided the affiliates in new directions without serious challenge from those who expressed doubts or reservations.

Characteristically these struggles involved disagreements over tactics that many criticized as disorderly or charges that the "middle class" chapter leadership was unwilling to actively concern itself with the black poor. The advocates of the ghetto orientation urged community organizing among black slumdwellers and such activities as rent strikes; by the middle of 1964 they had begun to criticize school integration campaigns as irrelevant to the needs of the poverty-stricken masses. The opposing faction usually contained those, both black and white, who felt untrained and unprepared for the new thrust, who questioned the denigration of white participation which sometimes accompanied it, and who charged the proponents of the new emphasis with "pushing the chapter into something" it was not ready for. Dissension often erupted when hesitant chapter leaders called for discussion or for time to study the implications of the changes in program. Denounced as "Black Bourgeoisie" and "White Liberals" in the recrimination which typically followed, they often countercharged that their critics had violated CORE's "nonviolent philosophy of respecting rather than attacking one's adversary." During the emotional controversy some members of both factions, disillusioned by the bitter personal attacks and the spirit of distrust, resigned or drifted away. In some cases, as in Columbus, where in 1964 Marlene Wilson led a dissident group that successfully challenged the leadership of chairman Arthur Zebbs for focusing on direct-action confrontation with city officials over school segregation rather than organizing the black community around problems which grass-roots people believed important, the cleavage was resolved through normal electoral procedures. When Olly Leeds faced a rebellion in Brooklyn CORE because he had at first accepted the black ministers' moderate settlement with public officials in the Downstate Medical Center demonstrations, he reversed his position and then astutely decided not to run for re-election as chairman but nevertheless continued to function as an important leader. In both cases the groups remained pretty well intact.[45] Several chapters, however, were marked by serious splits and even secessions. New Haven CORE was torn apart by a quarrel from which it never fully recovered; withdrawals from the Harlem affiliate, Queens CORE, and the Chicago group led to the creation of the East River, South Jamaica, and Metropolitan CORE chapters, respectively; in Los Angeles and Seattle the dissidents formed independent organizations unaffiliated with National CORE.

In New Haven, where the conflict centered upon the deliberate precipitation of violent incidents by a white Trotskyist who declared that only a revolution could solve the Negroes' problems, the affiliate was severely split over whether or not to conform to the Rules for Action, and was seriously weakened by the November 1963 "street riot." Not until the following February were other chapter leaders able to maneuver the Trotskyist from office and deprive him of significant influence.[46] In Los Angeles, a dissident faction advocated escalating tactics and opening an office in the ghetto. When the dominant group defeated the challengers' slate in an election in late 1963, the latter seceded to form Los Angeles Central CORE. Denied affiliation, this group became known as the Non-Violent Action Committee.[47] In New York City, a faction in Queens CORE, charging that the chapter, dominated by middle-class blacks living in integrated neighborhoods, was unwilling "to address itself to ghetto problems," seceded in the spring of 1964 and founded South Jamaica CORE "in the heart of the Negro ghetto in Queens." [48] In New York CORE an interracial group led by Velma Hill and Blyden Jackson similarly denounced chairman Gladys Harrington and the chapter's program. They criticized New York CORE's efforts "to integrate middle-class luxury apartments in Queens and Long Island that an overwhelming number of Negroes could not afford." Clarence Funnyé's TV image project was regarded as a symbolic cipher which did not help the black masses. The Jackson group began holding street-corner meetings in Harlem and successfully pushed the chapter to undertake rent strikes. In February 1964, after Jackson was defeated in his bid for the chairmanship of the Harlem affiliate, he and his followers formed East River CORE, and proudly called themselves the River Rats. As Jackson told the *New York Times,* "New York [CORE] was afraid of the guys downstairs—from the streets, the poolrooms, the gangs, the reform schools. We are not. We are from the streets." [49]

In Seattle, it was the dissident interracial Ad Hoc Committee, composed mainly of newer and younger members, which promoted the shop-in in the face of a reluctant leadership, and inaugurated the confrontation tactics at the fair-housing demonstrations against the Picture Floor Plans Company. In fact, the Ad Hoc faction wanted to court arrest in this project but was voted down by the membership which, a few weeks later, at a packed and heated meeting suspended the campaign entirely after obstructive tactics had precipitated a physical assault from an angry salesman. In the subsequent supermarket shop-in, two Ad Hoc members were accused of blocking the doors, contrary to instructions from the black leader in charge of the demonstration, and another was denounced for putting perishables in his shopping cart, in violation of the procedures agreed upon. Later, Ad Hoc members were charged with circulating "divisive and derogatory allegations" that the chapter leaders had conspired to thwart direct action projects and had "foisted a compromising agreement on the membership." Ad Hoc people attacked the chapter's black chairman and vice-chairman as "too respectable" and too fearful of losing their jobs and homes by participating in militant tactics. The Ad Hoc group also expressed an interest in the problems of the slumdwellers and opened a ghetto office for a brief period of time at the end of the summer. Defeated in its attempt to oust the chapter's established leadership in the next election and hoping to function independently as a ghetto-oriented organization, the Ad Hoc Committee withdrew, and soon after disintegrated. Meanwhile, amid the accusations and counteraccusations, a number of others left the Seattle Chapter, disgusted by the "lack of faith and trust we CORE people now have in each other." Thus the result of the conflict was to leave Seattle CORE seriously weakened.[50]

The tendency toward cleavage within chapters was sometimes reinforced by the frustration that arose when ambitious campaigns ended in defeat or in judicial repression. The morale of Los Angeles CORE was badly injured after the failure of the fair-housing project into which so much effort had been invested, and the chapter became weak and divided. In Seattle, where the cleavage over tactics originated largely as a generational difference in style, the disagreement turned into intense personal recriminations after the Picture Floor Plans fiasco. In Prince George's County, Maryland, CORE, which lacked the strength of the other affiliates already described, the schism was so severe that the chapter fell apart. The group, which heretofore had been united in its strategy—"one pack . . . who in the old days did not differ on what was violent and what was not"—became polarized after the convictions of those who had sat-in at the Levittown sales office. A faction led by the white chairman felt frustrated in doing things "the orderly way, which wasn't getting anywhere," and wanted to create a confrontation and fill the jails by defying the injunction which the Levitt management had obtained. In contrast, his opponents believed that progress, though slow, "would be lost if we got destructive." Mutual distrust and suspicion became rampant and the moderate faction dropped out, leaving the chapter greatly weakened.[51]

At St. Louis, CORE's top leadership was split in the aftermath of the Jefferson Bank project. The St. Louis chapter was exposed to hostile public opinion and a punitive court which meted out jail sentences ranging up to one year for violating the injunction against "physical interference" at the financial institution. The jailings had "a frightening and dampening" effect on many in the affiliate, and simultaneously increased the strength of a black-led faction headed by Lucian Richards, chapter chairman, and Percy Green, employment committee chairman, who called for more confrontations. In their efforts they were supported by Winston Lockett, a black field secretary, and Gene Tournour, his white colleague. The anger of the Richards-Green faction centered upon Charles Oldham, who having previously counseled against obstructive tactics at the bank, was accused of "selling out to the power structure." Oldham, for his part, had complained to the national office about the two field secretaries, and this had become common knowledge. Matters were only exacerbated when Lockett and Tournour were among those arrested for lying down under police vehicles during a Christmas boycott against downtown stores. They were jailed again on New Year's Eve for refusing to leave City Hall in a demonstration and then, upon being fined two days later, had to be dragged from the courtroom. In the climate of distrust St. Louis CORE was unable to mount another action program, and its disorderly meetings became occasions for vituperative attacks. One veteran

member described a chapter meeting in January 1964, the first one she
attended in five months:

> WOW! has it grown, and WOW! I recognized very, very few people
> from the old group. The chairman was in jail. . . . Well, Marian
> [Oldham] said it was the worst meeting to date. Several people were
> unable to express themselves without shouting, cursing, waving arms,
> and leveling accusations against other members; people who should
> know better ended up shouting back. . . . Charlie [Oldham] seems
> quite concerned one minute, rather weary and tired the next, and
> five minutes later he's laughing about growing pains and telling
> me not to worry. I saw him Tuesday afternoon, and he was in one
> of his better moods—made me feel like I was upset over nothing.
> Maybe a half an hour after I left Charlie the word reached me that
> Charles Oldham is now number one bad guy in CORE because "he's
> trying to get Gene and Winston fired." This little item was begun
> by a couple of girls Charlie got out of jail the day before with his
> own money because they were being threatened by their fellow in-
> mates and were scared.

The Oldham faction won the elections later in the year, and the dissidents led by Percy Green seceded to form their own group called AC-
TION.[52]

By the spring of 1964 the old consensus in CORE over tactics and
strategy had disintegrated. The revolution in expectations, the relatively
limited gains achieved, the outright failure of a number of ambitious
campaigns, and the growing tendency in the North to employ punitive
judicial sanctions all produced a crisis of confidence for many CORE
people. In this context some members, aware of the distance traveled
since 1960, still had faith in the organization's traditional approach. Others became increasingly alienated from American society, and in their
rejection of what they described as a totally racist system they advocated
further escalation of tactics to create serious confrontations and major social disorder. But after the fiasco surrounding the Brooklyn stall-in, they
began to have doubts that direct action provided a panacea for the black
man's problems. Others were coming to the conclusion that demonstrations were limited as a protest strategy, that direct action had all but
eliminated discrimination in public accommodations and had contributed substantially to increased employment in retail stores and con-
sumers-goods industries, but that new methods were needed to bring
about further progress, especially for the black poor. CORE members for
the most part still remained strongly committed emotionally to direct ac-

tion, but, as indicated previously, by the spring of 1964 its use was markedly on the wane in most parts of the country, and many were exploring the possibilities of organizing ghetto communities for other types of political and social action.

The tensions and cleavages within CORE—the black-white issue, the erosion of the commitment to nonviolence, the challenge posed by some chapters to the authority of the national office, the debate over tactics and program—reflected the fact that CORE, like the whole civil rights movement in the spring of 1964, was in a state of crisis. At the same time, CORE's financial debts were a serious problem, and efficiency at the national office was at an all-time low. Most important, the organization suffered from a lack of firm direction, involving both an uncertainty about how to deal with tactical radicalization on the one hand and the absence of a long-range program for tackling the problems of the slumdwellers on the other.

Most of these issues came to a sudden focus in three major conflicts which erupted in April 1964, and all of them posed serious personal problems for James Farmer. First, Brooklyn CORE's threatened stall-in aroused widespread emotional support among the chapters. Second, the NAC, disturbed at the inefficiency and lack of strong leadership in the national office, appointed an Evaluation Committee to investigate the conduct of Farmer's administration. Third, Norman Hill, concerned about what he called CORE's lack of programmatic direction, challenged Farmer by appealing to the NAC for approval of an appointment to the Program Department which Farmer strongly opposed.

During the spring and summer of 1964, Hill was a center of controversy that ended only with his resignation. Like Wally Nelson previously, he became a focal point in the debate over many of CORE's problems. The organization was in a state of flux; its future course had not been set. Hill articulated many of the newer tendencies in the organization at the same time that he vigorously rejected others. It is therefore instructive to examine his role and departure in some detail.

A shake-up in the national office in the fall of 1963 had elevated Hill to the post of program director, while Carey became assistant to the national director. At the area conferences that he directed during the following winter and spring, and at a February staff meeting in New Orleans that he helped to organize, Hill and his close friend Bayard Rustin articulated a strategy that called for a shift from street demonstrations to organizing a large grass-roots movement and engaging in partisan politics. Hill did not want direct action dropped from the arsenal of CORE weapons, but he was opposed to "the glorification of demonstrations as demonstrations," and believed that a far broader program was needed. Although some observers perceived a contradiction in Hill for supporting the Triborough Bridge demonstration but opposing the stall-in and expressing skepticism about the usefulness of direct action as a strategy, CORE's program director saw it as a question of emphasis and timing.[53]

Ever since the summer of 1963 when he had directed pilot community organization projects in Brooklyn and Newark, Hill had been in the vanguard of those attempting to employ new tactics to grapple with the problems of the black poor. Yet by no means was he alone in advocating community organization and partisan politics and an emphasis on the economic and social needs of the masses. He had a substantial influence on chapter leaders like Ruth Turner and Tony Perot in Cleveland, and George Wiley in Syracuse, who were enormously impressed by his plea that CORE shift its priorities and address itself to the concerns of the slumdwellers. One person prominent in Cleveland CORE recalled, "Hill helped turn the chapter around with the kinds of activities he was responsible for." [54] Others, especially on the southern staff, were moving quite independently in similar directions. In fact, in Mississippi and Louisiana, staff members had been establishing not CORE chapters but grass-roots community groups. By the spring of 1964 the thrust toward organizing the poor had become a major feature in CORE thinking. Rent strikes had been widely attempted throughout the Northeast. Intense discussion and even splits in some chapters had occurred over the need to redirect their program to benefit the black poor, and those who seceded from the Harlem and Queens chapters to form the East River and South Jamaica affiliates were close allies of Norman Hill. Nearly everywhere there was now general agreement—at least at the rhetorical level—that CORE must involve the "grass roots" and seek solutions to their basic problems. David Cohen, a leader in Cleveland CORE, who was strongly influenced both by Hill and by the chapter's executive secretary Ruth Turner, put it, "The great question confronting the Northern civil rights movement . . . is whether it can move from a . . . tactic [of crisis confrontation through nonviolent direct-action] which by itself may well spell political defeat, repression and further despair; whether it can evolve a program and tactic which offers greater hope of success." It was

hoped that the solution lay in creating "a much more cohesive and articulate black community" through building local organizations "around
the expressed needs of the slumdwellers." [55]

Originally, it had been anticipated that employment and education
problems would provide important levers for reaching and organizing
the black poor. However, job campaigns actually declined in much of the
country after the summer of 1963; and where they did occur, they were
not mounted as projects of slumdwellers but were instead the standard
kind of demonstrations involving the familiar types of activists, white
and black, who had participated previously. School boycotts temporarily
mobilized the whole black community, but they too failed to produce
sustained grass-roots organizing. Where real involvement occurred between CORE chapters and the black poor, it was associated with projects
to improve slum housing conditions. As we have observed, however, organizing slumdwellers and sustaining rent strikes proved far more difficult
than had been anticipated. Although in Detroit the CORE chapter's
ghetto program and rent strike projects were not inaugurated until the
summer of 1964, in most other places it had become clear by then that
rent strikes were no more effective as a tactic for solving housing problems than the earlier fair-housing campaigns.[56]

Moreover, National CORE's own major community action program,
held in Chicago during the summer of 1964, proved to be a disappointment. Instituted at Hill's urging, it was merged with an ambitious project which his friends in Metropolitan Chicago CORE had previously inaugurated in the southern part of the city. A staff of thirty black and
white task force workers operating three community centers in slum
neighborhoods set up children's tutoring, sports, and crafts programs,
and a planned parenthood clinic; community organization teams were
sent from door to door to determine housing code violations and to ascertain what other matters most concerned the local residents. While housing was the main focus, as one participant recalled, this was "a sort of
front"; task force workers were instructed to organize around any issue
relevant to the community. Unfortunately, CORE's substantial investment in the project produced only limited results, and no lasting neighborhood organizations. A number of the white workers were inept and
inexperienced, while some of the black ones had a defeatist, patronizing
attitude that the poor "couldn't be organized." A sit-in that some CORE
workers conducted in the office of the building commissioner, demanding
a rat extermination and housing inspection program, produced thirteen

arrests and a time-consuming court case that diverted the organizers from canvassing in the local neighborhoods. Some "grass-roots people" responded negatively to the centers: "They feel they will only get slapped down again. So they sit back passively and let the world happen to them. This is a survival technique," observed a member of the task force. In the end what was significant about the Chicago project was not tangible progress but the fact that it signified CORE's growing commitment to finding new ways to aid the slumdwellers.[57]

The limited successes with organizing the black poor and attracting them into CORE did not produce disillusionment with the theory of ghetto organization. What did develop, however, was considerable self-doubt about the practicality of middle-class-dominated CORE chapters choosing issues and tactics—such as rent strikes—for the poor to use in their struggle, and skepticism about the appropriateness of CORE members trying to bring the poor into the chapters altogether. Many felt that, instead, CORE affiliates should help slumdwellers create their own organizations around their own issues. Particularly illuminating in this connection was a discussion at the April 1964 West Coast Regional Conference:

> Some say that CORE is middle-class and afraid of the masses. But we need the masses. We have to let them know they are somebody, and not just by teaching Negro history. They need to see that the freedom movement is their struggle and that it gives them dignity. Their role in the movement needs to be defined. We need not expect them to participate in non-violent actions, but they [sic] are plenty of things they can do. They could conduct their own street meetings better than representatives from CORE who don't speak their language. We need to keep in close touch with the people, or we'll find them leading their own movement and leaving CORE behind. . . . CORE's most valuable contribution to the ghetto is to help them to organize themselves instead of trying to get them into CORE.

A few months later Bill Bradley, chairman of San Francisco CORE, which was organizing a community group in a Hunters Point housing project, insisted that CORE "must tell that community that we care enough to be here. We as an organization must assume the responsibility of engaging in a block by block organization campaign, in which our sole objective is to organize indigenous community organizations which are manned by and led by the community. . . . Under no circumstances should such organizations be controlled by CORE."[58]

While there was widespread agreement upon the importance of mobilizing the black poor in the struggle for their own freedom, there were divergences—implicit and not well-articulated in this period—stemming from separatist tendencies that were starting to emerge in CORE. For Norman Hill the program of ghetto organization was fully integrationist. From the start he had explicitly regarded his strategy as the best antidote to the threat posed by nationalists like Malcolm X.[59] Believing that dedicated and competent whites were as qualified as blacks for work among the black poor, he always appointed interracial staffs to his northern ghetto projects. Moreover, in explaining his approach, Hill often stated that CORE's goal should not be simply equality for blacks but the elimination of poverty for whites as well. Speaking at an area conference in St. Louis he said, "We have a clear task before us: . . . to begin to build the kind of movement which is a basic grass-roots movement, which involves all people, black and white in our struggle. . . . We need to talk about a movement which speaks to the everyday needs of our people, which speaks to why they don't have decent housing . . . why they can't get decent jobs at decent pay, why the children have to go to inferior schools. . . . It is when we build on this kind of movement that democracy will clearly be on the agenda not just for Negroes but for all people." [60]

In practice, however, the ghetto-orientation and community-organization thrust intertwined also with incipient nationalist tendencies. Because it substituted the aim of improving slumdwellings for the goal of achieving housing integration, it implicitly lent ideological legitimacy to a form of separatism. Implicit also in the emphasis on improving ghetto conditions rather than battling for integration was the realization that the lower-class black subculture had many positive attributes, a view that quite naturally converged with the message of race pride preached by men like Malcolm X. Moreover, the popularity of community organization grew in CORE at the very time that participation in the civil rights movement, and the movement's successes, also provided a new sense of black pride and identity. Simultaneously, the evident limitations in the strategies thus far employed, and the perception of how much yet remained to be done despite all the past sacrifices—in short, the whole spirit of impatience epitomized by the radicalization of tactics and the erosion of the commitment to nonviolence—heightened group consciousness by intensifying feelings of alienation from the larger society.

Paradoxically, at the very time that important strides toward integration had been made, many militants, feeling more and more isolated from that society, were beginning to question the value of this goal. They were starting to differentiate between equality and integration, and to doubt the wisdom of seeking to assimilate into the American middle class. SNCC activists were in the vanguard of those raising these questions, and a number of CORE militants agreed with them. By mid-1964 some people in CORE had concluded, for example, that the ghetto communities' concern was for immediate and radical improvement of their neighborhood schools rather than for school desegregation; and in fact, CORE's failure on the de facto school segregation issue would, in the long run, stimulate support for school decentralization and black community control of their own educational system. Thus the frustrating struggle for integrated schools actually encouraged separatist tendencies in CORE. In the spring of 1964 Farmer observed that for most blacks the problem was not "separation versus integration": "The real issue for them is getting the heel of oppression off their neck." Moreover, he declared that alienation had proceeded to the point where Negroes no longer "accept uncritically the assumptions and premises on which the predominantly middle-class American society is based." About the same time Ruth Turner articulated what many CORE people were increasingly feeling: "The melting pot has had a pretty homogeneous and uninteresting flavor to me. It has become a gray mass of mediocrity." Negroes, she frankly declared, would probably still choose to live together even if all the barriers were lifted.

Such observations were not new; what was new was that leaders in the movement were openly speaking in these terms, and were intimating that a pluralist society was in fact a desirable goal. Yet it should be emphasized that this view, when expressed by CORE people, was not at that time usually part of a consistently nationalist position. Ruth Turner, for example, though articulating both the desirability of a distinctive black culture and the necessity for black leadership, was still an advocate of integration, as her leadership in Cleveland's school desegregation campaign indicated.[61]

At the very time that the trend toward community organization among slumdwellers encouraged a changing role for whites, the idea that improvement of ghetto conditions was more important than racial integration appealed to those who were becoming disillusioned with CORE's failure to advance blacks more quickly into the American mainstream. For Norman Hill a ghetto orientation was grounded in economic class theory—helping "grass-roots people" to develop resources for mobility and integration in the larger society. But for those deeply concerned with black identity, the ghetto-reconstruction theme tended to become an end in itself, thus helping to pave the way for black separatism. Although these differences did not become clear until later, and although people who subsequently disagreed with Hill were at this time his sincere admirers, in retrospect the roots of ideological divergence were emerging by 1964.

Hill and his supporters also believed that the basic problems facing the black masses, and the white poor as well, required political solutions. Only government could guarantee employment, good education, and adequate housing for all, and pressuring elected officials to take appropriate action required extensive grass-roots community organization. Accordingly, Hill advocated the welding of black communities into cohesive units for partisan politics at the local, state, and national levels.[62] To demonstrate the value of activists participating in the political arena, he drew a pointed contrast between the "do-nothing" black aldermen of Mayor Daley's Chicago machine who were unresponsive to the black protest movement and the militant stance of William Clay, CORE leader and St. Louis city alderman. Hill's national political strategy, which he and Rustin developed out of their experience with the March on Washington, was based on the theory that the best hope for social change lay in maintaining the coalition of forces that had made the March a success —blacks, the traditional secular liberals represented by the ADA, moderate to liberal churchmen, and those in organized labor who were committed to racial equality. Given the insensitivity of the Republican Party to black needs, Hill believed that the Negro community, as a minority group, could achieve its broad goals only "in a political alliance with these elements" no matter how much "the inadequacy of their performance and commitment" could be criticized. Just as the Democratic Party, despite the power of selfish machine politicians and the reactionary southern wing, had been the political agent for racial progress since the 1930's, so now, in sustained pressure from progressive elements supporting the Party, lay the best opportunity for future advances. Hill and Rustin even hoped that the Negro-Labor-Liberal coalition could expel the "Dixiecrats" and "take control of the Democratic Party." [63]

Others, meanwhile, were independently coming to the view that CORE should turn to partisan political activity. In fact, the most important shove that CORE received in this direction came from MFDP and the challenge at the Democratic Convention. It was the Mississippi experience more than Hill's agitation that excited CORE people about the possibilities in partisan politics. Moreover, there were fundamental differences between Hill and the COFO-MFDP leaders. From the beginning the latter had a dual approach. If they failed to obtain recognition as the official Democratic Party in Mississippi, they were prepared to function as an independent political organization outside both major parties. Because they were operating in a southern context and possessed a millenarian outlook, they were more skeptical of the Democratic Party and less willing than Hill to accept a compromise. Thus, despite the common rhetoric about the need both for basic changes in the social structure and for political activism, the basic strategy assumptions underlying the two points of view were very different. Where Hill believed it possible—and necessary—to work within the system, the COFO enthusiasts were becoming disillusioned with it. This gulf became obvious as CORE prepared to back the MFDP's plans at the 1964 Democratic Convention and committed itself to direct action at Atlantic City. Hill relinquished the assignment of coordinating CORE's activities at the Convention because, while supporting the challenge, he believed that demonstrations on this occasion would antagonize the Democratic Party leadership upon whose good will the black man's cause depended so much.[64] To Dennis and most other COFO activists, on the other hand, the Democratic Party was part of the corrupt American establishment that had to be reformed, and, if this were not possible, then rejected as proof of the obdurate racism of American society.

As early as November 1963, at Hill's urging, the NAC had considered rescinding CORE's rule against partisan activity. Unpersuaded by Hill's doubts about the wisdom of "our getting people registered and then taking a neutral position," the Council had backed Gartner's motion to reaffirm CORE's "long-standing policy" of not endorsing political candidates. By the following summer, however, with the Freedom Democratic Party capturing the imagination of the militants, and with the nomination of the conservative Barry Goldwater at the Republican Convention all but assured, pressures mounted for CORE to rescind its ban. In fact, the subject was an important item of discussion during CORE's 1964 Convention. While Farmer at this point had not committed himself, national chairman Floyd McKissick openly advocated partisan politics as a necessary change in the organization's program. At the same time the NAC took up the question again. More members now favored dropping the ban, but, with some still fearing that this would invite co-optation by the political machines, a compromise was arranged. The Council authorized chapters to "conduct political education campaigns without specific endorsement of candidates." Right after the CORE Convention Farmer warned that, while the organization would remain nonpartisan, demonstrators would appear at the Republican Convention in San Francisco to demand that the party end its alliance with the Southern Democrats. And although Hill had reservations about leading direct action at the Democratic Convention, he, along with CORE's West Coast office, coordinated the vociferous demonstrations at the San Francisco conclave.[65]

Thus, while Hill was in the vanguard of CORE's new directions toward community organization and partisan politics, when it came to implementation he was at odds with others who advocated the same general thrust. By the spring of 1964 Hill found himself in opposition to what may be loosely described as CORE's left wing—a far from unified collection of individuals wedded, in varied ways and in different degrees, to separatist impulses, to lessening white leadership in CORE, to a radicalization of tactics that was often accompanied by a rhetorical justification of violent retaliation, and, in some instances, to revolutionary ideologies. Despite Hill's concern for the black poor, he was attacked for his democratic socialism, his skepticism about the Brooklyn stall-in, and his brand of coalition politics. For his part he now considered CORE to be in a serious crisis. Central to this crisis, he maintained, was a lack of programmatic direction in helping black slumdwellers, which had encouraged the emergence of nationalist and radical spokesmen outside CORE and had caused serious chapter problems within the organization. Hill charged that the "absence of a thorough knowledge of strategic and tactical nonviolence" had produced such misfortunes as "the tragic death of a CORE member in Cleveland and the confused, low level discussion of traffic stoppage at the World's Fair." In fact, to Hill the challenge posed by Brooklyn CORE, which he regarded as engaging in self-defeating tactics under the influence of revolutionary Marxist sympathizers, epitomized the dilemmas facing the whole organization. Both in marshaling opposition to the stall-in and in urging Brooklyn CORE's suspension, he played a leading role. Finally, Hill was also deeply troubled by the low morale of CORE's field staff, stemming from inefficiencies in the Organization Department, the lack of a training program, and the desperate need for more field secretaries.[66]

Hill's dissatisfaction reached a climax and an open confrontation with Farmer in April 1964, over Hill's efforts to appoint Tom Kahn, an official of the League for Industrial Democracy, as his assistant in the Program Department. Hill viewed Kahn, a white man who like himself was a young Socialist intellectual and close associate of Bayard Rustin, as an ideal person to help chapter leaders and field staff to develop a program around political action and economic issues. Farmer rejected Kahn's appointment because he did not want to strengthen what some charged was Hill's "Socialist bloc." In addition, Farmer was perhaps reacting to rumors that Hill was personally disloyal and was building a machine to bring in Rustin as national director. Afterward, Hill took the unprecedented action of appealing to the Steering Committee. And in an equally unprecedented action the Committee voted nine to three to overrule Farmer and appoint Kahn.

Although Kahn, lacking both Farmer's and McKissick's support, decided to decline the position, the Steering Committee's decision was nevertheless highly significant. It reflected a strong sense of disquietude over CORE's future, over the problems of debt, inefficiency, low morale, and program. In all of these matters Farmer's style of leadership was seen as playing a crucial role. The Committee agreed that he served CORE extraordinarily well as charismatic leader and public ambassador but had provided neither strong internal administration nor a firm sense of direction. In contrast, the Steering Committee, by no means Socialist-oriented, was impressed by Hill's coherent strategy. They politely but pointedly declared that "it might be wise to take a hard look at the present time-consuming demands being made on the National Director to see if revisions of his schedule, where possible, could leave more time to deal with these urgencies and give direction to the organization." Accordingly, they created an evaluation committee to look into CORE's administrative problems.[67]

Farmer was facing an unprecedented questioning of his leadership; for the first time, indeed, his position in CORE was being challenged. From all sides he was under attack—from Hill, from Brooklyn CORE, and from the Steering Committee. For the immediate future, however, the most pressing issue was the threat posed by the Brooklyn affiliate and the stall-in. The very Steering Committee meeting that rapped Farmer over the knuckles was the one that confirmed the suspension of Brooklyn CORE. For Farmer the stall-in issue was a serious personal dilemma. As a militant "mobilizing" leader it was desirable for him to support it; as an "articulating" leader working to retain the backing of white liberals and moderates, he was under strong pressures to oppose it.[68] His solution, as indicated earlier, was to side with the stall-in's opponents but personally to court arrest at the demonstrations held inside the Fairgrounds. At the same time Hill, who served as coordinator for the World's Fair project, secured the participation of some of his prominent Socialist friends like Rustin, Kahn, and Michael Harrington, who were also taken to jail. Afterward Hill and Farmer temporarily drew closer together. But the inherently unstable rapprochement was destroyed when fresh rumors reached Farmer that Hill and Rustin were plotting his removal.* Farmer now began to mend his fences with people to Hill's left. To limit Hill's influence at the 1964 Convention, Farmer forbade any "caucusing" by the staff. Several of Hill's backers were defeated for posts on the NAC in part because, as one CORE leader put it, "Farmer quietly put his weight with a different group of people," some of whom had previously been at odds with the national director.[69]

But Hill faced more than a renewed suspicion from Farmer. He found himself opposing popular sentiment in CORE regarding direct action and political strategy, so that his position would soon become untenable. In July, Hill and Rustin helped to arrange a meeting in which Randolph, Wilkins, King, and Young called for a moratorium on demonstrations until after the November elections. They were fearful that the white backlash which poll takers reported among blue-collar workers, and which was being fed by the recent New York City riots, might result in the victory of Goldwater. Farmer had also attended the meeting which drew up the manifesto calling for a moratorium and was reported to have agreed with its contents. But for CORE activists commitment to direct action was a highly charged emotional issue, and next day Farmer, under pressure from chapters across the country, repudiated the manifesto and directed them to continue with their plans for demonstrations. Hill deplored CORE's failure to support the moratorium.[70] Not only was Goldwater's defeat essential, but Hill also thought it imperative that Johnson be re-elected with the enthusiastic support of the black protest organizations and their labor-clergy-liberal allies. The Negro masses would back Johnson anyway, but if his black votes came through the political machines and over the opposition of the militant protest organiza-

---

* It is impossible to either substantiate or disprove this allegation. Many, including Farmer himself, believed it, but many other CORE leaders did not. The only person who actually claimed to have heard Hill and Rustin discuss such plans was their former close friend, Blyden Jackson, who at this time became involved in a bitter feud with Hill.

tions like CORE, "The prophecy that support of Johnson leads to loss of leverage would be self-fulfilling." [71] At this very juncture, however, with the MFDP about to mount its challenge at Atlantic City, CORE militants mostly agreed with the COFO leadership's view that the important thing was to secure the seating of the Freedom Party delegation, Johnson's opposition notwithstanding. For example, the future national associate director, George Wiley, who had backed Hill in the Tom Kahn episode, was a firm advocate of going along with COFO and MFDP, and mounting direct-action demonstrations at Atlantic City, which of course Hill opposed as counterproductive. In the end the events at Atlantic City, as already seen, only confirmed the movement's left wing in its skepticism about the Democratic Party leadership and the influential white liberals supporting it. But by then Hill had resigned from CORE. It had become clear that, however much he articulated CORE's thrust toward ghetto organization and partisan politics, his strategy differed substantially from those now gaining ascendancy in CORE.

The circumstances surrounding Hill's resignation in mid-August[72] were filled with ironies. First, despite the emotional groundswell against the moratorium, direct action had actually declined sharply, and CORE chapters undertook virtually no such campaigns in the months prior to the election.[73] Second, less than a week before Hill resigned, the Evaluation Committee vindicated his contentions about CORE's internal problems. Its report was highly critical of the performance of the national office, and along the lines of Hill's suggestions recommended the employment of both an associate national director and an overhaul of the Organization Department.[74] Finally, during the following months community organization became CORE's official new direction. Farmer answered criticisms of lack of programmatic focus by drawing up a carefully articulated analysis of community organization, which was presented to the NAC and staff that autumn and became the basis of CORE's future program.

The simultaneous impact of these two events—Hill's resignation and the Evaluation Committee's Report—was of the highest importance. As shall be seen in the next chapter, the Committee's recommendations produced critical staff changes and a searching discussion of CORE's future direction and program. Hill's resignation had undoubtedly been inevitable ever since he appealed to the NAC over Farmer's head. If this were not enough, his stance on the stall-in, the moratorium, and the Democratic Convention Challenge antagonized too many people in CORE.

Hill's pioneering advocacy of a ghetto orientation and partisan politics was soon forgotten because he did not conform to the mainstream of what CORE ultimately became. Yet, like his emphasis upon developing a program to benefit the black poor, Hill's resignation had incalculable effects on the organization. He had served as a sort of lightning rod, and absorbed considerable criticism from people to Farmer's left. As a dedicated integrationist he would have been an important influence against the separatist tendencies that were emerging in CORE.

V

CORE in Decline: The Road Toward Black Power 1964-1966

11

Community Organization: The Hope and the Reality

"The Civil Rights Revolution," A. Philip Randolph told a conference of prominent black leaders in January 1965, "has been caught up in a crisis of victory; a crisis which may involve great opportunity or great danger to its future fulfillment." The movement had secured a major triumph in the passage of the 1964 Civil Rights Act, yet so much remained to be done. The white South acceded only grudgingly; the concerns of the black poor everywhere had still barely been tackled. Given the enormity of the problems that remained unsolved, the crisis of victory was, in effect, a crisis of confidence, as activists floundered in their search for methods to bring about sustained and rapid progress. Randolph's epigram achieved even sharper relevance with the passage of the Voting Rights Act of 1965—an achievement that resulted from the SCLC-sponsored campaign at Selma, Alabama. Meeting in August, the SCLC convention found itself frustrated and uncertain where to turn; King's lieutenant James Bevel summed up the mood: "There is no more civil rights movement. President Johnson signed it out of existence when he signed the voting-rights bill."

The situation was ironic. In five years, the black protest movement had accomplished more than in all the preceding fifty. Yet with expectations outracing change, many militants had become cynical and bitter about American society—a mood of pessimism that was exhibited also among the masses in the North where civil disorders erupted annually. White support for the movement was greater than ever before, yet activists were growing increasingly hostile toward white liberals, suspicious of white participants, and more separatist in their outlook. Finally, at the very time that nonviolent direct action had become most fashionable—with thousands of Americans, black and white, converging on Selma, Alabama, during March 1965 in support of King's campaign there, and many thousands more marching with him a few days later in Montgomery—people in the most militant sectors of the movement considered the technique essentially obsolete. As Farmer, in his epigrammatic style, put it: "The old way" of direct action "won us the right to eat hamburgers at lunch counters and is winning us the right to vote, but has not basically affected the lot of the average Negro." [1]

Although CORE people were far from unified, the organization's basic answer to the problems posed by the "crisis of victory" was to shift away from direct action and voter registration to community organization. Because CORE had been floundering for lack of a well-defined sense of direction or an adequate program, the NAC, as we have seen had, as early as April, 1964, sharply criticized Farmer. In October, responding to this pressure, he presented to the National Action Council an ambitious set of proposals for what were called CORE's "New Directions." He articulated a program of community organization and political action that sought to provide both a sense of programmatic direction and a platform of unity for the disparate views among CORE activists. The basic task, of course, lay with the affiliates, but he proposed that this program be implemented at the national level by creating three new departments for economic, cultural, and political action. In the economic sector he wanted CORE to establish black producer and consumer cooperatives and to encourage small businesses. The Cultural Action Department would concern itself with "problems of 'identity,'" seeking "to develop in the Negro community a new self-awareness" through studying black history and culture. Most important of all as a means to strengthen the black poor was the achievement of political power. Farmer wanted CORE to adopt a flexible policy of pressing both from within and from outside the political establishment; basically the function of CORE chapters should be to help black communities develop local Freedom Democratic movements, operating pragmatically, making and breaking alliances as necessary. Only in this way would blacks achieve "maximum effectiveness in moving toward the goals we seek." "We must," he told the 1965 CORE Convention, "be in a position of power" before the political authorities would respond to the needs of the black community; demonstrations not backed by "political muscle" would yield only "diminishing returns."

Farmer thus allied himself with a ground swell of sentiment among CORE activists—and on the NAC in particular—for stimulating community organization, black identity, and political action. Farmer was careful, however, to take into account the sentiments of those, still numerous in the chapters, who wanted to emphasize CORE's traditional approach. He clearly did not exclude direct action from CORE's arsenal of weapons, although he did insist that, in view of the problems now being attacked, demonstrations would necessarily play a lesser role than previously.

In discussing his new program, Farmer also explicitly addressed himself to nationalist and separatist impulses that were both so important outside of CORE and also increasingly associated with the thrust within CORE toward black identity and community organization. With the slow pace of social change strengthening the appeal of nationalist spokesmen in the black community, Farmer's "New Directions" proposal was partly an attempt to counter their influential voices. One NAC member, for example, observed that Farmer's remarks about the need for CORE to help provide blacks "with identity" was one way to compete with the black nationalist emphasis on "thinking black." Farmer himself emphasized that the building of identity must be done without CORE's joining the "nationalist wing" of the protest movement. Both in his statement on "New Directions" and in his book *Freedom—When?*, written in early 1965, Farmer sought to bridge the gap within CORE between what with some oversimplification he described as the integrationist and the nationalist points of view, and to grapple with the issues raised by the growing "Mood Ebony" in the organization, which he observed was rooted in the pride flowing from the successes of the movement, the rising participation of lower-class blacks who never had integration or assimilation as their prime goal, and the propaganda of nationalists like Malcolm X, who "have influenced us perceptibly." To Farmer it was "clear that we must not, we cannot, leave the ghetto to the rabid nationalists." Yet "some form of nationalism is necessary and even healthy," for, "Like the nationalists, we must try to conquer the Negro sense of inferiority." Farmer agreed that "the old CORE idealists are correct when they warn that Negro group pride and group consciousness can deteriorate into the most narrow-minded chauvinism," but he cautioned against "The doctrinaire color-blind [who] often failed to perceive that it is *ideally* necessary for the black man to be proudly black today." Moreover, he aimed to reassure those in CORE who feared that a community organization program geared to rebuilding and revitalizing the black ghettos was "anti-integrationist, separationist, [and] reactionary." He thought it important for CORE to accept part of Malcolm X's "insight . . . rejecting the notion of some of the older civil rights organizations (and of the original CORE) that desegregation and integration in *itself* [sic] will accomplish miracles," and explained that the Negro community sought not integration per se but "Freedom and Equality," or "the right to exercise the prerogative of choice" in all areas of the nation's life, "unrestricted by race." In other words individual blacks should have the right to live either in mixed neighborhoods or in black neighborhoods "made livable through improvement of housing, employment, cultural and educational standards." Accordingly, CORE must continue to work for integrated education, open housing, and compensatory job opportunities as it had in the past, at the same time as it "enter[ed] the Negro community, working with those masses who couldn't care less about integration," helping them to "build a community life and a community spirit."[2]

Although CORE's fiscal difficulties precluded implementation of Farmer's proposals, the October 1964 meeting of the National Action Council gave formal approval to his recommendations, which, in effect, provided the platform for CORE's basic thrust through the rest of his administration. At the same time the NAC, addressing itself to the criticisms of CORE's internal operations which the Evaluation Committee had presented in August, inaugurated a series of important reforms at the national office.

The Evaluation Committee had censured top staff officials for permitting incompetence and inefficiency. Farmer's indecisiveness was obliquely noted: ". . . one of the major problems of the organization is that clear-cut, administrative directives have not been formulated and given to staff personnel by the National Director." Given the complexity of his responsibilities and his necessarily frequent absences from the office, it was "apparent that the duties of the National Director cannot be fulfilled by one person." The Organization Department was scored for lack of established procedures in the recruitment and training of field staff and the failure to service the chapters properly. The assistant to the National Director was criticized for not coordinating the various departments and for permit-

ting the breakdown in office discipline that produced the chronic ab-
senteeism and tardiness and the long delays in answering mail. The Evaluation Committee recommended the employment of a new administrator
to help Farmer, the removal or reassignment of inefficient executives, and
a substantial infusion of bureaucratic procedures: ". . . outline
specifications for each job position in organization; initiate a recruitment
program for field staff; . . . initiate training program for field personnel;
. . . establish screening procedures for recruitment of organization
personnel—testing, etc.; . . . professionals to set standards for office behavior and decorum; . . . initiate program for prompt reporting to work;
distribute mail before work day begins; . . . construct a table of organization with clear delineation of responsibilities." [3]

At its meeting in October 1964, the National Action Council approved
nearly all of the Evaluation Committee's report and recommendations.
That action symbolized the growing effort of the NAC to play a greater
role in the making of CORE policy. Indeed at the same meeting, the National Action Council spent considerable time discussing the nature of its
authority over the staff and concluded, "There is a close relationship between the NAC and staff; there is also a separation of NAC and staff; decisions can be originated by staff and agreed upon by NAC or [can be
originated] by the NAC itself; the staff is responsible to the National
Director but the NAC is also involved according to the Constitution in
hiring and firing; there is a real need for honesty in the relationship." [4]
Over the following months a series of important staff changes occurred.
Carey resigned and departed by the end of the year; McCain now spent
much of his time in South Carolina and delegated to Robert Gore, who
was named assistant director of the organization department, much of the
administrative burden.[5] To service the chapters more adequately, the
NAC appointed more staff, as the Evaluation Committee had urged.
Louis Smith, who had become northeastern field secretary late in the summer, opened a regional office and supervised three other field staffers.
Meanwhile, Mike Lesser worked with the midwestern chapters. In view
of CORE's continuing fiscal crisis, other key recommendations involving
recruitment and training were not implemented. After nearly ten months
on the job Smith complained, "I have yet to be told what was expected
of a Field Secretary. I was hired and left to grope. I have gotten by because I am basically chapter-oriented, but what happens when we get
field staff who are not?" Nor was the old problem of communication between the chapters and the Organization Department solved; as Smith re-

ported in the spring of 1965, the western chapters still suffered from "the national office's neglect and unwise counseling," and everywhere he found that the failure to obtain materials and information from national headquarters was a "major gripe." [6]

By far the most important change at the national office was the appointment of George Wiley as associate national director, to function as CORE's "primary administrator," and as "representative of the national organization in the absence of the national director." Wiley, who took office in January, was a chemistry professor who had been the principal spirit behind the very active Syracuse chapter; he had served for more than a year as an influential member of the NAC Steering Committee. In his new post, he was responsible for staff and program. He sought to tighten procedures—installing Edwin Day, a white Syracuse CORE associate, as office manager, insisting on reports, and reorganizing the work of the clerical staff.[7] He also went a long way toward restoring staff morale. He devoted considerable energy to reducing CORE's debts by instituting operational efficiencies and, toward the end of his tenure, by supplementing the activity of the fund-raising department with his own efforts among wealthy individuals and organizations. With Farmer on the road most of the time, Wiley handled staff placements, determined allocation of funds to a great extent, and made most of the day-to-day decisions.

Both by virtue of his position and the force of his personality, Wiley performed the functions which Rich had assumed informally in the early years of Farmer's administration. He worked hard at "keeping on top" of what CORE was doing, and he made special efforts to exchange ideas with staff and chapter leaders around the country. At the same time he attempted to see that the NAC was better informed than it had been previously. Nevertheless, given the complexity and spontaneity of CORE operations, the national staff was still the most important voice in the formulation of the organization's program.

To a considerable degree, Wiley's efforts to strengthen CORE were stymied by pressing financial problems. At one point he informed the NAC, "It has been practically impossible to do anything beyond caretaker activities. The most significant accomplishment I can record is that we have met payroll, and with a little luck we should make it again today." [8] What had happened was that despite the high debt with which CORE had been saddled in the spring of 1964, the national office, encouraged by the spurt in donations in June and July, anticipated optimistically that income would continue to rise. During the late summer and early autumn it substantially increased the field staff in both the North and the South. This expansion, however, coincided with a sharp drop in income; even though summer fund-raising had been unprecedentedly successful, there was a steep downturn in the fall, and for the seven months between June 1 and December 31, 1964, receipts fell nearly $60,000 from the $605,000 raised in the same period a year earlier. Conditions became so serious that in November and December the Steering Committee meetings were canceled because the travel agencies refused to extend more credit, and CORE was even having difficulty paying rent and phone bills. By the end of January the debt stood at $200,000.[9]

Several tactics were adopted to meet the crisis. First, in late 1964 and early 1965 loans totaling over $100,000 were obtained, guaranteed by philanthropists Stephen Currier and Andrew Norman.[10] Second, the CORE Scholarship, Educational, and Defense Fund (CORE-SEDF) was developed as a source of money for several programs. Originally established during the summer of 1962, and headed by Andrew Norman, who had previously lent CORE $60,000 for Freedom Ride bail money, the Fund now finally secured its tax-exempt status from the Internal Revenue Service. In early 1965 Rich resigned as Community Relations director to become CORE-SEDF executive director, and during the last year of Farmer's administration the Fund became a vital source of money, underwriting almost the entire legal program and assuming a major share of the responsibility for voter registration projects in the South.[11] Third, Farmer announced to the NAC in January 1965 that CORE was making some sharp economies—reducing staff in both the national office and the field. Under Wiley's watchful guidance, CORE's expenditures were trimmed to $60,000 a month. Significant savings resulted from closing the western and northeastern regional offices, as well as two of the expensive Chicago Freedom Centers.[12]

These measures notwithstanding, because of the expansion which had taken place in 1964, CORE spent a total of $1,023,000 during the fiscal year ending May 31, 1965—nearly $120,000 more than in the preceding fiscal year. Simultaneously, income had dropped to $803,000, a decline of nearly $100,000. By August 1965 the debt had reached nearly $295,000.[13] And receipts continued to fall off. Between June 1 and December 1, 1965, contributions totaled $433,000, over $100,000 less than in the corresponding period a year earlier. On the other hand, Wiley's tightening up on expenses, such as cancellation of three more Steering Committee meetings, began to show some effect. At the end of 1965 the debt had been cut to $233,000.[14]

Contributors were disenchanted by several developments: the past use of obstructive direct-action tactics; the cessation of dramatic news-catching demonstrations; the summer riots; the rejection of the compromise at the 1964 Democratic Convention; and the criticism by some chapter leaders of United States involvement in Vietnam. CORE's experience was not unique. While all the racial advancement organizations except the Urban League (which tapped large corporations) experienced a drop in income, the financial pinch was felt most severely by the activist organizations—CORE, SCLC, and SNCC—whose funding came mainly from white liberals.[15] Nevertheless, reduced though CORE's income was, its sources did not change. Direct mail still accounted for about half of CORE's funds, the mailing list having leveled off at a high point of about 75,000 names.[16] Most of the balance came from special projects and foundations. Contributions from labor unions began to drop in 1965, undoubtedly because of their disapproval of CORE's stand at the Democratic Convention, but their assistance had always proved disappointing, having reached a maximum of about $40,000 annually between 1962 and 1964. Approximately 95 per cent of the money still came from whites, with "Jewish contributions . . . predominant." [17] Money from the chapters continued to provide only a small part of the budget. Haley was appalled by how little they gave to the emergency appeals: "I have a real frustration from considering what seems to me to be an inability of most Northern chapters to respond effectively to this organization and crisis." [18]

Faced with a declining income, and increasingly attracted to the idea of black self-help, many CORE leaders found the notion of raising money from blacks appealing. In early 1965 the Steering Committee decided to make intensive efforts to seek substantial funds in the Negro community, where "there is no pattern of giving to CORE." William Bradley and Wilfred Ussery vigorously took up the theme at the 1965 Convention. By autumn, Farmer, McKissick, and Ruth Turner had already begun direct solicitations. But expectations for a major fund-raising campaign among blacks were not realized, and Gartner, who had become CORE's full-time fund raiser in June, informed the NAC, "We have not done anywhere near as well as we had hoped." In fact, as he informed Farmer, he had concluded that it was time to renew efforts among the group which had always supplied most of CORE's financial resources, "the much and properly maligned but nevertheless moneyed white liberal community." [19]

Four skilled fund raisers associated with the United Jewish Appeal trained Gartner and Wiley in fund-raising techniques. During late 1965 Farmer and Wiley spent considerable time making personal solicitations among "prestigious" white New Yorkers. The two conferred with Anna Rosenberg, former Assistant Secretary of Defense, who suggested prominent people she believed could be persuaded to aid CORE. And Franklin D. Roosevelt, Jr. agreed to help Farmer arrange a cocktail party for fifty wealthy people at a fashionable restaurant.[20]

Though faced with declining revenues, CORE did everything possible to maintain its program in the South. For the year ending May 31, 1965, $263,000, or about one-third of all expenditures, went to that region. The personnel connected with the southern regional office was greatly augmented. In September 1964 Dave Dennis was assigned to the New Orleans office as regional program director; during the following months the southern staff consisted of a dozen field secretaries and administrators and nearly fifty task force workers and unpaid volunteers. In the winter of 1965, when CORE's paid staff stood at an all-time high of 117, over half of the field personnel were stationed in the South.[21] CORE-SEDF also lent substantial assistance. During the summer of 1965 the southern staff ranks were swelled with over fifty college students financed by the Fund. More important, SEDF also greatly strengthened legal work in the South. It assumed responsibility for paying retainers to McKissick and Burt in North Carolina; Collins, Douglas, and Elie in New Orleans; and Murphy Bell in Baton Rouge; hired John Due to cover northern Florida; and secured other lawyers in Mississippi and South Carolina.[22]

Despite this support from SEDF, the sustained commitment to southern projects placed a great burden on National CORE, and it was never possible to finance them adequately. As Haley once put it, "The project in Louisiana is operating just as the National Office—on the good graces of its creditors. The project in Florida [exists] on the good graces of its friends in the community." Accordingly, Rich, who bore the brunt of fund-raising, was deeply concerned about the staff's tendencies to develop new programs which the organization could ill afford. In October 1964, when Haley, having secured NAC approval for additional personnel in Mississippi, transferred some of them to other locations, Rich expostulated, "I do know that we cannot continue to expand staff. Today, I negotiated a loan for $25,000 from the bank which was guaranteed by a private individual. One of the conditions of the loan was that we guarantee that we control the one variable we can control—our expansion. We made a commitment to retrench—this will mean primarily the laying off of clerical people in the national office. . . . We simply do not have the resources to do all that is needed. . . ." Similarly, he objected when Richard Jewett, who replaced Dennis as head of the work in Mississippi, opened a new project "at a time when we . . . are broke. We are not now paying our bills in Mississippi and every project is crying that we have been false to our obligations to them. To take on new obligations . . . is to open up ourselves to further justified criticism. . . ." [23] CORE's fiscal plight made it difficult even to sustain the task force, and the southern office began accepting unsalaried volunteers. On their part, for many months, task force workers in Louisiana and Mississippi were turning back to National CORE substantial portions of their meager $12.50 weekly salaries.[24] But such efforts provided only a temporary stopgap, and finally, beginning in the fall of 1965, financial realities forced a substantial trimming of the southern task force. By then, with the departure of Richard Jewett, only field secretary George Raymond and a handful of task force people remained in Mississippi. At the beginning of 1966 the situation in Florida and Louisiana reached a comparable point, and the southern regional office itself closed in May. Only modest grants for a renewed VEP program permitted a temporary, though limited revival of CORE activity in Mississippi and Louisiana during the middle of the year.[25]

Southern staff were "almost unanimous" in their "admiration for the COFO program," [26] and CORE's work in the South down to the end of 1965 operated in its shadow. Yet the impact of the Mississippi experience proved paradoxical. At first it stimulated proposals for an ambitious expansion of CORE's politically oriented southern program. However, it was not long before the community-organization thrust of the COFO experiment became dominant, and the staff was soon emphasizing the building of grass-roots organizations around the "felt needs" of local citizens. Even after passage of the 1965 Voting Rights Act, CORE leaders, except in South Carolina, usually pushed registration and politics into the background. In fact, militants on the Mississippi staff held that with the passage of the Act, COFO demands were "no longer radical," and that other approaches would be needed to "basically change the existing structure." As Ronnie Moore instructed the Louisiana staff in November 1964, "If the community wants to have a sewerage service above everything else we must organize them to meet that need. That organization can then work to reach long-range ends. By doing what the community wants, community leaders automatically will emerge. When these leaders come forward to work for the community, it's our responsibility to take a back seat and advise such community leadership. This is the only way we can permanently build self-supporting community units strong enough to stand on their own to solve their own problems." [27]

Philosophy notwithstanding, there was a degree of ambiguity in the manner with which community organization was carried out. Frequently, the staff operated as if it knew what was best, offering programs and tactics rather than assisting people in developing their own solution to their own problems.[28] Nevertheless, CORE field staff did help local communities attack a broad range of grievances. Although grass-roots organization could be developed around a variety of issues, in practice much of the work centered on using the leverage of federal power to exploit the "avalanche of new approaches" which the civil rights and antipoverty legislation of 1964 had opened up but "which most communities are not prepared to deal with." [29] Moreover, CORE's lawyers, pressed by Dennis, began to go beyond the defense of civil rights workers to what Rachlin called "affirmative legal action." Taking up a project in which Rachlin had long been interested, the organization's attorneys in Louisiana sought to force recalcitrant boards of education to desegregate by mounting an attack on tax-exempt construction bonds for jim crow public schools. Because bond purchasers usually demanded a certificate of nonlitigation and because of federal district court pressures, CORE obtained the reluctant consent of school boards in St. Tammany and East Feliciana Parishes and in Jonesboro and Monroe to begin desegregation.[30] Overall, however, the southern staff found, as northern CORE leaders had already discovered, that welfare issues proved less susceptible to attack than segregation and disfranchisement. Indeed, despite some notable successes, the final phase of CORE's work in Mississippi, Louisiana, and northern Florida became the most frustrating experience in the history of its southern efforts.

Demoralization appeared earliest in Mississippi, even though the liberating effects of the Convention challenge at first galvanized activists there into greater effort. To underscore the fact that it was the state's disfranchised blacks, rather than the whites, who were loyal to the national Democratic Party, and to strengthen the claims of the MFDP congressional candidates that they should be seated in the U. S. House of Representatives, a "Freedom Vote" was held in the fall of 1964 in which 68,000 people cast ballots for Lyndon Johnson and the Freedom Party's nominees. Yet, compared to the 82,000 who had voted for Aaron Henry in the first freedom election a year earlier, the turnout was disappointing. In CORE's Fourth District the "Freedom Vote" was small, even though staff resources had been poured into the area, Annie Devine of Canton was a candidate for Congress, and Farmer personally flew in to address a rally.[31]

This "very bad experience" in Canton [32] was symptomatic of the rest of COFO, which was coming apart at the seams. Dave Dennis departed in September, weary from the strain of two uninterrupted years of working in the state, feeling partly responsible for the deaths that had occurred, and unhappy because the local people were too dependent on him. For these and other reasons Robert Moses gradually withdrew from directing affairs and retired into obscurity. Simultaneous with this sudden and crucial loss in leadership, the coalition experienced a precipitous drop in income and faced internal problems and attacks from some organizations which had cooperated with it. The NAACP in particular and National CORE and the LCDC to a lesser extent complained that they were not consulted about important decisions. Many of the SNCC-oriented activists severely criticized the NAACP's Aaron Henry because he had wished to discuss seriously the possibility of accepting the compromise at the Democratic Convention.[33] By the end of 1964 COFO suffered a major breakdown of morale. The staff failed to do serious political organizing and instead expended time in meetings to discuss endlessly such matters as internal democracy, personality conflicts, and COFO's proper role in helping indigenous leaders make decisions for their communities. Epitomizing the situation were conditions at the Jackson headquarters, where interpersonal relations and black-white conflicts among the staff deteriorated to such a point that the office closed down completely for a week in November. In the following months COFO limped along. In April 1965, the NAACP formally severed relations with the coalition; CORE's connections with it grew ever more tenuous while even relations with SNCC's Mississippi staff grew tense and quarrelsome; and in September, the departure of Dick Jewett, CORE's top official in the federation, essentially signaled the demise of the COFO movement.[34]

With COFO's decline the focus of political attention rested upon the MFDP and its challenge to the seating of Mississippi's congressmen. Compared to the Convention challenge, this project received far less support from liberals, who argued that the strict constitutional procedures regarding the seating of congressmen did not apply to delegates at political party conventions. Eventually, in September 1965, the House of Representatives flatly dismissed MFDP's claims. Core's national office supported the efforts of MFDP throughout, lobbying with congressmen and urging its chapters to do the same.[35] There had been a brief upsurge of MFDP activity in June when it sponsored demonstrations at Jackson, where the Mississippi legislature met in special session to enact a law intended to circumvent the 1965 Voting Rights Act. Among those arrested for attempting to picket on the state capitol grounds was CORE associate director, George Wiley. Over the summer the political coalition which COFO had fashioned was completely sundered when NAACP forces, allied with the state AFL-CIO leadership, formed the Mississippi Democratic Conference from which COFO and FDP representatives were excluded.[36] In a few months, with CORE's staff almost entirely pulled out of the state, effective ties to the organization had ended.

With the diminishing fortunes of COFO and MFDP, the CORE operation in the state became essentially autonomous. And its thrust changed markedly, the CORE staff now focusing on building community organizations and consciously playing down its policy-making role. As a result, the staff spent much of its time in the autumn of 1964 sounding out local opinion. Dick Jewett reported that CORE staffers were listening to local people "with the expectation that some unknown program will actually emerge." As George Raymond said, "We are really trying to get a program developed with the community saying exactly what it will be. This will provide them with the feeling of 'I planned this and I'm going to work to see whether this program succeeds or fails.' . . . We feel that in Madison County at this point we must be advisory without a premade program." Talk and discussion largely replaced concrete program, and meetings were substituted for activity. By late 1964, there was much complaining about the MFDP leadership and its inability to relate to people in local community—even Annie Devine was criticized—and the projects in both Meridian and Canton were clearly going downhill. C. O. Chinn urgently reminded the task force workers in Canton, "We must draw in local people . . . get them to act," but few in the black community became involved. In Meridian there was so little participation at the community center and the freedom school that they soon operated on a skeletal basis. In Canton the center closed down after it became a hangout for "unruly youths." Even the political program foundered. The Meridian precinct organization fell apart, and weekly "mass meetings" drew as few as twenty-five people. In Canton, the weekly freedom rallies petered out altogether.[37] Not surprisingly, both projects suffered serious staff demoralization. In Canton, for example, the staff members blamed each other for shirking assigned duties and offending the black community with public displays of excessive drinking and sexual familiarity between black and white task force workers. A white task force worker who had joined the Canton project the preceding summer, was "very bothered by a general atmosphere of general aimlessness and unrest among the staff." In Meridian, where CORE encountered serious opposition from the local middle-class leadership, by mid-1965 the staff had departed in discouragement. This program, now run entirely by local people, continued to function only sporadically.[38]

CORE was able to muster its old enthusiasm for one activity—helping black farmers to vote in the Agricultural Stabilization and Conservation Committee (ASCS) elections in December 1964. Everywhere throughout the South these committees, operating under the Department of Agriculture's crop restriction program, discriminated sharply against black farmers, allowing them disproportionately smaller acreages to cultivate. COFO encouraged Negro candidates to run for election to the committees in twelve rural counties. The Madison County campaign was typical of the rest of the state—enormous effort, white violence, and very limited success. This overwhelmingly black county was crucial to COFO plans since, with 40 per cent of the land owned by small black farmers, it offered a real opportunity to elect a black majority to the ASCS committee. Accordingly, CORE committed extra cars and staff, Farmer wired Secretary of Agriculture Orville Freeman urging him to prevent voting fraud, and Marvin Rich was sent as an observer. On Election Day, however, white intimidation seriously interfered with Negro attempts to vote. George Raymond was arrested after identifying himself as a pollwatcher, while Eartiss Crawford, a black task force worker, was beaten, and Rich's nose was broken by a white gang loitering outside a polling place.[39] When the ballots were counted, seven whites and only one black were declared elected. CORE protested to the Agriculture Department and influential congressmen, and eventually the Department offered to hold new elections in two of the districts where whites had won. However, since this decision would have preserved white domination on the county committee even if Negroes won both contests, CORE's staff and the black farmers boycotted the new election.[40]

For several months afterward, CORE was able to stimulate a variety of activities in Madison County. With the help of northern financial contributions, a sewing cooperative was begun for women who had lost their jobs because of participation in the protest movement. Blacks tested places of public accommodations which flagrantly violated the Civil Rights Act, and in April 1965 they were admitted to the Canton theater on a nonsegregated basis. There was also a revival of interest in voter registration. One day in March, for example, fifty-four Negroes succeeded in registering. Later, in August, when the Department of Justice finally assigned federal registrars to the county in accordance with the Voting Rights Act, CORE workers raised the number of blacks on the voting rolls from less than 300 to well over 4000 in a whirlwind three-week campaign. Thereafter, however, activity became sporadic, and by the beginning of 1966 the project, wracked by personality conflicts, was a shambles.[41]

While attempting to maintain programs in Canton and Meridian, the CORE staff also branched out into several of the most rural counties in the Fourth District. Symbolically the most important of these was Neshoba County. A short time after the bodies of Chaney, Goodman, and Schwerner were discovered there, CORE workers established a varied program that included a freedom school, community center, distribution of food and clothing, voter registration and MFDP activity, and participation in the ASCS election. The most substantial direct action took place in Leake County, where CORE led an unsuccessful school boycott during August 1964 and a successful campaign to integrate a theater in Carthage. In Klan-infested Rankin County, fear and intimidation were rampant, but voter registration work was defiantly carried on. The home where the CORE staff lived was shot at, five churches were burned between November 1964 and April 1965, and the sheriff turned away a group which was trying to register and arrested its leaders. Nevertheless, the people continued to organize, and after the Justice Department filed suit against the registrar in April, voter registration efforts were stepped up. To dramatize the issue, in May George Raymond led 135 persons on a fourteen-mile protest march to the county seat, where Farmer addressed a rally on the courthouse lawn. The event was widely covered by the news media, and in the glare of national publicity the demonstrators were protected by police. After this public attention, and with authorities prodded by passage of the Voting Rights Bill, CORE workers were able to register 400 people by the end of the summer. Nevertheless, after these promising beginnings the projects in each of these communities, like CORE activity elsewhere in the state, lost momentum, and by the end of

1965 were virtually inactive.[42] In the end only the NAACP possessed the persistence and drive necessary to sustain viable activity; under the leadership of Aaron Henry and Charles Evers it would, before the end of the decade, develop a remarkable and well-known political-action program.

The work in Louisiana remained CORE's major southern project, and the organization continued to assign all the resources it could spare to the state. Fifteen task force members were retained after the summer of 1964, and several others were added in October. They were deployed in ten parishes under the direction of Ronnie Moore, who concentrated in the Sixth District, and field secretary Oretha Castle, former New Orleans CORE chairman, who in November assumed the responsibility for North Louisiana. By January 1965, because of CORE's fiscal crisis, the staff was cut by a third, although under a special SEDF program CORE substantially augmented its Louisiana summer task force and temporarily operated in seventeen parishes—more than ever before.[43]

In Louisiana, as in Mississippi, the CORE staff gave highest priority to building community organizations around the felt needs of local people, rather than maintaining programs of direct action and voter registration. Paradoxically, however, CORE's most dramatic and best-publicized activities were major direct-action campaigns in Bogalusa and Jonesboro, and its greatest accomplishments were obtained from voter registration drives.

In fact, the Louisiana staff's first undertaking during the autumn of 1964 was a vigorous voter registration project—the final phase of the VEP-funded program. Harassment was still common. In West Feliciana Parish, for example, some blacks were charged with perjury for making mistakes on their registration forms. In Monroe, on the evening before the November election, crosses were burned at intersections in the black community. Yet about 1200 new voters had been registered during the drive.[44] Afterward, the Louisiana program lost its momentum, and there was a virtual cessation of voter registration canvassing. Moore conceded, "One of our failures is that we have not developed approaches . . . to keep the people interested and active." The major achievement of late 1964 was the desegregation, with relatively little effort, of the Jonesboro library and of public accommodations in Alexandria, Baton Rouge, Plaquemine, and Monroe. In Monroe the results had been particularly striking. On November 11, following CORE testing, the city suddenly announced desegregation of all motels, hotels, and major restaurants; and at the end of December, the officials, following receipt of a letter from Oretha Castle, removed signs from fountains and restrooms in public buildings. Although the task force workers were discouraged by their inability to stir the local black communities, they did turn to making door-to-door surveys in several parishes to ascertain the "felt needs" of the people.[45] And during the first part of 1965 a wide variety of projects—ranging from testing public accommodations through working on job discrimination to securing mail delivery for a black neighborhood—were undertaken in an effort to create viable community organizations. In addition there were special action projects in Jonesboro and Bogalusa, which became major campaigns.

The most serious attempts to build around the expressed interests of the community occurred in North Louisiana. In Monroe, for example, the CORE staff continued a battle which they had begun a year earlier against discrimination at Olin-Mathieson. Although the chemical corporation had signed an equal opportunity agreement with the President's Committee, facilities were still completely segregated, no Negro had risen above the position of fork truck driver, and only one black man had been hired since 1956. CORE workers helped black employees file complaints with the President's Committee and make contact with sympathetic congressmen. Two investigations by army compliance officers followed, but the blacks denounced their findings as a whitewash. Nevertheless, some changes did occur: the paylines, time clocks, and restrooms were desegregated, and by the fall of 1965 some Negroes had entered the hitherto white lines of job progression.[46] Two other projects in the same city, set up as the result of interviews with residents in black neighborhoods, proved unsuccessful. Plans to rally the community through a campaign to eliminate the garbage dump near the Negro section never got off the ground. Nor did CORE achieve success with organizing a group of black welfare mothers who sought to obtain food stamps for which they were eligible. After protests were lodged with both federal and local officials, the parish board of supervisors agreed to confer with the mothers' representatives. But this effort also collapsed when the parish claimed lack of funds to operate the stamp plan.[47] On the other hand, in Jonesboro, CORE staff helped to obtain postal service for nearly three hundred black families forced to pick up their own mail because the city had refused to number the streets or erect street signs in their neighborhood. After considerable pressure on federal officials, including a personal appeal from Farmer to the Postmaster-General, the mayor of Jonesboro in April 1965 made the required improvements, and mail was finally delivered to the Negroes' homes.[48]

Meanwhile at Jonesboro and Bogalusa, CORE and local citizens inaugurated two major direct-action campaigns aimed at securing redress of a broad range of grievances, reminiscent of the demonstrations conducted in other southern cities during the summer of 1963. In the paper-mill town of Jonesboro tensions rose during January 1965, following the burning of two black churches used for civil rights rallies and the resegregation of four restaurants that had recently opened to blacks. Then, early in March, alarmed by rumors that a popular teacher who had been active in the movement would be fired, students boycotted and picketed the high school. In retaliation, police threw up a roadblock around the entire black community; Ernest Thomas, vice-chairman of the Deacons for Defense, was arrested and manhandled when he tried to cross the barrier. In defiance, CORE and the youths stepped up their protests, demanding improved facilities at the black schools and integration of the parish educational system, sponsoring Farmer's appearance at a mass rally, testing the resegregated restaurants, and leading daily marches on the school board. On March 26, the youngsters and parents blocked the school board office, and next day Governor John McKeithen arrived to meet with the protesting blacks. He promised to send a truckload of new textbooks, ordered the State Highway Department to pave the school's muddy playground and walkways, and created a local biracial mediation committee. The students returned to classes, but the modest victory produced by the governor's intervention was followed by a new escalation of protest. At a mass meeting the blacks set forth their demands for changes on a broad range of issues. A week after the governor's visit direct action was resumed with a march at the courthouse to protest police brutality, renewed attempts to secure restaurant service, and picketing of downtown merchants for refusing to employ blacks in nonmenial jobs. Enthusiasm was at a fever pitch, but after a climactic Easter Sunday prayer caravan to the two burned churches, the movement bogged down amid distrust and recriminations. The Deacons complained that most of the blacks on the biracial committee were elderly conservatives who regarded the activists as "hotheads," while those not in the movement pointed to the limited progress as a sign that things were indeed getting better. Although CORE-sponsored demonstrations were resumed in the summer, the staff had been withdrawn and activity at Jonesboro had practically ceased by the end of July.[49]

Better publicized was the campaign that occurred almost simultaneously in Bogalusa, a southeastern Louisiana town, about one-third black.

Economically dominated by a Crown-Zellerbach paper mill that maintained segregated lunchrooms and toilets and a jim crow "line of progression" relegating Negroes to lower-paying, unskilled jobs, Bogalusa boasted a powerful Ku Klux Klan that periodically whipped blacks and burned crosses. CORE workers had first entered the city in the spring of 1964 to conduct a voter registration drive with the Bogalusa Civic and Voters League, but in the succeeding months had twice postponed plans to return because black leaders, responding to the Klan-created climate of fear, urged giving the city's biracial commission more time to resolve the Negroes' grievances. Finally, in January 1965 the Voters League invited CORE for a brief stay to help test the extent of compliance with the public accommodations sections of the 1964 Civil Rights Act.[50]

CORE dispatched two white task force workers to Bogalusa. Action followed almost immediately—accompanied by violence from white hoodlums and a split in the local black leadership. On January 28, the two field workers and a group of black youths integrated the library and several restaurants amid threats and harassment which frightened the League's officers into urging suspension of the tests and the departure of CORE. Others, however, notably A. Z. Young and Robert Hicks, employees at Crown-Zellerbach and leaders in the local Pulp and Sulphite Workers Union, wished CORE to remain, and a rally held a few days later ended in pandemonium when the militants challenged the League's leadership. Arriving at Hicks' home after the meeting, the CORE workers were urged by the police chief to leave town at once because their lives were in danger; they remained, and fifteen armed Negroes stood guard throughout the night. In the succeeding days the Klan picketed the recently integrated restaurants, which quickly reversed their policies, and hoodlums assaulted the CORE staffers and local blacks. The angry blacks, spurred to greater militance, established a branch of the Deacons for Defense in March, and formally reorganized the League with Young as president and Hicks as vice-president. At a packed mass meeting, which has been described by two young CORE volunteers from Berkeley, Young assumed the mantle of leadership and called upon the adults to join the youth in their demonstrations:

> Mr. Young demanded to know from this audience where they stood: "Will you let your sons and daughters be hit by billy clubs, have live snakes thrown at them, have cigarettes put out on their bodies, and be chased by police dogs on picket lines and marches, while you sit at home? They are risking their lives; are you risking yours? . . ."

In a booming voice he proceeded to damn the total injustice of a system where a Negro lives with frustration 60 minutes of every hour, 24 hours of every day.

If there was any question regarding the status of the previous moderate leadership, Young settled it, "I am your leader; you are my followers." Deafening applause followed—the overwhelming endorsement of the new militant leadership. . . . A mass popular movement was born before our eyes. Smiles, handshakes—"yes, man" "set the record straight" shouted the audience. . . . We witnessed hope, belief and, more important, a lessening of fear and a new readiness to fight.[51]

By April the League was prepared to escalate its demands and invited Farmer to help begin the campaign's new phase. Presenting the mayor and city council with a petition that went far beyond the public accommodations issue, the League asked for equal opportunity in public and private employment, school desegregation, and lighting and paved streets for the black neighborhoods. The following day Klansmen shot into the home of Robert Hicks, and the Deacons promptly organized a permanent armed guard to protect the residence. Farmer and Ronnie Moore arrived in Bogalusa, and on April 9 they led a march of five hundred to City Hall, where Mayor Jesse Cutrer pledged to help solve racial problems. But negotiations collapsed when Cutrer insisted that half of the black negotiating team be drawn from those who opposed CORE's presence in town.[52]

This pattern of events—promises from the mayor, followed by acts of bad faith—was to be repeated twice more. Although this first rebuff, combined with fear of organized white violence, caused the movement to lose some momentum, the League found enough unintimidated people to man picket lines for jobs at the downtown stores. As the blacks continued their demonstrations, the governor sent in over three hundred state police to maintain order. On April 19, Wilfred Ussery, CORE's national vice-chairman who had organized a coalition of concerned California organizations to put pressure on Crown-Zellerbach's top national executives, led a march on city hall in the face of white harassment. Next day Farmer returned to Bogalusa to head yet another march, and announced that Louisiana would become CORE's leading target during the coming summer. With momentum thus building up again, talks with the mayor were resumed, and toward the end of May he promised that blacks would be permitted to use the city park immediately. When they entered the park, however, a white mob which included some policemen, drove them off, and the mayor ordered the facility closed. At the same time the League suspended demonstrations to avoid further violence.[53] Farmer flew back to the city to breathe new life into the local movement, amid Governor McKeithen's charges that Farmer "lives and thrives on trouble." On the same day, the mayor promised to grant Negro demands for sewers and water mains, to hire black police, and to have the City Council repeal segregation ordinances. Again, Cutrer, under Klan pressure, failed to keep his pledges.[54]

Picketing continued downtown, brief scuffles erupted as hundreds of both races milled around, and forty persons, including a number of whites, were arrested. Then on June 2, as the blacks were preparing for renewed demonstrations, a Negro deputy sheriff was murdered. The shock of the killing produced a temporary calm, but in July, under heavy police guard, the blacks conducted another march on city hall. More violence erupted, with pickets being attacked downtown, and a Deacon shooting a white man who had tried to hit him. In this critical situation McKeithen dispatched more state troopers, and on July 11 Farmer returned to lead yet another march. The following day, McKeithen sent his personal plane to fly Young and Hicks to the Executive Mansion, where he persuaded them to accept still another "cooling off" period. Moore and other CORE leaders, convinced that further demonstrations in Bogalusa would prove unproductive, supported the proposal. But when the two League officers returned to Bogalusa they found that the rank and file membership and the local CORE workers repudiated this arrangement; even McKeithen's arrival the next day to plead his case personally failed to prevent a renewal of the daily demonstrations. Disappointed, the governor pursued a new tactic, appointing a statewide biracial commission of black and white moderates which he hoped would destroy "trashy" groups like CORE. Moore, denouncing this "conspiracy among the so-called white moderates . . . and certain 'Negro leaders,' " warned, "It is time for the governor to realize that his biggest threat is coming from the grass roots people and not from the traditional good colored boys who dance with the winner." Meanwhile Young, recouping his leadership position, had militantly condemned McKeithen for threatening to confiscate weapons and warned that blacks would retaliate if violence persisted: "I do not advocate violence and we are going to do everything we can to keep down the civil war in the area. But, if blood is going to be shed, we are going to let it rain down Columbia Street [the main business street]—all kinds, both black and white. We are not going to send Negro blood down Columbia Street by itself, that's for sure." [55]

Bogalusa had long since seized the national headlines, forcing a minimal intervention from the Johnson administration that afforded at least some relief. In mid-April the Justice Department had filed suit in federal district court against six Bogalusa restaurants, and by mid-summer League members obtained service in nearly all eating facilities tested. At the same time the presence of John Doar, head of the Justice Department's Civil Rights Division and President Johnson's personal emissary, and a federal court order obtained by Collins, Douglas, and Elie produced a temporary cessation of police harassment.[56] Nevertheless, though daily marches and picketing continued into early August, the movement's energies were exhausted, and, all the effort invested by CORE and the League notwithstanding, the tangible accomplishments were few. At the end of the summer the major gains were the desegregation of the downtown restaurants and theaters and the employment—for the first time in the city's history—of two black policemen. In addition, the federal district court had ordered limited educational integration in response to a suit filed by CORE lawyers; in September eleven blacks were admitted to hitherto white schools. With a solution to this problem obviously far off, the League and CORE organized a brief boycott protesting the inferior educational facilities available to Negroes. The job campaign in the private sector similarly won little. The Crown-Zellerbach corporation accepted "in principle" a proposal urged by the Federal Equal Opportunities Commission to abolish the segregated line of progression in two of the plant's departments, but the downtown merchants adamantly refused to hire Negroes as clerks or cashiers, and at year's end the League was still boycotting the stores. Finally, the police department, though seemingly changed by the court order, reverted to form after a protest rally in October 1965 and "ran wild" in ghetto neighborhoods, clubbing and kicking any available black in what Richard Haley called a "night of terror in typical Bogalusa style." [57]

Meanwhile, during the summer of 1965 CORE had mounted ambitious programs in other parishes. Although, except for Ferriday (Concordia Parish), violence was minor compared to previous years,[58] accomplishments were limited by white intransigence. In Plaquemine, for example, CORE's energies were depleted in the unsuccessful campaign to pressure white political leaders to remove the town's garbage dump from its location near the black ghetto. In nine other parishes considerable effort devoted to assisting black farmers running for election to ASCS committees ended in complete failure.[59] In repressive Ferriday, which had not previously been touched by the militant activism of the 1960's, CORE task force workers at the end of July created the Ferriday Freedom Movement (FFM). Although most of the ministers and established leaders of the black community remained aloof, and fear of the Klan paralyzed much of the Negro population, the FFM nevertheless tested a drug store lunch counter, integrated the town library, began a voter registration drive, and under Ronnie Moore's leadership conducted a march to city hall to protest the rampant police brutality. Elsewhere CORE task force workers helped integrate some places of public accommodation, and in a few parishes conducted small job campaigns against retail stores.[60] The summer work was mainly geared, however, to pressing for benefits from the new federally funded programs. Not surprisingly CORE staffers wanted to do more than assure local black citizens a share of the federal largesse: they also sought to use the community action projects as vehicles around which to unite the black poor against the "white power structure." But these efforts seldom inspired the desired grass-roots organization, although they did produce some heated conflicts between CORE and the middle-class black leadership.

In several parishes CORE led the opposition to the policy of appointing elite blacks to act for the poor on the local antipoverty boards, and in Madison and Claiborne parishes federal officials ruled that funds would be withheld until all segments of the black community were represented. In Ferriday, Shreveport, and Homer, the CORE staff helped local blacks obtain federal grants for preschool education projects. But to CORE's dismay, the Ferriday project was totally controlled by middle-class blacks, while in Shreveport and Homer serious clashes developed with Negro administrative personnel whom CORE and its allies had originally selected to run the programs. CORE staffers, losing out in all three communities, sadly concluded that, rather than using the project as a tool for "challenging the present system," the middle-class blacks viewed it only as "an educational aid . . . to raise the Negro economically." [61]

In at least two parishes splits between CORE and the established civil rights leadership developed because the task force members were reluctant to engage in voter registration. In Tallulah, where CORE now entered a second time—and operated without interference—Zelma Wyche, president of the Madison Parish Get Registered and Voters' League, wanted to restrict activity to registration, while CORE people had other plans and proceeded to test public accommodations, work on the ASCS election, and fight the composition of the antipoverty board. CORE staff now termed Wyche "dictatorial," but finally agreed to cooperate with him on a campaign that ended with blacks becoming the majority of registered voters in the town. As a result, four years later Wyche himself became Tallulah's police chief.[62]

In Minden, CORE clashed with the nine-year-old Better Citizens and Voters League, headed by funeral director M. M. Coleman, who had originally welcomed the task force workers when they arrived at the start of the summer. However, he became disenchanted after discovering that the CORE staffers were eschewing voter registration to concentrate on antipoverty and job discrimination projects. Coleman cautioned that these efforts would be doomed to failure unless the League built up additional power by registering more Negroes. He charged that CORE was dictating to the local people and attempting to undermine his leadership. The task force members for their part concluded that "the people are ready but Coleman is not," and, encouraging what they called a "bourgeoisie-proletarian split," led a secession to form the Webster Parish United Christian Movement. The new organization bargained with city officials for municipal jobs, and when negotiations broke down, invited Farmer in to lead a mass march. But the Movement could neither mount sustained demonstrations against city hall nor initiate a threatened boycott of downtown stores. Belatedly the CORE staffers turned to voter registration exactly as Coleman had urged, and the only success they achieved was adding a thousand blacks to the rolls at the end of the summer. The factionalism did not disappear, but an appraisal by a CORE field worker in September reported that not only had a "superficial" unity been created in the joint registration campaign but Coleman's "bourgeois" group had "come to our rescue whenever we have had a real need," donating supplies, lending equipment, and hiring an attorney in the local school desegregation suit. Thus, as in many other communities, the rise of the militants, which first threatened to displace the old-guard leadership, ended with all of the protest groups existing in a complex relationship of coalition and competition. Minden was in fact almost an archetypical example of an organization like CORE or SNCC entering a community and, in the name of the masses, battling with the local leadership. As Haley put it, the story of factions in Minden was a "usual one." [63]

Overall, despite the rhetoric about organizing communities, the tangible accomplishments of the first part of the summer had deeply disappointed Haley at the southern CORE office. Consequently, during August a concentrated voter registration drive was undertaken in twelve parishes. Although the registrars still frequently used obstructionist tactics, the August drive produced over 11,000 newly registered voters. Nearly two-thirds of these came from Monroe and from East Feliciana Parish, where CORE had worked so long with meager results, but now at CORE's urging the Justice Department had supplied federal registrars. Even West Feliciana, where Negro registration had actually dropped from 85 to 25 between October 1964 and March 1965, and where the parish registrar would accept only 22 applicants a day, CORE's renewed drive resulted in 393 new registrants.[64] Thus ironically, the summer project that began with an orientation toward community action built around local welfare interest ended with its greatest achievement in voter registration.

Although beginning in the autumn of 1965 fiscal necessity forced serious curtailment of activities in Louisiana, viable work continued in several parishes through the winter. Appeals to Washington brought a federal registrar to West Feliciana Parish in October, enabling CORE to register a thousand people the following month. In New Orleans, CORE people enthusiastically supported Nils Douglas in his unsuccessful bid for election to the state legislature. In a few parishes where CORE had been active, blacks made "impressive showings" in the April 1966 primary elections. In Tallulah, Rev. Willie Johnson, chairman of the local voters league and a former New Orleans longshoreman who had been arrested in a CORE demonstration there, was elected to the Madison Parish Democratic Executive Committee. Working closely with NAACP leaders in St. Landry Parish, CORE fought the antipoverty board, and with wide community support, secured the election of several militant blacks to it. In Ferriday, despite incidents of violence ranging from the bombing of the home of the FFM's president to the burning of a Negro-owned gas station, the Movement picketed and boycotted downtown stores for jobs, demonstrated at a movie theater, tested restaurants, and with the assistance of Collins, Douglas, and Elie successfully brought a legal suit to begin desegregation of the public schools. However, the few who thus transferred to white schools met abuse from students and teachers. In East Feliciana the CORE staff helped the people establish their own pre-school education program. A task force worker assigned to St. Helena Parish focused on educational issues. He first helped the few youths who had integrated the white high school lodge protests with federal officials about the harassment they suffered at the hands of students and teachers. He then organized a protest against inferior conditions at the Negro school which involved three days of boycotting and sit-ins at the superintendent's office and the arrest of several students and CORE field personnel. By spring the school board, though still dragging its feet on integration, had met most of the demands for improving the physical facilities at the black school.[65] Such achievements notwithstanding, CORE activity in Louisiana was clearly tapering off.

As in Louisiana and Mississippi, CORE's north Florida project was bedeviled by a chronic lack of funds, operating as Haley put it, "on a kind of emergency status." Its new director, Spiver Gordon, who had been active with CORE ever since Ronnie Moore arrived in Plaquemine and who had played a key role in directing several Louisiana projects, urgently complained to Haley in December 1964: "We haven't received one red copper cent from National or your office." In January the eight CORE workers were reduced to four, and in April Gordon reported that lights at the Gadsden County Freedom House had been off for five days, the rent was two months overdue, and "voter registration has been very, very slow for the past weeks due mainly" to a lack of funds for cars and staff.[66] Yet Gordon and his staff undertook a broad program. In the weeks before the 1964 presidential election they stressed voter registration; in Gadsden County their work paid off when the outpouring of black voters led public officials to install new streetlights and promise to pave dirt roads in the Negro areas. Thereafter voter registration continued on a limited basis. In Liberty County, one of the last two counties in the state with an all-white voters list—and a place where previous black attempts to register had produced a "reign of terror, shootings, and burnings"—sixty-two Negroes peacefully registered in December.[67] By then, however, the CORE staff was giving most of its attention to other issues. Restaurants were tested in Tallahassee, where facilities generally opened, and in Gadsden County, where CORE workers were charged exorbitant prices in the few places that served them. They also set up a small community center in Gadsden County, and working with the local CORE chapter initiated "Operation Dialogue"—a door-to-door canvass to discover what problems the black community most wanted to see tackled.[68]

CORE in northern Florida generally acted through local adult organizations, but these relationships now began to produce problems. In Madison County, where CORE had operated closely with the NAACP Youth Council, the Association's adult branch pre-empted the young people's loyalties, and the ministers who had earlier welcomed CORE's assistance now wanted the organization to leave the county. In Gadsden County, where CORE had all along worked closely with the Civic Interest Group, Spiver Gordon found that the November election spurred into activity the more conservative Business and Civic League, led by the high school principal. This organization approached the white leadership "with a few washed down proposals and said either you do business with us or the outside element will take over." Even more disheartening, leaders in the Civic Interest Group now desired to operate independently, and breaking their close alliance with CORE, announced a program designed to compete with Operation Dialogue.[69]

Although the frustration stemming from lack of funds and problems with local black leadership created serious interpersonal conflicts within the CORE staff itself,[70] things picked up during the spring and summer. Gadsden County, where the most intensive work was done, was representative of the scope and success of this spurt of activity in northern Florida. Voter registration was conducted regularly. There was also a concerted effort to desegregate public accommodations, but only in the county seat of Quincy was CORE able to open most of the restaurants. Protests were lodged with the county school system, but black children were refused transfers from jim crow schools. CORE staff members pressed locally and in Washington to force hospitals at Quincy and Chattahoochie which received federal funds to integrate their facilities.[71] Finally, in their most successful operation, the CORE personnel fought to secure representation of the black poor on the local antipoverty board. Charging that most Negroes on the biracial body represented the middle-class Civic Interest Group and the even more elite Business and Civic League, they successfully petitioned Washington to withhold federal funds temporarily. By the time a federal investigator arrived, CORE had arranged a united front among the Negro organizations, and the official approved an arrangement under which lower-income families would choose their own representatives.[72] After the departure of the summer task force, activity again slowed down. Spiver Gordon desperately appealed to SEDF for funds, but Rich was unable to help until the following spring, when he scraped up $4000 for northern Florida. Gordon carried on, but CORE's program for Florida was really at an end, and in the summer of 1966 he himself joined the SEDF staff and returned to Louisiana.[73]

Paradoxically, it almost seemed as if by the time the Voting Rights Act of 1965 made massive voter registration feasible in the deep South CORE people had become disillusioned with the whole business. Only in South Carolina did CORE mount a concerted registration drive. In fact, the South Carolina project, directed by McCain and funded entirely by SEDF, ignored other forms of community organization activity. In April the campaign went into full gear with the arrival of eight task force workers and Farmer's appearance at a rally in Columbia. Even though all voter registration work in South Carolina was coordinated under a VEP coalition, state NAACP officials sought to undercut the impact of Farmer's appearance by informing the local press that CORE was not wanted in South Carolina.[74] Despite such interference, and the more serious problems created by county registrars who typically continued to open their books only one day each month, registration, which had been averaging between 300 and 400 a month at the beginning of the year, jumped to 1100 in April and over 1400 in May. The summer work of the South Carolina CORE staff, augmented by about 20 northern white volunteers, reached a climax when the books were opened on the first Monday in August. Some arrests occurred in Allendale County, and complaints of registrars' delaying tactics elsewhere were filed with the federal government. Nevertheless, beginning with August, registration averaged nearly 6000 a month.[75] McCain's staff was substantially aided by the new Voting Rights Act, which nudged many counties to provide additional registration days, and by agents of the Justice Department, whose presence at several courthouses led local officials to speed the registration process. Finally, after CORE's repeated requests, the Justice Department in November assigned federal registrars to Dorchester and Clarendon counties, where delaying tactics had been particularly notorious. By year's end, CORE-SEDF proudly announced that McCain and his associates had registered 37,000 blacks in 24 counties during 1965.[76]

CORE leaders like George Wiley, who had originally hoped that it might be possible to register enough blacks to defeat Republican Senator Strom Thurmond in his 1966 re-election campaign, decided at the end of 1965 that the goal had been "pretty unrealistic." Nevertheless, by then,

CORE had embarked upon "grassroots political organization" in five counties, with field workers laboring diligently to form blacks into a cohesive voting bloc. By March 1966 McCain reported that many Negroes had participated for the first time in Democratic Party precinct meetings, and in some instances were even elected precinct officers and delegates to the county and state conventions. In several communities, blacks ran for local office. In Clarendon County, where CORE, with the assistance of federal registrars, had raised the total number of black voters from 300 in June 1965 to 5000 in February 1966, two blacks ran for town council. They were defeated but obtained the enthusiastic support of the newly registered Negroes who turned out to vote. In June in Williamsburg County three blacks lost in the Democratic primary elections for the state legislature but one was victorious in his race for road commissioner. Finally, in the November 1966 elections, although Thurmond was re-elected to the Senate, the black vote proved to be the balance of power responsible for the Democratic victories in congressional and gubernatorial races.[77] Thus CORE's political work in the state was clearly a harbinger of things to come.

In the North, as in the South, there were some bright spots; yet there, too, the organization was quite clearly on the decline. A handful of chapters took on new life, and officially the number of affiliates actually rose from 114 in the summer of 1964 to 144 at the time of the 1965 Convention.[78] But since the Steering Committee had practically ceased disaffiliating chapters, a number of those listed were inactive, and, in fact, the 1965 Convention was the most sparsely attended one in half a dozen years.

The field secretaries during late 1964 and early 1965 found countless signs of demoralization. Mike Lesser, who toured several Ohio chapters in the fall, reported that Springfield CORE was "now defunct"; Toledo CORE had just reorganized after a long period in the doldrums; Cincinnati and Columbus were wracked by disruptive factional fights. The Columbus chapter's active membership fell from its height of about 100 in the spring of 1964 to 31 a year later. At St. Louis in December 1964, a columnist for the *Argus* asked, "What Happened to CORE?" and described the formerly militant chapter there as one that had "crept into obscurity." Across the river the once flourishing East St. Louis affiliate now had only four or five active members.[79] Louis Smith and Ike Reynolds arrived on the West Coast in the spring of 1965 to find most of the

western chapters simply limping along. San Diego, whose active membership stood at 75 at the conclusion of the Bank of America campaign in
the summer of 1964, had fallen to 30 five months later; Berkeley, claim-
ing 50 active members at the end of 1964, had only 36 by May; Seattle,
which at its peak in 1964 claimed 200 or more members—although the
distinction between the active and associate categories had broken down
—dropped to about 65 the following year, and by 1966 was drawing only
about 25 people to an average meeting. Early in 1965 one member of Los
Angeles CORE described its disintegration: "This chapter is no longer
able and/or willing to engage in meaningful direct action. We straggle up
Broadway to the Federal Building every now and then; we call off membership meetings so we can picket the Citizens Council, thus avoiding an
occasion for serious discussion of just what the hell we're doing." A year
later CORE's new director of the Organization Department, Herbert Callender, referred to Los Angeles CORE as "a total disappointment" and a
"paper chapter," a "group of middle-class snobs" who had failed to follow
the 1965 Convention mandate to organize the black community. The
chapter was "fragmented and uses most of its time having internal
fights." [80]

In the Northeast, where CORE had placed four field secretaries in the
autumn of 1964, the situation was somewhat better, but even there many
chapters were in a precarious condition, and compared to their activities
during 1963–64, most of the active ones were operating on a minimal
level. In January 1965, Philadelphia CORE chairman, James O. Williams, announcing that there was only one person left on the Education
Committee, said, "It is a sad day in the life of this organization when its
committees cannot function because of a lack of people." The Harlem
chapter in early 1965 had a $3500 indebtedness; it was so far in arrears
with the phone company that service was cut off. Downtown New York
CORE was similarly in deep difficulty; it was $3000 in debt, had "failed
to become a community-based organization," and appeared "on the road
to death." After a brief effort to begin community organization work, the
chapter died. Even the unusually effective Syracuse chapter, which continued to be a strong affiliate into 1965, declined disastrously in the aftermath of its discouraging Niagara Mohawk employment campaign, and
by July this once prospering affiliate had become so poor it could no
longer afford the $25.00 weekly salary it had been paying its executive
secretary.[81] A Boston CORE member recalled that by mid-1965 the chapter's meetings "became filled with the rhetoric of action . . . therapeutic

sessions for the membership." By autumn, a new field secretary for the Northeast, Walter S. Brooks, reported that most of the chapters he visited, even some recently affiliated ones, were in a badly deteriorated state, a number of them either "inactive" or "nonexistent." A half year after the 1965 Convention, Brooks found not a single affiliate in the entire northeastern region which had responded effectively to the conclave's "mandate" regarding community organization. By then, New Haven, which had a membership list of nearly seventy as late as the spring of 1965, had undergone such "disintegration and loss of personnel" that the affiliate's secretary described it as "in a real mess." Similarly, by early 1966 the Chicago chapter, which had continued quite active even though most of its energies were taken up with CCCO projects had become just a "paper chapter." [82]

The situation was complex. In some places CORE experienced something of a renaissance. Louis Smith and the other field secretaries worked energetically during the autumn of 1964 and the following winter to revive activity in the Northeast, and met with some temporary success. When Smith opened the northeastern regional office in the late summer of 1964, "We faced chapter problems and chapter rebellions," and "most of the Region was completely undeveloped." Over the following months a dozen new chapters from Providence, Rhode Island, to Buffalo, New York, and Pittsburgh, Pennsylvania, were affiliated, the majority of them in upstate New York.[83] At least two midwestern affiliates, Cincinnati and Detroit, were larger and more active than ever before. Cincinnati CORE held a rent strike, sponsored dramatic demonstrations against the buildings trades unions, and entered partisan politics. Detroit CORE, whose active membership rose from seventy-two in October 1964 to one hundred a year later, experienced its first arrests in a direct-action program for jobs, and organized a sustained tenant-organizing and rent-strike project. Baltimore CORE also enjoyed a vigorous revival, sponsoring major campaigns for open housing and better schools and assisting underpaid black workers to form their own union.[84] And a number of other chapters remained quite vigorous, carrying out significant action projects.

At the rhetorical level at least, the affiliates were now oriented toward community organization in the ghetto, "becoming increasingly involved with the people in the community," as they said. Time and again the chapter leaders urged CORE members to listen to the black poor who best knew their own "felt needs." Antoine Perot, who had directed the

Cleveland group's rent-strike program, maintained that, if CORE members were to employ their knowledge to help the poor, they must encourage grass-roots leaders "and involve them in all levels of power-sharing and decision-making. . . . We must make our assigned area a second home. We must become familiar with every street, barber shop, bar, restaurant, club, church, and whatever else we find where people are. When we develop the skills and the commitment to do this, we will be on the way to social change." Echoing the same theme, Bill Bradley told the Western Regional Convention late in 1964 that "the people in the ghetto have a much clearer idea of where they are and where they want to go than CORE people frequently do." [85]

Most chapters now met and had offices in the slums. Some, like Denver, Kansas City, Cleveland, and Oakland, established freedom houses to provide recreation, job-counseling, tutoring, and information on housing, black history, health, and voter registration. But these never even nearly fulfilled their expectations, for, as several NAC members noted, community organization programs were expensive and required an experienced full-time staff. In the spring of 1965 the Chicago chapter phased out two of the three centers established by the Program Department during the preceding summer because the national office could no longer continue to provide a subsidy; and even the remaining Southside Center was compelled to operate a greatly reduced program. Then Denver's freedom house closed its doors for what became the standard reasons: "One, it was becoming impossible to staff. Two, it was financially too much to maintain, and three, we were not successful in establishing communications with the people in the area." Even chapters that had less ambitious plans and merely attempted to staff walk-in offices on a six-day-a-week basis discovered that volunteers were hard to find. The difficulties in setting up a community center were illustrated by the experience of Columbus CORE, one of the most conscientious chapters, which under the leadership of chairman Marlene Wilson developed a singleminded commitment to community organization. Initiating their Everett Street project late in 1964, chapter members went from door to door for two months ascertaining the neighborhood's most immediate grievances. One grass-roots leader did emerge, but the high hopes for a center foundered on lack of money.[86]

In practice, community organization embraced a wide variety of programs. Some chapters focused on housing problems. New York CORE, for example, worked at forming tenants' councils, helping them forward complaints to proper authorities, and in some cases correcting code violations through court cases on their behalf. The Newark affiliate helped grass-roots people secure redress for individual grievances by interceding with employers and government agencies. A number of groups worked with young people. St. Louis established a program meant "especially for youth who had dropped out of school or gotten into trouble of some kind." Los Angeles organized the "Mighty Invincibles," which "has as its goal improvement of the neighborhood by participation in clean-up, beautification, and cultural programs." The Philadelphia chapter formed a Little Schools Corporation to provide preschool training for children from low income homes, and Long Island CORE set up its own program for sixty youngsters of the same age, stressing "cultural identification." Downtown New York CORE collected clothes for needy families and encouraged housewives to report complaints about price-gouging at local markets. Prince George's County CORE initiated a clean-up campaign as a start toward rehabilitating a Negro slum just outside Washington in Cedar Heights, Maryland.[87]

Other chapters attempted new approaches to employment problems. Long Island CORE established a job placement center, open in the evenings, at Wyandanch. In Los Angeles, during the autumn of 1965, Louis Smith, in addition to his duties as field secretary, cooperated with some secessionists from the local CORE chapter to establish Operation Bootstrap, which subsequently operated a highly successful job-training program.[88] And a few chapters undertook giving assistance to black workers in organizing for better pay and job conditions. In Detroit months of demonstrations by the affiliate helped Negro employees at a supermarket obtain a wage increase. The Rochester chapter in 1965 and the Boston chapter the following year both carried on intensive efforts among hospital workers. The successful three-month campaign in Boston, under the leadership of chapter chairman Frank Meranda, secured recognition of the union only after a picket line had been established at the home of the president of the hospital's board of trustees. The Rochester campaign, in which CORE people worked very closely with the union, ended in failure. At Baltimore in January 1966, the CORE staff began organizing the Maryland Freedom Union among black workers employed by small businesses such as retail stores, laundries, and nursing homes.[89]

Finally, with the passage of the War on Poverty Act, many CORE leaders became actively involved in the organization of—and the politics surrounding—the creation of local governing boards for the community action programs (CAP). Actually CORE proved to be ambivalent about the antipoverty projects. They helped to finance the sort of community organization work which CORE favored in its "New Directions," they appeared to provide a vehicle around which to create a power bloc of poor blacks, and they offered widening influence for CORE people who entered the antipoverty bureaucracy. On the other hand, despite the law's requirement that these federal projects operate with the "maximum feasible participation of the poor," CORE found them typically dominated by political machines or the black bourgeoisie; it soon became evident that chapters were weakened where their leaders accepted administrative jobs in the CAP programs; and, as CORE people involved themselves in the War on Poverty, the affiliates often tended to lose their identity as an independent organization.

Everywhere chapters pushed for representation and participation by the poor. CORE officials regarded this requirement as the "very heart" of the War on Poverty, the one thing that distinguished it from the "old inadequate and discredited welfare programs." Farmer protested to the agency's chief, Sargent Shriver, when signs appeared that this regulation was being relaxed, "We believe that the Anti-Poverty Program can go forward if, and only if, representatives of the poor, chosen by the poor, from the poor, play a significant role in the planning, direction and implementation of all anti-poverty programs." [90] In actual practice civil rights groups interpreted the phrase "maximum feasible participation of the poor" in two very different ways: (1) as a requirement that poor black people themselves be seated on the boards, and (2) as a stipulation that organizations who could speak for the black poor should be represented on the boards. CORE, along with other groups in the black community, often became involved in protracted battles against mayors who tried to use the federal money as a "political football," and who sought to prevent antimachine elements from developing a power base in the CAP programs. In this struggle against city halls, CORE helped to form coalitions which were often successful in obtaining more recognition for the poor and for organizations identified with the black protest movement. But once this happened, CORE frequently wrangled with the NAACP and similar groups over just exactly who was to represent the poor.

Some chapters employed direct action to dramatize their position. In Buffalo, thirty CORE pickets protested against the "silk-stocking" composition of the overwhelmingly white CAP board. In Los Angeles, CORE members sat-in at Mayor Yorty's office demanding representation of the poor. In Cleveland, where CORE joined with the NAACP and other groups in a coalition to fight the issue, chairman Grady Robinson and three others were arrested on a demonstration at City Hall. Across the country chapters appealed to Washington to delay funding of antipoverty programs in which the black poor were inadequately represented. Cleveland CORE pulled as many strings as it could; Marvin Rich, for example, pressed Vice President Humphrey's office to secure changes in the Cleveland CAP board, and eventually the chapter's demands were partially met. In Columbus, where only a few members of the board came from the poverty group, the chapter urged Washington to delay approval, organized a "People's Poverty Board" to press for more recognition of the poor, and finally secured a substantial representation of grassroots people. From Boston, chairman Alan Gartner personally went to Washington and was similarly able to hold up funds until poor blacks from Roxbury and Dorchester were placed on the board. And in San Francisco, CORE, led by Wilfred Ussery and William Bradley, played an instrumental role in the coalition which successfully fought Mayor Shelley until he agreed to change the composition of the antipoverty committee.[91]

In cities like Philadelphia, Newark, and Columbus, CORE chairmen were elected to the boards.[92] In a number of communities CORE people became paid personnel in the War on Poverty. Perhaps the most notable example of this occurred in San Francisco, where Wilfred Ussery served as the director of a district project. Several chapter members were on the board and a number of others on the staff. But once in office Ussery was embroiled in constant controversy until his resignation in 1967, being attacked by dissident factions on his board on the one hand, and himself challenging the moderate members of the central staff on the other. Such battling was not at all unusual. In Cleveland the coalition fighting for greater representation of the poor was split when CORE complained that the NAACP was making "private and separate negotiations . . . to get more NAACP representatives on the Board." Charging that the NAACP could not be trusted to represent the interest of low income people, Cleveland CORE declared that "Our role must be to 'watch dog' this federal program" so that "the money goes to the right people, in the right programs, and is controlled in the right ways."[93]

Participation in the War on Poverty was in several respects dysfunctional for CORE as an organization. Leaders who accepted the well-paying positions with CAP programs found it difficult to maintain active connections with their local affiliates, and since they were generally among the most experienced chapter members, the loss was substantial, especially in a period when most CORE groups were already weakened. Syracuse CORE members were so angered by this leadership drain that they considered voting to "toss out" anyone "making money off the poor" by accepting a War on Poverty job. People on the NAC even began to complain that the antipoverty program "has been used to buy off militant civil rights leaders." Equally important, CORE's efforts with the CAP projects absorbed considerable energy, thus deflecting activity away from specifically CORE projects. One leader in the Columbus affiliate recalled that the chapter's involvement in the antipoverty program "really blew the whole thing on CORE, which lost its identity." On both counts, the War on Poverty proved to be a significant contributing factor in the decline of chapter activity, and in retrospect some CORE people charged that "Johnson's War on Poverty killed CORE as much as anything." [94]

In the end, CORE failed to mobilize the potential power of the black poor through its participation in the War on Poverty. Nor in the long run did CORE's own community-organization efforts prove successful. The enormous problems encountered everywhere in organizing the poor, whose experiences made them fear to challenge the authorities, meant that substantial amounts of money and full-time experienced organizers were required if there was to be any chance of success.[95] Part-time CORE volunteers, usually characterized more by dedication and commitment than by expertise and training, and working with meager resources, faced an insuperable task. Many put forth an extraordinary amount of energy in organizing small groups of grass-roots people around specific grievances. In various communities they helped the poor obtain street lights at dangerous intersections or repairs in dilapidated tenements. Yet these achievements were limited and often temporary, and the community organizations which CORE chapters created usually withered away.

Simultaneously, a number of affiliates were experimenting with the second major programmatic emphasis of CORE's "New Directions"— partisan politics. Chapters were inspired by the example which had been set in Mississippi, and "independent political action" became a popular slogan all over the country. Rhode Island CORE noted, "Instead of merely supporting this or that political group we should build our own Freedom Democratic Movement." The leaders of Cleveland CORE, similarly influenced by MFDP, viewed politics as a necessary supplement to direct action. Thus rent strikes would "begin to solve the problems of slum housing," but only a politically mobilized black community could obtain the legislation needed to "finish the job"; it was now clear that, until the black community was "prepared to fight at the polls for the same things we have been fighting for in the streets, our success would be only partial." Indeed, even before the 1965 Convention removed, without controversy, the constitutional ban on partisan politics, CORE groups had entered the political arena.[96]

In a few cases CORE chapters chalked up some accomplishments. For example, in Englewood, New Jersey, where the City Council candidate backed by Bergen County CORE won overwhelmingly, and in Oklahoma City, where the CORE chairman Archibald Hill won handily over his white opponent in a race for the state legislature, the chapters registered concrete victories. More substantial was Boston CORE's participation in a highly successful strategy fashioned by Gartner and his old allies in the leadership of the Massachusetts Freedom Movement. Creating an anti-Goldwater coalition known as the Committee Against Political Extremism (CAPE), they first prevailed upon the black Republican Senator Edward Brooke to oppose openly his party's presidential candidate. Then, unhappy with the position of the Democratic candidate for governor, CAPE persuaded John Volpe, the Republican nominee, to issue a strong civil rights platform. CAPE saturated the black community with handbills endorsing Volpe, and the victorious Republicans credited CORE and the other CAPE organizations with swaying the election.[97]

Generally, however, CORE's foray into politics proved less rewarding. With few exceptions, the chapters backed losing candidates and often had difficulty with the details of day-to-day political organizing. For example, in April 1965, the New York City affiliates scheduled a march to dramatize their opposition to the re-election of Mayor Robert Wagner, but all together they were able to turn out only a hundred demonstrators. After Wagner decided not to run, they supported William F. Ryan in his unsuccessful bid for the Democratic nomination. They also endorsed Brooklyn CORE chairman Major Owens in his race for a seat on the City Council. For this campaign CORE created the Brooklyn Freedom Democratic Party, pledging that it would "not be tied to the various factions in the Democratic Party which have always frustrated the demands of the Negro people." Unfortunately few CORE people were willing to devote much time to the undramatic task of getting out the voters, and Owens lost.[98] In Newark, the chapter endorsed the United Freedom Ticket, a slate of candidates for the state legislature backed by a coalition of Negroes, Puerto Ricans, and white reformers in opposition to the

Democratic machine, which most blacks supported on Election Day. The slate was headed by former assemblyman George Richardson, whose once-promising political career had been badly damaged when he challenged the city administration and the Democratic Party county boss on police brutality and other issues. Despite a vigorous campaign in which CORE was intimately involved, the entire ticket went down in crushing defeat.[99] In Cleveland, CORE, like blacks generally, supported Carl Stokes in his first bid for mayor in 1965, when he ran as an independent. Stokes nearly won, but CORE's own strategy boomeranged. Chapter leaders prevailed upon the city's United Freedom Movement to remove its ban on political endorsements. This caused the angry resignation of several officers in the coalition, which included a number of non-partisan and tax-exempt organizations. Perceiving that the issue could completely destroy the UFM, the chapter did not press further for Freedom Movement endorsement but worked independently for Stokes and three black candidates on the City Council.[100] Cincinnati CORE's venture into politics also boomeranged, but for very different reasons, since this affiliate backed not an independent group but an established faction in the Democratic Party. The slate which it endorsed was headed by the president of the Cincinnati AFL-CIO and included only one of the three blacks running for the City Council. CORE chairman Leonard Ball explained that the two other blacks did not support CORE's position, while the white union leader did. Consequently, the chapter found itself in an awkward position, not only because all of its candidates lost but because the NAACP criticized CORE for opposing black office seekers and charged that it had sold out to the very group—the unions—it had fought in the construction demonstrations.[101]

Although national and chapter leaders alike articulated the importance of forming community-based organizations and engaging in partisan politics, in practice the affiliates around the country still engaged mostly in direct-action projects. Relatively few of these achieved victory, in part because many were more difficult or ambitious than those undertaken earlier, and in part because the chapters were now smaller and weaker. Moreover, the dramatic impact of direct action upon the general public had waned, and fewer non-CORE members were now willing to join the demonstrations.

In accordance with the thrust of CORE's New Directions, much of this activity was geared specifically to improving the quality of life in the ghetto rather than toward achieving integration, and often direct action was carried out as part of a deliberate effort to reach and organize the black poor. For example, in February 1965, Rochester CORE and a group of slumdwellers held a demonstration that obtained the installation of a traffic light for the safety of schoolchildren. A couple of months later, Baltimore CORE, protesting inferior educational facilities, conducted a twenty-six-hour sit-in at the school board and demanded not an end to de facto segregation but the replacement of one of the city's antiquated black high schools. Members of Washington CORE (which continued to negotiate with various firms on the issues of open housing and fair employment), in September 1965 chained themselves to the entrance of Shaw Junior High School protesting the substandard and unhealthy physical conditions in the building.[102] A number of chapters held demonstrations to protest police beatings and shootings and to urge the establishment of civilian review boards. Marches on city halls and police stations were conducted in St. Louis, East St. Louis—where CORE even held a sit-in at police headquarters—and Detroit. Brooklyn CORE led periodic picket lines, while Los Angeles CORE staged a sit-in at Mayor Yorty's office.[103] In the summer of 1965 both the Seattle and Los Angeles affiliates helped to establish "Freedom Patrols," which followed policemen to observe their behavior on duty. Newark CORE made police brutality its major focus during the spring and summer. In June, CORE protests brought the suspension of a patrolman who had killed a black, and the following month Farmer headed a march of more than 3000 demanding a civilian review board. Not long afterward, members of the chapter were arrested for sitting-in outside the mayor's office. The Policemen's Benevolent Association, seizing upon the fact that Newark CORE had circulated leaflets calling the suspended patrolman a "murderer," retaliated with a libel suit against Farmer, Robert Curvin, and other local CORE leaders, and the campaign against the police department collapsed.[104]

Several chapters sponsored housing campaigns on behalf of the slumdwellers. New Haven CORE, protesting the city's relocation of families from condemned urban renewal dwellings to other substandard housing, held an all-night vigil outside the mayor's house in April 1965, and a sit-in at his city hall office the following month. When the demonstrators, who tied themselves to chairs, refused to leave, police carried them out and arrested twelve, including chapter chairman Walter Brooks.[105] In June, Denver CORE picketed a slumlord's home and won a promise that extensive repairs would be made. In September, the Morris

County, New Jersey, CORE chapter staged a march protesting "unsafe and unsanitary" housing conditions in the "Hollow" section of Morristown. Between May and October, Long Island CORE, protesting a redevelopment project that would displace blacks, sponsored marches, conducted a sit-in at the Rockville Center urban renewal office, and picketed the mayor's home. The chapter also held a successful rent strike.[106] Most ambitious of all were the efforts of Detroit CORE, which during the summer of 1964 began organizing residents in the depressed 12th Street ghetto area. Tenant unions were formed in a number of buildings, and by early 1965 they had succeeded in forcing a few owners to make repairs. Seeking to publicize the issue, several chapter members were arrested in May, when they chained and padlocked themselves at the entrance to a construction site where a notorious slumlord was erecting a luxury hotel. Michigan law, however, severely hurt CORE's campaign. Those who engaged in the chain-in were prosecuted, landlords who had been compelled to make improvements simply raised their rents, and a number of tenants whom the chapter had organized for rent strikes were actually evicted. In the long run, chapter leaders could claim credit only for providing the original stimulus for a new and strongly worded housing-inspection ordinance which was later passed.[107] In a duplication of the organization's earlier experience, CORE still found tenant-organizing and rent strikes singularly unproductive of long-range gains, as was similarly discovered by Boston CORE members who mounted a futile two-week "dwell-in" to prevent the eviction of tenants who had participated in a rent strike sponsored by the chapter.[108]

A number of affiliates undertook direct-action projects which were neither involved with community organization work nor attracted the participation of many slumdwellers. Such activity carried out by chapter members and their sympathizers was directed at achieving integrated schools and housing and at opening new employment opportunities for blacks. The St. Louis, Missouri, and Southern Alameda County, California, chapters picketed at the sites of new housing developments which refused to sell to blacks. Long Island CORE, in a two-week campaign of picketing and sitting-in which produced five arrests, succeeded in obtaining housing for a black woman in a Hempstead apartment house. More impressive was the sustained campaign of Baltimore CORE in late 1965 and early 1966, led by the chapter's former chairman Walter Carter. On several occasions Baltimore CORE members were arrested for sit-ins at realtors' offices and construction sites. In November over 2000 participated in a march protesting discrimination at a new high-rise apartment house. When further demonstrations at this building produced counter-picketing by the KKK and the possibility of a violent confrontation, the city administration persuaded the owners to adopt an open occupancy policy.[109] Protests against school segregation, though now largely verbal, were still fairly frequent and sometimes provided the occasion for direct action. In Milwaukee, CORE engaged in daily sit-ins at the school super-intendent's office in the spring of 1965. During the summer, Chicago CORE participated in the CCCO's campaign of marches, street sit-downs, and mass arrests, calling for the dismissal of the school superintendent, and several times chairman Robert Lucas was among those arrested. James Farmer flew in and was himself carted off to jail, where he stayed an entire weekend rather than accept bail. As late as the spring of 1966 Seattle CORE helped lead a two-day boycott against de facto school seg-regation.[110]

Job campaigns were still the most popular activity among the affiliates, though their number was much smaller than in preceding years. Indeed in most places employment projects were small and often futile. The highly reputed Boston chapter, which had once successfully attacked major corporations, picketed a cab company without much enthusiasm, tried to persuade the Howard Johnson's chain to hire more blacks, and secured a compensatory hiring agreement from a supermarket.[111] Detroit CORE's major job campaign was directed at the Michigan headquarters of the Automobile Association of America. Picketing, which began in the summer of 1964, resulted in the chapter's first arrests a few months later when chairman Gloria Brown and others sat-in and refused to leave the building. The AAA management made only a vague agreement to en-gage in an active recruitment campaign. By the time Detroit CORE dis-covered how empty this promise was, the members' enthusiasm had waned, working in the ghetto had become the new watchword, and so the AAA project was dropped.[112] St. Louis CORE, riven by internal problems during the winter and spring of 1965, was able to conduct only a few small inconclusive job projects. At the end of the year the chapter briefly revived after the city's Public Service Board canceled the permits of about eighty jitneys serving the ghetto and allowed the routes to be absorbed by the metropolitan bus company. CORE called a bus boycott, organized a volunteer system of "Freedom Cars," and sponsored marches and picket lines at City Hall. But after three months of harassment by competing black companies and police summonses to Freedom Car drivers, CORE privately conceded defeat and reluctantly signed a face-saving agreement with the bus corporation.[113] In San Francisco, charging that downtown stores were failing to comply with the 1963 job agreement, CORE, with the cooperation of the United Freedom Movement, undertook renewed picketing toward the end of 1964. But unlike the previous year, the demonstrations were only sporadic, CORE was too weak to obtain a signed agreement even at the height of the Christmas shopping season, and by early 1965 the chapter was reduced to boycotting a single store.[114] Similarly, across the Bay in Berkeley, the Shattuck Avenue Christmas boycott, which had been fairly extensive in 1963, fizzled in 1964 with a half-hearted and unsuccessful action against one drugstore. Meanwhile, Berkeley CORE had failed to police the favorable agreement which it secured from Montgomery Ward's in 1963, and, when resignations occurred among the Negroes hired, they were often replaced with whites. By the time Berkeley CORE decided that the company was discriminating again late in 1964, the chapter was too demoralized to do anything about it.[115]

Epitomizing the weakness which characterized many chapters was the coordinated attack on the Trailways Bus Company sponsored in late 1964 by a number of northeastern affiliates. Charging that Trailways employed only a handful of black bus drivers in violation of its earlier agreement, CORE began the campaign with a noisy protest inside the Port Authority Bus Terminal in New York on November 7 that produced twenty-two arrests. But in the following weeks the project fell apart. New York demonstrations ended after Thanksgiving Eve when eleven New York area chapters could muster only fifty participants. Elsewhere the situation was even worse. Washington CORE was immobilized by factionalism, and the small Baltimore chapter was, at that point, unable to sustain interest in any project. In Philadelphia the Trailways campaign triggered another public feud with the local NAACP branch president Cecil Moore, who, insisting that the bus company had fulfilled previous job agreements with his organization, joined with the bus company in January to secure an injunction against CORE picketing. A short time afterward, CORE's regional field secretary Eric Mann pronounced the Trailways project a failure, his explanation revealing the loss of self-confidence within the organization. The project, he said, "was very difficult to pull off because of the racial antagonism of management; the size of the company; the amount of work it would take to truly mobilize the Negro community in any way; the lack of inherent emotionalism of the issue, which made it difficult to arouse the interest and enthusiasm of the 'man in the street,' . . . [and the fact that] the project involved CORE in a dispute with a discriminatory union." [116]

A few affiliates did undertake major employment campaigns, but these also either ended in failure or were viewed as failures because they did not achieve the ambitious goals originally set. In the spring of 1965 the Berkeley Campus chapter sought to obtain bartender and waiter jobs for blacks at the expensive restaurants in Oakland's Jack London Square. Capitalizing upon the mass enthusiasm engendered by the Free Speech Movement at the University of California in Berkeley, the chapter staged several gigantic demonstrations, drawing as many as 3000 pickets, chiefly students. With the restaurants proving adamant, the affiliate discussed the use of civil disobedience but drew back, intimidated by fear of the police. Seeking to obtain greater black participation on the demonstrations, it turned in April to attacking restaurants in downtown Oakland, but the black community showed little interest, and the project soon collapsed. [117] Nor were the results any better when a revived Cincinnati CORE tackled the building trades unions during the summer. The first demonstrations, held at a school construction site, brought the arrests of sixteen people, including chapter executive secretary Clyde Vinegar and chairman Leonard Ball, after police pulled demonstrators from the foundation forms. Authorities obtained an injunction barring further obstructive tactics at this location, but CORE's militance stimulated an NAACP sit-in at the building trades headquarters. Temporarily in accord, both groups held a twenty-seven-hour sit-in at the office of the president of the Cincinnati AFL-CIO Council. But the fragile unity was breeched when the NAACP publicly condemned CORE's plans to commit civil disobedience by staging a protest march without obtaining a required police permit. CORE thereupon applied for the permit, and Farmer personally arrived to lead the march. But by then CORE had held another construction site sit-in at the University of Cincinnati, in which fifteen were arrested, and had been slapped with another court injunction. In this context Farmer's presence, rather than symbolizing the expansion of the campaign, actually marked the end of it. [118]

Probably the two most ambitious employment projects undertaken by CORE chapters were Seattle's "Operation DEEDS" and Syracuse's attack on the giant utility, the Niagara Mohawk Power Company. Although during its three-year history the Seattle chapter had created a few hundred openings for blacks, it discovered that "the vicious circle of job discrimination" and black unemployment remained, completely overshadowing "modest gains made here and there." Concluding that "the frustrating failure to achieve a breakthrough in employment might be at least partly a result of dealing in piecemeal fashion with one employer at a time," the affiliate inaugurated a boycott of the entire downtown shopping area in October 1964, with a demand for 1200 jobs. Having set this high goal, the CORE members became frustrated and greatly disappointed when they failed to attain it, even though for this campaign they were acting alone, without the cooperation previously given them by the NAACP. Actually, judged by the yardstick which had been the measure until only a short time before, this project had been very successful, opening between one hundred and two hundred jobs for blacks in the downtown stores. Discouraged, and plagued by self-doubts, Seattle CORE engaged in intense discussions about the lessons to be drawn from Operation DEEDS: "How can we make a large complex campaign . . . more dramatically clear to the public? Was this project worth the financial expense involved? What can be done about the chronic problem that interest declines and manpower decreases for any project that continues over many months . . . ? Has [this] been *too big* a project for Seattle CORE, and if so how else can we produce significant change toward equal opportunity and an integrated society?" [119] Syracuse CORE's direct action against Niagara Mohawk, which employed six blacks out of 1500 workers, ended even more disastrously. When picketing, begun in March 1965, attracted little publicity, tactics were escalated. On one occasion, for example, four men, chaining themselves beneath automobiles, blocked the company's parking lot entrances. In subsequent weeks thirty-eight were arrested, and jail sentences ran as high as ninety days. The company added sixteen black employees, and in June a wearied CORE announced a six-month moratorium. A half-year later Niagara Mohawk reported no further increases in its black staff, but Syracuse CORE, by then ripped apart in factionalism, was in no position to do anything about it.[120]

Despite the overall decline of CORE activity around the country, this survey has shown that the organization nevertheless retained considerable vitality. The fiscal crisis notwithstanding, CORE's income for the year ending May 31, 1965, was over $800,000, the second highest in its history. Although community organization projects proved extraordinarily difficult to inaugurate and sustain, the staff in the South and the chapters in the North and West had carried out a significant number of voter registration drives and direct-action campaigns. It should be emphasized that the response of CORE chapters to the "Crisis of Victory" was highly varied and that while overall, the organization's situation was deteriorating, valiant efforts were made in many places to sustain a viable program.

12

A House Divided

By 1964 the black protest movement was becoming increasingly fragmented. The tendency toward a unity of strategy, if not between leaders, that was emerging during 1963 was dissipated, and after mid-1965 a coalition of the major protest organizations was no longer possible. People in the left wing of the movement—including those in SNCC and many in CORE—experienced a growing sense of isolation from American society, and became disdainful of the middle-class way of life. Viewing any compromise, even if employed as a temporary tactical device, as anathema, they spoke more and more of the necessity for "revolutionary" changes in the social structure and, especially after the Watts riot of August 1965, were inclined toward a rhetoric of violence. Increasingly critical of whites in the movement, they insisted that the organized power of the black community could by itself compel concessions from the "power structure" of capitalists, politicians, and bureaucratic labor leaders. For these militants, veering as they were toward a separatist ideology, Malcolm X became, after his assassination in 1965, a sacred symbol. In contrast, the right wing of the protest movement, which included a substantial group in the NAACP, was impressed by the changes which had occurred, and came to view its role as exercising influence within established institutions rather than fighting from outside. Encouraged by the legislation of 1964 and 1965 and by the selection of prominent protest leaders for high public office, they tended to view the Democratic Party not as an enemy but as an ally. Between these two poles were centrists like Rustin, Randolph, and King, as well as many in the NAACP, who recognized the new willingness of the Lyndon Johnson administration to move toward greater racial justice, but emphasized that continued pressure by a coalition of blacks and whites such as had backed the March on Washington would be needed to push for further gains.

King found it more difficult, and finally impossible, to maintain the symbolic role he had once played so effectively—serving, because of his charisma and the deliberate style of his campaigns, as a bridge between the movement's radical and conservative wings. As already noted, the events at the 1964 Democratic Convention not only discredited both the Democratic Party leadership and white liberal elements in the eyes of many militants, but indicated that the Negroes themselves were deeply divided. Subsequently, both the war in Vietnam and the Anti-Poverty Act of 1964 served to heighten the alienation of many militants and to complicate the cleavages in the protest movement. Some believed that the war diverted attention and funds away from solving the country's leading domestic problem. Others went further and regarded the war as cut from the same cloth as domestic racism, charging that both represented attempts of the "white power structure" to keep a colored race in a colonial status. At the opposite extreme were NAACP and Urban League leaders, who held that the Vietnam conflict was irrelevant to the black protest and mixing the two issues would only lose substantial support for the Negroes' cause. King, breaking with Johnson and centrists like Rustin, openly attacked United States policy in Vietnam, as did SNCC and a number of individuals in CORE. Meanwhile, the War on Poverty, while accelerating the shift to local community action led by the poor that was advocated by many militants, unintentionally increased the frustration and discontent of the slumdwellers by further escalating their expectations but failing to deliver anything substantial. At the same time, as indicated in the preceding chapter, contests for control of the community action programs often exacerbated the polarization between the more moderate middle-class leaders identified frequently with the NAACP and Urban League and those from CORE who claimed to speak more authentically for the black poor.

Not only was the protest movement polarized and fragmented, but CORE itself became greatly divided on a number of matters. The organization's diminishing activity was both a cause and a symptom of its malaise and was reflected in serious internal discussions over structure, membership, and direction. While the departure of Hill and many of his supporters signaled the end of any effective voice in CORE for his politically centrist position other key issues were vigorously debated. Members generally agreed about the importance of building CORE's program around the needs of the slumdwellers, but there were spirited debates within the chapters over the relative merits of direct action and community organization. There were overtly voiced disagreements about the value of maintaining CORE's integrationist traditions, the appropriate role for whites in the organization became an openly divisive issue, CORE's adherence to nonviolence came under increasing attack, and there was much difference of opinion about the stance CORE should take in regard to the Vietnam War. In short, the organization's old consensus on tactics and program had dissolved.

CORE members, of course, were not divided into monolithic blocs, and there was actually a broad spectrum of opinion concerning how far the organization should modify its program. Nevertheless, one can say that at one pole was a group which for tactical reasons felt that CORE should not publicly oppose the war and which remained basically attached to the organization's earlier ideology. At the other pole were those who wanted CORE to condemn the Vietnam War, defended the use of retaliatory violence, believed that blacks should dominate the organization and—turning away from CORE's previous integrationist orientation —came to advocate a program of black separatism. In between were peȯple who took a variety of stands on these issues. For example, there were many who supported the idea of community organization yet insisted that CORE should also continue to stress its traditional direct-action confrontation tactics. Moreover, many were enthusiastic about developing an emphasis on black identity but remained confirmed integrationists.

While these questions were debated in all parts of the country, there were differences in emphasis between the North and the South. CORE in the South, being chiefly a staff operation committed to community organization, did not experience the debates that prevailed in the North over the relative merits of the ghetto orientation versus direct action, or the self-criticism over the inability to attract grass-roots people. Yet just because it was a staff operation, the southern work was the segment of CORE activity most deeply affected by the organization's fiscal plight, and the source of serious challenge to the authority of the national office and the NAC. On the other hand, certain northern and western chapters supplied the principal thrust toward separatism and the defense of violence.

All over the North and West there was uncertainty and wrangling about tactics and strategy as CORE grappled with the problems of institutional racism—a debate which itself ironically contributed further to the declining amount of action. Tactically the discussion focused on the continued viability of direct action; in terms of direction the discussion centered upon whether CORE chapters should continue their thrust for integration or should work instead to improve living conditions in the ghetto. Conceptually the two disagreements were distinct, yet in practice they were frequently intertwined. Louis Smith pointed out that in most affiliates a split developed between those whose new emphasis was working with "street people" and those wedded to CORE's traditional program.[1] In Philadelphia the proponents of direct action denigrated the community organization-ghetto improvement approach as smacking of "social work." In Baltimore it was a group of long-time members, headed by ex-chairman Walter Carter, who questioned the new focus and finally in 1966 seceded to continue their fair-housing campaign. In Columbus during the autumn of 1964, field secretary Mike Lesser found the chapter "divided . . . concerning its role in the community [with] a free-for-all atmosphere at meetings concerning chapter activity." Former chairman Arthur Zebbs was still championing a downtown, direct action campaign for integrated schools, while the new chairman, Marlene Wilson, insisted that the group should work exclusively to help a slum area solve problems about which the residents were most concerned. Several weeks later, backed by Lesser, Wilson had established firm control, and the group had sent out survey teams to begin organizing a poverty-stricken neighborhood. In Detroit toward the end of 1965, the chapter, now much reduced in size, experienced a bitter election contest for chairman. The victor, Al Roberts, ran on a platform of continuing community organization in the 12th Street area as CORE's main function, while his opponent urged the chapter to expand its program and return to its earlier fight against citywide injustices in education and employment.[2] In Cincinnati, a small group of white radical youths in late 1964 stridently denounced the middle-class black leadership of the chapter, which Lesser described as containing many Negroes who resisted the idea of working in the slums, "because it is something they have recently escaped from and because community organization work is the fetish of the white kids who have alienated them." Cincinnati CORE was notable for mounting the kind of program which had been characteristic of CORE groups in 1963–64. Its most important campaigns in late 1964 and 1965 were a rent strike and mass demonstrations for jobs in the building trades. The rent strike—the project most closely related to community organization strategy—was accompanied by a week-long sit-in at City Hall in September 1964, which produced improved housing and health codes. Cincinnati CORE's approach in this case thus showed that a community organization thrust could be effectively combined with an old-fashioned direct-action confrontation downtown.[3]

Their desire to solve the problems of the slums notwithstanding, even chapters that were earnestly seeking to involve grass-roots people and relate to their needs found the goal still elusive. Late in 1964 a task force worker stationed in California informed McCain that "The Negro community, especially the lower economic segment, has been untouched by CORE." Several months later Berkeley Campus CORE despaired because it obtained no "significant involvement of Oakland's black community" in its job demonstrations there. Denver CORE, which established its Freedom House in a vacant store located in the city's poorest neighborhood, found that the residents were so hopeless that they could not take advantage of the help offered; moreover many of the middle-class blacks and whites in the chapter were reluctant to go to the area at night. Syracuse CORE deplored the fact that whites predominated among the pickets at the Niagara Mohawk demonstrations; even bringing in fifty grass-roots Negroes from Rochester to assist one Saturday did not move the Syracuse black community. Newark CORE worked hard to develop a base among the black poor, yet its City Hall sit-in against police brutality involved participants about equally divided between middle-class blacks and whites. Detroit CORE found that through its rent-strike projects some tenants joined the chapter, and a few became quite active, but most did not stay for long. In New Haven, where the chairman organized a group of "winos" who met at the CORE office, some of them briefly joined the chapter and came to meetings "fired up with wine," to the annoyance of most of the white and black middle-class members. In general, the few grass-roots people attracted to CORE were silent at meetings because of their limited education and expertise and soon drifted away. CORE's inability to relate effectively to the black poor became a matter of much soul-searching and self-criticism; as Farmer told the 1965 National Convention, despite the fact that affiliates had opened offices in the slums, "If we are honest we will admit that most have failed" in their efforts to organize the black poor. Earlier this problem had not prevented the development of effective action programs; now the ideological commitment to involving the poor was so strong that the failure to develop adequate techniques to do it, only added to the feeling of malaise.[4]

Because the community-organization orientation involved, however temporarily, a turning away from a direct struggle for integration, it converged as we have seen with separatist tendencies stemming from other sources. In addition, the talk of racial unity and power that underlay much community-organization theorizing lent itself to a nationalist interpretation; as one midwestern black CORE leader recollected, "The real rationale for community organization was to develop a base and get power to change things. For many people, this approach then gradually shifted into black power and separatism."[5] Indeed, some confirmed integrationists in CORE became concerned that the "New Directions" would tilt the organization in a separatist direction.

Perhaps the most articulate of these was Clarence Funnyé, the black chairman of New York CORE. In November 1964, a month after taking office, Funnyé held a press conference, where he unveiled his program for "deghettoization," or "the eradication of the ghetto." In his view it was shortsighted to rehabilitate dilapidated facilities in a manner that "just solidified the ghetto"; rather, Harlem must get schools and housing of such high quality that "other folks will want to live and go to school there." A professional city planner, Funnyé had already drawn up a proposal to use the St. Nicholas Park area for an urban renewal project that would upgrade the neighborhood to make it attractive for all, and thus maximize opportunities for "economic and ethnic residential integration." As he told reporters, "We have got to get across the idea that there's a common cause between . . . the white majority and the colored minority. . . . We must acquire allies, and sell the allies on the fact that they can get something out of working with us." Funnyé continued to agitate for his point of view, though it ran counter to the road CORE was taking, but he even failed to obtain wide-spread support among the interracialists in CORE, many of whom, like George Wiley, supported the community organization program. Funnyé wrote in a statement circulated at the 1965 Convention, a gathering that was anything but hospitable to his approach:

> It is my hope that this convention will grapple with what seems to me to be a basic conflict of aims. There are those among us who feel strongly that we must now turn our energies toward rebuilding and strengthening the ghetto to enhance black political power. There are those, on the other hand, who feel that our major thrust must be toward eliminating the ghetto, with all its attendant ills of slums, inad-

equate schools, high crime rates, poor police protection, inadequate services, and a feeling of hopelessness on the part of the inhabitants.

It seems to me that this deals in a very fundamental way with the question of CORE's continuing commitment to working for an integrated society. Can we work toward rebuilding the ghetto, and at the same time press for integrated schools? Can we seek to concentrate black political power, while ignoring the fact that all-white enclaves in our cities provide a breeding ground for bigoted pressure groups and prejudiced politicians? Can we, indeed turn our backs on the principle embodied in the 1954 school decision—that separation in itself is inherently unequal, and leads to a feeling of worthlessness among those who are so separated? [6]

Funnyé not only failed to affect the thinking of National CORE, but he was challenged in his own chapter by the avowed nationalist Roy Innis, who successfully opposed every program Funnyé attempted. As a result, the chapter was practically immobilized throughout Funnyé's term of office. Many of Innis' supporters were only partly in agreement with his views, and opposed Funnyé for a variety of reasons. Some of them charged that whites in Funnyé's faction were unduly influential in the chapter. This was an issue that began to achieve salience after the Harlem riot of 1964. Many black members—some out of embarrassment at the presence of white colleagues at the scenes of disorder, others out of resentment toward all whites whom they identified with the racist system that made such riots "inevitable"—openly questioned the usefulness of whites in the chapter altogether. Finally in November 1965, with the election of Roy Innis as chairman, a "black male caucus" became the group's chief policy-making body, and soon afterward the few remaining whites departed.[7] No other chapter went this far along the road to separatism during Farmer's administration. Yet elsewhere the skepticism about white participation in CORE, which had previously been raised in the course of carrying out community organization projects, became accentuated. One black integrationist, long active in CORE on the West Coast, put it, "Black separatism and community organization went hand in hand. Programmatically, community organization . . . fitted the needs of black nationalism because it was an activity that did not require much dealing with the white power structure—a task which whites had previously largely handled"—and because organizing the ghetto was one activity in which blacks "felt confident not only in excelling whites, but even being able to do without any whites at all." [8]

Columbus CORE illustrates the complexities and subtleties that arose as chapters sought to implement CORE's new directions and redefine the role of whites. Arthur Zebbs, who gave up the chairmanship in mid-1964, had earlier pressed for black leadership in the chapter. Yet his most influential adviser had been Jerry Zeller, a white man who was one of the affiliate's original members. Zebbs, moreover, encouraged white participation, and in fact his enthusiasm for maintaining a direct-action emphasis was based partly on the fact that it was a strategy in which whites could easily be utilized. On the other hand, his successor, Marlene Wilson, the chapter's leading advocate of a community-organization thrust, felt that, except for one or two special cases, white participation could be only in strictly supportive tasks such as doing research or typing. Within the chapter, some blacks charged that the whites were guilty of condescension. One black member recalled, "Whatever whites did would be interpreted as paternalistic." When a few whites assisted in canvassing a slum area for the chapter's first ghetto project, there was considerable ambiguity. A black critic of Wilson recalled, "Some black members felt they [the whites] *could* not work in the black community; some felt they could, but they *should* not. There was never clarity and there was a whole lot of vacillation. Many whites would ask what they could do. Marlene told them to paint a sign or be a fund-raiser, and they were not happy with this." A few did remain active, although they were excluded from leadership positions. Columbus CORE delegates at the 1965 National Convention pointedly referred to Zeller as a white person who knew how to follow black leaders. But for the most part, "whites did not know what to do and they dropped out of Columbus CORE." Yet it should be emphasized that the situation was highly complex, that black leaders dedicated to black control of the organization often displayed ambivalent attitudes. Marlene Wilson, though skeptical of the contribution whites could make, was distraught when in late 1965 Floyd McKissick ran against George Wiley for the post of national director, and the latter's opponents used as a weapon the argument that he had a white wife. As Wilson put it, "Dr. Martin Luther King says Love the white man, and I say he's out of his mind. NAC members say hate the white man and clear CORE of him, and though I am *committed* to the need for black people leading the movement, I cannot revert to an idea CORE taught me was wrong." [9]

By 1965 some people both on the NAC and in the chapters were indeed saying that whites should leave CORE. It should be stressed, of course, that there was a wide range of viewpoints in the organization, that there were still many blacks who disagreed with the thrust toward subordination of whites. In fact, in a number of chapters whites continued to play important roles. Moreover the blacks who wished to limit white participation were by no means united. A number favored complete white exclusion; others felt that whites should be permitted to remain on a restricted basis. Those who took the latter position defined the appropriate role for whites in various ways. Some blacks thought whites should supply only clerical and technical assistance; others held that in addition a few exceptional individuals might help in community organization. In either case, whites would be serving not as decision makers but strictly as followers. Some, permitting whites a wider role, believed that they could hold certain committee chairmanships but insisted that top posts and basic decisions must be in black hands. In Brooklyn CORE, as late as December 1964, five of the fifteen members of the chapter's executive board were white, though except for the housing committee chairman, white officers were limited to the essentially housekeeping posts of financial and recording secretary. Despite such diversity within CORE, the drift was clear. Sentiment for restricting the activities of white members was increasing, and for the first time there were overt demands for their complete exclusion.[10]

Whites continued to be divided in their response to this mounting and increasingly overt criticism. Some readily agreed that it was reasonable for blacks to control their own struggle for freedom and that whites made poor community organizers. Many, however, wrestled seriously with the question of what their appropriate role should be. For example, in Louisiana, Mike Lesser was among the first to articulate the issue. Fearing that because of his very effectiveness and expertise as a field secretary he might function, in effect, as a kind of paternalist, he entertained serious reservations about taking the responsibilities of leadership. Similarly Liz Fusco, the white CORE field worker who served as coordinator for the Mississippi freedom schools, was reportedly worried that the white task force people teaching in them "are not sufficiently sensitive to the problems of Mississippi Negroes and are therefore incompetent to deal with the people and inclined to do some kind of terrible damage." Some whites operated on the basis of a guilt complex and what a number of CORE people of both races regarded as masochism. For example, in San Fernando Valley CORE, which by late 1964 found itself without a program and rife with personality conflicts, the meetings had become "group therapy" sessions in which certain black members baited whites.

The chapter contained several whites who encouraged this, subscribed to the growing view that white members must take a back seat, and in some cases even agreed that whites did not belong in CORE. One white member recalled, "We had lots of white masochists—I remember one who got up and said, 'Every time I look in the mirror, I see that I'm white and I feel guilty. I can never know what it is like to be black.' Much of the time at meetings was taken up with oral confessions." Some whites romanticized the black world, as did the secretary of Marin County, California, CORE. After attending a regional conference in Los Angeles, she wrote that during her three days in the ghetto she had observed much evidence of depressing poverty, "but beyond these things I found something else. Truth. There does not seem to be the need for glamour or falseness that is so obvious in the white world. This truth and honesty are everywhere, in the food, the music, in the talk, and in the faces of the people. . . . Through all the things I saw and felt during these three days I have some strong feelings regarding the white role in the Civil Rights Movement. My feeling is that the role of whites should be one of almost silence." [11]

Despite the prevalence of such sentiments, the tendency over the next months was for large numbers of whites, confused and sometimes bitter, to withdraw in the face of quiet snubs, open attacks, and a constriction of their participation. In certain affiliates, tensions erupted into arguments, with blacks denouncing whites as insincere, domineering, or lacking in understanding of the black community. Even without such clashes, whites in many chapters sensed aloofness or brusqueness from some of their black colleagues. It became less frequent for black and white members to act as a cohesive in-group which socialized together. More and more of the whites drifted out of the organization as it became clearer that their views and contributions were less valued. Given the fact that white CORE members generally regarded blacks as a "reference group" whose approval was sought and needed, their withdrawal usually occurred without an open struggle against what seemed like an irresistible tide of growing nationalism.[12]

In such a context, few whites were attracted to CORE, and new members in this period were principally black. Gradually most of the chapters were losing their white majorities. Probably by the end of 1964 and certainly no later than the spring of 1965, CORE's active membership had become predominantly Negro. Among the chapters that had shifted to overwhelming black majorities were New York (Harlem), Columbus, Baltimore, and San Francisco. Syracuse, Boston, Long Island, Washington, and New Haven had become about half or slightly more than half black. Berkeley became mainly black by the middle of the year. Yet certain chapters were still predominantly white. This pattern was especially pronounced in suburban areas like Middlesex County, New Jersey, or Prince George's County, Maryland, which were almost completely white; but it also characterized chapters like San Diego and Seattle, which had slight white majorities, and Los Angeles, where the membership remained three-fourths white.[13]

The sharp drop in the proportion of white members was often interrelated with the simultaneous decline of chapter activity. On the one hand, antiwhite feelings often peaked when an affiliate was in trouble, with the whites functioning as an unconscious scapegoat for the chapter's problems. The presence of whites was frequently blamed for the movement's failure and for CORE's inability to relate to the black community. One white member long active in the Bay area observed,

> I have found that when victories are not happening, there is strife —there are more arguments at meetings—more of the charges that "we are superficial"—that "we should be concerned with making Negroes proud to be Negroes"; that "we should emphasize race history and Africa." It always begins like this—some Negro members go to the meeting after we have lost a project, or are losing it, and they say, "Why didn't we win? We didn't win because the Negro community is not behind us [our local CORE chapter]. We haven't gone out into the Negro community to really get it on our side, and the reason we haven't is that you whites are just a bunch of white liberals."

On the other hand, the withdrawal of large numbers of whites often coincided with the end of viable chapter programs. According to some black chairmen, with the departure of educated, upper-middle class whites who possessed skills and time many of the blacks lacked, it was extremely difficult to maintain day-to-day chapter routines. Yet these leaders had few regrets; to them it seemed necessary for blacks to have their own movement, even if, in the short run, efficiency and effectiveness were impaired. The causal sequence was often circular. Chapter decline produced hostility toward white members, and their departure meant the loss of manpower which further hurt the affiliate's program. Chapters varied greatly. Some affiliates like Newark and Seattle, although losing membership, suffering from sharp diminution in activity, and facing serious disappointment in their most important projects, did not witness attacks upon their white members. Moreover, withdrawal of whites did not necessarily spell inactivity. St. Louis, Cleveland, Brooklyn, and Philadelphia CORE groups had earlier experienced highly viable periods with overwhelmingly black membership and leadership, and the same was true of Cincinnati and Baltimore during 1964–66. Yet it was a symptom of CORE's malaise that in many instances, notably on the West Coast, frustration and discouragement polarized the chapters racially and intensified the thrust toward black separatism.[14]

CORE groups handled the black-white issue in diverse ways. In neither Boston, long a model of white participation and interracialism, nor in Cleveland, a predominantly black chapter with strong nationalist currents, did the problem achieve salience, although in both cases some of the whites felt rudely treated by some of the blacks. Several Negroes were quietly—but not openly—resentful of Alan Gartner's "white leadership" by the time he left Boston to join the National CORE staff in 1965. Cleveland CORE had explicitly committed itself previously to a policy of black leadership and policy-making; nevertheless, the chapter had at least one white person serving as chairman of a key committee through 1965. With dedication, expertise, and an unostentatious manner, he participated successfully in the chapter's hierarchy. Similarly, in Long Island CORE, where chairman Lincoln Lynch considered himself "a nationalist" and where black control was tacitly assumed to be a desirable goal, the issue rarely surfaced overtly, although occasionally a black person in disagreeing with a white would say, "I don't need any whites telling me what to do." In Pittsburgh, where Louis Smith visited in the autumn of 1964, the black members were "very suspicious of white people in the chapter and had even gone so far as to hold secret all-black meetings," but after his explanation of CORE philosophy, they elected a white vice-chairman. In St. Louis, on the other hand, the demoralization which plagued the chapter spilled over into attacks on whites. Even 'Charles Oldham was charged with selling out and making deals with the power structure. As a result most of the whites, including Oldham himself, departed.[15]

The well-integrated New Haven CORE did not experience overt racial tensions until the spring of 1965. Despite disparities in education, the whites, most of whom were connected with Yale University, had enjoyed close relations with their upwardly mobile working- and middle-class black colleagues. In March 1965, all the top officers except the corresponding secretary were Negroes; but five of the seven committee chairmen were white, making the chapter's executive committee about evenly divided between the races. Whites shouldered a great deal of the work, from performing clerical chores through participating in negotiations with city officials to organizing tenants; in part for this reason, whites continued to be very influential for a considerably longer period of time than they were in some chapters. Yet just here was an important source of difficulty. Underneath there was a basic distrust of educated white people who tried to participate in the black community, a resentment of their expertise and articulateness that was expressed first in jokes and jibes about their loquaciousness at meetings. In the spring of 1965 interracial socializing declined, and tensions surfaced. Several blacks began to ask openly, "Who are the whites to define the issues for us?" Chairman Walter Brooks, believing that the grass-roots blacks were kept out of the chapter by the intellectualizing of aggressive whites, wanted the latter "to do whatever they were told to do," and attempted to reduce their numbers and influence. By the summer of 1965 executive board meetings were taken up with arguing the issue of black control of the chapter, with Brooks making explicit his position that whites should be "faithful followers" rather than act as decision makers. Although the chapter remained slightly less than half black, the whites were thereafter edged out of the committee chairmanships; by March 1966, all the officers were black.[16]

It was in several California chapters that the black-white issue became most divisive. In the Bay area the tendency toward racial polarization was exacerbated by the demoralization which set in after the Sheraton-Palace Hotel and Auto Row demonstrations. Over two hundred of those arrested were convicted and a number were jailed; this fact, combined with the awareness that few blacks had actually been hired at the hotels and automobile showrooms, had a depressing effect on the local CORE chapters.[17] In this climate, the subsequent Bank of America project created disunity among Bay-area CORE people. To San Francisco chairman William Bradley and others the fact that blacks had obtained a few hundred jobs was beside the point; the number was well below the large goal originally set, and the financial institution had outmaneuvered CORE in making its agreement with the California FEPC rather than with the CORE negotiating committee. Bradley and Ussery wanted to continue the bank action and were resentful when most chapters refused to go along. Those who wanted to end the project believed that significant progress had been made, that to pursue the matter would be futile since only a handful of the chapters had done much direct action. Significantly, this disagreement tended to split the Bay-area groups along racial lines, with the black leaders insisting upon the importance of continuing the struggle, while a mostly white group regarded this as impractical. Ironically, a source of concern to some black chapter chairmen was the fact that the majority of those arrested in the Sheraton and Auto Row campaigns and most of the pickets in the Bank of America project had been white. Bradley charged that the whites were cowardly and insincere; for their part, Bradley's white critics considered him autocratic and unfair, if not downright racist.

Within the San Francisco chapter itself, where blacks occupied all the leadership positions and by early 1965 comprised about 80 per cent of the membership, the frustrating consequence of these employment campaigns produced a loss of vigor that became very evident in the lackluster retail store project at the end of 1964, and in the abortive effort to do community organization work in 1965. The chapter's project among the black poor at Hunter's Point coincided with—and precipitated—an overt attack upon white members. Bradley and the affiliate's black community relations committee chairman overruled plans to send integrated teams into the area. When opposition to this action was expressed, Bradley reportedly said, "Racism is the prevailing feature of the white mentality. . . . It doesn't make any difference who your ancestors are, you're still white." Other black executive committee chairmen declared, "Equality and integration are not the same thing." "Integration is a dirty word," Bradley asserted. "I never interpreted 'blacks and whites together' to mean that blacks and whites do everything together." For a brief period, San Francisco CORE's black teams worked at the Point, but Bradley was unable to revive the chapter through this attempt at community organization.[18]

Although Berkeley CORE, unlike San Francisco, had a white majority as late as the spring of 1965, the pattern was essentially similar. The declining affiliate was not even half as energetic as it had been a year earlier, and discouragement only exacerbated the racial polarization which had been present since the Bank of America project. Chapter members spent their time discussing how to sink roots in the black community, yet lacked confidence in themselves to do anything. Activity came to a standstill. Meetings became more unpleasant and argumentative, with certain black members charging that whites were afraid to pursue vigorously a downtown employment project because of "The Man." A number of blacks in the chapter regarded the whites as ignorant or insincere or both, declaring, "You don't understand us. You can't tell us what we want." "You can leave whenever you want, but we're in this for good." After one such incident, one white retorted sarcastically, "Well, why not give the white members half a vote?" Finally, about June 1965, a substantial number of members, mostly whites, left the chapter, which never recovered.[19]

In San Diego CORE, which as late as January 1965, was still 60 per cent white, resentment on the part of black chairman Harold Brown and others developed against a number of "organizationally sophisticated" whites who, it was felt, tended to dominate the chapter while many blacks, less educated and experienced, failed to speak up. He encouraged discussions of Negro history to instill race pride and experimented briefly with the use of a black caucus until criticism led to its discontinuance. The Bank of America campaign had a complex impact on the chapter. On the one hand, the victory gave confidence to blacks—proving that "we can do something—we are really somebody." On the other hand, it had been a hard project, success was limited and a number of people, including Brown, served jail sentences. Brown himself felt that in view of the minimal gains, none of which accrued to the black poor, the great effort and suffering had made such actions unlikely in the future. The repeal of the Rumford Fair Housing Law by popular referendum only added to the disillusionment, and his faith that whites would have a change of heart disintegrated. Brown himself bitterly warned of more militant methods to end housing discrimination: "the entire state of California must share the guilt, shame and burden of . . . a vote that has made segregation and bigotry legal. . . . If our moderate methods fail to gain significant results, then surely very shortly there will be others that will seek and practice much more extreme actions. . . . The 'streets' might not be the 'best' way, but—in our corrupted and warped and sick society—it is obviously the *only* way!" But the fact of the matter was that, as other members of the chapter recalled, "We petered out because the Establishment learned how to cope with direct action. Our energy was depleted—the jail sentences and court actions depleted us."[20] Unwilling to return to more limited direct-action projects, San Diego CORE stepped up attempts to recruit grass-root Negroes. As one black member recalled, "We were concerned about not reaching the guy on the street. We tried pool halls—everything. But to be active in CORE you needed leisure time—and grass-roots people didn't have it . . . and some resented us because we were middle class—they'd say, 'You mothers made it—CORE don't mean nothin' for me.' " Brown, disturbed that more whites than blacks had shown up on bank picket lines, and upset at the difficulties in recruiting the black poor, became outspoken in his criticism of assertive whites. Within the chapter he charged that overzealous "pushy white women" discouraged the participation of black female members, and he chastised blacks who voted contrary to his wishes: "How can you as a black man vote against me as a black man?" Yet many whites defended him. Although the interracial tensions were debilitating, San Diego CORE did not disintegrate until Brown secured the expulsion of two white Trotskyists in early 1965. This action brought the resignations of many anti-Brown activists, mostly white, who charged that the chairman persecuted people only because of their opposition to him, and the chapter lapsed into virtual inactivity.[21]

Such personality clashes were on the rise in CORE, but it should be emphasized that racial antagonisms were often not involved at all. In Washington CORE field secretary Herbert Callender found an "undercurrent of internal fighting" under black chairman and Freedom Rider Roena Rand, but the problem was tactical—whether or not the affiliate should work at community organization. "This group," he concluded, "does not particularly want to deal with the man in the ghetto." Complaints of autocratic chapter leadership were by no means new. Earlier Julius Hobson had been ousted from office in Washington CORE, the Dayton chapter had broken up amid recriminations over the chairman's dictatorial methods, and even Lincoln Lynch of Long Island CORE had faced a serious election challenge in the spring of 1964. Such cleavages now became more numerous. In San Diego, as just indicated, the magnetic Harold Brown, whose judgment had not previously been seriously questioned, found himself denounced by erstwhile supporters for high handedly ousting the Trotskyists. Factionalism in the Cincinnati affiliate during the fall of 1964 revolved around resentment over the strong personal leadership exercised by Clyde Vinegar, whom a CORE field secretary reported as being "very possessive" toward the chapter and as structuring things "so that all important decisions are his realm." The conflict was resolved when Vinegar resigned as chairman to assume the post of executive secretary. Under the joint leadership of Vinegar and the new chairman, Leonard Ball, the chapter went on to a period of unprecedented vigor that ended only after the debacle of its political efforts late in 1965.[22]

Cleveland, more than any other chapter, best illustrated the factionalism, infighting, and personality clashes that often accompanied a group's decline. Cleveland CORE's internal morale problems went back to Klunder's death and the affiliate's failure to reverse the school board's position on de facto segregation. The situation was exacerbated by the abortive effort against police brutality in the summer of 1964. In this context, the presence of a Trotskyist group, which had been previously accepted in the chapter, became a source of contention. The national office had long been concerned about infiltration by the Socialist Workers Party in Cleveland, and in the autumn Ruth Turner decided that their influence was harmful to her chapter. Because the incumbent chairman, Arthur Evans, although not a Trotskyist, was friendly with the SWP members, she backed an opposition slate against him in the hotly contested election in September. Other issues were also involved. Thus Evans, a founder of the chapter, believed that there was still substantial room for direct action, while many of his critics wanted to concentrate almost exclusively on community organization. Amid the atmosphere of mutual recriminations, both Evans and Turner were charged with dictatorial behavior by their opponents. Although the principal overt issue was concern about the influence exerted by the SWP members and their allies, the basic problem was that Cleveland CORE, unable to mount a significant program, turned to bitter internal fighting. The defeat of the Evans slate, and the exodus of the Trotskyists and many of their friends, brought peace but produced little revival in activity. Thus, in May 1965 the chapter fruitlessly picketed the school board for firing a teacher charged with membership in a black nationalist organization, but was easily upstaged by the NAACP, which on the very same day held a construction site demonstration that brought twenty-four arrests. As already mentioned, Cleveland CORE's foray into partisan politics boomeranged severely, and community organization work, even after the opening of the Bruce Klunder Freedom House in October 1965, lagged. By the end of 1965, the affiliate, like many others, was essentially moribund.[23]

Like many of the northern chapters, the CORE staff and national organization also suffered from considerable wrangling. This involved debates over the black-white issue and CORE's internal structure that would reach a climax at the time of the 1965 Convention.

In the South, black-white tensions were most severe in Mississippi, where the situation at the Jackson COFO office had become so critical in late 1964 that white staffers were "often subject to severe racial abuse and even violence from Negro workers." Within the CORE staff itself, although Jewett continued to play a prominent role until he left the state a year later, and although white volunteers often related well to the black community, conflicts between them and the black directors of local projects came up with painful regularity at staff meetings, as the following exchange indicates:

> Rev. [Clint] Collier [a black Mississippian, long a leader in CORE work]: "I hope we don't get the idea [from the preceding discussion] that out of state people don't have something to contribute. Sometimes some of those fellows understand these problems better than we do right here in it all the time. . . ."

> Theodus Hewitt [a black task force worker, native of Mississippi, head of the Harmony project]: "I didn't mean we don't respect the ideas of the white volunteers. But there needs to be a leader. And whites can't do all the things Negro workers can do. . . . There are white northerners who have come in here to push us around like the southern whites. . . ."

> Pat [a northern white task force worker]: "The problem is misunderstanding. Any white volunteer must have had a lot of leadership potential . . . to even be able to come down here. So when he came down here it was hard for him to adjust to not leading. He didn't mean to sound like the white bosses. But Negroes are so sensitive to being shoved around that they couldn't understand."

> Randy [Glenn, a southern black field worker and head of the Ofahoma project]: "This white-black question comes up at every meeting."

Even in Louisiana and Florida interracial tensions for the first time assumed serious dimensions. Thus at the orientation session for the 1965 summer task force, a new white volunteer was impressed by the "obvious resentment and friction" between the black and white staffers. Another, who had worked the preceding summer in Mississippi, recalled that the role of whites in the Movement "was endlessly discussed at the orientation," with pointed references being made to the objections that had been raised in southern black communities about the "demonstrative" behavior which white female CORE workers had exhibited when in the company of black males.[24]

For practical reasons both Ronnie Moore and Dave Dennis continued to be particularly anxious to attract young southern blacks to the task force. Thus in January 1965, at a time when the Louisiana task force consisted of five whites and eight blacks, Moore observed, "The racial ratio of staff is out of proportion. . . . More Negro staff members are needed." Dennis, as Southern Regional Office program director, with the leverage provided by SEDF money, was able to recruit a staff of summer workers in 1965 that was two-thirds black, in contrast to the summers of 1963 and 1964 when the majority of the task force had been white.[25] On the other hand, some white field workers were entrusted with important positions of responsibility. At the recommendation of Dennis and Moore, Mike Lesser and Richard Jewett had been accorded what was, because of CORE's financial straits, the rare honor of being promoted from task force workers to field secretaries during the summer of 1964. Other members of the task force were appointed to lead important projects, as in the case of Yates and Miller at Bogalusa. In certain instances interracial tensions arose as a result. In Florida, trouble centered upon a young white leader of the Gadsden County project, who worked well with field secretary Spiver Gordon, the head of the whole North Florida operation, but found himself in conflict with several local black staff workers. Resigning in January 1965, he stated that he was in full agreement with the "philosophy" that "whites should take a back seat in civil rights," and complained he had been unfairly charged with bringing in too many white staff members, with "attempting to dominate the project . . . [and] trying to establish a white leadership." The addition of new white staff people had been Gordon's decision; in fact the young man maintained that he had taken charge of the Gadsden County project only "by default," since when Patricia Due left, "no one was willing to assume the responsibility. . . . It is too bad that I am being condemned for assuming leadership just because there happened to be no Negro . . . who was willing to take the job." More serious were the problems of the white task force worker in charge of the Jonesboro project. In May 1965 he was dropped after accusations of "paternalism, poor staff relationships and some personal discrimination."[26]

Meanwhile there was also a conscious tendency to exclude whites from key positions in the national office. This became very evident in the debates which arose after Rich resigned as community relations director to take up his work with CORE-SEDF. In April 1965, the NAC accepted Farmer's decision to employ Alan Gartner as Rich's successor, only following considerable discussion, and only on a restricted and temporary basis. Despite Gartner's ability and availability, there was a feeling that his appointment should be reconsidered for several reasons: the fact that yet "another NAC member would be put on staff, the fact that once again a white person would be hired for a top position, the long acquaintance and friendship of Alan and the National Director and the former's influence upon the latter." [27] Ruth Turner presented a resolution to bar all whites from staff positions. The motion was dropped only after Peck heatedly denounced it as "discrimination-in-reverse . . . contrary to basic CORE principles" and after another NAC member advised that "It would look bad on paper." [28] Upon Ussery's motion, the NAC decided to separate the fund-raising and public-relations functions of the community relations department, giving the former to Gartner for only a year beginning June 15, with the understanding that he would withdraw if efforts to recruit a Negro were successful by then. Not long after, at a meeting in Farmer's office, Peck admonished the national director "for not standing up against a principle you know to be wrong." Farmer replied, "You'll simply have to put up with this sort of thing in the coming years; it's the trend," at which point Rich, who was present, objected and warned Farmer that if "the trend" was not fought, "They'll be getting after you next because you have a white wife." [29]

Meanwhile, two major structural problems had also arisen: a growing gulf between the southern field workers and the national organization on the one hand, and friction between the NAC and the national office staff on the other. Part of the difficulty was financial, stemming from CORE's inability to promote more than a handful from the task force to the higher paying and more prestigious post of field secretary. Some individuals had been performing duties similar to field secretaries for as long as two years, and undergoing the same dangers at a weekly subsistence pay of $15 to $25 that did not even include medical insurance.[30]

More important, many Southern staff members, committed to creating independent community organizations rather than to chapter formation and CORE's growth, developed an ideology extremely critical of organizational centralization. As Wiley discovered a short time after beginning his duties as associate national director, many of them lacked "an adequate CORE orientation." Haley, even though he sympathized with what his field workers were trying to do, warned that the community organization approach "can be completely honest only after staff has received considerable orientation in the nature of CORE." [31] For their part, southern staff had been deeply influenced by their own experiences. Dennis, Jerome Smith, and others who had been active in the early period of the New Orleans chapter, were imbued with a profound sense that CORE's growth and image were less important than helping local people organize themselves to fight their own battles. Dennis' views on the subject were confirmed by his work in Baton Rouge at the end of 1961 and early 1962, where National CORE and its staff basically set the strategy and obtained most of the publicity, thus in the end antagonizing local leadership. In Mississippi Dennis found that Moses was thinking along similar lines. Many of the southern staff absorbed Dennis' and Moses' faith in participatory democracy—in the ability of the poor to shape their own destiny—and the hostility which the two men shared toward centralized bureaucratic structures. Although the charismatic Moses in actual fact often made basic COFO decisions, he articulated the theory that "the people on the bottom don't need leaders at all. What they need is to have confidence in their own lives." Philosophically, therefore, many staff were committed not to the development of CORE chapters, but to organizing communities for their own advancement under leadership autonomous of CORE. According to one top official at national headquarters, southern staff members "had a mystical view of their relation to local people." [32]

The failure to organize local CORE affiliates was also partly based on certain practical realities, for, as CORE became involved with grass-roots blacks in southern towns, it reached people who, concerned about local problems, related directly to the courageous young staff activists who came to their communities rather than to a distant, impersonal national office. The policy of recruiting task force workers from among local youth only accentuated this tendency, while the fact that in many places CORE acted through existing local organizations also deterred the formation of chapters. In a town like Plaquemine or Bogalusa a CORE affiliate would have been viewed only as a threat to the voters leagues; it is probably no accident that in the Felicianas, where CORE did establish chapters, repression had been so severe that no voters league existed.

Thus for a variety of reasons a large group on the southern staff had concluded that CORE needed both democratizing and decentralizing. At the October 1964 NAC meeting, Rudy Lombard had explicitly questioned the desirability of developing new CORE chapters; at the same time he also argued that CORE-sponsored but autonomous local movements should somehow be able to articulate their interests in the CORE organization. Subsequently southern field people argued that such unaffiliated groups should be allowed voting representatives at CORE conventions. At the same time, they wanted to see the national structure revamped, the bureaucracy reduced to a skeleton, and the NAC stripped of much of its power. While Haley and Moore regarded such views as impractical, leaders like Dennis, Lombard, Jewett, Lesser, and Oretha Castle favored them. Thus, to Dennis the basic problem was, "we set up structure and slot people into it, [and therefore] we do not get community involvement." As he put it, "Our structure does not allow us to be open to new configurations. It excludes people from top to bottom. . . . We fight against the power structure because it excludes people and yet we do the same." [33]

While the southern staff thus felt alienated from the whole national structure—the New York headquarters and the National Action Council alike—the NAC's dissatisfaction with Farmer's style of operation and with the administrative staff's tendency to act autonomously, had not been resolved. After the 1964 Convention, in an attempt to diminish the influence of the organization's bureaucracy, the NAC and Steering Committee increasingly took to meeting in "closed session," excluding department heads from participating in important portions of their deliberations.

Rich in particular, as the most influential department head, was the object of resentment on the part of some NAC members. To some extent, this stemmed from his very control of the organizational mechanism and the effectiveness that he so often exhibited in influencing policy. One of Rich's warm supporters on the Council observed, "Rich was so damned good that he enveloped meetings and we had to go his way." On the other hand, his critics charged him with being a poor administrator, and with inefficiency and miscalculations that had permitted CORE to incur an unprecedented deficit—a record which one of them described as "fairly gross mismanagement." NAC members who desired to see the National Office give greater assistance to the chapters also charged him with favoring the southern program at the expense of the northern work. Rich had indeed been influential in encouraging the development of CORE's southern program, especially in Louisiana. It was the one program that could be truly called a project of the National Office, and given the fact that oppression in the South brought forth a strong emotional response from northern contributors, it was not surprising that he emphasized this aspect of CORE work. Ironically, however, Rich also aroused resentment from some of the southern staff who looked to him to finance their operations, because he was unable to fund the expanded program which they desired.

Some of the unhappiness with Rich stemmed from the fact that he symbolized CORE's old dependence on white leadership. Yet this was not a crucial factor, for subsequently the hostility of some NAC members toward the staff coalesced around Wiley, and later, a very differently constituted NAC would fight McKissick during his tenure as national director. Given CORE's many problems, tension between the NAC and staff was probably inevitable. Hard as the staff might try to consult the NAC and keep it informed, the crisis environment in which CORE operated required rapid decision-making. Policy therefore tended to be set by the staff, and the frustrated and often angry NAC found itself frequently dealing with relatively trivial matters.

Epitomizing the nature of the relationship between the National Action Council and the administrative staff was the argument over Alan Gartner's appointment to succeed Marvin Rich. The NAC was not involved in the original decision to hire Gartner, which was made by Farmer and Wiley, in consultation with Rich. It was only after the Council learned that Gartner had been offered the job and had accepted, that some members angrily forced a reconsideration of the appointment. The decisions about both Gartner and Peck marked an unprecedented assertion of power on the part of the NAC, which had previously accepted the wishes of the national staff on personnel affairs.[34]

Farmer's own position was becoming increasingly untenable. Nothing of course would have seriously jeopardized his tenure with CORE if the organization had not continued to decline in membership and activity. But when Farmer suddenly departed for a month-long African trip at the end of 1964, leaving CORE with an acute financial crisis and other unsolved problems, he antagonized the NAC. An infuriated Floyd McKissick called a special meeting of the Steering Committee which, for lack of funds, had not met since October. He criticized Farmer for taking the trip without consulting the NAC, especially in the face of "a number of disturbing developments which raise serious questions about the continued viability of National CORE." In an unprecedented attack, McKissick, asserting the authority of the NAC, also denounced the national staff and implicitly Farmer for ignoring the Council on many matters and failing to inform it of what was happening in CORE: "It is our feeling that the lack of communication from the National office has made it impossible for the NAC to effectively discharge" its constitutional responsibility of governing between conventions. Retrenchment was imperative, but it was "inexcusable" that the national staff, without consulting or even informing the NAC, had recently made the major policy decisions to reduce sharply operations in NAC-authorized projects in Mississippi and Chicago. Moreover, "the failure of department heads to keep the NAC informed on a regular basis makes it impossible for the NAC to make any sound policy decisions." [35]

At the special Steering Committee meeting held in Farmer's absence, Wiley agreed to inform NAC members regularly of staff decisions, departmental activities, and other important developments. Although in the following months Wiley did much to bring administrative efficiency into CORE's operation, the fundamental problems remained. This fact, combined with the continuing undercurrent of criticism against Farmer, undoubtedly convinced the national director that his skill could be used more advantageously elsewhere. Accordingly he entered into negotiations with the Johnson Administration to head a national literacy program funded by the War on Poverty, thus paving the way for his withdrawal from CORE at the end of the year.[36]

Another issue which continued to gain force was the legitimacy of the use of retaliatory violence. Both the summer riots of 1964 and 1965 in the North and West, and the physical intimidation that produced CORE's alliance with the armed Deacons for Defense in Jonesboro and Bogalusa, Louisiana, increased skepticism about CORE's continuing commitment to nonviolence. When Rustin publicly criticized the growing talk in CORE about the necessity of violence, Marvin Rich, while emphasizing that the organization was still nonviolent, admitted that in recent workshops CORE members had devoted long sessions to the whole question of violence versus nonviolence.[37] Part of the problem involved confusion over definitions—the distinction between nonviolence as a way of life and nonviolence as a tactic on demonstrations; the difference between violence as a weapon of self-defense against specific attacks, and the employment of violence as a strategy of offense. But there was indeed a genuine shift in sentiment within CORE.

Among staff members in Mississippi and Louisiana, continuing experiences with racist violence fueled the growing feeling that some sort of armed self-defense was necessary and legitimate. A task force worker at Ferriday, Louisiana, during the summer of 1965 noted that while nonviolence characterized official CORE activities, self-defense in protection of one's person and home was "taken for granted;" indeed "most projects here in the dangerous areas have arms in the house to protect against night attacks." [38] By then CORE's relationship with the Deacons for Defense, who had first appeared in Jonesboro, had produced a national controversy. This organization, which arose in the summer of 1964 to combat the intimidation of civil rights workers and local citizens, did not shrink from shooting at whites when necessary. Thus on one occasion, some of its members returned fire when a group of Jonesboro whites shot into a carload of civil rights workers in a Negro neighborhood. In the spring of 1965 the Deacons formed a chapter in Bogalusa and on at least one occasion there they had fired a volley of shots at a carload of toughs who had thrown a stone through the window of a staff member's car.[39] In both towns there was a substantial overlap between the CORE-allied movement and the Deacons. In Bogalusa, A. Z. Young and Robert Hicks both belonged to the defense group, while the Civic and Voters League's treasurer, Charles Sims, was president of the local chapter of the Deacons. Moreover, CORE workers in both cities were friendly with the Deacons and grateful for their protection.[40]

This connection compelled CORE leaders to grapple with the paradox of remaining nonviolent while accepting support from a movement dedicated to retaliatory violence. At the NAC meeting in February Dennis defended the relationship, explaining that the Deacons were community people who "support CORE in all respects except in our nonviolent approach." Clearly the southern CORE staff approved the alliance, and in fact the commitment to nonviolence was already eroded among many of them. In June, one task force worker assigned to the Canton, Mississippi, project observed that the staff was willing "to still be popularly characterized as nonviolent while feeling bound to nonviolence less and less in practice." About the same time Richard Haley noted privately that a great diversity of opinion had developed among the southern personnel, with some still committed to nonviolence either philosophically or tactically, some admiring but not practicing "the 'judicious use of violence' "; and others "readily express[ing] their willingness to use violence themselves." CORE had, in effect, laid aside the idea of "serious inquiry into the practicability of nonviolence for either new or old staff." Personally, Haley believed that CORE should "cooperate with the Deacons as a civic group and when necessary as a protective agency." [41]

By mid-1965 CORE was willing to acknowledge openly its association with the Deacons, justifying the relationship by arguing the constitutional right of self-defense. CORE's stance was dramatically symbolized when Farmer arrived in Bogalusa for the funeral of the black deputy-sheriff, O'Neal Moore, who had been killed by white hoodlums. Sims met

Farmer at the airport and drove to town with a pistol on the seat beside him. Farmer informed the press at the time: "CORE is nonviolent, but we have no right to tell Negroes in Bogalusa or anywhere else that they do not have the right to defend their homes. It is a constitutional right." Moreover, Ernest Thomas, a Deacon leader in Jonesboro addressed the 1965 Convention, and Farmer frankly told the delegates how much CORE workers valued the Deacons' protection in Klan-infested towns of Louisiana.[42]

Nevertheless the Deacons were a touchy subject. Martin Luther King criticized Farmer and CORE for being allied with them. Privately Farmer found it "hard to understand Martin Luther King's inconsistency in attacking the Deacons . . . when he accepts the defense offered by bodyguards." Publicly Farmer explained that the Deacons were a well-disciplined group who did not seek violence but arose to protect "an embattled Negro community." He personally believed that nonviolence was "the only practical mechanism at this moment in our history." Yet "Negroes in this nation are down to about their last ounce of patience. For all the hoopla and the speechmaking and legislation, very little has changed in the reality of Negro life in this country. . . . Now if you accept that as fact—then it's clear that violence may be on the horizon. And if violence is on the horizon, I would certainly prefer to see it channeled into a defense discipline rather than the random homicide and the suicide of rioting." [43]

Among northern chapter people, meanwhile, CORE's stance on violence was also a subject of increasing discussion, fed by both the summer civil disorders and the publicity over the Deacons. Some militant chapter leaders were openly justifying a shift away from nonviolence. Lincoln Lynch, for example, in February 1965, asserted that demonstrators should defend themselves if attacked, and he urged CORE to "re-examine and redefine" its position. A few months later, addressing a march protesting black exclusion from the Wyandanch volunteer fire department, he told a cheering crowd, "The bigots in the firehouse will learn that we're going to stop turning the other cheek. Nonviolence is coming to an end." In fact, the main thrust for a shift in CORE's position came from certain chapters in the North and West rather than from the South. For southern blacks working with CORE, self-defense was a practical necessity which did not contradict the use of nonviolent direct action on demonstrations. As Ronnie Moore put it, "I am and have always been in favor of self-defense of one's home, but I have always held that direct action, which includes picketing, mass demonstrations, etc., must be non-violent. Not only for philosophical reasons must this exist, but it must exist for practical reasons. I know the reality of non-violence because I have worked in the South and I have inhaled tear gas. I have witnessed police brutality; I have ducked bullets, therefore, I knew when it was wise to pick up guns and when it was wise to be non-violent." In contrast the northern CORE people who espoused retaliatory violence did not carry guns, but the issue was a highly emotional one for them, requiring official organizational approval. It was the Northeastern Regional CORE Conference which at the suggestion of Brooklyn CORE presented the 1965 CORE Convention with a resolution stating that "CORE accepts the concept of self-defense by the Deacons, and believes that the use of guns by CORE workers on a Southern project is a personal decision," permissible if approved by the regional director.[44]

During the summer of 1965 the Watts riot in Los Angeles revealed the full extent of latent sympathy for violence among northern CORE people, both black and white. In the publication of the predominantly white Berkeley Campus CORE chapter, sociologist C. Wright Mills was quoted with approval:". . . violence is the final support of power, and the final resort of those who would contest it." Field Secretary Louis Smith stated, "I find it amusing that those who are quickest to condemn the revolt of the people in Watts, who were only asking to share in the American dream, are the people who worship our revolt against mother England. . . . Watts was saying to white America [that blacks refuse to] walk peacefully to the gas chambers." Farmer, attuned to CORE's traditions, to the more militant thrust of many young blacks and whites within the organization, and to the general public, said: "I unqualifiedly condemn the suicide of rioting. This is not the bridge to freedom . . . [yet] we must remember that the outrage of unemployment and hopelessness that pervades the ghetto remains a prelude to the outrage of the rifle and the gasoline bomb. When will this country learn the lesson written on the streets of Los Angeles?"[45] Basically, the Farmer administration's solution to the issues raised by the Deacons and the riots was set forth by Haley. On the one hand, he was deeply concerned over persistent reports that southern staff members had weapons, and in November 1965 he sent a memo advising them that, while it was only realistic to accept protection from the Deacons, CORE people could not "really reconcile nonviolence" with carrying guns while going about their daily activities. The Deacons' "practices are not CORE's", and he insisted that staffers must resign if they were unprepared to follow the organization's policy. On the other hand, he maintained that "non-violence might well have been adopted by Los Angeles Negroes had they received convincing evidence of its effectiveness. Likely they saw, as we in CORE have learned, that the most persistent nonviolent campaign . . . can yield at best a puny gradualism. The laws we have won are grudgingly written, passed, and enforced." Haley himself personally remained committed to nonviolence; but his pessimism reflected CORE's increasing ambiguity on the issue.[46]

Most of these cleavages came to a head at the 1965 Convention. In one respect, the convention held in Durham, North Carolina, showed how much CORE and the civil rights movement had accomplished. For with CORE visitors staying in the leading hotel, and meeting at the town's convention auditorium, and with merchants displaying "Welcome CORE" placards, Durham's reception was a far cry from the one that had greeted the Journey of Reconciliation eighteen years before.[47] In other respects, however, the convention revealed the serious problems facing CORE. The conclave was the most sparsely attended one in half a dozen years, the participants were informed of the grim fact that the fiscal year had ended with a $220,000 deficit,[48] and Farmer confidentially informed the NAC of his intention to resign early the following year.* [49] Moreover, although delegates seemed unanimous behind CORE's New Directions, the gathering was, with the possible exception of the 1954 Convention, the most divisive CORE had ever held. The growing gap between the southern field staff and the national organization, the question of legitimacy of violence, the black-white issue, and the Vietnam War dominated the proceedings.

The distrust that had been growing for months between southern field personnel and the national organization was thoroughly aired both at a preconvention meeting of the staff and NAC and on the floor of the convention, with each side blaming the other for CORE's fumbling. Criticizing the whole "bureaucracy of CORE," Oretha Castle and Rudy Lom-

---

* In the end, however, the Johnson Administration refused to fund the project. (See *Times,* March 5, July 4, 1966; NAC, March 18–20, 1966, SEDF; Pittsburgh *Courier.* April 30, 1966; Sargent Shriver to Farmer, Aug. 4, 1966, Farmer Prs.) Because the intention was to have this Center for Community Action Education work closely with SNCC and CORE, and to give it an activist thrust similar to the CORE-inspired Headstart programs in Louisiana, the big-city mayors reportedly prevailed upon Johnson to withdraw the funds allocated for it. (Interviews.)

bard denounced the NAC for "politicking" at national conventions and operating without contact with the field staff or knowledge of its thinking. Mat Suarez complained that "Task force workers feel like step-children," while another southern staff member maintained, "The gripe is that the National Office has no consideration for the southern office." Field personnel in other parts of the country were also disaffected. Winston Lockett, who serviced the Midwest, protested that "Staff people feel that their basic integrity and loyalty to CORE is being questioned," while Mike Lesser, who was now working in the North declared, "I have no problems relating to individuals but have trouble relating to NAC and the national office." On the floor of the convention Richard Jewett, expressing his dismay at all the wrangling, broke down in tears, declaring, "CORE is in trouble. The movement is in trouble." [50]

There was much sentiment at the Convention in favor of a strong statement about the legitimacy of retaliatory violence. The Resolutions Committee "questioned severely" CORE's position on nonviolence, and the Constitution Committee debated deleting from the preamble the reference to nonviolent methods. The push for rescinding CORE's commitment to nonviolence was so strong that it was turned back only by the intervention of Deacon leader Ernest Thomas, who explained to key delegates that the Deacons and other southern blacks recognized the necessity of nonviolence on demonstrations. The Deacons, he said, would be prepared with guns to defend the demonstrators if necessary, but it was important for CORE to maintain its traditional position. His remarks and Farmer's careful distinction between the use of nonviolence on demonstrations, to which CORE's rules applied, and the constitutional right of self-defense, to which they did not apply, swayed the Convention to take no action. Nevertheless, the drift of sentiment was clear, and the stage had been set for the repeal of the constitution's nonviolent clause at the 1966 Convention.[51]

The varied impulses toward separatism, notably the growing skepticism about integration as a goal and the rising criticism of white participation also erupted during the Convention. No longer could CORE people take for granted that racial integration was a unifying purpose. Symbolically, the organization's shifting stance was epitomized by McKissick's inviting Black Muslims to be convention speakers for the first time in CORE's history. When one of them told the audience that all white men "were created evil," James Farmer "winced visibly." [52] At the NAC and staff meeting, Wilfred Ussery maintained that "desegregation as a goal is preferable" to integration, and Ruth Turner received considerable support for her categorical statement, "Developing the power of the community is the goal. . . . Integration is not a goal at this point." On the opening day of the Convention William Bradley took the floor to denounce white liberals and CORE's dependence upon them. Both he and Ussery insisted that it was imperative for CORE to develop fund-raising in the black community. Declared Bradley, "In fund-raising, until blacks support the movement we can't go anywhere. . . . We don't need professional fund-raisers. Start asking the people in the streets [for nickels and dimes]. . . . *Go* to the barroom. Talk to the people. *That's* where the money is." Other delegates declared that they resented the past help of whites, claimed that whites had never helped CORE much anyway, or asserted that they did not require the whites' future help.[53]

Reflecting similar sentiments, the NAC appointed Gartner to head the fund-raising department with the definite understanding that when a black was obtained for the job Gartner would step aside.[54] The Council also abolished the *CORE-lator,* officially because it did "not effectively portray the 'new' CORE." However, Peck, charging that this had been done only because he was white and had argued for CORE's interracial traditions, wrote Farmer denouncing the decision and reviewing his long history of dedicated service to the organization. Later when Peck was asked to consider handling a revamped *CORE-lator* on a temporary basis, he declined, since, as NAC member Olly Leeds informed him, the prevailing view was that the permanent editor must be black.[55] More explicit in its actions than the NAC, the Convention also moved to place definite limitations on the part that whites might play in CORE. The Constitution Committee, chaired by Bradley, even discussed the possibility of omitting from the description of CORE's purpose the statement that it was a multiracial organization. While discarding this proposal, the Committee did report an amendment that would have required all chapter leaders to be black. When the matter was brought to the convention floor, Harold Brown expressed surprise at the number of whites who disliked the proposal, and he accused them of revealing an inferiority complex. The new clause was passed, somewhat modified, providing that members from the minority community "shall substantially constitute the leadership" of the chapters.[56] Ironically, this amendment was pushed through at a time when blacks dominated the leadership in most chapters, and even more significantly on the NAC, where the only white member in 1965–66 was Ralph Rosenfeld, the Midwest Regional Chairman completing his two-year term. These actions at the National Convention intensified the tendency among black chapter leaders to limit white participation. It was after Durham, for example, that Walter Brooks, the chairman of New Haven CORE, openly began to discuss the idea of redefining the role of whites in his affiliate.[57]

The heated final session of the Convention was devoted to the Vietnam War. A week before the conclave, Martin Luther King had publicly denounced continued American involvement in Vietnam. The majority of delegates opposed the war, yet many believed that if CORE took such a position, a substantial number of the organization's supporters, both black and white, would be alienated. After a lengthy debate, a resolution was passed, condemning the Johnson Administration's "immoral policy of racism abroad" and demanding "an immediate withdrawal of all American troops" from Vietnam. Yet because of intense cross pressures, a majority had abstained from voting. Farmer who personally opposed the war but regarded the resolution as tactically imprudent, thereupon urged the Convention to reverse itself on the grounds that "this is not a point on which we would get the unanimous support of the ghetto community, and therefore, although individuals surely should support the move, organizationally we should not get out of step with the community." With CORE people emotionally committed to being in step with the black ghetto, the Convention thereupon tabled the Vietnam resolution, to the outrage of Olly Leeds, Lincoln Lynch, and other chapter leaders who had worked for its passage.[58]

Although all of CORE's problems received a thorough discussion during the Convention, none of them had been solved. In the following months conditions, if anything, grew worse. CORE's finances did not improve. Field staff needs remained critical, chapter activity continued to falter, and communications between the affiliates and the national office further deteriorated. Despite McCain's repeated requests since the Convention, by October only ten chapters had submitted reports on activities and current officer-and-address lists. The black-white issue grew more salient, the alienation of the southern field staff continued to simmer, and the NAC was wrestling unhappily with the organization's ineffectiveness, unsure of exactly what to do. At the end of the year, Ussery complained about the persistence of "a huge gap between the staff and the NAC in terms of information available to it with which to make decisions," and the Council's continuing failure to "solve the problem of how it shall move and discharge its responsibilities." [59]

CORE's malaise, its crisis of confidence, involved something far more profound than finances and structure, or even the disruptive relations between blacks and whites within the organization. As one behavioral scientist who observed the organization, concluded, CORE's basic problem was the uncertainty generated by its "changing mission," as it moved from attacking "overt discrimination to fighting more basic and murky areas like persistent unemployment, poverty, inadequate education, and so on. . . . A shift of the magnitude that CORE is attempting is very difficult, since this shift involves changing the organizational attitudes and expanding the human skills of the membership. In the transition period, the difficulties and frustrations involved lead people to blame each other, to feel guilty, and in general to react in unproductive ways." "Symptoms" such as resignations, inactivity, the collapse of individual chapters, "must be understood as *by-products of the changing mission.*" Similarly Ruth Turner, in evaluating CORE's problems, noted the shift "from pure civil rights issues to complex socio-economic issues. Past action against racism has become action to eliminate the effects of racism." Thus the chapters, which had known how to expose racial discrimination through direct action, now lacked the skills and patience to organize ghetto residents for dealing with complex socio-economic problems. "There is," she said, "an emotional hang-up of chapter members with 'Freedom Now.' Expecting instant freedom, they are unable to plan, think, study laws, and develop long-range proposals. Expecting instant results they are often unable to spend time in communities developing leadership there."

Turner believed that CORE's goal at this point should be building the power of the black community. Increasingly, in fact, CORE leaders had come to think more in terms of power than of moral appeals, thus adumbrating the popularity of the Black Power slogan. As William Bradley said, "unlike Martin Luther King, I do not feel we can appeal to the consciences of white America." Farmer's address to the Convention had been pitched in terms of placing blacks "in a position of power," a theme that had received considerable attention at the NAC and staff meeting just before. Harold Brown had summed up the feeling of many at the gathering when he said, "The Negro wants to share in power. We need to find the means for getting that power." Similarly, at the Northeast Regional Action Council meeting in August 1965, one delegate articulated the tenor of the conference when he asserted, "Organizing in low income areas is for power." [60]

Yet power was exactly what CORE lacked. Not only was the organization less influential than it had been at any time since before the Freedom Ride, but neither the chapters nor the national office had the resources or techniques for tapping the potential power of the black poor. Aside from financial insolvency, which prevented the hiring of full-time people to staff real community centers, the chapters were simply unable to sink roots in the ghetto. Ruth Turner charged them with " 'elitism' which holds us back. People who do not share *our* view of the struggle, exhibit *our* commitment, etc., simply cannot be on the 'in crowd.' Thus we leave out most of the community, and CORE chapters are often unrepresentative of the people they represent. Therefore chapters have often not involved people with the resources to solve organizational problems." In frustration CORE leaders became defensive and defeatist. Field Secretary Joyce Ware held that "CORE cannot define what is freedom for people. Work with the people, they will decide what they want. . . . We have nothing to say or do for the people in the ghetto, but we can try." In part this reflected an ideological commitment to building ghetto programs around "felt needs"; but it also reflected the failure of chapters to relate successfully to the black poor. As Washington CORE's chairman, Roena Rand said: "We must learn how to go into the community" without paternalistic benevolence. "We can no longer be leaders." Farmer himself maintained that "We made a mistake when we first started by recruiting Negroes in the middle class economic group and ignoring those in poverty areas. I hope it is not too late to communicate with those we have forgotten." And Wiley summed up the situation when he later recalled that "basically the problem really was going to center on building grass-roots community organizations and on having a substantial mass-based network of such organizations to deal with the political structure . . . [and mount] a direct assault on the problem of poverty. . . . Our people were professional and middle-class, very activist, but . . . unless CORE itself could become a grass-roots organization of poor people . . . it was going to be difficult for it to be the vehicle directly representative of those interests." [61] Thus the problem as seen by all CORE leaders, from interracialists like Wiley to separatists like Turner, was how to get a basically middle-class black organization to work effectively among the black poor.

In this crisis, intense conflict and bitterness were inevitable,[62] and these were strikingly evident in the circumstances surrounding the selection of Farmer's successor as national director in January 1966. The two leading contenders were Floyd McKissick and George Wiley. McKissick was the candidate of the separatist contingent on the NAC—notably Ussery, Bradley, Turner, and Lynch,—while Wiley, who was favored by most of the staff, also had substantial backing on the NAC among chapter leaders like Marlene Wilson, Robert Curvin, and Shirley Lacey. Although both candidates in their presentations to the NAC stressed that CORE must "get into the black community," Wiley's critics charged that he had "difficulty dealing with black people and surrounded himself with whites," meaning that he was still an integrationist who believed that whites could play an important role in the movement. Often underlying this line of argument was also resentment at his having a white wife. As one national staff member recollected, it was a choice between a "brilliant university professor married to a white woman, and a down-home lawyer who sounded black." Farmer, who had originally favored Wiley, wavered. After much agonizing he finally took the position that McKissick rather than Wiley had the "empathy and ability to articulate the feelings of the ghetto." In the end, with Ruth Turner having effectively laid the groundwork, and with Farmer swinging enough votes to clinch the outcome, McKissick was victorious, twelve to eight.[63]

The selection of McKissick was widely criticized in many of the chapters. It would, of course, be difficult to say how representative of the affiliates the NAC was at this point, though interview evidence suggests that the sparsely attended 1965 Convention, which had elected the Council, was disproportionately weighted with delegations from separatist-oriented chapters. Certainly it is clear that the chief support for him, and for the nationalist tendencies which he at this time represented, came from several chapters in California, Cleveland, and New York City, whose leaders played the key role in shaping the NAC's decision.

Dissatisfaction and rebelliousness at McKissick's election were angrily voiced at meetings of the Regional Action Councils over the next few months. Critics questioned the haste with which the decision was made, without giving chapters an opportunity to express themselves. They also deplored the $4000 increase in the national director's salary which McKissick had insisted on at a time when CORE was deeply in debt and when nothing had been done to alleviate the plight of the task force workers.[64] Some in the opposition, like Curvin, remained in CORE because of organizational loyalty; others drifted away. Moreover, a substantial loss of CORE staff followed. Wiley resigned soon after the election, as did people closely associated with him. Many field personnel also resigned. Mike Lesser, who denounced the national office for an insensitiv-

ity that had brought about the departure of individuals like Wiley and
Lombard, was dismissed after being charged by the new organization de-
partment director, Herbert Callender, with "conspiracy" to "disrupt"
CORE. Within a few months Gartner was also dismissed; Haley and
Dennis, facing ruinous cuts in the southern regional office budget re-
signed; and McCain took a position with SEDF. In the summer of 1966
Ronnie Moore, who was by then also working with Marvin Rich at the
Scholarship Fund, sadly called a roll of CORE's great leaders who had
resigned:

> Long before Floyd McKissick convened the 23rd Annual Convention
> of CORE, I had decided that the spirit, commitment, attitudes, and
> sacrifices that had made CORE, had long died. It started when mem-
> bers like Jim Peck, who was beaten in Alabama and ripped across
> the face with a knife necessitating 57 stitches, was fired without
> being notified. It continued when Jerome Smith, Freedom Rider,
> who received brain injuries in the McComb, Mississippi incident,
> was fired without notice. The list could go on and the names would
> include Rudolph Lombard; Dave Dennis; Richard Haley; and con-
> tinue with those who were fired or left CORE because they realized
> CORE was changing. [65]

Clearly an era in the history of the Congress of Racial Equality .had
ended. The way had now been prepared for CORE's espousal of Black
Power in the summer of 1966, and its ultimate shift toward an unequivocally nationalist ideology.

Epilogue

The change of administration solved none of CORE's problems. The financial crisis deepened. There were only a few viable chapters. CORE's leaders sought to again place CORE at the "cutting edge" of the black protest movement by taking an increasingly nationalist stance. Yet the longed-for welling of support in the black community eluded them. Schisms wracked the organization. Finally, when stability was restored two and a half years after Farmer's departure, what survived was essentially a small national office exercising tight control over a handful of active chapters and committed to a program of black separatism.

Under McKissick's leadership the national office pushed forward on the "New Directions." CORE leaders soft-pedaled integration and heightened their commitment to improving the conditions of ghetto life. As McKissick declared, "What the Negro wants is total equality. And that does not mean integration all the time. He wants his self-identity. He wants his culture." One of his very first actions after being elected national director was to move CORE's headquarters to Harlem in August, saving about $1000 a month in rent. More significant was the move's symbolic importance in promoting CORE's new black image and dramatizing its intense desire "to relate to the black community." [1]

In the spring of 1966 the national organization embarked upon a major "Target City" project in Baltimore, intended as a showcase demonstration of how the power of the black poor could be mobilized for their own advancement. While the Baltimore CORE affiliate continued its campaign to integrate a middle-income apartment house, the members of the interracial staff which the national office sent to the city created a highly varied program among the slumdwellers. They developed the Maryland Freedom Union, which sought better wages and hours for black workers in several white-owned ghetto stores; organized welfare mothers, who demanded more money from state and city officials; and started tenant groups, who hoped to obtain reduced rents and improved housing conditions. In politics, "Target City" embarked on a campaign to redistrict the city and create "a real base of power" for the election of more black councilmen. In November, with U. S. Department of Labor funds, it inaugurated a program to train high school dropouts as gas station attendants and managers. Despite all of these promising beginnings, "Target City" suffered from internal racial tensions, and because of inadequate funding foundered completely in the spring of 1967 when the director departed amid mutual recriminations with CORE's national headquarters concerning the financing and management of the project.[2]

Elsewhere CORE's activity amounted to relatively little. Herbert Callender, who replaced McCain as head of the Organization Department, visited the chapters and found his worst fears confirmed. Estimating that one-third of the affiliates had never seen a field secretary, he reported that many were either paper chapters or still lacked real roots in the black community and thus failed to "help the people organize themselves so that their economic and political power can ooze forward to eliminate 'the problems.'" In March 1966, at a training institute for northeastern chapter leaders, he observed that the conferees were baffled about "how to get into the community to organize the people in the ghetto." Privately, he noted, "A point brought out in the discussion around community organization by nearly everyone was that there are no longer available major issues around which communities can be organized. Goals are short-ranged; and local block associations, organized to fight housing problems, break up once their goals are accomplished. A question that was raised by a majority of the chapter people was 'Where do we go from here?'" Some months later, a Western Regional Convention similarly aired complaints that "Most of us do not know how to organize," that the chapters "are not dealing with the problems of the poor people. . . . It has been ourselves that is keeping us out of the ghetto." [3] Thus at the very time that CORE was most fully committed to the community action approach, the chapters, short of money, expertise, and manpower, found it enormously difficult to make a success of it. Yet, soon the intense self-criticism in which CORE members had engaged about their inability to relate to the black poor practically disappeared. It was as if CORE's internal crisis—itself partly a result of this failure to implement the "New Directions"—was so serious that leaders quarreled with one another and turned to a militant rhetoric of Black Power.

Farmer's departure not only came at a time when CORE activity was in serious decline but also coincided with a sharp drop in the organization's income. A short time after taking office, McKissick noted, "our main program for the next six months, by necessity, is going to be fundraising." Receipts toppled from $44,500 in January 1966 to $19,900 in February; by the end of April they had dropped "alarmingly" to $250 a day.[4] Total income during the fiscal year was probably about $400,000, but most of it was collected before Farmer left on March 1.[5] A few months later, by the time of the convention held in Baltimore, CORE had been forced to reduce its national office personnel by one-third, the Southern Regional Office had been closed, and the rest of the staff had not been paid in eight weeks. McKissick, in fact, became so involved in rescuing the organization from its financial morass that some associates felt he lacked time to develop a viable CORE program.[6]

Financial problems were intensified by a growing rupture with CORE-SEDF. The two organizations were undergoing an ideological divergence: CORE was moving in a more nationalist direction, while SEDF, though sponsoring community organization work, remained committed to interracialism, with Marvin Rich presiding as executive director over a mixed staff. The split was hastened in February 1966 when a black official of Mt. Vernon, New York, CORE publicly told a Jewish opponent in a de facto school segregation controversy that "Hitler . . . didn't kill enough of you." The incident alarmed many Jews, and in the ensuing furor the official resigned, while Farmer, condemning the remark as "intolerable," insisted that "There is no room in CORE for racism or bigotry of any sort." But Will Maslow, executive secretary of the American Jewish Congress, charging that CORE had failed to take prompt and decisive disciplinary action, angrily resigned from the Advisory Committee amidst considerable publicity.[7] Since Jews were, as the new associate national director Lincoln Lynch noted, "predominant" among CORE's contributors, the "Mt. Vernon incident" had "tremendous repercussions" for both CORE and SEDF.[8] A short time afterward, CORE-SEDF dropped CORE from its name and henceforth was known as the Scholarship Educational and Defense Fund for Racial Equality. Although SEDFRE continued to pay most of CORE's legal expenses and gave sub-

stantial assistance to CORE's 1966 southern summer program, misunderstandings continued to accumulate and culminated in November with
Rachlin's resignation as CORE's general counsel.[9]

Meanwhile CORE was deeply affected by the ebb and flow of sentiment among militant blacks and by the broader developments on the national scene. The swelling sense of pride stemming from the successes of
the black protest of the early 1960's, disappointment with the Johnson
Administration and the white liberals, the fragmentation of the movement, the enormous difficulties in overcoming the problems of the black
masses, and the riots that erupted spontaneously in 1964–65, all prepared
the way for the era of Black Power that emerged in 1966. The precipitating event that made the slogan famous was the June 1966 "Freedom
March" of James Meredith, who had achieved national fame in 1962 by
his successful effort to integrate the University of Mississippi. Meredith
had decided that a dramatic way to interest more Mississippi Negroes in
voter registration was to demonstrate that he could walk unharmed
through the state during primary election week. He had hardly begun
the journey when he was wounded by a would-be assassin's bullet. National civil rights leaders rushed to Meredith's hospital bedside in Memphis
and planned for a renewed march. There followed a disagreement over
strategy between Floyd McKissick and Stokely Carmichael on the one
hand and Whitney Young and Roy Wilkins on the other, with Martin
Luther King vainly attempting to play the role of conciliator. King,
Carmichael, and McKissick resumed the march amidst harassments and
taunts from jeering whites. A leadership schism of major proportions was
revealed, with King continuing to preach "black and white together" and
Carmichael calling for "Black Power." The latter received great public
attention with the electrifying phrase, and McKissick employed a similar
rhetoric. At the march's final rally in Jackson, CORE's new national
director declared, "1966 shall be remembered as the year we left our im-
posed status of Negroes and became *Black Men* . . . 1966 is the year of
the concept of Black Power. The year when black men realized their full
worth in society—their dignity and their beauty—and their power—the
greatest power on the earth—the power of *right*." [10]

The fact that CORE, like SNCC, became identified with black separatism, while the other leading civil rights organizations did not, was no accident. Contemporaries bracketed both organizations together as the left
wing of the movement, placing CORE somewhat to the right of SNCC in

militance. There were indeed several parallels between the two—their moralistic fervor, the extraordinary courage and total commitment exhibited by many of their members, their dislike of compromise, their concern with the problems of the poor, their inclination toward community organization, their suspicion of established leadership in the black middle class, in the Democratic Party, and among white liberals, and their tendency to view the future in millenarian terms.[11] These similarities stemmed from several sources. SNCC's militance and organizational charisma made it a reference group for many CORE members, who greatly admired the former's bravery and style. The two organizations recruited people, mostly youth, who were drawn by the militant image and by the opportunity for personal participation. Both SNCC and CORE thus attracted dedicated individuals with high expectations who experienced extraordinary frustration at the slow pace of social change, and in their disillusionment turned in a separatist direction.

It should be emphasized, of course, that in many fundamental respects the two were different. CORE was a federation of local groups, with a relatively weak national board and staff providing a moderate degree of coordination. SNCC, on the other hand, although originally a coalition of college groups, had become by 1963 an organization of staff people who initiated projects in local communities throughout the South. CORE, moreover, had begun as an explicitly interracial organization. SNCC, although attracting a number of whites to the staff, was from the start a black movement, and throughout its history the major officials were Negroes. Finally, CORE members were more varied in their degree of commitment to the cause and in the extent to which they would accept compromises on specific issues.[12] For the most dedicated CORE activists, as for SNCC people, the movement became a way of life, which took up practically every moment of time not spent in earning a living. But CORE, being a membership rather than a staff organization, included many who participated on a limited, part-time basis. More important, CORE, to a far greater degree than SNCC, included among its leaders those who mixed their moralism and idealism with a good dash of pragmatism, and a frank willingness to compromise when this seemed necessary. In addition there was still a sizable leaven of CORE members who were more tolerant of other viewpoints and organizations than the typical SNCC person. In short, SNCC members were more likely than CORE people to be True Believers. For all of these reasons CORE moved much more slowly than SNCC toward a black separatist position, and articulated an interpretation of Black Power notably less radical than SNCC's.

The 1966 CORE Convention met in Baltimore amid the excitement that had been precipitated by Stokely Carmichael's use of Black Power on the Meredith March. In three key respects the proceedings carried the thrust of the 1965 Convention to its logical conclusion—endorsing the Black Power slogan, discarding CORE's commitment to nonviolence, and reversing CORE's policy of eschewing an official organizational position on the Vietnam War. Although it should be emphasized that opinion was far from unified, the 1966 Convention clearly revealed the change which CORE had undergone in the preceding months. Carmichael himself addressed the conclave, helping to make Black Power its watchword. "We don't need white liberals. . . . We have to make integration irrelevant," he told his audience. Much confusion existed among the delegates —as among activists outside of CORE—regarding the meaning of Black Power. Interpretations ranged from "doing just what we have been doing," through black pride and unity, to complete separatism. Roy Innis, Harlem CORE chairman, led the battle that officially put the Convention on record as declaring "Racial co-existence through Black Power," rather than integration, constituted "the only meaningful way to total equality."

Yet the endorsement of Black Power did not go entirely unopposed. The small number of white delegates were a silent minority who "refrained as much as possible from participating in open discussions," but a few black delegates openly questioned CORE's uncritical embrace of Black Power. Robert Curvin, whose position represented the sentiments of a substantial minority at the Convention, maintained that the slogan's implications needed to be carefully considered. He held that a redistribution of power in America was needed so that "the poor both black and white can participate in the running of the country." In his view there did not exist in the black community the resources necessary for an organization like CORE to "go it alone," without white support.[13]

Considerable debate also occurred over CORE's position on nonviolence. McKissick himself described nonviolence as "a dying philosophy" that had "outlived its usefulness." While the Convention narrowly defeated a constitutional amendment to allow explicitly the affiliation of local groups which favored violence for self-defense during demonstrations, the delegates voted to delete the "technique of nonviolence in direct action" as a requirement for chapter affiliation. Moreover they approved a resolution which maintained that "the concept of nonviolence and self-defense are not contradictory," and that CORE's adherence to nonviolent direct action did not deny "the natural, constitutional, and inalienable right of self-defense." [14]

On the Vietnam War issue CORE's position had already been jelled by McKissick, who had become an outspoken critic of the war. In January, both he and Farmer had issued a joint statement declaring, "The escalation of that war is wrong, we believe. The war which must be escalated is the war against poverty and discrimination." In April the Northeastern Regional Action Council had overwhelmingly denounced the war as a racist and diversionary effort to stifle civil rights protest. The CORE Convention ratified this policy by not only condemning the American involvement in Southeast Asia but also pledging support to draft resisters. Afterward, McKissick joined a "Citizens' Mission to Cambodia" to investigate allegations of a Vietcong sanctuary there. When he returned, he declared there were no sanctuaries and denounced the United States for unprovoked raids on neutral Cambodian villages.[15]

At first Black Power articulated a mood rather than a program. Well on the way to becoming a household phrase by the time of the CORE Convention, it generated intense discussion about its real meaning, and a broad spectrum of ideologies and programmatic proposals emerged. SNCC and CORE, the two major groups to embrace the Black Power thrust, developed rather different interpretations. Although neither had a monolithic viewpoint, broadly speaking SNCC called for complete exclusion of whites from the movement; espoused independent political action outside the established parties; questioned the value of political alliance with other groups until blacks themselves built a substantial independent power base; and applauded the idea of guerilla warfare. CORE, while not disapproving of SNCC's strategy, was more flexible. At this point it still employed a few white staff members, advocated alliances with other groups and working within the Democratic Party to overthrow the established machine leadership, and, while justifying riots as the natural explosion of the oppressed against intolerable conditions, sanctioned violence only in self-defense. Although favorable toward economic cooperatives, it was more inclined toward job-training programs and developing a black entrepreneurial class based upon the market within the black ghetto. Basically, in the words of the 1966 CORE Convention resolution, Black Power meant "control of economic, political, and educational institutions and resources, from top to bottom, by black people in their own areas." [16]

McKissick justified "revolution" as a constitutional right and maintained that "Many good things have occurred for blacks as a result of violence," [17] but CORE's practical concerns lay elsewhere. For McKissick, the common goal underlying the divergent views among black people was "self-determination—the right to control one's own destiny." The black masses "have learned that integration is not possible in this society and the only alternative is for Black people to exercise the power over their own destinies." In accord with the 1966 Convention definition of Black Power, he called for local community control of schools, police, and courts; for the transfer of ownership of land and businesses in the ghettos to the blacks. Likewise, Ruth Turner, who became special assistant to the national director, defined Black Power as "the organizing of the black community for the purpose of promoting the interests and concerns of black people." Arguing that Black Power meant "the reaffirmation of the concept of a pluralistic American society," she contended that throughout American history other ethnic groups had united to obtain power without being forced to lose their identity. For CORE leaders this ideology was clearly reformist rather than revolutionary, and in application was anything but rigid. McKissick explained that "integrated quality education is still a desirable goal and there must be Federal action to insure integration wherever feasible," but in the major ghettos only community control of the schools would guarantee a high level of education. Politically he believed that Negroes needed to be opportunistic—moving where necessary to form a third political force outside the major parties; working within the Democratic Party where practical. Alliances with sympathetic white groups would be part of this strategy, but united blacks must be the dominant force in coalitions. Economically, McKissick's proposals ranged from entrepreneurial "black capitalism" through cooperatives and credit unions, to expanded federal antipoverty, housing, and employment programs. Ruth Turner pointed out that in CORE's program Black Power was exemplified by projects such as the Maryland Freedom Union, the marketing cooperative of sweet potato farmers organized by a task force worker in Louisiana, Louis Smith's job-training program known as "Operation Bootstrap" in Los Angeles, and the efforts to organize blacks into a united voting bloc in a number of communities.[18]

At the start of his term of office as national director, McKissick blurred the separatist implications of his remarks. At the final rally on the Meredith March he asserted, "Many men say they are afraid of what will happen when black power is fully accepted. But they *know* the black man's goals: they are the same as theirs." He charged that the Black Power philosophy was being "misinterpreted to mean violence and fascism." Actually, "Black Power . . . is a Movement dedicated to the exercise of American democracy in its highest tradition. . . . Black Power is not Black supremacy; it is a unified Black Voice reflecting racial pride in the tradition of our heterogeneous nation. Black Power does not mean the exclusion of White Americans from the Negro Revolution; it means the inclusion of all men in a common moral and political struggle." As the months passed, however, McKissick, pressed by leaders like Roy Innis and William Bradley, tended to become more explicitly separatist in his utterances. By the time he left office in 1968, he spoke of black people having detached destinies, living as a "nation within a nation." [19]

Having aligned CORE under the banner of Black Power, McKissick was only modestly successful in his attempts to reassure the dwindling number of CORE supporters who had been attracted by the organization's philosophy of interracialism and nonviolence. Homer Jack, one of CORE's white founders, enthusiastically endorsed the new thrust. James Farmer staunchly supported it. In an effort to counter the effect of Maslow's resignation, Farmer joined advisory board member Rabbi Arthur J. Lelyveld, president of the American Jewish Congress, in signing a fund-raising appeal designed to convince white contributors: "No true friend of CORE has ever failed to understand that the role of the white man in our struggle is more crucial now than ever before." [20] Lillian Smith, the southern white supporter who had served on the national advisory committee for two decades, promptly resigned, and, in a reference to her famous antiracist novel of the 1940's, condemned "the new *Killers of the Dream.*" A. Philip Randolph, who had served on the advisory committee since its inception, was similarly a critic of the new direction in which CORE was moving. [21]

The immediate result of the Black Power controversy was that more whites turned away from CORE. In a three-page appeal declaring that without financial help "CORE can die this year," McKissick acknowledged that the issue of Black Power had been "a wedge . . . driven between the Negro members of leading civil rights organizations and their traditional white liberal support." At first the impact of the Black Power approach produced another concerted effort to obtain major financing from within the black community. Lincoln Lynch, on the eve of the 1966

Convention, pointedly noted, "The black people cannot expect to ride to freedom on the purse strings of white people." But within a few months it became evident that the plans to raise substantial funds from blacks had failed. At year's end McKissick reported that appeal letters recently sent to a list of predominantly middle-class blacks "had given the poorest response." [22] By then, CORE faced bankruptcy—its monthly income from July through November having averaged only $22,000. McKissick, whose highest priority was to save the organization, decided to embark upon an austerity policy, even if that meant having to sacrifice a programmatic thrust. In January 1967 he announced that CORE's debt had been cut from $350,000—where it had stood at the end of the summer—to about $275,000—with economies effected by pruning the staff, curtailing national projects, and offering creditors settlements at twenty-five cents on the dollar.[23]

The chapters' immediate response to National CORE's adoption of Black Power was mixed. Although supported by separatist-oriented affiliates like Harlem, Cleveland, and San Francisco, there was ambivalence in some chapters and outright opposition in others. For example, at the post-convention discussions in Philadelphia CORE, some whites were perplexed and others bitterly resentful at what they regarded as rejection of their contribution. In endorsing the Convention's action, the Boston chapter issued a statement describing Black Power as an apt phrase for what the affiliate had been doing in housing, education, and employment all along. A black chapter in Winston-Salem, North Carolina, considered switching its affiliation to SCLC; while the white chairman of the predominantly white Binghamton, New York, chapter declared, "We're all [both blacks and whites] confused and very much alarmed by the new slogans and believe they need clarification." The predominantly Negro St. Louis CORE endorsed the Convention resolution on Black Power, "with the deletion of all reference to racial co-existence replacing integration as the philosophy and ultimate goal of the movement." Finally, there were those affiliates that were openly critical. Willie F. Williams, the black chairman of the mainly white Middlesex County, New Jersey, CORE, publicly asked whether the national organization had abandoned interracialism and nonviolence, and soon afterward the chapter ceased functioning, with its leaders deliberately turning instead to War on Poverty and human relations activities. And in Seattle, with its half-white membership, John Cornethan, the Negro chairman, pointedly declared that Black Power was not the position of his chapter, which passed a resolution that "there is still a vital role for Caucasians to play in CORE." [24]

There was, in fact, considerable sentiment in CORE for continued white participation. At the Convention some delegates had expressed the view that "Black Power in the ghetto is needed, but it is not necessarily needed in CORE itself." McKissick himself was not an advocate of white exclusion. He had expressed concern about the loss of white members, and employed a white woman as his secretary despite considerable criticism.[25] Several white task force workers remained on the national staff, and in March 1967 two were promoted to field secretary. The composition of the national advisory board remained nearly half-white, but except for Eugene Tournour, who succeeded Ralph Rosenfeld as North Central Regional Vice Chairman, the NAC was all black.[26]

Inexorable pressures were mounting to transform CORE into an all-black organization. After the Baltimore Convention whites steadily became a smaller minority in most chapters. Despite his "highest qualifications," Tournour's own Chicago chapter urged his recall from the NAC on the grounds that "in this era of the struggle the leadership *must* be a reflection of those communities we are endeavoring to reach." In Newark CORE there were heated discussions about the role of whites. Although no policy decision was explicitly spelled out, the whites, many of whom were already doubtful that they could participate effectively in the community organization thrust, had almost completely withdrawn by the end of 1966. After the 1967 CORE Convention deleted the word "multiracial" from the constitution, McKissick informed the *New York Times* that this would "let the world know the direction that CORE is going." [27] Subsequently, even in chapters like Boston, Kansas City, Missouri, and Seattle, which had operated very successfully as interracial groups, white participation practically disappeared. In Boston the withdrawal of almost all the remaining whites, who had continued to perform most of the routine and clerical duties and to provide the backbone of financial support, reduced an already weakened chapter to virtual inactivity by the middle of 1967. When Cornethan, who was still the Seattle CORE chairman, publicly criticized the Convention's action as a move to drive out the remaining whites, he was ousted from his post in September by a dissident faction.

Among the last affiliates to maintain consciously a policy of interracial membership was the predominantly black Kansas City CORE. One of the most active of the remaining chapters, it had an unusually successful job campaign with chain stores and downtown merchants during the summer of 1967. Shortly afterward, in the face of an attempt to limit the role of whites in the chapter, Kansas City CORE declared that the goals of Black Power could be won by an interracial group and "reaffirmed its policy of including whites in its membership and permitting them to hold office." Yet, at the end of 1968 majority sentiment in the chapter, which was by now more than 80 per cent black, had swung overwhelmingly in the opposite direction, and the group soon afterward ceased to function.[28] Actually, by the time National CORE officially excluded whites from active membership in the summer of 1968, they had already virtually disappeared from nearly all the chapters.

Meanwhile, chapter activity had not visibly increased, and the Baltimore Target City project was collapsing. Nevertheless, McKissick hopefully entered into negotiations with the Ford Foundation, and in July 1967 secured a $175,000 grant for voter registration, job-training, and leadership instruction in Cleveland. In the era of summer riots and the revolutionary rhetoric of SNCC, the Ford Foundation clearly sought to develop the potentialities inherent in CORE's moderate, reformist version of Black Power. National Program Director Antoine Perot, Jr., a former leader in Cleveland CORE, stated, "We hope to make Cleveland a model of what can be done in big cities to improve the lot of Negroes and forestall violence." The Cleveland chapter, whose membership had plummeted from its heyday in 1964, was rejuvenated by the grant. Its most publicized activities were voter registration and a youth leadership program emphasizing African culture, black pride, and race unity. After receiving an additional $300,000 in 1968, Cleveland CORE expanded its registration activities to include all of the newly created, predominantly black 21st Congressional District, and, working with other organizations, it placed 10,000 black citizens on the rolls prior to the November election which sent Louis Stokes, Cleveland's first black representative, to Congress.[29]

Cleveland CORE's renaissance was an exception to the bleak situation faced by National CORE. With the financial picture gloomy and absorbing so much of McKissick's attention, with few chapters conducting viable programs, and with the Baltimore project foundering, he was forced to cope with a serious crisis of confidence in his leadership only months after becoming National Director. Practically all at once, from several quarters, came challenges to the authority of the national office—from some staff people, certain chapters, and a number of NAC members.

Since the start of the McKissick administration, financial problems, in the words of one NAC member, "created such severe tension within the organization that no effort to establish a meaningful program has been attempted, and there are numerous personnel conflicts." At a Steering Committee meeting in August 1966, the participants made such personal attacks on each other and the national office that the chairman was instructed not to tolerate any more insults and to ask offenders to leave. The conferees agreed that "the source for the majority of the problem related back to 'lack of money.' " [30]

McKissick also faced resentment from a number of affiliates caused by attempts of national staff to exercise control over the chapters. For their part, many staff members felt impotent in relation to the NAC. They contended that organizational policy was being made by too few people, that the NAC was overbearing, and that "the lines of communication between staff and the National Action Council are broken." In turn, the NAC, whose communication difficulties with national staff were exacerbated because the organization's poverty prevented regular meetings, blamed McKissick for usurping its policy-making prerogatives and for failing to carry out its decisions. This unresolved structural problem of the relative power of staff and the NAC, which had surfaced in the final year of Farmer's administration, kept simmering and finally exploded in the spring of 1967. Dissident NAC members (mostly New York area chapter chairmen) charged that McKissick was ignoring their counsel. Demanding "recognition and understanding by staff of NAC function and position," they insisted that "better ties of communication *must be* established" between the national office and the NAC.[31]

By then there were two factions within the NAC on the brink of open warfare. The group headed by McKissick and national chairman Wilfred Ussery drew support from Roy Innis and several other chapter chairmen, mostly from the Midwest. The opposing faction was centered on the Northeast, and included Sol Herbert, Bronx CORE chairman and a national vice-chairman; Bonnie Barrow, national secretary and chairman of Morris County, New Jersey, CORE; Olly Leeds, chairman of Brooklyn CORE; and William Bradley, chairman of San Francisco CORE. Steering Committee meetings, usually held in New York, tended to reflect the alienation of the latter group. At one meeting in April, they charged that CORE "appeared to be a one man pyramid," with less sharing of authority than "even under Farmer with Marvin Rich." Angry that "the staff does not take the NAC seriously," the Steering Committee demanded "communication between NAC members and the national director immediately. . . . The NAC members are the governing body of this organization. . . . Under no circumstances will staff make decisions of policy affecting the entire organization." [32]

The feelings of frustration arising from CORE's decline erupted at an NAC and staff conference a month later. The conferees again exchanged recriminations, and Ussery observed, "If people are in a position of powerlessness, they tear at each other. The powerlessness of the NAC is a factor that keeps us fighting each other." At bottom was the feeling that most CORE chapters were "dead," "phony" organizations, as one delegate put it. Callender commented, "I am confused about statistics. We say we have 200 [chapters] when in reality we have 20 doing things we are supposed to do." In many instances, NAC members were officers of nonfunctioning groups and thus "represented nobody." The national director was chastised for failing to raise money and usurping the NAC's functions; and the Steering Committee in closed session even recommended that the NAC censure McKissick for ignoring directives. Roy Innis, although generally allied with McKissick in this period, denounced the staff as "a sacred cow in this organization." The level of morale at the conference was evident in such remarks as "CORE is dying," "Aren't we operating like a museum?," "Why hasn't Black Power stimulated money?," "CORE is run by bullshit!"

Some conferees were so discouraged that they proposed the national office and even the chapters be abolished, thus junking the organization's quarter-century structure. They suggested substituting one resembling SNCC's—with CORE restructured as "an organization of organizers" governing themselves through an administrative committee. "Maybe we don't need a national office," one participant declared. "We could operate, for example, out of projects." Some proposed using only unsalaried organizers "who will work voluntarily off the fat of the land." But Farmer, who attended the conference, thought this would "turn us into a different organization . . . and essentially write out anyone over 20," and Innis was "not so sure that the SNCC experiment is working so well." McKissick suggested that more centralization might be necessary to organize the black masses effectively. He pointed out that Marcus Garvey—whose reputation soared in the nationalistic context of the late 1960's—"was not a democratic leader, in fact, he was a dictator. He had ritual, discipline, and benefits for the membership. . . . We need to study his style." [33]

At the 1967 Convention, the anti-McKissick group demanded the ouster of the remaining whites and made an issue of CORE's application for funds from the Ford Foundation. They wanted a categorical rejection of any "white folks' money" to avoid a "sellout to whites." McKissick reminded the delegates that CORE, whose debt was now $400,000, could not raise significant sums from blacks and needed foundation grants until some other way of financing could be found. Innis, supporting McKissick, asked critics how CORE could remain alive without money, and asserted that if funds were obtained without restrictions, their source was unimportant. Ollie Leeds countered that only local chapters meant something in CORE, and that accordingly the national office, which had failed the affiliates anyway, needed neither money nor staff. McKissick's forces undercut their opposition by accepting a constitutional change eliminating the word "multiracial" from the description of CORE's membership and went on to defeat Bradley's drive to replace Wilfred Ussery as national chairman. Nevertheless, McKissick's days in office were numbered. Innis, whom the convention elected second national vice-chairman, provided key support for McKissick, and in December he was appointed to the post of associate national director, following Lincoln Lynch's resignation. By the summer of 1968, Innis was assuming the national director's duties, and in September the discouraged McKissick departed to establish his own consulting firm.[34]

Innis firmly believed that the organization's future lay in creating a tightly knit centralized structure, with CORE and its chapters clearly identified as a reform rather than a revolutionary movement. Both of these interrelated issues came to the fore at the 1968 Convention in Columbus, Ohio. Innis declared that CORE would build "a nation within a nation," attempting to develop black community corporations and "black ownership of capital instruments" to operate factories and businesses and provide job opportunities. His opponents, on the other hand, maintained that the American system was so oppressive that it had to be destroyed. The dissidents charged that CORE was now irrelevant to the black community and had, in effect, been co-opted by the white power structure, becoming, in the words of Brooklyn CORE chairman Robert Carson, "a simple tool to blind black people." He denounced the national office for accepting foundation grants and favoring black capitalism. Said Carson, "I believe that capitalism has to be destroyed if black people are to be free. We don't want anything to do with the white power structure as it is now." Innis moved to tighten national control over the loose federation of autonomous affiliates. As a symbolic assertion of the national office's authority, he attempted to enforce, for the first time, the $100 constitutional assessment on each chapter enacted by the 1965 Convention. Carson, declaring that "a few people who have a quest for power" were using CORE "for personal fame," denounced Innis' "strong arm tactics" that would bring the chapters under complete control of the national office. Innis charged that most of the dissident chairmen ("the local barons") who refused to give up power presided over "just paper chapters anyhow." [35]

After days of wrangling, Carson, Sol Herbert, and their followers largely from East Coast chapters, angrily seceded from the organization. The walk-out temporarily blocked ratification of a new constitution and the selection of Innis as national director to succeed McKissick, who had been on medical leave for months. Innis, however, consolidated his position at another convention held several weeks later in St. Louis, for the purpose of adopting a new constitution that would prevent future disruptions and "tighten up" the organizational structure. He informed the *Post-Dispatch* that the constitutional changes would "be the conversion of a document of the civil rights era to a document that suits the era of black nationalism." The delegates approved the new constitution and the Innis slate of officers headed by Ussery. This was not accomplished without further opposition, however. Insisting that CORE's needs required chapter autonomy and collective leadership rather than the concentration of power in Innis' hands, Robert Lucas, chairman of Chicago CORE and national vice-chairman for the North Central region, seceded with a number of delegates.[36] The victorious Innis stated that now with the local chapters far less independent, "We are moving away from separate little baronies." The small centralized organization that remained had no place for whites, who were now barred from active membership.[37]

One of Innis's first press releases as national director announced that CORE had become "once and for all . . . a Black Nationalist Organization," with "separation" as its goal. "Separatism," he averred, "is a necessary and pragmatic way of organizing two separate and distinct races of people"—a system under which blacks would control their own destiny. "When we have control of our own self-destiny, then we can talk about integration" for those Negroes who wished it, he said. But the traditional goal of integration, which "came to be viewed by the civil rights aristocracy not as a means to an end, but as an end in itself," was "as dead as a doornail." Innis demanded a new American constitution that would recognize blacks as a "nation within a nation." He envisioned "a nation-like structure created by a collection of black islands woven together as a 'separate political entity.' " [38]

The schisms in CORE had ended, but the new CORE—stable and centralized—had only a small staff, limited resources, and a handful of local chapters. With both SNCC and CORE weakened and in decline, the banner of Black Power and black nationalism passed to other groups, mostly locally based. SNCC eventually disappeared altogether.[39] But Afro-American Societies and Black Student Unions flourished at the predominantly white colleges and universities. Black caucuses proliferated in the predominantly white professional and church organizations. There was a general surge of community organization—of a spirit of self-help and racial solidarity, of uniting ghetto residents for concerted action, culturally, economically, and politically. The Black Panthers, founded in Oakland, California, in 1966 caught the public eye with their revolutionary ideology. Ironically, CORE, now unequivocally committed to separatism, proved unable to harness the surge of black nationalism. CORE stood transformed, but it was no longer at the cutting edge of the black revolt.

Twice CORE had flourished and twice CORE had fallen into decline. The first quarter-century of its existence can be divided into two distinct periods with parallel trajectories: the first extending from the origins in 1942–43, through the early flowering of CORE activity that came to a climax in the Journey of Reconciliation and in the subsequent work of St. Louis CORE and the Washington Interracial Workshop, to its nadir in the Wallace Nelson controversy in 1954; and the second period extending from the revival led by James Robinson in the late 1950's, through CORE's second flowering under James Farmer that encompassed the Freedom Ride, the VEP program, and the dramatic job and housing campaigns, to another nadir in the mid-1960's. What were the basic ingredients for CORE's periods of organizational success; what combination of factors accounted for its periods of decline; and how did its leaders attempt to cope with CORE's two organizational crises?

CORE was born in an era when public sentiment was slowly veering to a greater recognition of the legitimacy of the Negroes' demands for constitutional rights and equality in American society, and when black militancy, epitomized by the 1941 March on Washington Movement, was on the rise. In this context the small band of dedicated young CORE enthusiasts was able to break down some of the humiliating discriminatory barriers facing blacks in the cities of the North. Virtually all of their accomplishments involved places of public accommodations. These were a natural target of CORE activists for several reasons: the high visibility of this kind of discrimination; the vulnerability of the discriminators whose business could be hurt by CORE's tactics; and the fact that the right to service in hotels, restaurants, and amusement places enjoyed greater legitimacy in the eyes of whites than demands for equal job opportunity or housing desegregation. Such projects, with realistic prospects for victory, were well-suited to the CORE groups, which were composed of small numbers of dedicated people with little power in the community but who were filled with enthusiasm and were willing to spend enormous amounts of time and energy to dramatize the moral issue through direct action.

Only a small minority of white Americans subscribed to CORE's goal of a fully integrated, racially equalitarian society, and the sit-in tactics of CORE members as well as their commitment to interracial action were considered radical in many quarters at the time. Yet CORE's emphasis upon nonviolence and exhibition of optimistic good will toward discriminators, the meticulous adherence to the Rules for Action, and the activists' appearance of nonrevolutionary respectability, all operated to legitimize the organization's operations in the public mind, and thus to enhance the possibility for victory. At the same time the CORE ideology functioned to produce the cohesiveness and unity needed for effective group action. While some CORE people were pacifists who viewed nonviolence as a way of life, and others regarded it simply as a useful tactic, there was nevertheless a high degree of consensus among CORE members about the value of using interracial nonviolent direct action as the way to best achieve the goal of an integrated society based on racial justice. All these factors served to make CORE—small though it was—a viable organization.

When CORE revived and flourished anew in the late 1950's and early 1960's, it was again operating in a climate of increasing white recognition of the justice of Negro demands and a striking rise in black militance. CORE was able to capitalize upon these trends because of the bureaucratic structure and financial base which Robinson had created. CORE's further advance and its emergence as a major civil rights organization in 1961 were also facilitated by its bold use of new and dramatic direct-action tactics—the most notable being the jail-ins and the Freedom Ride —and the selection of the charismatic James Farmer as national director. Although the new climate of public opinion among both blacks and whites and CORE's own use of direct action produced a large influx of new members, organizational cohesiveness and the basic consensus over ideology, jobs, and tactics remained essentially intact into 1963. This was due to several factors: the inspiration and model provided by the nonviolent activists in the South; the enthusiasm and commitment—even millennialism—of the CORE members, with their optimistic expectations of victory and the rapid attainment of an integrated equalitarian society; the widespread public recognition in the North of the legitimacy of CORE's public accommodations and voter registration projects; and the highly visible and significant victories, mixed though they were with numerous defeats, in the southern desegregation campaigns and, to a lesser extent, in the northern job and fair-housing projects. The South had now become for the first time vulnerable to attack by civil rights organizations because of the trends in northern white public opinion and the growing leverage of the Negro vote, which forced the Kennedy Administration to intercede decisively after the Freedom Ride and later to endorse the thrust for a new civil rights law. With substantial successes having thus been achieved, CORE turned hopefully to attacking the economic and social problems of the northern ghettos.

Ironically, victories in specific campaigns had contradictory effects on the organization, both during CORE's first decade and again during the 1960's. On the one hand, success provided inspiration, attracted members, sustained chapter cohesiveness and morale, and encouraged attacks on other targets. On the other hand, success was sometimes demoralizing to chapters when, unsure of themselves, they floundered in the search for viable new projects. To undertake fresh programs quickly was essential; CORE was an action organization, and without an action project, chapters withered and died. Not only did success in the first years sometimes precipitate the disintegration of individual chapters, but, more important, the virtual elimination of segregation in public accommodations in northern and key border cities in the early 1950's produced a serious crisis for the whole organization. CORE found itself unable to move to other targets. It lacked the power to tackle northern employment and housing discrimination in a substantial way, in part because those issues, especially housing, enjoyed less legitimacy among whites, in part because the targets were less vulnerable, and in part because CORE lacked a significant base in the black community, whose active support would have been essential for success in job boycotts. CORE did exert effort to develop public accommodations campaigns in the South, but the repressive character of that region made such activity as difficult as the problems of the northern slumdwellers would prove to be in the sixties. Meanwhile CORE's problems were exacerbated by the McCarthyist anti-Communist hysteria, which all but made recruitment of new members and the development of new chapters impossible for an organization with CORE's radical image. In this frustrating and unproductive milieu, CORE leaders, while maintaining their consensus on nonviolence, interracialism, and ultimate goals, engaged in bitter disputes over specific tactics which in the end degenerated into a factionalism that nearly destroyed the organization.

CORE's second decline in the mid-1960's in many ways paralleled the decline in the early 1950's, but the pattern of events was far more complex, and unlike the earlier period involved a transformation of ideology and goals. The stirring events that began with the southern lunch-counter sit-ins generated an unprecedented escalation of tactics and expectations. CORE became more ambitious in its projects—raising its demands, often engaging in more radical forms of direct action, frequently choosing larger and more powerful targets, and turning to an attack upon the problems of the black poor. Simultaneously there was a shift in CORE's constituency. Not only did the organization recruit an increasing number of blacks, but it was also attracting people of both races who were drawn not by CORE's tradition of nonviolence and interracialism but by its militance.

As long as there were enough victorious projects for CORE members to feel that substantial progress was being made, the organization flourished—even in the face of serious administrative weaknesses. But the continuous rise of expectations demanded ever bigger victories; as a result, campaigns that would have been labeled successful in 1962 were regarded as failures by 1964. In addition, when CORE turned to dealing with the problems of the black poor several things became evident. It was harder to convince the white majority of the legitimacy of the new issues—compensatory employment, slum-housing, de facto segregated schools, and police brutality. To organize the poor was extraordinarily difficult and required enormous resources; in addition, most of the targets—school boards, slumlords, police departments, and discriminatory labor unions—were not responsive to demands for change. To many in CORE it soon became clear that at best direct action offered only limited possibilities for solving the basic concerns of the black slumdwellers or for securing the governmental intervention often needed to produce improvements in their daily lives.

Given the heightened expectations of many CORE veterans; given the impatient militancy of many of CORE's new recruits who were not socialized in the organization's traditional ideology; given the limited achievements of some of CORE's most ambitious job projects; given the repressive strategies of southern officials and the reluctance of the federal government to intervene there except under extraordinary pressure; given the failure of the mammoth direct-action campaigns against building trades unions, boards of education, and slumlords, CORE activists often became disillusioned. The very intensity of the commitment that characterized CORE enthusiasts, their dislike of compromise and halfway measures, accentuated their disappointment and bitterness. At the same time, outside of CORE, there was a resurgence of black nationalism, and the rise of the charismatic Malcolm X, who had an important impact on many black activists.

These interrelated factors produced in CORE a questioning of the organization's original ideology, tactics, and strategy—a breakdown in consensus and cohesiveness that took several different forms. There was a serious difference in opinion over the use of disruptive tactics that came to a climax in the debates over the stall-in. As many members, disillusioned with the limitations of direct action, espoused community organization and partisan political action, chapters became involved in acrimonious disputes over the relative merits of these different techniques. The commitment to two of CORE's other central values—nonviolence and interracialism—eroded. Finally, there was growing skepticism about CORE's original goal of an integrated society. Frustrated at the relative lack of progress and impressed by Malcolm X's nationalist pronouncements, many CORE activists came to despair of the possibilities of achieving a racially just, integrated society, and opted for separatist tactics and ultimately separatist goals. With the organization thus seeking to find a new mission and adapt to the changes in its environment and constituency, it became wracked with serious internal conflicts. As in the mid-1950's, CORE suffered a sharp drop in membership and in the number of active affiliates. Simultaneously, whites who had formerly responded generously to CORE's financial appeals were alienated by CORE's new thrust, and the decline in revenue that followed forced substantial cutbacks in the programs subsidized by the national office.

After each period of decline a greatly weakened CORE tried to maintain its organizational viability. In the 1950's CORE remained committed to its basic ideology, tactics, and goals, and successfully brought about a revival through vigorous fund-raising and the creation of a centralized bureaucratic structure, dominated by the paid staff. In the 1960's the process was less simple. Structurally there was an attempt to transfer power from the staff to the NAC; but the weakened secretariat proved unable to solve CORE's fiscal crisis or to reverse the decline in activity, and in the end the proponents of a centralized, staff-dominated organization assumed control. Unlike in the earlier period, however, CORE this time attempted to adapt through a transformation of its ideology and goals that would tap the ground swell of nationalist sentiment in the black community. It is too early to say whether or not this effort to revive the organization will eventually prove successful; at this point, however, CORE is a small organization, seeking to effectively relate itself to the black community and its needs.

From one perspective CORE in the 1960's had proven a failure. Many of its victories amounted to tokenism, and it consistently met defeat in campaigns against school boards, building trades unions, and police departments. Further frustrations followed the adoption of the "New Directions" program. Finally, CORE all but collapsed in the middle of the decade.

Yet had CORE really failed? In answering this question it is essential to make a distinction between *organizational* success and failure on the one hand and the success and failure of an organization's *goals* on the other. As we have pointed out on a number of occasions, the relationship between CORE's organizational vitality and its successes and failures in various campaigns was a complex one. In the end, CORE, despite numerous achievements, declined largely because of a sense of disillusionment with the pace of social change. On the other hand, while the organization itself became a shadow of its former self, considerable change continued to occur, particularly in the realm of politics and employment, which CORE's earlier activity had done much to initiate.

CORE's contribution to the black protest movement and to racial advancement had, in fact, been enormous. During the 1940's and 1950's it had pioneered in the use of direct-action techniques which later swept the country. CORE had played a major role in bringing about the desegregation of public accommodations from its first sit-in at Chicago through its single-handed campaign to desegregate public places in a border city like St. Louis and its help to the southern student demonstrators of 1960 to the Freedom Ride of 1961. These activities, followed by the upsurge of southern direct action in 1963, in which CORE took a leading part, culminated in the passage of the Civil Rights Act of 1964. In the North during the early 1960's CORE was pivotal in the battles for integrated housing, jobs, and decent dwellings for the black poor, as well as making a vital contribution to the attack on de facto school segregation and police brutality. Although many of these campaigns got nowhere, CORE was instrumental in helping to break down "whites-only" job barriers in dozens of cities. In addition, through its demonstrations CORE sensitized white elites to an awareness of the black man's problems, and thus helped pave the way for the gains that continued to be made even after CORE as an organization had moved to the sidelines. Finally, CORE's participation in the VEP program and the COFO experiment contributed to the passage of the Voting Rights Act of 1965 and, more directly, helped set the stage for the new political activism that sent a thousand individuals to public office in the South alone in 1972,[40] and made the black presence so important a feature of the 1972 Democratic Convention.

Despite discouraging disappointments, and at the cost of enormous sacrifices, CORE, both by itself and with other civil rights organizations, chalked up a significant record especially in public accommodations, voter registration, and employment. CORE members were always deeply aware of how very much more needed to be done before equality was achieved in American society. Yet CORE helped to set in motion waves of social change that have not yet run their course, and it played a pivotal role in arousing blacks to a greater militance that paved the way for the black activism of the seventies.

Note on Sources

The most important single source for a study of CORE is the organization's archives. The main body of these archives is now at the State Historical Society of Wisconsin (Madison). In addition to papers from the CORE national office, it houses the Western Regional Office Archives, the Southern Regional Office Archives, and the archives of the Scholarship, Education and Defense Fund for Racial Equality. Another valuable body of the CORE Archives is to be found at the library of the Martin Luther King Center, Atlanta, Georgia.

These holdings in Wisconsin and Atlanta are especially rich in materials dating from the 1940's to the administration of James Robinson, 1957–60 and in materials from the 1960's files of the legal, community relations, and organization departments. It should be pointed out that much of the correspondence of Norman Hill, George Wiley, Gordon Carey, and James Farmer has either been lost or destroyed. After the main body of materials was shipped to Wisconsin, however, we were able to consult at the national CORE headquarters in Harlem nearly three cabinets of records from the national director's office, principally from Farmer's and Wiley's files, as well as several other drawers of correspondence belonging chiefly to the department of organization. These materials, not sent to Atlanta or Wisconsin and most of them evidently since lost or discarded, are designated "CHQ" in our footnotes. The holdings

The civil rights materials in the Lyndon Johnson Library and James Forman's recollections of his experiences with SNCC, *The Making of Black Revolutionaries* (New York, 1972), became available too late to be consulted in the preparation of this book.

of the Scholarship, Education and Defense Fund, including the legal files of Carl Rachlin, and much of the material in the main body of the CORE Archives were consulted prior to being deposited with the State Historical Society of Wisconsin; possibly some of the records which we saw in New York were not sent to Madison.

There is also a substantial corpus of CORE materials in the Bancroft Library, University of California at Berkeley, and a few items are in the Library of the Institute of Governmental Studies at the same school. A large body of Seattle CORE records is at the University of Washington Library. The State Historical Society of Wisconsin also has several smaller groups of archival materials dealing with CORE chapters and CORE projects: the Columbus, Ohio, Vanguard League Archives, which we consulted while they were still in Columbus; the Milwaukee, Wisconsin, CORE Papers; the papers of the North Louisiana CORE office at Monroe; the records from the CORE project in Claiborne Parish, Louisiana; the East Feliciana Parish, Louisiana, CORE papers, which include some material on West Feliciana and St. Helena Parishes; the Jonesboro, Louisiana, Freedom House Papers; the Ferriday, Louisiana, Freedom House Papers, and the Bogalusa, Louisiana, Freedom School Papers.

Archives of several other organizations proved valuable for some phases of CORE's history. The records of the Fellowship of Reconciliation at Nyack, New York, were indispensable for a study of the founding of CORE. Two collections at the Library of Congress Manuscripts Division had useful records relating to CORE's early years: the NAACP Archives and the Nelson Jackson personal correspondence in the Southern Regional Office files of the National Urban League Archives. Two archival collections, those of the Southern Regional Council and of the Voter Education Project, were helpful in studying CORE's involvement in the southern voter-registration effort, 1961–66. We consulted three sets of papers at the John F. Kennedy Library—those of Burke Marshall, Assistant Attorney General for Civil Rights, and presidential assistants Lee White and Harris Wofford. White's papers were extremely disappointing, but those of Marshall and Wofford provided some useful information regarding CORE's southern project and the organization's relations with the Kennedy administration. A few relevant items are found in the correspondence of A. Philip Randolph in the Archives of the Brotherhood of Sleeping Car Porters, Library of Congress, and in the papers of Martin Luther King at Boston University.

We are indebted to nearly forty CORE national and chapter leaders for giving us access to manuscript materials in their personal possession.

Most of these still remain in private hands, although a few have since been placed in depositories as indicated below. They vary in extent from a few folders to a file cabinet or more of records. The papers of James and Lula Farmer provided a rich source of information about the first fifteen years of CORE's history. Documents in the possession of Eugene Stanley illuminated his role both in the Vanguard League and on the Journey of Reconciliation. Materials belonging to Herbert Kelman were helpful both in regard to early Baltimore CORE, and the attempt to revive CORE work in California in 1954–55. The files of Charles and Marian Oldham of St. Louis were exceedingly useful on both the St. Louis CORE and the national organization. Marvin Rich has some key documents relating to the period when he served at CORE's national office. George Wiley's papers illuminated both Syracuse CORE and the period when he was associate national director. Similarly the papers of Robert Curvin of Newark were helpful in connection with the activities of the chapter there and also for the period when he was on the National Action Council. Materials relating to National CORE, chiefly minutes, supplied by MaryLu Murphy, are now at the Wisconsin State Historical Society. Five small collections in the possession of former CORE field secretaries were also helpful: papers of Mary Hamilton Wesley and Fredricka Teer Kushner relating to National CORE and field staff matters; of Genevieve Hughes Houghton, chiefly concerning Berkeley, California, CORE; of Edward F. Hollander, dealing principally with the Southern Regional Office; and of James T. McCain (including his diaries), mainly concerning the work in South Carolina. Ollie Leeds' papers, important for the light they shed on the history of Brooklyn CORE, also supplied a few valuable items on the national organization, particularly the minutes of the 1966 Convention.

Other manuscript collections were concerned exclusively with individual chapters. Three sets of materials relating to Detroit CORE—the Ralph and Janice Rosenfeld Papers, the Gloria Brown Papers, and the especially complete papers of Leon De Meunier, chapter chairman in 1960–61—have been deposited at the Michigan Historical Collections, University of Michigan. The papers of Gene Schulze and Robert and Mimi Abramovitz, which are now on file at the State Historical Society of Wisconsin illuminate the history of New Haven CORE. David L. Cohen, Arthur Evans, and Bernard Mandel all have small but extraordinarily valuable manuscript collections relating to Cleveland CORE. There are two highly useful collections on Boston CORE: the papers of Richard Brown, which are now at Wisconsin, and the extensive papers of Phyllis

Ryan. Equally helpful were the papers of Frances White and of Edward and Joan Singler for Seattle, and the papers of Wanda Penny and Congressman William Clay for St. Louis. Materials formerly in the possession of Albert Mindlin, and now at Wisconsin, give a good picture of the Washington Interracial Workshop. Barbee Durham's papers, xerox copies of which are now at Wisconsin, enriched our picture of the Vanguard League, and Mary Coleman's Papers, which have also been placed at Wisconsin, were helpful in regard to the Baltimore and Washington chapters during the 1950's. Small collections of personal manuscripts belonging to Homer Randolph, Evelyn Rich, and Marian Merrill illuminate the history of the East St. Louis, Harlem (New York) and Prince George's County, Maryland, chapters, respectively. Virgil J. Vogel, Milton Davis, and Faith Rich all supplied helpful materials on various periods of Chicago CORE's history; Mrs. Rich's manuscripts have since been placed at Wisconsin. In addition, Alan Anderson and George Pickering let us see copies of their minutes of the Chicago Council of Coordinated Organizations. Items in the possession of four other individuals who did not belong to CORE were also of value: the late Robert Starobin, who while a student at Berkeley obtained materials relevant to CORE in the Bay area; Claude Ramsey, head of the Mississippi State AFL-CIO who has materials concerning COFO and Mississippi politics in 1964–65; Frank Stanley, Jr., of the Louisville *Defender,* who has documents relating to the history of Louisville CORE; and Pauli Murray, who possesses extensive materials concerning the Howard University sit-ins of 1943–44. Xerox copies of the last-named collection have been deposited at the Moorland Foundation Room, Howard University Library.

The Wisconsin State Historical Society has acquired several other personal manuscript collections relevant to CORE work in the South. Especially useful were those donated by Miriam (Mimi) Feingold Whitman, and Murphy Bell, concerning Louisiana; and of JoAnn Ooiman Robinson, and R. Hunter Morey relating to Mississippi. In addition there are some useful materials in the papers of William O. Reichert, of Lexington, Kentucky, CORE; of Mel Acheson, Charles G. Currier, and John Zippert, who were task force workers in Louisiana; and of Hank Werner and Howard Zinn, concerning Mississippi. Finally the State Historical Society of Wisconsin has two other collections that should be noted: correspondence of Milton Galamision, which gave some helfpful sidelights on Brooklyn CORE, and papers of Alan Gartner.

Three collections of clippings proved invaluable: those of Phyllis Ryan relating to the Boston civil rights movement; those kept by Long Island

CORE, which were consulted at the chapter's office in 1966; and those of Douglas Eldridge, reporter for the Newark *Evening News,* concerning black political insurgency within the Essex County, New Jersey, Democratic Party, and CORE's connection with it. There is also a small collection of clippings relating to Columbus CORE, catalogued as the Arthur Zebbs Papers, at the State Historical Society of Ohio.

Newspapers, both black and white, provided important sources of information, especially during the 1960's after CORE had become prominent. Most of them were particularly useful for studying the CORE chapters in the cities in which the individual papers were located; the *New York Times* and *Wall Street Journal,* both of which are indexed, were consulted for national coverage as well. We systematically studied the following black newspapers: Chicago *Defender* during the 1940's and again in the 1960's when CORE had an active chapter there; St. Louis *Argus,* 1948–66; and the following for the 1960's: Cleveland *Call and Post;* Louisville *Defender;* Michigan *Chronicle;* *Amsterdam News* (New York and Brooklyn editions); Philadelphia *Tribune;* Kansas City *Call;* Baltimore *Afro-American;* East St. Louis *Crusader;* East St. Louis *Monitor;* *California Eagle* (Los Angeles); and Los Angeles *Sentinel.* The *Mississippi Free Press,* a movement-oriented paper published at Jackson from December 1961 to August 1964, provided helpful insights into CORE's work with COFO. All of these, and the white dailies cited below helped to trace the history of a number of chapters and CORE-related local movements after 1960.

Libraries of the following newspapers opened their clippings collections: Seattle *Post-Intelligencer;* Seattle *Times;* Denver *Post;* East St. Louis *Journal;* Detroit *Free Press;* Detroit *News;* Philadelphia *Inquirer;* Columbus *Dispatch;* Columbus *Citizen-Journal;* Cleveland *Plain Dealer;* Cincinnati *Enquirer;* Newark *Evening News;* Kansas City *Star;* Kansas City *Times.* The Washington *Post* reader information service also supplied citations on CORE chapters in its area. The San Diego Public Library's card index to the San Diego *Union* made the coverage of the local CORE chapter in that newspaper easily accessible to us. In addition, a number of dailies were consulted to obtain details on specific local campaigns during the 1960's. Even biased Southern papers supplied important information which, judiciously employed, supplemented material from other sources. Especially extensive use was made of the following: Baton Rouge *State Times;* Chapel Hill *Weekly News;* Chicago *Tribune;* Durham *Morning Herald;* Durham *Sun;* Gadsden *Times;* Greensboro

Daily News; Jackson *Daily News;* Rock Hill *Evening Herald;* New Haven *Journal-Courier;* Philadelphia *Evening Bulletin;* Sacramento *Bee* (for the demonstrations at the state capitol in 1963); St. Louis *Post-Dispatch;* San Francisco *Chronicle;* and Tallahassee *Democrat.*

Other papers were consulted on a more restricted basis. The Baltimore *Sun,* the Dayton *Journal-Herald,* and the Oakland *Tribune* provided details on the CORE conventions held in these cities. The Baton Rouge *Morning Advocate* and the Shreveport *Times* supplied information on certain campaigns in the Louisiana parishes. The *News of Orange County* (North Carolina) was useful in connection with the Chapel Hill campaign. Unfortunately, the Madison County *Herald* (Mississippi), though studied for a two-year period, provided only occasional items about CORE's work in Canton. The Berkeley *Daily Gazette, Daily Californian* (University of California at Berkeley), Chicago *American,* Milwaukee *Journal,* Syracuse *Post-Standard,* and Los Angeles *Times* were helpful on their respective cities.

Several other serial publications were also exceedingly useful. Chief among these was CORE's official organ, the *CORE-lator;* a quite complete set was pieced together from issues scattered in the various archival holdings. The Fellowship of Reconciliation's journal, *Fellowship Magazine,* and the more fugitive *Equality,* edited by James Farmer in 1943–44 when he was the FOR's Race Relations Secretary, were important for understanding CORE's origins and early philosophy. The *Race Relations Law Reporter* proved helpful in studying some of the legal cases in which CORE was involved. *Ebony* during the 1960's had about eight or nine useful articles relevant to a study of CORE, ranging from descriptions of Brooklyn CORE's Ebinger Bakery demonstrations and the Deacons for Defense, to an article by the widow of Rev. Bruce Klunder and a feature on Roy Innis. *Integrated Education* contained data relating to CORE's participation in school protests. The *Southern Patriot,* organ of the Southern Conference Educational Fund, and *New South,* organ of the Southern Regional Council, supplied a few significant articles, as did *New Republic, Nation, Reporter, Commentary, Dissent, New Politics, Liberation,* and *New York Times Magazine.* These have been cited where appropriate. Finally, mention should be made of the Southern Regional Council's irregularly issued Special Reports, notably "The Student Protest Movement, Winter 1960" (SRC-13, Feb. 25, 1960, and revised April 1, 1960) and "The Freedom Ride, May 1961" (SRC-20, May 30, 1961).

Other important sources of information were confidential interviews held with 215 individuals; they ranged in length from brief sessions of fifteen or twenty minutes on restricted subjects to extended discussions lasting two or three hours; a number of people were interviewed more than once, a few as many as half a dozen times. All of these persons were interviewed with the understanding that the information they generously shared with us would not be for attribution.

The following fifty-one persons with whom we spoke were either national officers or staff members: Billie Ames [Tineau], Walter Brooks, Harold Brown, Gordon Carey, Val Coleman, Ronald Corwin, Robert Curvin, David Dennis, Mark Dodson, Nils Douglas, Barbee William Durham, James Farmer, Lula Farmer, Alan Gartner, Spiver Gordon, Richard Haley, Mary Hamilton [Wesley], Norman Hill, Velma Hill, Anna Holden, Edward Hollander, George Houser, Genevieve Hughes [Houghton], Roy Innis, Shirley Lacey, Ollie Leeds, Edward Lewinson, Winston Lockett, Rudy Lombard, Lincoln Lynch, James McCain, Floyd McKissick, Ronnie Moore, Juanita Nelson, Wallace Nelson, Charles Oldham, James Peck, Antoine Perot, Carl Rachlin, Richard Rapp, Marvin Rich, James Robinson, Ralph Rosenfeld, Bayard Rustin, Frank Shearer, Louis Smith, Eugene Stanley, Fredricka Teer [Kushner], Ruth Turner [Perot], Wilfred Ussery, George Wiley. Nearly all of those just named were also active at one time or another in local chapters. In addition, we interviewed other individuals who were either officers or active members of thirty-one affiliates and local movements. Finally, there was a group of twenty-five people outside of CORE who were knowledgeable about some phase of the organization's operations. These included several former Southern Regional Council officials, notably Leslie Dunbar, Harold Fleming, Paul Anthony, Vernon Jordan, as well as Pat Watters, who is still with the SRC; Al Hassler of the FOR; COFO leaders Aaron Henry, Charles Evers, and Robert Moses; LCDC officials Alvin Bronstein and Henry Schwarzchild; former assistant attorney-general Burke Marshall; and Timothy Jenkins, who as vice-president of the National Student Association played an influential role in encouraging the VEP.

Transcripts of two interviews which others have had with James Farmer were also helpful. One was an interview conducted by Albert Gollin of the Bureau of Social Research, of Washington, D. C., in connection with his research on the 1963 March on Washington. The other one was done by John F. Stewart as part of the oral history project of the John F. Kennedy Library, and the transcript is available there. Mention should also be made of the excellent tapes of speeches by

Farmer, Dave Dennis, and others in the possession of Edward F. Hollander of Washington.

There is only one book-length scholarly study of CORE—Inge Powell Bell's invaluable volume, *CORE and the Strategy of Nonviolence* (New York, 1968). There are a few books by CORE leaders that are important for an understanding of the organization's history. James Farmer, *Freedom—When?* (New York, 1965), is particularly illuminating about the early years and the organization in transition, 1963–65. James Peck, *Freedom Ride* (New York, 1962), discusses several early CORE campaigns as well as the famous foray into the South in 1961. Four other volumes based upon the recollections of participants should be mentioned: Debbie Louis, *And We Are Not Saved* (New York, 1970); Lewis Robinson, *The Making of a Man: An Autobiography* (Cleveland, 1970); Mwlina Imiri Abubadika (Sonny Carson), *The Education of Sonny Carson* (New York, 1972), and an extraordinary autobiographical volume by a young black Mississippian who served as a CORE Task Force worker in Jackson and Canton: Anne Moody, *Coming of Age in Mississippi* (New York, 1968). Two significant case studies of a local CORE chapter or a CORE-related local movement are Verda and Irwin Deutscher, "Cohesion in a Small Group: A Case Study," *Social Forces*, XXXIII (May 1955), 336–41, which deals with a chapter at Columbia, Missouri, in the early 1950's; and John Ehle's analysis of the Chapel Hill movement, *The Free Men* (New York, 1965).

The literature on the civil rights movement of the 1960's is enormous. We list here only the items we found to be most useful for a study of CORE. Robert Penn Warren, *Who Speaks for the Negro?* (New York, 1965), is based on a series of interviews with black protest leaders. Michael Lipsky's brilliant volume, *Protest in City Politics: Rent Strikes, Housing and the Power of the Poor* (Chicago, 1970), includes a lucid analysis of CORE's role in the New York rent strikes. Pat Watters and Reese Cleghorn, *Climbing Jacob's Ladder: The Arrival of Negroes in Southern Politics* (New York, 1967), describes the Voter Education project. Elizabeth Sutherland, ed., *Letters from Mississippi* (New York, 1965), offers some illuminating glimpses into CORE's participation in the COFO program. William Bradford Huie, *Three Lives for Mississippi* (New York, 1965), is the best account of the Chaney-Goodman-Schwerner murders. Victor Navasky, *Kennedy Justice* (New York, 1971), has a fine, succinct account of Robert Kennedy's handling of the southern black protest movement. Ralph Kramer, *Participation of the Poor: Compara-*

tive Case Studies in the War on Poverty (Englewood Cliffs, 1969); Edward Bentley and Frederick Wirt, eds., *School Desegregation in the North* (San Francisco, 1967); and Lynn Eley and Thomas Casstevens, eds., *The Politics of Fair Housing Legislation* (San Francisco, 1968), all contain case studies of campaigns in which CORE played an important role. William Keech, *The Impact of Negro Voting* (Chicago, 1968), discusses the political impact of the black protest movement in Durham. David Lewis, *King: A Critical Biography* (New York, 1970) is the best biography of Martin Luther King, Jr.

Several books and a number of analytical articles were especially useful for general background: Lerone Bennett, Jr., *The Negro Mood* (Chicago, 1964); Lewis Killian and Charles Grigg, *Racial Crisis in America: Leadership in Conflict* (Englewood Cliffs, 1964); Julius Lester, *Look Out Whitey! Black Power's Gon' Get Your Mama* (New York, 1968); Howard Zinn, *SNCC: The New Abolitionists* (Boston, 1964); Gary Marx, *Protest and Prejudice: A Study of Belief in the Black Community* (rev. ed., New York, 1969); Thomas Pettigrew, *A Profile of the Negro American* (Princeton, 1964); Charles Levy, *Voluntary Servitude: Whites in the Negro Movement* (New York, 1968); Alphonso Pinkney, *The Committed: White Activists in the Civil Rights Movement* (New Haven, 1968); Gary Marx and Michael Useem, "Majority Involvement in Minority Movements: Civil Rights, Abolition, Untouchability," *Journal of Social Issues,* XXVII (No. 1, 1971); N. J. Demerath, Gerald Marwell, and Michael Aiken, *The Dynamics of Idealism: White Students in a Black Movement* (San Francisco, 1971); Mark D. Naison, "The Rent Strikes in New York," *Radical America* (Nov.–Dec., 1967), reprinted in Fred Fox *et al.,* eds., *Strategies of Community Organization* (Itasca, Ill., 1970); Richard Rovere, "Letter from Washington," *The New Yorker,* XLI (Oct. 16, 1965), concerning the challenge to the seating of the Mississippi Congressional delegation; Marvin Rich, "Civil Rights Strategy After the March," *New Politics,* II (Fall 1963); Lewis Killian and Charles Smith, "Negro Protest Leaders in a Southern Community," *Social Forces,* XXXVIII (March 1960); Jack Walker, "The Functions of Disunity: Negro Leadership in a Southern City," *Journal of Negro Education,* XXXII (Summer 1963); Gerald McWorter and Robert Crain, "Subcommunity Gladiatorial Competition: Civil Rights Leadership as a Competitive Process," *Social Forces,* XLVI (Sept. 1967); Bayard Rustin, "The Meaning of Birmingham," *Liberation,* VIII (June 1963); and two articles by Donald von Eschen, Jerome Kirk, and Maurice Pinard: "The Disintegration of the Negro Nonviolent Movement," *Journal of Peace Research,* Issue No. 3 (1969), and "Processes of Recruitment in the Sit-In Movement," *Public Opinion Quarterly,* XXX (Fall 1969), 355–69.

Some master's theses and doctoral dissertations were also helpful in the preparation of this book: Harry Brill, "Black Militancy: A Case Study in Ego Politics" (Ph.D., University of California at Berkeley, 1969); Amon Burton, "The Politics of Fair Housing: A Case Study of the Movement to Enact a Fair Housing Ordinance in Wichita, Kansas" (M.A., Wichita State University, 1964); Edgar Chasteen, "Public Accommodations: Social Movements in Conflict" (Ph.D., University of Missouri, 1966); William Russell Ellis, "Operation Bootstrap: A Case Study in Ideology and the Institutionalization of Protest" (Ph.D., University of California at Los Angeles, 1969); Irving Goldaber, "The Treatment by the New York City Board of Education of Problems Affecting the Negro, 1954–1963" (Ph.D., New York University, 1964); Louis Goldberg, "CORE in Trouble: A Social History of the Organizational Dilemma of the Congress of Racial Equality Target City Project in Baltimore (1965–1967)" (Ph.D., Johns Hopkins University, 1970); Henry Holstege, "Conflict and Change in Negro-White Relations in Great Falls" (Ph.D., Michigan State University, 1966); James Laue, "Direct Action and Desegregation: Toward a Theory of the Rationalization of Protest" (Ph.D., Harvard University, 1965); Leslie Burl McLemore, "The Mississippi Freedom Democratic Party: A Case-Study of Grass-Roots Politics" (Ph.D., University of Massachusetts, 1971); Martin Oppenheimer, "The Genesis of the Southern Negro Student Movement (Sit-In Movement): A Study in Contemporary Negro Protest" (Ph.D., University of Pennsylvania, 1963); Ernest Patterson, "The Impact of the Black Struggle on Representative Government in St. Louis, Missouri" (Ph.D., St. Louis University, 1968); Anne Romaine, "The Mississippi Freedom Democratic Party Through August 1964" (M.A., University of Virginia, 1969); Jeffrey Smith, "The Omaha De Porres Club" (M.A., Creighton University, 1967); Emily Stoper, "Student Nonviolent Coordinating Committee: The Growth of Radicalism in a Civil Rights Organization" (Ph.D., Harvard University, 1968); Edward Tufts, "The Civil Rights Movement and Its Opposition" (Ph.D., Yale University, 1968); Paul Wehr, "The Sit-Down Protests: A Study of a Passive Resistance Movement in North Carolina" (M.A., University of North Carolina, 1960); Robert M. White, "The Tallahassee Sit-Ins and CORE:

A Nonviolent Revolutionary Submovement" (Ph.D., Florida State University, 1964; Ronald Corwin, "School Desegregation in Syracuse," (Ph.D., Syracuse University, 1968).

Finally, several studies by behavioral scientists have influenced our analysis of CORE as a social movement organization. In addition to the titles cited above by Inge Powell Bell, Lewis Killian and his collaborators, Verda and Irwin Deutscher, Gary Marx, Thomas Pettigrew, Jack Walker, and Donald von Eschen, Jerome Kirk, and Maurice Pinard, the following especially should be mentioned: James Vander Zanden, "The Nonviolent Resistance Movement to Segregation," *American Journal of Sociology*, LXVIII (March 1963); Ralph Turner and Lewis Killian, *Collective Behavior* (Englewood Cliffs, rev. ed, 1972); C. Wendell King, *Social Movements in the United States* (New York, 1956); Peter Blau, *Bureaucracy in Modern Society* (New York, 1956); Philip Selznick, "Foundations of the Theory of Organization," *American Sociological Review*, XIII (Feb. 1948); Selznick, *Leadership in Administration: A Sociological Interpretation* (New York, 1957); Charles Perrow, "The Analysis of Goals in Complex Organizations," *American Sociological Review*, XXVI (Dec. 1961); Perrow, *Organizational Analysis: a Sociological View* (Belmont, California, 1970); Michael Lipsky, "Protest as a Political Resource," *American Political Science Review*, LXII (Dec. 1968); John Roche and Stephen Sachs, "The Bureaucrat and the Enthusiast: An Exploration of the Leadership of Social Movements," *Western Political Quarterly*, VIII (June 1965); David Sills, *The Volunteers: Means and Ends in a National Organization* (Glencoe, Ill., 1957); Sheldon Messinger, "Organizational Transformation: A Case Study of a Declining Social Movement," *American Sociological Review*, XX (Feb. 1955); Joseph Gusfield, "Social Structure and Moral Reform: A Study of the Woman's Christian Temperance Union," *American Journal of Sociology*, XLI (Nov. 1955); Gusfield, "The Problem of Generations in an Organizational Structure," *Social Forces*, XXV (May 1957); Gusfield, "Functional Areas of Leadership in Social Movement," *Sociological Quarterly*, VII (Summer 1966); Gusfield, ed., *Protest, Reform and Revolt: A Reader in Social Movements* (New York, 1970); Mayer Zald, *Organizational Change: The Political Economy of the YMCA* (Chicago, 1970); Zald and Roberta Ash, "Social Movement Organizations: Growth, Decay and Change," *Social Forces*, XLIV (March 1966); James Geschwender, "Social Structure and the Negro Revolt: An Examination of Some Hypotheses," *Social Forces*, XLIII (Dec. 1964).

Notes

ABBREVIATIONS IN THE NOTES

In order to conserve space, certain abbreviated forms have been used. Minutes of Conventions, the National Action Committee, the National Action Council, and the Steering Committee are cited by simply giving the name of the body and the date—e.g. "1964 Convention;" "Steering Committee, Jan. 22–23, 1966." Short forms are also usually employed for staff reports, though in every case care is taken to give enough information so that the report can be readily identified in the archival and manuscript collections. Press releases cited are always those of the CORE national office, unless otherwise indicated; there is much duplication in the various archival sources, but the best collection of these releases is at Wisconsin.

In cases where a document lacks a date or the name of its author, and we have been able to supply this information, this has been indicated in brackets. Some undated documents are stamped with date of receipt at the CORE office and these are cited as "rec'd. . . ." Where the author or recipient of a letter cannot be identified we have used a question mark (?) to signify this fact.

A note is also in order as to the manner of citing the substantial amount of duplicated materials. Form letters and internal memoranda are cited as if they were typed or handwritten. Mimeographed or multilithed newsletters, reports, and pamphlets intended for general circulation are italicized. Printed pamphlets issued by CORE are cited using a standard form for books and pamphlets.

The following abbreviations have been used in the footnotes to designate certain frequently used sources:

Afro-American	Baltimore *Afro-American*
Argus	St. Louis *Argus*

CA	CORE Archives, Wisconsin
Call	Kansas City *Call*
Call and Post	Cleveland *Call and Post*
Chronicle	Michigan *Chronicle* (Detroit)
CHQ	CORE Archives, consulted in 1967 and 1969 at the national CORE headquarters, 200 W. 135th St., New York City.
Defender	Chicago *Defender* (In the 1960's the *Defender* published both a weekly and a daily edition; we consulted the weekly edition.)
Eagle	California *Eagle* (Los Angeles)
FOR	Fellowship of Reconciliation
MLK	CORE Archives, Martin Luther King Center, Atlanta
Monroe, La., MSS	CORE North Louisiana Office Archives, Wisconsin
NAACP Arch.	Archives of the National Association for the Advancement of Colored People, Library of Congress.
NAC	National Action Committee (prior to July 1962); National Action Council (beginning July 1962)
Rachlin Files	Legal Files of CORE Counsel, Carl Rachlin, part of the SEDF Archives
RRLR	*Race Relations Law Reporter*
SEDF	Archives of the Scholarship, Education and Defense Fund for Racial Equality, Wisconsin
Sentinel	Los Angeles *Sentinel*
SRC	Southern Regional Council Archives, Atlanta
SRO	CORE Southern Regional Office Archives, Wisconsin
Times	*New York Times*
Tribune	Philadelphia *Tribune*
UC	University of California, Bancroft Library
VEP	Voter Education Project Archives, Atlanta
WATS Line Reports	Reports phoned in to COFO and CORE Southern Office headquarters on Wide Area Telephone Service lines
WCO	CORE West Coast Office Archives, Wisconsin
WIW	Washington Interracial Workshop

CHAPTER ONE

1. For FOR interest in race relations, industrial conflict, and nonviolent direct action, see *Fellowship Magazine*, I (1935), ff, esp. "Statements of FOR National Council on Sit-Down Strikes," III (Jan. 1937), 14, and III (May 1937), 6; A. J. Muste, "Sit Downs and Lie Downs," III (March 1936), 5–6; James R. Robinson, "The Yogi and the Commissar," XII (Feb. 1946), 25–26; John Dillingham, "Our Racial Caste System," II (Dec. 1936), 13–14. In the FOR Minute Books, FOR Arch., see esp: Reports of the Southern Secretaries, 1939–40, *passim;* J. Holmes Smith, Report of Secretary of Committee on Non-Violent Techniques, March 28–May 25, 1941; Muste, Report to Annual Conference, 1941; James Farmer, Letter read at FOR National Council, November 29, 1941. For a discussion of Muste's role, overemphasizing somewhat his part in the founding of CORE, see Nat Hentoff, *Peace Agitator: The Story of A. J. Muste* (New York, 1965), 16–17, 106, 110–11.

2. To avoid identification with pacifism, CORE literature spoke of an informal discussion group rather than an FOR cell. Confidential interviews and materials in the FOR Archives revealed the crucial role of the cell in creating CORE. See George M. Houser, Report of Youth Field Worker, Sept. 30–Nov. 28, 1941, and Report of Youth Secretary, Sept. 12, 1942, FOR Minute Books.

3. Identification of the six was based on data obtained through interviewing and the following written sources: Houser, *CORE: A Brief History*, mimeographed pamphlet [1949], CA; Bernice Fisher, "Confessions of an Ex-Liberal," [ca. 1961], MS, Farmer Prs; and Houser to Juanita Morrow, July 7, 1948, CA.

4. On Farmer and Houser see *Fellowship Magazine*, VI (Feb. 1940), 30; VI (April 1940), 65; VII (Oct. 1941), 173; VII (Nov. 1941), 190; Farmer, Reports of Middle-Atlantic Student Secretary, 1939–1940, *passim*, and Report of Youth Field Worker, Sept. 30 to Nov. 28, 1941, FOR Minute Books; FOR National Council, Sept. 7, 1941, FOR Minute Books. On pacifism and Methodist church see Doniver A. Lund, "The Peace Movement Among the Major American Churches, 1919–1939" (Ph.D. dissertation, University of Nebraska, 1955), 131, 141; Muste to Walter White, April 18, 1941, NAACP Arch. Information on Robinson, Jack, and Guinn was obtained chiefly from interviews. On Guinn in jail, see *Defender*, Jan. 26, 1946. For Fisher see her "Confessions . . . ." On religious and student pacifism in general during the 1930's and early 1940's, see John Nelson, *Peace Prophets: American Pacifist Thought, 1919–1941* (Chapel Hill, 1967), esp. 25, 32–35, and Lawrence S. Wittner, *Rebels Against War: The American Peace Movement, 1941–1960* (New York, 1969), chaps. 1, 2, 3.

5. Interviews; Farmer, "The Race Logic of Pacifism," *Fellowship Magazine*, VII (Feb. 1942), 25.

6. Houser, *CORE: A Brief History*, 1; interviews; Fisher, "Confessions . . ."; *What is CORE?* leaflet [1943], CA; Krishnalal Shridharani, *War Without Violence* (New York, 1939); Houser, "We Say No to Jim Crow," *Fellowship Magazine*, XI (April 1945), 62.

7. Fisher, "Confessions . . ."; Houser, *CORE: A Brief History*, 1–2.

8. Farmer, "Memorandum to A. J. Muste on Provisional Plans for Brother-

hood Mobilization," Feb. 19, 1942, and "Additional Memorandum from James Farmer," March 9, 1942, FOR Arch. printed in Francis L. Broderick and August Meier, eds., *Negro Protest Thought in the Twentieth Century* (Indianapolis, 1966), 211–19.

9. Houser, *CORE: A Brief History*, 3; Farmer, *Freedom-When?* (New York, 1965), 55; interviews.

10. Houser, *CORE: A Brief History*, 4; Houser, *Erasing the Color Line*, third edition (New York, 1951), 37–38.

11. Houser, *CORE: A Brief History*, 5.

12. H. A. J. [Homer A. Jack], "Charter Members of CORE," 1942, Farmer Prs; Fisher, "Confessions . . ."; names of officers were obtained from the Chicago group's mimeographed newsletter, *CORE Comments*, 1942–43, *passim*, CA. Data on individual members and officers were obtained chiefly from interviews.

13. Fisher, "Confessions . . ."; Houser, *CORE: A Brief History*, 3.

14. Houser, "Report of Chicago Youth Secretary," Sept. 12, 1942, FOR Minutes Books; "CORE Statement of Purpose," leaflet [1942], Farmer Prs; "CORE Action Discipline," leaflet, 1946, Farmer Prs; Fisher, "Confessions . . ."; *CORE Comments*, 1942–43, *passim*; Minutes of the CORE Executive Committee, Feb. 28, March 3, 1943, and "Suggestions for the Discipline of Non-Violenteers," [ca. Feb. 1943], both in Nelson Jackson correspondence, National Urban League Archives, Southern Office Files, Library of Congress (hereafter cited as Urban League Arch.).

15. *CORE Comments*, 1942–43, *passim*.

16. Fisher, "Confessions . . ."; Farmer, *Freedom-When?*, 56–57.

17. Fisher, "Confessions . . ."; Farmer, "The Race Logic of Pacifism," 24–25; Bayard Rustin, "The Negro and Non-Violence," *Fellowship Magazine*, VII (Oct. 1942), 166–67.

18. Rustin, "The Negro and Non-Violence," 166; Fisher, "Confessions . . . ."

19. Rustin, "The Negro and Non-Violence," 167; Farmer to Fisher, Jan. 18, 1943, Farmer Prs; [Rustin], Lecture and Discussion, Oct. 17, for San Francisco Workshop on Race and Nonviolence, Oct. 9 to Nov. 17, 1943, FOR Arch.

20. Fisher, "Confessions . . ."; *CORE Comments*, March 13, 1943, CA; Minutes, CORE Executive Committee, Feb. 22, 1943, Urban League Arch.

21. Farmer to Fisher, Feb. 27, March 23, 1943, Farmer Prs. Farmer, "The Race Logic of Pacifism," 24; *Equality*, I (Nov. 1944), 2.

22. Shridharani, *War Without Violence*, 3–47; "CORE Action Discipline"; Farmer, *Freedom-When?*, 55–56; interviews.

23. Houser, *Erasing the Color Line*, 38; *CORE Comments* [Jan. 1943].

24. *CORE Comments*, Sept. 16 [1942], Aug. 25 [1942], Oct. [1942], Dec. 10 [1942], CA; *Defender*, Sept. 19, 1942.

25. "Discrimination at the University of Chicago: Background for Action, Pamphlet No. 2," [1943], CA.

26. Houser, *Erasing the Color Line*, 26–27; *CORE Comments*, Dec. 10, [1942], CA; Homer A. Jack, Report of interview with Mr. Harold, Nov. 18, 1942, CA.

27. Houser, "We Say No to Jim Crow," 61–62; Robinson to Night Manager

of Jack Spratt Coffee House, May 14, 1942, CA; "CORE Report Sheet," Oct. 9 and 13, 1942, CA; *CORE Comments,* Dec. [1942], Feb. 12, 1943, n.d. [Jan. 1943], and n.d. [May 1943], CA; Chicago *Bee,* May 16, 1943; William Lester and James Robinson to Cashier, Jack Spratt Coffee Shop, May 9, 1943, CA; Farmer, *Freedom-When?,* 60–62.

28. "Minutes of the First National Planning Conference of the Committee of Racial Equality," June 4–6, 1943, Farmer Prs; *Defender,* June 12, 1943; Houser, *Erasing the Color Line,* 24–25; Farmer, *Freedom—When?,* 62.

29. Pauli Murray, "Blueprint for First Class Citizenship," *Crisis,* LI (Nov. 1944), 358–59; "Pledge" of the Civil Rights Committee of Howard University NAACP, April 13, 1944, CA; and materials in Pauli Murray's Papers, esp. "Lesson Plan on Non-Violent Action," issued by Howard University NAACP Civil Rights Committee [1944]; mimeographed statement, "What Took Place on 11th and Pennsylvania, April 22, 1944"; Civil Rights Committee and others to President Mordecai Johnson, April 30, 1944, and Johnson to Leon Ransom, May 22, 1944.

30. Houser, "We Say No to Jim Crow," 61–62.

31. Houser, *Erasing the Color Line,* 31–34; Art Dole, untitled MS [1941], CA.

32. On Smith's role in Nonviolent Action Committee, see FOR Minute Books, 1941, *passim.* On Ashram, see *Fellowship Magazine,* VII (Jan. 1941), 2, and VII (July 1942), 118. On Pilgrimage, see *Fellowship Magazine,* VIII (Nov. 1942), 192; "The Spirit and Standpoint of the Interracial Pilgrimage to the Lincoln Memorial" [July 1942], and Smith correspondence with Madison Jones, June and July 1942, NAACP Arch.

33. On Farmer's and Rustin's work in general, see FOR Executive Committee, Sept. 29, 1942, April 27, 1943, and Report of A. J. Muste to FOR National Council Meeting, May 14–15, 1943, FOR Minute Books; *CORE Comments,* Dec. 10 [1942], CA. On Denver, see correspondence from Margaret Rohrer, Dec. 1942 to March 1943, CA. On New York and Syracuse, see "Syracuse CORE, Brief History," Feb. 19, 1943, CA; Farmer to Fisher, Oct. 14, Nov. 2, 1942, Jan. 16, March 17, 1943, Farmer Prs; Minutes of Non-Violent Action Committee Meeting, Oct. 26, 1942, FOR Arch.; "First National Planning Conference of Committee of Racial Equality, June 4, 5, 6, 1943," Farmer Prs.

34. Farmer to Fisher, Oct. 16, Nov. 24, 2, 5, 1942, Farmer Prs.

35. Farmer to Fisher, Nov. 2, 24, 1942; Feb. 27, March 5, 17, 23, 1943, Farmer Prs; CORE Executive Committee, Feb. 22, March 3, 1943, in Urban League Arch.; *CORE Comments,* Dec. 10 [1942], May [1943], June 25, 1943, CA; *Defender,* June 12, 1943.

36. Minutes of First National Planning Conference. . . .

37. Interviews; Cleveland *Gazette,* July 12, Aug. 2, 1941; and materials in the Vanguard League Arch., esp. Minutes of the Executive Board and Labor Committee, *passim,* and extensive correspondence with business officials; materials in the Barbee Durham Prs, esp. Durham to "the Editor," Feb. 15, 1941, "Report of Violations of the Civil Rights Law of Ohio in Columbus" [1941], "Supplement to the Vanguard League's Report on Civil Rights—Dealing with Thea-

ters" [June 1941], Durham to Dear Friend, May 26, 1941; and copies of the League's mimeo'd publication, *The Vanguard Bulletin*, 1941–42, Durham Prs, and *Vigilance*, 1942–45, esp. the issue of Feb. 18, 1943, Vanguard League Arch. On origins of the League, see Durham to "Russell" March 23, 1949, and attached clippings from *Ohio State News*, 1940, containing letters from "For More Civil Rights" [Barbee Durham] to Editor, April and May, 1940, Durham Prs.

38. Minutes of First National Planning Conference. . . .

39. *Ibid.;* Amended Constitution, 1945, CA; Houser to Dear Friends, Jan. 9, 1946, CA; Report on 1945 Convention, CA. We have been unable to locate a copy of the original constitution of 1944.

40. Fisher, "Confessions . . ."; Executive Committee, March 3–4, 1945, MLK; 1944 Convention and Report on 1945 Convention, CA.

41. On Rustin, see *Fellowship Magazine*, X (Feb. 1944), 30, and X (April 1944), 77; Rustin to New York Local Draft Board No. 63, Nov. 16, 1943, FOR Arch. On Farmer see Muste to Farmer [May 1945] in FOR Executive Committee, May 8, 1945, FOR Arch; and 1945 Convention, CA.

42. *Fellowship Magazine*, XII (July 1945), 132; Houser and Rustin to FOR National Council, May 30, 1947, FOR Minute Books.

43. Non-Violent Direct Action Committee, March 24, 1945, FOR Minute Books.

44. Houser, Report on West Coast Trip, March 15 to April 18, 1946, CA.

45. Minutes, National Planning Conference . . . ; Houser's column, "Non-Violently Speaking," *Equality*, II (March and July 1945).

46. Houser, "Memo on a Mass Non-Violent Interracial Movement," Sept. 1945, CA; Randolph to Houser, Jan. 4, 1945, CA; Houser to Randolph, Feb. 2, 1945, CA.

47. Farmer to Houser, Feb. 5, 1943, CA; Farmer to Fisher, Jan. 18, 1943, Farmer Prs; Houser to Farmer, Feb. 13, 1943, CA.

48. Houser, "Plan for Non-Violent Campaign Against Jim Crow," June 19, 1944, FOR Arch; Muste to Houser, June 28, 1944, CA; Fisher to Houser, July 12, 1944, CA; Houser, "Plan for a Two or Three Months Full-Time Campaign Against Jim Crow" [Sept. 1944], Farmer Prs; CORE Executive Committee, Oct. 14, 1944, MLK.

49. Houser to Muste, Feb. 21, 1945, and Muste to Houser, Feb. 28, 1945, CA; CORE Executive Committee, March 3–4, April 21, 1945, MLK; Non-violent Direct Action Committee, March 24, 1945, FOR Arch; Houser to Ruth Steele, May 11, 1945, CA; Houser, "Report on the CORE Summer Campaign," Sept. 1945, CA.

50. Houser, "Memo on a Mass Non-Violent Interracial Movement" [Sept. 1945], CA; CORE Executive Committee and Council Meeting, Dec. 8–9, 1945, CA; Houser to Wilkins, Nov. 23, Dec. 1, 1945, NAACP Arch; Houser to Executive Committee and Council, Jan. 9, 1946, CA; leaflet advertising summer workshop, "Volunteers for Interracial Action, June 17–Aug. 18" [ca. Feb. 1946], CA; Houser to Muste, June 8, 1946, CA; Houser to Eugene Stanley, March 14, April 15, May 14, 1946, Stanley Prs.

51. Houser, "Plan for a Two or Three Months Full-Time Campaign Against Jim Crow."

52. Houser, *CORE: A Brief History*, 7; CORE letterheads, 1945–47; Convention materials, 1945, 1947, CA.

53. *CORE Comments*, Sept. 1943, CA.

54. Philadelphia and Minneapolis Reports to 1947 Convention, CA; for Cincinnati, see Kathryn Veith to Houser, May 7, 1947, CA; for Kansas City, see Lawrence Scott to Houser, April 21, 1946, CA; for Lincoln see Bill Miller to Houser, Oct. 27, 1945, CA. Data on black chapter leaders from scattered sources. On Holmes and NAACP, see following in NAACP Arch.: Holmes to Oswald Garrison Villard [June 1915], May Childs Nerney to Holmes, June 29, 1915, and Holmes to Robert Bagnall, Nov. 10, 1926. On Durham, who obtained his job only after NAACP protest against discrimination, see *Crisis*, XLIV (Feb. 1937), 53, and Durham to Elliott Rudwick, Aug. 9, 1972, Durham Prs.

55. Interviews; William Barbee Durham to Houser, Nov. 8, 1948, CA.

56. Fisher to Houser, June 12, 1944, CA; Fisher, "Non-Violence in Principle and Practice," *CORE Comments*, Aug. 1944, Farmer Prs.

57. "History of the Committee on the Practice of Democracy, Kansas City, Missouri," n.d. CA; "History of Bartlesville CORE" [1947], CA.

58. Materials on New York CORE YMCA campaign in James and Lula Farmer papers, esp. New York CORE, "Open Letter to the Board of Directors of Brooklyn and Queens YMCA," Nov. 20, 1943, and New York CORE Minutes, June 1943 to June 1945, *passim;* Detroit *CORE-lator*, May 1944, CA; *CORE-lator*, May 1, 1945; 1944, Convention, CA; Fisher to Houser, June 6, 1944, CA; *CORE Comments*, June 1943 to Aug. 1944, *passim*, CA and Farmer Prs; Manuel Talley to Houser, Oct. 15, 1947, CA.

59. Claire Whitehead to Robert J. Kirschwing, Aug. 9, 1943, CA; Houser, *Erasing the Color Line*, 44–45.

60. *Defender*, Jan. 12, 19, Feb. 2, 16, 23, March 2, 9, 16, 1946; Warren Marks to Houser, Dec. 29, 1945, Jan. 7, 13, Feb. 2, 1946, CA; *CORE-lator*, May 1946.

61. Mrs. Henry Crawford, "Euclid Beach Incident" [1946], CA; Juanita Morrow to Houser, two undated letters [1946 and March 1947], CA. CORE Executive Committee, May 3, 1947, MLK.

62. Robert S. Vogel to Houser, Jan. 28, 1944; ? to Rev. Romig, May 10, 1944, both CA.

63. Correspondence of League officials with Columbus and Southern Ohio Electric Company and government agencies, 1943–45; Vanguard League Labor Committee Reports, Nov. 14, Dec. 13, 1944; *Vigilance*, Sept. 11, 1945, all in Vanguard League Arch.; interviews.

64. *CORE-lator*, May 1, 1945, March 1946; 1946 Convention Minutes; Gerald Bullock to Houser, May 30, 1947, CA; Homer Jack to Houser, Sept. 22, 1947, CA; Fisher to Houser, Oct. 1, 1945, CA; Detroit *CORE-lator*, March 1944, CA; Houser to John Hanly, Sept. 5, 1946, CA.

65. *Defender*, April 27, May 4, June 8, 1946, and Jan. 25, Feb. 8, May 8, 1947; Bullock to Houser, Oct. 22, Nov. 6, Dec. 26, 1946, CA; *Chicago CORE-News*, Nov.–Dec. 1946, CA; CORE Executive Committee, May 3, 1947, MLK.

66. ? to Rev. Romig, May 10, 1944, CA; Detroit *CORE-lator,* September, 1944, CA; Vanguard League Board Minutes, June 26, 1947, Vanguard League Arch.; *CORE Comments,* June 25, 1943, CA; *New York Corespondent,* Jan. 1947, Farmer Prs; 1947 Convention, CA.

67. Vanguard League pamphlets, *Democracy in Education,* 1943, and *Which September?,* 1944, Vanguard League Arch.; *Vigilance,* July 8, Aug. 13, Sept. 6, 1943, Durham Prs, and Oct. 18, 1943, Vanguard League Arch. Hospitals and Schools Unit of Chicago CORE, "Report on the Elementary and High Schools of Chicago" [March 1944], Farmer Prs; *CORE Comments,* March 27, May 1944, CA.

68. Chicago CORE, "Discrimination at the University of Chicago, Background for Action, Pamphlet No. 2" [1944], CA; *CORE Comments,* March 27, Aug. 1944, CA; "The Red Cross and its Jim Crow Policy," leaflet [1944], Farmer Prs; Syracuse CORE, "Progress Report of CORE's Campaign: Red Cross and Its Jim Crow Policy" [ca. Oct. 1943], Farmer Prs; *CORE Comments,* Aug., Nov., 1943; Jan. 24, May, Aug. 1944, CA; Robert Vogel to Houser, Jan. 28, 1944, CA; Oberlin *News-Tribune,* March 22, 1945, clipping, personal file and personal observations.

69. New York CORE Minutes, Nov. 1943 to May 1944, *passim,* James and Lula Farmer Prs; Fisher to Farmer, April 8, 1944, Farmer Prs; *Fellowship Magazine,* X (May 1944), 96; 1944 CORE Convention, CA.

70. Houser, "Non-Violently Speaking," *Equality,* I (Oct. 1944).

71. Marjorie Swann to Houser, Nov. 25, 1945, CA.

72. Ann Brown to Houser, June 12, 1946, CA; Minneapolis affiliation application [early 1947], CA.

73. Bob Hansen to Houser, Feb. 21, 1947, CA.

74. Marjorie Banks to Houser, April 27, Nov. 20, 1945, CA.

75. New York CORE Minutes, *passim,* James and Lula Farmer Prs.

76. Worth Randle to Houser, Aug. 14, 1947, CA; Kathryn Veith to Houser, March 1, 13, 1947, CA; Houser to Veith, April 10, May 26, 1947, CA.

77. Talley to Houser, Aug. 3, 1947, CA.

78. Fisher, "Confessions . . . ."

79. Interview; Tad Tekla to Houser, Sept. 29, 1946, CA.

80. Frank Shearer to Lillian Smith, Feb. 13, 1945 and Vanguard League Minutes, Feb. 12, March 5, 19, Dec. 4, 1947, all in Vanguard League Arch.; Durham to Houser, March 24, 1947, and June 8, 1948, both in CA; Group Reports to CORE Convention, 1947, CA; CORE Executive Committee, May 3, 1947, April 17–18, 1946, MLK; interviews.

81. *CORE Comments,* March 27, May 1944, CA; Fisher to Houser, June 6, July 12, 1944, CA; Homer Jack to Houser [ca. Feb. 1946], CA; Houser correspondence with Gerald Bullock, Warren Marks, Robert Gemmer, Marie Klein, 1946–47, *passim,* CA; *Chicago CORE-News,* Aug. 15, Sept. 15, 1946, CA; leaflets announcing rallies on Jan. 27 and Feb. 9, 1946, in Virgil J. Vogel Prs; Bernice Fisher to "Billie, Jimmy, and Jim" [ca. 1953], Lula Farmer Prs; James Robinson to Thomas Timberg, April 7, 1959, CA.

82. Houser, undated memo to chapters, quoted in Rudolph Lombard, "Staff Reorganization of CORE" [1962], CHQ.

83. CORE Executive Committee, Sept. 14, 1946, MLK; Houser to Wilson Head, Oct. 15, 1946, CA; Houser to Frank Shearer, May 15, 1947, CA; Houser to Lillian Smith, March 18, 1947, CA.

84. *CORE-lator,* Dec. 1945.

85. CORE Executive Committee and Council, Dec. 8–9, 1945, CA; Houser to Dear Friends, Jan. 9, 1946, CA; 1946 Convention, CA; CORE Executive Committee, Sept. 14, 1946, MLK; "On Motion Approving Field Executive—Report of Sub-Committee [Meeting], Sept. 15, 1946," memo dated Sept. 25, 1946, CA; Houser, "Memo on Full-Time Executive Secretary" [Oct. 1946], CA; Houser to Dear Friends, Feb. 26, 1947, CA; Juanita Morrow to Houser, Feb. 24, 1947, CA; Houser to Morrow, March 8, April 5, 1947, CA; Houser to Wilson Head, Oct. 15, 1946, CA.

86. Jack Greenberg, *Race Relations and American Law* (New York, 1959), 118–19; *Morgan v. Virginia,* 328 U. S. 373 (1946).

87. Rustin, "Journey of Reconciliation," undated report, FOR Arch.; interviews; CORE Executive Committee, Sept. 14, 1946, MLK; Houser to Wilson Head, Oct. 15, 1946, CA.

88. Houser and Rustin, "Memo on Bus Travel in the South" [Nov. 1946], NAACP Arch.; James Peck, *Freedom Ride* (New York, 1962), 16.

89. Houser and Rustin, Racial-Industrial Department Report in FOR Executive Committee Minutes, Jan. 10, 1947, FOR Arch.; Houser and Rustin, *We Challenged Jim Crow* (New York [1947]), 2; Rustin to C. J. Gates, June 8, 1947, and T. V. Mangum to Rustin, October 27, 1947, CA; Peck to Billie Ames, Oct. 29, 1954, Lula Farmer Prs; interview. On Stanley, see Houser to Stanley, April 4, 1947, and Stanley to Dear Friend [April 1947], both in Stanley Prs.

90. *Times,* Nov. 23, 1946; Houser to Dear Friend, Nov. 27, 1946, A. J. Muste to Walter White, Jan. 30, 1947, White to Muste, Feb. 13, 1947, Madison Jones to Muste, March 4, 1947, all in NAACP Arch.

91. Houser and Rustin, *We Challenged Jim Crow, passim,* supplemented with biographical data obtained from interviews and material in the CORE Arch. New York CORE chapter people were very close to Workers Defense League leaders. Also, interestingly enough, the League had filed a brief *amicus curiae* in the Morgan case. On Stanley see William Miles to Stanley, April 21, 1947, Stanley Prs, and interview.

92. Houser and Rustin, *We Challenged Jim Crow, passim;* "Background Statement on North Carolina Case" [1949], CA; Igal Roodenko to ? [addressee illegible] [April 1947], CA; Peck, *Freedom Ride,* 15–16, 21–23; Pittsburgh *Courier,* April 19, 1947.

93. Houser and Rustin, *We Challenged Jim Crow,* 10–11.

94. *CORE-lator,* April, 1948; "Background Statement on North Carolina Case"; CORE Press Release [March 1948], CA; Typed copy of N. C. Supreme Court decision, rendered Jan. 7, 1949, in *State v. Andrew Johnson et al.,* CA; on financing of the cases see extensive correspondence of Houser and C. J. Gates, T. V. Mangum, C. E. Boulware, and Herman L. Taylor, 1947–49, CA.

95. Robert Carter to Houser, Feb. 8, 1949, CA.

96. Andrew Johnson to Houser, March 12, 1949, CA. On experiences of the men in prison, see esp. Rustin to Muste, March 27, 1949, CA; Mrs. F. M. Fel-

met to Houser, April 9, 1949, CA; Mrs. Hugh Marshall to "Jessie," April 4, 1949, CA; and Rustin, "22 Days on a Chain Gang," mimeographed, [1949] FOR Arch.

97. Peck to Maurice McCrackin [1954], CA; George Engle to Rustin, Nov. 10, 1948, FOR Arch; Houser and Rustin, Report to FOR National Council About Racial-Industrial Work, in FOR National Council, May 30, 1947, FOR Minute Books. For example of press coverage, see *Argus*, June 27, 1947.

CHAPTER TWO

1. Report on 1947 CORE Convention, CA; 1947 Constitution, CA.

2. CORE Executive Committee, Sept. 13–14, 1947, MLK; Houser to CORE groups, Oct. 13, 1947, CA and n.d. [Oct. 1947], CA. *CORE-lator*, Oct. 1947; Houser, "Memorandum to CORE groups on plan for organization," Oct. 29, 1947, CA.

3. Manuel Talley to Houser, Dec. 6, 1947; Mary McLeod Bethune *et al.*, Appeal Letter, Dec. 3, 1947; Houser to Talley, Oct. 27, 1948, all CA.

4. 1949 Convention, CA; Report of Executive Secretary, June 1949, CA.

5. United financial statement [June 1947], CA; 1950 Constitution, CA; Catharine Raymond, Treasurer's Reports, June 1950, Charles Oldham Prs, and June 1951, CA; "Contributions of Sizeable Amounts, 1949–52" [1952], CA.

6. CORE Council, April 7–8, 1951, CA; 1951 Convention, CA; Houser to Farmer *et al.*, Sept. 18, 1951, Lula Farmer Prs.

7. Robinson, Report to CORE Council, Nov. 3–4, 1951, CA; appeal letters, *passim*, CA; Financial Secretary's Report to CORE Convention, 1953, in "Budget, 1953–1954," Mary Coleman Prs.

8. Treasurer's Report, June 1955, CA; "Comparison of 1953–54 Budget with Actual Amounts Received and Expended" [1954], Lula Farmer Prs; Houser, Report to CORE Council, Nov. 3–4, 1951, CA; Robinson to Billie Ames, Nov. 22, 1954, Lula Farmer Prs.

9. 1947 Constitution, CA.

10. Catharine Raymond to Edwin Irwin, Jan. 21, 1949, CA.

11. Correspondence of Houser with Talley, Orval Etter, Glenn Smiley, and Robert Cannon, 1948–50, *passim*, Minutes of Conventions and CORE Executive Committee and Council meetings, 1948–50, *passim*, CA; Houser, "A Proposal on Field Representatives," June 1949, Houser, "Memo on the Relationship of the National Office to the Field Representatives," June 1949, CA; *Western Correspondent*, March 15, 1950, Harriett A. Lane and Houser to CORE groups, April 20, 1950, CA; Houser to CORE groups, June 2, 1950, Houser to Bernice Fisher, Dec. 23, 1948, Fisher to Houser, Dec. 30 [1948], Jan. 27 [1949], Houser to Fisher, March 14, 1949, Talley, Report to CORE Executive Committee, April 4, 1949, CA; Talley, Report to CORE Council, March 10, 1950, all CA.

12. 1949 Convention, CA; 1949 Constitution, CA; Houser to CORE groups, Sept. 29, 1949, CA; interviews; for Houser's preference for the Executive Committee system, see Houser to Harriett Lane, Sept. 13, 1949, CA.

13. CORE Council, April 7–8, 1951, CA.

14. New York CORE, Memo to All Other Affiliates, CORE Locals, and Na-

tional CORE Officers, March 7, 1951, CA; Minneapolis CORE to Local CORE groups and National Office, May 29, 1951, Oldham Prs; CORE Council, April 7–8, 1951, CA; 1951 Convention, CA.

15. For biographical sketch, see Washington Interracial Workshop, *Brotherhood Bulletin*, July 13, 1954, CA. For New York CORE's ambivalence about Nelson, see James Farmer to Lynn [Kirk], June 1, 1951, Farmer Prs.

16. Robinson to Mrs. Robert Auerbach, Jan. 22, 1958, CA; Robinson to Billie Ames, Jan. 9, 1955, CA.

17. William Worthy, Memo to CORE Executive Committee on Universal Military Training [Oct. 1947], CA; Houser to William Hefner, Feb. 19, 1948, CA; CORE Executive Committee, Nov. 15–16, 1947, Oct. 23–24, 1948, MLK; Testimony of Randolph before Senate Armed Services Committee, March 31, 1948, printed in August Meier, Elliott Rudwick, and Francis Broderick, eds., *Black Protest Thought in the Twentieth Century*, revised edition (Indianapolis, 1971), 274–80; N.Y. *Amsterdam News*, April 24, 1948; 1948 Convention, CA; *Fellowship Magazine*, XIV (Oct. 1948), 34; interviews. On attitude of Minneapolis CORE see Houser to Ruth Little, Sept. 8, Oct. 22, 1948, and Little to Houser, Oct. 21, 1948, CA.

18. Worthy to Rustin, Nov. 5, 1947; Houser and Worthy, "Memo to CORE groups on Jim Crow Reserved Coach Train" [Nov. 1947]; Houser to William Hefner, Feb. 19, 1948; Houser, "Account of an Interview with Pennsylvania Railroad Officials," June 4, 1948, all CA.

19. Rustin to Peck, March 22, 1948, CA; *Tribune*, May 25, 1948; CORE News Releases, Dec. 22, 1949, May 16, 1950, March 21, 1951, May 20, Dec. 29, 1952, May 17, 1955; Conrad Lynn to Houser, March 18, 1952, CA; Houser to Lynn, April 17, 1952, CA; Houser to Peck, April 17, 1952, CA; Peck and Rustin, leaflet, "Why We're Picketing this Stockholders Meeting" [May 1950], CA; Peck to Houser, "Memo on Greyhound Situation" [April 1951], CA; "Report by James Peck to Greyhound Stockholders for Whom He and Bayard Rustin Acted as Proxy at Meeting" [May 1952], CA; Peck, "Minority Stockholders vs. Jim Crow —Continued," *Crisis* LIX (June–July 1952), 367–68.

20. Houser to Juanita Nelson, Dec. 6, 1948, CA; Houser to Harold Wilson, Oct. 24, 1950, CA; questionnaire on job discrimination sent to the chapters [Oct. 1950], Lula Farmer Prs; CORE Council, April 7–8, 1951, ÇA; Juanita Nelson to CORE groups and members, May 13, 1951, CA; 1951 Convention, CA.

21. 1950, 1952, 1954 CORE Conventions, CA; Houser to J. Waties Waring, Dec. 20, 1950, CA; A. Philip Randolph to Dear Friend, Feb. [sic] 1951, Oct. 31, 1951, CA; Houser to FOR staff, Oct. 14, 1953, FOR Arch.; CORE Council, March 21–22, 1953, Charles Oldham Prs; Oct. 10–11, 1953, James Farmer Prs; and Feb. 20–21, 1954, CA; Houser to CORE groups [Jan. 1954], Lula Farmer Prs.

22. See, e.g., discussion of Wichita CORE, 1947–49, in Amon Burton, "The Politics of Fair Housing: A Case Study of the Movement to Enact a Fair Housing Ordinance in Wichita, Kansas" (M. A. thesis, Wichita State University, 1964), 23.

23. Constitution of Baltimore CORE [1953], Mary Coleman Prs; Constitu-

tion and By-Laws of St. Louis CORE [ca. 1951], Wanda Penny Prs; see also, e.g., Constitutions of the Washington Interracial Workshop, Feb. 1949 and April 1950, Albert Mindlin—Washington Interracial Workshop Prs (hereafter cited as Mindlin-WIW Prs).

24. 1951 Convention, CA; Nelson, Reports to the 1952 and 1954 Conventions, CA.

25. Interviews.

26. Houser correspondence with Marjorie Kendrick, Aug. to Nov. 1944, CA; *CORE-lator*, Dec. 1945; Houser to Jack Flodin, Oct. 12, 1946, CA.

27. Interracial Workshop, *Progress Report* [July 1947], CA; Bob Kirk to "Galja," July 27, 1947, Mindlin-WIW Prs; Emily Josef to Dear Friend, Aug. 13, 1947, Mindlin-WIW Prs; *Argus*, Dec. 19, 1947; Interracial Workshop, *Progress Report*, April 1948, CA; Lynn Seitter to Rustin, Dec. 10, 1947, Mindlin-WIW Prs; Seitter to Houser, Jan. 8, 1948, Mindlin-WIW Prs; Don Coan to Houser, OCT. 5, 1948, CA.

28. Washington Interracial Workshop Minutes, March 4 and 7, 1949; Interracial Workshop, *Progress Report*, May 1950, all in Mindlin-WIW Prs.

29. Summer Interracial Workshop *Bulletin*, July 30, 1949, CA; Don Coan to Roland Robbins, Sept. 26, 1949, Mindlin-WIW Prs; Coan to Peck, Aug. 17, Sept. 18, 1949, Mindlin-WIW Prs; Coan to Houser, Sept. 30, Dec. 3, 1949, CA; Coan, Memorandum of Conference with Norman Elson, Nov. 18, 1949, Mindlin-WIW Prs; Coan to "Chris," Jan. 25, 1950, Mindlin-WIW Prs; Interracial Workshop Minutes, Dec. 1, 1949 and March 16, 1950, Mindlin-WIW Prs; Houser to Norman Elson, July 8, 1950, Mindlin-WIW Prs.

30. Washington Interracial Workshop Minutes, Oct. 1949 to April 1951, *passim;* Leon Whitt to Victor Orsinger, Oct. 17, 1950; Mindlin to Orsinger, April 10, 1951; Interracial Workshop to Orsinger, May 3, 1951; *Shop-Talk*, Nov. 1950, Jan., April, 1951, all Mindlin-WIW Prs. See also the following from CA: Al Mindlin, "History of the Playhouse Campaign" [ca. Jan. 1951]; Interracial Workshop to Orsinger, Nov. 17, 1950; Kirk to Houser, Feb. 18, 1951; Mindlin to Houser, April 28, 1951.

31. Washington Interracial Workshop Minutes, April 20, June 8, 1950, Mindlin-WIW Prs; Summer Interracial Workshop *News Bulletin*, July 17, 1950, CA; "Workshop Statement Concerning Action Project at Sholl's Cafe" [ca. July 1950], CA; "Workshop Report" [July 1950], Mindlin-WIW Prs; Lynn Kirk to Houser, Sept. 13, Oct. 25, 1950, CA. On Coordinating Committee being more vigorous than the Workshop see also Kirk to Catharine Raymond, Jan. 22, 1951, CA; Kirk to Peck, Feb. 20, 1952, CA.

32. Washington Summer Interracial Workshop *Bulletin*, July 31, 1951, Lula Farmer Prs, and July 21, 1952, CA; *Shop-Talk*, Feb. 12, April, May 13, Aug. 23, 1952, and April 25, 1953, all CA; Lynn Kirk to Jim [Peck], Feb. 20, 1952, CA; *Brotherhood Bulletin*, July 12, 1952, CA.

33. Mindlin, "Project Report Rosedale Playground Campaign, Sept. 1951 to Oct. 1952," dated June 6, 1953, CA; *Shop-Talk*, Dec. 15, 1951, Mindlin-WIW Prs; Mindlin to Houser, Sept. 3, 1951, CA.

34. The best account of the campaign, and the source of the above quota-

tions is Albert Mindlin, "Project Report Rosedale Playground Campaign Sept. 1951 to Oct. 1952," dated June 6, 1953, CA. In addition the following materials were helpful: Washington Interracial Workshop *Shop-Talk,* April [sic], May 13, Aug. 23, Oct. 25, 1952, CA; Summer Interracial Workshop *Bulletin,* July 21, 1952, CA; Lynn Kirk to Houser, Oct. 5, 1952, CA; Lillian Palenius to Houser *et al.,* Sept. 24, 1952, CA; Mindlin to Houser, Oct. 3, 1952, CA; and the following in the Mindlin-WIW Prs: Report of Mass Meeting, Oct. 23, 1951; Reports on Pilgrimages to Rosedale Playground, esp. those dated Oct. 30, Nov. 1, 5, 1951; Feb. 14, March 29, April 5, 1952; Minutes of Rosedale Citizens Committee Meetings, esp. Nov. 4, 5, 14, 21, Dec. 4, 1951; Jan. 15, Feb. 19, 1952; clippings from Washington *Afro-American,* June 24, 28, July 19, Sept. 13, Testimony of Helen Maddox before Recreation Board [1952]; Ruth Shirley to Henry Gichner [1952]; also interviews.

35. Summer Interracial Workshop *Brotherhood Bulletin,* July 13, 1953, Oldham Prs; and July 21, 31, 1953 and July 31, 1954, all CA; *Shop-Talk,* Feb. 1954, CA and March 26, 1955, Mindlin-WIW Prs.

36. Houser to CORE groups, Feb. 26, 1949, CA; [Irvin Dagen], "Report on St. Louis CORE" [June 1952], Lula Farmer Prs; Billie Ames to Houser, July 19, 1951, CA; *Argus,* Nov. 25, 1949; Ames to Delma Johnson, Feb. 16, 1955, Lula Farmer Prs.

37. *Up to Date* (publication of St. Louis CORE) Dec. 1950 and Dec. 1951, CA; Billie Ames to Houser, Aug. 17 and Oct. 8, 1949, CA; Questionnaire for National Council Meeting [ca. Spring 1952], CA; *Argus,* Oct. 22, 1948.

38. Correspondence of Billie Ames, Irvin Dagen, Joseph Ames, and Charles Oldham with store managers, 1950–52, *passim.,* Oldham Prs; *Up to Date,* March, April, and Dec. 1951, and Feb. 1953, CA; Marvin Rich to Houser, Feb. 6, 1950, CA; Ames to Houser, May 3, June 7, 1950, and Feb. 8, 1951, CA; Charles Oldham, "The Story of the Dimes" [1953], Oldham Prs; St. Louis CORE Minutes, June 19, 1951, Oldham Prs; *Argus,* Dec. 23, 30, 1949; Feb. 24, March 24, 31, May 12, 19, 26, June 9, Nov. 3, 1950; April 6, May 25, Aug. 17, 31, 1951; Leaflet, "Keep Score with CORE," May 1953, Oldham Prs.

39. Correspondence of Billie Ames with department store executives, Jan. to April, 1954, Oldham Prs; *Up to Date,* June 1954, CA.

40. Billie Ames to Raymond and Houser [April 1954], Mindlin-WIW Prs; Maggie Dagen to Houser, March 28, 1954, CA.

41. Billie Ames to Muriel Bluford, April 20, 1954, Lula Farmer Prs; St. Louis CORE Minutes, June 11, 1951, Oldham Prs; Ames to A. C. Thompson, Dec. 13, 1950, CA; CORE Chapter Questionnaire [ca. Spring 1952], CA.

42. Billie Ames to Houser, Nov. 11, 1952, CA; interviews.

43. Billie Ames to Dear Friend, Feb. 1954, CA.

44. *Up to Date,* Feb. 1954, CA; M. L. Bohanon to Billie Ames, July 1954, Oldham Prs; Ames to Muriel Bluford, July 27, 1954 and Ames to Maggie Dagen, Aug. 11, 1954, Lula Farmer Prs.

45. Billie Ames to Muriel Bluford, April 20, 1954, Lula Farmer Prs; Ames to Catharine Raymond, Feb. 11, 1954, CA.

46. *CORE-lator,* Oct. 1947, Nov. 1948, Mindlin-WIW Prs; Frank Stannard to

Houser, Feb. 13, 1948, CA; Stanley Kelley to Houser, June 11, 1948, CA; Lawrence CORE Report, Dec. 24, 1949, CA; Elmer Rusco to Houser, Dec. 10, 1950, CA. For Wichita, see Delores Day to Houser, Sept. 10, 1950, CA.

47. Nelson, Reports to CORE Conventions, 1953 and 1954, and to CORE Council, Feb. 20–21, 1954, CA; Billie Ames to Muriel Bluford, Aug. 3, 1954 and Jan. 14, 1955, Lula Farmer Prs.

48. Columbia CORE affiliation blank, n.d., CA; Columbia CORE *Bulletin,* Aug. 1, 1952, CA; Annual Project Report of CORE Groups, June 1953, CA; Verda and Irwin Deutscher, "Cohesion in a Small Group: A Case Study," *Social Forces,* XXXIII (May 1955), 336–41.

49. Baltimore affiliation application [ca. May 1953], CA; CORE Council, Oct. 10–11, 1953, CA; correspondence with members of Baltimore CORE, Nov. 1953 to March 1954, CA; Tom O'Leary to Billie Ames, May 17, 1954, Lula Farmer Prs; *CORE-lator,* March–April, June–July, Oct.–Nov. 1953; James Peck, *Non-Violence Against Jim Crow* [1959?], Mary Coleman Prs; *The Maryland Eagle,* August 8, 15, 1953, copies in Coleman Prs; *Afro-American,* May 8, 1954, clipping, Coleman Prs; interviews.

50. *Defender,* Dec. 6, 1947; Henry Lohman, "Review of Action Against Discriminatory University Medical Facilities and Instruction at the University of Chicago," Dec. 30, 1947, Virgil J. Vogel Prs; *CORE-lator,* Nov. 1948, Oct. 1950, June–July 1953; and the following in the Lula Farmer Prs: New York CORE minutes, 1952–53, *passim;* New York CORE *News,* Nov. 1953, March 1954; typescript of CORE Council Minutes, Oct. 10, 1953; and materials on TV campaign, 1952–53.

51. Correspondence with Manuel Talley, Feb. to Oct. 1948, *passim;* William J. Roberts to Houser, Nov. 19, 1948; Caroline Urie to Houser, Aug. 17, 1952, all CA.

52. *Times,* July 14, Aug. 14, 16, 21, Sept. 1, 1947; July 28, Sept. 6, 1948; *CORE-lator,* 1947–53, *passim;* and the following materials in the Lula Farmer Prs: New York *Corespondent,* Feb. 1949; New York CORE Minutes, April 25, Oct. 10, 1952, May 8, Sept. 18, 1953; and James Peck, "Report on New York CORE's Palisades Park Project" [1954].

53. Juanita Nelson to Peck, March 2, 1952, CA; CCHR, *News of Coney Island,* July 1952, CA; Juanita Nelson to Billie Ames, Jan. 9, 1953, Lula Farmer Prs; "Annual Project Report of CORE Groups," June 1953, CA; Mrs. Ernest Bromley to Peck, June 4, 1953, CA; James Robinson to Charles Oldham, Feb. 15, 1954, Oldham Prs; *Argus,* Aug. 13, 1954 and April 15, 1955.

54. *Defender,* May 10, July 26, 1947 and Feb. 28, 1948; Homer Jack to Houser, Sept. 23, 1947, CA; Chicago *CORE-News,* Oct. 18, 1947 and March 5, 1948, CA.

55. See e.g., Talley to Houser, Feb. 21, March 2, 9, 1949; Talley, Report to CORE Council, March 10, 1950, all CA.

56. Orval Etter to Houser, July 14, 1948, and clippings from San Francisco *Reporter,* April 30, Sept. 11, 1948, all CA.

57. *Tribune,* Dec. 30, 1947, Feb. 21, 1948; Orval Etter to Houser, Feb. 10, 1950; *Western Corespondent,* March 15, 1950; E. Lewis Branch to Houser, April 22, 1950, all CA.

58. *Western Corespondent,* March 15, 1950, CA; *CORE-lator,* Jan. and April 1950.

59. Talley to Houser, Sept. 17, 1948, May 24, 1949; Peck to Houser, Jan. 9, 1949; *Western Corespondent,* March 15, 1950; Orval Etter to Houser, April 17, 1950; Glenn Smiley to Houser, April 18, 1950, all CA.

60. Jeffrey Smith, "The Omaha De Porres Club," (M. A. thesis, Creighton University, 1967, *passim*); John Markoe, "Omaha De Porres Center," *Interracial Review,* XXI (Feb. 1950), 24–27; Denny Holland to Dear CORE members, July 30, 1951, May 9, 1952, CA; De Porres Club affiliation application, 1952, CA; Chapter Project Summary, June 1952, Oldham Prs; Jean Waite to Peck, Dec. 17, 1952, CA; Holland to Houser, Oct. 30, 1953, CA; *CORE-lator,* Jan.–Feb. and April 1954.

61. Houser to Billie Ames, July 8, 1950; E. Lewis Branch to Houser, Oct. 29, 1950; correspondence with Abraham Lincoln Fletcha, Orval Etter, Allen Willis, and Dixon Adams of San Francisco, Oct. 1947 to Jan. 1949, and Talley to Houser, March 15, 1949; correspondence with Marion Coddington of Pasadena, Sept. 1948 to Feb. 1954; Los Angeles *Corespondent,* May 6, July 25, 1952; Herbert Kelman, Report on CORE Field Work, 1955, all CA.

62. Correspondence with Frank Shearer, 1947–49, CA; Houser correspondence with Lorena Estlow of Chicago, 1950, CA; CORE Council, April 7–8, 1951, CA; Fred Fields to Peck, Dec. 10, 1952, CA; Annual Project Reports of CORE Groups, June 1952, Lula Farmer Prs; correspondence with Eroseanna Robinson, 1952, CA; data on disaffiliations obtained from Convention Minutes, *passim.*

63. Denny Holland to Houser, April 6, 1952 and Oct. 30, 1953; Houser to Holland, April 23, May 15, 1952; Bob Young to Houser, Jan. 11, 1954, all CA.

64. 1952 and 1954 Conventions, CA; CORE letterheads, 1950–54; interviews.

65. Lillian Palenius to Billie Ames, March 13, 1955, Lula Farmer Prs.

66. Houser to Mindlin, Feb. 4, 1954, Mindlin-WIW Prs; Houser, "Statement for Discussion on the Communist Problem at the CORE Conference . . ." [1948], CA.

67. *CORE-lator,* Nov. 1948; CORE Executive Committee, April 17–18, 1948, MLK; Houser, "Statement for Discussion on the Communist Problem at the CORE Conference and Pre-Conference Discussion in CORE Groups" [1948], CA; "Statement on the Communist Issue," adopted by 1948 Convention, CA.

68. Frank Condon to Talley, April 8, 1950, CA; Condon to Houser, March 11, 1950, CA; "The Friends of Miss Brown" to Dear Friend, Aug. 21, 1951, CA; Houser, "Impressions of Pittsburgh" [Sept. 1952], Carl Rachlin Files; Billie Ames to Houser, Oct. 1, 1952, CA; Houser to Ames, Oct. 9, 1952, CA; Al Mindlin to Houser, Aug. 21, 1952, CA; CORE Council, Oct. 18–19, 1952, and March 21–22, 1953, Oldham Prs.; Betty Beaver to Houser, Nelson and CORE groups [Oct. 1953], CA.

69. "Statement on the Communist Issue," adopted by 1952 Convention, CA; 1952 Convention, CA.

70. Robinson to Mindlin, Dec. 9, 1953, Mindlin-WIW Prs; Robinson to Oldham, Feb. 15, 1954, Oldham Prs; Nelson's Reports to 1952, 1953, 1954 Conventions, CA.

71. CORE Council, March 21–22, 1953, Oldham Prs; Nelson, Report to 1953 CORE Convention, CA; 1953 Convention, CA; CORE Council, Feb. 20–21, 1954, CA.

72. Robinson to Billie Ames, Lula Farmer, Bernice Fisher, Charles Oldham [ca. early 1954], Oldham Prs; CORE Council, March 21–22, 1953, Oldham Prs.

73. Neil Haworth, Lynn and Robert Kirk, Wallace and Juanita Nelson, Lillian Palenius and Catharine Raymond to CORE groups and leaders, Sept. 16, 1954, Lula Farmer Prs; Mindlin to Dear CORE member, Feb. 8, 1954, Mindlin-WIW Prs.

74. FOR Executive Committee, Sept. 21, 1951, FOR Minute Books, FOR Arch.

75. CORE Council, March 21–22, 1953, Oldham Prs; New York CORE Minutes, June 19, 1953, Lula Farmer Prs; 1953 Convention, CA.

76. Raymond to Billie Ames, Aug. 26, 1954, CA; Houser to Mindlin, Dec. 16, 1953, Mindlin-WIW Prs. Houser to Robinson *et al.* [ca. Jan. 1954], CA; Robinson to Billie Ames, Lula Farmer, Bernice Fisher, Charles Oldham [ca. Jan. 1954], Oldham Prs.

77. Houser to Robinson *et al.* [ca. Jan. 1954], CA; CORE Council, Oct. 10–11, 1953, CA; St. Louis and New York CORE to Dear Friends, Dec. 7, 1953, Oldham Prs; Oldham to Robinson, Dec. 11, 1953, Oldham Prs; Robinson to Oldham, Feb. 7, 1954, Oldham Prs. On Fisher's opposition to Nelson see Fisher to Farmer, June 8, 1953, Farmer Prs.

78. "Report on FOR Retreat," April 12–14, 1951, Minutes of National Staff Meeting, May 29–June 1, 1951, FOR National Council Meeting, May 14–16, 1953, FOR Executive Committee Meeting, April 5, 1954, all in FOR Minute Books; Houser to CORE groups, Feb. 5, 1954, CA; •Peck to Kelman, Jan. 7 [1955], Herbert Kelman Prs. Houser's departure from FOR was actually delayed until 1955.

79. Houser to Billie Ames, Feb. 15, 1954, Lula Farmer Prs; Robinson to Oldham, Feb. 15, 1954, Oldham Prs; CORE Council, Feb. 20–21, 1954, CA; Ames to Lillian Palenius, April 28, 1954, Lula Farmer Prs.

80. New York CORE National Problems Committee Meeting, June 4, 1954; Neil Haworth *et al.,* Memo to CORE groups and leaders, Sept. 16, 1954; Robinson to Ames, July 4, 1954, all in Lula Farmer Prs.

CHAPTER THREE

1. Billie Ames to Houser, June 28, 1954, CA; Catharine Raymond to Ames, Aug. 26, 1954, CA.

2. 1954 Convention, CA; Ames to Lula Farmer, June 25, 1954, Lula Farmer Prs; Ames to Catharine Raymond, Oct. 7, 1954, CA; Ames to Wallace Nelson *et al.,* Sept. 30, 1954, Lula Farmer Prs; Robert Carter to Ames, Oct. 2, 1954, Lula Farmer Prs; Ames to Carter, Oct. 26, 1954, Lula Farmer Prs; CORE Council, Nov. 27–28, 1954, CA.

3. Raymond to Robinson, June 14, 1955, Lula Farmer Prs; Nelson to James Peck, May 13, 1956, CA; Neil Haworth to Ames, March 24, 1955, Lula Farmer Prs; CORE Council, March 3, 1956, draft minutes, James Farmer Prs.

4. On Chicago, see: 1955 Convention, CA; Ames to Raymond, Aug. 10, 1954, Lula Farmer Prs; Joffre Stewart to Peck, n.d. Lula Farmer Prs; Lula Farmer to Charles Oldham, June 13, 1956, Oldham Prs; *CORE-lator,* Feb. 1957. On New York, see Robinson to Ames, Jan. 31, 1955, Lula Farmer Prs; New York CORE *News,* April 1955, and [early 1956], Lula Farmer Prs; *CORE-lator,* Spring 1955 and Feb. 1956; *Times,* Dec. 31, 1955; Robinson to Oldham, Nov. 17, 1956, Lula Farmer Prs; CORE Council, Jan. 27, 1957, James Farmer Prs.

5. *Up To Date* (publication of St. Louis CORE), 1955 *passim,* Oldham Prs; Billie Ames to H. Gaylord, Aug. 5, 1954, Lula Farmer Prs; Ames to Peck, Oct. 7, 1954, Lula Farmer Prs; St. Louis CORE Minutes, 1954–55, *passim,* Oldham Prs; Ames to Margaret Dagen, Oct. 20, 1954, Lula Farmer Prs; *Argus,* March 19, Sept. 17, Oct. 8, Dec. 17, 1954.

6. *Up To Date,* April 1955, Oldham Prs; M. Leo Bohanon to Billie Ames, July 19, 1954, Oldham Prs.

7. Ames to Houser, Nov. 5, 1954, CA; *Up To Date,* 1954–55, *passim,* Oldham Prs; Ames to Dear Friends, June 1, 1955, Oldham Prs; St. Louis CORE Minutes, Feb. 1, 8, 15, 1955, Oldham Prs; Oldham to Peck, Jan. 30, 1956, Oldham Prs.

8. Oldham to Peck, Jan 30, 1956, and Jan. 14, 1957, Oldham Prs; CORE Council, March 3, 1956, draft minutes, and Jan. 27, 1957, both in James Farmer Prs; Robinson to Oldham, May 16, 1957, Lula Farmer Prs.

9. *CORE-lator,* Feb. 1955, Feb. 1956; Lula Farmer to Charles and Marian Oldham, July 11, 1956, Oldham Prs.

10. *CORE-lator,* Fall 1955; Adah Jenkins to Lula Farmer, Dec. 19, 1956, Lula Farmer Prs; Jenkins, "Report to CORE Convention—Baltimore Chapter," July 1957, CA.

11. Lula Farmer to Oldham, July 11, Aug. 22, 1956, Oldham Prs; Lula Farmer to Joan Wertheimer, July 11, 1956, Lula Farmer Prs; Adah Jenkins to Robinson, March 1, 1957, CA; Robinson to Oldham, Nov. 3, 1957, MLK.

12. Herbert Kelman, Report on CORE Field Work [April], 1955, CA; Henry Hodge to District Manager of Fred Harvey Enterprises, Dec. 8, 1955, CA; *CORE-lator,* Fall 1955, Feb. and Spring 1956; Sayuri Buell to Robinson, March 16, 1957, CA; and the following materials in the Herbert Kelman Papers: Billie Ames to Kelman, July 27, Oct. 13, 1954, May 19, 1955; Kelman to Hodge, Dec. 5, 1954; Kelman to Marion Coddington, Dec. 5, 1954; Kelman to Ames, Feb. 1, May 15, 1955; Kelman to Gordon Carey, March 30, 1955; Carey to Kelman, April 5, 1955; Agenda for Los Angeles CORE Meeting, April 12, 1955; David McReynolds to Friends, May 10, 1955; McReynolds to Kelman, May 29, 1955; Kelman to Houser, May 30, 1955; Kelman to McReynolds, May 30, July 11, 1955; Kelman to Sayuri Buell, July 24, 1955; Buell to Kelman, July 27, 1955.

13. James Peck to Ames, Feb. 9, 1955, Lula Farmer Prs.

14. Peck to Ames, Nov. 10, 1954, and Robinson to Ames, Nov. 22, 1954, Lula Farmer Prs.

15. Peck to Ames, Feb. 9, 1955, Lula Farmer Prs.

16. Billie Ames to Muriel Bluford, Aug. 30, 1954, Jan. 14, 1955; Rabbi Fish-

man to Ames, March 11, 1955; Ames to Peck, Feb. 18, 1955; Ames to James Farmer, March 14, 1955, all in Lula Farmer Prs.

17. Ames to Houser *et al.*, March 29, 1955, CA; Robinson to Ames, May 15, 1955, Lula Farmer Prs; Billie Ames, appeal letter, June 1, 1955, CA.

18. Clothilde Burns to Esther Cannon, Jan. 10, 1956, Oldham Prs; LeRoy Carter, Report, Jan. to June 1956, CA.

19. David Lewis, *King: A Critical Biography* (New York, 1970), 72; Bayard Rustin, "Montgomery Diary," *Liberation*, I (April 1956), 7–10.

20. *CORE-lator*, Spring 1956; 1956 Convention, James Farmer Prs; Robinson to Martin Luther King, Sept. 23, 1957, and Robinson to A. Philip Randolph, Oct. 3, 1957, both in Brotherhood of Sleeping Car Porter Arch.

21. Carter, Report on Memphis [1956], Lula Farmer Prs; Carter, Field Report, Jan. to June 1956, CA; Esther Cannon to Robinson, Aug. 14, 1956, Lula Farmer Prs; Nashville group affiliation application, March 1957, CA.

22. Carter, undated report [1956], Lula Farmer Prs; Carter, Field Report, Jan. to June 1956, CA.

23. Carter to Oldham, June 7, 1956, Oldham Prs; Ralph Blackwood, "The Hutchinson Restaurant Campaign," Jan. 2, 1957, CHQ; and the following materials, all in the Lula Farmer Prs: Carter, Reports, Sept. 5–20, 1956; Nov. 12–Dec. 14, 1956; and Jan. 28–Feb. [sic] 1957; Carter to Lula Farmer, Nov. 28, 1956; Blackwood to Robinson, Jan. 2, 1957; Lula Farmer to CORE groups, Oct. 29, 1956; Robinson to Gordon Carey, Nov. 17, 1956; Peck to Blackwood, April 10, 1957; Blackwood to Peck, April 20, 1957; Robinson to Oldham, May 16, 1957.

24. Robinson to Gordon Carey, Nov. 29, 1956, and Wilson Riles to Robinson, Nov. 8, 1956, Lula Farmer Prs.

25. Robinson to Wilson Riles, April 23, May 18, 1957; Robinson to Houser, March 27, 1957; Robinson to Roy Arvis, May 30, 1957, all in Lula Farmer Prs.

26. Robinson, "CORE's New Directions. for 1956 and the Years to Come" [July 1956], CA; Oldham to Peck, Jan. 14, 1957, CA; *CORE-lator*, Feb. 1957; Finance Secretary's Report to 1957 Convention, CHQ; Robinson to Randolph, March 23, 1956, Brotherhood of Sleeping Car Porters Arch; Randolph Appeal letter, Jan. 7, 1957, CA.

27. Robinson to Billie Ames, Nov. 22, 1954, Lula Farmer Prs; Report of Executive Secretary to 1957 Convention, CA; Treasurer's Reports for fiscal years ending May 31, 1955, May 31, 1956, May 31, 1957, Lula Farmer Prs; 1956 Convention, James Farmer Prs.

28. Robinson, "CORE's New Directions for 1956 and the Years to Come" [1956], CA; CORE Council, March 3–4, 1956, CA; Robinson to Oldham, Nov. 17, 1956, Lula Farmer Prs.

29. 1957 Convention, James Farmer Prs; Constitution, March 22, 1958, CA.

30. See correspondence with Oldham, 1957–59, Oldham Prs and MLK.

31. Executive Secretary's Report to CORE Council, Feb. 21, 1959, CA.

32. Rich, Report of Community Relations Director to CORE Council, Jan. 23–24, 1960, CA.

33. Lula Farmer to Robinson and Oldham, Jan. 28, 1958, Lula Farmer Prs; Robinson to Mrs. Bert Seidman, Nov. 6 and 29, 1957, CA; Executive Secretary's

Reports to CORE Council, March 22–23, 1958, CA, and to 1958 CORE Convention, CHQ. On reason for changing title of CORE Discipline see Robinson to Billie Ames, Aug. 21, 1954, Lula Farmer Prs.

34. Gordon Carey to Howard R. Carey, March 18, 1959, CA; Rustin to King, March 12, 1958 and King to Rustin, March 19, 1958, Martin Luther King Prs; Boston University; King to Dear Friend, Aug. 1958 [sic], CA; NAC Agenda, Dec. 8, 1958, CA.

35. Robinson to King, Sept. 23, 1957, and Robinson to Randolph, Oct. 3, 1957, both in Brotherhood of Sleeping Car Porters Arch.; Robinson to Rustin, July 13, 1959, CA; Rich, Community Relations Director's Report to CORE National Council, Jan. 23–24, 1960, CA; Lula Farmer to all CORE Contacts, Oct. 4, 1957, Lula Farmer Prs.

36. Executive Secretary's Report to CORE National Council, Jan. 23–24, 1960, Oldham Prs; Jack Conway to Billie Ames, Sept. 1, 1954, Lula Farmer Prs; James Carey to Randolph, March 19, 1959, Brotherhood of Sleeping Car Porters Arch.; Robinson to Randolph, March 19, 1959, CA; 1959 Convention, CA; Rich, Community Relations Director's Report to CORE National Council, Jan. 23–24, 1960, CA.

37. NAC, March 2, 1958, James Farmer Prs; Robinson to Zimmerman, March 12, 1958, CA; Robinson to Oldham, May 5, 1958, Oldham Prs; Rich, Community Relations Director's Report to CORE National Council, Jan. 23–24, 1960, CA.

38. For example, see Robinson to Dear Friend, April 9, 1958, CA.

39. Executive Secretary's Report to 1958 Convention, CA; Robinson to Oldham, June 18, 1958, Oldham Prs; NAC, July 18, 1958, James Farmer Prs; Robinson to McCain, Aug. 18, 1958, CA.

40. Gordon Carey to Howard Carey, March 18, 1959, CA; Treasurer's Report, year ending May 31, 1959, CA; Executive Secretary's Report to CORE Council, Jan. 23–24, 1960, Oldham Prs.

41. Robinson to McCain, Aug. 11, 1958, CA.

42. Executive Secretary's Report to 1958 Convention, CHQ; NAC [Oct. 1958], Oldham Prs.

43. CORE Council, March 22–23, 1958, CA, and Feb. 21–22, 1959, Oldham Prs; Robinson to Charles and Marian Oldham, March 9, 1959, Oldham Prs; Carey, Report, March 22–April 19, 1959, CA; 1959 Convention, CA; McCain to Robinson, June 27, 1959, CA; McCain, Report, Sept. 23 to Oct. 21, 1959, CA; CORE Council, Jan. 23–24, 1960, James Farmer Prs.

44. Phil Roos to Carey, Nov. 18, 1959, CA; Carey to Bruce Haldane, July 31, 1959, CA.

45. Carey to Len Holt, March 10, 1959, CA.

46. Anna Holden, *A First Step Toward School Integration* (New York, June 1958); *CORE-lator*, Fall 1958 and Fall 1959.

47. McCain, Report on Alexandria, received Dec. 16, 1957, CA; Robinson to Oldham, May 5, 1958, Oldham Prs; Robinson to McCain, April 29, 1958, CA.

48. Robinson to McCain, Aug. 17, 1958, CA.

49. Robinson to McCain, Aug. 13, 1958; Carey, Report, Aug. 29 to Sept. 29,

1958; McCain, Report, Nov. 1958, all CA; McCain Diaries, Sept. 3–19, Nov. 11–25, 1958, McCain Prs.

50. Executive Secretary's Report to 1958 Convention, CHQ; Carey to Robinson, Nov. 22, 1958, CA.

51. Oldham to Carey, Nov. 28, 1958, CA; Walker to King, Nov. 26, 1958, CA; King to Dear Brother in Christ, Dec. 3, 1958, CA; NAC, Jan. 6, 1959, Marvin Rich Prs; Carey, Field Report, March 22–April 19, 1959, CA; Rich to Carey, March 3, 1959, Rich Prs; Robinson to Carey, April 2, 6, 1959, CA.

52. Executive Secretary's Report to 1959 Convention, Oldham Prs; Carey, Field Report, March 22 to April 19, 1959, CA; On Norfolk, see also, Carey to Harry Reid, July 8, 1959; Len Holt to Robinson, Oct. 18, 1959; Holt to Carey *et al.,* Jan. 26, 1960, all CA.

53. Oldham to Robinson, Nov. 25, 1957, MLK; Robinson to Irene Osborne, March 11, 1958, CA.

54. Howard Quint, *Profile in Black and White* (Washington, 1958), 51–54; Thomas Gaither, *Jailed-In* (League of Industrial Democracy Pamphlet, reprinted by CORE, April 1961, unpaged); "Dateline: Orangeburg, S.C.," *Fellowship Magazine,* XXII (Feb. 1956), 7–10; LeRoy Carter, Report [May 1956], CA; *Argus,* Aug. 23, 1957; Rock Hill *Evening Herald,* Feb. 26, 1960.

55. Robinson to Oldham, Nov. 29, 1957, MLK.

56. McCain to Robinson, Dec. 21, 30, 1957, CA; McCain, Report [Nov. 1958], CA; McCain Diaries, Dec. 20, 1957, to Nov. 3, 1958, *passim,* McCain Prs.

57. McCain Diaries, July 13, Feb. 21, 24, May 17, June 3, 6, 1958, McCain Prs; Robinson to CORE groups, Jan. 27, 1958, CA; Agenda for NAC Meeting, July 18, 1958, CA; James D. Rice, "Progress in Sumter" [1958], CA; Spartanburg CORE application for affiliation, rec'd Jan. 23, 1959, CA.

58. *Argus,* Dec. 4, 1959; McCain to J. S. Hall and A. J. Whittenberg, Nov. 11, 1959, McCain Prs.

59. Robinson to Charles and Marian Oldham, May 5, 1958, Oldham Prs.

60. Robinson to Irene Osborne, March 11, 1958, CA; A. Philip Randolph, appeal letter, May 1958, CA.

61. NAC, May 26, 1958, James Farmer Prs; McCain, Report, June 2–21, 1958, CA; 1958 Convention, Oldham Prs.

62. Robinson to McCain, July 11, 1959, CA; NAC, July 18, 1958, James Farmer Prs; CORE Council, Feb. 21–22, 1959, Oldham Prs.

63. NAC, Jan. 28, 1959, Rich Prs; Carey to McCain, Jan. 29, 1959, Oldham Prs; McCain to Carey, Jan. 30, 1959, CA; CORE Council, Feb. 21–22, 1959, Oldham Prs.

64. McCain, Diaries, Oct. 7, 1958, McCain Prs; McCain, Reports, Sept. 29–Oct. 14, Oct. 16–Nov. 6, 1958, and Jan. 3–31, 1959, CA; Robinson to McCain, March 8, 1959, CA.

65. Robinson to McCain, Oct. 28, 1959, CA; McCain, Report, Nov. 1–27, 1959, CA; *Argus,* Dec. 4, 1959; McCain, Report to CORE Council, Jan. 23–24, 1960, Oldham Prs; *Defender,* Jan. 16, 1960; and the following in the McCain Prs: J. S. Hall to I. P. Stanback, Nov. 24, 1959; Hall to "Dear Rev.," Dec. 17, 1959; "Program of the Emancipation Day Prayer Pilgrimage, January 1, 1960," interview.

66. Robinson to McCain, Dec. 23, 1959, CA; Executive Secretary's Report to CORE Council, Jan. 23–24, 1960, Oldham Prs; Everett Ladd, *Negro Political Leadership in the South* (New York, 1966), 109.

67. Mrs. Philip Stern to Dear Sir, Oct. 10, 1958; Robinson to Mrs. Stern, Oct. 13, Nov. 9, 1958, all CA.

68. Carey to Robinson, March 3, 1959; McCain, Report, Feb. 23–March 23, 1959; Shirley Zoloth to Robinson, July 14, 1959; Miami CORE application for affiliation, June 9, 1959, all CA.

69. Miami CORE Minutes, May 5, 1959; Miami *News,* June 14, 1959, clipping; Shirley Zoloth to Robinson, June 20, 1959, all CA.

70. Robinson, "Miami Interracial Action Institute," Jan 20, 1960, Oldham Prs; Robinson to Carey, Sept. 27, 1959, CA; Robinson to T. W. Foster, Oct. 16, 1959, CHQ; Carey to Patricia Stephens, Oct. 27, 1959, CA; John Brown to Carey, Nov. 24, 1959, CA; Miami CORE affiliation application [Nov. 1959], CA; A. D. Moore to Rich, Jan. 25, 1960, CA.

71. McCain, Report, Sept. 23, to Oct. 31, 1959, CA; Lewis Killian and Charles Smith, *The Tallahassee Bus Boycott* (New York, 1958); Richard Haley, "Tallahassee CORE, October 1959 to June 1960," CA; NAC, Nov. 12, 1959, Marvin Rich Prs; Robert M. White, "The Tallahassee Sit-Ins and CORE: A Nonviolent Revolutionary Submovement" (Ph. D. dissertation, Florida State University, 1964), 102, 105–11.

72. On Louisville see McCain, Report, Feb. 2–14, 1959, CA. On Lexington, see *ibid;* correspondence with William Reichert and Joy Quary, 1958–59, CA; Lexington CORE affiliation application [April 1959], CA; and materials in William O. Reichert Papers, 1959–60. On Charleston, see McCain, Report, June 23 to Aug. 15, 1958, CA; Carey, Report, March 22 to April 19, 1959, CA; correspondence with Elizabeth Gilmore, 1958–59, CA; and McCain Diaries, Aug. 8–15, 1958, McCain Prs.

73. Marian Oldham to Robinson, Sept. 6, 1958, and undated ms., "CORE Conquers Howard Johnson Discriminatory Practices," Oldham Prs; 1959 Convention, CA; CORE Council, Feb. 21–22, 1959, Oldham Prs; East St. Louis *Journal,* Nov. 16, Dec. 14, 1958; Jan. 16, July 21, Aug. 27, 1959; Feb. 1, 19, 1960.

74. CORE Council, March 22–23, 1958, CA; 1959 Convention, CA; correspondence with Adah K. Jenkins, Alexander Baron, and Helen Brown, 1957–59, *passim,* CA.

75. McCain Diaries, Sept. 22, 1958, McCain Prs; Carey, Reports, Aug. 29–Sept. 29, 1958, and March 22 to April 19, 1959; Robinson to Mary Schlossberg, Oct. 1, 1958; Schlossberg to Robinson, Nov. 17, 1958; Irene Osborne to James Farmer, June 4, 1959; Amy Cohen to Robinson, Dec. 21, 1959; "Washington CORE Activities," June 1959 to June 1960, all CA; and the following in the Mary Coleman Prs: Agenda for Washington CORE Workshop, June 13, 1959; "Active Membership List of Washington CORE, 1959;" and Washington *Afro-American,* clippings, March 17, 21, 1959.

76. Clay to NAACP National Youth Secretary, Oct. 16, 1955, Clay Prs; *Argus,* Aug. 12, Sept. 2, 9, 1955; Clay to M. Connor, Oct. 10, 1955, Clay Prs.

77. Oldham to Robinson, April 23, Sept. 9, 1958; Marian Oldham to Marian

Bardoff, July 29, Sept. 9, 1958; Oldham to William Clay, Sept. 14, 1959, all in Oldham Prs; *CORE-lator,* Fall, 1959; *Argus,* Aug. 14, 21, Sept. 11, 1959.

78. Robert Mack to William Clay, Sept. 14, 1957, Clay Prs; *Argus,* Oct. 4, 1957, Jan. 23, 1959.

79. Oldham to Peck [Jan. 1958], Oldham Prs; Joint Opportunities Council, "The A & P Story" [Jan. 1958], and "Report of Negotiating Committee" [Feb. 1958], Clay Prs; *Argus,* Jan. 10, 17, 24, May 16, Aug. 8, 15, 22, 29, 1958; Marian Oldham to Robinson, Sept. 25, 1958, Oldham Prs.

80. St. Louis CORE press release, Nov. 25, 1958, Oldham Prs; Eugene Tournour to M. Curry, Jan. 28, 1959, Oldham Prs; Oldham to Peck, April 18, 1959, CA; CORE, *Cracking the Color Line* (New York, 1962), 21–23; Rich to Len Holt, Jan. 28, 1960, CA; "St. Louis CORE Action Report, 1959–60," June 1960, Oldham Prs.

81. Carey, Report to CORE Council, Feb. 21–22, 1959, CA; Phil Roos to Robinson and Carey, Nov. 18, 1959, CA.

82. Robinson to Ellen Fisk, Oct. 27, 1959, CA.

83. Robinson to McCain, Sept. 25, 1957, CA.

84. Executive Secretary's Report to CORE Council, Jan. 23–24, 1960, Oldham Prs.

85. New York CORE Minutes, Aug. 6, 1958, Lula Farmer Prs; *CORE-lator,* Feb. 1958 and Spring 1959; Carey to Henry Hodge, July 10, 1959, CA; Tom Roberts to CORE Council, Jan. 20, 1960, CA.

86. Sayuri Buell to Carey, Jan. 26, 1959, CA; 1958 Convention, Oldham Prs, and 1959 Convention, CA; Earl Walter to Peck, April 13, 1958, CA; Buell to Robinson, May 12 and Oct. 10, 1959, CA; "Report on Survey Testing of Rental Units, December 20, 1959," CA; Carey to Thomas Roland, Oct. 7, 1960, CA; Robinson to Phil Roos, Nov. 25, 1959, CHQ; CORE Pamphlet, *Knock On Any Door* [ca. 1959], unpaged, UC; Los Angeles CORE Report to 1966 Convention, Oldham Prs.

87. On Boston, see Cynthia Carrington to Peck, Jan. 9, 1959; Michael Rice to Robinson and Carey, Feb. 14, 1959; undated typescript. "CORE Action on VA Housing, Boston, Summer, 1959," all CA; and draft of Boston CORE Constitution, Feb. 9, 1959, Herbert Kelman Prs. For Cleveland, see McCain to Robinson, Aug. 10, 19, 1959; McCain, Report, Aug. 4–28, 1959; Gregory Allen to Robinson, Dec. 11, 1959, all CA.

88. Hodge, Report on Seattle Trip [Fall 1958], and Hodge to Robinson, May 6, 11, 1959; Portland affiliation application, rec'd Sept. 3, 1959; Reuel Adair to Dear Friends, Sept. 17, Oct. 18, Nov. 1, 1959; Ellen Fisk to Peck, July 10, 1959; Fisk to Robinson, Sept. 26, 1959, all CA.

89. Beverly Walter to Peck, July 26, Sept. 25, 1959; Phil Roos to Robinson, July 20, 1959; *News of Berkeley CORE* [1959]; Robert Walter to Carey, Jan. 26, 1960, all CA.

90. Oldham appeal letter, Dec. 4, 1959, Oldham Prs; Statement of Income and Expenditures, June 1, 1959 through Dec. 31, 1959, CA.

91. Carey to Shirley Zoloth, June 23, 1959, CA; Robinson to Michael Rice, May 13, 1959, CA; Executive Secretary's Report to CORE Council, March 22–23, 1958, CA.

92. Rich to Oldham, July 16, 1959, CA; 1959 Convention, CA; CORE Council, Jan. 23–24, 1960, James Farmer Prs.

93. 1958 Convention, Oldham Prs; 1959 Convention, CA; Executive Secretary's Reports to 1958 Convention, CHQ, and to 1959 Convention, Oldham Prs; CORE Council, Jan. 23–24, 1960, James Farmer Prs.

94. Carey, Report to CORE Council, Jan. 23–24, 1960, Oldham Prs; NAC, April 21, 30, 1959, Oldham Prs.

95. Carey to Peter Clopfer, Dec. 2, 1959, CA.

CHAPTER FOUR

1. Southern Regional Council, *The Student Protest Movement, Winter 1960*, revised (April 1960), xix, xxiv; James Laue, "Direct Action and Desegregation: Toward a Theory of the Rationalization of Protest" (Ph.D. dissertation, Harvard University, 1965), 113–14.

2. James Farmer to Harry Golden, Oct. 24, 1963, CA; Miles Wolff, *Lunch at the Five and Ten: The Greensboro Sit-Ins* (New York, 1970), 24–27, 35–36; Gordon Carey to Estelle Wyckoff, Feb. 4, 1960, CA.

3. Rudolph Lombard, "Staff Reorganization of CORE" [1961], CHQ; Martin Oppenheimer, "The Genesis of the Southern Negro Student Movement: A Study in Contemporary Negro Protest" (Ph.D. dissertation, University of Pennsylvania, 1963), 58; Rich to all CORE groups, Feb. 9, 1960, CA; Rich to R. C. McLaren and Edward Harrigan, Feb. 11, 1960, CA; Rich to Karl Helfrich, Feb. 11, 1960, CA.

4. Robinson to CORE groups and advisory committee, Feb. 12, 1960, CA; Rich, Report to 1960 Convention, CA.

5. Robinson to McCain, Feb. 22, 1960, CA; *CORE-lator,* March 1960; Edward Rodman, "Portsmouth: A Lesson in Nonviolence," in CORE, *Sit-Ins: The Students* (New York, 1960), unpaged; Robinson to John Fleming, Feb. 17, 1960, CA; New York *Amsterdam News,* June 25, 1960.

6. Interviews.

7. Carey to Jesse Boston, April 5, 1961, CA; Greensboro *Daily News,* Feb. 9, 10, 1960; Durham *Sun,* Feb. 9, 10, 1960; Durham *Morning Herald,* Feb. 10, 1960; Paul Wehr, "The Sit-Down Protests: A Study of a Passive Resistance Movement in North Carolina" (M. A. thesis, University of North Carolina, 1960), 28; Carey to "Rich and Company" [ca. Feb. 12, 1960], CA.

8. McCain, Report, Feb. 8–29, 1960, CA; McCain to Robinson, Feb. 9, 23, 1960, CA; Rock Hill *Evening Herald,* Feb. 12, 1960; Florida State University *Flambeau,* March 15, 1960; Thomas Gaither, "Orangeburg: Behind the Carolina Stockade," in CORE, *Sit-Ins: The Students Report* (New York, 1960), unpaged; Southern Regional Council, *The Student Protest Movement, Winter 1960,* xxi, 5; McCain, Report to 1960 Convention, Oldham Prs.

9. Louis Lomax, *The Negro Revolt* (New York, 1962), 136; interviews with NAACP officials; Paul Wehr, "The Sit-Down Protests . . . ," 54; Robinson to McCain, Feb. 22, 1960, CA; McCain to Robinson, Feb. 19, 1960, CA.

10. Robinson, *The Meaning of the Sitins,* leaflet, Aug. 1, 1960, Oldham Prs; Robinson to Estelle Wyckoff, March 1, 1960, CA; *NAACP Annual Report for*

1958 (New York, 1959), 32; Anna Holden to Rich, Oct. 30, 1960 and Rich to Holden, Nov. 2, 1960, CA.

11. Helen Brown to Jim [Peck], June 6, 1960, CA; Robinson to Dear Student Leader, April 11, 1960, CA.

12. McCain, Reports, April 11–May 1, 1960, and May 3–June 1, 1960, both CA; McCain, Report to 1960 Convention, Oldham Prs; Rock Hill *Evening Herald,* Feb. 23–27, March 1, 15, 18, 22, April 1, 13, 25, 28, 30, May 5, 23, 27, 1960; Frank Robinson to James Robinson [June 1960], Oldham Prs.

13. Robert White, "The Tallahassee Sit-Ins and CORE: A Nonviolent Revolutionary Submovement" (Ph.D. dissertation, Florida State University, 1964), *passim;* Tallahassee *Democrat,* Feb. 14, March 13, 18, 21, 1960; Patricia Stephens, "Tallahassee: Through Jail to Freedom," in CORE, *Sit-Ins: The Students Report;* Florida State University *Flambeau,* March 15, 1960; *The CORE of the Matter* (Tallahassee CORE Newsletter), July 1960, CA; Richard Haley, "Tallahassee Core, Oct. 1959 to June 1960," CA; Robinson to Haley, March 28, 1960, CA. On speaking appearances see, Ben Stahl to Rich, May 27, 1960, CA; Allan Blackman to Robinson, June 23, 1960, CA; William Larkins to Rich, May 23, 1960, and Rich to Larkins, May 25, 1960, both CA; Brooklyn *Amsterdam News,* May 21, 1960; *Defender,* June 18, 1960; *Call and Post,* May 28, 1960; *Sentinel,* June 16, 1960; Rich to Paul Bennett, May 24, 1960, CA.

14. Baton Rouge *State Times,* March 29, 1960.

15. Major Johns, "Baton Rouge: Higher Education, Southern Style," in CORE, *Sit-Ins: The Students Report;* CORE, *Sit-Down Newsletter* July 11, 1960, William Clay Papers; McCain Report to National Convention, 1960, Oldham Prs; McCain, Report, March 29 to April 9, 1960, CA; Major Johns and Ronnie Moore, *It Happened in Baton Rouge, U.S.A.* (New York, 1962), unpaged; Baton Rouge *State Times,* March 29 to April 5, 1960.

16. Notes on NAC Meetings, April 19, May 24, June 10, 1960, Rich Prs; Major Johns, Report to 1960 Convention, CA.

17. On Norfolk, see Harry Reid to Rich, Feb. 15, 1960 and ? Dabney to CORE, May 4, 1960; on Nashville see Carey to Len Holt, March 1, 1960; on Atlanta, see correspondence with Estelle and Ben Wyckoff, Feb. to May, 1960; Len Holt, Report on Atlanta CORE, May 24, 1960; McCain, Report, July 10–22, 1960, all CA.

18. Columbia, Missouri CORE, affiliation application, March 1960, CA; Columbia CORE annual report, 1959–60, Oldham Prs; Miami CORE to CORE Council, Feb. 10, 1961, CA; *CORE-lator,* June 1960; Lexington CORE report to 1960 Convention, Oldham Prs; CORE, *Sit-Down Newsletter,* Aug. 22, 1960, Rich Prs; Julia Lewis to Robinson, Feb. 16, 1960, CA; Lexington, Kentucky, CORE *Newsletter,* March 1960, CA; Julia Lewis to Carey, May 11, 1960, CA; Lewis to Rich, June 8, Aug. 12, 1960, CA.

19. *Times,* Feb. 14, 17, 1960; *Argus,* Feb. 19, 26, 1960; New York *Amsterdam News,* Feb. 27, 1960.

20. Carey to Hodge, Feb. 24, 1960, CA; Robinson to CORE local groups, advisory committee, national officers, March 24, 1960, CA.

21. Robinson to Vivian Lang, March 2, 1960 and Lang to Dear Friends,

March 20, 1960, CA; *Tribune,* Feb. 20, 23, March 8, April 5, 1960; Ann Arbor Direct Action Committee affiliation application [ca. Nov. 1960], CA; Roger Moss to Carey, March 21, 1960, CA; McCain, report to 1960 Convention, Oldham Prs.

22. Chicago affiliation application [April 1960], CA; Faith Rich to Dear Friend, April 28, 1960, CA; interviews; *Defender,* March 19, May 28, 1960; Earl Walter, "Report of Los Angeles CORE, June 24, 1960," Oldham Prs; *Sentinel,* March 10, 17, 1960; *Eagle,* June 2, 9, 1960.

23. New York *Amsterdam News,* March 26, 1960; Oldham, Report to 1960 Convention, CA; Darwin Bolden to Dear Friend, May 18, 1960, CA: Robinson to Dear Friend, March 30, 1960, CA; *Times,* April 24, 1960; News Release, April 15, 1960; Carey to Roger Moss, May 23, 1960, CA; Robinson to Dear Friend, May 18, 1960, CA.

24. Roy Wilkins to all officers of NAACP State Conferences, Branches, Youth Councils, and College Chapters, March 16, 1960, copy courtesy of NAACP Labor Secretary Herbert Hill. On Berkeley, see Allan Blackman to Carey [April 1, 1960], and Anthony Salotto to Carey, Nov. 23, 1960, CA. On Philadelphia, see Martin Oppenheimer to Rich, Nov. 7, 1960 and Ben Stahl to Rich, Nov. 10, 1960, CA. For San Jose, see Eileen Hutchinson to Carey, June 23, 1960, CA.

25. Greater Boston Committee of Racial Equality, Annual Report, July 1960, Oldham Prs and interview; New York CORE Minutes, Feb. 24, March 9, 1960, Lula Farmer Prs; leaflet, "Suggestions for CORE Pickets," Feb. 26, 1960, CA.

26. Press Release [April 1960], and April 10, 1960; St. Louis CORE Action Report, 1959–1960, Oldham Prs; Minutes, St. Louis CORE Meeting, March 21, 1960, Wanda Penny Prs; CORE, *Sit-Down Newsletter,* July 28, 1960, Oldham Prs and Aug. 22, 1960, Rich Prs.

27. Carey, Report to 1960 Convention, Farmer Prs; *Argus,* July 8, 1960.

28. Special Announcement, May 14, 1960, Rich Prs; NAC, May 1, 1960, Rich Prs; 1960 Convention, CA.

29. "Miami Action Institute, 1960 Participants," CHQ; Untitled plan of Miami Action Institute [August 1960], CHQ; Carey to George and Walter McKelvey, Aug. 19, 1960, Oldham Prs; *Argus,* Sept. 9, 1960; St. Louis *CORE-lator* [ca. Dec. 1960], Oldham Prs; Ann Arbor Direct Action Committee newsletter, *The Picketer,* Sept. 1960, CA.

30. Carey quotation from his Report to 1960 Convention, Farmer Prs; for Gaither's views; see Gaither, "Where Does America Stand Today?" [Nov. 1960], attached to Gaither to Rich, Nov. 18, 1960, CA.

31. Carey to McCain, Oct. 29, 1960, CA; Carey to Rudolph Lombard, Oct. 12, 1960, CA.

32. McCain, Report, Sept. 8–25, 1960, CA; Clippings from New Orleans *Times-Picayune,* Sept. 10, 11, 12, 1960, and from New Orleans *Louisiana Weekly,* Sept. 24, 1960, CA; McCain to Marvin Robinson, Sept. 14, 26, 1960, CHQ; Carey to Marvin Robinson, Sept. 20, 1960, CA; James Robinson to Lombard [Sept. 1960], and Sept. 14, 1960, CA; Ruth Despenza, "Aid from Bishop F. D. Jordon and AME Ministers of the New Orleans AME Union" [Sept. 1960],

CA; New Orleans CORE, application for affiliation [Sept. 23, 1960], CA; *Lombard v. Louisiana,* RRLR, VIII (1963), 353 ff.; McCain to Carey, Oct. 2, 1960, CA; Lombard to Rich, Oct. 7, 1960, CA; Lombard to Carey, Oct. 8, 1960, CA; New Orleans CORE press releases, Oct. 12, Nov. 16, and [Nov. 28], 1960, CA; Lolis Elie to Rich, Oct. 18, Nov. 4, 1960, CA; Carey to Group Leaders, Advisory Committee, Student List, Nov. 18, 1960, CA; Gaither, Report, Nov. 11–28, 1960, CA; Hughes, "Report on School Situation in New Orleans," Nov. 28, 1960, CA. On origins of Consumers' League; see Daniel Thompson, *The Negro Leadership Class* (Englewood Cliffs, 1963), 138. On ideology of the New Orleans chapter, interviews and "Rudy's Statement at City-Wide Meeting, 9/60," attached to McCain to Rich, Sept. 28, 1960, CA.

33. McCain, Reports, May to July 1960, *passim,* CA; Rock Hill Evening *Herald,* June 7, 1960; Gaither, *Reports,* Oct. 1960, *passim,* Gaither to Carey, Oct. 12, 1960, CA.

34. McCain to Robinson, May 6, 1960, CA; Gaither Reports, Oct. to Dec. 1960, *passim,* CA, esp. Report of Oct. 17 to Nov. 1, 1960.

35. See, e.g., Carey to Napoleon Giles, Nov. 1, 1960, CA; Ann Arbor Direct Action Committee newsletter, *The Picketer,* Sept. 1960, CA.

36. Gaither to Carey, Nov. 4, 1960, Jan. 4, CA; Gaither, *Jailed-In* (New York, 1961), unpaged.

37. Gaither, *Jailed-In, passim.;* see also *Times,* Feb. 1, 2, 20, 21, 1961; Rock Hill *Evening Herald,* Jan. 31, Feb. 1, 2, 3, 21, March 2, 1961; *Afro-American,* Feb. 21, 1961.

38. Oppenheimer, "The Genesis of the Southern Negro Student Movement: A Study in Contemporary Negro Protest" 70, 95, 224; Gaither, *Jailed-In;* Rock Hill *Evening Herald,* Feb. 7, 11, 13, 1961; *Times,* Feb. 13, 1961. For an account giving greater credit to SNCC see Howard Zinn, *SNCC: The New Abolitionists* (Boston, 1964), 38.

39. Carey to CORE Groups, Officers, and Advisory Committee, Feb. 1, 1961, Oldham Prs; CORE Council, Feb. 11–12, 1961, CA; Rich to "Dear Brother," March 1, 1961, CA.

40. Zinn, *SNCC,* 39; *Afro-American,* Feb. 21, 1961.

41. Haley to Carey, Oct. 14, 18, Nov. 7, 10, 1960, CA. On St. Petersburg, see in addition, Carey to H. M. Nelson, July 28, 1960, CA; Carey to William Fleming, Jan. 11, 1961, CA.

42. On Huntington, see Perkins, Report, Oct. 16–23, 1960; Carey to Perkins, Oct. 25, 1960; Perkins to Carey, Nov. 2, 1960; on Richmond, Perkins, Report, Dec. 20, 1960, CA; on Covington, Barbara Cantril to Carey, May 17, 1961, CA; on Lexington, see Perkins, Report, Dec. 20, 1960, CA; Carey to Group Leaders and Members of Advisory Committee, Nov. 7, 1960, Rich Prs; Jane B. Stone to Carey, Nov. 15, 1960, CA; Perkins, "My 291 Days with CORE," Aug. 24, 1961, *passim,* Oldham Prs.

43. Interviews; Len Holt to Ulysses Prince, April 13, 1960, CA; Anne Braden to Rich, Feb. 28, 1960, CA; Braden to Robinson, Carey, and Rich, May 12, 1960, CA; Robinson to Braden, May 14, 1960, CA; Louisville *Times,* April 30,

May 3, 1960, and Louisville *Courier-Journal,* May 1, 1960, clippings, CA; Louisville *Defender,* June 2, July 28, 1960; Perkins, Report, Dec. 20, 1960, CA.

44. Louisville *Defender,* July 28, Aug. 4, 11, Nov. 17, 1960; Oldham to Rich, Aug. 25, 1960, CA; Perkins, Reports [ca. Nov. 1960], and Dec. 20, 1960, CA; Beverly Neal to Perkins, Dec. 6, 1960, CA; Lynn Pfuhl to Rich, Dec. 7, 1960, CA.

45. J. Aaron to Henry Hodge, Oct. 29, 1960, CA; *Sentinel,* Oct. 20, Dec. 15, 1960; Tom Roland to Robinson and Carey, Dec. 5, 1960, CA; Haley to Carey, Dec. 14, 1960, CA; "Washington CORE Activities, June 1959–June 1960," CA; Carey to Dear Friend of CORE, Dec. 8, 1960, CA.

46. On Philadelphia, see Carey to Ruth McIntosh, Oct. 8, 1960, CA; Hughes, "Descriptions of Persons Who Attended One or Both Organizing Meetings" [ca. Dec. 1960], CA; on Detroit, see Perkins, Report, Sept. 24–Oct. 9, 1960, CA; on Cincinnati and Columbus. see Hughes, Report, Oct. 9–25, 1960, CA; Perkins, Report, Dec. 21, 1960, CA; Hughes to Carey [Oct. 1960], CA; *The Freedom Line,* Cincinnati CORE Newsletter, mid-1961, CA.

47. Rich to Ben Stahl, July 23, 1960, CA; Oldham to Wanda Penny, Aug. 23, 1960, Penny Prs; Greater Boston Committee of Racial Equality, Annual Report, July 1960, Oldham Prs; Robinson to Sayuri Buell, June 8, 1960, CA; Faith Rich to Robinson, Nov. 28, 1960, CA.

48. Robinson to CORE Groups, National Officers, and Advisory Committee, Sept. 9, 1960, Rich Prs; Oldham to Roy Wilkins, Aug. 19, 1960, and Wilkins to Oldham, Sept. 16, 1960, Oldham Prs.

49. Judith Yesner to Carey, Nov. 12, 1960, CA; Richard Haley to Carey, Dec. 9, 1960, CA; Carey to Tom King, Jan. 20, 1961, CA.

50. U.S. Commission on Civil Rights, *1961 Commission on Civil Rights Report,* Vol. I, *Voting* (Washington, D.C., 1961), 36–37; Robert E. Boyd, Report on Fayette and Haywood Counties, July 11, 1960, CA; Richard Haley, Report to CORE Council, Feb. 11–12, 1961, Rich Prs; Haley, Reports and Correspondence, *passim,* Jan. to March 1961, CA; Carey to Mrs. Minnie Jameson, March 8, 1962, CA. On emergency relief work of the chapters, see Carey to Judith Yesner of Ann Arbor CORE, Jan. 20, 31, 1961, CA; Cleveland *Call and Post,* Jan. 21, 1961; Genevieve Hughes to Carey [ca. April 1961], CA; *CORE-lator,* Feb. and April 1961; Los Angeles *Sentinel,* Sept. 29, 1960, Jan. 19, March 2, 1961; St. Louis *CORE-lator,* Dec. 1960, Oldham Prs; *Defender,* Aug. 27, Sept. 10, Oct. 15–21, Dec. 10–16, Dec. 24–30, 1960; Jan. 28–Feb. 3, Feb. 25–March 3, 1961; Carey to Sterling Stuckey, Jan. 26, 1961, CA. On Eric Weinberger's project see Weinberger to Norman Hill, April 5, 1962, CA; Mary Hamilton to McCain, June 4, 1962, CA; Weinberger to Rich, June 9, 1962, CA; Weinberger to Carey, Sept. 21, 1962, CA; CORE, Transcript of "Commission of Inquiry into the Administration of Justice in the Freedom Struggle," May 25–26, 1962, mimeo'd, 1962, 162–80 CA; Carey to NAC, Dec. 19, 1962, CA. On developments in Fayette County in general, see Harry Holloway, *The Politics of the Southern Negro* (New York, 1969), chap. 4.

51. Cincinnati CORE newsletter, *The Freedom Line* [mid-1961], CA; Report

from East St. Louis CORE [ca. June 1960], Oldham Prs; Homer Randolph and Katherine Hairston to Dear Citizens, March 9, 1960, Homer Randolph Prs; Report of East St. Louis CORE Activities to National Council, Jan. 31, 1961, CA; East St. Louis *Journal,* Jan. 22, Feb. 1, 18, 19, June 19, 24, 26, 29, Nov. 7, 13, 16, 18, 1960; East St. Louis *Crusader,* Nov. 17, 1960; Columbia, Missouri, CORE Report, 1960–61, Leon De Meunier Prs; National CORE News Release, Oct. 26, 1960, Oldham Prs; St. Louis *CORE-lator,* Dec. 1960, Oldham Prs; Hughes, Reports, Oct. 9–25, 25–29, 1960, CA; Ann Arbor Direct Action Committee, *The Picketer,* Sept. 1960, Feb. 1961, CA.

52. New York *Amsterdam News,* July 30, 1960.

53. St. Louis CORE press release, April 25, 1960, Penny Prs; *Argus,* May 6, 1960; Oldham to Peck, June 1, 1960, Oldham Prs; St. Louis CORE Minutes, Feb. 14, 21, 1960, Oldham Prs; Minutes, March 27, April 4, 17, 1960, Penny Prs; St. Louis *CORE-lator,* Dec. 1960, Oldham Prs; East St. Louis *Beacon,* May 17, 1961; Report of East St. Louis CORE Activities to National Council, Jan. 31, 1961, CA; Evelyn Rich to Albert Barlow, Nov. 22, 1960 and Evelyn Rich to Dear Friend, Dec. 16, 1960, both Evelyn Rich Prs.

54. Brooklyn *Amsterdam News,* July 30, 1960; *Call and Post,* Aug. 13, 1960; Rich to Anna Holden, Aug. 3, 1960, CA; interviews.

55. Ann Arbor Direct Action Committee, *The Picketer,* Sept. 1960, CA; Brooklyn *Amsterdam News,* Aug. 20, 1960; New York CORE Minutes, Aug. 24, Sept. 14, 1960, Lula Farmer Prs; *Times,* Oct. 11, 1960.

56. Carey, Report to 1960 Convention, Farmer Prs; "State of Local CORE Groups," Nov. 13, 1960, Rich Prs.

57. Robinson, Appeal Letter, Dec. 14, 1960, Marvin Rich Prs; Treasurer's Provisional Report for year ending May 31, 1962, CA; Executive Secretary's Report to CORE Council, Feb. 1961, CA.

58. Executive Secretary's Report to the 1960 Convention, CA; Robinson, "Report on the Present Financial Status of CORE" [Dec. 1960], CA.

59. Robinson, Executive Secretary's Report to 1960 Convention, CA; 1960 Convention, CA; Robinson, "Some Remarks on the 1960 CORE Convention," July 20, 1960, CA; Robinson to Henry Hodge, Nov. 22, 1960, CA; William Larkins to Rich, May 23, 1960, CA; Rich to Larkins, May 25, 1960, CA; Allan Blackman to Robinson, June 23, 1960, CA.

60. 1960 Convention, CA; Robinson to CORE Groups, National Officers, and Advisory Committee, July 20, 1960, CA; Oldham to Henry Hodge, Aug. 8, 1960, Oldham Prs.

61. Robinson to Sayuri Buell and Henry Hodge, May 12, 1960, CA; *Eagle,* April 28, May 19, 26, 1960; interviews.

62. Hodge to Robinson, Aug. 3, 1960, CA; Robinson to Buell, June 8, 1960, CA.

63. Carey to Faith Rich, July 19, 1960, CA; NAC, July 19, 1960, Rich Prs; Hodge to Carey, Aug. 3, 1960, CA; 1960 Convention, CA; 1960 Constitution, CA; Robinson, "Some Remarks on the 1960 CORE Convention," July 20, 1960, CA.

64. Rich to Oldham, Nov. 10, 1960, and Oldham to Rich, Nov. 7, 1960, both

Rich Prs; Rudolph Lombard, "Staff Reorganization of CORE" [1961], CHQ: interviews.

65. Robinson to Rich, Oct. 4, 1960, Rich Prs; Lombard, "Staff Reorganization of CORE"; Rich to Oldham, Nov. 5, 10, 1960, Rich Prs; Oldham to Rich, Nov. 7, 1960, Rich Prs; also interviews.

66. Lombard, "Staff Reorganization of CORE"; Anna Holden, first draft of NAC Meeting Minutes, Dec. 4, 1960; "Redraft of Minutes of NAC, Dec. 4, 1960"; and final typed draft of minutes, all CA.

67. Interviews.

CHAPTER FIVE

1. *Boynton v. Commonwealth of Virginia*, 364, U. S. 454 (1960); Rich to Oldham, Dec. 28, 1960, Farmer Prs; *Times*, Feb. 1, 1961; *Defender*, Feb. 11–17, 1961; CORE Council, Feb. 11–12, 1961, CA; leaflet, "Freedom Ride 1961" [ca. March 1961], Oldham Prs; Gaither, Reports, March and April 1961, *passim*, CA.

2. "Freedom Ride, 1961—Participants," Oldham Prs; James Peck, *Freedom Ride* (New York, 1962), 115, 119, 122; John Lewis and Mr. and Mrs. Walter Bergman, application forms for Freedom Ride, CA; *CORE-lator*, May 1961; *Afro-American*, May 16, 1961.

3. Peck, *Freedom Ride*, 116–22; Walter and Frances Bergman to Leon De Meunier, May 4, 1961, and Bergmans to Dear CORE Friends, May 9, 1961, De Meunier Prs; *Afro-American*, May 9, 16, 1961; Joe Perkins, "My 291 Days With CORE," Aug. 24, 1961, Oldham Prs; Frances Bergman, "Freedom Ride Report," May 10, 1961, De Meunier Prs; Carey to Group Leaders *et al.*, May 11, 1961, CA.

4. *Afro-American*, May 16, 1961; *Defender*, May 27–June 2, 1961; *Times*, May 16, 1961; Testimony of James Peck and Albert Bigelow, in transcript of "Proceedings of Commission of Inquiry into the Administration of Justice in the Freedom Struggle, May 25–26, 1962," 112–21, 126–27, CA; interviews. On Bergman's brain damage see Detroit *Free Press*, April 18, 1971 (clipping, *Free Press* Library).

5. Southern Regional Council, *The Freedom Ride* (May 1961), ii; David Halberstam, "The Kids Take Over," *Reporter*, XXIV (June 22, 1961), 22; *CORE-lator* May 1961; *Time Magazine*, LXXVII (June 2, 1961), 15; Howard Zinn, *SNCC: The New Abolitionists* (Boston, 1964), 44–51.

6. Perkins, "My 291 Days . . . "; Carey, "Report of Meeting of the Freedom Ride Coordinating Committee," May 26, 1961, CA; Southern Regional Council, *Freedom Ride*, iv; Peck, *Freedom Ride*, 139–40; Larry Still, "A Bus Ride Through Mississippi," *Ebony*, XVI (Aug. 1961), 22–23, 26; Frank Holloway, "Travel Notes from a Deep South Tourist," *New South*, XXVI (July–Aug. 1961), 5–6; *Mississippi v. Farmer*, Jackson Municipal Court, May 26, 1961, in *RRLR*, VI (1961), 544 ff.

7. *Times*, May 25, 1961; Victor Navasky, *Kennedy Justice* (New York, 1971), 19; Farmer, "By phone from Montgomery, Alabama," to CORE leaders *et al.*, re: "Segregation in Interstate Commerce: Freedom Ride" [May 24, 1961], CA;

Farmer, *Freedom-When?* (New York, 1965); 69–70; John F. Stewart, "Oral History Interview with James Farmer," March 10, 1967, 7, (John F. Kennedy Library)

8. Carey to Chapter Chairmen and CORE Contacts, May 29, 1961, CA; Rich to Farmer, June 1, 5, 6, 1961; *Argus,* June 2, 1961; *Tribune,* June 6, 1961; *Defender,* June 10–16, 24–30, 1961; *Sentinel,* June 29, 1961; Robert Martinson, "Prison Notes of a Freedom Rider," *The Nation,* CXCIV (Jan. 6, 1962), 4.

9. Gaither, "Final Report on Freedom Rider Cases, Hinds County, Mississippi" [May 1962]; Genevieve Hughes, "Interfaith and Professional and Union Freedom Rides, June 12–17, 1961," CA; Robert McAfee Brown and Frank Randall, *The Freedom Riders: A Clergyman's View, An Historian's View* (CORE Pamphlet, reprinted from the Amherst College *Alumni News* [1961]).

10. Rich to Frank Weil, Sept. 8, 1961, CA; undated working scratch paper containing calculations at about the end of July, computing race, sex, and age of riders, CA; Cynthia Homire to Alfred Korn, Sept. 4, 1962, CA; Terry Sullivan, "What Is It Like to be a Freedom Rider?" *Interracial Review,* XXV (June 1962), 145; Charles Myers to Farmer, Sept. 2, 1961, CA.

11. Still, "A Bus Ride Through Mississippi," 28; Mary Hamilton, Statement in *Freedom Riders Speak for Themselves* (Detroit, 1961), 8 (pamphlet in Mary Coleman Prs); Oldham statement in *CORE-lator,* June 1961; Holloway, "Travel Notes from a Deep South Tourist," 7–8.

12. Executive Staff, Civil Rights Commission, "1963 Justice Report," Draft, July 16, 1963, Chap. 6, Jackson, Mississippi, 18, personal file; *Christian Science Monitor,* June 26, 1961.

13. "Commission of Inquiry into the Administration of Justice in the Freedom Struggle," Farmer Testimony, 338; *CORE-lator,* June 1961; Farmer, press conference, reported in Jackson *Clarion-Ledger* July 5, 1961; Martinson, "Prison Notes of a Freedom Rider," 6; Hamilton, Statement in *Freedom Riders Speak for Themselves,* 14–17; Farmer, "I will Keep My Soul," *The Progressive,* XXV (Nov. 1961), 21–22; William Wagoner, untitled statement [Aug. 1961], CA; interviews.

14. Rich to Farmer, June 19, 1961, CA; Lula Farmer to CORE Groups and Friends, July 27, 1961, CA; Farmer, *Freedom-When?,* 70–71; Testimony of Farmer and Louis Lusky at "Commission of Inquiry into the Administration of Justice in the Freedom Struggle," 340–43, 271–74, 280–90; Farmer to CORE Group Leaders and National Advisory Committee, Sept. 25, 1961, WCO; Farmer to CORE chapters and officers, Aug. 2, 1961, CA; *Times,* Sept. 2, 1961.

15. Rich to William Oliver, July 26, 1961, CA; Lula Farmer to George Wiley, Oct. 27, 1965, attached to which is document entitled, "Freedom Rider Loans—Schedule of Loans," CA; Lula Farmer to NAC, March 23, 1962, CA.

16. NAC, Sept. 8, Oct. 12, 27, 1961, CA; Rachlin to Louis Lusky, Oct. 10, 1961, Rachlin Files; Rich to Albert Gordon, Jan. 12, 1962, CA; Farmer to Larry Still, June 22, 1962, CA; *Henry Thomas v. Mississippi,* U. S. Supreme Court Decision, *RRLR,* X (1965), 42 ff.; briefs on the case in Rachlin files.

17. *Times,* May 30, Nov. 2, 1961; Rachlin to Rich, Aug. 16, 1961, Rachlin

Files; NAC, Sept. 8, 18, 1961, CA; [Carey], "Washington Project" [Sept. 1961], CA; Farmer to CORE Group Leaders, Sept. 25, 1961, CA.

18. Carey to CORE Groups *et al.,* Nov. 1, 1961, CA; Haley to Carey, Nov. 6, 1961, CA; Gaither to Carey [ca. Nov. 14, 1961], CA; McCain to Carey, Nov. 18, 1961, CA; Farmer and Carey, memo to Dept. of Justice and ICC, Nov. 7, 1961, CHQ; Jerome Smith, Testimony, "Commission of Inquiry into the Administration of Justice in the Freedom Struggle . . . ," *passim; Times,* Nov. 30, Dec. 1, 1961; Farmer to CORE leaders, *et al.,* Dec. 20, 1961, CA; New Orleans CORE, Summary of Activities, 1961, CA; Carey to NAC, Dec. 19, 1962, CA.

19. Rich, Report to 1961 Convention, CHQ; Farmer, *Freedom-When?,* 65; *Argus,* June 23, July 21, 1961, and personal notes on Farmer speech; Alan Gartner to Rich, Dec. 15, 1961, CA.

20. Interviews; James Laue interview with Ella Baker, quoted in Laue, "Direct Action and Desegregation" (Ph.D. dissertation, Harvard University, 1965), 169–70.

21. Rich, Community Relations Report, June 22, 1962, CA; Farmer quoted in Brooklyn *Amsterdam News,* Jan 6, 1962.

22. This analysis of Farmer's leadership and Rich's role is based mainly on interviews and personal observation. For certain of the specific incidents mentioned see Henry Holstege, "Conflict and Change in Negro-White Relations in Great Falls [Grand Rapids]" (Ph.D. dissertation, Michigan State University, 1966), 129; Milton Viorst, "The Blacks Who Work for Nixon," *New York Times Magazine,* Nov. 29, 1970, 66; Oldham to Peck, Sept. 21, 1962, Rich Prs; Oldham to Gartner, Sept. 21, 1962. Gartner Prs.

23. 1961 Convention, Oldham Prs; Treasurer's Report to 1961 Convention [Sept. 1961], CHQ; Apfel and Englander, "Official Financial Report," Sept. 7, 1961, CA; Rich, Report to 1961 Convention, Aug. 30, 1961, CHQ.

24. Robinson, Membership Director's Report to 1961 Convention, CHQ; NAC, Nov. 27, 1961, CA; Farmer to Dick Gregory, July 10, 1962, CA; Rich, Report to NAC, Oct. 26, 1962, CA; Lillian Smith to Rich, esp. Dec. 1, 1961, CA; [Rich], "Community Relations Department" [July 1963], CHQ.

25. "Statement of Income and Expenses (provisional), year ending May 31, 1962," CA; "CORE Income for the Year Ending May 31, 1963," CA; Rich to NAC, June 1, 1962, CA; Rich, Community Relations Department Report, Dec. 20, 1962, CA; [Rich], "Community Relations Department" [July 1963], CHQ. On Labor union contributions, see esp. Rich to Jacob Clayman, Feb. 28, 1962, CA, and Rich to James B. Carey, June 20, 1962, CA; also Farmer correspondence with Walter Reuther and Carey, 1962–63, CA and CHQ, *passim.*

26. Farmer to Dear Friend of CORE, Feb. 1962, personal file; Rich to Genevieve Hughes, May 3, 1962, CA; NAC, June 1, 1962, CA; Farmer to CORE Group Leaders, Aug. 31, 1962, WCO; Steering Committee, Nov. 30, 1962, and Feb. 22, 1963, CA; CORE Balance Sheet, May 31, 1963, CA; CORE Income for Year Ending May 31, 1963, CA.

27. Carey, Report to 1961 Convention, Oldham Prs; MaryLu Murphy to Rich, June 20, 1961, CA; Gartner to Rich [ca. mid-1961], CHQ; Evert Maki-

nen, Report on Detroit CORE, July 7, 1961, CA; Gladys Harrington to "Dear Friend," Oldham Prs; New York *Amsterdam News,* Aug. 12, 1961; "Proclamation on CORE's Fast for Freedom" [Aug. 1961], UC.

28. 1961 Convention, Oldham Prs; Lists of CORE Affiliates, titles vary, Oct. 1961, Feb., July 10, Dec. 17, 1962, n.d. [June 1963], all CA; CORE Council, Feb. 10–11, 1962, CA; National Action Committee, Feb. 23, April 27, 1962, CA; National Action Council, Dec. 22–23, 1962, CA; Steering Committee, March 29, April 26, June 7, 1963, CA.

29. Interviews and miscellaneous documents. On Chicago, see Jerome Smith, Report, April 21, 1962, MLK; Haley to McCain, Sept. 10, 1962, MLK; Charlotte Holliday, "Chicago CORE," Feb. 9, 1962, CA.

30. Minutes of Weekend Field Staff Meeting, Oct. 20–21 [1961], CA; "Sample Constitution and By-Laws for Local CORE Groups" [ca. 1962], CA; and the following constitutions: Baton Rouge [1962], MLK; Berkeley [1962] and San Francisco, Nov. 17, 1961, both UC; Chicago, revised March 1962, Faith Rich Prs; Detroit [Nov. 1961], Leon De Meunier Prs; see also Reginald Alleyne to Mr. and Mrs. Michael Davidson, Dec. 18, 1962, Seattle CORE Prs.

31. Farmer to CORE groups [ca. July 27, 1961], Rachlin Files; National press release, July 28, 1962; Rachlin to Robert Collins, May 2, 1962, CA; Farmer to Rudy Lombard, Gartner and LaVerne McCummings, May 9, 1962, CA; NAC, April 27, June 1, 1962, CA.

32. Farmer to CORE Groups, Advisory Committee [July 1961], Leon De Meunier Prs; NAC, Oct. 12, 1961, Oldham Prs; Carey to Dennis, Nov. 16, 1961, CA.

33. CORE Council, Feb. 10–11, 1962; National Action Committee, April 27, 1962; National Director's Report to 1962 Convention; Organization Department Report to Steering Committee, Feb. 22, 1963; Farmer to L. J. Eddy [June 1963], all CA.

34. Minutes of weekend field staff meeting, Oct. 20–21 [1961], CA; Steering Committee, Oct. 26, 1962; Program Department, Memo to Steering Committee, Oct. 26, 1962, CA; mimeo'd leaflet, "Task Force: Freedom," Nov. 13, 1962; Farmer to Carey, Dec. 19, 1962, all CA.

35. Oldham to Peck, Sept. 21, 1962, Rich Prs; interviews.

36. 1961 Convention, Oldham Prs.

37. New York CORE, "The Control of National CORE" [Sept. 1961], CA; Constitutions of Feb 12 and Sept. 4, 1961, both CHQ; 1961 Convention, Oldham Prs.

38. Oldham to Farmer, Oct. 7, 1961, Rich Prs; Harrington to Gartner, Jan. 6, 1962, CA; National Action Committee Minutes, Sept. 1961 to June 1962, *passim,* CA and Oldham Prs. On Gartner's role at convention, see Rich to Gartner, Sept. 6, 1961, CHQ and interviews.

39. CORE Council, Feb. 10–11, 1962, CA; Carey *et al.* to CORE National Officers and National Action Committee [Feb. 1962], CA; Oldham to Farmer, May 23, 1962, Oldham Prs; Gartner to Farmer, June 14, 1962, CA; National Action Committee, June 10, 1962, CA: 1962 Convention, CA; 1962 Constitution, CA; National Action Council, July 1, 1962, CA; Farmer to Rachlin, July 27,

1962, Rachlin Files. The discussion of the role of Oldham and Gartner is based chiefly on interviews; see also the thrust of the following correspondence: Oldham to Peck, Sept. 21, 1962, Rich Prs; Oldham to Gartner, Sept. 21, 1962, Gartner Prs; Fredricka Teer to Gartner, March 28, 1962, Gartner Prs; McCain to Gartner, May 3, 1962, Gartner Prs; and esp. Rich to Gartner, March 19, 1962, Gartner Prs.

40. McCain Diaries, Jan. 8, 1962, McCain Prs; Farmer to National Officers *et al.,* Feb. 20, 1962, CA; "Staff Report by the National Director," Feb. 10–11, 1962, CA; New York *Amsterdam News,* Feb. 24, 1962. On issue of greater black representation on national office staff, see Joseph Perkins, "My 291 Days With CORE," Aug. 24, 1961, Oldham Prs; Lombard, "Staff Reorganization of CORE," n.d. CHQ; interviews.

41. Rich to Anna Holden, Feb. 20, 1962, CA; Peck and Lombard, "Recommendations of the Budget Committee Appointed by NAC," June 1, 1962, CA; McCain to Gartner, May 3, 1962, Gartner Prs; Rich to Gartner, May 14, 1961, CA.

42. Carey, Report to 1961 Convention, Oldham Prs; 1961 Convention, Oldham Prs; Farmer to James Laue, Feb. 28, 1961, CA; Carey to Oldham, Oct. 6, 1961, CA; Minutes of Field Staff Weekend Conference, Oct. 20–21 [1961], CA; CORE Council, Feb. 10–11, 1962, CA; National Action Committee, Feb. 23, April 27, 1962, CA; Fredricka Teer to Henry Thomas, Feb. 22, 1962, CA; "Field Placement Plan" [Feb. 1962], CA; "Comments on State of the Chapters" [April 1962], CA; McCain, "Memo on Regionalization," July 18, 1962, CA; "Field Areas" [Dec. 1962], CA; National Action Council, Dec. 22–23, 1962, CA.

43. Minutes of Staff Meeting, Oct. 19, 1961; McCain, "Field Reporting," April 10, 1962; McCain to field staff, April 12, July 10, Oct. 24, 1962; McCain, "The Function of the Field Staff," June 1, 1962; Fredricka Teer to Mary Hamilton, May 7, 1962; Mary Hamilton, Report on CORE Staff Meeting, March 9–10 [1963], all CA.

44. McCain to Chairmen of Local groups, Feb. 19, Nov. 7, 1962, CA; Marcia McKenna to Eugene Tournour, Jan. 29, 1963, CA.

45. Gartner to Carey [Sept. 1961]; Teer to Norman Hill, Sept. 17, 1962; Teer to McCain, Feb. 5, April 1, 1963; Teer to Rich, Feb. 4, 1963; Teer to McCain and Marcia McKenna, April 4, 1963; all CA.

46. Carey to Farmer, April 20, 1962, CA; Farmer to Irene Palmer, Dec. 28, 1962, CA; Louis Englander to Farmer, Nov. 6, 1962, CHQ; Clora Coleman to Clerical Staff, e.g., Dec. 5, 1962, Feb. 12, 1963, CA.

CHAPTER SIX

1. Joint Statement of Rochester CORE and NAACP Youth Council, Aug. 21, 1961, CA; *Argus,* Jan. 27, Feb. 3, 1961 and East St. Louis *Journal,* May 21, June 20, July 5, 6, 7, 14, 16, 17, Sept. 2, 21, Oct. 9, 1961; Cincinnati CORE Newsletter, *The Freedom Line* [ca. mid-1961], CA, and *CORE-lator,* June 1961; Columbus *Citizen-Journal,* Jan. 26, 1961, July 20, 1962, and Columbus CORE *Corespondent,* Oct. 30, 1961, CA; *Call and Post,* Feb. 23, March 9, 16, 23, 1963, and interviews.

2. Carey, Report to 1961 Convention, Oldham Prs and *CORE-lator,* Oct. 1961; *Argus,* June 8, 15, 1962; Kansas City *Times,* Aug. 22, 23, Sept. 12, 14, 1963; Kansas City *Call,* Aug. 30, Sept. 13, 1962, March 7, 1963; July 3 and 10, 1964.

3. *CORE-lator,* Oct. 1961; *Afro-American,* Sept. to Dec. 1961, *passim;* NAC, Oct. 12, 1961, Oldham Prs, Nov. 27, 1961, CA; Dec. 15, 1961, CA; Juanita Mitchell to Julius Hobson, Oct. 27, 1961, CA; Minutes of Meeting on U. S. 40 Freedom Ride, Oct. 28, 1961, CA; Carey to Douglas Sands, Nov. 14, 1961, CA; Carey to CORE chapters and Advisory Committee, Nov. 15, 1961, CA; Carey to Clarence Logan, Nov. 14, 1961, CA; Carey to John Moody, Nov. 14, 1961, CA; Lincoln Lynch, Reports on Nov. 18, 1961 Baltimore Demonstration, and on Dec. 16, 1961 Route 40 Freedom Ride, both CA; Lee Hamalian, "Life Begins on Route 40," *The Nation,* CVIC (Jan. 27, 1962), 71–73; interviews.

4. Baltimore-Washington Coordinating Committee for Freedom Square Demonstration to Dear Friends, April 20, 1962, CA; Henry Sands to Peck, April 20, 1962, CA; Fredricka Teer to Sands, May 8, 1962; Minutes, Baltimore CORE, May 16, Aug. 8, 1962, CA; Minutes, Baltimore CORE Executive Committee, June 8, Aug. 3, 1962, CA; Baltimore CORE Newsletter, *The CORE Liberator,* Fall 1962 and Feb. 1963, personal file; Walter Carter to Norman Hill, April 1, 1963, CA; *Afro-American,* Feb. 6, March 6, May 15, 22, June 23, Aug. 7, 14, 1962, April 2, 1963; Carter to Carey, April 7, 1963, CA; press release, June 14, 1962; interviews, and personal observations.

5. NAC, Feb. 23, 1962, CA; Gartner to Farmer [April 1962], CA.

6. On Albany see Haley to Nick Louketis and Larry Gibson, Jan. 2, 1962, CA; on Baton Rouge see "Notes on a Biography of Dave Dennis" [1965], CA; for summary of McCain's views see Peck to Oldham, June 12, 1962, CA.

7. Joseph Perkins, Report on Louisville, March 22 to April 11, 1961, CA; Lynn Pfuhl to Carey, March 17, 1961, CA; Louisville *Defender,* Feb. 16–June 22, 1961, *passim;* interviews; plus following materials from files of Frank Stanley, Jr., of Louisville: Steering Committee Minutes, April 17, 22, 25, May 12, 19, June 2, 1961; Steering Committee Report on the Executive Board of the Louisville NAACP, n.d. [ca. April 30, 1961]; Integration Steering Committee, leaflet, "Official Results of Sit-ins, Testing and Re-testing 142 Downtown Restaurants," June 1, 1961; "Steering Committee Proposals to Mayor Bruce Hoblitzell," May 17, 1961; "Public Statement of the Mayor's Emergency Committee on Integration and the Steering Committee of the Negro Community," March 21, 28, 30, 1961.

8. CORE Council, Feb. 11–12, 1961, CA; Julia Lewis to Dear Friend, April 20, 1961; Carey to Gartner, March 1, 1961; Farmer to Jane Stone, March 24, 1961; Stone to Rich, April 3, 17, 1961; Bernard Diamond to Farmer, April 4, 1961; Stone to Diamond, April 26, 1961; Perkins, Report on Lexington, June 24, 1961; Buffalo CORE press release, May 4, 1961; press release, April 8, 1961, all CA.

9. James O'Rourke to Rich, May 17, 1961, CA; Genevieve Hughes, Report on Lexington, Feb. 13–March 1, 1962, CA; Margaret Smythe to Peck, April 6, 20,

1962, CA; Mary Hamilton to McCain, June 4, 1962, CA; Ed Blankenheim, Report on Kentucky-Tennessee CORE Chapters, Dec. 1961, CA; Haley to Carey, Nov. 6, 17, Dec. 4, 1961, CA; Haley to Pat Stephens, Nov. 29, 1961, CA; *CORE-lator,* June 1962.

10. Rock Hill *Evening Herald,* Feb. 25, March 13, 1961; *CORE-lator,* April 1961; McCain, Report, Nov. 18–Dec. 21, 1961, CA; Gaither, Report, Dec. 23, 1961, CA.

11. Henry Thomas, notebook on Alabama trip, late 1961, CA; Thomas to Carey, Nov. 20, 29, 1961, CA; Haley to Carey, Jan. 7, 1962, CA; Thomas, report on Huntsville [Jan. 1962], CA; Haley "Case History of A Failure" [March 1962], CA; *RRLR,* VII (1962), 533ff.

12. Gaither, Report on Jackson, July 11, 1961, to Feb. 2, 1962, CA; *Voice of the Jackson Movement,* Sept. 1, 1961, CA; Jackson Nonviolent Movement affiliation application [Dec. 1961], and Chapter Report [ca. Feb. 1962], CA; Gaither to Fredricka Teer, Feb. 25, 1962, CA; Gaither to McCain, April 12, 1962, CA; NAC, June, 1962, CA; Peter Stoner, untitled statement, June 20, 1962, CA; *Mississippi Free Press,* June 23, 1962; David Dennis, Reports, July 25 and Aug. 14, 1962, MLK, and Oct. 25, 1962, CA; Dennis to McCain, July 3, Aug. 21, Sept. 26, 1962, MLK.

13. "Notes on a Biography of Dave Dennis" [1964], CA; Transcript of "Commission of Inquiry into the Administration of Justice in the Freedom Struggle, May 25–26, 1962," 327–32, CA; David Dennis to Cyril Simon, Nov. 10, 1961, Rachlin files; LaVert Taylor, Report, April 1962, CA; McCain to Marvin Robinson, June 13, 1962, CA.

14. Dennis to Carey, Nov. 1961 [sic], CA; Dennis to Fredricka Teer, Feb. 24, 1962, MLK; *Garner v. Louisiana,* 368 U. S. 157 (1961); Farmer to CORE leaders *et al.,* Dec. 20, 1961, Oldham Prs; Executive staff, Civil Rights Commission, "Civil Rights U.S.A., Justice 1963," Chap. 3, Baton Rouge, Draft, April 19, 1963, personal file; Ronnie Moore and Weldon Rougeau, Testimony, "Commission of Inquiry into the Administration of Justice in the Freedom Struggle," 4–10, 49–51; Baton Rouge *State Times,* Dec. 11, 15, 19, 20, 1961; Decision of U.S. Supreme Court in *Elton Cox v. Louisiana,* Jan. 18, 1965 in *RRLR,* IX (1964–65), 1911; McCain, Report, Nov. 18–Dec. 31, 1961, CA.

15. Willie Bradford, Treasurer of Baton Rouge CORE, untitled memo [Jan. 1962], CA; Baton Rouge *State Times,* Dec. 18, 19, 27, 1961, and Jan. 4, 6, 19, 23, 26, Feb. 1, 2, 1962; Moore and Rougeau Testimony at "Commission of Inquiry into the Administration of Justice in the Freedom Struggle," 19–29, 12–14, 52–54; *New York Times,* Jan. 27, Feb. 1, 2, 3, 1962; Farmer to Friends of CORE, April 23, 1962, CA.

16. Baton Rouge *State Times,* Feb. 1, 12, 1962; Farmer to Dear Friend of CORE, Feb. 23, April 23, 27, 1962, CA; Burke Marshall to St. John Barrett, Feb. 7, 1962, Marshall Prs; press releases, April 3, 1962, Feb. 27, 1964; materials relating to State of Louisiana vs. Ronnie M. Moore, Murphy Bell Prs, Reel No. 3.

17. RRLR, IX (1964–65), 1911 ff.; *Time Magazine,* LXXXV (Jan. 29, 1965),

30; Rachlin to all CORE Counsel, April 28, 1965, Rachlin files; Nils Douglas to Rachlin, May 7, 21, 1962, and other materials on the case in Murphy Bell Prs., Reel No. 2.

18. Rich to Eleanor Roosevelt, May 1, June 20, 1962, CA; Rich to CORE Group Leaders, April 21, 1962, CA; "Commission of Inquiry into the Administration of Justice in the Freedom Struggle," *passim;* and in the Burke Marshall Prs: Farmer to Marshall, May 1, 1962; Marshall to Ed Guthman, May 8, 1962; Guthman to Marshall, May 9, 1962; Marshall to Farmer, May 10, 1962; Theodore Newman to Marshall, May 28, 1962.

19. Press release, Aug. 8, 1962. On injunction, which was ultimately overturned in the federal courts see Baton Rouge *State Times,* Dec. 27, 1961, Feb. 2, 1962; *RRLR,* VII (1962–63), 153ff., and VIII (1963), 854ff.

20. C. T. Smith to McCain, Feb. 22, 1962, CA; Haley to New Orleans CORE, March 13, 1962, CA; Inge Bell, *CORE and the Strategy of Non-Violence* (New York, 1968), 100–101; Marvin Robinson to Fredricka Teer, May 22, 24, 1962, CA; Robinson to McCain, Sept. 25, 1962, CA. On decline, see, e.g., Mary Hamilton to McCain, Jan. 3, 1964, CA.

21. Communications from Mary Hamilton, July 1962 to April 1963, CA and Mary Hamilton Prs; and from Winston Lockett, Dec. 1962 to March 1963, CA; Arlean Wilkes to Carey, June 24, 1963, CA; Lebanon CORE *Freedom-News,* Oct. 1, 1962; Lebanon CORE Report, rec'd Jan. 28, 1963, CA. On Memphis and Chattanooga, see Hamilton to McCain, April 27, May 31, 1963, Hamilton Prs.

22. CORE Council, Feb. 10–11, 1962; Program Department, Report to NAC, March 23, 1962, CA; Carey to Active CORE Members, June 1, 1962, CA; press release, May 4, 1962; 1962 Convention, CA; Carey to Genevieve Hughes, May 31, 1962, CA; NAC, June 1, 1962, CA; Cox, Reports, June 2, 11, 23, 1962, CA; Farmer to Wilkins, June 20, 1962, CA; Wilkins to Farmer, June 25, 1962, CA.

23. Press release, Aug. 10, 20, 1962; *CORE-lator,* Sept. 1962; Carey, *The City of Progress,* pamphlet on Statesville (New York, 1962); Carey to Farmer, Sept. 7, 1962; Carey, Report on Freedom Highways Project, Jan. 11, 1963, CA; *Chronicle,* Aug. 18, 1962; *Afro-American,* Sept. 4, 1962; Steering Committee, Sept. 7, 1962, CA; Peck, "A Carolina City—15 Years Later," *CORE-lator,* Nov. 1962.

24. Farmer to Rabbi Roland Gittelsohn, Aug. 31, 1962, CA; Farmer to Anna Holden, Aug. 31, 1962, CA; Farmer to Dear Member, Sept. 4, 1962, personal file.

25. Carey to CORE Chapters *et al.,* Oct. 10, 1962, Faith Rich Prs; Howard Johnson, Roy Wilkins and James Farmer, "Joint Statement and Progress Report," Oct. 30, 1962, CHQ; Carey to Farmer, Nov. 29, 1962, CA; Steering Committee, Nov. 30, 1962, CA; Carey to NAC, Dec. 19, 1962, CA; NAC, Dec. 22–23, 1962, CA; Howard Johnson to Supervisory Personnel, Nov. 20, 1962, CA; Carey to Richard Graham, March 1, 1963, CA; press release, April 3, 1963; Steering Committee, June 7, 1963, CA.

26. Moon Eng, Report, Dec. 26, 1962; Claudia Edwards, Reports, Dec. 18, 23, 1962, and Jan. 13, 1963; Carey to Jerome Smith, Jan. 4, 1963; Carey to Farmer, Jan. 14, 1963, all CA.

27. Carey to McKissick, June 7, 1963, CA; Carey, Report on Freedom Highways, Jan. 11, 1963, CA.

28. C. O. Simkins to Carey, Sept. 19, 1962, CA; Durham NAACP-CORE, Agenda for Oct. 10, 1962 meeting, CA; interviews.

29. Wendell Scott to Dear Reverend, Nov. 13, 1962; Carey to C. O. Simkins, Oct. 10, 1962; undated boycott circular [Oct. 1962]; McCain to Farmer, Oct. 31, 1962; clippings from High Point *Enterprise,* Nov. 17, 23, 1962; McKissick to Carey, Nov. 24, 1962; Carey to William Thomas, Dec. 7, 1962; George Raymond to Carey, rec'd Feb. 8, 1963; press releases Oct. 18, Nov. 18, 29, 1962, March 21, 1963; Greensboro CORE press release, March 9, 1963, all CA.

30. Harold Fleming, "The Federal Executive and Civil Rights," in Talcott Parsons and Kenneth Clark, eds., *The Negro American* (New York, 1965), 373; Transcript of "Oral History Interview with Harris Wofford," by Larry Hackman, May 22, 1968, John F. Kennedy Library; Louis Lomax, *The Negro Revolt* (New York, 1963), 246–48; Pat Watters and Reese Cleghorn, *Climbing Jacob's Ladder: The Arrival of Negroes in Southern Politics* (New York, 1967), 45, 47; Howard Zinn, *SNCC: The New Abolitionists* (Boston, 1964), 48; Burke Marshall's notations regarding views of SRC leaders on memorandum, "Those Invited to Attend Luncheon with the Attorney-General, Monday, March 6th . . . ," Marshall Prs; interviews. On Currier's earlier interest, see Stephen Currier to Martin Luther King, Jr., Jan. 5, 1961, King Prs, Boston University; James Wood to Currier, Jan. 13, 1961, King Prs; King and Wyatt Tee Walker to Currier, May 3, 1961, King Prs.

31. The foregoing discussion was based largely on interviews. On NAACP, see Roy Wilkins, Report of Executive Secretary for May 1961, NAACP Board of Directors Minutes, NAACP Office, New York; Wilkins to Burke Marshall, May 17, 1961, Marshall Prs; Marshall to Wilkins, May 18, 1961, Marshall Prs; Wilkins to Robert Kennedy, June 30, 1961, Marshall Prs. On dating of Capahosic meeting, see Marshall to F. D. Patterson, May 12, 1961, and Marshall to George Barrett, May 23, 1961, both in Marshall Prs. On meeting at Justice Department a key document was a memorandum by a representative of the National Student Association, who was present: Robert Walters, "Re: Meeting at Department of Justice, June 16, 1961," addressed to Richard Rettig and Tim Jenkins, copy in Edward Hollander Prs. For Farmer's recollection of what CORE representatives told him about the meeting, see transcript of "Oral History Interview with James Farmer, March 10, 1967," 13–14, John F. Kennedy Library.

32. Leslie Dunbar, "Notes on the Morning Session at the Taconic Foundation, July 28, 1961," memo dated Aug. 11, 1961, SRC Arch; Burke Marshall, Memorandum, July 31, 1961, Marshall Prs; Dunbar to members of SRC Executive Committee, July 31, Sept. 13, 1961, SRC Arch; Farmer to Stephen Currier [Aug. 17, 1961], CA; 1961 CORE Convention, Oldham Prs; Rich, Report to NAC, April 27, 1962, Oldham Prs; interviews.

33. Minutes of Weekend Field Staff Meeting, Oct. 20–21 [1961], CA; Zinn, *SNCC: The New Abolitionists,* 59; CORE Council, Feb. 10–11, 1962, CA; interviews. For McCain's view, see Steering Committee, March 29, 1963, CA.

34. Burke Marshall, Memorandum, Sept. 1, 1961, Marshall Prs; NAC, Oct. 27, 1961, Oldham Prs; Farmer to Leslie Dunbar, Oct. 16, 1961, SRC Arch.; Dunbar to Stephen Currier, Oct. 5, 1961, SRC Arch; Roy Wilkins to Currier, Oct. 17, 1961, SRC Arch.; Watters and Cleghorn, *Climbing Jacob's Ladder,* 47, 49; Marshall to John Siegenthaler, Oct. 23, 1961, Dec. 18, 1961, Marshall Prs; Adrian DeWind to Marshall, Dec. 14, 1961, Marshall Prs; Dunbar to Farmer, March 17, 1962, CA; Dunbar to Marshall, March 27, 1962, Marshall Prs; Mitchell Rogovin to Marshall, March 28, 1962, Marshall Prs; Marshall to Dunbar, March 30, 1962, Marshall Prs, NAC, May 4, 1962, CA.

35. G. E. Barrett, Notes on April 17, 1962, meeting of VEP Cooperating Agencies, SRC Arch. On negotiations for and awarding of grants, see NAC, March 23, 1962, MLK; Wiley Branton to Farmer, May 4, Aug. 15, 1962, VEP Arch.; Farmer to Branton, March 28, 1962, CA; Rich to Farmer, April 20, 1962, CA; Rich to Branton, April 19, 1962, CA; Steering Committee, Sept. 7, 1962, CA; Branton to Rich, Dec. 14, 1962, Rich Prs. On registration statistics for the first years of the VEP grants, see Rich to Branton, May 10, 1963, CA.

36. McCain, *The Right to Vote* (New York, 1962); "Summary of Reports from NAACP, CORE, and SNCC" [1962], VEP Arch.

37. J. C. Givens and A. Glover, Sumter CORE Report [Feb. 1962], CA; Frank Robinson, Reports, April 1–14, July 12, 1962, CA; Sumter CORE Office reports, April 20, Aug. 1–18, 1962, CA; [Jack Minnis], Report on South Carolina, Oct. 22–24, 1962, VEP Arch; SRC, "First Status Report, Voter Education Project," Sept. 20, 1962, CA; [McCain], Report to 1963 Convention, CA; Frank Robinson to McCain, March 5, 1963, VEP Arch.; [Minnis], Memo for Branton, March 13, 1963, VEP Arch.; Minnis to Branton, April 2, 1963, VEP Arch.; Rich to Branton, April 10, 1962, CA. On percentage of blacks registered in Williamsburg County, see Burke Marshall to Ernest Hollings, Oct. 6, 1961, Marshall Prs.

38. U.S. Commission on Civil Rights, *1961 Commission on Civil Rights Report,* Vol. I, *Voting* (Washington, D.C., [1961]), 41–46, 50; "Proposed Schedule for CORE Participation in VEP Program for period Aug. 1, 1962 through March 31, 1963," CA; "Negro Registration in Louisiana" [July 1962], Rachlin files.

39. Dennis to Fredricka Teer, Feb. 24, March 6, May 19, 1962, MLK; Dennis, Report, May 3, 1962, CA; McCain to Organization Department, May 11, 1962, CA; Ronnie Moore to Rich, May 16, 1962, CA; "Schedule of Voters' Education Clinics, July 23–28, 1962," held in Baton Rouge, UC; Branton to Farmer, Aug. 15, 1962, CA; W. W. Harleaux to Branton, Oct. 16, 1962, CA; Steering Committee, Oct. 26, 1962, CA.

40. Ronnie Moore, Draft of Letter to Community Facilities Administration, Dec. 3, 1964, CA; Mimi Feingold to Parents, Dec. 3, 1963, CA; *Task Force Chronicle* (Plaquemine), July 23, 1963, WCO; Moore to McCain, March 22, 1963, CA; Branton to Carey, Nov. 27, 1962, CA.

41. Moore to McCain, rec'd March 28, 1963, CA.

42. McCain to Burke Marshall, April 10, 1963, and Spiver Gordon to McCain, June 21, 1963; Moore to Justice Department [April 1963]; McCain to

Marshall, April 2, 1963; Moore to McCain [April 1963], all CA. On McCain's trip to Washington, see McCain diaries, Oct. 7, 1962, McCain Prs.

43. Farmer to Branton, March 25, 1963, MLK.

44. Zinn, *SNCC: The New Abolitionists,* 62–78; NAC, Oct. 12, 1961, Oldham Prs; Minutes, Field Staff Meeting, Oct. 20–21 [1961], CA; SRC, "First Status Report, Voter Education Project," Sept. 20, 1962, CA; Dennis, Report, July 25, 1962, MLK; Dennis to McCain, June 3, 5, 10, 30, Aug. 13, 1962, MLK.

45. Watters and Cleghorn, *Climbing Jacob's Ladder,* 63; [Dennis], "Mississippi," Feb. 20, 1963, CA, and esp. Dennis, Report, Aug. 29, 1962, CA; interview.

46. Dennis, Reports, Oct. 25, Dec. 3, 1962, MLK; Dennis to McCain, Sept. 26, Oct. 3, 25, 1962, MLK; [Dennis], "Mississippi," Feb. 20, 1963, CA; Zinn, *SNCC: The New Abolitionists,* 102.

47. Dennis to McCain, Sept. 5, 1962, CA; Dennis, Reports, Aug. 29, Oct. 15, 1962, rec'd Jan. 14, 1963, all CA, and Report, Oct. 25, 1962, MLK; Dennis to CORE contacts, Nov. 26, 1962, MLK and Dec. 3, 1962, CA; Dennis to Marcia McKenna, Nov. 11, 1962, MLK; Dennis to McCain, rec'd Jan. 9, 1963, MLK.

48. Dennis, Reports, Oct. 25, 1962, MLK, and March 1–31, 1963, CA; Dennis to McCain, March 15, 1963, CA; Rich to Ed Hollander, April 22, 1963, CA; Dennis to Marcia McKenna, March 24, 1963, MLK; *Mississippi Free Press,* April 20, May 18, 1963.

49. In general, see [Dennis], "Mississippi," Feb. 20, 1963, CA; Quotes from Dennis, Report, Aug. 29, 1962, CA; Dennis to McCain, Oct. 12 and Dec. 6, 1962, CA.

50. [Haley] "Report of Meeting with Attorney-General Robert Kennedy, Aug. 2, 1962," CA and *Times,* Aug. 4, 1962; Rich to Lillian Smith, Sept. 26, 1962, CA; Rich to Farmer, June 6, 1962, CA; Alan Gartner to Rich, rec'd June 22, 1962, CA; Farmer to Genevieve Hughes, Dec. 6, 1962, CA. For general discussion of whole issue, see Watters and Cleghorn, *Climbing Jacob's Ladder, passim,* esp. 47, 55, and Chap. 8. On district judges, see relevant chapters in Leon Friedman, ed., *Southern Justice* (New York, 1965); Carl Rachlin to Eleanor Roosevelt, April 16, 1962, Rachlin files; Robert Kennedy to Roosevelt, May 22, 1962, Burke Marshall Prs; Roosevelt to Rachlin, April 26, 1962, Rachlin files. For other examples of CORE protest to the White House, see Harris Wofford to Farmer, Feb. 2, 1962, CA; Lee White to Farmer, Aug. 11, 1962, CA; Farmer telegram to John Kennedy, March 7, 1963, CA.

51. Farmer to Branton, March 25, 1963, CA.

CHAPTER SEVEN

1. 1961 Convention, Oldham Prs; Tony Salotto to Carey [Spring 1961], CA; Genevieve Hughes, Report, Dec. 1961, CA; Greater Boston CORE Report [ca. Feb. 1962], CA.

2. Santa Clara Valley CORE, *Northwest Area Newsletter,* Dec. 1961, CA; Agenda, CORE Housing Institute, July 29–Aug. 8, 1961, CHQ; "1962 CORE

Employment-Housing Institute Summary" [July 1962], CA; Carey to Farmer, memorandum, "Discussion of National or Regional Conference Workshop. . . . ," July 16, 1962, CA; McCain, "Memo on Regionalization," July 18, 1962, CA; Steering Committee, Oct. 26, 1962, CA; NAC, Dec. 22–23, 1962, CA; McCain, Organization Department Report to 1960 Convention, Marylu Murphy Prs.

3. New York CORE press release, Oct. 8, 1961, CA; Grand Rapids *Press,* April 13, 1962.

4. On Long Island, see Long Island CORE Report to 1962 Convention, CA; *Times,* Aug. 7, Oct. 11, 1962; Brooklyn *Amsterdam News,* Aug. 11, 1962. On Seattle, see Joan Singler to Carey, Aug. 6, 1962, CA. On Philadelphia, see *Tribune,* May 26, 1962; Elizabeth Lynes to Rich, July 9, 1962, CA; Philadelphia CORE Report to 1962 Convention, UC, and quote from William Fischer to Rich, June 27, 1962, CA. On Los Angeles, see Los Angeles CORE Report to 1962 Convention, UC, and *Sentinel,* July 19, 1962. On Syracuse, see Alice Tait to McCain, [April 1962], CA. For other Operation Windowshop projects, see, e.g., "Background Information for [Cleveland] CORE Members" [1964], Arthur Evans Prs; Detroit CORE Report to 1962 Convention, UC; and leaflet, "Columbus CORE Announces Operation Windowshop" [1962], Ollie Leeds Prs. For discussion of factors inhibiting middle-class blacks from moving into white suburbs, see Lewis Watts *et al., The Middle-Income Negro Family Faces Urban Renewal* (Waltham, Mass., 1964), *passim.*

5. *CORE-lator,* Aug. and Dec. 1961; "Lefrak Report," Dec. 1961, CA; leaflet, "End Discrimination in Housing by the Lefrak Organization" [1962], Ollie Leeds Prs; *Times,* Oct. 5, 7, 1961; Brooklyn *Amsterdam News,* Oct. 14, Nov. 25, 1961, Dec. 22, 29, 1962; press release, Dec. 20, 1962; Brooklyn CORE *North Star,* Dec. 1962, Leeds Prs.

6. *Defender,* Jan. 27–Feb. 2, 1962; *CORE-lator,* April 1962; Chicago *Tribune,* Jan. 23 to Feb. 6, 1962, *passim;* Chicago South Side CORE unit, *Civil Rights News Review,* April 1962, CA; Debbie Meier, "Chicago Sit-Ins Attack Jim Crow," *New America,* Feb. 23, 1962.

7. On Philadelphia, see *CORE-lator,* Nov. 1962, and Louis Smith to Rich, Oct. 15, 1962, CA; on Newark, see *Times,* Sept. 16, 1962; on Washington, see Washington *Post,* Nov. 11, 1962, March 16, 1963; on Bergen County, see *Wall Street Journal,* March 7, 1963 and *CORE-lator,* Feb. 1963; on Syracuse, see *Times,* Dec. 4, 1962 and *Call and Post,* Dec. 15, 1962.

8. Holden to Farmer, Nov. 10, Dec. 12, 1962, CA; "Profile of Ann Arbor Fair Housing Association" [Feb. 1962], CA; AAFHA press releases, Jan. 28, April 9, 1962, CA; AAFHA-CORE, Report [late 1962], CA; Holden to Rich, March 7, 1963, CA; Lamar Miller to Farmer, March 14, 1963, CA; Miller to Dear Friend, March 31, 1963, CA; Lynn Eley, "The Ann Arbor Fair Housing Ordinance," in Eley and Thomas Casstevens, eds., *The Politics of Fair Housing Legislation* (San Francisco, 1968), 307–8, 318.

9. Denver CORE affiliation application, Dec. 1, 1961, CA; Hughes to Carey, Dec. 28, 1961, CA; Los Angeles CORE Report to 1962 Convention, UC; *Eagle,* Feb. 22, March 1, 8, 15, April 2, July 26, Aug. 2, 16, Sept. 27, Oct. 4, 18, 25,

Nov. 8, 15, 1962; Jan. 10, March 14, April 11, May 9, 1963; *Sentinel,* Aug. 2, 16, Nov. 8, 15, 1962; Jan. 17, Feb. 7, 14, May 9, 1963.

10. New Haven *Journal-Courier,* Sept. 18, 19, 29, Nov. 10, 1961, Feb. 7, 1962; Gloster Current to Farmer, Oct. 3, 1961, CA; [Haley], Memoranda on New Haven, Sept. 29, Oct. 7, 1961, CA; New Haven NAACP *Voice,* Sept. 22, 1961, CA; Libby Palmer to Carey, Oct. 27, 1961, CA; Mary Hamilton to McCain, Feb. 23, March 1, 1962, CA; New Haven CORE Report [March 1962], CA; Norman Hill to New York Area Contacts, April 30, 1963, CA.

11. Tony Salotto to Carey, June 1, 1961, CA; "Summary of Employment Survey of Merchants—Shattuck Avenue [Berkeley]" [1961], CA; Libby Palmer, Report on New Haven CORE, March 26, 1962, CA.

12. Genevieve Hughes to Carey, Jan. 17, 1961, CA; William Fischer to Carey, April 2, 1961, CA; Evert Makinen, Report on Philadelphia CORE, July 24, 1961, CA; Philadelphia CORE to CORE Council, Feb. 10–11, 1962, CA; Philadelphia CORE, "A Report to the Community on Horn and Hardart Employment Practices" [Spring 1962], CA; *CORE-lator,* Nov. 1962; *Tribune,* April 4, 11, 25, Nov. 18, 1961, March 20, April 7, 1962.

13. Brooklyn *Amsterdam News,* Feb. 10, 1962; New York *Amsterdam News,* April 21, 1962; Edward Mollette and Evelyn Rich to F. M. Flynn, Jan. 4, 1962, and "Statement Made by General Manager of New York Daily News," Feb. 2, 1962, both in Evelyn Rich Prs; New York CORE Report to NAC, Feb. 1962, Alan Gartner Prs; East St. Louis *Beacon,* March 22, May 31, 1962; East St. Louis *Journal,* May 6, 1963; *Eagle,* Oct. 26, Nov. 2, 9, 16, Dec. 7, 14, 1961, March 15, April 5, Aug. 16, 1962; Berkeley *Corespondent,* Dec. 1961, UC; Washington *Post,* Jan. 22, March 9, April 27, May 18, 29, June 14, July 15, 25, Sept. 19, Oct. 14, 15, 20, 22, 23, Nov. 11, 12, 1962; Greater Boston CORE Report [ca. Feb. 1962], CA; Farmer to CORE Groups [Aug. 1961], CA; Boston CORE *Newsletter,* Jan. 1962, and [March 1963], CA; *Chronicle,* Jan. 5, 1963, and Detroit CORE *Newsletter,* Feb. 1963, CA.

14. Joan Singler, Report on Selective Buying Campaign, Jan. 13, 1962, CA.

15. On Seattle, see: Joan Singler, Report on Selective Buying Campaign, Jan. 13, 1962, CA; Edward Singler, "Seattle CORE," Feb. 6, 1962, CA; "Safeway's Policy of Racial Discrimination," Oct. 21, 1961, CA; Report from Seattle CORE Meeting of Nov. 8, 1961, CA; "Status Report on the Selective Buying Campaign" [Nov. 1961], CA; Genevieve Hughes to Carey, Dec. 23, 1961, CA; interviews. On Denver, see Jean Walzer to McCain, May 30, July 26, 1962, CA; Fact sheet from Denver CORE employment committee, rec'd May 21, 1962, CA; Hughes to James Reynolds, May 23, 1962, CA; Mary Rapp to Rich, June 1, 11, 1962, CA; Rapp to McCain, June 11, 1962, CA; Denver *Post,* June 9, 1962.

16. Walzer to McCain, July 26, 1962, CA, and Denver *Post,* July 14, 17, 19, 20, 23, 31, Aug. 22, 26, 1962; Seattle *CORE-lator,* [May 1962], CA; Joan Singler to Rich, May 27, 1962, CA; Ed Singler to Carey, Dec. 6, 1962, CA; Henry Hall to J. C. Penney, Oct. 8, 1962, Seattle CORE Prs; Negotiators Meeting with Penneys, Sept. 6, 1962, Seattle CORE Prs; Negotiators Report, J. C. Penney Company [May 1962], Seattle CORE Prs; Joan Singler, Report on Selective Buying Campaign, Jan. 13, 1962, CA; Joan Singler to Carey, April 13, 1962, CA; Seattle

CORE newsletter, Dec. 13, 1962, CA; Ed Singler to Carey, April 5, 1962, Seattle CORE Prs.

17. *Argus,* May 26, 1961; March 30, July 6, 20, 27, Sept. 21, 1962; undated "Fact Sheet" [Fall 1962], CA; Farmer to CORE Group Leaders, July 19, 1962, CA; McCain to CORE chapter contacts, Dec. 4, 1962, CA; NAC, Dec. 22–23, 1962, CA; St. Louis *CORE-Action* (chapter newsletter), April 1963, Oldham Prs; Columbus *Citizen-Journal,* Sept. 24, 1962; Arthur Zebbs to Zev Aelony, Nov. 6, 1962, CHQ; Barbee Durham to Zebbs, Oct. 17, 1962, CHQ; Mary McKnight to Durham, Oct. 24, 1962, CHQ; Durham, "Report on Supermarket Conference," Oct. 26, 1962, CHQ; Gloster Current to Farmer, Nov. 26, 1962, CHQ; Farmer to Current, Nov. 29, 1962, CHQ; Durham to Farmer, Dec. 10, 1962, CHQ; Rich to MaryLu Murphy, Dec. 17, 1962, CA; Murphy to Rich, March 11, 1963, CA.

18. News release, Feb. 22, 1962; Charleston, West Va. CORE report [ca. Summer 1962], CA; Mary Hamilton to McCain, June 4, Dec. 15, 1962, CA.

19. On Louisville, see Reports and correspondence from field secretaries Haley, Hamilton, Henry Thomas, and Don Wendell, Feb. to June, 1962, CA; quotations from Thomas, Report on Louisville, May 17, 1962, and Hamilton to McCain, June 22, 1962. On New Orleans see Oretha Castle to Rich, March 26, 1963, and Lolis Elie to Rich, May 31, 1963, CA. On Durham, see Claudia Edwards, Reports, March 3, April 14, 1963; Isaac Reynolds, Report, Feb. 2–March 1, 1963; Walter Riley, Quinton Baker, Isaac Reynolds to Dear Sir, Feb. 18, 1963; the same three to Dear Fellow Citizen, March 5, 1963; press release of Durham NAACP and CORE, March 1, 1963; "Don't Buy for Easter," leaflet [ca. March 3, 1963], all CA.

20. CORE Council, Feb. 10–11, 1962, CA; [Carey and Don Wendell], Guidelines for Employment Negotiation" [Nov. 1962], CHQ; Carey to Richard Rapp, Dec. 12, 1962, CA; Summary of Dec. 11 [1962] New York chapters meeting on Sealtest, CA; untitled document, CORE proposals, Dec. 13, 1962, CA; Minutes, Sealtest Negotiations Meeting, Jan. 23, 1963, CA; Brooklyn CORE *North Star,* Feb. 1963, CA; "CORE's Agreement with Sealtest," Feb. 14, 1963, CA; NAC, Dec. 22–23, 1962; Robert Curvin to Farmer, Jan. 3, 1963, Curvin Prs; interviews. On role of college students, see Alan Rosanes to Fredricka Teer, May 28, 1962, and Columbia *Spectator,* Oct. 30, 1962, clipping, CA.

21. Eugene Tournour to McCain, March 29, 1962, CA, and *Argus,* Oct. 13, 1962, and March 9, 1962; Brooklyn *Amsterdam News,* Jan. 26, Feb. 16, 23, 1963, and Long Island CORE Report to 1963 Convention, CA; Philadelphia *Bulletin,* April 14, 17, 19, May 14, 15, 1963; *Tribune,* March 30, April 16, 27, 1963; Louis Smith to James Tate, March 24, 1963, CA.

22. Fredricka Teer to New York Area Contacts, July 30, 1962, CA; "Declaration of Intention between Brooklyn CORE and Ebinger Baking Company," August 17, 1962, CA; Rich to MaryLu Murphy, Dec. 17, 1962, CA; Brooklyn *Amsterdam News,* Aug. 18, 1962; New York *Amsterdam News,* Oct. 27, 1962; "Civil Rights Battle: Northern Style," *Ebony,* XVIII (March 1963), 96–98, 100, 102; and materials in the Ollie Leeds Prs, esp. Brooklyn CORE Minutes, May 21, June 4, Aug. 6, 1962; Notes on Meeting of Negotiations Committee and Ebin-

ger Bakery, May 25, 1962; "Ebinger Campaign Memo," Aug. 6, 1962; "Background Information on Brooklyn CORE-Ebinger's Negotiations" [1962].

23. 1961 Convention, Oldham Prs; 1962 Convention, CA; Farmer, Report to 1962 Convention, CA.

24. *Eagle*, June 14, Aug. 30, 1962; Philadelphia CORE Testimony before Philadelphia Board of Education, rec'd Dec. 4, 1962, CA; Philadelphia *Inquirer*, Oct. 11, 1962.

25. Chicago CORE, Reports, Feb. 1961, and n.d. [fall 1962], CA; *Defender*, Sept. 3 and 24, 1960, Sept. 2–8, 16–22, 1961; Faith Rich to Board of Education and Len O'Connor, Aug. 22, 1961, Faith Rich Prs; Fred Fields to Farmer, Dec. 30, 1961, CA; *Integrated Education*, I (Jan. 1963), 22–23; Samuel Riley to Dear Alderman, Jan. 17, 1963, Faith Rich Prs; Chicago South Unit Report, rec'd Nov. 20, 1962, CA, Oakland *Tribune*, May 2, Sept. 19, 1962; *Integrated Education*, II (April-May 1964), 43; Berkeley CORE press releases, May 1 and Sept. 19, 1962, CA; Berkeley CORE, presentation to Berkeley Board of Education, May 1, 1962, WCO; Berkeley *Corespondent*, Oct. 1962, CA.

26. For Englewood, see *Times*, Feb. 7, 17, 1962, and *CORE-lator*, April 1962. For Malverne, see *Times*, Aug. 1, 3, 1962, and Brooklyn *Amsterdam News*, July 27, 1962. For San Francisco, see San Francisco CORE, Statement to Board of Education, Sept. 1, 1962, WCO; Fredricka Teer, Report, Sept. 24, 1962, CHQ; San Francisco *Chronicle*, Sept. 19, 20, 1962.

27. For Brooklyn, see New York *Amsterdam News*, Sept. 8, 22, 1962; *Times*, Sept. 19, 1962; Brooklyn *Amsterdam News*, Oct. 27, Nov. 17, Dec. 9, 1962, and Feb. 2, 9, 16, 1963; Brooklyn CORE *North Star*, Nov. 1, 1962 and Feb. [sic] 1963, Leeds Prs; "The Bibuld Case Fact Sheet," Dec. 3, 1962, Leeds Prs; Brooklyn CORE press releases [Oct. 1962], Leeds Prs, and Jan. 7, 1963, CA; Irving Goldaber "The Treatment by the New York City School Board of Problems Affecting the Negro, 1954–1963" (Ph.D. dissertation, New York University, 1965), 216–19. For Syracuse, see Ronald D. Corwin, "School Desegregation in Syracuse" (Ph.D. dissertation, Syracuse University, 1966), *passim*; Syracuse *Post-Standard*, June 19, Aug. 30, Sept. 26, 1962; and the following materials in the George Wiley Prs: Wiley, "History of De Facto Segregation Negotiations and Action in Syracuse," Oct. 1962; Statements by Syracuse CORE, the Civil Rights Committee of IUE Local 320 and Syracuse NAACP, Sept. 14, Oct. 21, 1962. For Englewood, see Sally Elliott to Don Wendell, May 22, 1962, CA; undated circular, "Englewood Movement" [Summer 1962], CA; David Spengler, "The Englewood-Teaneck, New Jersey Experience," in T. Bentley Edwards and Frederick Wirt, eds., *School Desegregation in the North* (San Francisco, 1967), 202–41.

28. Joint Statement released by Rochester CORE and NAACP Youth Council, Aug. 21, 1961, CA; *CORE-lator*, Dec. 1961; East St. Louis *Journal*, Nov. 11, 1962; Eugene Tournour to McCain, Nov. 9, 1962, CA; National Action Council, Dec. 22–23, 1962, CA.

29. Minutes of Weekend Field Staff Meeting, Oct. 20–21 [1961], CA; Genevieve Hughes, Report, June 14, 1962, CA; Carey to Theodore Alpen, May 16, 1961, CA; *Ohio State Lantern*, April 24, 1961, cited in James VanderZanden,

American Minority Relations (New York, 1963), 314–15; John Schopp to Rich, Jan. 6, 1962, CA; Chicago Southside Unit Report, rec'd. Nov. 20, 1962, CA; Zev Aelony to Marcia McKenna and McCain, March 25, 1963, CA; Noel Day, "The Freedom Movement in Massachusetts" [mid-1963], George Wiley Prs; also interviews.

30. Genevieve Hughes, Report, April 11–15, 1962, CA; Minutes of Metropolitan Area Coordinating Council, Jan. 11, 1962, CA; 1962 CORE Convention, CA; Inge Powell Bell, *CORE and the Strategy of Non-Violence* (New York, 1968), 74, 67–69; Brooklyn CORE Officers, Sept. 1962, Leeds Prs; Rochester *Times*, June 3, 1961, clipping CA; interviews. For suggestive treatments of the social-psychological aspects of recruitment of blacks into the nonviolent direct-action movement, see Bell, *CORE and the Strategy of Non-Violence*, 71–76, and Maurice Pinard, Jerome Kirk, and Donald Von Eschen, "Processes of Recruitment in the Sit-In Movement," *Public Opinion Quarterly*, XXX (Fall 1969), 355–69 and Gary Marx, *Protest and Prejudice: A Study of Belief in the Black Community* (New York, 1967), chap. 2. For discussion of the participation of a particular Jewish sub-group of young females, the so-called "Bagel Babies," see Debbie Louis, *And We Are Not Saved: A History of the Movement as People* (Garden City, New York, 1970), 38–42.

31. Mary Hamilton to McCain, Dec. 15, 1962, CA; Edgar Chasteen, "Public Accommodations: Social Movements in Conflict" (Ph.D. dissertation, University of Missouri, 1966), 141–44; interviews.

32. Interviews.

33. New York CORE, "Yesterday—Today, Progress Report, Oct., 1963," CA; New York *Amsterdam News*, April 21, 1962; interviews.

34. Blyden Jackson to Farmer, March 20, 1962; Libby Palmer, Report on New Haven CORE, March 12, 1962; Ann Arbor CORE, Report [late 1962], CA; interviews.

35. On Brooklyn, interviews, and Brooklyn *World-Telegram*, April 16, 1963 (interview with Ollie Leeds), clipping, Leeds Prs. On Philadelphia, see Hughes, "Descriptions of Persons Who Attended One or Both Organized Meetings" [Dec. 1960], CA; Beryl Radin to Rich, Oct. 26, 1960, CA; Philadelphia CORE Annual Report, July 1, 1962, CA; interviews. On Syracuse, Evert Makinen to Rich, Feb. 8, 1963. On St. Louis, interview.

36. Various materials in Leeds Prs regarding Beth-El Hospital strike, esp. Brooklyn CORE Minutes, June 4, 1962, and Leeds, "Statement of Brooklyn Congress of Racial Equality Protesting Beth-El Hospital Discrimination Against its Negro and Puerto Rican Employees," June 24, 1962; Brooklyn *Amsterdam News*, Sept. 22, 1962; Ollie Leeds to Farmer, Sept. 18, 1962, CA; and materials on Operation Cleansweep in Leeds Prs, esp. Leeds, Memorandum to Kings County and New York City Authorities, Aug. 24, 1962, and Brooklyn CORE *North Star*, Oct. 1, Dec. 1962; Hill to Fredricka Teer, Oct. 30, 1962, CA.

37. Farmer to Robert Miller, Feb. 26, 1962, CA; Adah Jenkins to Farmer, Jan. 31, 1962, CA.

38. For example, Rich to Rachlin, Nov. 3, 1961, CA; Teer to McCain, Feb. 3, 1963, CA; interviews.

39. Lou Smith to James Tate, March 24, 1963, CA.

40. Minutes of Field Staff Meeting, Oct. 20–21 [1961], CA.

41. Greater Boston CORE Report, rec'd Nov. 15, 1962, CA; Philadelphia CORE Report [summer], CA.

42. On Williams generally, see Julian Mayfield, "Challenge to Negro Leadership," *Commentary*, XXXI (April 1961), 297–305; Robert F. Williams, *Negroes With Guns* (New York, 1962). For overall summary of events of Aug. 1961 and their aftermath, see *The Southern Patriot*, XIX (Oct. 1961), 1–3, and XXII (March 1964), 1–3. On involvement of Freedom Riders and CORE, see Paul Brooks to Nashville Christian Leadership Conference, Aug. 17, 1961, CA; "Freedom Riders Presently in Monroe, North Carolina, 20 August '61," CA; Minutes, Monroe Nonviolent Action Committee, Aug. 19, 1961, CA. On Lowry case, see John Lowry to Farmer, Aug. 24, 1964, and Carl Rachlin correspondence with Richard J. Scupi and William Kunstler, Sept. and Oct. 1964, all Rachlin files.

43. Farmer to CORE groups and national officers, April 12, 1962, CA; Farmer to Greensboro CORE, Sept. 26, 1962, CA; interviews.

44. Culbert Rutenber to Farmer, March 23, 1962, and Farmer to Rutenber, April 23, 1962, CA; Clipping from *Princetonian* in John Ernest to Farmer, May 24, 1962, CA; Farmer to Dear Friends, May 29, 1962, CA; "Summer Action Bulletin," July 23, 1962, CA; Brooklyn CORE *North Star*, Nov. 1, 1962, personal file.

45. Interview with Fredricka Teer and Genevieve Hughes cited in Inge Bell, *CORE and the Strategy of Non-Violence*, 57; San Francisco *Chronicle*, Sept. 19, 1962; Haley to Staff Members, March 1, 1963, and Hill to Steering Committee, April 26, 1963, both CA.

46. Interviews for Newark and Harrington's view on Farmer; J. W. Franklin to McCain, Feb. 28, 1962, CA for New York; Brooklyn CORE *North Star*, Nov. 1, 1962, personal file; list of Brooklyn CORE chapter officers, Sept. 1962, Leeds Prs; Teer, Report, May 11, 1962, CA; Haley to Charlie Butts, July 17, 1962, CA.

47. On Detroit, see 1961 CORE Convention, Oldham Prs; NAC, Sept. 18, 1961, CA, and Oct. 12, 1961, Oldham Prs; Leon De Meunier to Oldham, Sept. 13, 1961, Oldham Prs; and the following in De Meunier's papers: Carey to Bill Goode, Sept. 21, 1961; Carey to Detroit CORE and Metropolitan CORE, Oct. 3, 1961; De Meunier to Anna Holden and Carey, Nov. 6, 1961; and Carey to De Meunier, Nov. 14, 1961; also interviews. On New Orleans, see Bell, *CORE and the Strategy of Non-Violence*, 83, 100–101.

48. Robert Gore, "Black on Black" [1962], CA. On Gore's pacifist ideology, see Gore, "Nonviolence," in Glenford Mitchell and William Pearce, eds., *The Angry Black South* (New York, 1962), 128–51.

49. Farmer to Alton Lemon, March 15, 1962, CA; Grand Rapids *Press*, April 13, 1962.

50. Interviews; Bell, *CORE and the Strategy of Non-Violence*, 48; Farmer to Faith Rich, Oct. 25, 1942, CA.

51. Jean Krentz to Malcolm X, July 16, 1962, CA; Durham *Morning Herald*, April 1, 20, 1963; Malcolm X and James Farmer, "Separation or Integration: A Debate," *Dialogue Magazine*, II (May 1962), 14–18, reprinted in August Meier,

Elliott Rudwick, and Francis Broderick, eds., *Black Protest Thought in the Twentieth Century,* 2nd edition (Indianapolis, 1971), 387–412.

52. J. W. Franklin to McCain, Feb. 28, 1962, CA; Hartford CORE Report, rec'd April 24, 1963, CA; interviews; Bell, *CORE and the Strategy of Non-Violence,* 100.

53. Hughes to Rich, July 19, 1962, CA; interviews.

54. San Francisco *CORE-lator,* July 1962, CA; interview.

55. Hughes, Report, June 11, 1962, CA; Farmer, *Freedom-When?,* 88; Bell, *CORE and the Strategy of Non-Violence,* 49. Farmer erroneously recollected the date as 1964.

56. Bell, *CORE and the Strategy of Non-Violence,* 47; Hill to Fredricka Teer, Oct. 30, 1962, CA; interviews.

57. Farmer, National Director's Report to 1962 Convention, CA; Farmer, *Freedom-When?,* 77–78.

CHAPTER EIGHT

1. Dayton *Journal Herald,* June 28, 1963.

2. *Wall Street Journal,* May 17, 1963.

3. Farmer, "The New Jacobins and Full Emancipation," in Robert Goldwin, ed., *100 Years of Emancipation* (Chicago, 1963), 100; Dayton *Journal Herald,* June 27, 1963; Columbus *Citizen-Journal,* June 28, 1963; Lerone Bennett, "Mood of the Negro," *Ebony,* XVIII (July 1963), 30.

4. Bayard Rustin, "The Great Lessons of Birmingham," *Liberation,* VII (June 1963), reprinted in August Meier, Elliott Rudwick, and Francis Broderick, eds., *Black Protest Thought in the Twentieth Century,* 2nd edition (Indianapolis, 1971), 332.

5. On CORE's role in Birmingham, see esp. interview with Isaac Reynolds in *New America,* May 31, 1963; on CORE's role in the Jackson demonstrations which culminated in the assassination of Medgar Evers, see esp. *Mississippi Free Press,* June 1, 8, 15, 22, 1963; Anne Moody, *Coming of Age in Mississippi* (New York, 1968), 263–85; *Times,* May 31, 1963; Farmer to CORE Leaders, May 31, 1963, WCO.

6. On Moore, see esp. Farmer to CORE Group leaders, April 24, 1963, CA; Moore to Peck, Feb. 24, 1963, CA; Peck to Moore, Feb. 27, 1963, CA; Moore, Open letter to Mississippi Governor Ross Barnett [April, 1963], CA. On the Memorial Walk, see Steering Committee, April 26, 1963, CA; Bob Gore, "Moore Memorial Trek Diary," May 1963, CA; Carey to Chapter Chairmen, May 3, 1963, WCO; Haley, from Kilby State Prison, to Rich, May 23, 1963, CA; Howard Zinn, *SNCC: The New Abolitionists* (Boston, 1964), 175–80. On second group of marchers, see Claudia Edwards, Report, June 2, 1963, CA; Mary Hamilton to McCain, Aug. 9, 1963, CA. See also letters from jail: Edwards to Carey, May 23, 1963, CA; Gordon Harris to Parents, May 25, 1963, CA. On CORE's hopes for the project and being overshadowed by Birmingham, see *Times,*

April 28, 1963, and Gartner to Rich, May 7, 1963, CA. On ultimate reversal of the walkers' convictions, see press release, Nov. 6, 1964.

7. Press release, May 9, 1963.

8. Marvin Robinson to Carey, May 31, 1963, CA; Mary Hamilton to McCain, Aug. 9, 1963, CA; Claudia Rawles, "The Gadsden Report" [1963], CA; Robinson to McCain [Aug. 1963], CA; Gadsden, Alabama, *Times,* June 11, 14, 16–19, 22, 27, Aug. 4, 1963; *Times,* June 13, 15, 16, 21–24, 28, July 2, Aug. 4, 1963; Burke Marshall, Memorandum, July 17, 1963, and Carl Gabel to Marshall, July 20, 1963, Burke Marshall Prs.

9. Gadsden *Times,* June 26, 1963; *Hamilton v. Alabama,* U. S. Supreme Court Decision, in *RRLR,* IX (1964), 56; Oscar Adams to Mary Hamilton, March 31, 1964, Hamilton Prs.

10. Press release, Nov. 6, 1964; Gadsden *Times,* July 4, 6, 1964.

11. Frank Robinson, Report, Aug. 11, 1963, CA; Robinson to McCain, Sept. 7, 1963, CA; McCain, Memo to Farmer on Trip to South Carolina, Sept. 20 to Oct. 30, 1963, MLK; Catherine Patterson to McCain, Nov. 29, 1963, CA; Jane Rogers to CORE, March 2, 1964, CA. On desegregation of lunch counters, see Durham *Sun,* June 19, 1963.

12. See esp. Jerome Smith to Carey, Jan. 22, 1963, CA; B. Elton Cox to McCain, March 9, April 23, 1963, CA; Floyd McKissick to Carey, Feb. 9, 1963, Rachlin Files; R. Hunter Morey, "CORE in High Point," May 11, 1963, and Morey to "Steve," April 7, 1963, Morey Prs.

13. NAACP-CORE Negotiating Committee to Mayor of Durham, May 23, 1963, CA; William Thomas *et al.,* Report on Greensboro CORE, June 7, 1963, CA.

14. On Greensboro, see Greensboro *Daily News,* May 14–26, 31; June 3, 5–8, 14–19, 26; July 1, 4, 8, 9, 25; Aug. 9, 24, 26, 28; Sept. 5–7, 18, 30; Oct. 8–10, 1963; *Times,* May 16–19, 21–23, 25, 26, June 7, 8, 15, 1963; press releases May 16, 20, 23, 1963, May 28, 1964; *The Candle* (mimeo'd, Greensboro), No. 1, May 23, 1963, No. 5 [June 1963], and No. 6 [June 1963], all CA; William Thomas to McCain, Sept. 2, 1963, CA. On Durham, see Durham *Morning Herald,* May 19–25, June 3, 5, 7, 9, 19, 1963; Durham *Sun,* May 20, 23, 30, 1963; press release, May 20, 1963; Bruce Baines, Report, May 25, 1963, CA; *Times,* May 20–24, 1963; Allen Sindler, *Negro Protest and Local Politics in Durham, North Carolina* (New Brunswick, 1965), 15–20. On work of Durham Interim Committee, see also William Keech, "The Negro Vote as a Political Resource: The Case of Durham" (Ph.D. dissertation, University of Wisconsin, 1966), 198–206. On High Point, see R. Hunter Morey, "CORE in High Point," May 11, 1963, Morey Prs; press release, May 29, 1963; clippings from High Point *Enterprise,* June 5, 11–13, CA; Mrs. D. Z. Mitchell, circular letter, July 22, 1963, CA; Greensboro *Daily News,* Aug. 24, Sept. 25, 1963; *Times,* Sept. 5, 10, 12, 15, 1963. Quotations from Farmer in Greensboro *Daily News,* May 20, 21, 1963. For disposition of street-blocking cases, see McKissick to Morey, June 18, 1964, Morey Prs. For complete desegregation of Greensboro and High Point not taking place until Civil Rights Law of 1964 went into effect, see Greensboro *Daily News,*

July 4, 10, 1964. On Chapel Hill, see *Chapel Hill Weekly*, May 26, 29, June 9, 16, 19, 23, 26, July 10, 21, 24, Aug. 4, 14, 18, Dec. 18, 22, 26, 1963, Jan. 5, 15, Feb. 23, 26, March 1, 22, April 22, 26, 1964; *News of Orange County*, Dec. 19, 1963, Jan. 16, April 9, 1964; Chapel Hill CORE, "Activity Report," No. 1 [Dec. 1963], MLK; Claudia Edwards, Reports, Oct. 27, Dec. 22, 1963, Jan. 4, 1964, CA; B. Elton Cox to McCain, Dec. 9, 1963; John Dunne to Rich, Dec. 17, 1963, and rec'd March 24, 1964, both CA; Steering Committee, Jan. 24, 1964, CA; Dunne to McCain, Feb. 20, 1964, CA; McKissick to Rich, May 19, 1965, MLK; press releases, Dec. 19, 1963, Jan. 2, Feb. 13, 1964; *Times*, Feb. 2, 9, May 21, 1964. For McKissick's dismissal of Sanford's invitation, McKissick to Farmer, Jan. 18, 1964, MLK. In general on the whole Chapel Hill Movement (with a somewhat critical view of the role of National CORE), see John Ehle, *The Free Men* (New York, 1965).

15. *CORE-lator*, Nov. 1962; Haley, "Tallahassee: A Tale of One City" [Jan. 1963], CA; Tallahassee *Democrat*, Sept. 26, Oct. 26, Nov. 13, 1962; May 29–31, June 1, 2, 4, 12, 14, Sept. 15–17, 19–21, 25, Oct. 25, 1963; "Statement of Pat Due Concerning Arrest in Tallahassee, Florida, January 23, 1963," CA; press release, May 29, 1963; Haley to McCain, June 5, 1963, CA; Tobias Simon to Carl Rachlin, Sept. 24, 1963, Rachlin Files; Pat Due, Report to NAC, Nov. 7, 1963, CA; Haley to Farmer *et al.,* Oct. 10, 1963, CA. For chapter decline, see Due to Rich, June 1, 1964, CA; Judy Benninger to McCain and Haley, June 15, 1964, CA. On final desegregation of theaters, see Tallahassee *Democrat*, July 3, 4, 1964.

16. Ronnie Moore, "The Story of Plaquemine," Sept. 6, 1963, CA; Baton Rouge *Morning Advocate*, Aug. 20–22, 1963; Farmer, *Freedom-When?* (New York, 1965), 5–15; Farmer, *The Louisiana Story* (New York, 1963), unpaged pamphlet; Jack Minnis to Wiley Branton, Aug. 30, 1963, VEP; Mary Hamilton to McCain, Oct. 14, 1963, CA; David Marlin to Burke Marshall, Aug. 20, 21, 22, 23, 26, 1963, and St. George Barrett to Marshall, Sept. 2, 1963, CA; Farmer, Address at Clinton, La., Aug. 4, 1964, taped interview in Edward Hollander Prs. On restraining orders, see *RRLR*, VII (1963), 863 ff., and documents in Murphy Bell Prs, Reel No. 3. On near riot on Sept. 1, see AP dispatches in Baton Rouge *State Times*, Sept. 2, 1963, and Philadelphia *Bulletin*, Sept. 2, 1963.

17. Farmer, *Freedom-When?*, 15; Farmer, telegram to John F. Kennedy, Sept. 6, 1963, CA; Burke Marshall to Farmer, Sept. 9, 1963, CA.

18. Rich, "Civil Rights Strategy after the March," *New Politics*, II (Fall 1963), 45; Farmer quoted in *Afro-American*, March 17, 1964.

19. *Afro-American*, May 21, July 9, 16, Aug. 30, 1963; interviews and personal observations.

20. Randolph to Farmer, March 26, 1963, CA; Steering Committee, March 29, 1963, CA.

21. The preceding discussion is based chiefly on interviews and personal observations. For Farmer's recollections of the evolution of March strategy and the coolness of many CORE chapters to the less militant tactics, see transcript of John F. Stewart, "Oral History Interview with James Farmer, March 10, 1967,"

20–21, John F. Kennedy Library, and transcript of Albert Gollin's interview with James Farmer, June 9, 1967, courtesy of Albert Gollin. For pressure on King, see also Charles Diggs to King, June 27, 1963, CHQ. Gollin's interview with Farmer and Rich, "Civil Rights Strategy After the March," 49, summarize CORE's view of the consequences of Randolph's coalition strategy.

22. Interviews; Rustin to March on Washington co-chairmen, Sept. 27, 1963, Alan Gartner Prs; Steering Committee, Aug. 30, 1963, CA; Haley to Farmer, Sept. 3, 1963, CA. See also discussion of coalitions at NAC, Nov. 8–10, 1963, CA.

23. Rich to Haley, March 27, 1963, CA; interview with Turner in Robert Penn Warren, *Who Speaks for the Negro?* (New York, 1965), 380; interview.

24. Statement of Income for Year Ending May 31, 1964, CA; Rich to NAC, June 1, 1963, CA; Haley to John Gillis, Aug. 20, 1963, CA.

25. Rich to Inge Bell, July 28, 1966, SEDF; "Extra Special Specials" [1964], and "Tip-top Contributors in New York City Area" [1964], both CA.

26. See, for example, Val Coleman to Oretha Castle, Oct. 14, 1963; Coleman to Farmer, June 24, 1964; Willard Alexander to Farmer, Nov. 21, 1963; Helen Major to Rich, Jan. 9, 1965, all CA. On Artists, see Brooklyn *Amsterdam News,* July 6, 1963; press release [July 1963].

27. Financial statement, month ending Nov. 30, 1963, CA; Statements of Income for Fiscal Year Ending May 31, 1963, and May 31, 1964, both CA.

28. Farmer to L. J. Eddy [June 1963], CA; Steering Committee, Jan. 24, 1964, CA.

29. Chet Duncan to McCain, July 22, 1963, CA; Steering Committee, Aug. 30, Sept. 27, 1963, CA; Marcia McKenna, Report to NAC, Nov. 8–10, 1963, CA; "Affiliated CORE Chapters, 6/22/64," personal file; on Los Angeles, *Wall Street Journal,* May 17, 1963, and *Sentinel,* July 11, 1963; on Brooklyn, Brooklyn *World-Telegram and Sun,* April 16, 1963, clipping, Leeds Prs and interview.

30. On Toledo, Inez Boyd to McCain, Sept. 13, 1963, CA; on Kansas City, Constance Timberlake to Farmer, Sept. 25, 1963, CA; on Seattle, Georgia Martin to Rich, Oct. 1, 1963, CA, and interviews; on Berkeley, "Western Regional CORE Chapters Report," July 29, 1963, CA; on Boston, interviews.

31. Since chapters only rarely submitted membership statistics to national, these are knowledgeable estimates made by CORE officials. See Haley to John Gillis, Aug. 20, 1963, CA; *Times,* July 30, 1964; Karen Berg to Morris Richards, Nov. 20, 1964, CA.

32. Membership lists of Detroit CORE, 1963–64, Ralph Rosenfeld and Gloria Brown Prs; Membership List of San Diego CORE, Sept. 24, 1964, MLK; "Active Voting List, Washington, D. C. CORE," March 24, 1964, MLK; Newark CORE Membership List, March 16, 1964, Curvin Prs; "Resolution on New Haven CORE Unity" [January 1964], Gene Schulze Prs; "Background Information for [Cleveland] CORE Members" [ca. Spring 1964], Arthur Evans Prs; Haley to Members of New York CORE, Jan. 18, 1964, CA; William Ellis, "Operation Bootstrap: A Case Study in Ideology and the Institutionalization of Protest" (Ph.D. dissertation, University of California at Los Angeles, 1969), 79–80. For

case of deliberate exaggeration of chapter membership for public consumption,
see admission of Julius Hobson, former chairman of Washington CORE, in
Washington *Post*, July 4, 1972.

33. Inge Bell, *CORE and the Strategy of Non-Violence* (New York, 1968),
21 n.

34. Seattle *Post-Intelligencer*, June 16, 1963; Seattle CORE newsletter [Sept.
1963], CA; Cleveland *Plain Dealer,* July 15, 1963. For St. Louis, Berkeley, and
Los Angeles, see accounts of campaigns given below.

35. Hughes to Rich, June 17, 1963, CA.

36. Newark *Evening News,* July 20, 1963; Kansas City *Times,* Aug. 22, 1963.
For Long Island, New York, and California, see discussions of campaigns below.

37. Evert Makinen to Carey, May 23, 1963, CA; Henry Holstege, "Conflict
and Change in Negro-White Relations in Great Falls [Grand Rapids]" (Ph.D.
dissertation, Michigan State University, 1967), 157–61; Chet Duncan, Report,
July 9, 1963, CA; Ann Arbor CORE press release, Oct. 25, 1963, CA; St. Louis
Post-Dispatch, Sept.-1, 1963; San Francisco *CORE-lator,* Nov. 1963, Ollie Leeds
Prs; Hughes to Rich, rec'd June 3, 1963, CA, June 17, 1963, CA.

38. For Seattle, see Georgia Martin to Farmer, March 24, 1964, CA; for St.
Louis, "Facts on Jefferson Bank" [late 1963], Oldham Prs, and St. Louis *Post-
Dispatch,* Dec. 6, 1963; for Philadelphia, Philadelphia *Bulletin,* May 27, 28, 31,
June 1, 2, and esp. June 3, 1963. Other data were secured from interviews and
personal observations.

39. The preceding discussion was based principally on interviews and personal observation. For Berkeley, however, see Chet Duncan, Western Regional
CORE chapter report, Nov. 4, 1963, CA and Berkeley CORE Minutes, Sept. 3,
Dec. 4, 1963, WCO. On Cleveland, see also Louis Masotti and Jerome Corsi,
Shoot-Out in Cleveland (New York, 1969), 6–7; Lewis Robinson, *The Making
of a Man* (Cleveland, 1970), 64–65. On Brooklyn, see also *Times,* June 22, 1964,
and Bernice Fisher to Farmer, Aug. 11, 1963, CA; and the following in the Milton Galamison Prs: Ollie Leeds to Galamison, Aug. 12, 1963, and [Aug. 1963]
and Galamison to Nelson Rockefeller, Aug. 13, 1963.

40. Newark *Evening News,* July 10, 1963; Program transcript of WCBS-TV,
Newsmakers, July 14, 1963. CHQ; summary of Farmer's Reports to 1963 Con-
vention in preliminary minutes of 1963 Convention, MaryLu Murphy Prs;
Farmer, National Director's Report to 1964 Convention, Farmer Prs.

41. *Times,* June 29, 1963, and summary of Farmer's remarks in preliminary
minutes of 1963 Convention, MaryLu Murphy Prs; [Dayton CORE], "Objec-
tives" [Spring 1963], CHQ and Dayton CORE to Haley, April 23, 1963, CA; St.
Louis *Post-Dispatch,* Aug. 25, 1963; San Francisco *CORE-lator,* Nov. 1963, Ollie
Leeds Prs; and for Syracuse: Evert Makinen to Carey, June 19, 1963, CA; ? to
Rich, [Aug. 1963], CA; ? to Bob Gore, Aug. 17, 1963, CA. See also, "The Protest Movement North: The Syracuse Story," George Wiley Prs.

42. For Lexington, see press releases, Aug. 5, 22, 1963; Louisville *Defender,*
July 25, Aug. 1, 1963. For Dayton, see Dayton CORE *Bulletin,* March 16, 23,
Nov. 30, 1963, CHQ; Dayton CORE to Haley, April 23, 1963, CA; W. S. McIn-

tosh to Bob Gore, Aug. 11, 1963, CA; Dayton *Journal Herald*, June 29, July 4, 1963. For Berkeley, see *Daily Californian* (University of California at Berkeley), Nov. 8, 21, Dec. 3, 1963; Berkeley *Daily Gazette*, Nov. 8, 21, 26, 1963; Lawrence Gurley to Gentlemen, Dec. 11, 1963, UC; press release, Dec. 19, 1963, and interviews. For San Francisco, see Memorandum of Understanding with San Francisco Retailers Community Relations Group, Dec. 17, 1963, CA; San Francisco *Chronicle*, Dec. 18, 1963. For St. Louis, see *Argus*, Dec. 6, 13, 1963; St. Louis *Post-Dispatch*, Dec. 5, 6, 8, 14, 1963.

43. Berkeley CORE, "Discrimination in Employment: The Case of Montgomery Ward" [1963], Fredricka Teer Kushner Prs; Berkeley *Corespondent*, May 10, 1963, CA; Genevieve Hughes to Rich, rec'd June 3, 1963, CA; Berkeley and Oakland CORE circular [May 1963], UC; Fredricka Teer to Hill, July 3, 1963, Kushner Prs; Duran Bell to Rich, July 18, 1963, CA; Minutes, Berkeley CORE Meeting, Aug. 20, 1963, WCO; Berkeley Campus *CORE-lator*, Sept. 1964, UC.

44. Western Regional CORE Chapters Report, Aug. 26, 1963, CA; Denver *Post*, July 16, 26, Sept. 8, 27, 1963; Detroit CORE newsletter, Feb. 1963, Ralph Rosenfeld Prs; *Chronicle*, July 6, Aug. 3, 1963; Harry Douglass to Dear Friend, Spring [sic] 1964, Detroit *News* Library Files; Seattle *Post-Intelligencer*, June 22, Aug. 7, 1963; "Seattle CORE Conference, August 17, 1963," Seattle CORE Prs; *Afro-American*, Sept. 24, Oct. 22, 29, Nov. 13, 1963, Jan. 14, 1964; Edward Chance to H. Warren Buckler, Dec. 13, 1963, CA; ? to John Schaefer, rec'd Feb. 6, 1964, CA; Long Island CORE Clipping books, March 10, 20, 1964; Lincoln Lynch to Dear Friend, Nov. 13, 1963, CA; press release, Nov. 21, 1963; Long Island CORE newsletter, March 26, 1964, CA. Velma Hill, "Report on A & P Negotiations and Settlement" [Dec. 1963], CA; Rich to Frances Bergman, Dec. 23, 1963, CA.

45. On San Francisco, see Western Regional CORE Chapters Report, Aug. 12, 1963, CA: Minutes, Safeway Negotiating Meeting, Aug. 21, 1963, WCO; R. A. Hillis to Chet Duncan, Sept. 18, 1963, WCO; Duncan to Bryan Stokes, Sept. 6, 1963, WCO; "Transcription of CORE Negotiating Team Meeting with Lucky Stores, Feb. 3, 1964," CA; Bay-area chapters press release, Feb. 12, 1964, CA; press release, Feb. 27, 1964; San Francisco *Chronicle*, Dec. 18, 1963, Feb. 18, 20, 27, 29, March 1, 1964; "Lucky Stores Final Agreement, Feb. 28, 1964," WCO. On Seattle, see esp. reports of negotiating meetings and correspondence with A & P and Tradewell chains, Nov. 1963 to Aug. 1964, *passim*, in Seattle CORE Prs; Seattle *Daily Times*, Oct. 22, 1963, March 21, 22, July 12, 1964; Seattle CORE newsletters, Oct. and Nov. 1963, WCO; Seattle *CORE-lator*, July and Aug. 1964, CHQ.

46. Philadelphia *Bulletin*, May 14, 15, 19, 22–28, 31, June 1–3, 21–28, Aug. 9, 20, 1963; *Tribune*, May 4, 7, 11, 14, 18, 21, 25, 28, June 4, 22, 29, Aug. 20, 1963, May 5, 1965; Newark *Evening News*, July 3, 10, 14, 18, 30, Aug. 3, 6, 7, 15, 16, 1963 and interviews.

47. *CORE-lator*, Sept. 1963; *Times*, June 14, July 14, 16, Aug. 8, 10, 23, 25, Sept. 30, Oct. 2, 1963, May 1, 8, 13, 14, 15, 16, 1964; Brooklyn *Amsterdam News*, July 20, 27, Aug. 3, 17, Sept. 28, Oct. 5, 12, Dec. 14, 1963; May 23, 1964; New

York *Amsterdam News,* July 13, 27, Aug. 10, Sept. 14, 21, 1963; New York CORE, Report to 1963 Convention, Alan Gartner Prs; New York CORE, "Yesterday-Today, Progress Report," Oct. 1963, CA; press release, May 23, 1964.

48. East St. Louis *Journal,* Aug. 12, 15, 16, 18, 1963; East St. Louis *Crusader,* Aug. 13, 22, 1963.

49. "Facts on Jefferson Bank" [ca. late 1963], Oldham Prs; CORE and the Bank" [ca. 1964], Oldham Prs; St. Louis CORE press release, Dec. 5, 1963, Oldham Prs; press releases, Oct. 31, 1963, Jan. 14, 30, March 5, April 2, 1964; St. Louis *Post-Dispatch,* Dec. 6, 1963, Jan. 14, March 31, 1964, and Aug. 2, Sept. 20, 21, 1965; *Argus,* Aug. 30, Sept. 6, Oct. 11, Nov. 1, 8, 1963, Jan. 10, March 6, 27, April 3, 17, 1964; Ernestine Patterson, "The Impact of the Black Struggle on Representative Government in St. Louis, Missouri" (Ph.D. dissertation, St. Louis University, 1968), *passim;* Virginia Brodine, "The Strange Case of Jefferson Bank vs. CORE," *FOCUS/Midwest,* II (Nov. 1963), 12–15, 24; Jules B. Gerard, "Jefferson Bank Dispute Rocks St. Louis," *FOCUS/Midwest,* V, No. 36 (1967), 13–15; *Jefferson Bank and Trust Co. vs. Robert B. Curtis et al., RRLR,* IX (1964), 82 ff.

50. Boston CORE press releases, Feb. 15, April 8; Boston *Globe,* clipping, Feb. 19, 1964; Boston *Corespondent,* Feb. 19, April 27, 1964; Richard Brown to Alan Gartner, Feb. 2, 1964; "Minutes of Meeting Between Richard Brown and John H. Stetson," April 16, 1964; all in Richard Brown Papers.

51. Minutes, California CORE Conference, Jan. 17–19, 1964; "Demands—Bank of America," March 16, 1964; CORE Negotiating Team to Frank Young, May 12, 1964; Bill Bradley and Wilfred Ussery, Report, June 10, 1964; Bradley to California chapters, May 12, 1964; Negotiating Team to CORE chapters, May 20, 1964; Chet Duncan, "Bank of America," May 26, 1964; Bradley, "Bank of American Report" [Nov. 1964]; Bruce Hartford, "Report of Bruin CORE's Action against Bank of America," rec'd July 30, 1964; Los Angeles CORE press release, Aug. 31, 1964; Negotiating Team press release, Sept. 1, 1964, all WCO. Also: San Francisco *Chronicle,* March 17, 24, April 21, May 22, 23, 26, 30, June 2, 6, 13, 17, 20, 27, July 3, 4, 16, 22, Sept. 2, 23, 1964; *Sentinel,* June 4, July 16, Sept. 3, 24, Oct. 8, Dec. 3, 1964; San Diego *Union,* June 6, 13, 20, 27, 30, July 7, 8, 18, Aug. 1, 8, 13, 21, 22, 29, 1964, and July 30, 1965; San Diego CORE press release, Jan. 30, 1966, MLK.

52. *Times,* July 4, 5, 1963; "Long Island CORE and the Civil Rights War, 1963," Jan. 1964, CA.

53. Interviews; on arrests at Hayes-Bickford Restaurants, see also Boston *Globe,* July 11, 1964, clipping, Phyllis Ryan Prs.

54. MaryLu Murphy to Rich, July 21, 1963, CA; Marian Oldham to I. C. Steinlarge, Aug. 14, 1963, and Richard Kerckhoff to Marian Oldham, Aug. 20, 1963, in Charles Oldham Prs.

55. San Diego *Union,* Dec. 11, 24, 25, 28, 1963, Jan. 1, 3, 10, 18, May 26, 1964; San Diego Gas and Electric Co. vs. San Diego CORE, *RRLR,* XI (1966), 1401 ff. St. Louis *Post-Dispatch,* Oct. 30, 1963, and East St. Louis *Journal,* April 30, July 11, 17, Oct. 30, 1963.

56. Velma Hill to Dear Sir, April 2, 1964, CA; Shaefer Fact Sheet No. 2, is-

sued by National CORE, March 23, 1964, CA; *Times,* March 21, 1964; New York *Amsterdam News,* Dec. 28, 1963, March 28, April 4, 1964; plus personal recollections of Newark and World's Fair.

57. "New York CORE, Yesterday-Today, Progress Report," Oct. 1963, CA; New York *Amsterdam News,* Sept. 28, 1963. On Lever Brothers, see also Abe Fortas to Farmer, Aug. 15, 1963, CA.

58. The discussion concerning Newark was based chiefly on interviews and personal observations; on Western Electric and N. J. Bell, see also the following in Robert Curvin Prs: Curvin to C. Cuthbertson, Feb. 29, 1964; Notes relating to negotiation meetings with N. J. Bell executives [1963–64]; Minutes, Newark CORE, Nov. 21, 1963, April 13, 1964. On San Francisco, see: press releases, April 17, 24, 1964, and San Francisco *Chronicle,* March 1–3, 7–12, 14, 15, 18, April 5, 12, 13, 16, 19, 1964; William Barlow and Peter Shapiro, *An End to Silence: The San Francisco State College Student Movement in the Sixties* (New York, 1971), 43–48.

59. *Eagle,* March 14, June 27, July 4, 18, Aug. 1, 29, 1963, March 19, 1964; *Sentinel,* July 4, 11, 18, Aug. 1, 8, 15, 22, 29, Sept. 5, 1963; Minutes of California Conference of CORE Chapters, July 20, 1963, WCO; Western Region CORE Chapters Report, July 29, 1963, CA; Western Region CORE Report, Aug. 8, 1963, CA; Western Field Secretary Report, May 20, 1963, CA.

60. Chet Duncan, Western Region CORE Chapters Report, Sept. 30, 1963, WCO; Seattle *Post-Intelligencer,* July 28–31, Aug. 4, 1963, March 10, 1964; Seattle *Daily Times,* March 23, April 5, May 15, 16, June 22, Sept. 5, 1964; Edward Singler to Rich, July 31, 1963, CA; Seattle CORE, "A Statement of Principles," March 22, 1964, CA; interviews; and the following in the Seattle CORE Papers: Joan Singler to Dear Friend, July 8, 1963; Seattle CORE Minutes, March 26, April 23, May 11, 1964; "A Report on Seattle CORE'S Direct Action Housing Project Protesting Racial Discrimination Practices at Picture Floor Plans, Inc." [mid-1964].

61. On Prince George's County, see "Belair Demonstration, Fact Sheet," July 29, Aug. 3, 12, 1963, all CA; Clipping, Baltimore *Sun,* Oct. 1, 1963, CA; Alfred Ochs to Dear Sir, Nov. 9, 1963, CA; *Afro-American,* Aug. 6, Nov. 19, 1963; Washington *Post,* Aug. 16, 18, 19, Sept. 8, 22, Oct. 7, 25, Nov. 14, 1963, Jan. 5, Feb. 14, 1964; interviews; Alfred Ochs to Dear Friend, Nov. 9, 1963, Marian Merrill Prs; flyer, "March for Freedom of Residence," Nov. 1963, Merrill Prs. On Washington, see Washington *Post,* June 11, Aug. 17, 1963, June 21, 24, July 2, 1964.

62. Lynn Eley, "The Ann Arbor Fair-Housing Ordinance," in Eley and Thomas Casstevens, eds., *The Politics of Fair Housing Legislation* (San Francisco, 1968), 335, 339, 341–46, 349; *Chronicle,* Aug. 10, 24, Nov. 2, 1963, Jan. 25, April 4, 1964; Ann Arbor CORE press releases, June 26, Oct. 25, 1963; Anna Holden to McCain, Sept. 22, 1963; Ann Arbor CORE, NAACP, Catholic Interracial Council press release, Feb. 6, 1964, all CA.

63. Columbus *Citizen-Journal,* June 12, 14, 15, 18, 19, 20, July 11, 13, 16, 17, 30, 1963; Myron Q. Hale, "The Ohio Fair-Housing Law," in Eley and Casstevens, *The Politics of Fair-Housing Legislation,* 158; interviews.

64. *Sentinel,* June 13, 29, 1963, Jan. 2, 16, May 28, June 4, Aug. 20, Sept. 3, 1964; Sacramento *Bee,* May 29 to June 22, 1963, *passim;* Chet Duncan to Marcia McKenna, Jan. 20, 1964, CA; Duncan to Organization Dept., June 13, 1964, MLK; MaryLu Murphy to Rich, Aug. 24, 1964, CA; Duncan to Rich, Sept. 10, 1964, CA; Western Regional Office press release, Aug. 14, 1964, WCO.

65. Denver CORE newsletter, Jan. 30, 1964, CA; Denver *Post,* Jan. 15–18, 1964.

66. For New Haven, see New Haven *CORE-lator,* Sept. 1963, CA. For Philadelphia, see *Tribune,* Aug. 20, 24, Sept. 3, 1963, and Philadelphia *Bulletin,* Aug. 18, 1963. For New York, see *Times,* Aug. 22, 1963; press release, Aug. 22, 1963; Carey to Farmer, Oct. 15, 1963, CHQ. For Long Island, see press releases, July 2, Aug. 6, 1964, and Long Island CORE clipping books, June 18, 24, 29, 1964. On New Haven, see New Haven *Register,* Oct. 5, 6, 1964 clippings in Robert and Mimi Abramovitz Prs, and New Haven *Journal-Courier,* Sept. 19, 26, Oct. 4, 1963, June 5, 1964.

67. On Syracuse, see Rich, "Civil Rights Strategy After the March," *New Politics,* II (Fall 1963), 45; "The Protest Movement North: The Syracuse Story" [1964], Wiley Prs. On Philadelphia, see: *Tribune,* Sept. 21, 24, Oct. 29, 1963; Philadelphia CORE press release, Oct. 3, 1963, CA; Philadelphia *Bulletin,* Aug. 25, Sept. 18–21, 1963; "CORE Goes Slumming," *Greater Philadelphia Magazine,* LIV (Sept. 1963), 79–87. On New Haven, see New Haven CORE press release, Nov. 2, 1963, CA; New Haven *Register,* Oct. 10, 11, 1963, clippings in Abramovitz Prs; New Haven *Courier-Journal,* Oct. 25, 30, Nov. 1, 4, 1963.

68. On Long Island and Syracuse, see notes 66, 67. On New Haven, see New Haven *CORE-lator,* Sept. 1963, CA; Gene Schulze to Haley, Oct. 12, 1963, and Schulze to Richard Jackson, Oct. 9, 1963, Schulze Prs; "Statement of New Haven CORE Concerning the Unilateral Break-off of Negotiations by Charles Henchel and the Guerra Brothers" [Oct. 1963], Abramovitz Prs; New Haven *Journal-Courier,* Nov. 7, 1963. On Philadelphia, see Philadelphia *Bulletin,* Aug. 7–9, 28, 1963; Philadelphia *Inquirer,* Oct. 5, 1963.

69. Mark D. Naison, "The Rent Strikes in New York," *Radical America,* Nov.–Dec. 1967, reprinted in Fred Cox *et al.,* eds., *Strategies of Community Organization* (Itasca, Ill., 1970), 226–38 (quotation, p. 230); Michael Lipsky, *Protest in City Politics: Rent Strikes, Housing and the Power of the Poor* (Chicago, 1970), esp. 53–83, *passim; Times,* June 4, Sept. 28, Nov. 2, Dec. 1, 2, 1963, April 21, 1964; New York *Amsterdam News,* Nov. 9, 1963, Feb. 29, April 4, 1964; Joel Freedman to Commissioner Birns, Aug. 7, 1963, CA; George Schiffer to Val Coleman, Sept. 19, 1963, CA; Schiffer to J. Gribetz, Nov. 21, 1963, CA; Schiffer to CORE Distribution List, Dec. 17, 1963, CHQ; Peter Myers to Housing Committee Chairmen, Oct. 1, 1963, CA; Irving Lesnick to Carl Rachlin, Oct. 29, 1963, Rachlin files; Downtown CORE Bulletin, rec'd March 30, 1964, CA; and the following in MLK: Allan Hoffman, Report on Brooklyn CORE, Dec. 15, 1963; East River CORE Progress Report, rec'd April 9, 1964; Johnny Valentine to National CORE, Sept. 10, 1964; New York CORE, "Tenant Council News," July 14, 1964; Arthur Williams to McCain, April 29, 1964; East River CORE

Application for Affiliation [Spring 1964]. The denouement of the Eldrige Street Project is given in Frances Piven and Richard Cloward, "Rent Strike: Disrupting the Slum System," *New Republic,* CLVII (Dec. 2, 1967), 12.

70. For Cincinnati, see "Cincinnati CORE Activities, July 1964 to June 1965," CA. For Cleveland, see Circular of Cleveland CORE [Dec. 1963], CA; Ruth Turner to McCain, Dec. 20, 1963, CA; *Cleveland CORE Guide to Action, 1963–1964,* WCO; "Roaches and Ulcers: The Cleveland Rent Strikes" [early 1964], Bernard Mandel Prs; *Call and Post,* Jan. 18, Feb. 1, June 6, 20, 1964; "Summary of Activities, Cleveland CORE, July 1963 to June 1964," Arthur Evans Prs; Cleveland CORE *Action Letter,* Feb. 1964, David Cohen Prs; Cleveland *Plain Dealer,* Dec. 12, 1963, Jan. 13, 19, April 12, 1964. For Boston, see Alan Gartner, Testimony Before the Low Cost Housing Study Commission, Nov. 24, 1964, Rachlin files; Boston *Corespondent,* April 27, 1964, Richard Brown Prs; Boston CORE News Release, July 11, 1964, Brown Prs; and the following clippings, all in the Phyllis Ryan Prs; Boston *Herald,* March 13, 1964; Boston *Globe,* March 16, April 1, 1964; Brookline *Chronicle,* June 23, 1964; Roxbury *City News,* June 11, 1964.

71. Milton Davis to McCain, Oct. 26, 1964, Davis Prs. See also Westside Chicago CORE *CORE-lator,* Feb. 1964, Faith Rich Prs; [Tournour], "CORE Northern Project: Chicago" [Fall 1964], CA; *Defender,* April 11–17, June 13–19, 1964.

72. Farmer, Report of National Director to 1964 Convention, CHQ.

73. Robert Crain *et al., The Politics of School Desegregation* (Chicago, 1968), 19–20; *Integrated Education,* I (Aug. 1963), 48–49.

74. John and Laree Caughey, *School Segregation at our Doorstep: The Los Angeles Story* (Los Angeles, 1966), 6, 18, 21, 24–28; Los Angeles CORE press release, Sept. 18, 1963, CA; *Sentinel,* Sept. 19, 26, Oct. 10, 31, Nov. 7, 1963; "CORE Demands to the [Los Angeles] Board of Education, Sept. 3, 1963," CA.

75. *Times,* June 20–24, 27, July 6–10, 1963; Brooklyn *Amsterdam News,* June 21, 29, July 13, 1963; Irving Goldaber, "The Treatment by the New York City Board of Education of Problems Affecting the Negro 1954–1963" (Ph.D. dissertation, New York University, 1964), 228–33; "Long Island CORE and the Civil Rights War, 1963" [Jan. 1964], CA; and *Times,* Sept. 15, 1963.

76. *Defender,* July 20–26, July 27–Aug. 2, Aug. 17–23, 24–30, Aug. 31–Sept. 6, Sept. 7–13, 1963; Chicago *Tribune,* July 11–24, Aug. 1, 3, 13–15, 20, 24, 29, 1963; "Chicago CORE School Integration Proposals" [July 1963], Faith Rich Prs; B. Elton Cox to McCain, July 10, 1963, CA; Genevieve Hughes to Rich, July 6, 1963, CA; Florence Field to Norman Hill, Aug. 13, 1963, CA; Frank Ichishita, "A Neighborhood Demonstrates," *Integrated Education,* I (Dec. 1963–Jan. 1964), 35–39.

77. On Cincinnati, see *Integrated Education,* II (April–May 1964), 4–5; Farmer to CORE Contact List, Feb. 21, 1964, WCO; Clyde Vinegar, "The Cincinnati School Boycott," in Cincinnati CORE Report to 1964 Convention, personal file; on Kansas City, see press release, April 24, 1964, and *Integrated Education,* II (June–July 1964), 8; on Milwaukee, see Milwaukee *Journal,* May 18,

19, 1964, and the following in the Milwaukee CORE Prs: "Facts About the Freedom Day School Withdrawal, May 18, 1964," and Richard McLeod, "Summary of CORE Education Committee Activities, 1963–1964."

78. Noel Day, "The Freedom Movement in Boston," *Integrated Education*, II (Dec. 1964–Jan. 1965), 13–19; Massachusetts Freedom Movement, *Freedom's Journal* [Jan. 1964], CA, and [Feb. 1964], Phyllis Ryan Prs; and the following materials in the Ryan Prs: press releases of Freedom Stay-Out Day Committee, Feb. 12, 14, 23, 1964, and clippings from Boston *Globe*, June 18, 19, 1963, Feb. 26, 1964.

79. Minutes of CCCO, Nov. 1963 to Feb. 1964, *passim*, courtesy of Alan Anderson and George Pickering; Milton Davis to Farmer, Oct. 28, 1963, Davis Prs; Chicago CORE Statement at Dec. 18, 1963, School Budget Hearing, in Faith Rich Prs; *Defender*, Nov. 2–8, 1963, Feb. 15–21, Feb. 22–28, 1964.

80. David Rogers, *110 Livingston Street* (New York, 1968), 26–27, 111–16; Minutes of Meeting New York CORE Committee Chairman, Nov. 30, 1963, CA; NAC, Jan. 24, 1964, CA; "Statement of New York CORE Chapters on School Integration," Jan. 16, 1964, CA; Minutes of Feb. 26, 1964, Meeting of New York CORE Chapters, CA; Norman Hill Press Conference Statement, Feb. 27, 1964, CA; Documents relating to the school boycott movement in New York City, Jan. and Feb. 1964, Milton Galamison Prs, Reel No. 2; *Times*, Feb. 3, 4, 28, March 5, 15, 16, 1964; "Statement of Policy by the Congress of Racial Equality on Public School Education in New York City" [Jan. 1964], CHQ; New York *Amsterdam News*, Feb. 8, 14, March 21, 1964.

81. Cleveland CORE *Action Letter*, Feb. 1964, David Cohen Prs.

82. David Zuverink, "Moses and Pharoah in Cleveland," *Integrated Education*, II (June–July 1964), 35–37; Allan Hoffman to National Office Staff, Feb. 6, 1964, MLK; "Summary of Activities of Cleveland CORE, July, 1963 to July, 1964," Arthur Evans Prs; press release, April 24, 1964; Cleveland CORE *Action Letter*, June, 1964, CA; *Call and Post*, Sept. 14, 1963, Jan. 25, Feb. 1, 8, 15, March 21, 28, April 4, 11, 18, 25, Sept. 19, 1964; Cleveland *Plain Dealer*, Aug. 17, Sept. 24, 25, 28, Oct. 1, 1963, Jan. 24–Feb. 5, March 29, April 6–9, 14, 17, 1964; Robinson, *The Making of a Man*, 70–73, 92–94, 106–9.

83. On St. Louis, see Crain *et al.*, *Politics of School Desegregation*, 22–28; on Cincinnati, see Cincinnati *Enquirer*, March 4, 18, April 7, 8, May 2, 8, 11, 14, 18, 21, 28, 1964. On New York, see "NAACP and CORE Statement to the New York City Board of Education and Superintendent of Schools on Commissioner Allen's Report," May 28, 1964, WCO; Rogers, *110 Livingston Street*, 27–28. On Los Angeles, see Caughey, *School Segregation At Our Doorstep*, 28; on Boston, miscellaneous materials in Phyllis Ryan Prs.

84. On this point, see Crain *et al.*, *Politics of School Desegregation*, 114–17, where the distinction is made between civil rights leaders who advocated integration and community leaders who wanted to improve the quality of ghetto schools.

85. For example, Val Coleman to Farmer *et al.*, April 6, 1964, CHQ.

86. Brooklyn *Amsterdam News*, Aug. 3, 1963; *Times*, Nov. 20, Oct. 17, 1963; *Argus*, Oct. 11, 1963; Chicago *Tribune*, July 23, 1963; *Sentinel*, Aug. 15, 1963.

87. San Francisco *CORE-lator,* Nov. 1963, Ollie Leeds Prs; Syracuse CORE, Report on Police Procedures [March 1964], and Syracuse CORE news release, March 18, 1964, George Wiley Prs. Cleveland *Plain Dealer,* Feb. 6, June 20, July 21, 23, 1964; Cleveland CORE *Action Letter,* Feb. and April 1964, David Cohen Prs; Allan Hoffman to National Office Staff [Feb. 1964], MLK; *Call and Post,* June 27, July 4, Aug. 1, 8, 1964. *Times,* March 21, 1964, and materials relating to *People of State of New York vs. Frances Crayton et al.,* 1964, in Rachlin files.

88. Arthur Williams to McCain and Rich, April 13, 1964, CHQ; Farmer to Dear Friend, May 18, 1964, CA; Brooklyn *Amsterdam News,* May 23, July 25, 1964; *Times,* June 10, July 19, 1964; George Schiffer, "The Gilligan Case: Report of the Congress of Racial Equality," Sept. 2, 1964, CA; press release, May 28, 1964; Farmer, "The Riots and CORE," *CORE-lator,* July–Aug. 1964; "The Ways and Means Committee to Deter [sic] Demonstrations," Minutes of Meeting held July 26, 1964, James Farmer Prs; Carl Rachlin, "This is CORE's Report on the Gilligan Case," Sept. 2, 1964, Rachlin files.

89. For description of Mel's Drive-In project, see San Francisco *Chronicle,* Nov. 3, 4, 7, 9, 1963, and University of California *Daily Californian,* Nov. 2, 11, 1963. Quote from Jack Weinberg, untitled article, Berkeley *Campus CORE-lator,* Sept. 1964, UC.

90. Weinberg, untitled article, Berkeley Campus *CORE-lator,* Sept. 1964, UC; Bill Bradley, newsletter addressed to San Francisco CORE, March 27, 1964, WCO.

91. *Times,* March 7, 8, 1964; Farmer, *Freedom-When?,* 37–38.

92. *Times,* Jan. 16, 17, 1964; Brooklyn *Amsterdam News,* Jan. 25, 1964; Steering Committee, Jan. 24, 1964, CA.

93. Farmer, telegram to Isaiah Brunson, April 9, 1964, CHQ; Farmer and McCain to Steering Committee, April 11, 1964, MLK; Steering Committee, April 11, 1964, CA; McCain to Brunson, April 15, 1964, MLK; Farmer to Dear Friend, April 16, 1964, MaryLu Murphy Prs; interviews. On length of Steering Committee meeting, see McCain Diaries, April 11–12, 1964, McCain Prs.

94. Brooklyn *Amsterdam News,* April 18, 1964; *Times,* April 23, 1964.

95. Steering Committee, April 11, 1964, CA; *Times,* April 23, 26, 1964; Rachlin to Farmer *et al.* [April 1964], Rachlin files; interviews and personal observations.

96. For Farmer statements see McCain Diaries, April 17, 1964, McCain Prs, and Farmer to A. Philip Randolph, April 9, 1964, Brotherhood of Sleeping Car Porters Arch. For representative statements by Landry and Carmichael, see, for example, Pittsburgh *Courier,* May 2, 1964, and Washington *Post,* May 16, 1964.

97. Mark Dodson to Carey, Oct. 24, 1963, CA; Ruth Moskowitz to Farmer, Oct. 16, 1963, CA; Jack Weinberg, untitled article in Berkeley Campus *CORE-lator,* Sept. 1964, UC; Teer, Summary Report and Schedule, April 1–7, 1963, CA; and Teer to Rich, June 1, 1963, Fredricka Teer Kushner Prs; *Defender,* July 27–Aug. 2, 1963.

98. Rich to Mrs. David Mellor, Dec. 19, 1963, CA; interviews.

99. McCain to Farmer, Memo on West Coast Trip, Oct. 13 to Nov. 12, 1963,

CA; Rich to Ruth Moskowitz, Dec. 24, 1963, CA; Rich to David Johnson, March 12, 1964, CA.

100. *New York Times Magazine,* Sept. 4, 1963; Genevieve Hughes to Rich, June 17, 1963, CA; Farmer speech in Cleveland, quoted in Cleveland *Plain Dealer,* July 15, 1963; Program transcript of WCBS-TV *Newsmakers,* July 14, 1963, CHQ; *Times, March 8, 1964.* On Carey, see, for example, Carey to Mrs. George Wislicki, March 24, CHQ.

101. Rich to Betty Lou Valentine, April 1, 1964, CA.

102. Interviews.

103. Steering Committee, April 11, 1964, CA; Long Island CORE newsletter, April 30, 1964, CA; personal observation on New Jersey; New Haven *Journal-Courier,* April 16, 1964 and Edward Campbell to Steering Committee, April 19, 1964; Mimi Feingold to Parents, April 26, 1964, Miriam Feingold Whitman Prs; CORE Western Regional Conference, April 16–18, 1964, WCO.

104. NAC, May 1–3, 1964, CA; Carey to Bookkeeping Department, Aug. 13, 1964, CA; Steering Committee, Sept. 26, 1964, WCO.

105. Steering Committee, April 11, 1964, CA; Farmer to chapter chairmen, April 16, 1964, MLK; on Brooklyn's queries to national, interviews; Gartner statement in Boston *Corespondent,* April 27, 1964, Richard Brown Prs; Warren, *Who Speaks for the Negro?,* 197–98.

CHAPTER NINE

1. David Dennis to Wiley Branton, April 5, 1963, May 20, 1963, both VEP; James McCain to Dennis, April 8, 1963, MLK; Dennis to McCain, rec'd May 1, 1963, MLK, Aug. 8, 1963, MLK, and Oct. 19, 1963, CA; Dennis to James Farmer and Norman Hill, Jan. 15, 1964, CA; Dennis to Farmer, Marvin Rich, and McCain, Jan. 24, 1964, CA; interviews.

2. Quotation from Ike Reynolds, Report, Jan. 18, 1964, CA; also Dennis to NAC, "Concerning: An Abortion for a Pregnant State" [Nov. 1963], CA; McCain to Farmer, re: Visit to Louisiana, South Carolina, and North Carolina, Nov. 25 to Dec. 5, 1963, CA; unidentified white staff member from West Coast, MS notes on New Orleans National Staff Conference, Feb. 12–17, 1964, WCO; Minutes, Staff Meeting, March 21, 1964, CA; Ed Hollander to Rich, April 2, 1964, CA.

3. Frank Robinson to McCain, Sept. 7, 1963, CA; McCain to Farmer, Report for period Sept. 20 to Oct. 30, 1963, MLK; "CORE Voter Registration—1963–1964," CA; Rich to Branton, June 17, 1964, CA.

4. "CORE Voter Registration, 1963–1964," CA; Randolph Blackwell to Branton, Dec. 3, 1964, VEP; Weldon Rougeau to Rich, March 27, 1964, CA; Rougeau to McCain, Nov. 3, Dec. 19, 1963, CA.

5. Pat Due to NAC, Nov. 7, 1963, CA; Pat Due to McCain *et al.,* Sept. 6, 1964, Rachlin files. On violence in North Florida, see esp. Richard Haley to Burke Marshall, Aug. 31, 1964, SRO.

6. Due to Gordon Carey, Jan. 31, 1964, CHQ; Due to McCain, Branton, Rich, Feb. 1, 1964, CA; Due to Rich, March 14, 1964, CA; Due to Haley, April 2, 1964, SRO.

7. Due to McCain *et al.*, Sept. 6, 1964, Rachlin files. For the summer project, see also Due to McCain *et al.*, July 31, 1964, Aug. 14, 1964, CA; Field reports, North Florida Citizenship Project, July–Aug. 1964, *passim*, SRO; Judy Benninger to Rich and Haley, July 23, 1964, SRO.

8. NAC, Nov. 8–10, 1963, CA.

9. Carey to Participants in Louisiana Summer Project, June 24, 1963, and attached list of participants, CA; *Task Force Chronicle* (Plaquemine), June 23, 1963, WCO; Mimi Feingold to Parents, July 23, 1963, Miriam Feingold Whitman Prs; [Ronnie Moore], Summer Field Report [1963], CA; Untitled tabulation of CORE Voter Registration Statistics, 1963 and 1964 [Nov. 1964], CA; Moore to McCain, Aug. 15, 1963, CA.

10. [Feingold], Field Report, Aug. 1–4, 1963, CA; Feingold to Parents, Aug. 5, 19, 1963, Whitman Prs; [Moore], Summary Field Report [Sept. 1963], CA; lists of people attempting to register, 1963, voter registration complaints, 1963, and East Feliciana CORE affiliation application [1963], in East Feliciana CORE Prs. On arrest of Lesser, who remained in jail for nearly three weeks until CORE produced $2000 bond, see also Baton Rouge *Morning Advocate*, Aug. 3, 22, 23, 1963.

11. Nils Douglas, "The United States Supreme Court and Clinton, Louisiana" [1965], CA; Documents and correspondence on the restraining order in Murphy Bells Prs, reel No. 1; Mary Hamilton, Report to McCain, Nov. 14, 1963, CA; Ed Vickery to Moore, Sept. 18, 1963, CA; undated handwritten report, no author [Oct. 11, 1963], CA; [Moore], "Louisiana in Brief," May 1964 version, CA; Baton Rouge *State Times*, Oct. 14, 1963; and the following in the East Feliciana CORE Prs: Corrie Collins *et al.*, to school board, to Judge John Rarick, to District Attorney Richard Kilbourne, all Sept. 19, 1963; Clinton CORE press releases, Dec. 3, 9, 1963; Vickery, "Complaint Regarding Violation of Constitutional Rights," Dec. 5, 1963.

12. On legal maneuverings, see *CORE et al., vs. Town of Clinton and Parish of East Feliciana*, Decision in U. S. District Court, Sept. 22, 1964, copy in Rachlin files; William Kunstler to Rachlin, Dec. 3, 1963, Rachlin files; Baton Rouge *Morning Advocate*, Aug. 23, 29, Sept. 14, 1963. Also opinions of federal district court and state court in *Town of Clinton and Parish of East Feliciana vs. CORE et al., RRLR*, IX (1964), 1132–33.

13. Moore, "The West Feliciana Story," 1963, CA; "V. R. Meeting," Sept. 24, Oct. 1, 1963, East Feliciana CORE Prs; Bud Adelman, "Birth of a Voter," *Ebony*, XIX (Feb. 1964), 88–98; Robert Penn Warren, interview with Joe Carter in *Who Speaks for the Negro?*, 3–9; Baton Rouge *State Times*, Sept. 20, Oct. 17, 18, 1963. On Carter's suit see materials relating to *Joseph Carter vs William Percy and Fletcher Harvey*, 1963, Murphy Bell Prs, reel No. 1.

14. Moore, "The West Feliciana Story"; Adelman, "Birth of a Voter"; no author, Weekly Report for Iberville and the Felicianas, Nov. 4–10, 1963, CA; "New Persons—St. Francisville Clinic," Nov. 12, 19 [1963], East Feliciana CORE Prs; Baton Rouge *State Times*, Oct. 18, 21, 23, 24, 29, 30, 1963; Moore, telegram to Robert Kennedy, Dec. 2, 1963, CA; Lesser to Terry Perlman, Nov. 4, 1963, CA; voter registration complaints, 1963, East Feliciana CORE Prs.

15. Baton Rouge *State Times,* Oct. 21, 1963; Lesser to Perlman, Nov. 4, 1963, CA.

16. Mary Hamilton to Rich, Sept. 30, 1963, CA; Minutes, Sixth Congressional District Staff Meeting, Nov. 7, 1963, CA.

17. *CORE-lator,* Nov. 1963; press releases, Oct. 7, 10, Dec. 23, 1963; Moore, telegram to Robert Kennedy, Oct. 9, 1963; statement of Kenny Johnson [Oct. 1963], all CA; Baton Rouge *State Times,* Sept. 11, Oct. 5, 7, 8, 10, 11, 12, 14, 16, 1963; Edsell Brown *et al.,* Statement, Oct. 9, 1963, and other documents in Murphy Bell Prs, reel No. 3.

18. Moore, Summary Field Report [Sept. 1963], CA; Hamilton to Rich, Sept. 30, 1963, CA; Baton Rouge *State Times,* Sept. 25, Oct. 4, Dec. 10, 1963; Feingold to Parents, Oct. 15, 1963, Whitman Prs; Moore, "VEP Summary Field Report, January, 1964," Jan. 19, 1964, CA; taped recording of Farmer's address at Clinton, La., Aug. 4, 1964, Edward Hollander Prs. Moore, Summary Field Report [Sept. 1963], CA; Hamilton to Rich, Sept. 30, 1963, CA; Baton Rouge *State Times,* Sept. 25, Oct. 4, Dec. 10, 1963.

19. Rich to McCain, Jan. 3, 1964, CA; "CORE Voter Registration—1963," CA.

20. On Shreveport, see LaVert Taylor to McCain, Aug. 6, 1963; Ike Reynolds, Report, week of Sept. 28, 1963; Bruce Baines, Report, Oct. 26, 1963; William Douthard, Report [Nov. 9, 1963]; Reynolds to McCain, Nov. 6, Dec. 18, 1963, all CA. For descriptions of activity in New Orleans, see Hamilton to McCain, Jan. 12, 1964, CA; Haley to McCain, May 10, 1964, CA; New Orleans CORE press releases, Feb. 22, March 30, 1964, CA; Doris Castle, "CORE on Canal Street" [Spring 1964], CA; Hollander to Rich, July 18, Aug. 5, 1964, CA; CORE Southern Office press releases, July 20, Aug. 4, 1964, SRO.

21. Minutes of Louisiana Staff Meeting, Nov. 7, 1963, CA.

22. Bertrand Tyson to Carey, Oct. 20, 1963, CA; Bill Brown, Report, Dec. 6–15, 1963, CA; Mimi Feingold to Parents, Dec. 3, 1963, CA.

23. [Moore], "A Proposed Voter Education Program for Louisiana: Rural and North" [Oct. 1963], CA; Minutes, Louisiana Staff Meeting, Nov. 7, 1963, CA; Bill Brown, Report, Dec. 6–15, 1963, CA; Mike Lesser, Report, Dec. 9–12, 1963, CA; "CORE Voter Registration—1964," CA and "CORE Voter Registration—1963," CA.

24. Spiver Gordon, Reports, Iberville Parish, Jan. to June 1964, *passim,* CA and SRO.

25. Field Reports for East Feliciana, West Feliciana, and St. Helena Parishes, Jan. to April 1964, *passim,* CA; on library incident, see also typed press release from Clinton, March 7, 1964, CA and Spiver Gordon, telegram to Burke Marshall, March 11, 1964, CA; Feingold to Parents, March 7, 10, 16, April 24, 1964, Whitman Prs. For court cases arising out of this demonstration, producing Supreme Court victory in Feb. 1966 (*Brown v. Louisiana*), see Rachlin to Pierre Tonachal, March 3, 1966, Rachlin files. Rachlin to James Cook, April 19, 1966, Rachlin files; copy of U. S. Supreme Court decision, Feb. 23, 1966, Rachlin files; documents, 1964–66, in Murphy Bell Prs, reel No. 1.

26. Mimi Feingold to William Bey, March 7, 1964, CA; Feingold to Fay Ben-

nett, March 3, 1964, CA; Farmer to Steering Committee, Aug. 7, 1964, CA; Farmer to Frank Reeves, Aug. 25, 1964, CA; Reeves to Princeville Canning Co., Sept. 1, 1964, CA; Jordan Truitt to H. C. Carter, Sept. 1, 1964, CA; Truitt to Farmer, Sept. 7, 18, 1964, CA; Carey to Ronnie Moore, Sept. 9, 1964, CHQ; press release, Sept. 24, 1964; Steering Committee, Sept. 26, 1964, WCO.

27. Moore to McCain, May 16, 1964, CA.

28. [Lesser], Field Report, Ouachita Parish, Dec. 9–12, 1963, CA; [Lesser], "VEP Activities 1 Jan.–12 Jan., 1964, Monroe, La.," in Monroe La. MSS; Lesser, VEP Field Reports for Ouachita Parish, Jan. 14, 1964, Jan. 12–31, 1964, CA; McCain Diaries, Feb. 26, 1964, McCain Prs; Lesser, CORE–VEP Report, North Louisiana, Feb. 1–March 14, 1964, CA; Lesser, VEP Field Report, April 1–30, 1964, CA; Claudia Edwards, Voter Registration, Monroe, Louisiana, May 11–25, 1964, CA.

29. On Tensas Parish: Moore to Barbara Whitaker, May 21, 1964, CA; Lesser to Moore, May 14, 1964, CA; VEP Report, Feb. 1 to March 31, for Tensas Parish, CA. On Madison Parish: [Lesser] CORE–VEP Report, North Louisiana, Feb. 1–March 14, 1963, CA.

30. [Lesser], CORE–VEP Scouting Report, Jackson Parish, Feb. 5, 1964, CA; Danny Mitchell, VEP Field Report, Jackson Parish, June 24, 1964, CA. On harassment, see "Chronology on Jonesboro" [1965], CA; Newark *Star-Ledger,* July 12, 1965 (feature article on Lesser), clipping, CA: *CORE-lator,* July–Aug. 1964; Rich to Drew Pearson, Aug. 14, 1964, CA; documents relating to Ronnie Moore and *Michael Lesser vs. James O. Smith et al.,* Murphy Bell Prs, reel No. 3. On purge and proportion of blacks registered in Jackson Parish, see Burke Marshall to Jack Gremillion, Sept. 1, 1961, Marshall Prs.

31. Moore, "Summary Report Louisiana Freedom Summer, June 10–June 25, 1964," June 27, 1964, SRO; Moore to Louisiana Task Force, July 24, 1964, SRO; "Staff Assignments, June 29–August 9, 1964," SRO; Ronnie [Rowena] Sigal and Mimi Feingold, Field Report, West Feliciana, June 23–24, 1964, CA; Moore, telegrams to Kennedy, June 29, July 25, 1964, SRO.

32. Moore, Louisiana VEP Report, June 27, 1964, CA; Lesser and Ruthie Wells, VEP Field Report, Ouachita Parish, June 19–24, 1964, SRO; Ronnie Sigal and Mimi Feingold, Field Report, West Feliciana, June 23–24, 1964, CA; Moore, "Voter Registration in Louisiana" [Sept. 1964], CA; W. C. Flanagan, president of the Progressive Voters League to Registrar Estelle Wilder, July 23, 1964, and Jonesboro project press release, June 23, 1964, both in Jonesboro, La., Freedom House Prs; quotation from Feingold to Parents, July 10, 1964, Whitman Prs.

33. Memos of Judy Rollins, to no one, usually undated, July 1964, and Aug. 3, 1964, SRO; Matthew Battieste to Farmer, July 24, 1964, CA; Lawyers Constitutional Defense Committee, "Status of Active Cases—Louisiana, as of September 10, 1964," CA; Ed Hollander, typescript report of messages phoned in July 29, 1964, SRO: Frederick Brooks, Field Report, Jackson Parish, Oct. 5–15, 1964, SRO; Ouachita Parish Field Report, June 28–July 14, 1964, Monroe, La., CORE, MSS; Lesser to Rich, July 13, 1964, CA; Affidavits of Dave Washington, July 13, 1964, Jimmie Donald Andrews, July 12, 1964, and Ronnie Roy Brass,

July 11, 1964, all SRO; materials on Monroe Library cases, Murphy Bell Prs, reel No. 4; and the following in the Jonesboro, La., Freedom House Prs: Willie Lee Jackson, statement, Aug. 3, 1964; Earlene Knox, complaint [July 1964]; Larry Robinson, untitled statement [ca. July 28, 1964]; Daniel Mitchell, CORE testing form, July 16, 1964; and Will Palmer, CORE testing form, July 20, 1964; and various reports and press releases, SRO, including SRO press releases of July 21, 28, 1964.

34. "Lunch Counter Testing Report," for Plaquemine [July 1964], SRO.

35. On CORE posts, see COFO letterhead, Feb. 1964, CA; Dennis to Farmer and Hill, Jan. 15, 1964, CA. On Core's share in COFO headquarters budget, see Dennis to Farmer and Hill, Jan. 15, 1964, CA; Dennis, Memo, "Politics" rec'd May 1, 1964, Wiley Prs; COFO, "Financial Report," May 6 to July 31, 1964, CA; Rich to Dennis, June 18, 1964, CA.

36. Lois Chaffee to Norman Hill, Feb. 3, 1964, MLK; Dennis to Branton. April 5, 1963, VEP. A discussion of this issue, from COFO's viewpoint, can be seen in COFO Executive Committee Minutes, July 10, 1964, R. Hunter Morey Prs.

37. Interviews; quotations from Haley, "CORE in the South (September to December, 1964)," Jan. 28, 1965, CA; McCain to Haley, March 23. 1964, CA; Lois Chaffee to Hill, Feb. 3, 1964, MLK.

38. Mary Hamilton, Report on Staff Meeting, McIntosh, Georgia, March 9 and 10, 1963, dated March 19, 1963, CA; interviews.

39. Paul Harrell, "Report on Civil Rights Cases in Louisiana" [July 1964], Rachlin files; John Due to Jack Greenberg *et al.*, April 2, 1964, Rachlin files; Bob Moses to Greenberg, rec'd April 2, 1964, Rachlin files; Haley to Rich, March 20, 1964, CA; interviews. On political-ideological grounds for hostility of Rachlin and LCDC to Guild, see esp. explicit references in the following, all in papers of R. Hunter Morey, COFO's legal coordinator: Morey to Arthur Kinoy, April 13, 1964; COFO Executive Committee Minutes, July 10, 1964; Victor Rabinowitz to Kunstler & Kunstler, Bob Moses *et al.*, Aug. 5, 1964.

40. Haley to McCain, March 18, 1964, MLK.

41. On fourth district funding, see McCain, "Recommendations for Mississippi," Feb. 20, 1964, MLK; McCain to Haley, March 23, 1964, MLK. On contributions to Jackson office, see Note 35, above. On staff, see Dennis to Farmer and Hill, Jan. 15, 1964, CA; Dennis to McCain, May 27, 1964, MLK; Rudolph Lombard to Haley, July 20, 1964, SRO; Haley to McCain, Aug. 21, 1964, SRO; "Field Staff Personnel" [end of Aug. 1964], SRO. On Dennis getting additional funds by appealing directly to the NAC, see Steering Committee, Dec. 6, 1963, CA; NAC, May 1–3, 1964, CA; "Resolutions passed by the NAC at the Philadelphia Meeting, May 1–3, [1964]," CA; and esp. interviews.

42. Rachlin to Farmer, Nov. 12, 1963, Rachlin files; "Minutes Constitutional Rights Defense Committee," April 2, 1964, SEDF; LCDC news release, May 20, 1964, SEDF; LCDC Minutes, June 12, 1964, Rachlin Files; Memo of Meeting, April 23, 1964, Rachlin Files; Rachlin to Farmer, May 11, 1964, Rachlin files; Rachlin to Hill, Rich, Carey *et al.*, April 13, 1964, CA; Morey to SNCC Person-

nel Committee and COFO Executive Committee, Oct. 30, 1964, Morey Prs; Rachlin, "Report on Various Local Installations Visited During the Week of July 20, 1964" [July 1964], Rachlin files.

43. Branton to Dennis, May 29, 1964, CA; U. S. Commission on Civil Rights, *1961 Commission on Civil Rights Report,* Book I, *Voting* (Washington, 1961), 272–73.

44. George Raymond to Carey, two letters [June, 1963], CA; Raymond, Reports, June 23–30, 1963, CA; June 16, and June 16–22, 1963, both VEP; Dennis, Reports, June 16, 24, 1963, VEP; Annie Mae Moody, Reports, June 21–29, 1963, VEP, and Aug. 15, 1963, CA; Anne Moody, *Coming of Age in Mississippi* (New York, 1968), chap. 23; Dennis to McCain, "Mississippi in Motion," Oct. 19, 1963, CA; *Mississippi Free Press,* June 22, July 6, 1963; Jackson *Daily News,* June 25, 26, 1963; Madison County *Herald,* June 20, 27, 1963; Mat Suarez, Report, June 22–27, 1963, VEP. On Chinn's second arrest and conviction, see Hollander, "Canton, Mississippi," March 9, 1964, CA; Hollander, Reports, March 9–15, March 16–22, 1964, CA; Hollander to Rich, May 14, 1964, SRO; Haley to Mrs. C. O. Chinn, June 15, 1964, SRO; Haley to L. H. Rosenthal, June 15, 1964, SRO.

45. Annie Moody, George Raymond, and Gene Thompson, "Committee on Registration Education, June 11–August 9," VEP; Dennis to Branton, Aug. 22, 1963, VEP; Dennis to NAC [Nov. 1963], "Concerning: An Abortion for a Pregnant State," CA; Dennis to McCain, "Mississippi in Motion," Oct. 19, 1963, CA; *Mississippi Free Press,* Aug. 24, 31, Sept. 21, Oct. 5, 12, 1963.

46. Various materials issued by Committee to Elect Aaron Henry Governor of Mississippi, CA; Dennis to NAC [Nov. 1963], "Concerning: An Abortion for a Pregnant State," CA; on Yazoo City incidents, see esp. Freedom Vote Headquarters, "Summary of Events in Yazoo City, October 24 to November 10, 1963," CA; also Raymond, Report [Nov. 1963], MLK; Robert Gore to Farmer *et al.,* Memo on Jackson Trip, Oct. 31 to Nov. 5, 1963, MLK.

47. Moody, *Coming of Age in Mississippi,* 340–43; Dennis to NAC, "Concerning: An Abortion for a Pregnant State" [Nov. 1963], CA; *Mississippi Free Press,* Nov. 16, 1963.

48. COFO, "Outline for COFO Programs—1964" [Dec. 1963], accompanying Dennis to Farmer and Hill, Jan. 15, 1964, CA; Minutes of COFO meeting, Dec. 15, 1963, JoAnn Ooiman Robinson Prs; on plans, see also *Mississippi Free Press,* Nov. 18, 1963; Leslie Burl McLemore, "The Freedom Democratic Party of Mississippi: A Case-Study of Grass Roots Politics" (Ph.D. dissertation, University of Massachusetts, 1971), 16.

49. Dennis to McCain, Aug. 8, 1963, MLK; Dennis to CORE groups and members, Aug. 9, 1963, MLK; Dennis to Benjamin Brown, Oct. 14, 1963, MLK; Dennis to Rich [Oct. 1963], CA; Steering Committee, Dec. 7, 1963, CA; COFO, "Outline for COFO Programs—1964" [Dec. 1963], CA; quotations from Dennis to NAC, "Concerning: An Abortion for a Pregnant State" [Nov. 1963], CA.

50. Charlie Cobb, Memorandum to Mississippi COFO staff and COFO Summer program committee, Feb. 20, 1964, CA; COFO Summer Project Staff to All

Friends of the Mississippi Movement [June 1964], WCO; quote from Cobb, "This Is the Situation," in COFO, *Notes on Teaching in Mississippi,* June 1964, CA.

51. Dennis, "An Awakening City," Jan. 23, 1964, CA; *Mississippi Free Press,* Jan. 25, Feb. 1, 1964; Ed Hollander, "Report on Canton," Feb. 26, 1964, CA; Report of Mat Suarez in "Minutes of COFO Convention," Feb. 9, 1964, JoAnn Ooiman Robinson Prs.

52. Dennis, "An Awakening City," Jan. 23, 1964, CA; Hollander, "Report on Canton," Feb. 26, 1964, CA; Hollander, "Report on Defendants in Canton, Mississippi," Feb. 4, 1964, CA; press release, Feb. 6, 1964; *Mississippi Free Press,* Feb. 15, 1964; Jackson *Daily News,* July 30, 1964.

53. Organization Dept. Report, Feb. 20, 1964, CA; *Mississippi Free Press,* Feb. 29, March 7, 1964; Jackson *Daily News,* Feb. 29, 1964; Hollander, "Largest Mississippi Voter Registration Attempt in Canton," March 2, 1964, CA; *Madison County Citizen* (mimeo'd), March 9, 1964, CA; Claude Sitton, "Negro Queue in Mississippi is Symbol of Frustration in Voter Registration Drive," *Times,* March 2, 1964; Jackson *Clarion-Ledger,* March 6–8, 1964; Hollander to Beryl Radin, March 11, 1964, Hollander Prs.

54. *Madison County Citizen* (mimeo'd), March 9, 1964, CA; Hollander, "Canton, Mississippi," March 9, 1964, CA; Students at Rogers High to D. M. Allen *et al.,* March 1, 1964, CA; press release, March 5, 1964; *Mississippi Free Press,* March 14, 1964.

55. *Mississippi Free Press,* March 28, 1964; *The Madison County Citizen* (mimeo'd), March 16, 1964, CA; Hollander, "Canton Weekly Report," March 9–15, March 16–22, 1964, CA; copy of Judge Cox's order, CA.

56. Hollander, "Canton Weekly Report," March 16–22, 1964, CA; COFO, "Anti-Picketing Law Passed in Mississippi to Combat Civil Rights Activity" [April 1964], CA; Farmer, telegram to J. Edgar Hoover, May 29, 1964, CA; Hollander to Rich, April 23, 1964, CA; Haley to McCain, June 5, 1964, CA; Haley to Raymond, June 15, 1964, CA.

57. *NOW: The Voice of Freedom* (Jackson, mimeo'd, May 25, 1964, CA; press release, June 4, 1964; Moody, *Coming of Age in Mississippi,* 368–75; Burke Marshall to Robert Kennedy, June 2, 1964, Marshall Prs.

58. Dennis, taped recording of speech at political rally, Dearon Farm, Sharon, Miss., May 23, 1964, Hollander Prs.

59. Lois Chaffee to Hill, Feb. 3, 1964, MLK: SRO press release, March 14, 1964, CA.

60. William Bradford Huie, *Three Lives for Mississippi* (New York, 1965), 46–49, 55–59, 70–71; press release [June, 1964].

61. Mickey Schwerner, Report, Feb. 2–7, 1964, CA; Rita Schwerner, Reports, Jan. 5 to June, 1964, *passim;* see also Huie, *Three Lives for Mississippi,* 93–94, 77–78, 97–103.

62. SRO press release, May 14, 1964, SRO; Rita Schwerner, Report, June 6, 1964, CA; Haley to Mickey Schwerner, June 10, 1964, SRO.

63. Press releases, June 4, 11, 1964; Haley to Allen Adams, June 12, 1964, CA; Burke Marshall to Robert Kennedy, June 2, 5, 1964, Marshall Prs; Testi-

mony of George Washington, Jr., in *Hearings Before the United States Commission on Civil Rights, 1965,* Vol. II, *Administration of Justice* (Washington, 1965), 216–22.

64. Rachlin to Rich, Hill, Carey *et al.*, April 13, 1964, CA; Minutes of LCDC meeting, June 12, 1964, Rachlin files; Farmer to Parents of Civil Rights Workers in Mississippi, June 29, 1964, CHQ; Rich to Haley, June 12, 1964, CA; Farmer to Robert Kennedy, June 12, 1964, and Burke Marshall to Farmer, June 23, 1964, both in Marshall Prs; Haley to Rich, June 9, July 10, 1964, CA.

65. Mickey Schwerner, Report, Feb. 2–7, 1964, CA; *Times,* July 5, 1964; Affidavits of Junior and Beatrice Roosevelt in COFO, "Affidavits" [Summer 1964], CA; Steering Committee, Aug. 8–9, 1964, Rachlin files.

66. *Times,* Aug. 9, 1964; Huie, *Three Lives for Mississippi,* 228–29.

67. COFO, *Mississippi: Handbook for Political Programs* [June 1964], Ca; "COFO Freedom Centers—September, 1964," CA. On Leake County, see also Reports of Dorothy Teel, July 6, 10, 19, 28, 29, 31, 1964, Hank Werner Prs.

68. Elizabeth Sutherland, ed., *Letters from Mississippi* (New York, 1965), 11–12; interviews and personal observation; [COFO], "A List of Mississippi Churches Destroyed or Damaged, June 15 to September 20," CA.

69. Robert Gore to Rich, July 22, 1964, CA; Gore, "COFO Project in Meridian, Mississippi, Summer, 1964" [Aug. 1964], CA; *Mississippi Free Press,* July 18, 1964; Liz Fusco, "Freedom Schools in Mississippi" [Fall 1964], CA; Noel Day, *Curriculum Guide for Freedom Schools* [1964], personal file; Staughton Lynd, "The Freedom Schools: Concept and Organization," *Freedomways,* V (Spring 1965), 309; Sue Sanford, Peter Praetz, and JoAnn Ooiman, Report on Pleasant Green Freedom Schools, July 4 [1964], JoAnn Ooiman Robinson Prs; Sutherland, ed., *Letters from Mississippi.* (Lynd was state coordinator for the Freedom Schools.)

70. COFO, *Mississippi: Handbook for Political Programs* [June 1964], CA; Washington Office MFDP, *The Mississippi Freedom Democratic Party* [July 1964], CA; no author, "To COFO Staff, re: Statewide Political Program" [April 1964], CA; SRO press release, June 2, 1964, SRO; affidavits of Annie Devine and Leonard Clay in COFO, *Mississippi: How Negro Democrats Fared,* Part II [June 1964], CA; Reese Cleghorn, "Who Speaks for Mississippi?," *The Reporter,* XXXI (Aug. 13, 1964), 32.

71. Minutes, COFO meeting, Dec. 15, 1963, JoAnn Ooiman Robinson Prs; Robert Gore to Rich and McCain, July 22, 1964, CA; Sutherland, ed., *Letters from Mississippi,* 206–07, 210–13; Gore, "COFO Project in Meridian, Mississippi, Summer, 1964" [Aug. 1964], CA.

72. Joseph Rauh *et al., Brief Submitted by the Mississippi Freedom Democratic Party to the Democratic Convention Credentials Committee,* 1964, 19, CA; COFO, "Running Summary of Incidents," Aug. 6, 1964, CA.

73. *Times,* May 6, 1964; Hill to all CORE chapters, June 25, 1964, WCO; NAC, June 30–July 2, 1964, CA; Steering Committee, Aug. 8–9, 1964, CA.

74. Rauh *et al., Brief Submitted by the Mississippi Freedom Democratic Party . . . ;* Farmer, "Testimony Before the Democratic Platform Committee," Aug. 19, 1964, CA; *Times* and Washington *Post,* Aug. 19–25, *passim;* Suther-

land, ed., *Letters from Mississippi,* 220–22; Len Holt, *The Summer That Didn't End* (New York, 1965), 155–57, 163–78; McLemore, "The Mississippi Freedom Democratic Party," 134, 149, 152–55; Anne Romaine, "The Mississippi Freedom Democratic Party through August, 1964" (M.A. thesis, University of Virginia, 1969), *passim;* press release, Aug. 27, 1964; interviews. On Farmer's position, see Sutherland, 222, Holt, 175, and esp. Romaine, 228, 241, 294; also interviews.

75. Mississippi and Louisiana Staff, "Proposed Plan of Action for CORE" [Sept. 1964], accompanying Dennis and Mississippi staff to NAC members and national office of CORE, rec'd Sept. 21, 1964, CA.

CHAPTER TEN

1. 1963 Convention, CA; James Farmer to Weldon Rougeau, March 31, 1964, CA; Alan Gartner to CORE Group Leaders, March 13, 1964, CA.

2. Carl Rachlin to Morris Abram, Dec. 26, 1963, Rachlin files; Rachlin to Farmer, Nov. 12, 1963, May 12, 1964, Rachlin files; Minutes of SEDF Program —Executive Committee, Oct. 7, 1964, SEDF; George Schiffer, "Report to the CORE Lawyers," Dec. 21, 1964, Rachlin files; Minutes of Chapter Executives' Meeting with Farmer, March 8, 1964, CA; Minutes of MACC Drafting Comittee, March 21, April 5, 1964, MLK and March 29, 1964, CA; Fredricka Teer, Reports, Jan. 11, and April 1–7, 1963, CA; Chet Duncan to James McCain, July 22, 1963, CA; Minutes, California Conference of CORE Chapters, July 20 and Dec. 7–8, 1963, WCO; Minutes, CORE Regional Conference, April 17–19, 1964, WCO; interviews.

3. Marvin Rich to Editor, *New York Times,* March 20, 1964, CA; Floyd McKissick to Farmer, March 18, 1964, and Farmer to McKissick, March 24, 1964, MLK; Statement of Income for Fiscal Year ending May 31, 1964, CA; Farmer to Field Staff, May 5, 1964, WCO; NAC, Aug. 8, 19, 1964, Rachlin files; CORE Financial Statement for four months ending Sept. 30, 1964, CA; interview.

4. Robert Penn Warren, *Who Speaks for the Negro?* (New York, 1965), 190–91: Rich to Community Relations Staff, July 13, 1964, MLK; Clora Coleman and Carey to Staff, Aug. 21, 1964, MLK.

5. McKissick and McCain to all field secretaries, Feb. 4, 1964, CA; McCain to Winston Lockett, Oct. 18, 1963, CA; McCain to Field Staff, Aug. 5, 1963, CA; McCain to all Field Staff Personnel, Dec. 16, 1963, Mary Hamilton Prs.

6. McCain to Task Force Workers, Oct. 2, 1963, Mary Hamilton Prs; McCain to Gartner, Sept. 17, 1963, CA; Duncan to McCain, Aug. 26, 1963, CA.

7. Josetta Brown to Norman Hill, Sept. 17, 1963, CA; Constance Timberlake to Farmer, Sept. 25, 1963, CA; McCain to Timberlake, Dec. 16, 1963, CA; McCain, Memo to Field Secretaries, March 24, 1964, CA. For NAC's concern with internal chapter problems see, for example, Steering Committee, Jan. 24, 1964, and NAC, Feb. 21–23, 1964, both CA.

8. Haley to Staff, Sept. 10, 1963, MLK.

9. Genevieve Hughes to Rich, June 17, 1963, CA; Steering Committee, June 7, 1963, CA; MaryLu Murphy to Robert Curvin, July 17, 1964, Curvin Prs; interviews.

10. Columbia University CORE newsletter, March, 1963, CA; Minutes of the Proposed Greater New York Metropolitan Area Coordinating Council, Dec. 7, 1961, CA; Hill to New York Area Chapter Chairmen, Sept. 24, 1963, CA.

11. NAC, May 1–3, 1964, CA; Steering Committee, May 22, June 19, 1964, CA; 1964 Convention, CA; Washington *Post*, June 21, 22, 24, 29, July 7, 29, 1964.

12. Farmer, Report to 1964 Convention, MaryLu Murphy Prs; 1964 Convention, CA; also personal observations and Malcolm Burnstein, "CORE National Convention, 1964," Berkeley Campus *CORE-lator*, Sept. 1964, UC.

13. This analysis is based primarily on interview materials.

14. David Dennis to McCain, "Mississippi in Motion," Oct. 19, 1963, CA; Ed Hollander to Marvin Rich, April 2, 1964, CA; Mimi Feingold to Parents, Aug. 19, 1963, July 10, 1964, Miriam Feingold Whitman Prs; Charlotte Greenup to Mimi Whitman, Oct. 12, 1966, Whitman Prs; interviews.

15. Interviews; quotation from Howard Zinn, *SNCC: The New Abolitionists* (Boston, 1964), 186.

16. Zinn, *SNCC: The New Abolitionists*, 188; Dennis quoted in *Times*, Aug. 9 and 10, 1964; Moses quoted in Warren, *Who Speaks for the Negro?* 99. See also Robert Moses' statements in Anne Romaine, "The Mississippi Freedom Democratic Party through August, 1964," (M.A. thesis, University of Virginia, 1969), 69–72.

17. Interviews; Sutherland, ed., *Letters from Mississippi*, 3, 5, 10, 14, and quote, p. 202. For discussions of the Mississippi summer experience highly critical of the white volunteers, see Alvin Poussaint, " 'White Problem' Spawned 'Black Power,' " *Ebony*, XXIII (Aug. 1967), 88–94, and Allan Keller, *et al.*, "Summer 1964: The White 'Freedom Fighter' in the South," *Kansas Journal of Sociology*, I (Summer 1965), 119–22.

18. Interviews; Inge Bell, *CORE and the Strategy of Non-Violence* (New York, 1968),14.

19. Interviews; quotation from Warren, *Who Speaks for the Negro?*, 381.

20. "CORE Goes Slumming," *Greater Philadelphia Magazine*, LIV (Sept. 1963), 79; Minutes, California CORE Conference, Jan. 17–19, 1964, WCO; Leonard Cohen to Marshall England, June 24, 1964, CA; interviews.

21. Interviews; Bell, *CORE and the Strategy of Non-Violence*, 16; "Summary of Activities, Cleveland CORE, July, 1963 to July, 1964," Arthur Evans Prs.

22. The foregoing discussion was based chiefly on interviews. For Chicago, see also B. Elton Cox to McCain [Oct. 1963], CA; for Washington, see *Afro-American*, June 23, 1964, and Washington *Post*, June 22, 1964; for New York, see also Minutes of Meeting at National Office on Trusteeship for New York CORE, Jan. 19, 1964, MLK; Tina Lawrence to Farmer, Jan. 23, 1964, MLK, and quotation from Blyden Jackson in *Times*, June 22, 1964.

23. *Times*, April 22, 1963; Farmer, *Freedom—When?* (New York, 1965), 90; interviews.

24. Gartner to Farmer, rec'd July 5, 1963, CA; *Times*, Sept. 4, 1963; Richard Haley to Alfred Ochs, Nov. 14, 1963, CA; Schedule of 1963 Convention Workshops, CA; Haley to Staff, Sept. 18, 1963, MLK.

25. Warren, *Who Speaks for the Negro?*, 193–94.

26. The preceding discussion is based largely on interviews. For Baltimore, see Vera Lynn to Hill [Oct. 1963], CA; on Klunder, see her article, "My Husband Died for Democracy," *Ebony*, XIX (June 1964), 35; for Farmer's reference to whites as "rabid black nationalists," see *Freedom—When?*, 88.

27. Philadelphia *Inquirer*, June 16, 1963; Gladys Harrington quoted in Dayton *Journal-Herald*, June 29, 1963; *Times*, June 28, 1963; on nonviolent workshop, see Gordon Carey to Rudy Lombard, June 21, 1963, CA; "1963 CORE Convention Workshops," CHQ, and Dayton *Journal-Herald*, June 29, 1963; preliminary draft, 1963 Convention Minutes, MaryLu Murphy Prs.

28. *Times*, June 29, 1963; Farmer, "The New Jacobins and Full Emancipation," in Robert Goldwin, ed., *100 Years of Emancipation* (Chicago, 1963), 96. (This paper was written about Sept. 1963.)

29. Haley to Farmer *et al.*, Nov. 20, 1963, CA; Steering Committee, Jan. 24, 1964, CA.

30. Rich to Genevieve Hughes, July 16, 1963, CA; National Director's Report to the 1964 Convention, MaryLu Murphy Prs; unidentified CORE field worker, Notes on New Orleans National Staff Conference, Feb. 12–17, 1964, WCO.

31. On Malcolm X's influence, see Bayard Rustin, "Nonviolence on Trial," *Fellowship Magazine*, XXX (July 1964), 5, 8.

32. On King, see Rustin, "Montgomery Diary," *Liberation*, April 1956, reprinted in *Down the Line: The Collected Writings of Bayard Rustin* (Chicago, 1971), 55. On Aaron Henry, personal observation. On Dennis, see telegram to Robert Kennedy and Lyndon Johnson, Jan. 30, 1964, CA; interviews. On Jerome Smith, see George Plimpton, *American Journey: The Times of Robert Kennedy* (New York, 1970), 121; *Times*, May 26, 1963; interviews.

33. The preceding discussion draws ideas from Bell, *CORE and the Strategy of Non-Violence*, 26–27, 37–43, and from Donald von Eschen, Jerome Kirk, and Maurice Pinard, "The Disintegration of the Negro Non-Violent Movement," *Journal of Peace Research*, No. 3 (1969), 216–34. However, the particular formulation employed here is our own. On Long Island CORE, see Long Island CORE Clipping Books, July 21, 31, and Aug. 6, 1964; on Chicago, interviews; on Cleveland, interviews and Cleveland *Plain Dealer*, Feb. 5, 1964; on New Haven, interviews, New Haven *Journal-Courier*, Nov. 3 and 4, 1963, and Rich to Mrs. David Mellor, Dec. 19, 1963, CA; on West Coast Conference, see Thomas Cummins to Farmer, April 20, 1964, CHQ.

34. *Times*, March 15, 1964, for Malcolm X's proposing gun clubs; Malcolm X, "The Ballot or the Bullet," in George Breitman, ed., *Malcolm X Speaks* (New York, 1965), 23–24; "Cleveland CORE Guide to Action, 1963–1964," WCO; Cleveland *Plain Dealer*, April 4, 5, 6, 8, 1964; Lewis Robinson, *The Making of a Man*, 78–79, 102; interviews; Turner quoted in Warren, *Who Speaks for the Negro?*, 384.

35. *Sentinel*, July 2, 1964; NAC, June 30–July 2, 1964, CA.

36. *Times*, July 19, 20, 21, 1964; New York *Amsterdam News*, July 25, 1964; Farmer, *Freedom—When?*, 28–29.

37. San Diego *Union,* July 31, 1964; New Haven *CORE-lator,* Aug. 1964, MLK; Farmer, *Freedom—When?,* 33.

38. Rich to Ed Singler, Aug. 6, 1963, CA.

39. Interviews; "Activities of Queens CORE, July, 1963 to May, 1964," WCO.

40. Interviews; NAC, Nov. 8–11, 1963, CA; Haley to Downtown CORE, Nov. 13, 1963, CA.

41. Carey to Marty Cahill, Dec. 2, 1963, CA; Bell, *CORE and the Strategy of Non-Violence,* 14.

42. The preceding discussion was based almost entirely on interviews. In the few instances where membership lists were available it proved possible to obtain precise racial breakdowns through interviews: see Detroit membership list [May 1964], Ralph Rosenfeld Prs; Newark Membership list, March 16, 1964, Robert Curvin Prs; Berkeley membership lists [ca. Spring 1964], and Nov. 1964, Genevieve Hughes Prs. For Cleveland, see also Mary Hamilton to McCain, May 19, 1962, CA, and Haley to McCain, March 17, 1963, CA; for Los Angeles and California, see *Sentinel,* Aug. 15, 1963; Los Angeles *Times,* Sept. 25, 1963, clipping, CA; Minutes of California Conference of CORE Chapters, Jan. 17–19, 1964, WCO.

43. On Cleveland, see Untitled MS [1964], Arthur Evans Prs; and for date of opening of office, "Summary of Activities, Cleveland CORE, July, 1963 to July, 1964" [1964], Evans Prs. On Syracuse, see: George Wiley to Dear Jim, July 17, 1963, CA; Evert Makinen to Carey, May 23, 1963, CA; "The Protest Movement North: The Syracuse Story" [1964], Wiley Prs; Syracuse CORE, *In the Wind,* Aug. 1964, CHQ; Ronald Corwin, "School Desegregation in Syracuse" (Ph.D. dissertation, Syracuse University, 1968), 150, 172–73; interviews. For Newark: Newark *Evening News,* July 12, 1963, and personal observations. On Philadelphia, see Ada Countee to Norman Hill, March 17, 1964, CA; Philadelphia *Inquirer,* March 17, 1964. On New Haven, see Allan Hoffman to McCain, June 15, 1964, CA. Marlene Wilson to Farmer, July 8, 1964, MLK; "Cleveland CORE Guide to Action, 1963–1964," June 1964, WCO.

44. Interviews.

45. Interviews; quotation from Gene Schulze to Haley, Oct. 12, 1963, Schulze Prs; on Leeds, see also Leeds to Milton Galamison, Aug. 12, 1963, Galamison Prs.

46. Eleanor Holmes to Winston Lockett, Feb. 8, 1964, MLK, and the following in the Gene Schulze Prs: Schulze to Velma Hill, Dec. 17, 1963; Schulze to Haley, Oct. 12, 13, 1963; Schulze to New Haven CORE Executive Board, Oct. 13, 1963; Schulze to William Winnick, Nov. 16, 1963; Schulze to Katherine Holmes, Dec. 26, 30, 1963; Schulze to Grace Lockett, Dec. 30, 1963; "Resolution on New Haven CORE Unity" [Jan. 1964]; Schulze to Burl Towles, Dec. 31, 1963; Grace Lockett to Zeke Abelson *et al.,* Jan 3, 1964.

47. Woodrow Coleman to McCain, Nov. 29, 1963, MLK; Chet Duncan, Report on Los Angeles CORE, Dec. 18, 1963, MLK; Steering Committee, Jan. 24, 1964, CA; Carey to Arthur Silvers, March 23, 1964, CA. On N-VAC activities, see *Eagle,* Jan. 2, 9, June 11, 1964; *Sentinel,* March 22, 1964, July 22, 1965; Wil-

liam Ellis, "Operation Bootstrap: A Case Study in Ideology and the Institutionalization of Protest" (Ph.D. dissertation, University of California at Los Angeles, 1969), 79–84.

48. Wallace Murphy to Velma Hill [Feb. 1964], CA; Allan Hoffman to McCain and NAC, April 10, 1964, CA.

49. "Action NOW for Jobs and Freedom—A Program for New York CORE" [late 1963], CHQ; interviews; Blyden Jackson and Tina Lawrence, "East River CORE, A Progress Report," rec'd April 9, 1964, CHQ; *Times,* March 14, 1964.

50. Seattle CORE Minutes, April 23, May 12, 1964; "Violations of the CORE Rules for Action" [Aug. 1964]; Seattle CORE Executive Committee Minutes, May 11, 1964; Tim Martin *et al.* to Dear Active Member [Aug. 1964], all in Seattle CORE Papers; interviews.

51. Interviews.

52. Oldham to McCain, Dec. 20, 1963, CA; St. Louis *Post-Dispatch,* Dec. 5, 15, 1963, Jan. 2, 3, 1964; MaryLu Murphy to Rich, Jan. 8, 1964, CA; Marian Oldham to McCain, Nov. 3, 1964, CA.

53. Agenda for Connecticut Area Conference, Dec. 13–15, 1963, CA; draft agendas for Midwest Area Conference, April 10–12, 1964, and Michigan Area Conference, May 1–3, 1964, CA; Feingold to Parents, Feb. 16, 1964, Whitman Prs, and Agenda for New Orleans Staff Conference, Feb. 1964, CHQ; *Times,* May 3, 1964; Hill to Farmer, Aug. 14, 1964, CA; on press regarding Hill's stand as paradoxical, see *Times,* Sept. 4, 1964.

54. Interviews.

55. David Cohen, "Notes Toward a Civil Rights Strategy for Religious Groups," presented at Religious Research Association, Cleveland, June 19, 1964, copy, courtesy David Cohen.

56. Cohen, *ibid.;* for Detroit, interviews and *Chronicle,* June 6, 13, 1964.

57. NAC, Feb. 21–23, 1964, CA; *Defender,* April 11–17, June 13–19, July 11–17, 1964; Steering Committee, June 19, 1964, CA; Farmer, Report to 1964 Convention, MaryLu Murphy Prs; Milton Davis to McCain, Oct. 28, 1964, Davis Prs; Debbie Meier to Rich [late 1964], Davis Prs; Winston Lockett to McCain, Aug. 12, 1964, MLK: Jo Adler, "Chicago," Aug. 21, 1964, CA; quotations from interviews. For a more favorable assessment of the accomplishments of the North and West Side projects, see [Eugene Tournour], "C.O.R.E. Northern Project: Chicago, Ill." [Sept. or Oct. 1964], Alan Gartner Prs.

58. Minutes, CORE Regional Conference, April 16–18, 1964, WCO; San Francisco CORE newsletter [Aug. 1964], WCO.

59. Hill to Fredricka Teer, Oct. 30, 1962, CA; Hill to New York Area Chapter Chairmen, Sept. 24, 1963, CA.

60. Hill, Address to the St. Louis Area Conference, April 4, 1964, printed in August Meier, Elliott Rudwick, and Francis Broderick, eds., *Black Protest Thought in the Twentieth Century,* 2nd ed. (Indianapolis, 1971), 442–43.

61. Farmer, Report on 1964 Convention, MaryLu Murphy Prs, and Farmer, quoted in Warren, *Who Speaks for the Negro?,* 386–87; Turner, quoted in Warren, *Who Speaks for the Negro?,* 191, and interview.

62. Hill, Address to St. Louis Area Conference; Cohen, "Notes Toward a Civil Rights Strategy for Religious Groups."

63. Quotes from Hill to Farmer, Aug. 14, 1964, CA; see also Bayard Rustin, "From Protest to Politics: The Future of the Civil Rights Movement," *Commentary*, XXXIX (Feb. 1965), 25–31.

64. Interviews. For fragmentary documentary evidence on Hill's and Rustin's course in this period, see Hill and Rustin, memo to Ella Baker, Farmer, James Forman, Martin Luther King, John Lewis, Robert Moses, A. Philip Randolph, and Andrew Young [June 1964], CHQ; NAC, June 30 to July 2, 1964, CA; Hill to all CORE Chapters, June 25, 1964, WCO; Steering Committee, Aug. 8–9, 1964, CA.

65. NAC, Nov. 8–10, 1963, June 30–July 2, 1964, both CA; Kansas City *Times*, July 4, 6, 1964; interviews; Chet Duncan, Bill Brown, and Frank Glover, "CORE Operation at the Cow Palace" [July 1964], WCO; San Francisco *Chronicle*, July 15, 16, 1964.

66. Hill to Steering Committee, April 10, 1964, George Wiley Prs; also interviews.

67. Steering Committee, April 11, 1964, CA; interviews; Tom Kahn to Farmer, April 16, 1964, Farmer Prs.

68. Joseph Gusfield, "Functional Areas of Leadership in Social Movements," *Sociological Quarterly*, VII (Summer 1966), 137–56.

69. Interviews.

70. San Francisco *Chronicle*, July 31, 1964; Berkeley Campus *CORE-lator*, Sept. 1964, UC; *Times*, July 20, 31, 1964.

71. Hill to Farmer, Aug. 14, 1964, CA.

72. *Ibid.*

73. Transcript of Farmer Interview, WABC-TV, Nov. 15, 1964, CHQ.

74. Report of the Evaluation Committee, appended to Minutes of Closed Session of Steering Committee, Aug. 8–9, 1964, CA.

CHAPTER ELEVEN

1. Opening Remarks by A. Philip Randolph at Conference of Negro Leaders, New York, Jan. 30–31, 1965, copy in George Wiley Prs; James Bevel quoted in Charles Silberman, "Beware the Day They Change Their Minds," *Fortune*, LXXII (Nov. 1965), 150; James Farmer quoted in Whitney Young's Column, "To Be Equal," *Tribune*, Oct. 30, 1965.

2. Farmer, "A Few Guidelines for Organizational Expansion," Oct. 9, 1964, CA; Farmer, Suggested Guidelines for Future Organizational Expansion," April 3, 1965, CA; Farmer, Report to the 1965 CORE Convention, printed in August Meier, Elliott Rudwick, and Francis Broderick, eds., *Black Protest in the Twentieth Century*, rev. ed. (Indianapolis, 1971), 460–66; Farmer, *Freedom—When?* (New York, 1965), 91–92, 103, 121. For impact of nationalists outside CORE on New Directions, see NAC, Oct. 10–12, 1964, Rachlin files, and Rudy Lombard, "NAC Retreat" [Oct. 1964], CA.

3. Report of Evaluation Committee, appended to Minutes of Closed Session, Steering Committee, Aug. 8–9, 1964, CA.

4. NAC, Oct. 10–12, 1964, Carl Rachlin files.

5. On Gore, see Richard Haley, untitled statement for staff, Oct. 15, 1964, CHQ; James McCain to Farmer and Wiley, March 16, 1965, MLK; Wiley to NAC members and staff, Sept. 8, 1965, MLK.

6. Lou Smith, Report, Sept. 1964 to Jan. 1965, dated Jan. 25, 1965, CA; Smith to Joyce Ware *et al.* [ca. late 1964], CA; Smith to Farmer *et al.,* May 3, 1965, MLK; Smith to Ike Reynolds, March 18, 1965, WCO.

7. Typescript of Directions for Press Conference, Nov. 23, 1964, Wiley Prs, and *Times,* Nov. 24, 1964; Report of Evaluation Committee, with Minutes, Closed Session, Steering Committee, Aug. 8–9, 1964, CA; Wiley to Clora Coleman, Sept. 20, 1965, MLK; Wiley to NAC Members, June 16, 1965, Wiley Prs; interviews.

8. Wiley to NAC, June 16, 1965, MLK.

9. Wiley to NAC, Feb. 2, 1965, CHQ; Floyd McKissick to NAC, Nov. 14, 1964, Curvin Prs; Wiley to NAC, Dec. 11, 1964, Robert Curvin Prs; interviews.

10. Marvin Rich to Farmer, Nov. 4, 1964, MLK; Clyde Bergen to Rich, March 18, 1965, SEDF; Rich to Stephen Currier, March 22, 1965, MLK; Rich and Rachlin to Andrew Norman, Jan. 8, 1965, Rachlin Files; Rich to Lula Farmer, March 11, 1965, MLK; Lula Farmer to Rich, March 11, 1965, Rich Prs.

11. Steering Committee, Sept. 7, 1962, CA; Minutes of Special Meeting of CORE-SEDF Board of Directors, Feb. 21, 1963, SEDF; "Freedom Rider Bond Loans—Schedule of Loans," attached to Lula Farmer to Wiley, Oct. 27, 1965, Rachlin Files; Rich to Farmer, Nov. 30, 1964, Rich Prs; Steering Committee, Jan. 15, 1965, CA; "Summary and Conclusion of [SEDF] Legal Committee Meeting, Aug. 17, 1965," SEDF; Andrew Norman to McKissick, Feb. 23, 1967, Rich Prs; National Office Monthly Budget, Oct. 1965, SEDF; Wiley to NAC Members, Oct. 22, 1965, MLK; Farmer to NAC, Jan. 7, 1965, CA; "Citizenship Education Projects Expenditures, Jan. 1, 1965–Oct. 31, 1965," Nov. 5, 1965, Rich Prs; Edwin Day to Rich, Dec. 16, 1965, SEDF.

12. Farmer to NAC, Jan. 7, 1965, CA; Wiley to Chapters, Staff and NAC Members, Sept. 8, 1965, Wiley Prs; see also "National CORE Staff Meetings, November–December [1964], Decisions," MLK; on closing of western and northeastern regional offices, see Ike Reynolds to McCain, April 29, 1965, WCO and Wiley to Reynolds, May 21, 1965, CA; Minutes, Northeast Regional Action Council, Sept. 11, 1965, Curvin Prs; Wiley to Chapters, Staff and NAC, Sept. 8, 1965, CA.

13. Statement of Income and Expenditures for the Year Ending May 31, 1965, CHQ; Wiley to NAC, Jan. 20, 1966, Curvin Prs; "History of CORE Debt," Oct. 22, 1965, SEDF; "History of Debt and Income" [ca. Dec. 1965], CHQ.

14. Untitled financial report for NAC, Jan. 1966, CHQ; McKissick to NAC, May 17, Sept. 29, 1965, MLK; Wiley to NAC, Jan. 20, 1966, Curvin Prs.

15. *Times,* Jan. 24, 1965, July 24, 1966.

16. Alan Gartner to McKissick, March 3, 1966, CHQ; on size of mailing list,

see Farmer, Report to 1964 Convention, MaryLu Murphy Prs, and Gartner to NAC, Aug. 15, 1965, Rich Prs.

17. Rich to Inge Bell, July 28, 1966, SEDF; Lincoln Lynch, associate national director, quoted in *Times,* July 25, 1966.

18. Haley to Gartner, Nov. 19, 1964, CA; see also NAC, June 30, 1965, Curvin Prs; Wiley to McKissick, Jan. 30, 1966, Wiley Prs.

19. Steering Committee, Jan. 15, 1965, CA; Gartner to NAC [ca. Oct. 1965], SEDF; Gartner to Farmer, Wiley, McKissick, Sept. 27, 1965, CHQ.

20. Interview; Minutes, "Fund Raisers Meeting," Sept. 29, 1965, CHQ; Farmer to Franklin Roosevelt, Jr., Dec. 15, 1965, CHQ; Wiley, "Anna Rosenberg—Dossier," Sept. 27, 1965, CHQ; also Wiley "dossiers" on Jane Mayer, Amory Houghton, James Slater, Marvin Kratter, Sol Linwitz, Dec. 1965, CHQ; on xerox, see also E. K. Damon to Wiley, April 7, 1966, CHQ, enclosing $2000 as pledged.

21. Statement of Income and Expenditure for Year Ending May 31, 1965, CHQ; "Field Staff Personnel" [Sept. 1964], SRO; "Southern CORE Staff and Locations" [Jan. 21, 1965], SRO; "CORE Southern Payroll," March 3, 1965, CHQ. On CORE's total staff and its deployment, see Charles G. Currier to Wiley, Feb. 26, 1965, Currier Prs, and 1966 Convention, Ollie Leeds Prs.

22. Dennis to Rich, March 18, 1965, SEDF; "Report on Recruitment," May 18, 1965, SRO; *Times,* Aug. 15, 1965; Rachlin, Report of General Counsel to NAC, Oct. 1964, Rachlin Files; Rachlin to Wiley, Jan. 18, 1965, Rachlin files; Wiley to NAC, Oct. 22, 1965, SEDF.

23. Haley to Rich, Nov. 19, 1964, SRO; Haley, "Mississippi CORE Staff" [Oct. 1, 1964], SRO; Rich to Haley, Nov. 9, 1964, CA; Rich to Dick Jewett, Dec. 10, 1964, CA.

24. Haley, "CORE in the South, September–December, 1964," Jan. 28, 1965, CA; Ronnie Moore to Haley, Dec. 4, 1964, SRO; Moore to Staff Members, Dec. 10, 1964, SRO; Minutes, Mississippi 4th District Meeting [Dec. 1964], SRO; Jewett to Rich and Farmer, June 15, 1965, CHQ.

25. "Southern Monthly Budget" [Oct. 1965], SEDF; Haley, "Personnel Administered by CORE Southern Office," Jan. 12, 1966, SEDF; Haley to Herbert Callender, April 12, 1966, MLK. On Jewett and Raymond, see Wiley to NAC and Staff, Sept. 8, 1965, and New Orleans *Times-Picayune,* Dec. 12, 1965, clipping Wiley Prs; on SRO office, Haley to McKissick, May 24, 1966, MLK. On new VEP, see Dennis to McKissick, Jan. 22, 1966, MLK; Gartner to McKissick, Feb. 18, 1966, MLK; Vernon Jordan to Haley, April 14, 1966, VEP; Haley to Jordan, April 22, 1966, VEP.

26. Haley to McCain, Aug. 20, 1964, SRO.

27. Mississippi and Louisiana Staff, Memorandum [Sept. 1964], attached to Dennis and Mississippi staff to NAC and national office, rec'd Sept. 21, 1964, CA; "Staff Discussions, Canton COFO Office," April 2, 1965, JoAnn Ooiman Robinson Prs; Moore to Louisiana Staff, n.d. attached to another memo dated Nov. 3, 1964, SRO.

28. Mike Lesser, "Let's Have a People's Conference," a paper prepared for the May 1965, Louisiana Staff Conference, CA.

29. Southern Regional Office to Department of Organization and NAC, April 9, 1965, SRO.

30. On prior interest, see esp. Farmer to Chase Manhattan Bank, Nov. 30, 1962, CA; Farmer to Counsel and Staff, Dec. 27, 1962, CA; "Background Information on CORE's School Bond Campaign," Feb. 1963, Rich Prs; Steering Committee, March 29, April 26, 1963, both CA. On genesis of "affirmative legal action" program, see esp. Lolis Elie to Rachlin, Dec. 4, 1964, CA; Rachlin to Farmer, Wiley and Rich, May 10, 1965, Rachlin Files; Rachlin to Collins, Douglas, and Elie, Feb. 24, 1965, Rachlin Files. On Louisiana cases, see esp. Rachlin to David Dennis, March 15, 17, 1963, Rachlin Files; "Facts Relating to Complaint Filed in St. Tammany Parish School Case," April 6, 1965, Rachlin Files; Nils Douglas to Rich, April 30, May 24, 31, SEDF; Rachlin to Collins, Douglas, and Elie, July 14, 1965, SEDF; Lolis Elie to Rich, July 28, 1965, SEDF; Rachlin to Rich, Aug. 12, 1965, Rachlin Files; Rachlin Report to NAC, Oct. 20, 1965, SEDF; *Wall Street Journal,* April 7, 30, June 2, 4, Aug. 5, 1965; Rachlin to Farmer, Wiley, Gartner, Rich, Sept. 9, 1965, MLK; Ed Hollander to Bruce Baines, Nov. 18, 1965, Hollander Prs. On other litigation to desegregate parish schools, see extensive materials in Murphy Bell Prs on East Feliciana (reel No. 2) and West Feliciana (reel No. 4) parishes; and relevant documents, 1965, in East Feliciana CORE Prs.

31. MFDP Fact Sheet, Press Conference, Washington, Nov. 16, 1964, CA; Minutes MFDP Executive Committee, Sept. 13, 1964, CA; George Raymond, "Canton CORE," Jan. 1965, MLK; COFO, "Running Summary of Incidents during the 'Freedom Vote' Campaign," Oct. 18–Nov. 2, 1964, CA; see also various Meridian Field Reports by Sandra Watts and Frank Wright, Oct.–Nov. 1964, CA; and Minutes, Canton Staff Meeting, Sept. 21, 1964, CA.

32. Dick Jewett, "Mississippi Field Report," Jan. 19, 1965, CA.

33. "Rough Minutes of a Meeting Called by the National Council of Churches to Discuss the Mississippi Project, September 18, 1964," copy, CA; Henry Schwarzschild to LCDC Board of Directors, Sept. 11, 1964, Rachlin Files; on Henry, see *Times,* April 14, 21, 1965, interviews and personal observations.

34. Minutes of 4th Congressional District Staff Meeting [Dec. 1964], CA, and January 15–17, 1965, JoAnn Ooiman Robinson Prs; Jewett, "Problems Facing COFO" [Oct. 1964], CA; Minutes, Staff Meeting, Jackson COFO, Nov. 23, 1964, CA; Hunter Morey, "Crossroads in COFO" [late 1964], Morey Prs; *Times,* April 14, 21, 1965; *Call,* April 23, 1965; New Orleans *Times-Picayune,* Dec. 12, 1965, clipping, Wiley Prs. On Dennis, interviews; on Moses, see Bruce Payne, "SNCC: An Overview Two Years Later," in Mitchell Cohen and Dennis Hale, eds., *The New Student Left* (Boston, 1966), 96, and Pat Watters, *Encounter with the Future* (Atlanta, 1965), 8–9. On SNCC-CORE problems, see Minutes of Staff Meeting, April 1, 1965, Robinson Prs.

35. Richard H. Rovere, "Letter from Washington," Oct. 10, 1965, *The New Yorker,* XLI (Oct. 16, 1965), 233–44; miscellaneous material from Washington office of MFDP, Dec. 1964 to Sept. 1965, CA; Wiley to All CORE Chapters, April 7, 1965, CA; Dennis to Office Staff, May 4, 1965, CA; "Statement of James

Farmer, National Director, CORE," press release May 17, 1965; Farmer, telegrams to 17 Congressmen, Sept. 9, 1965, CHQ; Farmer to All CORE Chapters, Sept. 9, 1965, CA; Lawrence Guyot to Farmer, Sept. 24, 1965, CHQ.

36. Farmer, "The CORE of It," New York *Amsterdam News*, July 3, 1965; *Times*, June 17, 1965; Affidavit by Wiley to FBI Agents, July 12, 1965, Wiley Prs; Wiley, notes made in Jackson jail, June 1965, Wiley Prs. On Mississippi Democratic Conference and COFO objections to it, see substantial materials in both the R. Hunter Morey Prs and the Claude Ramsey Prs, esp. COFO leaflet, "The Mississippi Democratic Conference is a Fraud;" also interviews.

37. Jewett, "Mississippi Field Report, September, 1964 to January, 1965," Jan. 19, 1965, CA; Raymond, "Canton CORE," Jan. 1965, MLK; Minutes, Fourth District Staff Meeting, Sept. 21, 1964, CA; Meridian COFO Weekly Reports, Sept. to Dec. 1964, *passim* and Rich to Haley, Jan. 12, 1965, CA; Canton COFO, Two Weeks Report, Sept. 10, 1964, CA; Canton and Rankin Counties Report [Nov. 1964], SRO. On criticism of MFDP, see Minutes, Fourth District Staff Meeting, January 15–17, 1965, and Minutes, Staff Meeting, April 1, 1965, both in JoAnn Ooiman Robinson Prs.

38. On Canton, see Minutes, Canton Staff Meeting, Sept. 21, 1964, CA, and Jewett, "Mississippi Field Report, September, 1964 to January, 1965," Jan. 19, 1965, CA; quotation from JoAnn Ooiman to George Raymond, Oct. 10, 1964, JoAnn Ooiman Robinson Prs. On Meridian, see weekly Meridian field reports, Sept. 1964 to Jan. 1965, CA; Catherine Crowell to Dear Sir, May 15, July 2, 1965, CA; Crowell, Meridian Project Report, May 15–June 15, 1965, CA; George Smith, Assistant Project Director's Report, May 15–June 15, 1965, CA. On problems with community leaders, see esp. Eric Weinberger to Rich, March 11, 1965, MLK, and Weinberger to Farmer, March 18, 1965, CA. On later activity, see SRO press release, Nov. 22, 1965, SRO; Joe Morse, Meridian Project Report, July 5, 1966, MLK.

39. *COFO News*, Dec. 11, 1964, CA; Jewett, Weekly Report, Nov. 9–15, 1965, CA; Raymond, "Canton," Jan. 1965, MLK; Farmer, telegram to Orville Freeman, Dec. 1, 1964, CA; "Madeleine" to Rich, rec'd Dec. 14, 1964, CA; New York *Amsterdam News*, Dec. 19, 1964; *Times*, Dec. 4, 1964; Rich to Lester Condon, Inspector General of Agriculture Dept., Dec. 9, 1964, CA.

40. See extensive correspondence—esp. Rich to Lester Condon, Dec. 9, 1964; Condon to Rich, Dec. 18, 1964; Rich to Orville Freeman, Feb. 17, 1965; Walter L. Bieberly to Rich, March 1, 1965; Rich to Bieberly, March 3, April 20, 1965; Rich letters to Freeman, Hubert Humphrey, Jacob Javits, Robert Kennedy, William Fitts Ryan, April 20, 1965; Javits to Rich, May 8, Kennedy to Rich, May 10, 1965, all CA; affidavit of George Raymond to Office of Inspector General, U. S. Department of Agriculture, Jan. 7, 1965, SRO; Canton CORE to CORE Southern Regional Office, Feb. 8, 1965, SRO. On whole matter of ASCS election, see also testimony in *Hearings Before the United States Commission on Civil Rights*, 1965, Vol. II, *Administration of Justice* (Washington, 1965), 231–65. On new elections and CORE's response to it see F. W. Please to Rich, April 26, 1965, CA; W. H. Forsyth, Untitled mimeo'd statement [April 1965],

CA; *COFO News,* May 2, 1965, CA; Raymond, "Latest Developments in ASC elections in Madison County" [March 1965], JoAnn Ooiman Robinson Prs; *Madison County Citizen,* May 1, 22, 1965, Robinson Prs.

41. Canton Project Report [March 1965], CA; *Madison County Sewing Firm,* mimeo'd pamphlet [June 1965], CA; Report from Canton, rec'd April 5, 1965, by telephone at Southern Regional Office, SRO; "Fact Sheet on Voter Registration and Freedom Days," Feb. 7, 1965, JoAnn Ooiman Robinson Prs; Minutes of Staff Meeting, Madison County COFO, March 22, 1965, Robinson Prs; press releases, April 1, Aug. 30, 1965; Raymond to Wiley, Ed Day and Haley [late Aug. 1965], MLK; Herbert Callender to McKissick, Oct. 11, 1966, MLK.

42. For Neshoba County, see press release, Aug. 27, 1964; Hollander to Alvin Adams, Oct. 22, 1964, CA; Neshoba Project Report, ca. Dec. 1964, CA; press release, New Orleans Office of CORE, Oct. 20, 1964, CA; COFO WATS Line Report, Oct. 11, 1964, CA; Haley to Vonnie Jones, May 18, 1965, SRO; Raymond to Wiley, Ed Day, Haley, [late Aug. 1965], MLK. On Leake County, see esp. Harmony Project, Daily Reports, Aug. 17, 22, 23, 24, 25–29, 1964, CA; Citizens and Parents Committee for Equal Schools in Leake County to J. T. Logan, Aug. 10, 1964, Hank Werner Prs; "Leake County," a statement prepared for Dec. 4–6 COFO Staff Conference, CA; Randy M. Glenn, "Ofahoma Report," ca. Jan. 1965; Haley to Jewett, Jan. 13, 1965 SRO; SRO press release, Nov. 22, 1965, SRO. On Rankin County, see Raymond, Report on Rankin County [Jan. 1965], MLK; Rankin County Project, "Bi-Annual Report" [May 1965], CHQ; WATS Line Reports, April 12, May 26, 1965, SRO; *CORE-lator,* May–June 1965; Farmer, "The CORE of It," New York *Amsterdam News,* June 12, 1965; May 29, 30, 1965; Raymond to Wiley, Day and Haley [late Aug. 1965], MLK.

43. Louisiana Staff Assignments, Oct. 1964, Nov. 8, 1964, SRO; Moore to McCain, Jan. 16, 1965, CA; Louisiana Staff Assignments, Jan.–May 1965, CA; [Moore], "Louisiana Summer Project Field Report—1965." [Fall 1965], SEDF.

44. "West Feliciana Intimidations and Harassments" [Oct. 1964], CA; Monroe Staff to Moore, Nov. 3, 1964, SRO; Moore, "Field Report, September, 1964 to January, 1965," Jan. 19, 1965, CA.

45. Haley to McCain, Dec. 1, 1964, SRO; Moore, "Field Report, September, 1964 to January, 1965," Jan. 19, 1965, CA. On Monroe, see Alvin Culpepper to Monroe Negro Leaders, Nov. 16, 1964, Monroe, La., MSS; Oretha Castle, Field Report, Dec. 13, 1964, to Jan. 24, 1965, SRO; Castle, letters to Monroe and Ouachita Parish officials, Dec. 14, 1964, SRO.

46. CORE-VEP Field Report, North Louisiana, Feb. 1–March 14, 1964, SRO; Ouachita Parish Field Reports, 1964, *passim,* Monroe, La, Mss; Thomas Valentine, William Brown, and Mike Lesser to Hobart Taylor, March 2, 1964, MLK; Farmer to Taylor, March 3, 1964, and Taylor to Farmer, March 9, 1964, both MLK; Farmer to Adam Clayton Powell, March 3, 1964, and Powell to Farmer, March 6, 1964, both MLK; Paul Douglas to Farmer, March 17, 1964, MLK, and Dec. 4, 1964, CHQ; Augustus Hawkins to Farmer, March 24, 1964, MLK and July 27, 1964, CHQ; Ward McCreedy to Hawkins, July 21, 1964, CHQ; McCreedy to Farmer, July 23, 1964, MLK; Roscoe Young *et al.* to Farmer, Aug. 19, 1964, CHQ; Young *et al.* to McCreedy, Aug. 15, Sept. 25, 1964, CHQ.

47. *Programs for Change* (mimeo'd pamphlet), Feb. 25, 1965, Monroe, La., MSS; *CORE Freedom News* (Monroe), Jan. 16, 28, 1965, SRO; Field Reports, Ouachita Parish, Jan. to May 1965, Monroe, La., MSS; Lillie Flynnroy to Secretary of Agriculture, May 5, 1965, to U. S. Commission on Civil Rights, March 16, 1965, and to Monroe Department on Public Welfare, March 16, 1965, all in Monroe, La., MSS.

48. Haley to Postmaster General John Gronouski, Jan. 7, 1965, MLK; J. L. Pearce to Haley, March 15, 1965, Jonesboro Freedom House Prs; Pearce to Haley, March 21, 1965, SRO; Farmer, telegram to Gronouski, March 23, 1965, MLK; Gronouski, telegram to Farmer, March 24, 1965, CHQ; Haley to Pearce, March 24, 31, 1965, SRO; Oretha Castle, memo, March 25, 1965, SRO; Ernest Thomas to Pearce, March 30, 1965, Jonesboro Freedom House Prs; Gronouski to Farmer, April 5, 1965, MLK; Pearce to Thomas, April 5, 9, 1965, SRO; LeRoy Collins to Gronouski, April 14, 1965, SRO; Thomas *et al.* to Mayor Tate, May 12, 1965, SRO; Haley to Bruce Baines, Sept. 8, 1965, SRO.

49. Oretha Castle, Report, Dec. 13, 1964, to Jan. 24, 1965, CA; "Activities in Jonesboro, La." [April 1965], Monroe, La., MSS; [Charles Fenton], "The Jonesboro-Bogalusa Project" [March 1965], SRO; Ernest Thomas, affidavit, March 1965, SRO; Glenn Johnson and Annie Johnson to School Superintendent J. D. Koonce, March 19, 23, 1965, Jonesboro Freedom House Prs; Haley to John McKeithen, March 30, 1965, SRO; "Jonesboro Chronology" [1965], CA; unsigned statement from Jonesboro Negroes to City of Jonesboro and Parish of Jackson, March 28, 1965, Monroe, La., MSS; Hollander, "Jonesboro Summary," April 15–18, 1965, SRO; Hollander, "Draft Louisiana Summer '65 Brief Summary" [sic] [Sept. 1965], SRO; WATS Line Reports for Jonesboro, July 11–24, 1965, SEDF; Baton Rouge *State Times*, March 24–26, 29, April 5, July 14, 15, 18, 21, 28, 1965; Shreveport *Times*, March 26, April 16, 17, 19, July 16, 22, 1965; *Louisiana CORE Newsletter* [late July 1965], and *CORE Southern Regional Newsletter* [July 1965], both in East Feliciana CORE Prs; Patsy Boone, "Summary of Community Meeting, August 1, 1965," Jonesboro Freedom House Prs.

50. Farmer to NAC, March 23, 1965, CA; Carl Hufbauer, "Bogalusa: Negro Community vs. Crown Colony," Berkeley Campus *CORE-lator*, I (Spring 1965), 18–21, UC; "Crown Zellerbach in Bogalusa," March 31, 1965, typescript, CA; Vera Rony, "Bogalusa: The Economics of Tragedy," *Dissent*, XIII (May–June 1966), 234–37; Loria Davis, Mimi Feingold, Howard Messing, "Summer Parish Scouting Report, Washington Parish" [ca. April 1965], CA; Haley, "CORE in Bogalusa" [March 1965], SRO.

51. Moore, Louisiana Field Report, Jan. to June 1963, CA; Farmer to NAC, March 23, 1965, CA; "Fact Sheet on Bogalusa," Feb. 17, 1965, Wiley Prs; "Bogalusa, Louisiana, Incident Summary," Jan. 25 to Feb. 28, 1965, SRO; Oretha Castle [?], unsigned statement, March 25, 1965, SRO; Rony, "Bogalusa: The Economics of Tragedy," 239; Anita Levine and Becky White, "The Problem in Focus," Berkeley Campus *CORE-lator*, I (Spring 1965), 24, WCO.

52. Bogalusa Civic and Voters League Demands, April 6, 1965, SEDF; *Times*, April 8, 1965; Baton Rouge *State Times*, April 8–10, 1965; CORE Southern Re-

gional Office, "Summary of Incidents in Bogalusa, Louisiana, April 7–9," Wiley Prs; "Bogalusa Summary, April 13–20, 1965," SEDF; memo of meeting of April 14, 1965, with Mayor Jesse Cutrer, SEDF; Hollander, memo of phoned reports from Bogalusa, April 13, 1965, SEDF.

53. Joel Rubenstein to Hollander, April 28, 1965, SEDF; press release April 15, 1965; Shreveport *Times,* April 13, 15, 20, 21, 1965; Baton Rouge *State Times,* April 14, 15, 19, May 20, 21, 24, 1965; Wiley, "Louisiana Situation Report," May 20, 1965, CHQ; Sam Barnes, Incident Report, May 19, 1965, Bogalusa Freedom School Prs.

54. Shreveport *Times,* May 23, 1965; press release, May 27, 1965; Washington Parish Field Report, May 15 to June 15, 1965, SEDF; Statement of A. Z. Young, May 25, 1965, Bogalusa Freedom Schools Prs.

55. Shreveport *Times,* May 29, 31, July 3, 8, 9, 18, Sept. 7, 1965; Baton Rouge *State Times,* June 1, 2, 3, July 7, 9, 15, 16, 20, 21, 22, 24, 31, Aug. 2, 5, 7, 1965; *Times,* July 9, 12, 14, 1965; *Call,* July 16, 1965; *Call and Post,* Aug. 7, 1965; WATS Line Report, July 13, 1965, SEDF; Bogalusa Civic and Voters League press release, June 3, 1965, Bogalusa Freedom School Prs. For quotations, see Baton Rouge *State Times,* July 22, 1965 (McKeithen), and July 17, 1965 (Young), and *Louisiana CORE Newsletter* [July 1965], East Feliciana CORE Prs (Moore). For support of McKeithen proposal among CORE leaders, interview.

56. Baton Rouge *State Times,* April 20, July 16, 17, 20, 27, 28, 30, 31, Aug. 2, 1965; Alan Gartner, "A Report on Bogalusa," July 22, 1965, CA; Rachlin to Collins, Douglas, and Elie, July 14, 1965, Rachlin files; *Gregory Hicks et al. vs. Claxton Hight, Jesse Cutrer et al.,* complaint, June 24, 1965, Rachlin files.

57. Untitled chronology on Bogalusa, Oct. 20, 1965, CHQ; Baton Rouge *State Times,* Aug. 5, Sept. 2, 1965; "Washington Parish Public Schools, 1964–65," CHQ; SRO press release, Oct. 26, 1965, Wiley Prs, and "List of Demands Presented to the Bogalusa School Board, 18 October, 1965," CHQ; *Wall Street Journal,* Dec. 20. 1965; SRO press release, Dec. 20, 1965, SRO; press release, Nov. 2, 1965.

58. Haley to Rich, Sept. 8, 1965, SEDF; on Ferriday, see WATS Line Reports, Concordia Parish, June 28 to July 24, 1965, SEDF; Ronnie Moore to John McKeithen, July 5, 1965, SRO; Baton Rouge *State Times,* July 28, 1965; Mel Acheson to Garry Greenberg, July 27, Aug. 17, 1963, Acheson Prs.

59. Haley to Moore, July 28, 1965, SEDF; WATS Line Reports, Iberville Parish, June 28 to Aug. 17, 1965, SEDF; Mike Lesser to Haley, Aug. 12, 1965, SRO; Hollander, "Draft Louisiana Summer '65 Brief Summary" [Sept. 1965], SEDF; Henry Brown *et al.,* Weekly Field Reports for the Felicianas, July–Aug. 1965, *passim,* East Feliciana CORE Prs.

60. WATS Line Reports, June–Aug. 1965, *passim,* SEDF; on Ferriday, see also Mel Acheson to Garry Greenberg, July 27, Aug. 17, 1965, Acheson Prs; *FFM Newsletter,* Aug. 15, 1965, Acheson Prs; "Record Book of the Ferriday Freedom Movement," July and Aug., *passim,* in Ferriday Freedom House Prs.

61. For antipoverty boards, see esp. Louisiana Community Action Program Report [ca. June or July 1965], SEDF; Louisiana WATS Line Reports, July

1965, *passim*, SRO and SEDF; Brown *et al.*, Weekly Field Reports for the Felicianas, July–Aug. 1965, East Feliciana CORE Prs; and Richard Thomson, "Final Field Report for Claiborne Parish," Oct. 14, 1965, Claiborne Parish MSS. For "Head-Start" pre-school programs, see Nancy Gilmore, compiler, "Field Report–State of Louisiana," Aug. 15, 1965 (containing quotation); Judith Fleiss and Mike Lesser to Freddie Mack [July 1965]; Minutes, Meeting of Coordinating Committee for Project Headstart in Caddo, Claiborne, and Concordia parishes, May 23, 1965, SEDF; Pam Smith, Claiborne Parish Field Report, June 21 to July 17, 1965, Claiborne Parish MSS. For detailed discussion of CORE strategy in using Headstart programs as a base for social action, see esp. "CORE Summer Project Orientation–Educational Program Workshop," June 1965, East Feliciana CORE Prs.

62. Madison Parish WATS Line Reports, May 29 to July 24, 1965, SEDF; "Louisiana Summer Project Field Report—1965," SEDF; Louisiana Community Action Program Report [ca. June or July 1965], SEDF; SRO press release, Nov. 25, 1964, CA; *Times*, Oct. 3, 1965; *Time Magazine*, VC (March 2, 1970), 17.

63. "A Petition" [July 30, 1965], SEDF; Ronnie Moore to CORE SRO, National CORE and SEDF, re: Voter Registration Campaign in 12 Parishes, Aug. 6–Sept. 1, 1965, SEDF; WATS Line Reports, Webster Parish, June 29 to Aug. 17, *passim*, SRO and SEDF; Hugh Robbins, Field Fellowship Report, July 28, 1965, SEDF; Moore, "Webster Parish Scouting Report," March 17, 1965, SRO; on Farmer and the mass march, see Baton Rouge *State Times*, Aug. 6, 7, 8, 1965; [Eddie Scott], Report on Minden [Sept. 1965], SEDF; Haley to Scott, Sept. 20, 1965, SEDF.

64. Haley to Moore, July 28, Aug. 1, 1965, SRO; Moore, Louisiana Summary Field Report, Oct. 1965 through April 1965, CA; Moore to CORE SRO, National CORE and SEDF, re: Voter Registration campaign in 12 parishes, Aug. 6 to Sept. 1, 1965, SEDF; Brown *et al.*, Reports on East Feliciana Parish, Aug. 8–15, Aug. 18–22, 1965, East Feliciana CORE Prs.

65. On West Feliciana Parish, see "The People, West Feliciana Parish" to Louis Mitchell of U. S. Civil Rights Commission, Aug. 18, 1965, SEDF; Bernice [Noflin] to Mimi Feingold, Sept. 20, 1965, in Miriam Feingold Whitman Prs; Henry Brown and Christine Wright, Reports, Oct. 5, Nov. 24, 1965, SEDF; SRO press release, Dec. 20, 1965, SRO. On New Orleans, see Hollander to Gartner, Jan. 18, 1966, and SRO press release, Jan. 25, 1966, Hollander prs; *The Douglas Statesman*, March 19, 1966 and *The Douglas Victory Special*, Feb. 12, 1966, personal file; also interviews. On Madison Parish, see SRO press release [April 1966], Hollander Prs. On St. Landry Parish, see John Zippert, Reports on St. Landry Parish, Sept. 1965 to April 1966, *passim*, SEDF, and Zippert to Callender, April 16, 1966, SEDF. On Ferriday, see the following in the Ferriday, La., Freedom House Prs: David Whatley to Robert Vann, Nov. 23, 1965; SRO press release, Nov. 23, Dec. 19, 1965, March 29, 1966; Robert Louis to Dear Sir, Nov. 28, 1965; Harris David to Whatley, Dec. 1, 1965; Concordia Parish Report, Feb. 15, 1966; John Hamilton to Haley, May 18, 25, 1966. On East Feliciana, see Henry Brown, Reports, Nov., Dec. 13, 1965, Feb. 10, April 5, June 2, 1966, all SEDF. On St. Helena, see Fred Lacey to Dear Sir, Oct. 5, 1965, SEDF; Lacey,

"Student Movement on the Schools, St. Helena Parish, Fall 1965–Winter 1966" [Feb. 1966], SEDF; Haley to John Doar, Nov. 25, 1965, SEDF; Lacey, Reports, March 8, April 22, 1966, SEDF; Ellis Howard *et al.* to John Doar, Jan. 19, 1965, East Feliciana CORE Prs; and extensive materials relative to *St. Helena Parish School Board v. Fred Lacey,* 1966, and *Fred Lacey and Bruce Baines v. State of Louisiana,* 1966, Murphy Bell Prs, reel No. 3; also Freedom Day Action Committee, untitled document listing demands on school board, Jan. 1966, Bell Prs, reel No. 3.

66. Haley to Maxine Skurka, Oct. 19, 1964, SRO, and Haley to Steve McVoy, Oct. 30, 1964, SRO; Spiver Gordon to Haley, Dec. 15, 1964, SRO; Gordon to Wiley, Jan. 15, 1965, Wiley Prs; Gordon to Haley and McCain, April 30, 1965, SRO.

67. *Gadsden County Free Press,* Aug. 22, 1964, CA; *Florida Free Press,* Oct. 9, 1964, SRO; Haley, "CORE in the South, September–December, 1964," Jan. 28, 1965, CA; *Florida Free Press,* Dec. 18, 1964, CA (for quote) and Gordon to Haley, Dec. 15, 1964, SRO.

68. Sadie Jones, Report, Jan. 1–15, 1965, SRO; *Florida Free Press,* Dec. 4, 11, 18, 1964 CA; Stuart Wechsler to Gordon and Haley, Dec. 15, 1964, SRO; On Operation Dialogue, see David ("Steve") McVoy to Gordon and Wiley, Nov. 16, 1964, CA.

69. Sadie Jones to Gordon and Haley, Nov. 18, 1964, SRO; Gordon to Haley, Nov. 25, Dec. 14, 1964, SRO; Scott McVoy to Gordon, Dec. 18, 1964, SRO; David McVoy to Gordon, Dec. 15, 1964, SRO.

70. See esp. Stuart Wechsler to Haley [April 1965], SRO, and discussion of black-white relationships in Chapter 12.

71. On restaurants, see Stu Wechsler, Report for Feb. 1–16, 1965, SRO, and Wechsler to Haley and Gordon, April 30, 1965, MLK; on schools, see Gadsden County Task Force Field Report, July 4–10, 1965, SEDF and John Due Report, July 11–25, Rachlin Files; on hospitals, see Gordon to Haley and McCain, April 30, 1965, MLK; Due to Hayden Burns, Shelton Granger *et al.,* May 14, 1965, SRO; Gadsden County Task Force to Gordon and Haley, July 3, 1965, SRO.

72. John Due, Reports, Feb. 22 to March 27, 1965, and July 11–25, 1965, Rachlin Files; Gordon to Haley, March 15, 1965, SRO; Gordon, Reports, Feb. 1–15, March 1–15, and March 15–31, 1965, MLK; Stuart Wechsler, Report, Feb. 15–28, 1965, MLK.

73. Gordon to Rich, Oct. 20, 1965, SEDF; Rich to Gordon, Nov. 3, 1965, SEDF; Rich to McKissick, May 19, 1966, SEDF; Gordon to Haley and Herb Chandler [i.e., Callender], Jan. 8, March 20, 1966, MLK; Gordon to John Doar, March 7, 1966, MLK; Ronnie Moore to Gordon, July 27, 1966, SEDF.

74. "Confidential News Letter" from Andrew Norman and Ann Singer, SEDF, Feb. 5, 1965, SEDF; Rich to SEDF Board Members, March 23, 1966, SEDF; on NAACP's reaction, see McCain to National CORE and staff, April 28, 1965, SEDF.

75. McCain to National CORE and SEDF, rec'd July 23, 1965, SEDF; press

release, Aug. 3, 1965; statistics from "1965 SEDF South Carolina Voter Registration Report" [Jan. 1966], SEDF.

76. McCain to CORE and SEDF [Oct. 1965], and Nov. 6, 1965, SEDF; Henry Di Suevero to John Doar, Oct. 18, 1965, SEDF; Wiley, Report on South Carolina Trip, Nov. 21–22, 1965, Wiley Prs; Rich, Report of SEDF Executive Director, April 1, 1965, to March 15, 1966, SEDF.

77. Wiley, Report on South Carolina Trip, Nov. 21–22, 1965, Wiley Prs; McCain to CORE and SEDF [Jan. 1966], SEDF; Robert Stover, "Resume of the South Carolina Voter Registration Project," Feb. 1966, in Rich to SEDF Board Members, March 23, 1966, SEDF; McCain to SEDF and National CORE, March 14, 1966, Curvin Prs; McCain to Rich, May 21, 1966; "South Carolina Democratic Primary," June 1966, SEDF; McCain, untitled manuscript [Nov. 1966], SEDF.

78. List of chapters, prepared for the 1965 Convention, personal file, and Minutes of the NAC afternoon session, June 30, 1965, CA.

79. Mike Lesser to McCain, Jan. 25, 1965, Curvin Prs; on Cincinnati, see also Robert Gore to Cincinnati CORE Executive Board [Sept. 1964], MLK; on Columbus, interviews, and Marlene Wilson to Maxine Skurka, May 12, 1965, MLK; *Argus,* Dec. 11, 1964; Callender to Lou Smith, Nov. 4, 1964, MLK.

80. Reynolds to McCain, April 29, 1965, WCO; Smith to Farmer *et al.,* May 3, 1965, CA; San Diego CORE membership lists, Sept. 21, 1964, and Feb. 17, 1965, MLK; Berkeley CORE membership list, May 1965, Genevieve Hughes Prs; interviews for Seattle; "Bruce" to Lois Rogers, March 2, 1965, WCO; Callender to Lincoln Lynch, May 2, 1966, SEDF.

81. Philadelphia *CORE-lator,* Dec. 1964 to Jan. 1965, CA; New York *Amsterdam News,* Jan. 23, 1965; Joyce Ware, Report on Downtown CORE, Jan. 28, 1965, MLK, and Clora Coleman to Wiley, Oct. 20, 1965, MLK; Ed Day to McCain, Oct. 9, 1964, MLK; list of Syracuse CORE members, March 1965, MLK; and John L. McDowell to Syracuse CORE members [July 1965], MLK.

82. On Boston, interviews; Walter Brooks to Joyce Ware, Oct. 21, 1965, CHQ; Brooks to Callender [Jan. 1966], Wiley Prs. For New Haven, see New Haven membership list, March 1965; Brooks to Virginia Louis [Jan. 1966], and Naomi Burns to Dear Friend, April 22, 1966, all in Robert and Mimi Abramovitz Prs. On Chicago, see Callender to McKissick and Lynch, May 2, 1966, CA.

83. Louis Smith to Farmer *et al.,* May 3, 1965, MLK; scattered data in MLK plus NAC Minutes, June 30, 1965, CA.

84. See below for discussions of campaigns; on Detroit membership, see chapter membership lists, Oct. 1, 1964, and Oct. 1, 1965, both MLK.

85. Quotations from Washington *Afro-American,* Aug. 28, 1965; Donald Roberts, chairman, Detroit CORE, to Chapter Chairmen, April 20, 1965, WCO; Tony Perot, "What is Community Organization," in *Cleveland CORE News* [late 1964], David Cohen Prs; Western Regional Convention, Nov. 27–29, 1964, WCO.

86. For Denver, see "Project–Denver, Colorado Freedom House" [1964], MLK; Denver *Post,* Nov. 16, 1964, and Robert De Luxe to Ronnie Moore, Sept.

30, 1965, MLK. For Kansas City, see Carl Randolph and Lela Shank to McCain, Nov. 14, 1964, MLK; NAC and Staff Meeting, June 29, 1965, CA. On Chicago, see Robert Gore to Wiley, Jan. 27, 1965, MLK; McCain to Bookkeeping, Oct. 1, 1964, MLK; McCain Diaries, Nov. 21–25, 1964, McCain Prs; "National CORE Staff Meetings, November–December [1965]," MLK; Charles Smith to Wiley, April 23, 1965, MLK; "Chicago CORE Information Service," April–May 1965, Faith Rich Prs; Beth Wise, "Report from the Southside CORE Freedom Center, July–August, 1965," Faith Rich Prs. For Columbus, interviews.

87. New York CORE, Report to 1965 Convention, CA; on Newark, interviews; *St. Louis Review,* May 21, 1965, MLK and Bob Gore to McCain, Dec. 1, 1964, MLK; Los Angeles *Sentinel,* Sept. 16, 1965; on Philadelphia, see press release, Jan. 7, 1965, and James Williams to Lou Smith, Dec. 14, 1964, MLK; Long Island CORE press release, Aug. 26, 1965, MLK; Joyce Ware, Report on Downtown CORE, Jan. 28, 1965, MLK; on Prince George's County, see press release, Dec. 17, 1964, and the following in the Marian Merrill Prs; flyer, "Poverty in Prince George's County" [Dec. 1964], and offprint from Baltimore *Evening Sun,* "The Story of Cedar Heights," Oct. 14, 1964.

88. *CORE Scores,* II (Feb. 1966), MLK, for Long Island; William Ellis, "Operation Bootstrap: A Case Study in Ideology and the Institutionalization of Protest" (Ph.D. dissertation, University of California at Los Angeles, 1969), *passim.*

89. On Detroit, see Detroit *Free Press,* May 29, 1965; *Chronicle,* June 5, 12, 1965; Detroit CORE press releases, Feb. 10, 27, 1965, Ralph Rosenfeld Prs. For Rochester, see Anthony Riley to Farmer, March 1, 1965, Rachlin files; Wiley to Max Greenberg, April 15, 1965, CHQ; Wiley to NAC, May 5, 1965, Curvin Prs; Wiley to All Department Heads, May 27, 1965, CHQ; interview. On Boston, interviews and materials in Jewish Memorial Hospital Folder, May to July 1966, Phyllis Ryan Prs; on Baltimore, see Louis Goldberg, "CORE in Trouble: A Social History of the Organizational Dilemmas of the Congress of Racial Equality Target City Project in Baltimore (1965–1967)" (Ph.D. dissertation, Johns Hopkins University, 1970), 17, 24, and chap. II.

90. Wiley, quoted in press release, Nov. 8, 1965; Farmer to Sargent Shriver, Aug. 12, 1965, MLK.

91. For Buffalo, see press release, Feb. 25, 1965. For Los Angeles, see *Times,* May 29, 1965. For Cleveland, see *Cleveland CORE News,* Feb. 1965, UC; undated clipping CHQ; Rich to Ruth Turner, Jan. 29, 1965, CA; press release, Nov. 8, 1965. For Columbus, interviews. For San Francisco, Ralph Kramer, *Participation of the Poor: Comparative Case Studies in the War on Poverty* (Englewood Cliffs, 1969), 25–30, 33–34.

92. Mike Lesser to McCain, Nov. 18, 1964, MLK; Newark *Evening News,* Aug. 20, 1965, clipping, CHQ; press release, Feb. 25, 1965.

93. Kramer, *Participation of the Poor,* 38–41; *Cleveland CORE News,* Feb. 1965, UC.

94. Interviews; NAC, April 10–11, 1965, CA.

95. For excellent discussion on this point, see Harry Brill, "Black Militancy: A Case Study in Ego Politics" (Ph.D. dissertation, University of California at Berkeley, 1969), 40–48.

96. *Rhode Island CORE News* [July 1965], MLK; Ruth Turner, "Politics and the Future of the Civil Rights Movement," and Tony Perot, "What is Community Organization?" in *Cleveland CORE News* [late 1964], David Cohen Prs; "CORE National Convention . . . Constitutional Changes," July 1965, CHQ.

97. Bergen County CORE newsletter [Nov. 1964], MLK; press release, Nov. 19, 1964; and the following in Phyllis Ryan Prs: CAPE press releases, Sept. 11, 17, 24, Oct. 29, Nov. 2, 1964; James Breeden to Dear Friend, Oct. 31, 1964; and clipping from *Christian Science Monitor,* Nov. 5, 1964.

98. *Times,* April 17, 1965; Joyce Ware to City-Wide CORE Chapters, May 12, 1965, CHQ; New York Area CORE chapters, untitled paper, Aug. 30, 1965, CHQ; New York *Amsterdam News,* May 1, Sept. 4, 11, 1965; Brooklyn *Amsterdam News,* Aug. 14, 1965; "Brooklyn CORE—1965—A Brief Review" [ca. June 1965], personal file; Northeast Regional Action Council Minutes, Nov. 13, 1965, Curvin Prs.

99. Interviews; clippings on Richardson and United Freedom Ticket, Newark *Evening News,* April 22 and Sept. to Nov. 1965, *passim,* courtesy of *Evening News* reporter, Douglas Eldridge.

100. Cleveland *Plain Dealer,* Aug. 27, Sept. 11, 19, 27, 1965; *Call and Post,* Aug. 28, Sept. 18, 1965; Ruth Turner to Dear Friend, Oct. 10, 1965, MLK.

101. Cincinnati *Enquirer,* Oct. 29, 30, 1965; *Call and Post,* Nov. 20, Dec. 4, 1965; North Central Regional Action Council Meeting, Feb. 4–6, 1966, MLK; Cincinnati CORE newsletter, Nov. 6, 1965, MLK.

102. Louis Smith, untitled memo to Northeast Regional Office, Feb. 17, 1965, MLK; *Afro-American,* Jan. 19, March 30, April 6, May 11, June 15, July 13, Aug. 24, Oct. 5, Nov. 2, Dec. 14, 1965, and *Times,* April 10–11, 1965; Washington *Post,* Jan. 19, 22, April 29, Sept. 9, 1965.

103. St. Louis *Post-Dispatch,* Aug. 26, Sept. 16, 1965; Callender to Louis Smith, Nov. 4, 1964, MLK; Detroit *News,* May 16, 1965; Brooklyn *Amsterdam News,* July 25, Nov. 28, 1964, July 31, 1965; *Times,* Aug. 20, 1965.

104. Seattle *Post-Intelligencer,* July 11, 21, 25, Aug. 5, 1965, and Seattle *CORE-lator,* Aug. 1965, CHQ; *Sentinel,* Sept. 3, Nov. 25, 1965; undated materials regarding Newark patrolman, Rachlin files and Newark *Evening News,* July 22, 30, Aug. 14, 1965, and personal observations.

105. Gene Schulze to Maxine Skurka, April 6, 1965, MLK; New Haven *Journal-Courier,* April 29, May 11, 1965; New Haven *Register,* May 10, 11, Oct. 6, 1965; various materials in the Robert and Mimi Abramovitz Prs, March to May 1965, including Minutes of CORE Meeting with New Haven Redevelopment Agency, March 6, 1965, and Minutes of CORE Meeting with Mayor Richard Lee, April 8, 1965.

106. Press release, June 10, 1965, and Denver *Post,* June 6, 1965; Newark *Star-Ledger,* Sept. 9, 1965 and Newark *Evening News,* Sept. 30, 1965, clippings in CHQ; Long Island CORE clipping books, May 12, Aug. 30, Sept. 14, 28, Oct. 25, 1965.

107. Interviews; press release, June 10, 1965; undated CORE [Detroit] Tenant Notice [early 1965], Gloria Brown Prs; Detroit *News,* April 5, May 27,

1965; Detroit *Free Press,* May 17, 28, 1965; Detroit CORE, *Tenant Council News,* June 4, 1965, Ralph Rosenfeld Prs; Minutes, Detroit CORE Membership Meeting, July 7, 1965, Brown Prs; *Chronicle,* Aug. 15, 1964, March 13, April 24, 1965; Detroit CORE, *The Newspaper,* Feb. 21, 1966, Gloria Brown Prs; Leither Barnes and Clyde Cleveland to George Romney, Oct. 28, 1966, Brown Prs.

108. Boston *Corespondent,* Nov. 29, 1965, Richard Brown Prs.

109. St. Louis *Post-Dispatch,* Aug. 28, 1965; Southern Alameda County *CORE-lator,* May and June 1965, MLK; clippings in Long Island CORE clipping books, Jan. 30, Feb. 8, Feb. 9, 1965; Baltimore Housing Committee Newsletter, rec'd Aug. 25, 1965, CHQ; McCain to NAC, Oct. 21, 1965, MLK; *Afro-American,* June 15, July 27, Aug. 17, 31, Oct. 12, Nov. 2, 1965; Louis Goldberg, "CORE in Trouble: A Social History of the Organizational Dilemmas of the Congress of Racial Equality Target City Project in Baltimore (1965–1967)" (Ph.D. dissertation, Johns Hopkins University, 1970), 9, 59–61, 86–89.

110. *Times,* June 6, 1965; *Defender,* June 12–18, Aug. 7–13, 1965, and *Times,* June 13, July 11, 1965; Seattle *Post-Intelligencer,* Feb. 20, March 31, April 1 and 2, 1966; "Do You Want Action on School Integration?" [1966], Frances White Prs; Seattle CORE Minutes, Feb. 17, April 28, 1966, Seattle CORE Prs.

111. Boston CORE press release, April 13, 1965, Richard Brown Prs; Louise Cameron to Brown, March 1, 1965, and "A" to Brown, July 12, 1965, Brown Prs; "Memorandum" [Jan. 1966], MLK; interviews.

112. *Chronicle,* Aug. 15, 22, Sept. 26, Oct. 3, 10, 1964; Detroit CORE press releases, Sept. 27, Oct. 1, 1964, Gloria Brown Prs; Detroit *Free Press,* Oct. 31, Nov. 21, 28, Dec. 5, 1964; Farmer to G. B. Phillips, Oct. 7, 1964, Curvin Prs; undated Fact Sheet on AAA, Ralph Rosenfeld Prs; interviews.

113. *Argus,* Jan. 28, April 16, June 25, Dec. 3, 10, 24, 1965, Jan. 14, Feb. 4, 18, 25, March 11, 1966; North Central Regional Action Council Minutes, Feb. 4–6, 1966, MLK.

114. San Francisco *CORE-lator,* Dec. 1964, March 1965, WCO; San Francisco *Chronicle,* Nov. 21, Dec. 16, 24, 1964; leaflet, "Why Boycott Sears" [Feb. 1965], WCO.

115. Virginia Burton and Lawrence Gurley to Dear Sir, Nov. 5, 1964, UC; Larry [Gurley] to "Ginger" [Sept. 1964], CA; interviews.

116. Northeast Regional Headquarters to Chapter Chairmen, Oct. 7, 1964, MLK; Northeastern Regional Office press release, Dec. 17, 1964, MLK; *Afro-American,* Nov. 24, 1964; Philadelphia *Inquirer,* Dec. 31, 1964; *Tribune,* Jan. 9, 12, 19, 23, 1965; Philadelphia *Evening Bulletin,* Jan. 6, 1965; materials relating to *NAACP and Safeway Trails vs. CORE and Williams et al.,* Jan. 1965, Rachlin files; James O. Williams to Smith, Jan. 24, 1965, MLK; Philadelphia *CORE-lator,* Dec. 1964–Jan. 1965, CHQ; Eric Mann to Smith, Jan. 18, 1965, Curvin Prs.

117. Berkeley Campus *CORE-lator,* April 21, 1965, Robert Starobin Prs; Berkeley CORE newsletter, May 1965, MLK; interviews.

118. Cincinnati *Enquirer,* July 27, Aug. 5, 10–14, 26, 27, 1965; Cincinnati

CORE newsletter, Nov. 6, 1965, CHQ; Cincinnati *Post and Times-Star,* July 28, Aug. 13, 1965, clippings in CHQ; *Call and Post,* July 31, Oct. 9, 1965.

119. Charles Valentine, "DEEDS: Background and Basis. A Report on Research Leading to the Drive for Equal Employment in Downtown Seattle," Oct. 1964, Edward Singler Prs; Seattle *Post-Intelligencer,* Aug. 13, Oct. 17, 24, Nov. 26, 1964; Seattle *Daily Times,* Oct. 6, 19, 25, 1964, Jan. 13, 1965; Seattle *CORE-lator,* Feb. 1965, CA, and [Sept. 1965], CHQ; Walter Hundley to Peck, March 18, 1965, Seattle CORE Prs; final quotation from Seattle *CORE-lator,* Feb. 1965.

120. Fern [Freel] to Wiley, Jan. 20, 1965, Wiley Prs; "Comprehensive Report—Niagara Mohawk Happenings to April 1965," April 1965, Wiley Prs; *Times,* April 30, June 19, 1965; Press release, June 17, 1965; Faith Seidenberg to Rich, May 25, 1965, SEDF; Civil Rights Foundation of Syracuse, "Fact Sheet in Niagara Mohawk-CORE Matter" [late 1965], Wiley Prs; Wiley, untitled memorandum, Dec. 29, 1965, Wiley Prs; J. J. Ehlinger, vice-president, Niagara Mohawk Power Corporation to Elliott Rudwick, Aug. 12, 1971, enclosing copy of G. V. Watters, executive vice president Niagara Mohawk to Ralph Kharas, Oct. 28, 1965.

CHAPTER TWELVE

1. Interviews; Louis Smith to Northeast Regional Office, Feb. 17, 1965, MLK.

2. Interviews. On Baltimore, see also Louis Goldberg, "CORE in Trouble: A Social History of the Organizational Dilemmas of the Congress of Racial Equality Target City Project in Baltimore (1965–1967)," (Ph.D. dissertation, Johns Hopkins University, 1970), 97. On Columbus, see also Mike Lesser to James McCain, Oct. 15, Nov. 18, 1964, MLK; Lesser, Report to Columbus CORE Executive Committee, Sept. 15, 1964, MLK. On Detroit, see also *Chronicle,* Nov. 6, 1965.

3. Leonard Ball, "Urban CORE: A View from Cincinnati," in Columbia University CORE, *The Movement* [Spring 1965], UC.

4. Le Faucette to McCain, Nov. 9, 1964, MLK; Berkeley Campus *CORE-lator,* April 21, 1965, Robert Starobin Prs; untitled document regarding Syracuse CORE [1965], MLK; interviews; Farmer, Report to 1965 Convention, printed in August Meier, Elliott Rudwick, and Francis Broderick, eds., *Black Protest Thought in the Twentieth Century,* rev. ed. (Indianapolis, 1971), 463.

5. Interview.

6. *Times,* Nov. 17, 1964; Clarence Funnyé, "New Directions for the Civil Rights Movement," Nov. 16, 1964, MLK; Funnyé, "Outline of a Demonstration Project to Devise Methods for Deghettoization of Harlem," Oct. 1964, MLK; New York CORE, Report to the 1965 Convention, CA See also Funnyé "Deghettoization," *Architectural Forum,* CXXX (April 1969), 74–77.

7. Interviews; on the black male caucus, see also Alex Poinsett, "Roy Innis: Nation-Builder," *Ebony,* XXIV (Oct. 1969), 173.

8. Interview.

9. Interview; Marlene Wilson to Floyd McKissick, Jan. 17, 1966, MLK.

10. Interviews; *Brooklyn CORE's Action* [title sic], Dec. 1, 1964, Ollie Leeds

Prs; William Gellerman, "My CORE Program Experience and Some Ideas on Training with Civil Rights Organizations," Oct. 1965, SEDF.

11. Interviews; JoAnn Ooiman to Martha, Sally and Arlene, Oct. 2, 1964, JoAnn Ooiman Robinson Prs; San Fernando Valley CORE, "Activities, Needs, and General Progress, June–July, 1965," Wiley Prs; and Robert Bailey, "Why My Chapter Failed," Nov. 27, 1965, Genevieve Hughes Houghton Prs; Diane Callaghan to ? [Dec. 1964], WCO.

12. Interviews.

13. Interviews; for Prince George's County, see Herbert Callender to Joyce Ware [Aug. 1965], CHQ.

14. Interviews.

15. Interviews; on Pittsburgh, see Louis Smith, Report [Oct. 1964], CHQ.

16. Interviews.

17. San Francisco *Chronicle*, April 17, 18, May 13, 14, 27, June 2, 4, 9, 13, July 14, 15, 16, 31, Aug. 1, Dec. 23, 1964; A. Lenske and S. Shumer, "A Fact Sheet on the Injustices in the San Francisco Civil Rights Cases," July 8, 1964, WCO; *Sentinel*, July 16, 1964; Berkeley Campus *CORE-lator*, Sept. 1964; "The San Francisco Civil Rights Trials, Prepared by Committee for Justice in Civil Rights Cases," July 18, 1964, Starobin Prs; William Barlow and Peter Shapiro, *An End to Silence: The San Francisco State College Student Movement in the Sixties* (New York, 1971), 47–48. On failure of hotels to live up to agreement due to union resistance, see *Times*, July 24, Nov. 29, 1966.

18. Interviews; Walter Riley to Farmer and McKissick, May 30, 1965, CHQ; "Minutes of Education Conference on Urban Problems," May 18–22, 1967, CHQ.

19. Interviews.

20. Interviews; on court actions and jail sentences, see San Diego *Union*, Sept. 2, 15, 1964, Feb. 20, Oct. 30, 1965; for Brown's response to repeal to Rumford Act, see Brown, "Major Position Paper—CORE Reaction to Passage of Proposition 14" [Nov. 1964], WCO.

21. Brown to McCain, Jan. 25, Feb. 20, 1965, MLK; Ambrose Broadus to McCain, Feb. 19, 1965, MLK; Frederick Cawley to CORE, Feb. 25, 1965, MLK; Mildred Gustafson to McCain, Feb. 27, 1965, MLK; John Porter to Brown, March 11, 1965, CHQ; Rosemary Laws *et al.* to McKissick, March 29, 1965, CHQ; Smith to McCain, Wiley, McKissick, Farmer *et al.*, March 29, 1965, CHQ; Porter to Carl Rachlin, Aug. 2, 1965, CHQ; interviews.

22. Callender to Joyce Ware [Aug. 1965], MLK; exhibit prepared by a faction of Dayton chapter, entitled "Inside Dayton CORE," and other extensive materials on Dayton controversy, 1963–64, CA; interviews for Long Island CORE; and on Cincinnati: Lesser to McCain, Nov. 2, 1964, MLK, and Minutes, North Central Regional Action Council, Feb. 4–6, 1966, MLK.

23. Interviews; on National CORE's concern about Trotskyists in Cleveland, see also Steering Committee, Jan. 24, 1964, CA; on chapter election, see also Lesser to McCain, Sept. 9, 1964, MLK; on school board picketing, see *Call and Post*, May 8, 1965; on opening of Freedom House, see *Call and Post*, Oct. 9, 1965.

24. R. Hunter Morey, "Crossroads in COFO," Dec. 3, 1964, Morey Prs; Minutes, Fourth District Staff Meeting, Jan. 15–17, 1965, JoAnn Ooiman Robinson Prs; Martin Fassler, Report to CORE-SEDF [Sept. 1965], SEDF; Beverly Lee, Field Fellowship Report, June 27, 1965, Bogalusa Freedom House Prs.

25. Ronnie Moore, Field Report, Jan. 19, 1965, CA; Dave Dennis to Marvin Rich, March 18, 1965, SEDF; Dennis to Southern Staff [1965], SRO; [Dennis], "Report on Recruitment," May 18, 1965, SRO; *Times,* Aug. 15, 1965.

26. David "Steve" McVoy to Haley, Dec. 28, 1964, Jan. 18, 1965, SRO; Moore to Haley, May 17, 1965, SRO; Haley to Henry Amos, telegram, May 25, 1965, SRO.

27. NAC Closed Session, April 10–11, 1965, Robert Curvin Prs.

28. James Peck to Farmer, July 27, 1965, CA, and Dec. 6, 1965, MLK.

29. NAC Closed Session, April 10–11, 1965, Curvin Prs; Wiley to NAC, April 22, 1965, CHQ; Peck to Farmer, Dec. 6, 1965, MLK.

30. George Raymond *et al.* to Farmer [June 1965], CA; see also Haley, "Comments on the Petition submitted by Task Force to James Farmer and NAC" [June 1965], CA; 1965 Convention, CA; NAC, July 7, 1965, CA.

31. Wiley's remarks in NAC, Feb. 6–7, 1965, CA; Haley, "The Proposed Southern Program to Begin in Autumn, 1964," [Sept. 1964] SRO; see also Haley, "CORE in the South, (September-December, 1964)," Jan. 28, 1965, CA.

32. Interviews; for quotation from Moses, see Payne, "SNCC: An Overview Two Years Later," 97.

33. Interviews; Rudy Lombard, "NAC Retreat" [Oct. 1964], CA; Dennis remarks in 1965 Convention, CA, and in NAC and Staff Meeting, June 29, 1965, CA.

34. Interviews.

35. McKissick to NAC, Jan. 8, 1965, Curvin Prs.

36. Steering Committee, Jan. 15, 1965, CA; interviews; Farmer to Lyndon Johnson, "Proposal for Implementing a National Literacy Program," Feb. 5, 1965, MLK.

37. Rich to Alfred Hassler, Nov. 12, 1964, CA; Bayard Rustin, "Nonviolence on Trial," *Fellowship Magazine,* XXX (July 1964), 8.

38. Mel Acheson to "Hi-y'all," July 30, 1965, Acheson Prs.

39. *Times,* June 6, 1965.

40. Haley, Memo on CORE-Deacon Relationships [June 1965], SRO. On overlapping officers of Voters League and Deacons in Bogalusa, see *Times,* July 9, 1965; *Afro-American,* April 13, 1965; *Wall Street Journal,* July 12, 1965. On Deacons' outlook and methods, see interview with Charles Sims in Joanne Grant, ed., *Black Protest* (New York, 1968), 357–65.

41. NAC, Feb. 6–7, 1965, CA; Joanne Ooiman to Richard Haley, June 6, 1965, SEDF; Haley, memo on CORE-Deacon Relationships [June 1965], SRO.

42. *Times,* June 10, 1965; Personal observations at convention. For Farmer making point about constitutional right to self-defense, see also, for example, *Chronicle,* May 22, 1965, and Transcript of News Conference of Farmer, McKissick, and Wiley, June 30, 1965, CA.

43. *Tribune,* July 17, 1965; *Chronicle,* July 17, 1965; Farmer to Jackie Robin-

son, Aug. 31, 1965, CHQ; Farmer, letter to editor, published in *Call and Post,* July 17, 1965.

44. Long Island CORE clippings books, Feb. 18, June 14, 1965; Moore to Rich, Aug. 8, 1966, SEDF; Brooklyn CORE, Proposed Resolutions for 1965 Convention, June 1965, personal file; Northeast Regional Action Council, Proposed Resolutions for 1965 Convention, June 26, 1965, Curvin Prs.

45. Berkeley Campus *CORE-lator,* Sept. 9, 1965, UC; Louis Smith, "Watts: Burning of the American Dream," *idem;* press release, Aug. 17, 1965.

46. Haley to CORE Staff, Nov. 23, 1965, Monroe, La., CORE MSS; SRO press release, Aug. 23, 1965, MLK.

47. *Times,* July 2, 1965; personal observations.

48. *Times,* July 5, 1965; financial documents distributed at convention, CHQ.

49. Interviews. For public announcement of Farmer's resignation to assume direction of literacy program, see *Times,* Dec. 28, 1965, and *Afro-American,* Dec. 28, 1965.

50. NAC and Staff Meeting, June 30, 1965, CA; 1965 Convention, CA; personal observations.

51. 1965 Convention, CA; personal observations.

52. *Times,* July 4, 1965.

53. NAC and Staff Meeting, June 29, 1965, CA; 1965 Convention, CA.

54. NAC, July 6, 1965, CA.

55. NAC, June 29, 1965, CA; Peck to Farmer, July 27, 1965, CA, and Nov. 11, 1965, MLK.

56. 1965 Convention, CA; "CORE National Convention . . . Constitutional Changes," 1965, CHQ; personal observations.

57. Interviews.

58. 1965 Convention, CA; *Times,* July 6, 1965; personal observations. See also Brooklyn CORE Proposed Resolutions for 1965 Convention, June 1965, personal file; Northeast Regional Action Council, proposed resolutions for 1965 Convention, June 26, 1965, Curvin Prs; Lincoln Lynch to Julian Bond, May 22, 1966, CHQ. On Farmer's opposition to the war, see also Farmer, "The CORE of It," New York *Amsterdam News,* Oct. 30, 1965.

59. McCain to NAC, Oct. 21, 1965, CA. Ussery comments in NAC, Dec. 31, 1965 to Jan. 2, 1966, CA.

60. Eugene Nadler, "Organizational Consequences of CORE's Changing Mission" [1965], SEDF; NAC, Dec. 31, 1965, to Jan. 2, 1966, CA; Northeast Regional Council Minutes, Aug. 14, 1965, Curvin Prs; for quotation from Bradley, see San Diego *Union,* Jan. 31, 1965.

61. Turner quoted in NAC, Dec. 31, 1965 to Jan. 2, 1966, CA; Ware and Rand in Minutes, Northeast Regional Action Council, Aug. 14, 1965, Curvin Prs; Farmer in Cleveland *Plain Dealer,* Oct. 13, 1965; Wiley in Hobart Burch, "A Conversation with George Wiley," *The Journal,* IX (Nov.–Dec. 1970) 10.

62. For a discussion of this point, see William Gellerman, "My CORE Program Experience and Some Ideas About Training with Civil Rights Organizations," Oct. 1965, SEDF.

63. NAC, Dec. 31, 1965 to Jan. 2, 1966, CA; Wilson to McKissick, Jan. 17, 1966, MLK; interviews.

64. Wilson to McKissick, Jan. 17, 1966, MLK; Cathy Rosen to Wilfred Ussery, Jan. 18, 1966, CHQ; Lesser to Callender, Feb. 28, 1966, SEDF; Callender to McKissick and Lynch, May 2, 1966, SEDF; Moore to Rich, Aug. 8, 1966, SEDF; Northeast Regional Action Council Minutes, Jan. 29, 1966, Curvin Prs; Midwest Regional Action Council Minutes, Feb. 4–6, 1966, CA; Louis Smith, Memo to Western Region CORE Chapters, Subject: Minutes of Regional Convention, May 21–22, 1966, MLK. On NAC voting salary increase, see NAC, Dec. 31, 1965, to Jan. 2, 1966, CA.

65. *Times,* Jan. 5, 1966; Mike Lesser, "The Movement—Where It's At, and Where We (CORE) Are In It," paper delivered at Midwest Regional Action Council Meeting, Feb. 4–6, CHQ; Herbert Callender to Lesser, Feb. 18, 1966, Curvin Prs; Alan Gartner to NAC, March 4, 1966, Farmer Prs; Callender to Richard Haley, March 8, 1966, Edward Hollander Prs; Hollander to Charlie Currier, April 20, 1966, Hollander Prs; Dennis to CORE National Office, April 30, 1966, MLK; Haley to McKissick, May 24, 1966, CHQ; Moore to Rich, Aug. 8, 1966, SEDF. Also interviews.

EPILOGUE

1. *Defender,* Jan. 15–21, 1966; *CORE-lator,* [late 1966], CHQ.

2. *CORE-lator* [late 1966], CHQ; "The State of the Organization" [Spring 1966], CHQ; Herbert Callender to Floyd McKissick and Lincoln Lynch, May 2, 1966, CHQ; *Breaking the Noose* [1966] (pamphlet on Target City Project), CHQ; Callender to McKissick, "Proposed Budget for Baltimore Project" [1966], Marvin Rich Prs; *Afro-American,* March 29, April 26, June 14, July 5, 12, 1966; Minutes of Baltimore Target City Project Board of Directors, 1966–67, *passim,* CHQ; "Report on Financial and Organizational Crisis" [May 1967], CHQ; McKissick to NAC, May 9, 1967, CHQ; Lynch to McKissick, May 14, 1967, CHQ; McKissick to Walter Brooks, May 18, 1967, CHQ; NAC, May 20, 1967, CHQ; Louis Goldberg, "CORE in Trouble: A Social History of the Organizational Dilemmas of the Congress of Racial Equality Target City Project in Baltimore (1965–1967)" (Ph.D. dissertation, Johns Hopkins University, 1970), *passim.*

3. Callender to McKissick, NAC and staff [Jan. 1967], George Wiley Prs; Callender to Chapter Chairmen, Jan. 27, 1966, Robert Curvin Prs; Callender to McKissick, NAC and Department Heads, March 18, 1966, Curvin Prs; Callender to McKissick and Lynch, May 2, 1966, SEDF; Minutes, CORE Western Regional Convention, Sept. 3–4, 1966, WCO.

4. McKissick to Marlene Wilson, Feb. 3, 1966, MLK; NAC, March 18–20, 1966, MLK; Lynch to Curvin, April 29, 1966, Curvin Prs.

5. For varying estimates made by CORE leaders, ranging from about $250,-000 to $600,000, see "The State of the Organization" [Spring 1966], CHQ; Draft Minutes, 1966 Convention, CHQ; *Times,* March 2, July 25, 1966.

6. NAC, March 18–20, 1966, MLK; Lynch to McKissick, May 3, 1966, CHQ;

Lynch to Curvin, April 29, 1966, Curvin Prs; Baltimore *Sun,* July 3, 1966; Curvin to Rich, July 11, 1966, Rich Prs; interviews.

7. Press release, Feb. 9, 1966, CHQ; *Times,* Feb. 9, 1966; Statement of Synagogue Council of America, Feb. 10, 1966, Curvin Prs; Carl Rachlin to Shad Polier, Feb. 10, 1966, Rachlin Files.

8. Lynch, quoted in ⋅ *Times,* July 25, 1966; Rich to Richard Haley, Feb. 11, 1966, SEDF; Rachlin to Robert Drinan, March 3, 1966, Rachlin Files; NAC, March 18–20, 1966, MLK.

9. On this whole question of the growing rupture between CORE and SEDF, see SEDF Board Minutes, March 23, May 17, 1966, SEDF; Andrew Norman to Rich, Jan. 23, 1966, SEDF; McKissick to Rich, March 25, 1966, SEDF; Alan Gartner to McKissick, March 2, 1966, CHQ; Rich to McKissick, April 13, 1966, Rich Prs; Rich to SEDF Staff, May 18, 1966, SEDF; NAC, March 18–20 and Sept. 10–11, 1966, MLK; Rachlin to McKissick, Nov. 23, 1966, Rachlin Files; Rich to McKissick, Dec. 16, 29, 1966, SEDF; McKissick to Rich, Dec. 19, 1966, SEDF; McKissick to Rachlin, Feb. 8, 1967, Rachlin Files; Norman to McKissick, Feb. 27, 1967, Rachlin Files; Rachlin to McKissick, March 3, 1967, Rachlin Files.

10. *Times,* June 13, 15, 16, 1966; National CORE office to CORE chapters, re: Meredith March [June 1966], CHQ; "Minutes of Meeting of Meredith March—Lorraine [sic] Motel," June 10, 1966, CHQ; "McKissick Statement on Meredith Shooting," June 6, 1966, CHQ; McKissick to CORE Friends, June 20, 1966; quotation from McKissick, "Speech for Meredith Freedom March Rally," June 26, 1966, CHQ.

11. For discussions of SNCC, see Howard Zinn, *SNCC: The New Abolitionists* (Boston, 1964); Lerone Bennett, "SNCC: Rebels with a Cause," *Ebony,* XX (July 1965), 146–53; Emily Stoper, "Student Nonviolent Coordinating Committee: The Growth of Radicalism in a Civil Rights Organization" (Ph.D. dissertation, Harvard University, 1968); Bruce Payne, "SNCC: An Overview Two Years Later," in Mitchell Cohen and Dennis Hale, eds., *The New Student Left* (Boston, 1966), 86–103; Allen Matusow, "From Civil Rights to Black Power: The Case of SNCC, 1960–1966," in Barton Bernstein and Allen Matusow, eds., *Twentieth Century America: Recent Interpretations* (New York, 1969), 531–36; Gene Roberts, "From Freedom High to 'Black Power,' " *New York Times Magazine,* Sept. 25, 1966.

12. See Minutes of CORE Southern Staff Conference, New Orleans, Feb. 6–7, 1966, MLK, for varied views among staff concerning accepting compromise.

13. 1966 Convention, Ollie Leeds Prs; Curvin to Rich, July 11, 1966, Rich Prs; C. A. Valentine, Notes on "Resolutions Put Forward at the CORE National Convention, Baltimore, 4 July, 1966," Edward Singler Prs; Baltimore *Sun,* July 5, 1966; *Times,* July 2, 5, 1966; interviews.

14. Baltimore *Sun,* July 3, 5, 1966; *Times,* July 3, 1966; Draft Minutes for 1966 Convention, CHQ; "Report of Elections at CORE National Convention, July 4, 1966," with notes taken at convention by Valentine, Singler Prs.

15. *Times,* Jan. 9, 1966; Minutes, Northeastern Regional Action Council, April 23, 1966, Curvin Prs; Baltimore *Sun,* July 5, 1966, and *Times,* July 5,

1966; McKissick, unsigned memorandum [Aug. 1966], CHQ; Alvin Simon, "Black Power and Cambodia: A Dialog with Floyd B. McKissick," *American Dialog,* III (Nov.–Dec. 1966), 17.

16. Copy of Convention Resolutions in C. A. Valentine, Notes on "Resolutions Put Forward at the CORE National Convention, Baltimore, 4 July, 1966," Singler Prs.

17. McKissick, *Genocide USA: A Blueprint for Black Survival* (New York, 1967); San Diego *Union,* Nov. 8, 1967.

18. McKissick, "McKissick Offers Resolutions and Programs," July 31, 1967, MLK; McKissick, *Constructive Militancy: A Philosophy and a Program* (New York, [1967]), 4–5; Baltimore *Sun,* July 3, 1966; Steering Committee, Aug. 16, 1966, MLK; Oakland *Tribune,* June 30, 1967; *Wall Street Journal,* April 5, May 21, 1968; McKissick's Remarks to Chicago Freedom Rally, July 10, 1966, CHQ; interview; Ruth Turner [Perot], "Black Power: A Voice Within," *Oberlin Alumni Magazine,* LXIII (May 1967), 17–19, reprinted in John Bracey, August Meier, and Elliott Rudwick, eds., *Black Nationalism in America* (Indianapolis, 1970), 465–70. For point of view of another leader close to McKissick, national chairman Wilfred Ussery, see his testimony in *Hearings Before the United States Commission on Civil Rights,* held in San Francisco and Oakland, May 1967 (Washington, 1967), 266–73. See also McKissick, "Programs for Black Power," in Floyd Barbour, ed., *The Black Power Revolt,* (Boston, 1968), 179–81.

19. McKissick, "Speech for Meredith Freedom March Rally," June 26, 1966, CHQ; McKissick, Speech at Chicago Freedom Rally, July 10, 1966, CHQ; McKissick, "Black Power," *Interracial Review,* XXXIX (July 1966), 127–28; McKissick, *Three-Fifths of a Man* (New York, 1969), 101–3, 137, 157; National Broadcasting Company, *Meet the Press,* XII (July 14, 1968), *passim.*

20. Homer Jack to McKissick, July 11, 1966, CHQ; Farmer and Arthur Lelyveld to Dear Friend [Feb. 1967], CHQ.

21. Lillian Smith, telegram to McKissick, July 5, 1966, CHQ; interviews.

22. *Wall Street Journal,* July 22, 1966; McKissick to Dear Friend [Autumn 1967], CHQ; Lynch quoted in Baltimore *Sun,* July 2, 1966; NAC, Dec. 17, 1966, MLK.

23. Minutes, CORE National Advisory Committee, Jan. 26, 1967, CHQ; *Afro-American,* Sept. 6, 1966; *Wall Street Journal,* Nov. 4, 1966.

24. For Philadelphia, interviews; Minutes of Boston CORE Meeting, July 6, 1966, Phyllis Ryan Prs; for Winston-Salem and Binghamton, see *Wall Street Journal,* July 22, 1966; for St. Louis, see typed notation on "Report of Elections at CORE National Convention, Baltimore, 4 July, 1966," in C. A. Valentine's Notes on 1965 Convention, Singler Prs; for Middlesex County, see clipping from *Daily Home News* enclosed in Ronald Copeland to McKissick, July 11, 1966, CHQ, and interviews; for Seattle, see Minutes, Western Regional Convention, Sept. 3–4, 1966, WCO, and Seattle *Post-Intelligencer,* July 24, 1966.

25. Draft Minutes, 1966 Convention, CHQ; Minutes, Northeast Regional Action Council, April 23, 1966, Curvin Prs; personal observations and interviews.

26. *CORE-lator,* April 1967, CHQ; Minutes, National Advisory Committee,

Dec. 17, 1966, CHQ, and Farmer and Lelyveld to Dear Friend [Feb. 1967], CHQ; Fred Shapiro, "The Successor to Floyd McKissick May Not Be So Reasonable," *New York Times Magazine,* Oct. 1, 1967, 100.

27. Chicago CORE to North Central Regional Delegates [Autumn 1966], Ralph Rosenfeld Prs; interviews for Newark; McKissick quoted in *Times,* July 6, 1967.

28. For Boston, interview; Seattle *Times,* July 19, 28, 1967, and Seattle *Post-Intelligencer,* Aug. 26, Sept. 9, 14, 15, 1967; Kansas City *Star,* July 23, Sept. 1, 1967, and Kansas City *Times,* July 19, 21, 25, Aug. 2, Sept. 1, 1967, and Dec. 18, 1968.

29. *Call and Post,* Aug. 5, 19, Dec. 16, 1967, Jan. 20, March 23, Aug. 10, Sept. 28, Oct. 5, 1968; Cleveland *Press,* July 25, 1967; Cleveland *Plain Dealer,* July 14, 25, 1967; *Times,* July 14, 15, 1967.

30. Curvin to Rich, July 11, 1966, Rich Prs; Steering Committee, Aug. 16, 1966, MLK.

31. Draft, 1966 Convention Minutes, CHQ; Minutes, Western Regional Convention, Sept. 3–4, 1966, WCO; NAC, Dec. 17, 1966, MLK; C. A. Valentine, Notes on 1966 Convention, Singler Prs; Bonnie Barrow to McKissick, March 28, 1967, CHQ.

32. Kenneth Marshall, Memorandum [ca. July 1967], CHQ; Reports on 1967 Convention in Oakland *Tribune,* July 4, 5, 1967; Steering Committee, April 8–9, 1967, MLK.

33. "Minutes of Educational Conference on Urban Problems, held at Lexington, Kentucky, non-NAC Sessions, May 19 through 22, 1967," CHQ; Steering Committee, May 22, 1967, MLK.

34. Oakland *Tribune,* July 4, 5, 1967; *Times,* July 6, Dec. 26, 1967; interviews; Lynch to McKissick, July 28, 1967, MLK; *A Brief History of the Congress of Racial Equality,* Feb. 1969, personal files; *Times,* June 26, 1968.

35. *Times,* June 26, July 4, 8, 1968; Columbus *Citizen-Journal,* July 8, 1968; Columbus *Dispatch,* July 8, 1968; Philadelphia *Inquirer,* July 9, 1968; *Call and Post,* July 3, 1968; Mwlina Imiri Abubadika (Sonny Carson), *The Education of Sonny Carson* (New York, 1972), 182–86.

36. McKissick to Robert Lucas, July 11, 1968, CHQ; Columbus *Dispatch,* July 5, 6, Oct. 21, 1968; Columbus *Citizen-Journal,* July 8, 1968; *National Guardian,* July 13, 1968; St. Louis *Post-Dispatch,* Sept. 15, 16, 1968; *Times,* Sept. 17, 1968; Alex Poinsett, "Roy Innis: Nation Builder," *Ebony,* XXIV (Oct. 1969), 174; *A Brief History of the Congress of Racial Equality;* press release, Sept. 26, 1968, Rich Prs.

37. *Times,* Sept. 17, 1968; press release, Sept. 26, 1968, Rich Prs; *A Brief History of the Congress of Racial Equality, 1942–1969.*

38. Press release, Sept. 28, 1968, Rich Prs; St. Louis *Post-Dispatch,* Sept. 15, 1968; *Time Magazine,* VC (March 9, 1970, 14); Innis interview in *U. S. News and World Report,* LXV (Nov. 25, 1968), 60; *Newsweek,* LXXIII (June 30, 1969), 26. See also Roy Innis, "Black Self-Determination," *New Generation,* LI (Summer 1969), 18–22, and Innis, "Separatist Economics: A New Social Con-

tract," in William Haddad and C. Douglas Pugh, eds., *Black Economic Development* (Englewood Cliffs, 1969), 50–59.

39. For good discussion of SNCC's decline as its rhetoric grew more radical, see Gene Roberts, "The New SNCC: Weaker, Fierier," *Times,* Aug. 20, 1967.

40. Voter Education Project, Inc., *Black Elected Officials in the South, February 3, 1972* (1972).

Index